"The language of 'covenant' floats through the universe of contemporary Christian ethics like the element helium floats through the physical one: it is abundant, lofty, necessary for telling a coherent origin story, and yet surprisingly inert. Contemporary discussions about covenants are, after all, far more likely to attend to their significance in the history of Christian ethics than to make covenant language do much work in the present. In *Christian Ethics: A New Covenant Model*, though, Hak Joon Lee performs an impressive alchemical feat: he transforms reasons to attend to the significance of covenants in the history of Christian ethics into arguments for their applicability in contemporary Christian social ethics. Building from his telling of a biblically and historically informed theo-drama in which covenants are central to the movement from liberation to restoration, Lee fashions a Jesus-centered 'new covenant ethic' that can catalyze social imaginations capable of addressing matters as varied as economic inequality, war, marriage, racism, and the environment. In doing so, he reminds us that covenant language has been significant because it is still potent."

— **Mark Douglas**
Columbia Theological Seminary

"Hak Joon Lee informs, instructs, and inspires in this wide-ranging, challenging, and compelling text in Christian ethics. The work takes seriously the current context, contemporary political theologies of liberation, and Christian tradition. *Christian Ethics: A New Covenant Model* should be obligatory reading not only for theological ethicists but also for those who desire to live in and love the world faithfully as followers of Jesus."

— **Patrick T. Smith**
Duke University Divinity School

"In *Christian Ethics: A New Covenant Model*, Hak Joon Lee convincingly argues that 'covenant' is the most comprehensive image on which a rich Christian ethical vision and practice can be centered. He shows that a new covenant vision, far from being a stale offering from an irrelevant past, steers the Christian moral conversation between secular liberal and conservative biblicist options, integrates and organizes the most important methodological conversations of the past century, and helps Christians respond in a biblically grounded yet passionate and culturally open way to the most pressing social issues of our day—politics, economics, criminal justice, race, and sexuality among them. We are in Lee's debt!"

— **David L. Stubbs**
Western Theological Seminary

Christian Ethics

A New Covenant Model

Hak Joon Lee

William B. Eerdmans Publishing Company
Grand Rapids, Michigan

Wm. B. Eerdmans Publishing Co.
4035 Park East Court SE, Grand Rapids, Michigan 49546
www.eerdmans.com

Published 2021
Printed in the United States of America

27 26 25 24 23 22 21 1 2 3 4 5 6 7

ISBN 978-0-8028-7687-4

Library of Congress Cataloging-in-Publication Data

Names: Lee, Hak Joon, 1958– author.
Title: Christian ethics : a new covenant model / Hak Joon Lee.
Description: Grand Rapids, Michigan : William B. Eerdmans Publishing Company, 2021. | Includes bibliographical references and index. | Summary: "A broad introduction to Christian ethics based on a covenantal understanding of Christian life rooted in Scripture"—Provided by publisher.
Identifiers: LCCN 2021015722 | ISBN 9780802876874 (hardcover)
Subjects: LCSH: Christian ethics. | Covenants—Religious aspects—Christianity.
Classification: LCC BJ1251 .L367 2021 | DDC 241—dc23
LC record available at https://lccn.loc.gov/2021015722

Unless otherwise noted, Scripture quotations are taken from the New Revised Standard Version of the Bible.

To Jackie

and

the late E. J. Emerson

Contents

Preface

We are living in a post-Christian (even anti-Christian) society. The Christian worldview, along with its values, is losing influence, and its moral credibility and authority are being challenged. For decades, many intellectuals and educated people have claimed that the world has "come of age"; it no longer "turns to religion for frameworks of meaning and explanation as it once did."[1] Secularity has seemingly reached new heights and all forms of institutionalized religion are rejected, while the credibility of Christianity is now hitting new lows. Anti-Christian sentiment stems from disappointment and anger at judgmental, anti-intellectual, misogynistic, and politicized forms of Christianity. Out of shame, young people en masse are leaving the churches.

In today's cultural milieu, being a Christian is no longer socially attractive.

On the other hand, humanity faces a crisis. Recent political and economic developments (the rise of ethno-nationalism, identity politics, authoritarian regimes, global pandemic, global warming) reveal the fragility and vulnerability of life on this planet.

Culturally, the forces of fragmentation and authoritarianism threaten democracy, human rights, and the very sense of life together (symbiosis).

Economically, the splendid technological advances of the past century have translated into the common good and enhancement of the quality of life. However, they have also intruded on individual privacy and widened the gap between the rich and the poor, leading to the concentration of power into the hands of the rich few.

Socially, globalization has resulted in confusion, poor governance, global disarray, and disorderliness, as seen in the refugee and migrant crisis, rather than common flourishing.

These negative effects are culminating in the US government's miserable failure in handling the COVID-19 pandemic.

1. Bonhoeffer, *Letters and Papers from Prison*, 478.

All these demonstrate how vulnerable freedom is without public-spiritedness, how fragmenting a society is without shared moral vision and values, and how fragile a democracy is without spiritual depth.

This book presents new covenant ethics as a plausible paradigm of Christian ethics that is biblically faithful, methodologically coherent, socially relevant, and transformative in this era of globalization, digitization, and neoliberalism. New covenant ethics draws its ethical form, content, and characteristics from Jesus and the new covenant of Jesus. Covenant is an especially compelling option in today's pluralistic society in the global era.

A book on covenant ethics may sound outdated at a time when the idea of covenant is losing cultural currency. Even among young Christians in the Reformed tradition, the attraction of covenant as a constructive theological vision and moral imagination is receding in the face of competing theological models such as postliberal theology, neo-Augustinianism, Radical Orthodoxy, and feminist and liberationist theologies.

There are roughly three distinctive postures toward covenant among Christians in our culture: First, many in the West are very familiar with it, as the idea of covenant has been secularized to the extent of being indistinguishable from contract. People frequently use the term to describe daily business and personal transactions involving two or more parties. Thus, many may wonder whether there is anything new or special about covenant. Even among Christians, the idea is unattractive because it is perceived as overly forensic, procedural, or transactional—too outworn and obsolete to capture people's moral imagination and inspire them for the transformative action that our society needs.

Second, for many young Christians, the idea of covenant represents a shameful part of Christian history, when white Christians used the concept to justify dehumanizing and reprehensible systems of racial segregation and oppression, notably in the United States and South Africa (supporting the ideologies of the "redeemer nation," Manifest Destiny, and apartheid). The suspicion and reluctance are reinforced today because the idea is claimed by ultraconservative Jewish Zionists in Israel to justify the occupation of the West Bank and other Palestinian lands. When memories of colonialism and racism are still fresh, why should we bring covenant back? It is too tainted or corrupted to recover its credibility. In the growing liberal cosmopolitan society that celebrates inclusiveness, tolerance, and acceptance, and in the cultural milieu that is increasingly apathetic or hostile to Christianity, it takes more than a strong stomach to publicly use a symbol that is reminiscent of such a shameful past.

Third, most Christians from non-Reformed heritages dismiss covenant as the specific parlance of the Reformed tradition that often prioritizes God's universal law (based on creation and the Ten Commandments) over the particularity of Jesus's teachings, narratives, and community. Its ethical approach seems impertinent in a postmodern culture where historical and cultural particularity, identity, and self-construction are celebrated over claims of rationality, law, and universality. There is a mistaken perception among Christians that covenant is more central to the Old Testament than to the New Testament: that it is only remotely related to Jesus and his moral teachings because he mentioned covenant only on a few occasions, most notably at his Last Supper.

In short, covenant is a morally ambiguous and ambivalent concept at best, and a hostile and tainted one at worst. To use such a term, especially in a culture where secularization excels and Christians find themselves intellectually and morally defensive, seems counterproductive, rather than attractive, to young Christians.

The reluctance, suspicion, and emotional resistance to covenant are understandable. However, these problems are not intrinsic to covenant. The misuse or abuse of a biblical symbol or idea is not confined to covenant alone. Central biblical ideas such as kingdom, God the Father, grace, heaven, and hell have also been misused and abused. Furthermore, the abuse/misuse of covenant occurred through the illicit assimilation of covenant to a white racist ideology that justified ethno-racism, nationalism, and colonialism over against religious and racial outsiders and indigenous people in order to promote political and economic interests. Just as the solution to bad religion is not atheism but good religion, the solution to the misuse of biblical symbols or ideas is not their abandonment but their restoration and rehabilitation. One should not throw out the baby with the bathwater.

Covenant cannot simply be dismissed as an outdated idea or a racist ideology. Contrary to criticisms and popular reluctance, the biblical idea of covenant, in fact, has rich, robust, and radically liberating impulses within it. The covenant embodies the biblical vision of a highly egalitarian, just, and communal society in God. Covenant exercises a subversive power toward unequal structures of power while imparting revolutionary social ideals and imaginations. For example, the Sinai covenant was revolutionary in its critique of the Pharaonic system of oppression and exploitation, as well as in its presentation of an alternative form of society. The ideas of tribal confederacy (as opposed to kingship), Sabbath, and Jubilee in the Torah—all informed by covenant—were revolutionary in the historical and cultural context of the ancient Near East. Similarly, the new covenant of Jesus Christ was radical, subversive, and egalitarian. Jesus's life and ministry were extremely unconventional; he redefined the boundaries, structure, and meaning of the community by including people previously excluded.

Covenant is liberating because covenant is about fair and right "relationships"—"to put things right." Covenant intends to make right and reconciled relationships happen. Because of this liberative thrust, covenant has been crucial in providing a theological and moral basis for the projects of democracy, constitutionalism, human rights, and civil society. Furthermore, covenantal polity includes a self-correcting, reforming power, as shown in the examples of US social movements for abolition, women's suffrage, civil rights, and labor. These movements have appealed to and called for thorough and consistent implementation of the democratic ideals and values embedded in the Declaration of Independence and the Constitution, which were inspired by the covenantal tradition of colonial America, especially New England.

The covenantal drama of liberation-restoration is at the heart of the biblical plot and theo-drama that run through both the Old and New Testaments. Covenant embodies a unique vision that balances the passion for freedom and justice with community and peace. A biblical concept of covenant embodies a particular way of organizing just and right relationships on the basis of freedom. In God's reign, covenant offers the scaffold of a common life—organizing it in a just, organic, and complex way, in institutional diversity and constant dynamic interactions and transactions. Covenant aims at shalom, which describes the wholeness, integrity, and joy of creation.

I believe that the new covenant offers the most faithful, relevant, and transformative way to read the Bible for Christian ethics. New covenant ethics attempts to renew and restore a liberative vision and the healing message of covenant on a new biblical and theological ground. It takes Jesus and his new covenant (not the Sinai covenant and its narrative of Canaan conquest) as the starting point.

The new covenant of Jesus is the climax of God's covenantal organizing of creation. It is inclusive, ecological, egalitarian, and nonviolent. New covenant ethics empowers grassroots organizing, communicative engagement, just peacemaking, and democratic rule making as primary mechanisms of reorganizing a society. It corrects the abuse/misuse of covenant.

It is my hope that the ethics of Jesus obtains a new democratic horizon and relevance and that democracy gains a new spiritual depth and moral ground. New covenant ethics translates Jesus's shalom message and just peacemaking ministry into our own social and political contexts.

Acknowledgments

Every book has its own distinctive character. While it is mostly shaped by the intellectual and biographical story of the author, more often than not its character is also influenced by hidden voices that usually come in the form of inspirational ideas, clarifying thoughts, inquisitive questions, comments, and suggestions during the process of preparing and writing the book. These hidden voices are often no less important in determining the final form of the book.

This book is no exception. A number of kind and faithful people have helped to shape this book into its final form, and their contributions are a hopeful sign of covenantal care and fidelity still alive in our society despite the erosive power of individualism, fragmentation, and liquidity.

Many thanks go to Joshua Beckett for his assistance with research, proofreading of the entire manuscript, and helpful comments on sexual ethics; to the late E. J. Emerson and Jae Yang for their thorough proofreading of the manuscript at different stages of this book; to Melanie Dzugan for her page proof and indexing work; to Seung Woo Lee for his methodical work on the bibliography and assistance with the indexing; to my doctoral students Diana Kim, Phil Allen, Melanie Dzugan, and Candice Perkins for their thoughtful discussion of the manuscript and their encouragement; to Jessica Joustra for her careful scholarly comments on Part I; to Kirk Nolan for reading the entire manuscript and sharing helpful insights; to Ron Sanders, John Mustol, and Nick Brown for their constructive comments on the chapters on politics, creation care, and medical ethics, respectively; to James Ernest for his trust in this project, expressed through his patience and generous moral support; and finally, and most importantly, to my wife Jackie for faithfully journeying with me in my ministry and scholarly life, reminding me of the importance of covenantal commitment for our shared life on both sunny days and rainy days.

I dedicate this book to Jackie, for her wisdom, abiding personal support, and sacrifices for the family, and the late E. J., to celebrate her life and remember her modeling of friendship that this book hopes to inspire.

Introduction

> For theological reflection on social matters, much more significant than the "original covenant" on which the federalist tradition builds is the "new covenant," which remains almost completely neglected as a resource for political thought.
>
> —Miroslav Volf, *Exclusion and Embrace*

Friends is a classic American sitcom that remains popular among many young people despite the passage of more than two decades since it first appeared in 1994. Based in Manhattan, it is the story of six friends (Rachel Green, Ross Geller, Monica Geller, Joey Tribbiani, Chandler Bing, and Phoebe Buffay) who are all quirky in one way or another—spoiled, compulsive, weird, immature, desperate, and wimpy—reflecting their early childhood family trauma or personal complexes. They struggle to achieve professional success and romantic happiness, but their lives are never straightforward. Over the course of eight years, these friends go through family crises, numerous personal mistakes, failures, conflicts, laughter, tears, and surprises. The message of the sitcom is that these six young people learn what it really means to be friends as they experience various challenges. They are discouraged and frustrated by past hurts and wounds, but they also find a resting and healing place in friendship. They stick together, accepting and caring for each other, finding grace among each other.

There are several reasons for the tremendous popularity of *Friends*. The show superbly describes a widespread moral ethos among young people—nonjudgmental, tolerant of different lifestyles, expressive, feeling imperfect and vulnerable, but also longing for acceptance, trust, and belongingness.[1] In hilarious ways, the sitcom asks

1. Unfortunately, this ethos is in stark contrast with the public perception of Christians as

a very serious question: What is friendship? This question is pressing and poignant for young people who live in a society where traditional communities are disappearing and social life is increasingly stressful and lonely. They look for an alternative community where they can find acceptance and support.

Friends raises several important questions for Christians: Does the church offer good company like those six friends? How would the church accept persons of wildly different personalities like the six characters? Would the church provide a space (like Central Perk, where they frequently gather) where Christians can find acceptance, forgiveness, empowerment, and the joy of sharing life? What resources does Christianity have for meeting the growing needs of young people that *Friends* seems to portray? These are not easy questions to answer, and we know that churches today are often more religious institutions than places that provide friendship and grace where lives are shared together.

This book is about Christian ethics based on covenant. In this post-Christian era, many people do not fully comprehend what covenant is; they typically conflate it or confuse it with contract—a legal agreement between different parties—and are unaware of its deep biblical meaning. However, covenant, as we will see shortly, is central to the Bible. More importantly, covenant, in a nutshell, is about God's friendship with humanity. Indeed, God called Abraham "my friend," just as Jesus called his disciples "friends" (John 15:15). The Bible is the drama of friendship: from creation of humanity as God's partner, to the unexpected betrayal of humanity that leads to alienation, to God's constant efforts to restore friendship, which climax in God's incarnation in Jesus and dwelling in us as the Spirit. Surprisingly, however, the biblical idea of covenant celebrates core values that *Friends* depicts: trust, acceptance, commitment, honesty, affection, and self-sacrifice for other friends. The message of the Bible is that God never gives up on friendship with humanity. Just as Joey becomes a member of the new family that Chandler and Monica form at the end of the show, we are invited to become permanent members of God's family.

Ethics

Then what is ethics, and why do we need ethics? How is ethics related to covenant, and how is ethics based on covenant different from other forms of ethics? While having a forceful (even if often distracted) passion for justice and individual rights, many young people in the postmodern era have negative or sullen reactions to the word "ethics." It conjures up images of dry rules, courts, intolerant religious groups, or

---

mostly judgmental, hypocritical, narrow-minded, and proselytizing. See Kinnaman and Lyons, *UnChristian*.

rigid parents or teachers. Whatever the postmodern bias or disenchantment about ethics may be, it is an indispensable aspect of human life. Friendship and genuine romantic love—emotional qualities that our popular culture promotes and young people highly value—are moral in nature. Maintaining them well requires certain moral norms and virtues such as trust, honesty, loyalty, and sacrifice.

Ethics is part of our very nature as human beings. The questions of fairness, right, and good always loom large, whether spoken or not, when we interact with others and make our decisions regarding marriage, school, work, voting, shopping, etc. We always rely on certain normative standards to assess and evaluate our decisions and actions.

If ethics is indispensable to human life, then what is it and what is its role? Broadly speaking, ethics has to do with the quality of life: how to live a *good*, happy, or excellent life. Indeed, ethics is a unique human endeavor to live life well, in a fulfilling way. Specifically, we rely on ethics to secure predictability and stability in our life;[2] that is, ethics helps to protect us and society from chaos (survival) and to find reliable guidance toward flourishing (thriving). Because of its necessity for common human survival and thriving, some form of ethics is found in every society, even a global society, although the question of how to best achieve thriving has never been settled in human history.

This book defines ethics as a normative endeavor to organize human life toward goodness, happiness, and thriving, while avoiding or mitigating confusion and chaos. We organize and order our personal and social life using certain ideals, norms/values, and rules, which are typically based on reason, experiences, cultural tradition, or religion.[3] These ideals, rules, and values provide a road map for a good, excellent, and thriving life.

This normative organizing effort is critical and reflective, not impulsive or arbitrary. It is not confined to one area of life or one moment in time but encompasses the entire human life. Personally, ethics has to do with the ordering of one's life toward excellence while keeping integrity; socially, it concerns organizing and arranging institutional and social life in a just and orderly way, so that people may live with

2. The correlation of ethics and stability is found in the Greek etymology of ethics (*ta ēthika*). The noun *ēthos* means "dwelling" or "stall," a place that houses animals and protects them from wild animals. The verb form *eiōtha* means "to act according to custom." Ancient Greeks believed that social custom provided security for society in the same way a stall provides security for animals. Based on the etymology of "ethics," one may say that ethics as an academic discipline studies what brings stability to human life and "what holds human life together." Lehmann, *Ethics in a Christian Context*, 25.

3. The question of what is the authoritative ground of these goals, norms, and virtues is increasingly controversial in a pluralistic society. Some find the ground in a specific religion, some in a cultural tradition, while others find it in reason.

a sense of security, predictability, and trust. The individual and social dimensions are never separate because a society constitutes the context of an individual life, and the quality of a social relationship affects individuals. In summary, one may say that ethics is the art of organizing human life that aims at life's stability (minimally) and flourishing (maximally).

Like other world religions, Christianity takes ethics very seriously. It claims that God is a moral, righteous God. One can find lists of rules, norms, virtues, and moral teachings in both Testaments of the Bible. Christianity also promises flourishing, well-lived lives (excellence) and a right and peaceful community for humanity in God. However, a Christian view of morality goes beyond rules and commandments. In fact, rules and commandments are only secondary to God and God's relationship with humanity. Christianity teaches that a good relationship with God and with others is the ultimate source of happiness and goodness. Rules are subjected to and guided by the cosmic vision of just, peaceful, and harmonious relationships, called shalom. Christianity claims that only such relationships offer the condition for genuine human flourishing and happiness.

Covenant as a Key Metaphor of Christian Ethics

This book introduces the biblical idea of covenant as a divinely designed framework for the flourishing of humanity and the planet and as a key metaphor of Christian ethics.[4] That is, covenant renders a compelling account of the Christian moral life that is designed to lead to the common thriving. Let me first explain what a key metaphor is and why it is important for Christian ethics, and then how covenant is a key metaphor of Christian ethics.

According to Richard Hays and Sallie McFague, human knowledge is metaphoric. Humans understand and organize the world around them relying on various metaphors. Among them, key metaphors play central roles in guiding a person's perception and interpretation of reality by providing focus, clarity, and coherence.[5] According to David Kelsey, the choice of a key metaphor in reading Scripture represents "a single synoptic, imaginative judgment"[6] as it encapsulates the core vision and conviction of Scripture.

Christian ethics also relies on certain key metaphors in explaining the distinctive nature and dynamics of the Christian moral life and obligations. The choice of a key metaphor inevitably reflects one's worldview—one's view of God, humanity, and

4. "Key" here does not mean "exclusive" or "exhaustive" but rather connotes "primary" or "central."

5. McFague, *Metaphorical Theology*.

6. Kelsey, *Use of Scripture*, 159, quoted in Hays, *Moral Vision*, 194.

the world, and their interrelationships. A particular model or paradigm of Christian ethics (often called a "school" or a "tradition") is built through a coherent and systematic conceptualization of a key metaphor in order to explain God's moral character, demand, and human moral responsibility. Relying on a key metaphor, Christian ethics attempts to render "both a compelling account of why things are the way they are and a portrait of how they ought to be."[7] In short, a key metaphor directly and indirectly informs our ethical vision, values, and practices, namely, the shape and contours of Christian ethics.

Various Christian ethical traditions (e.g., liberationists, Reformed, evangelicals, communitarians, Anabaptists, Catholics) have developed their ethics on the basis of key metaphors that are related to their unique understandings of God's character, will, and relationship with the world. For example, liberationists take God's liberation of the oppressed (in terms of race, gender, and class) as a key metaphor, while Catholics take God's natural order of creation (given in natural law) as a key symbol. Reformed Christians embrace divine commands (available through creation and Scripture, most notably the Ten Commandments) as a focal metaphor, while for Anabaptists, the God who revealed Godself on the cross is a central symbol. The choice of key symbols typically leads to the selection of or emphasis on particular teachings or literature in the Bible as the central texts of Christian ethics. Some prominent examples of such authoritative texts are the exodus story (liberationist), the Ten Commandments (Reformed), the Sermon on the Mount (Anabaptists, Mennonites), the passion narrative, and epistolary passages on the cross of Jesus.

Scripture presents such a variety of metaphors and symbols for Christian ethics that one may rightly ask, "By what criteria do we determine which symbols are key root metaphors?" For Christians, I suggest, the criteria for a key metaphor include faithfulness, comprehensiveness, relevance, and practical efficacy (motivation). That is, a key ethical metaphor is faithful to Scripture and its theological convictions and encompasses the diverse texts of Scripture; it is capacious enough to address complex social issues with coherence and relevance; and, finally, it is capable of motivating moral actions.[8]

This book presents covenant as the key biblical metaphor that meets the criteria above. That is, covenant is faithful to Scripture in properly describing God's moral character, demands, and relationship with humanity and nature; it is comprehensive with its wide representation in the diverse texts and literary genres of the

7. Stackhouse, *Ethics and the Urban Ethos*, 80.

8. Similarly, in his study of NT ethics, Richard Hays offers three criteria in evaluating the appropriateness of focal metaphors: inclusivity ("a textual basis" with wide representation in Scripture), coherence (securing unity among diverse documents without serious tension), and faithfulness ("central and substantial ethical concerns" of the Scripture). Hays, *Moral Vision*, 195.

Bible (see chap. 1), capacious in dealing with a variety of social issues with coherence, and efficacious in motivating Christians for moral actions. In short, covenant captures the rich moral vision and thick ethos of the Bible more accurately than other metaphors.

Here are several more reasons why covenant is central to the biblical worldview and a key metaphor of Christian ethics: Covenant constitutes the basic story line, a narrative plot, and a central drama of Scripture holding together the unity between the Testaments. Christian redemptive history is framed in terms of covenant. The stories of Israel, Jesus, and the church would not make sense outside the covenantal plot. Major biblical events and stories can be interpreted as covenant itself or covenant related, and accordingly, covenant is found in every critical moment of God's dispensation and in major turning points in biblical history.

Scripture offers numerous references to covenant. The word "covenant" appears 287 times in the OT (*bᵉrît* in Hebrew) and 33 times in the NT (*diathēkē* in Greek). However, the significance of covenant in Scripture transcends sheer arithmetic. The motif of covenant reverberates throughout Scripture; it is presupposed in many passages. Walther Eichrodt notes, "Even where the covenant is not explicitly mentioned the spiritual premises of a covenant relationship with God are manifestly present."[9]

According to Kevin Vanhoozer, the Bible is an unfolding theo-drama—a script of God's actions in and for the world.[10] He claims that covenant is "not simply one biblical or theological theme among others. The God/world distinction and relation alike is ultimately a matter of covenantal drama."[11] From the beginning, creation and the human life in it are covenantally designed by God. Covenant is a metaphor that best portrays the free, intimate, and reciprocal relationality that characterizes the divine-human interaction and the interdependence and solidarity among all creatures. The biblical drama of covenant is not fictional but realistic;[12] it offers an apt device to account for various events, incidents, and data in the Bible.

9. Eichrodt, *Theology of the Old Testament*, 36–37. Most biblical scholars are aware that major important biblical notions such as covenant, reign, and righteousness are implied or presupposed even when specific references to those terms are not made in Scripture. Covenant is one of them.

10. Vanhoozer, *Faith Speaking Understanding*, 20.

11. Vanhoozer, *Remythologizing Theology*, 68.

12. The idea of drama offers a more accurate interpretation of biblical stories and parables than narrative or story. Drama looks similar to narrative (which connotes a fictional quality) but is different from the latter because of its participatory and performative nature. For Christians, biblical stories and parables make realistic, not fictional, moral claims; they not only describe or explain the events but also call for appropriate performative responses on the part of the audience. That is to say, Christians not only read and share the biblical stories but also are required to perform them as participants in the ongoing salvific drama of God. One would not actually perform the drama

It does not gloss over the struggles and failures of people in history. It deals with the sinful but beloved people of God and their real-life stories, which include moral flaws, betrayals, power struggles, and temptations as well as their moral aspirations and endeavors.

Covenant is the modus operandi that God takes in interacting with humanity and the world, and God fulfills God's purpose for humanity and creation through covenant. In the Bible, covenant is central to God's reign, which is by nature ethical and manifested in the calling and formation of God's community.[13] To be covenanted means to be God's people; it is to enter into and stay under God's reign of love, righteousness, peace, and joy.

Covenant holds the key to the question of the distinctiveness of Israel and the church.[14] The term "covenant" itself was consistently applied by the Israelites to their relationship with God from the earliest times.[15] Standing in a deep covenantal tradition of Israel, Jesus's identity and ministry were deeply covenantal. The early Christian community considered itself the new Israel, a universal community of covenant comprising the entire humanity of Jews and gentiles, male and female, slaves and slave masters.[16] There is a broad consensus that Paul's understanding of the Christ event and Paul's ethical teachings—Jewish apocalyptic understanding of God, election, and community—are informed by covenant. Hence, covenant provides the window through which we gain a deeper and more accurate knowledge of God and God's interactions with humans.

As ethics has to do with the normative organizing of human life, covenant is the art or method of God's organizing a community toward shalom.[17] God uses covenant to organize God's community, including creation. In the Bible, the coming of God's reign is intimately connected with the covenantal organizing of people.

---

if one did not truly believe it was real. The performative nature of the biblical drama comes from its covenantal plot and structure. See Stassen, *A Thicker Jesus*, 12.

13. "Kingdom and covenants go hand in hand because covenants were the means by which God ruled over his kingdom. They were God's kingdom administrations, leading the kingdom of God toward its destiny of expanding to the ends of the earth." Birmingham Theological Seminary, "Kingdom, Covenants and Canon of the Old Testament."

14. Nicholson, *God and His People*, 191.

15. Freedman, "Divine Commitment and Human Obligation," 419.

16. The significance of covenant is found in the enduring interest on it in NT studies, especially in the ongoing debates around the so-called new perspective on Paul, sparked by the monumental study of E. P. Sanders on "covenantal nomism." The debates have offered new insights on Pauline theology, especially the continuity between the OT and the NT, Judaism and Christianity, while provoking heated debates on the doctrine of justification. However, the insights of these discussions have not been adequately translated into Christian ethics.

17. For a detailed discussion, see Lee, *God and Community Organizing*, chap. 1.

Gerhard Lohfink notes: "The rule of God presupposes a people of God, in whom it can become established and from whom it can shine forth."[18] God's covenantal organizing, which is the manifestation of God's reign, is ethical in nature. The organizing happens through a covenanting process that morally binds different parties into a new moral community, and it entails the redefinition and reworking of social relationships, that is, the transformation of unjust social arrangements and structures.

Covenantal organizing is intimately related to the three key motifs of ethics: rules, goal, and virtue. A new community is formed on the basis of the agreed-upon rules between the parties (covenantal stipulations); it aims toward a shared goal (telos); the parties should be reliable and trustworthy beyond external regulations (specified by covenantal stipulations) in order to sustain a covenantal relationship, hence the formation of virtues and character is a necessary concern here.

The central quest of Christian ethics—how we ought to live as God's children—cannot be separated from God's moral purpose (shalom), God's normative demands, and God's character. In the Bible, it is in a covenant relationship that humans find God's purpose, learn God's will, and freely commit to and bind themselves with God to be God's partner and imitate God's character. Karl Barth aptly notes: "How can it be Christian ethics if it does not know and take into account the fact that the divine covenant of grace with man is the beginning of all God's ways and works, and that the human situation grounded in this covenant is, therefore, the situation of every single man?"[19]

Covenant explains the distinctive and dialectical nature of the Christian moral life better than other biblical metaphors (such as love, liberation, law, or the cross). For example, it effectively captures the dialectic relationship of the indicative and the imperative in Christian ethics. As we see in the exodus story and in Jesus's redemptive ministry, human moral obligation takes form as a response to God's initiating salvific actions (liberation or deliverance). It is indicative because humans participate in God's ongoing organizing actions in history. However, humans are not just passive observers of God's action but God's coworkers. Covenant precisely accounts for this dialectic relationship in which the imperative flows from the indicative.

The brief observations above show that although covenant does not exhaust all the moral ideas and motifs of Scripture, it is a central drama and key moral metaphor of the Bible. Its centrality for Christian ethics is unparalleled. Christian moral life and obligations are primarily structured and informed by covenant. As we will elaborate further in the book, the inherent theological potency and ethical capacious-

18. Gerhard Lohfink, *Jesus and Community*, 27.

19. Barth, *Church Dogmatics* II/2, 643.

ness of covenant set it apart from other biblical metaphors or concepts. Without accounting for covenant and its distinctive theological-ethical dynamics, any study of Christian ethics would be unable to fully and accurately account for the Christian moral life that is covenantally designed by God.

Thesis and Rationale

Claiming that Christian ethics derives its distinctive content, shape, and characteristics from covenant in general, and the new covenant of Jesus in particular, this book constructs a coherent and plausible form of Christian ethics (its method, practices, and social ethics) centered on the new covenant of Jesus: new covenant ethics.

Theological interest in covenant is nothing new. Noticing its centrality in the Bible, Reformed theologians have upheld covenant as a comprehensive biblical paradigm of human life that applies to every type of relationship (with God, fellow human beings, and other creatures) and every level (personal, institutional, and societal) of human relationships. Numerous books and articles on covenant have been published over the centuries, and scholarly research continues today among Jewish and Christian theologians, ethicists, historians, and biblical scholars.

Despite these efforts, however, no one has developed a coherent and compelling form of a Christian ethic based on the new covenant of Jesus. The studies of covenant in Christian ethics have focused on general patterns, key theological motifs, and ethical norms of covenant (e.g., divine-human relationality, reciprocity, law, divine commandment, rule making, nature of Christian obligation, structure and pattern of human life, and constitutive principle of society), with the Sinai covenant (in a close association with the creation covenant) as its primary model. Christian ethicists have examined covenant as the constitutive and organizing principle of a society, the better understanding of various modern institutions—their structures and patterns—and social issues associated with them (e.g., family, business, politics, congregation, medicine, law, education, and international relationships).[20] On the other hand, historians and social scientists have studied the influence of covenant theology on the development of modern constitutional democracy, human rights, and other enduring political and social legacies.[21]

This book is different from traditional covenantal ethics in that it takes the new covenant of Jesus as its starting point and foundation. Jesus and his new covenant

20. May, *The Physician's Covenant*; May, *Testing the National Covenant*; Mount, *Covenant, Community, and the Common Good*; Stackhouse, *Covenant and Commitments*; Allen, *Love and Conflict*.

21. Walzer, *The Revolution of the Saints*; Moot, *Politics Reformed*; Bradley, *Religion, Revolution, and English Radicalism*; Wolfe, *Leveller Manifestoes*; Weir, *Early New England*.

are the center of Christians' spiritual and moral life. Worship, ethical decisions, and spiritual practices take place in the knowledge of their covenant relationship with God in Jesus. Jesus is the content of their doxology, spiritual growth, and moral endeavors. However, traditional covenantal ethics does not explicitly and sufficiently take Jesus and his new covenant as the starting point and center of Christian ethics, usually attributing more centrality to the Sinai covenant, with the law or divine commandments as its key metaphors!

The claim that covenant is the center of biblical drama and the heart of a biblical paradigm of the moral life is incomplete without fully grasping and explicating the significance of the new covenant of Jesus. This failure to take the covenant of Jesus as the center and crux of the entire covenant drama has created moral confusion, inconsistency, and the abuse/misuse of covenant.

On the other hand, Anabaptists and Mennonites have historically upheld Jesus (and the Sermon on the Mount) as the starting point and center of their ethics, but without taking covenant (the new covenant) as the narrative framework, historical background, and theological contour of Jesus's ministry and teachings. As many scholars argue today, the Jewish background of Jesus and the NT is critical in understanding the worldview of the NT and the early church and in overcoming white racism.[22] Jesus and his moral teachings cannot be properly understood apart from the covenantal history of God's interactions with humanity and Israel.

Consequently, both traditional covenant ethics and Anabaptist/Mennonite ethics are limited in establishing the proper narrative and theological continuity between the OT and the NT, and the OT covenants and the new covenant of Jesus—the former forgetting the centrality of Jesus for the Christian moral life, and the latter ignoring the covenantal matrix of Jesus and the Sermon on the Mount. This book interprets Jesus's ethics in a covenantal framework and the fulfillment of covenant in Jesus. Matthew 5:17–18 offers a key interpretive clue in dialectically connecting the OT covenants and the new covenant.

New covenant ethics is a paradigm of Christian ethics based on Jesus and his new covenant, which is the climax of the covenantal drama of the Bible. While it shares common moral features and characteristics of the biblical idea of covenant in general, the new covenant intensifies, expands, and eschatologizes them in a cosmic scope fulfilling the promises of the OT covenants. The new covenant is a covenant ad infinitum.

With the goal of organizing God's shalom community, new covenant ethics is Trinitarian in its theology; eschatological in its scope; and nonviolent, ecological, and just peacemaking in its nature, compared to the other covenants.

22. J. Kameron Carter, *Race*; N. T. Wright, *Paul and the Faithfulness of God*.

Method

In constructing new covenant ethics, typology plays an important role. Typology is a hermeneutical technique employed in the study of literature, history, archaeology, and the social sciences to secure reliable epistemological reference points and to expand the explanatory power of social phenomena, historical events, and textual meanings. In biblical hermeneutics, a typology helps see the continuity in God's redemptive history and acts across a long span of history. "Typology is the meaning of theo-dramatic unity, the principle that accounts for the continuity in God's words and acts, the connecting link between the history of Israel and the history of the church, the glue that unifies the Old and New Testaments."[23]

For example, in the Bible, Adam is a type for Noah, Abraham, Israel, and Jesus, while Eden is a type for the ark, Canaan, and new creation. As the divine drama unfolds through the tumults of history, typology helps to discern God's actions without losing narrative coherence and theological continuity. It is essential to see how the past is connected with the present and the future. Biblical writers relied on typology to interpret various events, and they attempted to understand what God was doing in their times in light of the past types (patterns) of God's work. Types are constant but not fixed; they adapt to new contexts through analogical imagination and reasoning.

Typology is useful in understanding the biblical covenants and in constructing new covenant ethics; covenant describes a particular type of God's organizing of humanity and nature. A typological reading of covenant helps to clearly see how God interacts with God's creatures and how God achieves God's purpose through covenants from the beginning (prototype) to the end (antitype). Its typology permeates the Bible. It is a repeated pattern of God's interaction with humanity and other creatures in the Bible. Covenant serves as a theological constant in the divine drama across history despite the ongoing moral failures of God's people. Covenant is a divinely designed type (the prototype of God's creation) that anticipates the fulfillment in the antitype (the new covenant). The biblical drama gains the unity through covenantal typology that integrates prototype and antitype.

A figural reading, typology, is inextricably tied with analogical thinking—similarity in difference. Analogy describes an intellectual process on which we rely when we attempt to explain a certain complex or ineffable reality by comparing it to some familiar or already well-known entity or phenomenon. In describing rich, complex experiences or in explaining mystery, we constantly borrow symbols, metaphors, and figurative language because "no single image can define reality."[24]

23. Vanhoozer, *The Drama of Doctrine*, 223.

24. Spohn, *Go and Do Likewise*, 57. It is more so with Christian faith that deals with the divine

Analogy presupposes and relies on a typological thinking, and vice versa. This affinity between analogy and typology helps us see how biblical covenants are similar with each other in their differences. The coherence between protype and antitype (consequently the canonical unity as well) is achieved through typological-analogical interpretation of biblical covenants. In the Bible, "typology is the study of analogical correspondence among revealed truths about persons, events, institutions, and other things within the historical framework of God's special revelation, which, from a retrospective view, are of a prophetic nature and are escalated in their meaning."[25]

Typology (and analogy) operates through the memory-hope (promise-fulfillment) pattern of the Bible, which is also one of the constitutive dimensions of covenant. Diverse biblical covenants are typologically and analogically related in their continuity and discontinuity to previous covenants, with the new covenant as their fulfillment. "If we neglect typology, we risk missing some truth that the divinely inspired author intended. Anticipatory symbols are introduced into the biblical narratives with divine intention in order to set up the pedagogical relationship of type and antitype, promise and fulfillment."[26]

In other words, covenant is a typological paradigm in the Bible. Typology renders not only internal dramatic coherence but also external adaptability (analogical imagination). Because of these qualities (coherence and adaptability), covenant serves as a wonderful paradigm for Christian ethics. It keeps faithfulness, capaciousness, and a broad relevance and applicability in diverse historical and cultural contexts, as we see not only in ancient Israel and the early churches but also in the rise of modern democracy and constitutionalism in Europe and the organizing of the international order in the post–World War II era.

This book claims that covenant and its patterns (types) are at the heart of the biblical paradigm of ethics. Through a careful exegesis of divine covenants in the Bible, it identifies several key patterns (types) of the covenant: externally, the covenantal drama of liberation-restoration; internally, the threefold operational patterns.

1. God's covenantal organizing is framed by an overarching pattern of "liberation" (judgment against oppression, sin, death) and "restoration" (re-creation of a new, just community [shalom]). Constituting the rubric of God's covenantal drama, this pattern appears in major biblical covenants: God delivered the universe from chaos to cosmos (the creation covenant), Israel from the Egyptian oppression to

---

reality and its mystery. Christian theology relies on the use of analogy because its subject matter is the God who is transcendental, mysterious, and ineffable beyond human description.

25. Beale, *Handbook on the New Testament Use of the Old Testament*, 14, cited in Estelle, *Echoes of Exodus*, 52.

26. Estelle, *Echoes of Exodus*, 42.

the promised land as a priestly kingdom (the Sinai covenant), and humanity from sin and death to a new creation (the new covenant of Jesus).

2. In moving toward shalom, God's covenant operates by a threefold dialectical pattern: unilateral-bilateral, communal-communicative, and memory-hope (chap. 3). Together, the three dialectics exhibit the distinctive nature and operating pattern of divine covenant: what covenant is (its unique nature and moral characteristics), how covenant is established and sustained, and how it unfolds in history.

Displaying God's intention and method in building a moral community, the covenantal drama of liberation-restoration and the threefold dialectics are crucial for understanding the distinctive nature, grammar, and characteristics of the biblical covenants in general and the new covenant of Jesus in particular. They help elucidate the logic, pattern, and purpose of covenant as God's organizing method, and consequently the Christian moral life.

The methodological importance of these patterns and dialectics cannot be overemphasized; they demonstrate the capaciousness, performative power, and problem-solving capability of new covenant ethics in resolving the tensions in several key binary ethical categories, such as divine-human agency, norm-context, worship-ethics, and unity-diversity (chap. 5), in reorganizing various discrete ethical motifs, notably goal, law, virtue (chap. 7), and norms/values in a coherent way (chap. 8), let alone accurately elaborating the reigning biblical ethos and the performative nature of the Christian morality and accountability.

Grounded in Jesus and his new covenant, the Christian moral life is liberative, restorative, indicative, communicative, contextual, and eschatological.

The Order of the Book

This book has two parts: method and social ethics. Part 1 is more theoretical in constructing the method of the new covenant ethics, while part 2 is practical in testing the relevance of new covenant ethics in critical engagements with various social issues of our time. Part 1 has three subparts.

Chapters 1–2 offer a brief overview of the major divine covenants in the OT: covenants with creation/Adam, Noah, Abraham, Moses, and David. The objective is to show how the biblical narrative and redemptive history run through a covenantal plot and story line, forming a distinctive and coherent worldview, how these covenants are interrelated (across the Old Testament and New Testament) with their final climax in the covenant of Jesus Christ, and how the latter is distinct from the others.

Chapters 3–6 study the distinctive patterns, characteristics, and strengths of covenant. Chapter 3 studies the pattern of the covenantal drama and the threefold dialectics of covenant: unilateral-bilateral, communal-communicative, and memory-hope (promise-fulfillment), while chapter 4 examines the distinctive nature, characteristics, and practices of new covenant ethics (communicative engagement, just peacemaking, community organizing, and nonviolent direct action) derived from the new covenant of Jesus and the three dialectics. Chapter 5 studies how new covenant ethics creatively harmonizes the tensions between divine and human agency, norm and context, the being and becoming of Christian identity, worship and ethics, and unity and diversity. Chapter 6 briefly compares new covenant ethics with other major forms of Christian ethics (traditional Reformed ethics; the ethics of Reinhold Niebuhr, John Howard Yoder, and Stanley Hauerwas; and liberation ethics), to highlight its strengths and distinctiveness.

Chapters 7–10 examine the moral values, sources, and method of new covenant ethics. Chapter 7 studies several core moral values and norms of the new covenant and their interrelationships structured under the threefold dialectics: gratitude, trust, hospitality, truth and truth telling, love, justice, freedom, solidarity, rights, and hope. Chapters 8–9 analyze the three classical motifs of ethics (goal, rule, and virtue) and the four moral sources of Christian ethics (Scripture, tradition, experience, and reason) from a covenantal perspective. Chapter 10 develops a methodology of covenant ethics that is communal, communicative, and analogical.

Part 2 begins with a covenantal approach to Christian social ethics (chap. 11) and discusses a covenantal theory of distributive justice: equality, need, merit, and capability (chap. 12).

Chapters 13–20 explore various social issues in our globalizing, digitizing, and neoliberal society in a critical conversation with secular liberal ethics and conservative evangelical ethics: politics (chap. 13), economics (chap. 14), creation care (chap. 15), criminal justice (chap. 16), race (chap. 17), sex and marriage (chap. 18), human life at its beginning and end (chap. 19), and war and peace (chap. 20).

The book concludes with a brief summary of what new covenant ethics is and what its distinctive contributions are today for Christian discipleship and public discourse in an era of globalization.

Definition

Christians generally define the divine covenant as the agreement made through the exchange of pledges between God and humans, whose fulfillment leads to blessings but whose breach leads to retribution. The agreement is typically (but not always) concluded by a covenantal ritual (e.g., cutting animals, sharing meals), which emphasizes the solemn nature of the pledges. This understanding is based on the Sinai covenant, which most scholars claim resembles ancient Near Eastern suzerain-vassal treaties.

This book defines covenant as God's organizing mechanism of a community, which is established when humans accept God's invitation to enduring fellowship, typically following God's deliverance or promise of future blessings (royal grant). It consists of the three moral components: love, justice, and power, and is instituted and operated by communicative interaction between the participants. In short, covenant is a communicative mechanism that *justly* organizes the *powers* and commitments of people into a *loving* fellowship, with shalom as the ultimate goal.

Scope

Scripture discloses different forms of covenants (divine-human, human-human, divine–other creatures) with different foci and emphases. Among these covenants, the divine-human covenant is logically prior to and more authoritative than the human-human covenant. The latter is guided and stipulated by the former. My primary (but not exclusive) focus in this book is the divine-human covenant in the Bible, found particularly in major biblical covenants that are theologically connected to the new covenant of Jesus both directly and indirectly. My strategy is to study the nature, meaning, and logic of the divine covenant and explore their implications for the Christian moral life, because the Christian moral life is a response to God's grace—the outworking of our covenantal relationship with God in every realm of a social life.

Like other major metaphors in the Bible, covenant is multifaceted and fertile, with many layered meanings. "There is no single covenant tradition or single meaning of the covenant."[27] My discussion of covenant is not exhaustive in the sense of including the contributions of various kinds of biblical criticisms, nor does it examine every covenant mentioned in the Bible.

Contribution

Grounded in the covenant of Jesus and his teachings, new covenant ethics presents a faithful, capacious, and coherent form of Christian ethics for the global era. It is biblical in its foundation, communicative in its method, and liberative in its praxis. Despite centuries-long, extensive discussions of covenant, no one has developed a coherent Christian ethic that is explicitly centered in Jesus and his new covenant. The failure to identify Jesus and his new covenant as the center and starting point of the Christian moral life has resulted in the confusion, misunderstanding, and misuse/abuse of covenant. In a clear distinction from traditional covenant ethics and

27. Allen, *Love and Conflict*, 19.

other paradigms of Christian ethics (e.g., Christian realist, Anabaptist/Mennonite, liberationist), new covenant ethics offers a faithful and plausible approach to Christian ethics with wide applicability today in addressing various moral challenges in our society. It offers a form of Christian ethics that enables a complex moral thinking (instead of a reductionistic, partisan ethic) and that instills a passion for justice and hope for the renewal of a society (instead of despair and hopelessness). Equipped with this holistic ethical framework, Christians may confidently engage with popular culture and the public realm, both of which are increasingly fragmented and polarized under the impact of globalization, digitization, and neoliberal economy.

1

New Covenant Ethics

Biblical Foundation, Features, and Method

CHAPTER 1

A Brief Survey of the Old Testament Covenants

> The covenant is the goal of creation and creation is the way to the covenant.
>
> —Karl Barth, *Church Dogmatics* III/1

> If creation was the external basis of the covenant, [the covenant] is the internal basis of [creation].
>
> —Karl Barth, *Church Dogmatics* III/1

This chapter and the next establish covenant as the root metaphor and the divine drama of Scripture. Through a brief survey of the major covenants in the OT (with creation/Adam, Noah, Abraham, Israel, and David), this chapter shows how the biblical story line moves through various covenants, anticipating its climax in Jesus Christ. This survey of the OT covenants is important to understand the full meaning and implication of the new covenant of Jesus Christ because it is the consummation of the preceding covenants. Furthermore, the patterns and types of the OT covenants are crucial to understand the moral nature of God and God's interactions with humanity and other creatures.

The survey of the biblical covenants in this chapter is far from exhaustive; it is only representative. Even the study of each covenant focuses only on its basic moral contours and characteristics. Special attention will be given to the patterns and types of God's work in covenant—how God continuously uses covenant to organize God's community and what patterns and types are discernible in the process. Let us now examine the major covenants in the Bible, starting with the covenant with creation.

Covenant with Creation

The Westminster Confession, a major theological document in the Reformed tradition, reads: "The first covenant made with man was a covenant of works, wherein life was promised to Adam, and in him to his posterity, upon condition of perfect and personal obedience."[1] Despite Reformed theology's creative application of the idea of covenant to Adam, called the covenant of works, there is still considerable dispute among scholars on whether God's relationship with creation and Adam could be defined as covenantal. One major reservation centers on the fact that the term "covenant" does not appear in the creation story (Gen. 1–3).

Despite the absence of the term in Genesis 1–3, I claim that the overall ethos—the theological and ethical premises of the creation story—is covenantal in nature.[2] A covenantal interpretation offers more plausibility and explanatory power for the text than other interpretations. Any reasonable reader of Scripture recognizes that certain key motifs and ideas, such as covenant or God's reign, are assumed in many places of the text without explicit reference. This happens because biblical writers communicate to a faith community that already shares certain core theological and moral assumptions. This practice applies to covenant: there are several plausible reasons to consider God's relationship with creation and the first humans in covenantal terms.

William J. Dumbrell offers a sensible explanation for why God's relationship with creation should be understood as a covenant. According to him, the term "covenant" first appears in the OT in Genesis 6:18. Interestingly, in describing God's covenant with Noah, the author of Genesis chose the verb *heqim* ("to establish a covenant") rather than the verb *krt* ("to cut a covenant"), which is typically employed to portray the initiation of a covenant (cf. Gen. 15:18; 21:27, 32; Exod. 23:32; etc.). He claims this verb choice is not incidental; it implies that God's covenant with Noah (Gen. 6:18) is not a newly initiated covenant[3] but a reestablishment of the old covenant, which had already existed, namely, God's covenant with creation.[4] His claim is substantiated in the other uses of *heqim* in Genesis 17:7, 21; Exodus 6:4; Deuteronomy 8:18; etc.

Several passages in Scripture directly refer to creation as a covenantal event. For example, Job 5:19–22 directly refers to the covenant with creation. Additionally, the prophet Hosea mentions God's covenant when he says, "I will make for you a covenant on that day with the wild animals, the birds of the air, and the creeping things of the

1. "Chapter VII of God's Covenant with Man," *Westminster Confession of Faith*, Briarwood Presbyterian Church, PCA, https://briarwood.org/resources/westminster-confession-of-faith/chapter-vii-of-gods-covenant-with-man/.

2. For a similar claim, see Spykman, *Reformational Theology*, 259–65; Kline, *By Oath Consigned*.

3. Dumbrell, *Covenant and Creation*, 20–33.

4. Dumbrell, *Covenant and Creation*, 32.

ground" (Hos. 2:18),[5] reminiscing about the creation story and Noah's covenant. Likewise, Psalms 3:9–22 and 89:19–37 compare the firmness of God's covenant with David and Levitical priests to God's "covenant with the day and night." Similarly, Jeremiah 31:35–36 states that the sincerity of God's promise to Israel is as firm as his sustenance of the natural order of creation.[6] All these references show that creation is God's covenantal work and that God maintains its order through God's covenantal fidelity.

The ordering of the universe in Genesis 1 signifies a covenantal underpinning of creation. The creation story reveals the patterns and motifs that typically characterize the covenant: ordering or righting of things through separating and binding. The first three days of God's creation consist in the repeated ordering acts of God that set up the boundaries among different entities, forces, and structures, while the last three days fill it with all kinds of creatures. An orderly and harmonious creation emerges step-by-step as God rules over chaotic and disorderly forces. Through differentiation and binding, God is ordering by putting all things right. God assigns and fills each realm with living creatures and distributes dominion (including rights and responsibilities). The assignment and distribution of spaces become the precondition for the survival and flourishing of all creatures. God's orderly work has the effect of turning a disordered chaos into a harmonious cosmos. Establishing the order through differentiating and fettering is a typical covenantal motif.[7]

> Despite the mystery and virility, Genesis 1 is really about order. Chaos is untangled into light and darkness, inchoate ground is divided into water and land, and a firmament is erected to hold the rainstorms above at safe distance from the ground water below. Most of the language is about separating and dividing, like the task of one doing laundry. . . . It takes three days to create earth's spaces and three days to fill them with correlating animate and inanimate creatures. . . . Every day fits the scheme. And poetic repetition of phrases like, "It was good" infuse Genesis 1's spatial proportion with a moral aesthetic.[8]

The rhythm, constancy, and regularity of the natural order are the result of God's covenant with creation. Likewise, in correlation with the physical order, Genesis 1

5. Unless otherwise indicated, Scripture quotations in this book come from the New Revised Standard Version.

6. "Thus says the LORD, / who gives the sun for light by day / and the fixed order of the moon and the stars for light by night, / who stirs up the sea so that its waves roar— / the LORD of hosts is his name: / If this fixed order were ever to cease / from my presence, says the LORD, / then also the offspring of Israel would cease / to be a nation before me forever."

7. Elazar, *Covenant and Polity in Biblical Israel*, 44, 65, 101.

8. Lilly, "Developing a Moral Vision for Climate Change."

implies that a certain moral order is embedded in God's creation, testifying to the integrity and moral coherence of God's creation. Mary Douglas comments, "Being moral would mean being in alignment with the universe, working with the laws of creation, which manifest the mind of God."[9] This motif of the covenantal ordering of creation appears in wisdom literature and in the prophets as well. This order serves as the stabilizing force and the moral reference point of human activities.

As the opening story of the Bible, the creation covenant has a profound ethical meaning and profound implications. It is more than cosmogony (the birth of the world), as it touches nature, humans, family, and economy in their intersections. Importantly, the creation covenant has profound ecological implications for our global society and the planet today, which faces looming threats from global warming, pollution, and water shortage—all human-made ecological disasters based on a myopic anthropocentric worldview of the West. It counters this worldview by presenting creation as the default, antecedent community for all creatures and all human communities. As Isaiah's eschatological vision of shalom portrays (Isa. 11:6–9), creation constitutes a single moral community under God in which every living creature is a member with certain rights.

The covenantal character of creation becomes even clearer with God's covenant with Adam.[10] Covenantal patterns and motifs are pervasive in Genesis 1–2, which discloses the typical covenantal pattern (differentiating and fettering), premises (unity in diversity), and motifs (sonship, moral obligations, and rest).[11] Genesis 2 depicts Adam as the archetypal representative of humanity, namely, God's covenantal partner. Made in the image of God (which indicates sonship), Adam is endowed both with the power to represent God to the rest of creation and the responsibility to care for creation. Although God is the ruler of creation, God yields and grants space for humanity as partners in God's ongoing organizing of creation. In a pattern similar to the differentiation of the spaces and dominions of the cosmos in the first three days, God sets the moral boundary for human freedom/power and responsibility by placing a stricture on human behavior. The tree of knowledge symbolizes the boundary of human power in relation to God (the specific term of relationship between God and humanity), while the tree of life (eternal life) points

9. Mary Douglas, *Leviticus as Literature*, 44.

10. Thomas E. McComiskey writes: "In the relationship that God established with mankind and the created world, certain strictures were placed on creation that obtain to this day. Thus the emphasis on 'creation' rather than 'works' in the mere designation *covenant of creation* is more consonant with the intent of the context. Adam thus functioned as a representative of all mankind as he received the announcement of the divine disposition." McComiskey, *The Covenants of Promise*, 220. Also see Vogels, *God's Universal Covenant*; Galloway, "Creation and Covenant," 108–18.

11. Christopher Baker, *Covenant and Liberation*, 46.

toward the future promise of blessings and reward for Adam's covenantal faithfulness. Violation of the stipulation leads to death, while obedience leads to eternal life and Sabbath—peace and harmony in creation (Gen. 1:26). Even more importantly, Hosea 6:7 offers a direct reference to Adam's covenant ("Like Adam they transgressed the covenant; / there they dealt faithlessly with me"), which compares the apostasy of Israel to Adam's disobedience in Eden and speaks of both incidents in terms of a breach of covenant.

Furthermore, Genesis portrays the relationship between Adam and Eve in a typically covenantal framework. God created them as differentiated persons (male and female) in unity, whose relationship was characterized by freedom, equality, reciprocity, and union (Gen. 2:23)—unity in diversity and diversity in unity, reflecting the triune life of God.

God's covenant with Adam becomes further evident in light of the close typological continuity and parallel pattern between the creation story and Noah's story. The creation mandate reappears in Noah's covenant (Gen. 9:6–7);[12] typical covenantal motifs (such as kingship, rest, and obligations) are found in the creation story (Gen. 2:16–17) and then repeated in Noah's story.

Genesis 1–3 serves as a classic, covenantally oriented typology of salvation history. As much as the positive metaphors of covenant, such as sonship and blessings, are present, the negative metaphors of the covenant—temptation, disobedience, broken relationship, and, finally, expulsion from the garden—are also found there. These are repeated throughout the OT in the apostasy, disobedience, disloyalty, and exile of Israel. All these observations show that the idea of God's covenant with creation/Adam is not far-fetched at all; it is consistent with the other covenants in the Bible in pattern, logic, and moral characteristics.[13] As we will discuss in chapter 3, the patterns of gift-task, reciprocity, and remembrance-hope are notable here.

The covenant with creation/Adam is foundational and normative for the subsequent covenants, as it sets the plot and the typological pattern and gives impetus for the rest of salvation history. The subsequent biblical covenants, in the final analysis, take the creation covenant as their reference point. They point toward the restoration of the covenant of creation/Adam. In other words, the subsequent covenants are God's rescue operations to fix the negative consequences caused by human disobedience.

The linking of covenant and creation runs deep throughout the entirety of Scripture, rendering a universalistic scope and impetus as well as a transcendental moral

12. "When Gen 8:22–9:7 is taken as a prelude to the covenantal promise of 9:8–17, the latter has clear verbal connections with the story of creation, especially as in Gen 1 (cf. 9:1 and 1:28; 9:2–3 and 1:29; 9:10 and 1:20–25)." McConville, "בְּרִית," 749.

13. Dumbrell, *Covenant and Creation*, 33–39.

ground to its narratives and moral teachings.[14] This cosmic covenant is the default mode of human existence. Every human social arrangement and structure in history is circumscribed by this cosmic (universal) covenant of creation. Human society cannot override or contravene this covenant. There is no redemption without the redemption of creation; for redemption is creation restored.

Covenant with Noah

Genesis 6 describes the human moral condition after the Fall. Corruption and violence reached their peaks as humans constantly threatened God's order to the extent that the integrity of creation was compromised (Gen. 6:5, 11–12). The flood was God's intervention to save humanity from self-destruction as well as God's judgment against sin. God ordered Noah to build the ark, and he responded in obedience.

After the flood receded, God established a covenant with Noah, his family, other creatures, and the earth itself. Noah's covenant is closely tied with the creation covenant. Like the creation covenant, Noah's covenant is a universal covenant of God that concerns all creatures and creation; it is explicitly ecological in nature, thus checking the anthropocentrism and ethnocentrism often associated with other covenants in the OT.

Several crucial creational motifs are reiterated in Noah's story: Noah represents the head of humanity, as Adam did; he was given the same creation mandate (Gen. 8:17); and God commanded Noah to steward all species, which is reminiscent of Adam's task in the garden (Gen. 9:1–7). As Noah was the symbol of humanity, the ark was a microcosmic symbol of Eden—a carrier of God's promise and blessings and hope for the creation. God's covenant with Noah was intended to restore the basic order of creation (threatened by human sin).

What is notable and ecologically important is that God specified nonhuman creatures and the earth as God's covenant partners, reiterating this reality four times (Gen. 9:15–17).[15] God promised to protect Noah and his dependents (i.e., future humanity), other creatures, and the earth from the instability of the natural order. To ease the fear and anxiety of Noah, God gave a rainbow as a sign of God's fidelity. Through the covenant with Noah, creation and humanity received another chance, and the goodness of creation and God's firm commitment to its well-being were reaffirmed.

14. For example, in Leviticus, God's command to be holy is aligned with the laws of creation, which involve respecting a proper, rightful place for animals and plants; to violate their places is declared profane. Ellen F. Davis, *Scripture, Culture, and Agriculture*, 94–95.

15. "I will make for you a covenant on that day with the wild animals, the birds of the air, and the creeping things of the ground; and I will abolish the bow, the sword, and war from the land; and I will make you lie down in safety" (Hos. 2:18).

In terms of its moral intention and nature, Noah's covenant is often called the covenant of preservation. It preserved the earth and humanity from the raging torrents of the flood and the surging sea; it protected humanity from self-destruction due to violence and corruption; and it preserved animals from human aggression. Herman Bavinck is helpful in elaborating the ethos of preservation in Noah's covenant: "It limits the curse on the earth; it checks nature and curbs its destructive power; the awesome violence of water is reined in; a regular alternation of season is introduced. The whole of the irrational world of nature is subjected to ordinances that are anchored in God's covenant."[16]

Noah's covenant lays out more clearly circumscribed moral parameters for humans in relating to others and animals, with a new focus on violence. Noah's covenant also reveals God's adjustment to a changed human condition (violent passion and temperament) following the Fall (Gen. 8:21, "the inclination of the human heart is evil from youth"). Humans had become a serious threat both to fellow humans and to animals (Gen. 9:2). One example of a moral adjustment is God permitting human consumption of animal flesh, but with a clear restriction on the consumption of blood (9:3–4). God reemphasizes the sanctity of human life by warning of retribution against anyone who violates it (9:5–6). However, the message of Noah's covenant should not be interpreted as anthropocentric. The event of the ark (hosting all living creatures there) and God's reiteration of a covenantal relationship with animals had the effect of reminding Noah and his offspring (who have now become a threat to other species) of the sanctity of all living creatures and the earth by saying that they too live in a covenantal relationship with God. Noah's covenant delicately balances the reality of sin with God's original intention for creation. It adjusts God's laws to a new situation of human rebellion and sinfulness. The basic sanctity of both creation (including nonhuman creatures) and human life (the *imago Dei*) was assured again, despite the changed condition of life after the Fall and God's judgment.

Although it often receives less attention than other covenants in Scripture, Noah's covenant is extremely important for Christian social ethics. It offers a theological ground for common grace, which God makes available to all human beings despite sin. God's common grace operates to preserve the basic natural order of creation (e.g., seasonal rhythms and stability, seedtime and harvest), the basic rights of humanity, and the life of animals from further deterioration, violence, and abuse. Until the final consummation of creation in the eschaton, "Noah's covenant is the pivot around" which God's preserving work of justice revolves.[17] As an eternal covenant, it

16. Bavinck, *Reformed Dogmatics*, 3:218.

17. Dell, "Covenant and Creation in Relationship," 131.

still has a binding moral power over all of humanity, including Christians. As we will discuss later, technically speaking, Christians live simultaneously under the binding authorities of the Noachian covenant and the new covenant of Jesus, and this doubling-binding nature is crucial to properly understand the scope and parameters of Christian social ethics (chap. 11).

Covenant with Abraham

God made covenants with Abraham twice, in Genesis 15:18 and in 17:2.[18] If Noah's covenant is a kind of a safety-net covenant that intended to preserve creation from further deterioration, then Abraham's covenant indicates God's initiative of redemption that counters human depravity and sin in order to restore the brokenness of creation. God's response to the global plight of sin at the tower of Babel was the global blessing of Abraham for all of humanity:[19] Abraham's covenant is multidimensional in its meaning and quite comprehensive in its scope. It encompasses a nation (Israel), ecology (the land), and the global community (blessing to the nations).

Abraham's story also has some resonance with the creation story. Just as chaos, darkness, confusion, corruption, and violence were in the background of the creation covenant, the chaos and confusion following the collapse of the tower of Babel (Gen. 11) serve as the context for Abraham's election and calling. Instead of punishing humanity in a catastrophic way as he did in Noah's time, God calls Abraham, another Adamic figure (type), to do something new. God's blessings and promises to Abraham included flourishing (both descendants and fame), the gift of the land (as opposed to the expulsion from Eden), and the restoration of all peoples (as opposed to their scattering after Babel).

Creation mandates are repeated in this covenant. As Adam was given the garden to tend, Abraham was promised a new garden (Canaan) where he would fulfill God's initial blessings for humanity: land, seed, a blessing to be fruitful and multiply, and a blessing to the nations by undoing the curses of Adam in Genesis 3—toil of labor, pain of childbirth, and physical death. As Adam had been created in the barren soil and placed into the garden of Eden (Gen. 2:4–15), so too was Abraham sent from his native land to Canaan. Now Canaan is God's new Eden, just as Abraham is God's new Adam. Overall, Abraham remained faithful to God's covenant, despite his occasional mistakes and weaknesses. Accordingly, Abraham was later presented

18. Gen. 22:16–18 also ratifies the covenant in Gen. 17 through God's oath. However, God's initial calling already has a covenantal nature. God commands Abraham to go to Canaan, together with the promises of rich blessings, and Abram responds to God.

19. Christopher Wright, *Old Testament Ethics*, 49.

as a universal example of faith and obedience for future believers. God's redemptive plan for humanity and God's covenant continue across generations, from Abraham to Isaac, to Jacob, and later to Israel through Moses.

Covenant with Israel: The Sinai Covenant

Among all the biblical covenants, the Sinai covenant occupies a special place. It provides the most detailed ritualistic and ethical instructions and directives. It is at the heart of the Torah (the first five books of the Bible), a collection of stories leading to the Sinai covenant, and its expositions and commentaries. Compared to other biblical covenants, the Sinai covenant offers the most systematic explication of covenant and its requirements through clearly delineated stipulations (the Ten Commandments and covenantal codes, statutes, and ordinances) and elaborate rituals binding Israel as God's covenantal partner in every realm of its life. In this covenant, God promises to make Israel his special possession among the peoples—a kingdom of priests and a holy nation to the world.

This covenant indicates a partial fulfillment of God's covenant with Abraham (a great nation) and continues Abraham's calling (to be a blessing to the nations) through Israel on a far more extensive and broader scale, namely, as a covenanted people and nation. Like Abraham, Israel represents a restored humanity. Israel was called to be a paradigmatic model of a new community for other nations that embodies God's compassion, righteousness, and justice in the entirety of its social life.[20] They were expected to display what a redeemed people would look like as "a light to the nations" that shines forth God's glory and as "a priestly kingdom" to which all other nations come and learn God's ways. It was required to become a model for other nations not only in its piety, religious practices, or moral life but also in its entire social system and institutions (family, law, economy, politics, etc.). The moral quality of Israel's personal and social life mattered to God because Israel, as a community (a collective entity), was to be the vessel of God's revelation and blessing to all the nations.

The Sinai covenant first appears in Exodus 19 through 24, chapters that detail the covenantal ceremony at Mount Sinai. If we examine the narrative structure of the Sinai covenant, we see the covenanting event taking place against the immediate historical background of God's deliverance of the people of Israel from Egypt. The covenant making begins with a historical prologue—the narration of God's past deliverance: "I am the Lord, your God, who brought you out of the land of Egypt" (Exod. 20:2). The prologue offers the historical context of the covenantal relation-

20. Christopher Wright, *Old Testament Ethics*, 62–63.

ship that is about to be instituted. It places the subsequent commands, laws, and ordinances in their proper historical and theological contexts. In addition, it has the effect of embedding the rules and norms in the relational, narrative framework.

The Ten Commandments are related to the creation covenant (and the Noachian covenant); while they were given to Israelites, who experienced YHWH's redemption, their moral message was universal because they describe God's expectation and moral demand for humanity, with Israelites as the representative.[21] As "abiding moral laws,"[22] the Ten Commandments disclose God's plan and will for humanity in a more detailed manner than the creation covenant and the Noachian covenant.

There are two parts to the Ten Commandments, indicated by two tablets: the first tablet has to do with worship of God, while the second has to do with the ethical life of the people of God in community. The very structure of the Ten Commandments shows the unity and order between worship and ethics in the covenantal life of Israel. Denoted in the same document, worship and ethics can be understood as inseparable in Israel's life. This structure and order imply that ethical life is rooted in Israel's relationship with God (embodied and practiced in worship). At the same time, their moral sanctification is a crucial barometer of the state of the people's internal (spiritual) relationship with God. That is, those who love God and worship him genuinely are to live uprightly and justly.[23] Through their worship and moral life, their covenant with God was renewed and reenacted in everyday life. The Ten Commandments teach what the pious, righteous, and just life should be—piety toward God and justice toward other human beings.[24] Both piety and justice are indispensable for the building of a community.

In Israel's life, the Sinai covenant operated as a comprehensive moral framework within which the Ten Commandments served as the summary of the moral law and the constitution of Israel as a unified political body. Detailed moral demands were stipulated through numerous other statutes and ordinances. Covenant regulated and guided every aspect of Israel's life from worship to family, from economics to agriculture, and from tribal politics to international relationships. Every member of the community believed that he or she was individually covenanted with God; thus no activity was exempt from the obligations specified by the covenant.

21. Smedes, *Mere Morality*, 6–10. This claim is not far-fetched because similar laws/commandments, the fifth through tenth commandments in particular, are found across many other ancient societies with variations.

22. Smedes, *Mere Morality*, 10.

23. Wright notes: "there was . . . an inseparable link between the kind of society Israel was (or was supposed to be) and the character of the God they worshipped." Christopher Wright, *Old Testament Ethics*, 58.

24. Althusius, *Politica*, 142.

Covenantal spirituality was expressed in rituals and spiritual practices as well as in laws and commandments. In the Torah, Leviticus details the spiritual practices that covenant requires. Israelites were required to exercise covenantal faithfulness in every domain and every aspect of their lives—in their eating (selecting proper animals that are properly slaughtered), in their treatment of strangers, in their relationships to the land and to neighbors, and in their ordering of time (Sabbath).

Torah offers numerous stipulations that guide and regulate sacrificial rituals (Lev. 24:3–8), covenantal meals (Lev. 24:9–11), the erection of the tabernacle (Exod. 25–27; 35–40), and the consecration of Aaron and his sons as priests (Exod. 28–29).[25] The Covenant Code is an application of the fundamental principles of the Ten Commandments to specific matters of daily conduct. The Covenant Code seeks to make the principle of the Ten Commandments practical by distinguishing various moral situations in which the principle is applied.[26] It illustrates in detail what the way of life under God's covenant should look like. Such extensive application indicates the seriousness with which Israel took the covenant.

Throughout the rest of the OT, the exodus story and the Sinai covenant consistently serve as a key metaphor and a central moral reference point for Israel by which Israel's religious and social practices are inspired and critically examined. The Ten Commandments and the Covenant Code serve as a plumb line not only for Israel's moral actions but also for the behavior of other nations.[27]

For example, the prophets relied on the Mosaic covenant in their social criticism in parallel with the Torah law, a connection reminiscent of Deuteronomy (cf. Deut. 31:26).[28] Specifically, the prophets charged the people's sins and apostasy by referring back to the Mosaic laws, especially the Ten Commandments.[29] They passionately pointed out the repeated human failures to live up to their promises. Amos, Hosea, Isaiah, and Jeremiah presented stinging indictments against the people of Israel for their breach of covenant with God. The list of violations included idolatry, sexual promiscuity, oppression of the poor, and violence. They alerted the people that neither the temple and its rituals nor biological lineage would protect Israel, but only their covenant fidelity to God and God's order. The prophets warned their contemporaries about the moral complacency and self-righteousness through which

25. McConville, "בְּרִית," 749.

26. Flanders, Crapps, and Smith, *The People of the Covenant*, 203.

27. "And I will make justice the line, / and righteousness the plummet; / hail will sweep away the refuge of lies, / and waters will overwhelm the shelter" (Isa. 28:17).

28. McConville, "בְּרִית," 751.

29. In their social criticism, the Hebrew prophets relied on the election traditions (Amos 2:9–11; 3:2), certain of the Mosaic laws (Amos 2:7–8; cf. Lev. 18:8, 15; 20:11–12; Deut. 24:12–13), and the covenantal curses (Amos 4:6–10; cf. Deut. 28:21–22, 24).

they distorted God's election into an unconditional guarantee of their security and protection while ignoring their obligations and loyalty to God's law—especially the violation of the rights of the poor, the orphans, and the widows. They called them to return to the Lord from idolatry and follow the ways of justice and righteousness stipulated by the covenant. Their rhetoric frequently employed the "lawsuit pattern" in which God calls Israel into a kind of legal tribunal (Hos. 4:1–3 and Mic. 6:1–5).[30]

The prophets used the Sinai covenant as the moral frame of reference for their criticism, assessing major historical events in terms of moral cause and effect. In light of the covenant, they warned that apostasy, idolatry, injustice, and social exploitation would invite God's punishment. For example, Isaiah, Jeremiah, and Ezekiel claimed that the destruction of the temple and the captivity occurred because Israel violated the covenantal promises. Given Israel's violation of the covenant, it was inevitable and sensible for God to punish Israel. However, in light of God's boundless grace, they never forgot to preach the hope for restoration, despite Israel's sin of apostasy and injustice, and God's judgment of them.

Covenant with David

The Davidic covenant is found in 2 Samuel 7, established between God and David and his descendants with the promise that God would continue the lineage of his kingship through him and his offspring.[31] Interestingly, it is a reversal of the narrative trajectory of the Bible, as it moves from Israel (a collective body) to David (an individual king).[32] One may wonder why the Davidic covenant is necessary in addition to the Sinai covenant when God's covenants with the patriarchs are partly fulfilled (absorbed) in the Sinai covenant.

One cannot understand the meaning of David's covenant without understanding the changed political and social contexts of Israel. David's covenant is a response to a developing monarchy after the era of the judges: "The purpose of the covenant with David . . . was to engraft the developing monarchy into the existing Israelite covenantal structure. To this extent, the Davidic covenant is a modification of the Sinai Covenant, and is, as we shall see, presented as being within the process of the fulfillment of the Abrahamic covenant."[33]

30. McConville, "בְּרִית," 751.

31. The Davidic covenant is similar to the Abrahamic covenant in that its efficacy extends to the descendants beyond David.

32. Delbert R. Hillers comments: "If the older [Sinai] covenant spoke of blessings for obedience and curses for disobedience on the part of all Israel, this covenant now strikes the motif that Israel's history will henceforth be determined by the character of her king." Hillers, *Covenant*, 112.

33. Dumbrell, *Covenant and Creation*, 127.

With the Davidic covenant, Israel is now placed in a different theological framework. It is an implicit understanding of the Bible that the rise of monarchy indicated a political failure of the Sinai covenantal project (which envisioned a confederal model among the twelve tribes rather than a hierarchical monarchy), and that the Davidic covenant is God's adjustment to Israel's failure. Instead of counting on the precarious and fragile faith of Israel, God now takes David as his primary covenant partner to achieve God's purpose; "[God's] bond to the people of Israel is through this [Davidic] line of monarchs."[34] God is now determined to carry out God's plan through David and his lineage, rather than through the people of Israel; in God's eyes, David represents the people of Israel.

David, like Abraham, is considered to be a symbol (type) of covenantal loyalty, as 1 and 2 Kings continuously refer to him as a faithful covenantal exemplar for all other kings of Judah. Through David, a reliable figure is provided that pleases God's heart and thus allows the covenantal relationship to continue. God promised him and his descendants an eternal blessing, and Israel could now safely participate in God's blessings on the basis of God's promise to David.[35]

Unfortunately, the history of covenant under David's offspring, the kings of Judah, was not a happy one either. The covenant did not prevent the collapse of Judah. Consequently, David's covenant underwent further theological modifications in the exilic and postexilic periods, which we examine below.

The New Covenant in Isaiah, Jeremiah, and Ezekiel

With the destruction of Judah in 587 BC and the subsequent exile, the biblical drama of covenant faced another turning point: it shifted from a national covenant (Israel) to a universal covenant with a strong eschatological tone. The exile was a shocking, traumatic event for Israel in every aspect—politically, economically, culturally, and theologically. The exile forced them to undergo a deep soul-searching, asking of their faith fundamental questions: How were they to understand the covenant between God and Israel in the exile when the covenant seemed utterly broken and when the temple, Jerusalem, and the land—the most eminent covenantal symbols—were all gone? A radical theological recalibration was necessary if the idea of covenant were to remain relevant for understanding Israel's identity as the people of God.

A shared recognition emerged that since Israel had broken the covenant, God would have to decide whether the covenant continued or not. In addition, there was a deep awareness of the indescribable depth of human depravity—idolatry, injus-

34. Hillers, *Covenant*, 117.

35. Oswalt, *The Book of Isaiah*, 438.

tice, and violence—that made human covenantal partnership with God no longer conceivable. Prophets searched for new theological options to address the depth of human sinfulness. Subsequent theological responses were to reimagine the covenant in radically different terms by shifting the focus of the covenant toward God's side—God's unconditional love, mercy, and faithfulness that transcend human depravity. Israelites now put their entire hope in God's unfailing love out of their belief that God would not desert God's people despite their sinfulness and disobedience, and that God would grant the Israelites a new beginning after the judgment. This rude awakening led to the reimagination of covenant itself.

The prophets dreamed of a future time when the covenant would no longer be broken and defiled by disobedience. They put their hope completely in God's new initiative and fidelity in forming a new covenant that would transcend human failure.[36] This new theological reconstruction was most evident in the prophetic ministry of Jeremiah, Ezekiel, and Isaiah. They carefully studied and knitted together previous covenants (especially the Abrahamic, Sinai, and Davidic covenants) and developed a new idea of the covenant. These prophets revised and reconstructed biblical motifs and themes such as the new exodus, restoration, creation, the call to address spiritual concerns, and the needs of the community in exile. For example, they reinterpreted the Davidic covenant because David was the ideal, morally paradigmatic figure in Israel's history. He was understood as a type (prefiguration) of the Messiah—the symbol of a high political hope for Israel,[37] who would fulfill the covenantal obligations on behalf of humanity. Israel in the exile believed that "on the foundation of the Davidic house, the new community of the return [would] take shape."[38]

Jeremiah and Ezekiel introduced a radically novel understanding of the covenant—"the new covenant."[39] The new covenant has at least two unparalleled characteristics. First, it has a supreme efficacy on human life, as the metaphor "circumcision of the hearts" indicates. God's law is no longer external to the people but is written on the heart of each individual, thus guaranteeing an intimate, harmonious moral relationship between God and each person. This implies that human obedience is

36. Hahn, "Covenant in the Old and New Testaments," 270.

37. Dumbrell, *Covenant and Creation*, 162.

38. Dumbrell, *Covenant and Creation*, 161. For example, Isaiah prophesied that the Prince of Peace would reign from the throne of David (9:6–7), and he introduced the idea of the suffering servant as "the agent and guarantor of God's covenant for Israel and nations." Rata, "Covenant," 104. One finds a similar Davidic motif in Jeremiah (Jer. 23:5–6; 33:15–26), Ezekiel (Ezek. 34; 37), and the Minor Prophets.

39. Instead of "new covenant," Isaiah uses the term "covenant of peace" or "everlasting covenant" (55:3; 61:8).

voluntary, motivated through God's intimate personal presence, and for the first time in history, humans are able to fulfill their covenantal responsibilities.

Second, the new covenant is eschatological; its application moves beyond the boundary of Israel, anticipating universal peace, justice, and rest in a manner that is consistent with the original creational order (Jer. 31:35–37). The new covenant is the "everlasting covenant." It does not fail, and the reign of God will finally be completed through it. It is encompassing because the knowledge of God will be universal, and through this covenant creation, Israel, and gentiles will form one covenantal community.[40] In addition, it anticipates the advent of shalom: "[The new covenant] will usher in the period that will be characterized by the absence of divine wrath. The peace aspect of this covenant is more than just the absence of war or hostility; it also has the connotation of the sum total of covenant blessing."[41] Despite its eschatological nature, the new covenant is neither ahistorical nor suprahistorical; it is historically achieved through God's faithfulness in history while representing a comprehensive solution to the human predicament.

Covenant in the Wisdom Literature

One may wonder how the idea of covenant is associated with wisdom literature in the Bible, because the term "covenant" is found there the least among biblical genres.[42] Proverbs, Job, and Ecclesiastes do not mention Israel's election, covenant rituals or rules, the land of Israel, or even the individual names of people or places associated with the covenant. However, the concept and premises of covenant are assumed and continue to operate in this literature in a subtle way, forming its background worldview. Jamie Grant claims: "Literary interaction is often much more subtle than the simple repetition of a word or words. Covenant may not be the focus of attention in the [wisdom literature], but the concept of covenant subtly influences the didactic thrust of the Wisdom books and if we are unaware of this interaction then we skew the message of these books."[43]

A few examples will suffice. Among the wisdom literature, the book of Proverbs relies on Solomon, David's son, as its major source of moral authority. This reveals an awareness of God's covenant with David and his lineage. Likewise, the book of Job is rich with covenantal themes and motifs that are essential to its moral message. Specifically, the book depicts the relationship between God and Job in covenantal

40. Jocz, *The Covenant*, 238–39.

41. Rata, "Covenant," 103.

42. There are two references to covenant in Job, one in Proverbs, but none at all in Ecclesiastes.

43. J. A. Grant, "Wisdom and Covenant: Revisiting Zimmerli," 109.

terms: "the description of Job's 'blamelessness,' along with the blessings and curses which he experiences produce a plausible case for viewing the bond between Job and Yahweh as a covenantal one."[44] The book is plotted as a grand test on the covenantal fidelity of Job. Satan questions the very nature of the relationship between God and Job, and he is allowed to test how far Job's relationship with God can go despite Job's calamities and misfortunes. Job defends his integrity against his friends' false accusations of his unfaithfulness. "The root of Job's 'complaint' then is that he views himself as one who apparently has not been treated fairly by God, according to the terms of the covenant."[45] Job's lamentation and protest toward God are typical characteristics of a covenantal relationship built upon communicative action (see chap. 3 below).

The covenantal nature of the wisdom literature becomes more evident when we examine these books in light of the covenants with creation/Adam and Noah. Although creation stories in these works (e.g., Prov. 8) are different from those of Genesis, they address the same themes: creation, order, fidelity, wisdom, and humanity's place in creation. The wisdom books stress the stability of the cosmos, the basic integrity of creation, and the predictability of the natural order as signs of God's fidelity to the creation. That is, a certain cosmic moral order is embedded in the regularity of nature, which is critical for human well-being.

The above observation demonstrates that wisdom is a vehicle for grasping this order, and it does not have to come directly through God's supernatural revelation but is universally available for careful human observation and thoughtful reflection. There is no contradiction between "the cosmic and social order of justice set forth by the creator and sustainer of reality, which serves as the basis of the shared communal life. All human beings participate in the cosmic social order."[46]

While the emphases of the wisdom literature and the covenantal texts are often contrasted (such as the election of Israel versus universal humanity, and special revelation versus general revelation), the two genres share the same premises: first, that God is the creator, establisher, and preserver of the universal order; and second, that though this creational order is inscrutable, it is not automatically given but is sustained by God's faithfulness because God is covenantally committed to it. Duane Garrett nicely sums up the relationship: "The fear of God, the rejection of temptations to easy gratification, and the acknowledgment that the world is God's creation are the foundations. The theological presuppositions in wisdom are the same as those of the covenantal texts. Covenant and wisdom are therefore in theological agreement but belong to different genres and have distinct purposes."[47]

44. Rogland, "The Covenant in the Book of Job," 55.
45. Rogland, "The Covenant in the Book of Job," 55.
46. Perdue, *Wisdom Literature*, 29.
47. Garrett, *Proverbs, Ecclesiastes, and Song of Songs*, 56.

Moreover, these literatures share the same moral messages with the Sinai covenant: the fear of God, humanity's dependence on God, and the emphasis on social justice.[48] Many passages in the Bible link Israel with the rest of creation. For example, Deuteronomy 4:6 connects the law and proverbs.[49] Hosea and Jeremiah also remind Israel of the permanence of God's *hesed* in reference to the natural order. While the Sinai covenant focuses on the particularity of Israel, it never loses the purpose and mission of Israel for the rest of humanity. It reminds Israel (and the church) that God is not a parochial God but is the maker of heaven and earth and the ruler of all lives. In other words, despite their different emphases, in an important way, wisdom literature complements covenantal literature.[50] By doing so, it vastly expands the horizon and applicability of covenant. Importantly for our project, by adding a cosmic scope, public relevance, and transcultural pertinence, the covenantal themes found in the wisdom literature offer important moral resources for Christian public theology and social ethics (see chaps. 4, 11, 12).

Summary

Our brief survey shows how covenant is central to the biblical drama of the OT, constituting its plot and story line. Its scope is quite comprehensive, as it is found across diverse genres of the OT, not only in the revelatory documents of Israel, but also in wisdom literature in general. We also see how its key patterns and motifs are repeated across different covenants and their related stories: the use of covenant as God's organizing mechanism, God's ongoing initiative despite human failures, consistent patterns of differentiation binding, rule making in covenants, and emphasis on human moral response and fidelity.

Having surveyed major covenants in the OT, we now turn our focus to the new covenant of Jesus. The next chapter will discuss how the NT also unfolds under the same divine drama set off in the OT but expands and intensifies its patterns and types in the eschatological context of God's reign in Jesus Christ.

48. J. A. Grant, "Wisdom and Covenant," in *Dictionary of the Old Testament Wisdom, Poetry and Writings*, 858–63.

49. Cf. Deut. 10:12–13.

50. Ps. 8 claims that a human being is the crown of creation. However, Job and Ecclesiastes challenge this anthropocentric assumption by suggesting that there is nothing special about humanity, and humans are no better than other creatures.

CHAPTER 2

The New Covenant of Jesus Christ

> The Bible is not flat; Christ is its peak and its center. No moral issue should be addressed apart from consideration of the meaning of Jesus Christ for reflection on that issue.
>
> —Glen Stassen and David Gushee, *Kingdom Ethics*

Among many covenants of Scripture, the new covenant of Jesus constitutes the foundation of the Christian spiritual and moral life. It distinctively shapes and guides Christian ethics, although many Christians do not recognize it. In fact, most Christian ethicists, including the Reformed ones, have not paid close attention to the covenantal matrix of Jesus's ministry and teachings, and have thus failed to fully understand the scope, ethical meanings, and implications of his new covenant in its relationship to the entirety of Jesus's life and ministry.

This chapter begins with a short overview of the covenantal background and content of Jesus's life, ministry, and teachings, and then studies the new covenant, asking: What is the new covenant of Jesus? How is it related to the OT covenants? How is it similar to and different from them? What does it mean that the new covenant is the climax of the biblical covenants?

My objective is to explain the moral nature and features of the new covenant and what they mean for the Christian moral life.

The Covenantal Background of the NT

Unlike the proliferation of covenant language in the OT, the NT contains only thirty-three references to covenant. Moreover, the Synoptic Gospels seldom discuss it. However, the NT presupposes the OT and its covenantal drama, plot, and theological perspective in interpreting Jesus's birth, life, teaching, death, resurrection, and the ministry of the early church, though often without explicitly naming it or elaborating on it.[1] Major theological themes and motifs of the NT—such as God's reign, righteousness, election, reconciliation, atonement, and church—cannot be properly understood without acknowledging their underlying covenantal presuppositions.

According to biblical scholars, covenant was a dominant theological motif among the Jews during the Second Temple period,[2] constituting the religious worldview, practices, and thought patterns of Jews living in Jesus's time.[3] Under the harsh and oppressive rule of the Romans, Jesus, his disciples, and even his contemporaries, the pseudomessiahs, perceived themselves as exiles while still inhabiting the territory of the promised land. Their eschatological vision awaited the full restoration of Israel and its return from said exile. They prayed for God's active intervention in history in order to liberate his people.[4]

This collective viewpoint of Jewish hopes and expectations was expressed in the framework of the exodus tradition that shaped their imaginations, religious behaviors, and literature.[5]

Jesus was no exception. Firmly standing within the exodus-Sinai tradition he inherited, he preached the reign of God and built a new community around him. The norms of justice, mercy, nonviolence, and faith, which Jesus emphasized in his parables and moral teachings, were covenantal in nature. He gave himself as the covenantal sacrifice and bond between God and humanity. The climax of Jesus's covenantal action was the cross. A new, inclusive, and egalitarian community was formed around his body as the new covenant (the church). Jesus fulfilled the covenant and has become the new covenant itself. His new covenant is eternally celebrated in the key ritual of Christianity, the Eucharist.

Following Jesus, early Christians interpreted God's deliverance of the people through Jesus with the imagination and language of covenant. They proclaimed

1. Michael Horton says: "The New Testament, by its very designation, is understood as a ratification of this gracious covenant and the inauguration of its new covenant administration, with the apostles as 'ministers of a new covenant' (2 Cor. 3:6)." Horton, *Covenant and Eschatology*, 135.

2. See Sanders, *Paul and Palestinian Judaism*; Gorman, *Inhabiting the Cruciform God*; N. T. Wright, *Paul and the Faithfulness of God*.

3. For example, the idea of election, a core covenantal idea, was at the center of theological debates and conflicts between Jesus (and his followers) and Jewish leaders. The Qumran and early Christian communities believed that they were participating in the "new covenant" that Jeremiah and Ezekiel had promised.

4. N. T. Wright notes that there was "the anguished longing of Israel for her covenant god to come in his power and rule the world in the way he had always intended." N. T. Wright, *Jesus and the Victory of God*, 203.

5. N. T. Wright, *Jesus and the Victory of God*, 155.

Jesus as the promised Messiah and understood themselves as the new Israel.[6] Such self-awareness and identity were forged in covenantal terms and practiced through two distinctive covenantal sacraments: baptism and the Eucharist. They took up prominent covenantal themes and motifs in the OT—such as election, exodus, deliverance, atonement, the people of God, exile, return from exile, suffering servant, and prophetic promises—and reworked and reinterpreted them in light of God's revelation in Jesus Christ.[7] Distinctive Christian identity and practices developed out of these intense covenantal reworkings and reinterpretations.

Among the marks and motifs of the covenant, a covenantal pattern of "promise-fulfillment" is prominent in the NT. Early Christians understood Jesus as the fulfiller of all previous covenants and their promises (the covenants of creation, Noah, Abraham, Moses, David, and the "new covenant" of Jeremiah/Ezekiel). For example, "the repeated stress on promise and fulfillment is a distinctive and foundational motif of Luke-Acts; consequently, Lukan ethics becomes comprehensible only as an aspect of his larger vision for the people of God as the bearers of the fulfilled promise."[8] This pattern is equally prominent in Matthew. For example, Matthew begins his gospel with a genealogy that portrays Jesus as a descendant of Abraham and David, which demonstrates God's fulfillment of God's promises to them. "There are more than a dozen such 'formula quotations' in Matthew."[9]

Similarly, Paul refers to the Abrahamic covenant in claiming that Israel's pledge—to be a light to the nations and God's priestly kingdom—is now realized in the church through Jesus Christ. The Davidic covenant is also important in validating Jesus's messiahship through his identification as a descendant of David. The covenant of Jesus fulfills what the prophets (Isaiah, Jeremiah, Ezekiel, and others) foretold when they took the creation and all nations as the final reference of the covenant in its scope and application. On the other hand, the Epistle to the Hebrews discusses in detail the relationship of Jesus's death and the covenant (Jesus gave himself as

6. Paul Hanson finds an "unbroken continuity" between the Jewish tradition and Jesus in the NT, for example, in the double love commandment; the Lord's Prayer (which was influenced by traditional Jewish prayers); his mission to the Jews and the restoration of Israel symbolized in his calling of the twelve disciples; Paul's presentation of the gentiles as "Abraham's offspring" (Gal. 3:29); Matthew's portrayal of "the early history of Jesus as a recapitulation of the exodus and settlement events, and then presents him as the new Moses"; and so on. Hanson, *The People Called*, 386–87.

7. The apostle Paul's ideas of the righteousness of God, the union with Christ, justification, eschatological hope, and the church take on strong covenantal tones and meanings.

8. Hays, *Moral Vision*, 114. Luke reports that the prophecy of Isaiah (42:6b; 49:6b) is fulfilled now in Jesus (Luke 2:32; Acts 13:47; 26:23): God's purposes of salvation would finally extend to the whole world beyond Israel.

9. Hays, *Moral Vision*, 96.

a sacrificial lamb for the eternal atonement of sin for humanity), while in terms of ethics Jesus Christ fulfilled all the requirements of the law by obeying God and living out the obligations as a covenantal partner of God.

The prevalence of promise-fulfillment typology is found in the fact that various titles of Jesus are related to the previous covenants. Jesus is the new Adam (recapitulating the Genesis story); he is the Messiah King (in the lineage of King David); he is a blessing to the nations (fulfilling Abraham's call and the prophecy of Isaiah); and he brings a radical internal renewal of people, the "circumcision of the hearts" (actualizing the prophecies of Jeremiah and Ezekiel about the new covenant). This also means that the covenant offers a hermeneutical key to studying Jesus's life and ethics.

In light of this observation, it is appropriate to define Jesus's ministry as one of covenantal renewal.[10] After all, the renewing of the covenant is the reapplication, or the recontextualizing, of God's covenant, the Sinai covenant in particular, in a variety of historical contexts.[11] In renewal, the historical events of God's salvation are retold and reappropriated, rules and ritual are revised, and the people of God rededicate themselves to God. Jesus, in his own context, also retold historical events, revised rules and rituals, and rededicated himself and his followers to God.[12] Jesus's covenantal renewal, theologically speaking, was not an ordinary renewal but the final, climactic renewal. Jesus and his disciples eschatologically reapplied the rich, dynamic, and lengthy covenantal tradition of Israel to their own living context.[13] Blasting all moral complacency, spiritual pretension, and listless ritualism,[14] Jesus elaborates on what the real heart and true spirit of the Torah are. The radical nature of Jesus's covenantal renewal is found in his Sermon on the Mount.

The Covenantal Ground of the Sermon on the Mount

Covenantal renewal offers a crucial insight for properly understanding Jesus's Sermon on the Mount, and it clarifies any potential confusion and misunderstanding about

10. Horsley, *Covenant Economics*.

11. There are many parallels to the exodus story in the Gospels. For instance, the gathering of God's people in the exodus parallels Jesus's gathering of the Twelve; the forty years of wilderness wandering are remarkably similar to the forty days Jesus spent fasting in the desert; likewise, God's daily provision of manna and quail is reminiscent of Jesus's miraculous feeding of thousands in the wilderness. The continuity is also visible in the ritual of the Eucharist. Jesus's word "My blood . . . poured out for many" is reminiscent of what Moses did at the covenant ceremony in Exodus (Exod. 24:6–8).

12. Jesus was not the only covenant renewer. In the history of Israel, covenant renewal is recorded in Deuteronomy, Joshua, Nehemiah, Jeremiah, Isaiah, and Ezekiel.

13. Hanson, *The People Called*, 396.

14. Allison, *The Sermon on the Mount*, 13.

its moral content and meaning. Although the covenant is not explicitly named in the Sermon, its covenantal premise is clearly evident. Biblical scholars, notably Richard Horsley, underscore the parallels between the Mosaic covenant (Exod. 20; Deut. 5) and the Sermon on the Mount (Matt. 5–7). That is, the Matthean Jesus is a new Moses. Or perhaps Moses is a typological prefiguration of Christ. For example:[15]

- Jesus's ascension of the mountain in the opening two verses of Matthew 5 ("He went up the mountain; and after he sat down, his disciples came to him. Then he began to speak, and taught them") is similar to Moses ascending Mount Sinai to receive the law from God and giving it to the Israelites.
- Each clause of the Beatitudes is structured following a promise-fulfillment pattern, linked by the conjunction "for" (*hoti* in Greek). This pattern frequently appears in OT covenant documents. The kingdom of heaven is promised "for" those willing and eager to live in the way of Jesus.
- The covenantal logic of divine-human reciprocity (gift-task) is found in both the Sinai covenant and the teachings of the Beatitudes.[16]
- A covenant lists various blessings and curses. The Sermon on the Mount, despite a different format, maintains the material similarity of both blessings and curses (Matt. 7).
- Fidelity and trust to and in God ("no one can serve two masters"; "do not worry") are norms and values covenantal in nature.
- Jesus, like Moses, preaches on murder, adultery, divorce, almsgiving, oaths, revenge, forgiveness, prayer, and fasting. Indeed, Jesus both reaffirms and reinterprets Moses's words on these topics.
- Jesus, like Moses in the OT, is reported by Matthew as the "one having authority."
- At the end of the Sermon, Jesus heals the people after coming down from the mountain. This is similar to Moses's act of healing in Exodus 34:29.[17]
- Just as the Ten Commandments were given to those freed from slavery, Jesus was already liberating the people from the power of Satan when he preached

15. The discussion in this section draws upon Lee, "Covenant as a Historical Drama."

16. This covenantal pattern of reciprocity appears in several places in the Sermon on the Mount (5:44–48; 6:4, 6, 18, 25–33). Consider especially: "Love your enemies and pray for those who persecute you, so that you may be children of your Father in heaven; for he makes his sun rise on the evil and on the good, and sends rain on the righteous and on the unrighteous. For if you love those who love you, what reward do you have? Do not even the tax collectors do the same? And if you greet only your brothers and sisters, what more are you doing than others? Do not even the Gentiles do the same? Be perfect, therefore, as your heavenly Father is perfect" (5:44–48).

17. Allison, *The Sermon on the Mount*, 17.

> the Sermon. This means that "all the demands which follow presuppose that God's salvation is already in advance as absolutely free gift" and "the liberating and salvific reality of the reign of God is in principle a presupposition of all [his] demands."[18]

These examples demonstrate that Matthew introduces Jesus as a new Moses[19] delivering the people from the power of Satan and giving a new Torah on the mountain.[20] Just as Moses typologically gave the law to the liberated Israelites, Jesus gives the new teaching to the new covenant community freed from Satan. His community adopted and practiced Jesus's Sermon on the Mount as a new charter of their community, in a way analogous to the Ten Commandments. The parallels made between the Sermon and the covenant at Sinai demonstrate that the former is a kind of covenant renewal speech prior to the inauguration of the kingdom of God. Jesus's reinterpretation of the Torah is particularly found in the six antitheses (two triadic sets) of the Sermon (Matt. 5:21–48) that begin with "You have heard that it was said. . . . But I say to you." But Jesus's renewal is far more radical and intensive than the Mosaic form, as the moral transformation involves the human desires and the heart.[21]

A covenantal interpretation of the Sermon helps to address confusion and misunderstanding about its moral teachings (e.g., that the Sermon is too idealistic or unpractical, even counterintuitive; or, as some feminist theologians charge, that the Sermon unintentionally inculcates passivity and servility that undermine women's agency and self-love).[22] As we discuss in the next chapter, in a covenantal context, God's moral commandments and laws (including the teachings of the Sermon on the Mount) are first indicative before imperative. Like other covenantal teachings, the Sermon presupposes God's initiating deliverance and the outpouring and presence of the Spirit in Christian life as the immediate background of these teachings. As the Decalogue was given to those who were liberated from slavery, Jesus's teach-

18. Gerhard Lohfink, *Jesus and Community*, 59; Lee, "Covenant as a Historical Drama," 95–96.

19. The exodus typology is prevalent in the Gospel of Matthew. For example, Herod's order to kill all the boys in Bethlehem in Matt. 2:16–18 closely resonates with Pharaoh's edict to slaughter male Hebrew babies in Exod. 1:15–22.

20. Hanson, *The People Called*, 386.

21. Glen Stassen's idea of "the transforming initiatives of the Sermon on the Mount" (the fourteen triads) helps us understand the radical nature of Jesus's covenantal renewal (Stassen and Gushee, *Kingdom Ethics*, 141–43).

22. Stassen and Gushee note: "We believe that [in the interpretation of the Sermon on the Mount] people have put too much emphasis on the virtues (poverty of spirit, purity of heart, peacemaking and so on), and not enough emphasis on what Jesus was emphasizing—God's presence, God's active deliverance, God's giving us a share in that deliverance and so blessedness and joy." Stassen and Gushee, *Kingdom Ethics*, 35.

ings are for those who are already delivered from sin by God's power. Matthew 4:23–5:2 tells us that before Jesus preached, he first cured people and unleashed the power of kingdom, the presence of God defeating the power of Satan. Nothing was demanded of the crowd before they were healed and redeemed; it was an unconditional act of God, just as in the exodus story. Lohfink notes: "The Sermon on the Mount in Matthew and Luke has a programmatic introduction intended to make clear that all the demands which follow presuppose that God's salvation is already in advance as absolutely free gift. It is all the more true of Jesus himself that the liberating and salvific reality of the reign of God is in principle a presupposition of all demands."[23]

At the same time, a covenantal interpretation of the Sermon is critical for a proper understanding of Jesus's ethics, in particular his relationship with the Mosaic law (the Sinai covenant), and by implication other moral teachings and wisdom of the OT in general (the creation covenant and the Noachian covenant, and others). How to understand the relationship of the Sermon on the Mount to the Mosaic law defines the shape and content of Christian social ethics, as we see, for example, in the historical and ongoing controversies between Christian pacifists, on the one hand, and Catholics and mainline Protestants, on the other. The new covenant ethics that this book develops explores a third option between the above two camps. This section explores this option (which is grounded in the Sermon on the Mount and the covenant of Jesus but embraces the Mosaic law and other moral teachings and wisdom of the OT). I find the biblical ground for this new option in Matthew 5:17–20. In particular, the idea of "fulfillment" provides a clue to what Jesus's ethics was and how he was thinking of the OT (the law and the prophets) and his new ethics. These verses disclose Jesus's attitude toward the OT in general. Along with the covenantal tone and background of the Sermon, they explain the relationship of the OT to Jesus—how Christian ethics should approach the law and the prophets in light of the Christ event.

> "Do not think that I have come to abolish the law or the prophets; I have come not to abolish but to fulfill. For truly I tell you, until heaven and earth pass away, not one letter, not one stroke of a letter, will pass from the law until all is accomplished. Therefore, whoever breaks one of the least of these commandments, and teaches others to do the same, will be called least in the kingdom of heaven; but whoever does them and teaches them will be called great in the kingdom of heaven. For I tell you, unless your righteousness exceeds that of the scribes and Pharisees, you will never enter the kingdom of heaven."

23. Gerhard Lohfink, *Jesus and Community*, 59.

What does Jesus mean by "fulfill" the law and the prophets? How would the "fulfillment" look? Simultaneously, what does Jesus mean by "not one letter, not one stroke of a letter, will pass from the law until all is accomplished"? How is this statement compatible with "fulfillment," as they look incommensurable with each other?

The contrast between "fulfill" and "abolish" reveals Jesus's intention clearly. Given that "abolish" means "destroy," with the legal connotation of annulment or invalidation,[24] Jesus definitely does not declare any divorce between himself and the OT. Matthew's choice of the Greek word fits the context of Jesus's speech because the law and the prophets (referring to the Scriptures) had a legal binding power over Jews. In fact, Jesus sternly warns against any possible ignoring or breaking of the Scriptures and the commandments found therein. Jesus recognizes the binding authority of Scripture and implements "God's previously revealed, salvific will in his proclamation" and ministry.[25] Jesus's point is that the authority of Scripture will be relevant and binding until God's purpose is finally fulfilled. The legitimation formula "Truly I tell you" and the hyperbolic tone emphasize the unwavering authority of the Old Testament.

Hence, "fulfillment" is neither abolition nor replacement, but rather enhancement and perfection. It is "more" than the law and prophets, but not in contradiction to them. There is a certain continuity and discontinuity between Jesus and them. The following verse (20) is intimately associated with verses 17–19. The demand that the justice and righteousness of Jesus's followers should surpass those of the Pharisees is parallel to 5:17, just as "exceeding" is to "fulfillment." This reinforces verse 17: what Jesus emphasizes is not the abolition (annulment or destruction) of the law and the prophets, but the exceeding of them!

On the other hand, verse 18 connotes the eschatological nature of Jesus's fulfillment in relation to the law and the prophets. "Now that the scriptures are being fulfilled in Jesus' ministry, the passing away begins, but not yet fully because heaven and earth have not yet passed away. This process means that some parts pass away, but others do not."[26] Some parts of the law and the prophets are passing away as they are being fulfilled in Jesus himself, but others remain valid until heaven and earth pass away. In fact, in the Sermon and in Jesus's ministry, some laws of Moses are abrogated, or transformed, while others remain valid. Through his own radical renewal of the Sinai covenant, Jesus abrogated the ceremonial laws (regarding Sabbath, sacrifices, diet, etc.) once and for all, as his incarnation and atoning death have

24. Warren Carter, *Matthew and the Margins*, 140.
25. Warren Carter, *Matthew and the Margins*, 141.
26. Warren Carter, *Matthew and the Margins*, 142.

fulfilled the requirements of these laws. But moral laws were transformatively reinterpreted in the Sermon or eschatologized through his personal example (servant leadership, care ministry, sacrificial love) and the double love commandment. Some moral teachings, notably the Ten Commandments, and marriage were reaffirmed in a new eschatological context.

Jesus envisions the new moral life in deep continuity with the OT. When Jesus begins each antithesis, he refers to Mosaic law, precisely. This is more evident in the first two antitheses, where he does not reject the Mosaic law but rather focuses on the intention of the laws. Through these passages, Jesus communicates what the law and the prophets mean for his community. Continuity is also found in his emphasis on justice, mercy, faithfulness, and the double love commandment, which are all core norms and values of the Sinai covenant and the Mosaic law. Jesus still teaches the Golden Rule, *but he reinterprets and enhances it.* The Golden Rule is not based on the merits of other humans; it is a response to the Father's love. That is, Christians should reciprocate the good that others have done to them, but especially what God has done for them.

In short, Jesus teaches his followers to approach the Mosaic laws (and the OT) in a transformative way (by transvaluing them in light of Jesus's death and resurrection) in the context of his final covenantal renewal. "Jesus is the key to interpreting them (so 5:21–48), to determining what is already passing from the law and what is not."[27] Jesus, through the mouth of Matthew, invites Christians to exercise careful theological discrimination and moral deliberation of the teachings of the OT, rather than hastily jumping to total rejection or blind obedience.

The moral life transformed in Jesus is characterized by a deep love of God and others, nonviolence, and nonretaliation. In these ways, it is more faithful to the intention of the moral laws and the core norms of the prophets. In his ministry, Jesus himself embodied a kind of love that was inclusive, forgiving, and generous. He welcomed and ate with the unclean and tax collectors (Matt. 9:13). He forgave, and he did not retaliate.

The idea of "fulfillment" in Matthew 5:17 has a theological significance beyond Matthew; it is consistent with the typological-analogical pattern of covenant in the Bible in general, the NT in particular: "promise-fulfillment." In the NT, the promise-fulfillment typology is found in various titles of Jesus related to the previous covenants: New Adam, Second Adam, Last Adam, Great High Priest, Lamb of God, Messiah King, Son of Abraham, and David. For example, Luke reports that the prophecy of Isaiah (42:6b; 49:6b) is fulfilled now in Jesus (Luke 2:32; Acts 13:47; 26:23):

27. Warren Carter, *Matthew and the Margins*, 142.

God's purposes of salvation would finally extend to the whole world beyond Israel.[28] The opening genealogy of Matthew, which portrays Jesus as a descendent of Abraham and David, also implies God's fulfillment of God's promises to Israel, especially the Davidic covenant, which is important in validating Jesus's messiahship.

In summary, then, despite a relative dearth of references to "covenant," the reigning assumptions and ethos of the NT are unquestionably covenantal. Jesus and his disciples stood in a long, rich, and dynamic covenantal tradition of Israel that was reinterpreted through strong eschatological sentiments of the Second Temple period.[29] The spirit and rubric of Jesus's ministry and the early church were covenantal in nature. The covenant serves as the background and framework from which to understand the meaning of Jesus's incarnation, ministry, death, resurrection, and return.

There cannot be any fundamental moral contradiction between the new covenant and the other covenants; the NT was the reworking of the OT covenants in light of the Christ event. The old and the new covenants are related as "promise and fulfillment," "preparation and accomplishment," "shadow and substance," and "particular and universal."[30]

The New Covenant of Jesus

Despite its continuity with the previous covenants, the covenant of Jesus is different from them because of its consummating and eschatological nature. The covenant of Jesus accomplishes the original purpose of God for creation while integrating various strands of God's covenantal promises, and thus it is the covenant of consummation.[31] Eschatology indicates the new, radical moral impetus and cosmic scope of the new covenant. Paul Hanson highlights the radicality of the new covenant: "In light of the eschatological reality of the Kingdom, all traditions and customs pale before the new reality. And it is this new reality that evokes the fitting response."[32] In this sense, it is properly called *the new covenant* that the prophets dreamed of.

The covenant of Jesus is the eschatological covenant that signifies God's shalom community. Heralding the dawning of the new creation, the new covenant situates the entire creation under God's reign in Jesus Christ. In Jesus Christ, the fullness of time has arrived and history is reaching the consummation. In the new covenant,

28. Hays, *Moral Vision*, 114.
29. Hanson, *The People Called*, 396.
30. Bavinck, *Reformed Dogmatics*, 3:223.
31. Robertson, *The Christ of the Covenants*, 272.
32. Hanson, *The People Called*, 402.

the entire creation is waiting for its final redemption—the final victory of God—in its cosmic groaning and sighing. Jesus's resurrection becomes a proof for the future renewal of the entire creation. That is to say, "In the present time, the new creation already appears, but only proleptically; consequently, we hang in suspense between Jesus' resurrection and *parousia*."[33]

Instituting the new covenant has profound moral implications. In a biblical worldview, the establishment or renewal of the covenant usually meant the reorganizing of the moral and religious life of a community—not only its identity and membership but also its cult and ethics, entailing both inward and outward transformation. As the covenant was eschatologized, religious and moral stipulations and identity markers related to the previous covenants were also changed; circumcision, Torah, temple, repentance, election, and cult were radically reinterpreted or redefined. God's restoration now extends from Israel to all nations, and to the entire creation. The mission of the church as a new covenant community is to share God's blessings with all nations, fulfilling God's promise to Abraham. It is to continue the calling of Israel as the priestly kingdom, as the salt and light to other peoples.

This eschatological nature has ecological implications as well. Just as Israel's covenant involved not only the people but also the land, the new covenant of Jesus Christ involves not only humanity but also the other creatures and the planet. God has become human to rescue creation itself, not just humanity.

> Salvation in cosmic terms expresses the fact that human life is not only dependent upon fellowship with others but moves within the wider circle of creation at large. The new order initiated by the Messiah affects not only human relationships but also every other relationship in which man is involved. It is only when God is truly our Father that the cosmos becomes, in spite of its immensity, an ally and not a crushing weight. Human life takes place in a double context: within history and within the cosmos; both history and creation stand under the providence of God's covenant with man.[34]

Colossians 1:16 describes the cosmic scope of the covenant of Jesus.

One distinctive characteristic of the new covenant as the eschatological covenant is that Jesus Christ is not only the representative of humanity in the covenant with God, but he himself is also the basis and content of the covenant. Jesus identified

33. Hays, *Moral Vision*, 198.
34. Jocz, *The Covenant*, 235.

himself as the new covenant at the Last Supper when he declared: "for this is my blood of the covenant, which is poured out for many for the forgiveness of sins" (Matt. 26:28). Jesus wrought reconciliation and shalom through his crucified and resurrected body. He presents himself (symbolized by his blood and flesh) as the ground of the atonement and reconciliation (establishment of the covenant) between God and humanity. In other words, he *is* the God-human covenant—the site and the terms of the covenant simultaneously. The Christian idea of redemption is not comprehensible without the covenant of Jesus, in which the divine-human exchange takes place. God has become a human in Jesus Christ and has invited humans into a covenantal relationship in him. Jesus's flesh is the covenantal flesh, the site of the exchange and communion between God and humanity. Whoever participates in the covenant of Jesus is adopted as a child of God and cleansed and sanctified and guided by the Spirit. This is a radical departure from the previous covenants, while indicating the concluding (consummate) nature of his covenant. Covenantal rituals and ethical practices and theology converge in the person and work of Jesus. The form and content and the theory and practices of the new covenant are not separable from Jesus. Jesus's flesh is the covenantal flesh, the site of the exchange and communion between God and humanity. His body is the basis of human fellowship with God. God's will and desire to be in full communion with humans are fulfilled in Jesus Christ through his obedience to God. The OT promise that "I will be your God and you will be my people" is now actualized in an even higher form: "This is my Son, the Beloved, with whom I am well pleased" (Matt. 3:17).[35]

A great divine-human exchange happens in his body. His status and glory become a human's—and human sin becomes his own. As Athanasius said, "He took what is ours so that we might have what is his."[36] Jesus is the Son of God, and in Jesus we are adopted to be God's children. God loves us as he loves his Son. The Son is the future of humanity and creation. Human destiny and fate and future are hidden and united with the Son. His body is a covenantal body both ritually and ethically.

Because of this Jesus-constitutive nature, the covenant of Jesus is dramatically different from the previous covenants, and it is scandalous and blasphemous to the eyes of many of the Jews of his day. Every aspect of Jesus's life—from his incarnation, ministry, and death to his resurrection—now has covenantal meanings and implications. His body is a new temple, just as his death has atoning power for human sins. His resurrection indicates God's victory over the power of Satan that

35. The Matthew text recapitulates Ps. 2 and Isa. 42.

36. Paul says, "Though he was rich, yet for your sakes he became poor, so that by his poverty you might become rich" (2 Cor. 8:9).

had been frustrating God's plan for humanity, and his second coming promises the consummation of God's reign in the community of shalom.

If Jesus *is* the new covenant, then what is the stipulation of the new covenant? What are the right ethical behaviors required for the newly elect people of God?

The NT has no neatly delineated covenantal stipulation in the form of concise lists of the laws or commandments like the Ten Commandments. "The newness of the commandment of love is really related to the theme of covenant at the Last Supper—the 'new commandment' . . . is the basic stipulation of the 'new covenant' of Luke xxii 20."[37] The tone and content of NT ethics tend to be more communal and aretological than deontological or judicial, as in the Torah, relatively speaking. The NT shows several strands or directions in interpreting the stipulations of the covenant of Jesus. For example, instead of enumerating a list of commandments, Paul emphasizes "life in Christ," "walking with the Spirit," and principles such as love and righteousness. However, there is a shared focus among the NT documents. The double love commandment remains the central ethic of the new covenant as the foundational attitude and disposition of believers.[38] Christians are called to love God and others in a manner that reciprocates God's love (1 John 4:19). In the Gospel of John, the love commandment is reiterated in the context of the inauguration of the covenant of Jesus.[39]

As we discuss in chapter 6, Jesus's parables, moral teachings, and actions provide more detailed knowledge on how to live as covenanted people. The earthly ministry of Jesus shows how Jesus lived out his covenant relationship with God and others in faithfulness of trust, love, justice, and hope. In particular, Jesus's life, ministry, and teachings show us what moral life in the new covenant should be like and how disciples should live as the new covenant people of God.[40]

However, given the dialectic relationship between the new covenant and the OT covenants in Matthew 5:17, it is safe to say that the rules, laws, values, and moral teachings of the OT are relevant insofar as they are coherent with (or do not contradict) the vision of the new covenant. If they are not, then they should be reevaluated and reworked in the context of the new covenant, as Jesus and the early churches did.

37. Raymond E. Brown, *The Gospel according to John 13–22*, 614.

38. Cf. N. T. Wright, *Paul and the Faithfulness of God*, 727. Both the Fourth Gospel and Paul emphasize the double love commandment, conformity to Jesus, and union with Christ.

39. Christopher Baker, *Covenant and Liberation*, 260.

40. The idea of covenant helps to show theological continuity between Matthew and Paul; whereas Paul explains the new covenant from a soteriological perspective, Matthew shows how redeemed people (disciples) should live under the new covenant.

Concluding Observation of Chapters 1 and 2

This brief survey of biblical covenants in this and the previous chapter has shown that covenant is a constitutive plot and a running drama of Scripture. God creates, liberates, restores, and governs humanity and the world through the covenants, climaxing in the new covenant of Jesus. Although its framework is sometimes hidden from our modern view, covenant forms the architectural structure of the rich and diverse biblical narratives, and its goal is to create the conditions of flourishing for every life to the glory of God.[41]

Each biblical covenant is different from the others in terms of the historical time and context of its establishment, human partner(s), and purpose. Despite differences in partners and historical contexts, a common trajectory and message runs through all the biblical covenants. The covenantal drama in the Bible moves from liberation (deliverance) toward shalom—the full and wholesome communion between God, humanity, and creation. Covenant is an ordering mechanism that God uses to organize a new, just community based on God's justice, love, and power. Through the covenant, God desires and constantly seeks reconciliation and friendship with humanity. We hear the constant refrain of the covenant formula throughout the Scriptures: "I will be your God and you will be my people" (cf. Gen. 17:8; Exod. 6:7; Rev. 21:3). Some recurrent motifs and patterns (types) are shared by the biblical covenants, such as election, Eden, Adam, sonship, obligations, reciprocity, etc., revealing certain reliability and consistency in God's dealing with humans.[42]

The OT and the NT are unified in terms of the covenantal drama and the purpose of shalom that all the covenants intend to achieve. All divine covenants have one single source in God, even as they refract differently. The God of Noah and Israel and the God of Jesus is the same God, who is just, loving, and powerful. Together they show what God's preserving, ordering, redeeming, and perfecting work looks like.

Each covenant is related to the others under God's overarching covenantal drama, while playing its own distinctive role in God's redemptive history.[43] Hence, one cannot properly understand a particular covenant without understanding the preceding and subsequent covenants.[44] For example, a proper understanding of

41. "Like the architecture of most buildings, the framework is largely hidden from view." Horton, *God of Promise*, 13.

42. This means that typology plays an important role in studying the covenant.

43. Excepting the covenant with creation, all other covenants build upon previous covenants.

44. The following are some examples of the links and overlaps between the biblical covenants: Sinai covenant and the Abrahamic promises (Exod. 6:2–8; Deut. 7:7–9); Davidic covenant and

Noah's covenant is not possible apart from the covenant with creation, as well as other covenants. Likewise, apart from the stories of the other covenants in the Bible, the full significance, meaning, and implications of the covenant of Jesus cannot be comprehended.[45] Misunderstandings and distortions are inevitable when Christian understandings of Jesus's life, ministry, death, and resurrection are discussed apart from the covenants of the OT. John H. Walton observes this interrelatedness of the covenants in the Bible: "Each [covenant] is part of a single, unified program of revelation. The enactment or primacy of one does not mean the nullification or subordination of another. None of these covenants replaces the one before it—each supplements what has come before. In the same manner, if each covenant supplements the previous covenant(s), then each has a unique contribution to make: thus, the discontinuity. Rather than see each covenant as a separate entity, they are here considered to be phases of development; subagreements to the main agreement."[46]

The interrelatedness of the covenants shows that God's creational intention and purpose and God's redemption and salvation history do not contradict each other. "They share the same concern: how does one live life well before the living God? Both sets of literature come to the conclusion that it is impossible to do so apart from real, and therefore inevitably covenant, relationship with God."[47] Bavinck's summary is also helpful: "The road was the same on which believers in the Old and the New Testaments walked, but the light in which they walked was different."[48] They all work together toward the same destination of God's glory and shalom in Christ.

Among the biblical covenants, the creation covenant and the new covenant of Jesus—both universal in scope—serve as the beginning and end of the entire biblical narrative. The former is the first foundational covenant, while the latter is its final fulfillment. The new covenant, as the salvific plan of God in Jesus, has a protological

Sinai covenant (2 Sam. 7:22–24); new covenant and Sinai covenant (Jer. 31:33; Ezek. 36:26–28); new covenant and Davidic covenant (Ezek. 34:23–27); new covenant and Abrahamic covenant (Ezek. 36:24–28); interlinks among all four covenants (Ezek. 37:24–28). Walton, *Covenant*, 51. This applies to the new covenant of Jesus as well.

45. J. Kameron Carter affirms this point by saying, "To be drawn into the scriptural witness to Jesus is to be drawn into the Torah and the words of the prophets, which he sees symbolized in the figures of Moses and Elijah who are on Mt. Tabor with Jesus. Thus between [Maximus's *Epistle*] 2 and [*Ambigua*] 10, Christ becomes intelligible only in relationship to Abraham, Moses, and the prophets, or the people of Israel in their relationship to YHWH the Triune God. Therefore, what is Jewish about Jesus is essential to his divine identity as the Son of God in the economy of redemption. His relationship to Israel is not superseded." J. Kameron Carter, *Race*, 346.

46. Walton, *Covenant*, 49–50.

47. J. A. Grant, "Wisdom and Covenant," in *Dictionary of the Old Testament Wisdom, Poetry and Writings*, 861.

48. Bavinck, *Reformed Dogmatics*, 3:223.

underpinning and a cosmic, eschatological telos. The creation covenant sets the tone and plot of Scripture. All other covenants after the Fall had been God's attempts to remedy the problems of human sin and corruption of creation. Jesus recapitulates the story of creation and Adam (Rom. 13:9; Eph. 1:10). He has finally undone Adam's disobedience, just as Mary undid Eve's through her obedience (Luke 1:38), and he has fulfilled God's purpose for the entire creation.[49]

Figuratively speaking, among many peaks in the mountain of the Bible, the new covenant of Jesus is the apex, while the creation covenant is the initial peak. Like a grand, tortuous mountain with many different peaks, various biblical covenants are parts of the unifying drama of God's liberation-restoration. From a Christian perspective, all the other covenants between the creation covenant and Jesus's covenant presume the former while heading toward the latter. Bookended by these two covenants, each of the others serves a distinctive role in God's providence.

Among all the covenants in the Bible, the covenant of Jesus has the final, though not exclusive, authority. All the preceding covenants are, in the final analysis, subordinate to it, although it does not override or forfeit the other covenants. Since it is the final covenant, all Christian moral decisions and actions must take place in light of it. This means that moral laws and teachings and liturgical stipulations of the OT are to be assessed and reworked in its context, which is, in fact, what Jesus and the NT writers did, as we discussed.

With this note, we now turn to the covenantal drama and relational dialectics of covenant that will help to clarify the nature, content, and purpose of the Christian moral life grounded in the new covenant of Jesus.

49. Gorman, *The Death of Messiah*.

CHAPTER 3

Covenantal Drama and Threefold Dialectics

We love because [God] first loved us.

—1 John 4:19

Come now, let us argue it out, says the LORD.

—Isaiah 1:18

Scripture presents the variety of God's covenants with different partners (humans, other species, Earth) in diverse historical or geographical contexts with different scopes and purposes.[1] Despite their diversity of historical contexts, forms, and participants, exegetical studies of various divine-human covenants in the Bible help us to identify a distinctive trajectory and distinctive patterns of God-human interactions.

This chapter studies the typological patterns of covenant, namely, the covenantal drama of liberation-restoration; the triad of love, justice, and power; and the patterns of unilateral-bilateral, communal-communicative, and memory-hope. A proper understanding of this drama and these patterns is crucial to grasp the moral nature, logic, and characteristics of a biblical idea of covenant, including the new covenant, and accordingly to construct new covenant ethics.

1. Covenant in the Bible appears in the forms of divine election, treaties, alliances, legal contracts, loyalty agreements, and marriage agreements. Specific examples include the following: international treaties (Josh. 9:6; 1 Kings 15:19), clan alliances (Gen. 14:13), personal agreements (Gen. 31:44), legal contracts (Jer. 34:8–10), loyalty agreements (1 Sam. 20:14–17), and marriage agreements (Mal. 2:14). Walton, *Covenant*, 14.

Covenantal Drama: Liberation-Restoration

A covenantal drama has the trajectory of liberation-restoration. When we carefully examine major biblical covenants in their narrative contexts, it is clear that God's organizing work in history unfolds from "liberation" (from chaos, injustice, sin/death) to "restoration" (building of a new, just community), with covenant mediating the two phases.[2] Constituting the rubric of the divine drama, this pattern appears in major biblical covenants: God's deliverance of the universe from chaos to cosmos (the creation covenant), Noah and his family from the flood, Israel from the pharaoh to the promised land (the Sinai covenant), and humanity from the power of sin/death to a new creation (the new covenant of Jesus). In these covenants, Eden, the ark, the ancient nation of Israel (the promised land of Canaan), and the church (the new creation), respectively, indicate the new community of shalom opposed to disorder, corruption, oppression, sin, and death.

This means that in the Bible, covenant is not a mere judicial agreement between two parties; it is God's organizing principle to de-organize an old community and re-create a new, just community. God's covenantal organizing, broadly speaking, has the following three stages: (1) liberation (or deliverance), (2) covenant (entering a committed relationship), and (3) restoration (or building of an alternative community). Covenant is preceded by God's liberation (deliverance) but followed by the collaborative work of restoration between God and human partners. All three stages are inextricably interrelated, as they constitute the overarching pattern of God's organizing of a community.

This overarching pattern is intimately associated with God's reign, which is manifested through God's judgment against evil (liberation) and God's building of a new, just society (restoration). God's reign is not arbitrary but has a clear telos (shalom) and a moral trajectory (liberation-restoration), and it occurs through God's organizing of the shalom community.[3] Reign is a political as well as an ethical concept, and liberation-restoration is a pattern that describes God's reign and organizing work in which covenant serves as a constitutive and transformative principle.

As mentioned in the previous chapter, the new covenant finally fulfills the drama of liberation-restoration in a new eschatological community whose scope is cosmic and whose moral nature is radically nonviolent, inclusive, egalitarian, and caring, thus fully reflecting the moral ethos of God's reign.

2. Not every divine covenant in the Bible exactly displays this overarching pattern; yet, one may say, every covenant indirectly serves the same goal of restoring God's shalom. In the biblical canon, some covenants, such as the Abrahamic and Davidic covenants, serve as bridges to the two major covenants.

3. For a detailed discussion, see my book *God and Community Organizing.*

Justice, Love, and Power: The Triadic Components of Covenant

Closely related to God's organizing work from liberation to restoration, covenant is constituted by three moral components: love, justice, and power.[4] Justice and love are respectively associated with liberation and restoration, while power denotes raw energies and resources that require moral guidance and purpose for its proper use and actualization.

If liberation-restoration indicates the overarching historical pattern of God's organizing, the triad describes the inherent organizing impetus of covenant: a just and right ordering of power toward love. That is, covenant is a relational mechanism that justly organizes the powers of different parties toward deeper loving fellowship, with shalom as its ultimate goal.

In Scripture, the three refer to God's core attributes in relating to creation. There is no separation among the three in God: the God of love is the God of justice and righteousness (Ps. 36:10) and the God of power (God the almighty, God the warrior). They are always closely interrelated in God's action (Ps. 36:5–6).

1. *Justice.* Covenant is based on justice because covenant itself denotes the righting of a previously alienated relationship—"putting things right." To put things right is to give each party its due, including the respect of the rights of each person. Covenant assumes that every person is endowed with certain inalienable rights and that everyone has a duty to respect them. Justice serves as the minimal moral condition for human flourishing. In the covenant, the demand of justice is codified in the form of covenantal stipulations (or terms). The immediate goal of covenant is to secure a right relationship, but the ultimate goal is the building of the beloved community, love embodied in shalom.

Viewed from a different angle, covenant is a mechanism of differentiation and binding, separation and fettering between the participants. While justice has to do with differentiation (protecting the identities and rights of each party through fair distribution of power), love is concerned with binding them into a new community.

4. These three concepts are the key structural (architectonic) components that constitute covenant. While the three dialectics (unilateral-bilateral, communal-communicative, memory-hope) are concerned with operational dynamics (describing multidimensional aspects of the divine-human relationship), the triad constitutes the conceptual composite of covenant. While the former is operational, the latter is anatomical.

They are closely associated with the second dialectic (communal-communicative). The communal-communicative is a mechanism of fellowship that manages powers (life forces and claims) arranged in justice and commitment toward the fulfillment in love.

2. *Love*. While justice makes relationships right with God and others, love perfects this righted relationship into a deeper communion. In the divine covenant, the entire covenant is motivated by the triune God's love to restore the creation into the beloved community of shalom. Daniel Migliore notes: "From the foundation of the world, the purpose of the triune God has been to share life with others, to create a community of holy love in which all are united without loss of enriching differences."[5] Love fulfills justice, but the fulfillment is not possible without first meeting the demands of justice. While love is other-regarding and self-sacrificing in building a new community, it does not disregard the power of the self and others, nor justice—the rights, fairness, and legitimate self-interest of each party.

3. *Power*. Covenant presupposes the power (energy and capability) of each participant. Power refers to the capability of a moral agent to exercise free decisions and actions. In its basic form, power is the right to survival (to protect oneself) and the capability of pursuing one's fulfillment. Here the power includes not only external resources (force, money, land) but also an invisible, internal capability of a moral agent (in the form of character and virtue). Power is essential to moral agency. Covenant recognizes the importance of power in building a good society: "Without proper exercise of power, justice is not possible";[6] without healthy self-love, other-love is not conceivable; without the full development of moral capability of each member, a healthy, flourishing community is unimaginable.[7]

While affirming the necessity of power, covenant justly and rightly guides the exercise of the power of people toward the love of others. That is, justice offers a formal moral guideline for the use of power, while love serves as its motivation and purpose. A moral use of power is protecting the rights of others and building a just, trusting fellowship with them. As the composite of love, justice, and power, covenant is the constitutive principle of a just community that maximizes the potential of each person while striving toward perfect fellowship of love.

Shalom is the complete cosmic actualization of love, justice, and power of all creatures, namely, the perfection of covenantal organizing. Without a proper balance and full actualization of the three, shalom is not possible. Shalom describes the state where the capability of each creature is fully maximized in voluntary participation, right arrangements and fair exchanges are actualized, and mutual care and love are practiced. All three are necessary for common flourishing.

5. Migliore, *Faith Seeking Understanding*, 358.

6. De Gruchy, *Reconciliation*, 202.

7. Justice as capability is based on the same insight. Chapter 12 discusses this aspect in further detail.

In their combination, the triad of love, justice, and power helps us to see what God's organizing reign (liberation-restoration) looks like in history. God exercises power according to the principles of justice and love. God does not rule the cosmos arbitrarily and whimsically, but always through justice and love. While the three are never separate, the combination of justice and power is expressed primarily in God's judgment against injustices, and the combination of love and power is manifested in God's healing and restorative work. God exercises the three in building a covenantal community. Love, justice, and power are integral to God's reign, and together they serve to achieve God's purpose, that is, shalom.

These components are found in all major biblical covenants with different scopes, degrees of balance, and levels of harmony. However, as we discuss in the next chapter, only the new covenant has achieved complete integration, harmony, and perfect balance among the three.

Threefold Dialectics

Under this rubric of liberation-restoration, we find in the biblical covenants a recurring triadic pattern that appears in their establishment (entering), sustenance (staying), and journey (striving): unilateral-bilateral, communal-communicative, and memory-hope (promise-fulfillment).[8] The unilateral-bilateral dialectic describes the divine initiative and human response, while the memory-hope (promise-fulfillment) dynamic is related to future blessings as well as sanctions (the consequences of one's actions) grounded in God's past redemptive event. While the unilateral-bilateral dialectic is formal and structural in nature, the communal-communicative dialectic is interactive and dialogical in its dynamics. Finally, the memory-hope dialectic is temporal or historical. Together these three features describe the multifaceted, dynamic, and organic nature of the divine covenant.

The three dialectics are not neatly divided and organized; rather, they are interrelated and overlap with each other to some degree. However, together they constitute the distinctive contours and dynamics of the covenant, explaining how the covenant is established, operates, and unfolds toward a shared vision of God and humanity. Harmonizing the seemingly opposite ethical ideas or dynamics of gift and task (unilateral-bilateral), indicative and imperative, unity and diversity (communal-communicative), memory and hope (promise-fulfillment), they offer an interpretive key for understanding the shape, nature, and character of the Christian moral life.

8. The question how these dialectics operate in God's interaction with nonhuman creation is beyond the scope of this work, although one cannot deny that some similar pattern is possible through God's ecological design and ongoing evolutionary process in creation.

Unilateral-Bilateral

Among these three dialectics, the unilateral-bilateral has to do with the way a covenant is established.

As aforementioned, covenant is preceded by a unilateral (unmerited) redemptive act of God, in the form either of liberation (or deliverance) or the promise of future blessings, that is, a royal grant (e.g., God's promise of blessings for Abraham or God's promise of eternal succession of kingship to David and his descendants). Then God offers human beings a covenantal relationship on the basis of God's benevolent act or blissful intent. However, once a covenant is established, the relationship takes on a bilateral character (that is, it becomes mutual), with certain obligations entailed. In other words, every biblical covenant is unilateral in God's unmerited act of redemption and God's free offer of enduring fellowship, but then takes on a bilateral form and character once established.[9] To demonstrate my point, I examine two sets of covenant, traditionally contrasted as "conditional" (the covenants with Adam

9. Traditionally, Christian and Jewish scholars have categorized the biblical covenants into two rival groups: unilateral versus bilateral covenants and unconditional versus conditional covenants. A unilateral covenant is one in which God is the sole initiator and establisher of the covenant, and thus human response is not required. Conversely, in a bilateral covenant both God and human beings equally participate in its establishment. Similarly, but with a different focus, the categorization of unconditional versus conditional covenants has to do with the presence or absence of legal or moral conditions (specified in the covenant stipulations) to enter the covenant. If there is no specific obligation that binds human partners, it is called an unconditional covenant; if there is a specified obligation, then it is named a conditional covenant. Typically, the covenants of Abraham, David, and Jesus Christ are considered unconditional covenants, while the Adamic covenant (called "covenant of works" in the Reformed tradition) and the Sinai covenant are treated as conditional covenants.

However, this classical categorization of the covenants (unilateral versus bilateral, unconditional versus conditional) is problematic, unhelpful at best, and possibly distortive and misleading at worst. The idea of a bilateral covenant mistakenly conveys the impression that human obedience is required (as a precondition) to enter into a covenant relationship with God, while an unconditional covenant is misunderstood to entail no human obligation at all to enter into or stay in the covenant relationship with God.

As a result of this misplaced categorization, there is a profound misunderstanding among many Christians that while the old covenant (the Sinai covenant) is conditional, as its fulfillment depends on human obedience to the law, the new covenant of Jesus is unconditional without any obligation other than faith, since it is a sheer gift from God. This has led to deleterious moral consequences for the Christian life, which Bonhoeffer rightly criticized as "cheap grace."

It is my claim that both elements (unilateral and bilateral, unconditional and conditional) are neither separate nor mutually exclusive, but are found in every biblical covenant, whether the covenant is offered in the form of a royal grant or a mutual agreement, when we carefully examine each covenant holistically in its full narrative scope and context of the divine-human interactions.

and Israel) and "unconditional" (the covenants with Noah, Abraham, David, and Jesus Christ).

1. In God's covenant with Adam, Adam did not attempt to earn his salvation. He already had a right relationship with God in Eden.[10] Adam's image (sonship) was already given to him with his creation; he was not required to earn it. In other words, he was endowed with God's gift/blessing to be God's viceroy with access to all resources except the tree of knowledge that served as a moral boundary (stipulation). The condition (not eating the fruit of the tree of knowledge) was added later to the already-existing covenantal relationship between God and Adam as the creator and God's viceroy, respectively, not the other way around.[11]

2. Although typically considered unilateral, the Noachian covenant has a strong bilateral dimension.[12] Noah received God's favor as he was told to build the ark. He obeyed all of God's commands, including hosting every pair of animals in his ark. This means that God's promise of deliverance from the flood (a unilateral initiating grace) was reciprocated by Noah's obedience in building the ark. The bilateral aspect becomes even more evident later when God reaffirmed his covenant. "The note of command is also present in the prohibition both of murder (vv. 5–6) and of the consumption of blood (v. 4), which is to play an important role in the OT's ritual laws (Lev 17:11) and which even continues in the NT (Acts 15:20). In reality, therefore, both promise and command belong within the covenantal thought of Gen 1–11."[13]

3. Similarly, the Abrahamic covenant is not solely unilateral. Although God's election and promise of blessings for Abraham were pure acts of grace, as implied in Genesis 12:1–3, God's election and blessings are contingent upon Abraham's obedience to God's call to go to Canaan. Even if Abraham's verbal assent is not recorded in the text, one can easily deduce that his obedience to God's call implies his assent. There are other references to the bilateral aspects of the Abrahamic covenant: God demands Abraham to be blameless before him (Gen. 17:1, 9–14).[14] This implies that

10. Gentry and Wellum, *Kingdom through Covenant*, 612.

11. Furthermore, there is his making a public oath. Covenant with Adam does not fit the formula of a conditional covenant exemplified by the Sinai covenant.

12. Steven Mason, in his book *"Eternal Covenant" in the Pentateuch*, 70, argues that the literary structure of Gen. 6:17–21 and Gen. 9:1–7, usually overlooked, shows the bilateral nature of the Noah's covenant. It has two sides, in a way that is consistent with the construction common to the covenant cutting that specifies "the responsibilities of the two parties in a single direct discourse." In other words, Noah's covenant in Gen. 9:7–9 is structurally similar to Abraham's covenant in Gen. 17:4–9. Mason concludes that human obligation is intrinsic to Noah's covenant.

13. McConville, "בְּרִית."

14. "It would be going too far to say that [the covenant with Abraham] represents a religious idea contradictory to the Sinai covenant. As we saw, a pact like that reported in Exod. 20 lays obli-

despite the unilateral nature of God's call and promise of blessings (royal grant), God expects a reciprocating response from Abraham.[15]

4. The Sinai covenant, with its detailed stipulations of heavy human obligations (legal and ritualistic), may appear to be conditional, especially given its lack of a strong promissory aspect. However, this is a misunderstanding. The preceding exodus event (God's deliverance of Israel from Egyptian slavery) set the historical and theological basis for the Sinai covenant. This fact is attested by the preamble that narrates God's past deliverance as the basis of the covenant making: "I am the Lord your God, who brought you out of the land of Egypt" (Exod. 20:2). This historical prologue strongly indicates that the Sinai covenant is based on God's preceding gracious act and is not conditional in an a priori sense. Accepting God's invitation and entering the covenant through oath taking were only responses to God's initiating act. The conditions (summed up in the Ten Commandments) had to do, not with entering the covenant, but with staying in it. This observation is consistent with the predominant consensus of OT scholars that the Israelites' moral obligations arose from gratitude toward what God had done, which took the form of free acceptance of God's commandments.

5. David's covenant also shows a pattern similar to the covenants of Noah and Abraham. God first showed mercy to David and promised to establish him and his descendants as permanent rulers over Israel (Ps. 89:3–4). But God also required their loyalty and warned of the consequences of disloyalty (Ps. 89:30–32).[16] This shows that God's unilateral promise is balanced with God's requirement of obedience (1 Kings 2:4; cf. Ps. 132:11–12).[17]

---

gations only on the subjects, and yet the Lord, it is assumed, will also behave in a just and righteous way. It is not an instrument for establishing a tyranny. Conversely, even though a covenant like that with Abraham does not spell out how Abraham is to behave, it is assumed in the relation—that of having Yahweh as God—that Abraham will continue to trust God and walk righteously before him. Yet, granting all this, the emphasis in each of the two is so different that they come very close to being opposites." Hillers, *Covenant*, 104–5.

15. McConville, "בְּרִית," 749.

16. "If his sons forsake my law / and do not follow my statutes. . . . / I will punish their sin with the rod, / their iniquity with flogging" (Ps. 89:30–32 NIV). King Solomon's prayer at the dedication of the temple reveals that David's relationship with God was not solely unilateral but bilateral when he says, "You have shown great kindness (*hesed*) to your servant, my father David, because he was faithful to you and righteous and upright in heart" (1 Kings 3:6 NIV). Then Solomon, in the same spirit, prays about his own covenantal relationship with God: "There is no God like you . . . you who keep your covenant of love (*hesed*) with your servants who continue wholeheartedly in your way" (8:23 NIV).

17. "The fact that there are no conditions mentioned in the original proclamation of the Davidic covenant in 2 Samuel 7 does not necessarily mean that it is an unconditional covenant. . . . One of the key issues to be decided is whether succession to the throne is a benefit of the covenant or

6. The covenant of Jesus Christ is regarded as the supreme example of a unilateral, unconditional covenant. Nothing other than faith is required to enter into the covenant. However, is there no binding obligation or expectation at all for believers to maintain a covenantal relationship with God in Jesus Christ? Though not as elaborate as the Ten Commandments, the stipulation is still included in the covenant in the form of a new commandment: "Love one another as I have loved you." This obligation fulfills all the laws, and its demand is even higher than that of the Sinai covenant because it expects a change in one's heart and internal motivations as well as in one's external behaviors. This bilateral nature is found in baptism, the initiation rite of covenant. Baptism is granted not only on the basis of one's profession of faith but also on one's (or one's parents') public pledging (an oath taking) to trust and follow Jesus in every situation.

Furthermore, a very broad or general stipulation or a public pledge in baptism does not mean that the new covenant of Jesus completely lacks a punitive clause against disobedience. The writer of Hebrews sternly warns of the danger of apostasy when he says:

> "Today, if you hear his voice,
> do not harden your hearts as in the rebellion." (Heb. 3:15)

This citation from Psalm 95:8 calls to mind the tragedy that happened to the first-generation Israelites who had left Egypt and then entered the covenant at Mount Sinai but fell in the wilderness because of their disobedience.[18]

---

the essence of the covenant. If it is a benefit, then it can be withheld even though the covenant itself continues to be maintained. But, if succession to the throne is simply a benefit, how can one describe the essence of the covenant?" Walton, *Covenant*, 115.

18. Bavinck also noticed the shift of the focus within the covenant of grace: "In the covenant of grace, that is, in the gospel, which is the proclamation of the covenant of grace, there are actually no demands and no conditions. For God supplies what he demands; Christ has accomplished everything, and though he did not accomplish rebirth, faith and repentance in our place, he did acquire them for us and the Holy Spirit therefore applies them. Still, in its administration by Christ, the covenant of grace does assume this demanding conditional form. The purpose is to acknowledge humans in their capacity as rational and moral beings; still, though they are fallen, to treat them as having been created in God's image; and also on this supremely important level, where it concerns their eternal weal and eternal woe, to hold them responsible and inexcusable; and, finally, to cause them to enter consciously and freely into this covenant and to break their covenant with sin, and enable him, consciously and freely, to enter into the covenant and break with sin. The covenant of grace, accordingly, is indeed unilateral, it proceeds from God; he has designed and defined it. He maintains and implements it; it is a work of the triune God and is totally completed among the three Persons themselves. But it is destined to become bilateral, to be consciously and voluntarily accepted and kept by humans in the power of God." Bavinck, *Reformed Dogmatics*, 3:230.

Many scriptural teachings in the NT reflect this pattern of shift from the unilateral (indicative) to the bilateral (imperative). For example, the Pauline letters show this pattern when they begin with a discussion of what Christ has accomplished for us, then move to moral admonitions to Christians in light of the accomplishment of Christ. That is, the imperative follows the indicative. The pattern shows that Christ's atoning work (justification) is to be followed by our response (faith) and ethics (sanctification), not the other way around. A driving force of Christian moral life is gratitude; obligation is the grateful response to it.

Covenantal stipulations, the formal agreement between the parties, represent the emblem of this bilateral relationship. They concretely spell out how the people of God should live. This bilateral dimension is the heart of human responsibility, and it describes the distinctive nature of Christian ethics. The moral life begins with the free human response to God's unconditional love (grace) and invitation into the divine project to restore shalom, and it grows through human fidelity in staying in and journeying with God in the covenantal fellowship (communal-communicative, memory-hope) toward God's shalom. Without this bilateral dimension, the covenant loses its very relational quality and moral nature, and God's grace becomes cheap grace.

Under the rubric of the covenantal drama of liberation-restoration, the unilateral and the bilateral are not antithetical. While the unilateral sets sinners *free from* the power of sin or oppression, the bilateral sets them *free toward* a sanctified and fulfilled life in fellowship and communion with God and others. The purpose of the covenant is to establish communion, and communion presupposes genuine freedom between the two partners that is freely granted by God's liberative acts.

This implies that love in its perfection is always mutual, not unilateral. God's intention in the covenant is a mature human understanding and reciprocation of God's love. God works patiently toward our maturity. This divine intention is even further evident when we look at the institution of the atonement mechanism within the covenant. When humans fail to fulfill their obligations, they have recourse to this atonement system to receive forgiveness and be restored to a covenantal relationship.

In summary, this pattern of initiating divine grace reciprocated by free human response renders a defining character to Christian worship and ethics: the indicative precedes the imperative. Task (imperative) flows from gift (indicative). "A gift propels toward a task. A charge moves toward a discharge," says William May.[19] Just as a tree is sustained by its root, the Christian life is fed and sustained by God's grace.

The indicative nature of covenant explains why the motif of "response" (or responsibility) is prominent in the Christian life. It better explains the central biblical

19. May, *Testing the National Covenant*, 91.

ethos of the Bible.[20] Karl Barth notes that "the being of man is an answer, or more precisely a being lived in the act of answering the Word of God."[21] Hence, obedience in covenant is more a kind of "harkening"—a response corresponding to God's gracious action toward us: "Our action corresponds in kind to God's action. . . . The content, the nature of God's grace determines the content and nature of our acts. Our response is love because God's grace is manifest as love. . . . With our actions we are to render account to [God's grace]."[22]

This pattern appears consistently in the Bible, demonstrating that the Christian moral life depends on God's grace. "We love because [God] first loved us" (1 John 4:19). The starting point of the Christian life is not being good or right, but living freely and responsibly as the ones who are first loved and reconciled by God in Jesus Christ. Hence, in covenant, obedience is not a blind or involuntary compliance but a free, self-conscious, informed, moral act out of gratitude.

However, this priority of the indicative does not mean that the imperative is to be abandoned. The imperative is necessary to guide and spell out in concrete terms how the people of God should ethically live out their new identity in the various relationships and realms of society. This imperative typically has two distinctive parts—obligations toward God (worship) and obligations toward others (ethics), as we see in the two parts of the Ten Commandments and in the two love commandments: love of God and of one's neighbors.[23] A right relationship with God restored in Jesus Christ naturally and simultaneously flows to our relationship with others. Set free by Christ *from* the power of sin and death, we are now free *for* a sanctified life, corresponding to the liberation-restoration pattern.

Furthermore, as we discuss in the next chapter, evoking gratitude in human hearts, the indicative creates a powerful incentive and motivation for the imperative. The two are seamlessly unified in covenant; covenant effectively explains the logic and rationale of the sequence and unity between the indicative and the imperative.

Communal-Communicative

While the unilateral-bilateral dialectic focuses on how a covenant is established, the communal-communicative dialectic describes how a bilateral relationship between

20. Informed by covenantalism, H. Richard Niebuhr, in his posthumously published book *The Responsible Self*, articulated this responsive nature of the human moral life. That is to say, human moral life is shaped by the motif of "response" even more than by a goal or a rule.

21. Barth, *Church Dogmatics* III/2, 175.

22. Mott, *Biblical Ethics and Social Change*, 28.

23. In addition to worship (God) and ethics (others), one may add mission/evangelism (the world).

God and humans actually operates in the covenant. The covenant relationship is the ongoing exchange between God and human partners that grows toward a deeper fellowship. Life in the covenant is not static but dynamic and animated.

This dialectic derives from a covenanting process itself.[24] The etymology of covenant and ancient rites of covenant (e.g., animal cutting and meal sharing) disclose how the communal-communicative dialectic is intrinsic to the covenant. Two Akkadian words are related to the Hebrew word *brit, biritum* (meaning "space between") and *beriti* (indicating "fetter" or "binding agreement").[25] The word *lichrot brit,* literally to cut a covenant, derived from a religious ceremony in which an animal is halved and participants pass between the divided parts—the act symbolizing the reunion of the parts (Gen. 15:10; Jer. 3). On the basis of this etymological background, *brit* implies the "fettered freedom" or "liberating bondage,"[26] unity in difference, difference in unity, namely, communal-communicative.[27] The integral nature of the communal-communicative dialectic to the covenant is found in the fact that it is parallel to the "cutting (of an animal)" and "binding" ceremony (a shared meal) of a covenantal ritual. "Cutting covenant" involves not just a separation but, paradoxically, the preparation of each party to be newly bonded in free commitment and deep loyalty.

Communal

In general, the term "communal" connotes "common," "shared," and "conjoined," characterizing the nature of a good community. The communal in the covenant describes the sticky, affectional, solidaric aspect of a relationship between the parties, namely, the deep affection and bond that the parties have toward each other, which goes beyond calculations of self-interest or the prescription of moral duties alone. This communal quality is exactly what distinguishes covenant from contract.

The "communal" in the covenant is grounded in God's *hesed,* which is usually translated "steadfast or unfailing love," love that is generous, faithful, and compassionate. It reflects the inner Trinitarian life in which the Father, Son, and Spirit communicate and exchange among themselves in love. God's communal love is relational and aims at fellowship and community. The communal indicates the very purpose that the triune God aims at with the covenant: communion (*koinōnia*). The

24. The communal and the communicative are respectively correlated with the love and justice components of covenant, confirming the dynamic moral nature and centrality of covenant for the Christian moral life.

25. Elazar, *Covenant and Polity in Biblical Israel,* 44.

26. Elazar, *Covenant and Polity in Biblical Israel,* 44.

27. Circumcision, known as *berit milah,* is reminiscent of this cutting ceremony.

covenantal mantra repeated throughout Scripture, "I will be your God and you will be my people," succinctly presents this communal purpose of the covenant.[28]

The communal aspect of the divine covenant is expressed by several prominent metaphors in Scripture that are intimate, personal, even erotic in nature, such as sonship (Gen. 1:26; Exod. 4:22; Deut. 32:8–9; Rom. 8:15; Heb. 12:7), blood (Exod. 24:6–8; Luke 22:20), the common meal (Exod. 24:11), and marriage (Hosea; Jer. 31:32; Mal. 2:13–16; Eph. 5:23; Rev. 19–22). Among these metaphors, the metaphor of marriage is the most powerful in conveying the depth, personal intimacy, and exocentricity of the communion between two different parties in the covenant, while the filial image has the merit of emphasizing an onto-solidaric dimension of the divine-human relationship. The relationship is not artificial but quasi-biological like the parent-children relationship, and to enter a covenantal relationship with God means to restore and reclaim the original primeval bond between God and humanity.

The ritual of shedding or sprinkling blood in a covenant ceremony indicates the depth and seriousness of commitment and the sanctity of bond established in the covenant. It is based on the belief that blood is the essence of life (Gen. 9:4). Therefore, shedding or sprinkling blood in a covenant ritual symbolizes that each party commits to the relationship with a seriousness that risks, even bets on, his or her own life. On the other hand, the common meal emphasizes friendship and fellowship between the covenant parties.[29]

The communal dimension of the covenant gets even stronger in the new covenant of Jesus Christ. In addition to the metaphors of marriage and sonship, the NT introduces other communal metaphors, such as "the vine and branches" and "the body of Christ," and articulates them in a new theological framework to describe a believer's participation in and union with Jesus Christ. Baptism and the Eucharist also take on a strong organic, corporal nature to emphasize the depth of the communal love and intimacy between God and the human partner in Christ. While baptism depicts the solidarity of a believer with Christ in both death and life, the Eucharist emphasizes the mystical union between a believer and Jesus through partaking of his flesh and blood, anticipating the future messianic banquet and eternal communion between God and his people. Christ himself is communicated to us in the Eucharist through the Spirit. In addition, the Eucharist speaks of our daily reliance on the subsistence of God's grace in Christ's flesh and blood, while it foreshadows

28. God's communal love indicates God's consistent "gesture of outgoing friendship" toward humanity (Jocz, *The Covenant*, 241).

29. One can find other communal metaphors in "dwelling" and "the companionship of God in tabernacle."

the eschatological wedding banquet of Christ with his bride, the church. The church as the body of Christ is found in Paul's understanding of the members' relationship with Christ, the head of the body.

In a diverse way, these communal metaphors describe the depth of mutual commitment between God and humans in a covenant relationship beyond legal transactions. To be covenanted is to be completely committed to each other, as God has demonstrated in Jesus Christ. Claimed by God as God's own, we are called to live in love, loyalty, and service to God. There is no partial, lukewarm involvement in the covenant. The communal metaphors explain why God is so jealous, unrelenting, and passionate toward God's people: God is so committed and cares so much about the relationship with humanity.

The communal quality in the covenant is nurtured through worship, sacraments, and fellowship that serve as the means of communication between God and us. Through these means we freshly experience God's grace, and in turn we grow in our love of God and others.

Communicative

While affection, intimacy, and solidarity characterize the communal aspect of covenant, freedom, alterity, and justice highlight its communicative dimension.[30] The term "communicative," in general, refers to the dialogical or discursive aspect of our social life, with the connotation of willing or eager communicating engagement. It is directly associated with the bilateral dimension of the covenant, where the covenant partners freely engage with each other around various issues.

Communication in covenant is not merely dialogical but also performative. The idea of communicative action is extremely helpful in understanding God's communication and God's interaction with humans in covenant.[31] God's action in covenant is neither general nor abstract but personal and embodied. God rules the world not with mechanical causality but through communicative interaction with humans while respecting their freedom. For example, God's revelation is essentially

30. Although these characteristics may sound very similar to those of a contract, covenant is different from contract because of its communal nature.

31. Human communication uses nonverbal or symbolic forms (e.g., shaking hands, exchanging gifts, eating together) in addition to speech. This nonverbal, symbolic action also has a performative force. Regarding the performative nature of symbolic actions, Donald Evans says, "Sometimes an institutional act can be performed not only verbally but also non-verbally. I acknowledge status by bowing or saluting; I welcome by shaking hands; I bless by laying on of hands; I marry by mingling blood; I command by pointing; or I mourn by rending garments. Each action, like a performative utterance, has a performative force." Evans, *The Logic of Self-Involvement*, 75.

a communicative event, thus both informational and performative.[32] When God reveals, God not only communicates but also does something with God's words. God addresses a particular person or a group with a specific intention or purpose (call, warning, blessing, etc.).[33] Regarding the communicative (performative) nature of God's revelation, Clark Pinnock writes, "Revelation is not primarily existential impact or infallible truths but divine self-revelation that both *impacts and instructs*. The mode of revelation is self-disclosure [self-communication] and interpersonal communication. As such it is pregnant with significance and possible development."[34] Similarly, God's commandments and laws are communicative because of the living, performative nature of God's words.

This communicative dimension (dialogical and performative) of God's action is crucial for properly understanding the moral nature and function of covenant, in particular its coordinating, performative, binding nature. Covenantal partners rely on communicative action to enter into the covenant and to stay in it. Achieving covenant stipulations (through mutual agreement) is a communicative process that typically includes the deliberative process of inquiring, contesting, and validating the claims of and exchanging promises (pledges) between the parties.[35] While staying in the covenant, the parities hold each other accountable through communication actions. In other words, the communicative action theory helps to grasp the performative nature of moral accountability and fellowship intrinsic to covenant.[36]

32. In congruence to our argument, Barth rightly locates revelation in the theology of the Word of God, on the basis that God addresses human beings through his Word.

33. A communicative approach addresses the problem of a traditional theism, which, framed in terms of supernatural causality, such as God as the unmoved mover or immutable God, faces difficulties in answering the question of how God relates to the world, especially a human that has its own free will and decision-making capacity.

34. Pinnock, *Flame of Love*, 226 (emphasis added).

35. Dale Patrick notes: "Covenant making is a verbal action with illocutionary force." Patrick, *The Rendering of God*, 96. For further discussion, see Vanhoozer, *Remythologizing Theology*, 213–14.

36. The theory of communicative action is helpful for elucidating a coordinating function of human language and its performative nature. It is built upon the speech-act theory, which was first developed by John L. Austin and J. R. Searle. It was refined through other theorists, including Jürgen Habermas, whose magnum opus, *The Theory of Communicative Action*, has made a huge contribution to discursive ethics and democracy.

Austin defines utterance (or a speech act) as the most elementary unit of human communication. According to him, to understand a particular speech means to recognize not only the meaning of words but also the intentions behind the words; for to utter something is not just to "say" something, but rather to "perform" something in a certain circumstance. The meaning of a language (speech) is not found in its propositions but in its use by speech actors, that is, meaning as a "language in use."

The speech-act theory distinguishes between three dimensions of utterance: locution, illo-

The communicative dynamic of the covenant is predicated on (1) the freedom, alterity, and rights of human beings as God's image-bearers and (2) their communicative competence. Created in the image of God, humans are able to think, judge, and reason with God and others. Covenant does not call for humans' blind obedience to God but rather a free response.[37] In God's relationship with human beings, God does not swallow up human agency but rather empowers it, and God's authority is exercised through communicative actions. A communicative approach is necessary because the genuine fellowship that God seeks with humans is possible only on the basis of freedom and respect, not coercion. When coerced, humans cease to be free moral agents, and their decisions lose moral validity. In a divine-human relationship, covenant plays a significant role because it protects and enhances human freedom. Despite a huge imbalance of power between God and humans, covenant gives human beings a safe space to argue, reason with, and even protest against God, and this space is given through God's free self-emptying (*kenōsis*) and love toward humanity.

Scripture shows numerous examples of individuals who freely and communicatively engaged with God on various issues of life. Abraham, Jacob, Job, Moses, and Jeremiah are but a few of the humans who reasoned with, pleaded to, and sometimes argued with and protested against God. Among the many descriptors of communicative engagements in Scripture (e.g., pray, confess, plead, argue, protest), perhaps the image of "wrestling" best portrays what happens in the covenant between God and humans. The image is from the account of Jacob wrestling with God alone until dawn, when God finally yields to his request and blesses him, while also striking

---

cution, and perlocution. While locution is concerned with what language generally describes, illocution is concerned with the actional intent implied in a speech, and perlocution has to do with the impact or influence of a speech act on its hearer. Put in a different way, locution refers to the proposition of the statement; illocution refers to the performative aspect of a speech; and perlocution is concerned with the impact of a speech.

Among these three dimensions, the illocutionary is especially important in a speech act because it illuminates the social and performative nature of a speech. One can do several things with one's words—promising, asserting, commanding, and questioning; illocution refers to how words and signs are performatively employed in a speech (how they are used or performed) to accomplish a particular intention of a speaker on a hearer. The same proposition, for example, eat, is interpreted in different ways (as an assertion, a question, or a command, etc.), depending on the context of a discursive interaction. Therefore, locution (proposition) alone does not constitute a speech. It becomes a meaningful speech only when it is interpreted in relation to the intention of a speaker addressed toward her hearer in a particular social context. This theory has a direct relevance to Christian theology and ethics.

37. Elazar notes, "The act of hearkening is an act of hearing, considering, agreeing, and then acting. It is a human sign of freedom, of free will, whereby in order to act human we must consciously decide to do so, even in response to God." Elazar, *Covenant and Polity in Biblical Israel*, 70.

and dislocating his hip joint (Gen. 32:22–32). *Israel,* Jacob's new name from God (meaning "the one who strives with God") and later a collective name of his descendants, indicates that communicative engagement is the central feature of the people of Israel's relationship with God, permanently marking their national character.

Although our communication with God takes many different forms, Walter Brueggemann identifies "yielding" and "assertion" as the two typical modes, with "praise" and "lament" as their respective liturgical expressions. Lament and praise show how high and how far our communication with God can go. They indicate that a covenantal relationship is neither excessively resistant nor excessively submissive, but communicative. Lament and praise are interrelated in our spiritual life; lament without praise is graceless, bleak, and depressing, while praise without lament is blind, mechanical, and triumphalistic.[38] Through yielding and assertion, lament and praise, our covenant relationship with God becomes "a living intercourse."[39]

The communicative dynamic indicates that a covenantal bond is maintained and renewed by constant open discursive interactions with God. A free, open, truthful engagement is the sign of a healthy, trusted, and living relationship. The work of the Spirit is very important for the communicative fellowship in the covenant. Just as the Spirit works as the bond of love between the Father and the Son, the Spirit mediates our union with God. That is, through reciprocal and intersubjective communication, the Spirit works to unify the parties while respecting the alterity and identity of each, simultaneously.

Through the exercise of the Spirit's own distinctive *kenōsis,* the Spirit is fully present in each creature and comprehends the depth of God in every creature. The Spirit is able to communicate in millions of different ways in respect to the conditions and realities of every creature. As the Pentecost event shows (Acts 2:1–12), the Spirit communicates with humans by respecting their personal particularity and cultural diversity. In the new covenant, the Spirit works in a way that respects the alterity (freedom and otherness) of each person. The communicative work of the Spirit is very important in understanding how the divine and human will cooperate in the new covenant through the Spirit; it explains how God persuades and empowers human partners to freely do God's will.

A covenantal bond between God and believers in Jesus grows through daily fellowship in the Spirit—open, sincere, and truthful communication and exchange of affection and goodwill. Furthermore, through communication, a covenantal

38. Brueggemann, *The Covenanted Self,* 19.

39. Heschel, *The Prophets,* 50. Like lament and praise, confession is another form of communicative action prevalent in covenant; admitting one's sins or mistakes, confession intends the restoration of fellowship that is estranged or broken.

relationship is never static but always responsive to the changes of time and our surrounding environments. Communication is indispensable as we walk with God in the Spirit.

Summary

The communal-communicative dialectic constitutes the heart of covenantal sociality. It has a deeper basis in the triune God as it reflects the very life of the Trinity, where endless and perfect communication mediates divine unity and diversity, oneness and threeness in the Godhead. God's communication with humanity repeats the pattern of God's inner Trinitarian communication, which is communal and communicative in nature.[40]

This dialectic shows how God actually works with humans in the covenant. As an ongoing mechanism of a covenantal life, the communal-communicative dialectic characterizes the intersubjective nature of Christian worship, prayer, and fellowship. As we discuss in chapter 11, the communal-communicative dialectic constitutes the heart of the covenantal method of ethical reasoning.

In the covenantal relationship, the communal and the communicative are not mutually contradictory but complementary, and always in a creative tension. The latter is the more rational side of the covenant, while the former is the more affectional side. While the communal emphasizes the intimate, solidaric aspect of the covenant, the communicative stresses truth, freedom, and justice.[41] The communal forms the desire as well as the goal of the communicative, while the communicative serves as the method and process for achieving the communal. Communication is a mechanism that mediates and reconciles the differences between covenantal partners in achieving unity. As its Latin etymology indicates, communication is a process and mechanism that "makes common" between different parties.

40. Along with the works of social Trinitarians (such as Jürgen Moltmann, Leonardo Boff, Miroslav Volf, and Daniel Migliore), Herman Bavinck's work on the Trinity is also helpful in understanding the archetype/ectype relationship between the Trinity and the creation. According to James Eglinton, in Bavinck, "God as the archetypal (triune) unity-in-diversity is the basis for all subsequent (triniform) ectypal cosmic unity-in-diversity." See Eglinton, *Trinity and Organism*, 54.

41. One should note, however, that the communal dimension logically precedes the communicative dimension in the covenant in a manner analogous to the way the unilateral is antecedent to the bilateral. This is because the covenant is initiated by God, motivated by God's love to enter eternal communion with humanity, which is actualized through communication (fellowship) of the Spirit in Jesus Christ. This sequence (order) is crucial not only soteriologically but also ethically. Soteriologically, it speaks that God's love is the source of our redemption and goal; ethically, it entails that we should aim for love (the communal) as the goal in all our moral endeavors and attempts.

Thanks to the communicative dimension, the covenant never confuses or intermingles the identities of two partners. It does not absorb a weaker party even when a mystical union occurs. Thanks to the communal dimension, the relationship is never contractual or solely judicial. Together the covenantal parties form a deep, living, dynamic, and reciprocal bond. Through the two dynamics, covenant preserves the balance, harmony, and creative tension between intimacy and publicity, solidarity and freedom, and love and justice between the parties.

A good and trusted communication is the life energy of the covenant. The covenant erodes when communication stops. When the covenant loses the communal dimension, it degenerates into a contract, where only communicative exchanges of rights prevail. When only the communicative prevails, the covenant may become overly contentious or contractual. Just as a conflictual or contentious tendency of the communicative is checked and balanced by the communal, so is the mystical, uninformative, or collectivistic danger of the communal checked by the communicative. By virtue of its communicative dimension, the covenant is not distorted by blind submission or irrational trust. Conversely, by virtue of its communal nature, covenant is neither fragmented nor reduced into a contract. Each party has a responsibility to contribute to the deepening of the fellowship.

Memory-Hope

If the first two dialectics explain how covenant is established and justly maintained between the parties, then the third dialectic, memory-hope, explains how covenantal partners work together to approximate shalom in history. The memory-hope pattern literally describes how the covenant is tied with the past experience of God's liberation (memory) and the future completion of restoration (hope). Memory-hope is embedded in the divine drama (liberation-restoration). Memory and hope correspond to liberation and restoration, respectively. In the new covenant, memory pertains to the "already" of God's salvific work in Jesus Christ, while hope is related to the "not yet" of the resurrection of the body. The dialectic characterizes a distinctive temporal trajectory of covenant and the outlook of people living under it.

Obviously, this temporal pattern is no longer unique to Christians;[42] a person's life (biography) is typically framed and interpreted in terms of memory and hope. The pattern plays an important role in granting a person the meaning and purpose of identity, as well as a unique sense of identity. However, the pattern takes a far more coherent form when it is laden with a thick theological meaning in covenant.

42. This sense of temporality in fact originated from the linear imagination of time in Israel informed by the covenant.

Like the other two dialectics of covenant, memory and hope are separate, but they are dialectically related in the covenant. In the covenant, memory and hope reinforce each other. Memory gives the ground for hope, just as hope animates memory by giving it direction and purpose. In the covenant, God's future helps persons see new transforming realities beyond the present confinement and limitations, while God's past act of deliverance continues to provide a sense of assurance and comfort. That is to say, memory and hope provide a motivating power for ethics and mission. Memory pushes and hope pulls people on the journey toward God's promised land: the past experience of God's grace offers us reason to persevere, while the future pulls us with inspiration and hope anchored in God's promise. The future is not visible, and the present may be confusing and uncertain, but a believer finds direction and comfort in God's past salvific event and assuring future promise.

In a covenantal context, memory is not nostalgic, but nourishing and empowering, as it is connected to the present and the future as the formative and promissory event to be remembered and rehearsed. Allen Verhey notes:

> That remembered past is not simply a series of events that can be described objectively but rather events to be celebrated in repentance and jubilee, to be rehearsed in ritual and festival. The past, moreover, is not simply gone; we do not live in the past, but it lives in us. . . . By remembering we interpret the present, make sense of it. And remembering we sustain certain possibilities and nurture certain expectations; by remembering we learn to hope. Without memory there is no hope. We are not "fated" by our past (not as long as repentance remains a possibility sustained by our memory, at any rate).[43]

Just as covenant grants a distinctive meaning to memory, it also provides hope with moral substance. In the new covenant, the content of hope is God's shalom, where all lives flourish and live in right and peaceful relationships with one another. Shalom describes the perfection of the covenant that God intended for creation, which has already advanced in the new covenant of Jesus. It embodies the health and wholeness (encompassing the physical, emotional, and spiritual dimensions) of all creation in God's blessing. Shalom is the historical realization of the triune communion in which God's fellowship with humanity and other creatures is finally and fully actualized. All human aspirations and activities point toward this goal.

The hope dimension is closely associated with that of promise-fulfillment, which frequently appears in the Bible in relation to covenant. Promise-fulfillment is a subcategory of memory-hope, with its inextricable tie with hope. That is, Christian

43. Verhey, *Remembering Jesus*, 67.

hope is energized not only by the memory of the past but also by God's promises. In fact, the new covenant and the covenantal drama, because of their eschatological nature, always carry in them a strong promissory thrust. Framed by the promise-fulfillment pattern, a covenantal life is forward-looking. Covenant is established on the basis of the exchange of mutual promises. In the new covenant of Jesus, God has promised the future resurrection and full restoration of creation, which are sealed in the broken body of Jesus Christ (the Eucharist) and in the outpouring of the Spirit. Covenant is hence hope-filled because, in making a promise, God commits Godself to its fulfillment with fidelity.

Because of hope, covenant is not nostalgic; because of its rootedness in memory, it is not utopian. The Christian life is, rather, to join God's ongoing liberative-restorative work today. Christians cannot be morally complacent because they still have kingdom work to do, and forgetting or ignoring this remaining task (for example, by focusing solely on individual or spiritual salvation) is tantamount to spiritual amnesia and moral negligence. Entering a covenant with God means agreeing to join God's liberative-restorative work in pursuing shalom.

This pattern of memory and hope appears in many places in Scripture. For example, consider Jacob's confession when he is returning home from Laban's house after twenty years of labor. Having left Laban but soon to be confronted by his alienated brother, Esau, Jacob has no place to go. At this moment of impasse, Jacob remembers God's promise, his covenant with God, and the memories of God's provision, protection, and blessings at Laban's house. Out of this memory of God's past faithfulness and promise of Bethel, he finds new strength in his journey despite the uncertain future.

This theme of memory-hope is distinctive in the book of Deuteronomy. In a sense, Deuteronomy is the book of memory and hope. It consists of Moses's sermons for the Israelites who journeyed with him for forty years in the wilderness and were now on the plains of Moab, shortly before crossing the Jordan. Moses told the stories that reminded the postexodus generation of Israelites of God's great deliverance and faithfulness, to assure their faith and strengthen their ongoing commitment to God's promise.

This pattern continues in the NT as well. Christians live in the memory of God's salvific love demonstrated in Jesus Christ while waiting for the redemption of their bodies and the entire creation in the future. Christians, like ancient Israel, are the people of this memory; they are called to remember Christ's incarnation and cruciform passion as they wait for his return in glory.

This dialectic of memory-hope in covenant is closely tied with worship and liturgy. Just as the Passover and other festivals did for Israelites, Advent and the Eucharist liturgically and sacramentally connect the memory and hope grounded in the new covenant of Jesus. Joseph Cardinal Ratzinger, later Pope Benedict XVI, explains how memory and hope are inextricably connected in the Christian celebration of Advent:

> Advent is concerned with that very connection between memory and hope which is so necessary to man. Advent's intention is to awaken the most profound and basic emotional memory within us, namely, the memory of the God who became a child. This is a healing memory; it brings hope. The purpose of the Church's year is continually to rehearse her great history of memories, to awaken the heart's memory so that it can discern the star of hope. . . . It is the beautiful task of Advent to awaken in all of us memories of goodness and thus to open doors of hope.[44]

Through storytelling and liturgy that recapitulates the story, the memory-hope dialectic strengthens a covenantal bond within a faith community as it provides a communal biography and a shared vision. Like a suspension bridge that connects both banks of a big river, together memory and hope form a coherent drama filled with a meaning and a sense of direction. The dialectic and its drama serve as a shared frame of reference that guides the ethical discernment, discipleship, and public ministry of the community. Christopher Wright writes: "The context in which Israelites made ethical decisions, and carried on ethical reflection or critique, was the belief that there was both a past to which they had to respond (God's redemption of Israel from Egypt) and a future for which they were in part preparing (God's blessing to the nations)—and all of it under the sovereign purpose of the Lord as God."[45] In the covenant, a faith community obtains a coherent historical framework and a moral horizon to assess its decisions and actions.

Memory-hope helps people cope with historical contingencies with principled creativity and openness. It grants hermeneutical creativity as well as responsibility for people to live out their callings and obligations in their own historical contexts. This dialectic offers a crucial theological foundation for analogical reasoning. Christians interpret and assess moral issues in light of past events and teachings as well as future hope in God. Memory-hope helps each generation of Christians to hear God's calling and find its responsibility in the changing cultural contexts.

Located in the matrix of memory-hope, Christian identity and moral life are neither static nor rootless. To be rooted in the past does not make one self-enclosed, nor does being open to the future make one relativistic. Christian identity and moral life

44. Ratzinger, *Seek That Which Is Above*, 16.

45. Christopher Wright, *Old Testament Ethics*, 35.

are dynamic, embodied, and evolving (see chap. 6). With a clear sense of rootedness and purpose, the memory-hope pattern sustains and deepens Christians' identity as God's people as they journey with the Spirit in history.

In summary, this pattern has greatly affected Christian worship and education. Storytelling based on shared memory has the power to bind people together, if the shared hope gives a sense of the same purpose—enhancing the inner unity and mutual commitment among the members of a group. Telling the story of God's redemptive event (such as the exodus) has the effect of inviting younger generations into the same event and folding them into God's covenant community, sharing the same collective memory and the same hope and expectation of the future. In fact, the Passover haggadah reminds all around the table to say, "We were there."

Summary and Implications of Three Dialectics

Together the three dialectics illuminate the dynamic, multifaceted, relational nature of the covenant: how the covenant is established (unilateral-bilateral), operates (communal-communicative), and unfolds toward shalom (memory-hope) in the divine-human partnership. They show that the covenant is a grace-based, dialogical and performative, and hope-driven event. The covenantal drama and the three dialectics offer a proper moral vision, orientation, and concrete directives of the Christian life. In covenant, God's people find the balance and complementary nature of liberation and restoration, gift and task, freedom and solidarity, memory and hope. The threefold dialectics are found in major biblical covenants, but they take a far more radical and intensified form in the covenant of Jesus because of its Trinitarian and eschatological nature and the work of the Spirit (see chap. 4).

Furthermore, the three dialectics are pertinent in explaining how covenant is efficacious in motivating moral actions, as the above discussion of memory-hope has already indicated. The numerous "motivational clauses" in the Bible reveal how the ethical motivations in the Bible are associated with covenant and its three dialectics. Usually "prefaced with some syntactic indicator, such as 'for/because,' 'for the sake of,' 'so that,' or, 'lest,'"[46] these motivational clauses offer rationales as to why believers should be faithful to God and others.

Among all these motivations, gratitude (first dialectic) is primary and foundational because gratitude is a proper motivating force that corresponds to God's initiating grace and act of deliverance. The rationale is that since God has been gracious to us, we should be gracious toward others. It is frequently found in legal codes

46. Patrick Miller, *Israelite Religion and Biblical Theology*, 337. These clauses indicate the transition from the indicative to the imperative.

that stipulate generous treatment of the poor, aliens, widows, and orphans, while appealing to empathy or evoking a sense of shame in a believer.

In the Bible, motivations are intimately associated with a believer's intimate *communal* relationship with God (second dialectic). In covenant, humans experience God neither as an impersonal power nor as a principle, but as a personal *Thou*. A covenantal God is active, initiating, engaging, and responsive, unlike the remote, reticent god of deism. The God of the covenant is a faithful companion in our life. This God listens to our prayers and sings, rejoices, weeps, and dances with us.

These motivational clauses are *communicative* in nature as they intend to persuade believers to do moral actions by providing various plausible reasons for the actions (second dialectic). These clauses create powerful incentives for a believer to be faithful to her covenantal commitments. The moral clauses and their rationales, as part of God's communicative action, make obedience to God informed, reasonable, and attractive, appealing to the intellect, affection, and desire of a believer.

These motivational clauses can be categorized in terms of temporality: past, present, and future. If gratitude is a motivation based on the memory of God's action in the past (pushing force), then hope in the future blessings is a motivation grounded in the future (pulling force—third dialectic), while God's abiding love in our present life operates as a stabilizing and invigorating force.[47] This pattern appears in Paul's letters; he always frames his ethical admonitions on the basis of what God does for believers in Jesus Christ (and why believers should be grateful and live morally) and what the Spirit is currently doing in their lives, while always reminding others of God's faithfulness in fulfilling God's promises in the future and why Christians should not lose hope even in difficult circumstances.

In the new covenant, the Spirit is the power who gives us the succor and strength to remain faithful to God and others by evoking and instilling gratitude, love, and hope in us. Worship also plays a major role in motivating God's people for moral actions. By recapitulating the story of God's deliverance, worship invokes in believers the memory of God's deliverance in the past and assurance of God's future promise, together with a renewed sense of God's abiding presence and companionship in the present.

Conclusion

The covenantal drama; the composite of love, justice, and power; and the three dialectics tell what covenant is. Obviously, it is more than a fair agreement between different parties. It constitutes the free, reciprocal, dynamic, and graced nature of the

47. The idea of the Spirit as the advocate and the comforter strongly connotes this abiding nature of God's presence in the life of a believer.

Christian life. Covenant embodies God's design and plan for creation. Embedded in the divine drama of liberation-restoration, covenant denotes a divinely designed moral condition for creational flourishing, which is finally fulfilled in the new covenant of Jesus. Without a proper understanding of this dramatic nature and telos, covenant is indistinguishable from contract.

The meaning and implications of our discussion in this chapter are tremendous. The telos, key norms, and method of Christian ethics derive from these patterns and logic of the covenant. The covenantal drama and three dialectics are crucial in developing a constructive Christian ethics based on the covenant, as they explain the foundation, logic and grammar, and telos of the Christian moral life. They disclose who God is, what God's character and purpose are, how God relates to humanity and the world, and what God expects from God's human partners. Simultaneously they illuminate what kind of creature we are; what our identity, obligation, and future destiny are; and how we are to live in relation to God and other creatures.

On the basis of the findings of this chapter, the next two chapters study the distinctive moral nature, characteristics, and ethical practices of new covenant ethics. They demonstrate the plausibility and fertility of new covenant ethics by clarifying the frequently confused or misunderstood theological or ethical notions in Christian ethics such as love, justice, and power and the relationships between law and gospel, norm and context, unity and diversity, worship and ethics, and so on.

CHAPTER 4

The Distinctive Nature, Characteristics, and Practices of New Covenant Ethics

> Power at its best is love implementing the demands of justice, and justice at its best is power correcting everything that stands against love.
>
> —Martin Luther King Jr.,
> "Where Do We Go from Here?"

The objective of this chapter is to study new covenant ethics and its distinctive nature, characteristics, and practices. New covenant ethics is grounded in the covenant of Jesus and its moral features. The previous chapter identified key moral features of covenant through the study of the covenantal drama (liberation-restoration) and the three dialectics: unilateral-bilateral, communal-communicative, and memory-hope. Building on these findings, this chapter explores the distinctive characteristics of new covenant ethics. It claims that while new covenant ethics shares the above features, it substantially expands and intensifies them. Compared to the other covenants, new covenant ethics is Trinitarian in its theology, cosmic and eschatological in its scope, and resolutely nonviolent, just peacemaking, and ecumenical in its moral nature. The chapter demonstrates how the Eucharist epitomizes the crux and tenets of new covenant ethics.

Drawing upon these characteristics of new covenant ethics, the chapter also proposes the four moral practices of new covenant ethics: (1) communicative engagement, (2) just peacemaking, (3) grassroots community organizing, and (4) nonviolent action. These four practices are instrumental in organizing God's covenantal community today and in implementing the moral vision and norms/values of God's reign embodied in Jesus and his new covenant.

The Characteristics of New Covenant Ethics

Certain moral characteristics directly inform and shape the social practices of new covenant ethics. Below, we explore them individually.

Trinitarian

New covenant ethics is Trinitarian. Theologically, the covenant of Jesus Christ is the collaborative work of the Father, Son, and Spirit.[1] The NT interprets the Christ event (Jesus's incarnation, ministry, death, and resurrection) and the new covenant in relation to the Father and the Spirit. Jesus is not an ordinary person (e.g., merely a prophet); he is the Lord, Son of God, Messiah, incarnate Logos, and new Adam. The Father sent Jesus; Jesus's ministry was driven and guided by the Spirit; Jesus fulfilled the Father's will through his obedience by giving his life as the sacrifice for humanity; the Spirit conceived Jesus and raised Jesus from death and now brings the whole creation to its fulfillment to glorify the Father through the Son.

Naturally the new covenant is also the work of the Trinity. The new covenant of Jesus is Jesus centered but not Jesus exclusive; all three Trinitarian persons are equally involved in the making, sustaining, and fulfilling of the covenant. In the new covenant, the triune God is the source, content, power (efficacy), and goal for the organizing of the world.[2] If Christ is the content of the new covenant, then the Spirit is its effecting power and fulfiller, and the Father is the source (fountain).[3] Shalom, the historical actualization of the triune life (*perichōrēsis ad extra*), is the purpose of the covenant. The new covenant is protological as it fulfills the Father's intent at creation, christological since Jesus Christ is its very content and bond, pneumatological because the Spirit now directly mediates and actualizes the Word

1. This does not imply that the OT covenants lack a Trinitarian ground or that all three persons were not involved in them at all. The economy of the three Trinitarian persons in history coheres and revolves around the covenantal drama, soteriologically and ethically. However, the covenant of Jesus is distinctive from them, as it is established and operates on the basis of far more explicit Trinitarian assumptions and articulations. A Trinitarian reading of the OT covenants (how the Father, Son, and Spirit were involved in them) is possible only in light of the covenant of Jesus.

2. According to Vanhoozer, the three persons of the Trinity are involved in the communication, and their economy corresponds to three dimensions of communicative action: the Father is the origin of communication, the Son is its content, and the Spirit is its effective power. He contends, "Father, Son, and Spirit may be expressed in terms of tripersonal communication: voice (speaker; author); word/discourse (formed sounds/content); breath (medium; channel; power)." Vanhoozer, *Remythologizing Theology*, 28.

3. The Trinity helps us see the rich, dynamic, multifaceted theological dimensions of the new covenant of Jesus: protological, christological, pneumatological, and eschatological.

in believers, as prophesied by Jeremiah and Ezekiel, and eschatological as it is the consummation of all other covenants.

In particular, the active role of the Spirit is distinctive in the new covenant. As the perfecting power, the Spirit mediates and actualizes the Word in specific situations in a manner that is analogous to the incarnation of the Son. In God's self-communication in history, the Word and the Spirit always work together as the two hands of God. Because of the Spirit, the Word is neither abstract nor cerebral but concrete and embodied. Conversely, because of the Word, the Spirit is not arbitrary or enigmatic but rather enlightening and illuminating.

Thanks to the work of the Spirit, God's communication has a different kind of performative power. God's communication is not simply informative but is also transformative. God's grace "does not merely 'inspire' the response, it actually creates the ability to respond—it is both the reason and the power for the response."[4] The Spirit brings about a change in our hearts (Isa. 55) by convicting, compelling, and convincing us to turn from self-centeredness. The Spirit transforms and regenerates humans and builds the body of Christ in the context of the new covenant. Through the Spirit's ongoing communicative work, the Spirit enlivens the new covenant and our fellowship in it.

Eschatological

As mentioned in chapter 2, the new covenant of Jesus is the final eschatological covenant. It is the most inclusive covenant that encompasses every person and creature, even Earth itself.[5] Now the whole creation constitutes a single moral community.[6] Joseph Allen notes, "The inclusive covenant has to do with all living creatures, whether they can covenant or not, in that it affirms their value as God's good creatures and places on human beings the responsibility of caring for them."[7]

Reflecting the cosmic scope and inclusiveness of the new covenant, new covenant ethics is ecological. The new covenant grants membership to every creature. As will be discussed in chapter 15, each creature has an intrinsic value and a right, thus deserving protection, care, and support for its survival and thriving.

While the scope of the new covenant coincides with that of the creation covenant and the Noachian covenant, the moral meaning and nature of the new covenant are

4. Mott, *Biblical Ethics and Social Change*, 32.

5. While the covenant of Jesus is more inclusive than the Sinai covenant, the inclusivity of the latter was radically revolutionary by its contemporary standard. For example, Deut. 29:10–13 shows that the assembly of Israelites gathered to renew the Sinai covenant included women, aliens, and children as the equal covenantal partners of elders, officials, and men under God.

6. Allen, *Love and Conflict*, 39.

7. Allen, *Love and Conflict*, 39.

different from the latter. With its emphasis on just peacemaking, love, nonviolence, and righteousness, the covenant of Jesus, of all the biblical covenants, most closely embodies shalom. Also, the Spirit is now directly working as a mediator between God and humans along with the Son.

Liberative-Restorative

Following Jesus, new covenant ethics is liberative and restorative. The liberative-restorative drama is found in many places in the gospel stories. Jesus started his ministry with the announcement that "the kingdom of God is near," which indicated judgment against oppressors and the restoration of Israel. Richard Horsley supports this claim: "The Gospel has two complementary aspects, the renewal of Israel and the condemnation of the rulers."[8] Like the prophets, Jesus in his public ministry confronted the corrupt and oppressive rich, the proud, and the powerful, and labored to build a new covenant community among his followers (see chap. 14). The Jubilee, the divine political-economy, was at the center of his message.

Jesus was critical of the abuse of power by the rich and the privileged. The Sermon on the Mount is not completely peaceful but is also confrontational. The Sermon preaches God's judgment against the wealthy, the proud, and the powerful,[9] while it proclaims the promises of God's blessing to the poor, the hungry, the meek, and the mourning.

The Nazareth manifesto (Luke 4:18–19) best summarizes this liberative-restorative covenantal ministry of Jesus. Recapitulating the exodus and the Jubilee story, Jesus proclaims God's liberative-restorative work for the marginalized. We see the motif of liberation in the words "release" and "let the oppressed go free," and that of restoration in the phrases "recovery of sight to the blind" and "to proclaim the year of the Lord's favor." Proclaiming good news and the year of the Lord's favor (Jubilee) functions as an *inclusio*, enclosing the message of liberation and restoration.

Similarly, Jesus's exorcism was another sign of God's reign—the performance of liberation-restoration. Exorcism is not mere shamanistic conduct but is profoundly theological-ethical in the context of the covenantal drama; it liberates people from the evil forces possessing them. These evil forces encompass all de-creational powers, principalities, and evil spirits that rebel against God's love and justice, including Roman military power (Luke 8:26–39).

Through his table fellowship, Jesus built a new community where human dignity and equality were affirmed and communal ties and trust were strengthened through

8. Horsley, *Jesus and Empire*, 78.

9. For example, Jesus warns against ecclesiastical elitism and patriarchal domination (Matt. 23:8–12). Lee, *God and Community Organizing*, chap. 3.

mutual aid and care among people. Tax collectors and zealots became friends; Samaritans, Jews, and Romans participated equally in God's new community (Luke 7:1–10; 17:11–19; Matt. 8:5–13; John 4:7–26). The parable of the wedding banquet (Luke 14:16–24) demonstrates the inclusive and egalitarian nature of his community, where the poor, the crippled, the blind, and the lame were welcomed.

Finally, through his death on the cross and resurrection, Jesus has defeated the power of Satan, delivering humanity from sin and death, and by doing so has restored God's creatures to their rightful places and relationships with God and others. In the eschatological inbreaking of God's reign, all of history and the world are now the theater of God's covenantal organizing, and humans are called to be God's partners in this endeavor. The Eucharist is the occasion where a new community of liberation and restoration celebrates God's reign in the memory of Jesus's ministry and the hope for the heavenly banquet.

The covenantal drama still unfolds today through the work of the Spirit, and God invites people to the new covenant community. In God's covenantal drama, humans are not just passive observers of the divine drama but the coactors. Living between memory and hope, Christians join the liberative-restorative ministry of the triune God, who is already working in history.

With the new covenant as its organizing method and locus, new covenant ethics organizes God's new eschatological community today in various cultural contexts. It radically redefines the membership of God's people and their relationships. It is open to every person, transcending all human boundary markers and artificial social barriers (family, race, gender, religion, nationality, etc.), fulfilling God's original intent at creation. "There is neither Jew nor Gentile, neither slave nor free, nor is there male and female, for you are all one in Christ Jesus" (Gal. 3:28 NIV). Anyone who responds to God's deliverance in Jesus Christ in faith is now welcomed to the community.

This community is no longer ruled by privilege, status, and power, which Jesus identified with paganism (Matt. 20:25), but by equality, trust, and care (Mark 10:42–45). The members become brothers and sisters in God. Human power, honor, and prestige are radically relativized because they ultimately belong to God ("for the kingdom and the power and the glory are yours forever" [Matt. 6:13 mg.]). Built upon the new covenant, this community aims to be an alternative to the hierarchical, patriarchal, exploitative social system and divisive and fragmenting forces.

Composite Ethics of Love, Justice, and Power

New covenant ethics is the composite ethics of love, justice, and power in their dialectical balance and harmony. The ideas of love, justice, and power are often perceived to be mutually conflicting or incompatible. However, new covenant ethics provides a cohesive theological framework that integrates love, justice, and power in their dialectic balance and harmony. Unlike pacifists who choose love over justice, liberationists who prioritize justice over love, and Machiavellians who choose power over love and justice, new covenant ethics embraces justice, love, and power in their integral balance. It aptly describes what God's reign in Jesus looks like: God's reign is the reign of love, justice, and power in their perfect balance and harmony.

Like the other covenants, the new covenant is the composite ethics of love, justice, and power, but in the new covenant, its composite nature and scope are now eschatologized. That is to say, the other biblical covenants have the three components, but usually with narrower scopes or disproportionate balance and integration among them. For example, in the Noachian covenant, despite its cosmic scope, the love dimension is relatively weak compared to the justice and power aspects; the Sinai covenant displays all three components in a relatively good balance, but its scope was limited to Israel. However, in the new covenant, the composite expands to a cosmic horizon and reaches its complete integration and perfect balance among love, justice, and power. In particular, the love dimension is far more prominent and intense compared to the other covenants.[10]

In the new covenant, love does not abrogate but nurtures the power of everyone in just and right relationships. The exorcism, moral teachings, and healing ministry of Jesus were empowering. They helped liberate people from destructive forces and restore their freedom and agency as God's children. Every work of social justice requires the use of collective power (moral, spiritual, political, economic) to correct and dismantle injustices and unjust social structures. This means that a covenantal community is the community of not only love and justice but also power that nurtures and enhances the capability of each member and the community.[11]

In new covenant ethics, because of love, justice is not purely judgmental but is also delivering and restorative.[12] Because of justice, God's love is not sentimental but liberative and orderly.[13]

10. The creation covenant (the covenant with Adam), before its breach, was closest to the new covenant in terms of the integration, balance, and scope of the three components.

11. Chapter 11 discusses the tension between justice and shalom (and love) in social ethics, as the former is enforceable while the latter is not.

12. Lewis Smedes notes: "Justice and love form a kind of moral counterpoint in life. Justice holds us back in respect; it tells us to let people be what they are and have what they have. Love pushes us toward people in care; it tells us to get into people's lives so that we can help them be what they ought to be and get what they ought to have. Justice tends to urge us to keep the rules, especially the 'Thou shalt not's.' Love translates the negative commands into positive invitations to creative helpfulness. Justice and love are the absolute of life to which the other commandments point; the other commands are valid because they direct us to embody justice and love in the complex realities of human life." Smedes, *Mere Morality*, 240.

13. In a similar spirit, divine commandments on justice included in Lev. 29 are the examples

Because of its relational nature and connection to justice and power, a covenantal love is different from a typical notion of *agapē* love as self-abnegation. It is other-regarding but not completely self-denying; it is volitional, agential, and reciprocal. New covenant ethics upholds the healthy self-love of a person because it is the foundation for a meaningful moral agency and the precondition for other-love.

Because of love and justice, power is neither abusive nor arbitrary. Because of its connection to justice, power in new covenant ethics is corrective against injustices; justice offers necessary rules and norms that guide the use of power. Because of its relation to love, power is neither instrumental nor utilitarian but nonviolent and communal; it is to build the beloved community. Martin Luther King Jr.'s aphorism sums up the relationship in an excellent way: "Power at its best is love implementing the demands of justice, and justice at its best is power correcting everything that stands against love."[14]

Just Peacemaking

The balance and harmony of love, justice, and power in new covenant ethics are directly related to another major moral characteristic: just peacemaking.

Just peacemaking, literally speaking, has justice-making and peace-making (shalom-making) dimensions—rectifying injustices and reconciling alienated relationships. To put it differently, it restores a trusted, peaceful relationship on the basis of justice. Justice and peace are never separable in covenant; covenant "carries with it the demand to do justice and seek peace."[15] If covenant is God's method to "put things right," to put things right always includes the restoration of peace (reconciliation) between the parties. In other words, to "put things right" inevitably includes the liberative work of justice as well as the reconciling work of peace building. Covenant is God's invitation to peace (shalom) through the removal of injustice, alienation, and enmity between the parties. Until peace is achieved, the relationship is never "right."

A recurring message of the Bible is that righteousness and justice are indispensable in bringing genuine peace to a society (Ps. 96:10–13; Isa. 9:2–7; 32:16–17; 48:18; 60:17). Peace grows on the firm basis of right and just relationships. There is no shortcut to peace that ignores or avoids justice. Any peace that lacks justice is intrinsically flawed and usually defends the status quo of oppression and injustice.

---

of love with the double love commandment as the summary, not the replacements, of commandments on justice.

14. King, "Where Do We Go from Here?," 247.

15. De Gruchy, *Reconciliation*, 188.

Just peacemaking corresponds to the covenantal drama of liberation-restoration. Just peacemaking is a concrete moral embodiment and practice of the divine drama. The Bible reiterates a theological motif or idea in different terms or languages to communicate its complex meanings and nuances. For example, reconciliation, atonement, and justification describe God's forgiveness of sin with different emphases and nuances. Likewise, liberation-restoration, love-justice-power, and just peacemaking are similar to each other in the context of the new covenant. Peace describes the content of restoration—what restoration finally brings forth. At the same time, it portrays the state where the composite of love, justice, and power is fully actualized in the new covenant. While distinctive, peace is closely associated with love. In the new covenant, peace indicates not merely the absence of enmity or conflict but the active presence of friendship, trust, and care for others—the qualities of love.

New covenant ethics is just peacemaking; it aims to achieve justice and peace together. The idea of just peacemaking describes what the new covenant is about. The new covenant is God's final, perfecting act of just peacemaking with humanity through God's gracious initiative in Jesus Christ. While just peacemaking is an integral aspect of the biblical covenants, it becomes far more explicit in the new covenant of Jesus because of its clear and unrelenting commitment to peace, love, and nonviolence. In a clear distinction from the other covenants, new covenant ethics unequivocally rejects violence and aggression (e.g., the holy war) and champions justice and peace (shalom). In the Sermon on the Mount, Jesus teaches, more explicitly than in any other passage in the Bible, that peacemaking is a primary calling of God's people: "Blessed are the peacemakers, for they will be called children of God" (Matt. 5:9).[16] The core teachings of the covenant of Jesus and the Sermon on the Mount—such as nonviolence, nonretaliation, dialogue, care, and restorative justice— are all contributive (conducive) to peacemaking.

Nonviolent

New covenant ethics is nonviolent. Covenant is deeply tied with nonviolence because, by definition, covenant indicates a commitment to a nonviolent resolution of conflict among the participants. It relies on communicative engagement in establishing and maintaining a just and peaceful relationship between the parties. To enter covenant means publicly declaring the rejection of violence and war to resolve political conflicts. This commitment helps to build mutual trust and understanding,

16. This passage resonates with Gen. 1, which describes humanity as God's image-bearer, God's royal representatives toward creation, and God's companion in shalom-building work.

and the agreement serves as the framework for future negotiations when new needs for adjustments arise.

Expanding and intensifying this nonviolent nature of the covenant, the new covenant of Jesus is radically nonviolent, nonretaliatory, and communal not only toward its members but also toward others. It calls for proactive peacemaking and demonstration of goodwill toward others, including one's enemies. Such a radical moral stance is demanded by God's own goodness and mercifulness, which was demonstrated toward us in the life, ministry, and suffering of Jesus. Nonviolence is consistent with the eschatological vision of the new covenant, namely, the full restoration of love and peace (shalom). Only through nonviolence can God's love and peace be actualized.

However, a commitment to nonviolence does not come at the expense of justice and power. Jesus's command to turn the other cheek is not acquiescence to evil, but a firm commitment to active nonviolent resistance to injustice. Turning the other cheek is the assertion of one's equal dignity, which covenant ethics advocates. Influenced by Jesus's Sermon on the Mount, Mahatma Gandhi was the first person to apply nonviolent action (through marches, demonstrations, and sit-ins) for political change. In the twentieth century, nonviolent action gained a political and moral importance among peacemaking traditions[17] and demonstrated its effectiveness for meaningful political change in many parts of the world.

Ecumenical

Surprisingly, new covenant ethics is ecumenical; it is a particular ethic with public relevance. While rooted in the particular historical drama of Jesus and his new covenant, it is able to engage in the public realm with relevance and competence. An ecumenical approach is possible because new covenant ethics offers an organizing method that applies to not only the church but also society and its institutions with the same final vision, norms/values, and constitutive logic.

Specifically, new covenant ethics' ecumenical and public engagement takes place through its dialectic relationship with the Noachian covenant. With its focus on justice (the stipulation of minimal moral obligations), the Noachian covenant has direct public relevance. It is given to all of humanity, living in the condition of sin, without any religious prerequisite for membership.[18] That is, its primary purpose is to preserve the minimal order of justice and human flourishing. Despite human disobedience, God is faithful to God's creation, and God's common grace is work-

17. Cortright, *Peace*, 20.

18. VanDrunen, "The Protectionist Purpose of the Law," 106.

ing in the world to restrain the power of sin and destruction, to preserve necessary minimal order and condition for the flourishing of all creatures.

Technically speaking, while they are members of the new covenant, Christians are still under the Noachian covenant's binding authority because it is the eternal covenant (thus valid for the rest of history) and the power of sin in history is not yet completely done away with. Christians are responsible to work to promote justice in a society. This means that Christians are double bound by the Noachian covenant and the new covenant;[19] they are caught between the two, and their ethics is characterized by just peacemaking—pursuing both justice (under the Noachian covenant) and peace (under the new covenant) in every realm of life. Justice is necessary but not sufficient. Christians are called to pursue shalom, but without overriding the concern of justice. This means that new covenant ethics takes a form of rooted cosmopolitan ethics.[20]

The ecumenical nature of new covenant ethics (and the meaning and implications of the dialectic relationship of the Noachian covenant and the new covenant) will be further explored in the next chapter and in chapter 11 (when we discuss covenantal social ethics).

Eucharistic

New covenant ethics is eucharistic. Baptism and the Eucharist are the sacraments of the new covenant that God uses to organize a new, just community. Both are integral to the new covenant; if baptism has to do with entering the new covenant (beginning), the Eucharist is concerned with staying in it (sustenance).

Baptism is the initiation rite that indicates the beginning of a new life in Christ. The ritual (immersion into water) portrays dying and living with Christ. It enacts the drama of liberation and restoration in the transformation of the baptized—liberation from the old, sinful way of life and restoration to a new, flourishing life in the Spirit.

It is Trinitarian, which is made explicit in its Trinitarian formula; the three persons are communicatively involved in the cleansing and rebirth of a believer. It is eschatological. It signifies a new peoplehood (a global tribe) and the foretaste of a new creation. As the firstfruits, a believer is called to the life of service and discipleship for the renewal of creation in solidarity with creation and others, especially the

19. The new covenant, the creation covenant, and the Noachian covenant are the work of the same triune God. The perichoretic unity among the three persons of God provides the basis of unity and coherence among these covenants. The unity exists between common grace in creation and special grace in Jesus Christ because the God of redemption is none other than the God of creation.

20. On rooted cosmopolitanism, see my book *The Great World House*, chap. 4.

poor and the oppressed, in the manner in which Jesus demonstrated his solidarity with creation and humanity in his enfleshment and ministry.

Although baptism displays key moral features of new covenant ethics, it is the Eucharist that embodies ethics in a comprehensive, dynamic, and succinct manner. In a simple but profound way, the Eucharist epitomizes what the new covenant is about. Strikingly, the Eucharist displays all the major dialectical patterns of the new covenant and their moral features that we have discussed: liberation-restoration; the triad of love, justice, and power; the three dialectics; and the covenant's nature as Trinitarian, eschatological, ecological, and ecumenical along with just peacemaking.

The Eucharist is *Trinitarian*. In a worship service, we thank the Father for the fruit of his creation and his self-donation in Jesus Christ; we partake in the flesh and blood of Jesus; and we invoke the coming of the Spirit (*epiclesis*) for his communicative presence at the table so that the elements are made our own through his work.

The Eucharist signifies a new community of a liberated and restored humanity in Jesus. The table represents the gathering of people liberated from greed, domination, separation, and accumulation to be restored into gratitude (first dialectic), sharing (second dialectic), and hope (third dialectic). It is a covenantal practice that represents a new eschatological community, where the communicants live in the hope of the final reign of shalom promised by the triune God.

The Eucharist represents the community where God's justice and righteousness are restored, power and resources are shared, and love and care are practiced among the members. Its ceremony integrates God the creator (the source of all lives and materials) with God the liberator and restorer. Hence, those who participate in this ceremony are reminded of their responsibility to do neighborly love and justice. By reflecting God's moral character, egalitarianism, respect, trust, mutual sharing, and empowerment, they characterize its lifestyle.

The Eucharist is a peace meal that symbolizes just peacemaking and reconciliation between God and humans, humans and humans, and humans and nature. It is ecological. Bread and wine are gifts from the earth. Their presence on the table reminds us of the shared destiny and solidarity between humanity and nature, as members of God's creation. We receive them with thanksgiving for God's generosity and fidelity, and we recommit ourselves to good, caring stewardship of God's creation and other creatures.

The Eucharist is also ecumenical; all people are invited and eat together—from east and west, from north and south, regardless of their racial, gender, economic, and national backgrounds.

Its various names (Eucharist, Lord's Supper, Holy Communion, Christian Passover meal) reveal how the sacrament is associated with the covenantal drama of liberation-restoration and the three dialectics.

(1) *Eucharist.* It is a thanksgiving meal to God for God's initiating grace, the gifts of creation and God's giving of Jesus Christ for our redemption. By receiving God's gifts with gratitude, we are charged to continue the ministry of just peacemaking by joining the liberative and restorative work of God.

(2) *Holy Communion.* The sacrament is a communion meal between God, humans, and creation, which draws the communicants deeper into God and others. When communicants partake together in the same broken body of Christ, God's gifts strengthen the bond among them. Embodying the shared life (*koinōnia*) in Christ, the sacrament points to the eschatological vision of shalom in which peace, harmony, and unity are actualized.

(3) *The Lord's Supper.* This name is associated with the third dialectic of covenant, which is memory and hope. The Eucharist is the memorial as well as an expectant meal—a meal of joy and hope. It remembers Jesus's last meal with his disciples, as Jesus commanded ("Do this in remembrance of me"), while anticipating the messianic banquet with Jesus that is promised with his return.

(4) *Christian Passover meal.* The meal is historically connected to the covenantal drama, in particular, the Passover meal of the exodus event in which Hebrew slaves ate paschal lambs and half a dozen other foods before they left Egypt. The event collectively celebrates the divine judgment against Pharaoh. Overlapping with the Lord's Supper, it reinforces God's liberative-restoring work in history, the memory and celebration of God's triumph over unjust powers and the hope for the restoration of the shalom community. Recapitulating the Sabbath economics of Israel (see chap. 13), the sacrament ritually represents Jesus's vision of political economy. It connects the story of his table fellowship with the practice of the daily sharing of basic subsistence with others.

The above brief observation exhibits how intimately the Eucharist is related to the new covenant and its various patterns. It expresses the wide range and diverse aspects of new covenant ethics and all its major moral characteristics, thus proving the validity of new covenant ethics and its faithfulness to theological convictions. In this sense, we may declare that new covenant ethics is eucharistic ethics.

Practices of New Covenant Ethics

The moral characteristics discussed above (Trinitarian; eschatological; liberative-restorative; the triad of love, justice, and power; nonviolent; and just peacemaking) directly inform and shape the social practices of new covenant ethics. There are at least four different moral practices that embody the triad of love, justice, and power: (1) just peacemaking, (2) communicative action, (3) grassroots organizing, and (4) nonviolent action.

Grounded in the new covenant of Jesus, these practices are guided under the rubric of the covenantal drama (liberation-restoration). These practices achieve God's covenantal organizing (putting things right) that is manifested in justice for the oppressed (liberation), reconciliation (just peacemaking), healing-remedy (rehabilitation and renewal) of people from the effects of sin, and their full restoration into a just, peaceful, and loving community. This means that Christians fight against injustices, corruption, and distortion (liberation) and pursue just peacemaking by restoring broken relationships (reconciliation). Finally, Christians build new organizations and a new society working together to approximate shalom.

These practices aim to contribute to the covenantal organizing of the shalom community. These practices are all nonviolent, which is consistent with the spirit of the covenant of Jesus. Together they seek to reduce human evil through the implementation of justice and to restore trust and peace. Specifically, they engage and pursue the following:

1. conflict resolution (which entails mutual agreement) through communicative action and just peacemaking
2. transforming social structures and conditions (which entails new rule making) through communicative action (moral persuasion), nonviolent direct action, and grassroots organizing
3. creating a shared structure and full inclusion (which entails new moral and constitutional transformation) through communicative action and structural-institutional organizing.

In short, these practices help to "overcome and heal the past, restructure power relations, restore justice and develop a common vision for the future."[21]

Just Peacemaking Practice

It is natural that new covenant ethics identifies just peacemaking as one of its core practices. Just peacemaking is an important practice to approximate shalom. Just as the biblical ideas of reconciliation and atonement are descriptors of peacemaking, confession, dialogue, covenanting, and forgiveness are part of peacemaking practices.

In peace studies, just peacemaking is a well-known genre of conflict resolution in domestic and international relationships. The new covenant and just peacemaking theories share the same insight and motivation: conflict resolution. Peacemaking

21. De Gruchy, *Reconciliation*, 183.

theories seek a peaceful resolution of the conflicts in the short term and lasting peace in the long term, just as covenant seeks a just and reconciled relationship between the formerly alienated parties. A voluntary agreement between the parties in the covenant is a sign that the conflict has been resolved. Not many theories of just peacemaking explicitly acknowledge covenant as their theoretical ground and framework, but Pierre Allan and Alexis Keller's definition of just peacemaking almost precisely describes its implied covenantal nature: it is "a process whereby peace and justice are reached together by two or more parties recognizing each other's identities, each renouncing some central demands, and each accepting to abide by common rules jointly developed."[22] A more detailed discussion of the similarities and differences between the just peacemaking practice of new covenant ethics and other peacemaking theories will be offered in chapter 20.

Just peacemaking practice is proactive in the new covenant. "Peace, like war, must be waged. It must be waged courageously, persistently, creatively, with imagination, heart, and wisdom."[23] New covenant ethics is neither otherworldly nor sectarian. It rejects violence, withdrawal from society, and acquiescence or blind support of the government. It is active but peaceful, political but not partisan, militant but civic.

The proactive nature of just peacemaking in the covenant of Jesus corresponds to God's own initiative in just peacemaking. In inviting humanity to a covenantal bond, God is proactive toward us. A consistent message of the Bible is that God is continually and relentlessly reaching out to us to restore the broken relationship with us by liberating us from the power of sin. Through God's just peacemaking (justification), we, former enemies of God, become God's friends (Rom. 5:10). We are obligated to respond to God's proactive grace through our own proactive just peacemaking toward others (as the first dialectic indicates). In response to God's drama of liberation-restoration, we are called to engage in just peacemaking.

Compelled by God's love, we keep expanding the work of just peacemaking further within and without a covenantal community. In covenant, peacemaking leads to peace growing, peace deepening, and peace expanding. Just peacemaking continues in a covenantal relationship in the form of the communal-communicative dynamic. The communal-communicative dynamic denotes the life of a covenantal community that is just, peaceful, reciprocal, and loving. Just peacemaking is nurtured in a covenantal fellowship.

This approach of just peacemaking is consistent with Jesus's commandment to

22. Allan and Keller, *What Is a Just Peace?*, 7. Just peacemaking theory and practices are already well known among political scientists, peace activists, and Christian ethicists, but there is a dearth of studies done on them from a covenantal perspective. As we discuss in chapter 20, new covenant ethics is able to embrace its purpose, core values, and emphases in a covenantal framework.

23. Stassen, *Just Peacemaking*, 18.

be yeast, salt, light, and mustard seed—the metaphors of transformative nature at a grassroots level (not imperial, coercive, or hierarchal, but local and spreading). In his life and teaching, Jesus embodied just peacemaking; likewise, discipleship in the early church was characterized by righteousness and peacemaking.

Just peacemaking practice is applicable to all levels of social relationships, including intergroup and international peacemaking. It has profound meaning and profound implications for Christian social ethics, for example, in criminal justice (chap. 16), race relationships (chap. 17), and war and peace (chap. 20).

Communicative Engagement

As discussed before, covenant is built and maintained through communicative actions between different parties. Free, equal, and reciprocal communication serves as a key mechanism to reach mutual understanding, collaborative deliberation, and cooperation. Communicative engagement is a key practice in building and renewing solidarity (unity-in-diversity) among members. New covenant ethics relies on communicative engagement in two major interrelated areas: conflict resolution and rule making.

Covenant has been used in the Bible and human history as a method of cooperative conflict resolution and trust building in various historical situations. This affinity of covenant with conflict resolution is found throughout history when people in the Near East and other parts of the world relied on covenant, or a similar process, as a mechanism to avoid war and conflict and to build peaceful and trusted relationships.

Dialogue and negotiation between opposing parties, as common sense indicates, are a more constructive way to address conflicts than resorting to violence. The process of conflict resolution typically relies on communicative engagements between the parties, which occur through dialogue, acknowledgment of mistakes and negotiation of guilt, and reparation. New covenant ethics is well equipped for conflict resolution through its emphasis on nonviolence, truthful confession, and forgiveness.

A major role of communicative engagement in covenant is rule making. Rule making is an integral part of covenant because covenant is based on an agreement that typically includes certain rules. These rules are called covenantal stipulations, and they are reached through communicative engagement between different parties. In short, the process to reach an agreement is the process of rule making.

When made on the basis of an agreement, rules represent a communal solidarity that mediates individual members and a community. They are not permanent but open to revision through ongoing communicative engagements of a community. Rule making plays a crucial role for covenant in organizing or renewing a community. A common life (and governance) relies on certain shared rules, and any new form of governance, such as global governance or a major social reform, entails a rule-making process.

With its rule-making role, new covenant ethics is methodologically well poised to deal with the challenges of pluralism and diversity in the global era. Through the influx of immigrants, advances of technology, and changing cultural values, a contemporary society faces immense challenges to reconstitute itself, culturally and morally. Creating a new form of unity out of diverse groups is a major task for every society in the global era, and it cannot be achieved through coercion, such as is practiced by authoritarian regimes and illiberal governments. As the art of organizing life together (symbiosis), new covenant ethics can address this challenge with the practice of communicative engagement and its rule-making method.

Communicative engagement and rule making with non-Christians are possible on the basis of the Noachian covenant. As mentioned above, all human beings, including Christians, are bound by the Noachian covenant. As the source of all truth, God's self-communication is not confined to the Christian community. Jesus Christ is God's final revelation, but he is not the only revelation. Wisdom literature in the Bible substantiates and validates this fact; it does not specify Israel or the church as the sole source of wisdom.

Wisdom indicates a set of knowledge obtained from human experiences for general relevance and moral enlightenment. It is instructive that moral statutes and ordinances were already available in the form of community wisdom/tradition or general human moral experiences before the special revelation on Mount Sinai. Some of the Ten Commandments are in continuity with the laws of surrounding nations. This point is reinforced in the story of Jethro's advice to Moses (Exod. 18:13). The book of Exodus treats the prudence of Moses's father-in-law, which probably resulted from his long administrative experience, as being as valid as the direct divine revelation.[24] The very fact that Jethro's advice was given on the "mountain of God" (18:5) is quite stunning. The implication is that common moral wisdom can serve as a valid moral source for Christians, and Christians do not have to be afraid of learning from non-Christians in seeking the justice and peace of a society.[25]

On the basis of the Noachian covenant, it is possible for Christians to participate in the process of rule making with other groups, which is called making a compact. Like a covenant, a compact is based on mutual agreement, but it is a secular phenomenon. While a covenant is an agreement where God is a direct party to, or a

24. Fretheim, *Exodus*, 199–200.

25. Braaten, *No Other Gospel!*, 65–82.

guarantor of, a covenantal relationship, a compact "rests more heavily on a legal, though still [universally] ethical, grounding."[26] It is neither as expedient as a contract nor as explicitly theological as a covenant. As in covenanting, communicative engagement is indispensable in a compacting process.[27]

Hans Küng's Global Ethic project exhibits an example of compact. In particular, the document "Declaration toward a Global Ethic" was created on the basis of an agreement among the representatives of various religions regarding shared moral principles and values for humanity: the Golden Rule, justice, human dignity, freedom, equality, human rights, and sustainability. Max Stackhouse also notes the covenantal nature of morality in general. "People and nations, cultures and religious traditions are often covenantal in some respects, and that is why we can find agreement on many things that are morally wrong. Every language has terms for sacrilege, disrespect, lying, cheating, stealing, murder, rape, exploitation, etc.; every nation has laws against these, every culture disapproves of them, and every known religion recognizes these as opposed to divine law—even if there are some differences of tradition as to how these are applied to particular cases."[28]

Conflict resolution and rule making are interrelated because the former typically entails the latter, resulting in an agreement between the parties that specifically delineates the content of the resolution. Communicative engagement is a constructive practice of new covenant ethics for conflict resolution and rule making. Its importance is growing exponentially in a globalizing society where a social need for addressing alienation and enmities between diverse groups and new rule making is increasing.

Grassroots Community Organizing

As mentioned, organizing has been intrinsic to God's covenant project from the beginning. God organizes a new, just community through covenant. History shows God's reign as an ongoing labor to organize the shalom community with the covenant as its means. Israel and the church are the products of God's covenantal organizing.

In general, community organizing refers to a method that intentionally gathers and builds people into an organization of collective identity around shared concerns

26. Elazar, "Federal Models of (Civil) Authority," 250–51.

27. Lisa Sowle Cahill notes: "The foundations of morality are not best understood as innate structures of consciousness or rationality which are self-evident at an abstract level, but as broad areas of agreement about human needs, goods, and fulfillments which can be reached inductively and dialogically through human experience." Cahill, *Sex, Gender, and Christian Ethics*, 2.

28. Stackhouse, "A Covenantal Justice in a Global Era," 210.

about justice. While related to God's covenantal organizing, grassroots community organizing here has a narrower scope and meaning. Although its ultimate purpose is to organize a shalom community (which is eschatological), its immediate purpose describes a local practice of community organizing (which is political-social) in a manner similar to Saul Alinsky's method.[29] Developed and popularized by Saul Alinsky (1909–1972) and his disciples, community organizing has been used for political change in many different forms. It is democratic and grassroots oriented, and it shares many sensibilities with covenantal organizing. Along with nonviolent resistance, it has become an indispensable method of grassroots democracy today.

Of the four practices, grassroots community organizing embodies covenantal organizing in the most encompassing manner. It actually organizes with the aim of transforming (by liberating and restoring) a local community from injustice to justice. Toward this end, it relies on the three other practices of new covenant ethics. It depends on communicative engagement in building trust and relationships among members, internally, and in building coalitions with other organizations, externally. It resorts to nonviolent action as a collective action for political change, while resorting to just peacemaking as a means of conflict resolution and democratic negotiation.

Community organizing begins with the identification of a shared concern about justice among the participants; then it builds trust and mutual cooperation using various mechanisms of one-on-one, communicative deliberation, small group meetings, coalition building, etc.; finally, it engages in collective action. That is to say, community organizing attempts to achieve two immediate moral-political objectives: first, to build a reliable community of mutual trust, support, solidarity, and hope (i.e., social capital), and second, to translate the accumulated social capital (mutual trust, support, solidarity, hope) into organizational power to change unjust social relationships. While community organizing may have immediate political objectives (legislation and implementation), its goal is larger than that. It aims at community renewal, the revitalization of civil society.

Grassroots community organizing in new covenant ethics is another employment and enactment of the triad of love, justice, and power. Grounded in a passion for justice (in its critique of imbalance of power and structural evils), it is a method that generates power (political capability) among the members (by relation building and collective identity, and mobilization of resources) in order to build a just society. Achieving justice includes correcting injustices and protecting people from oppres-

29. See my book *God and Community Organizing*. However, covenantal organizing is different from Alinsky in its emphasis on love in balance with justice and power. Saul Alinsky's method focuses on the two concerns of power and justice, often at the expense of love.

sion, exploitation, and abuses, and such correction is not possible without mobilization of people and resources. It is politically realistic in its recognition of self-interest and the importance of power accumulation, but love is its motivation and goal.

In general, grassroots community organizing has two dimensions in expanding power and building an organization: bonding and bridging.[30] In terms of bonding, covenantal organizing nurtures trust and mutual understanding among the members and accumulates collective power to work for targeted social change in local communities. In terms of bridging, Christians are tasked with the responsibility to work with others in order to organize institutions and society afresh. Christians do not have to rely on their own power and organization alone. To approximate shalom and increase their power base and resources, they need to build coalitions with non-Christians. Bridging work in community organizing is a concrete way to practice the covenantal principle of unity-in-diversity, the vision of a life together.[31]

The method of grassroots community organizing is shareable between Christians and non-Christians in building coalition. New covenant ethics relies on moral persuasion and communicative engagement in building bridges and networks with others. All concerned groups join and collaborate with each other in achieving justice and enhancing the common good. Participants may share the rich memory of past struggles for justice and peace (triumphs and suffering) and refresh the shared hope for the better future of humanity. Through mutual inspiration and communication, they may reach mutual agreements for trusted relationships and shared actions.

Nonviolent Action

Nonviolent action for political change is the morally consistent, politically effective way of exercising power according to the vision and principles of the new covenant. The covenantal drama, and its triad of love, justice, and power, and just peacemaking, offer a coherent theological moral framework for the use of nonviolent action (e.g., peaceful marches, sit-ins, demonstrations, civil disobedience, sanctions).

New covenant ethics takes the question of power seriously in its social engagement because power inequality is at the center of social injustice and oppression. For example, colonialism, slavery, and segregation were the result of an imbalance of power. Without the accumulation and application of power, the removal of social evil is impossible.[32] Nonviolent action builds collective power through

30. The two are interrelated as in Aristotle's ethics and politics. Covenant ethics and covenant politics are both aspects of God's reign.

31. Cf. Walzer, *Thick and Thin.*

32. Power used in nonviolent resistance does not have to be political or economic only but can also be moral and spiritual.

grassroots community organizing and peacefully uses it to correct injustice and implement justice.

The use of collective power is based on the recognition that the privileged never voluntarily give up their privileges and power and only do so when challenged by a countervailing power. Reinhold Niebuhr writes, "Whenever men hold unequal power in society, they will strive to maintain it. They will use whatever means are most convenient to that end and will seek to justify them by the most plausible arguments they are able to devise."[33] Moral persuasion alone is not sufficient to bring about systematic political change; hence the exercise of collective power is necessary. Nonviolence actively aims to change the unjust laws and unequal political power relationships that are the source of injustices.

In the context of the new covenant, the ultimate aim of mobilizing and exercising power is to build the beloved community of shalom. Nonviolent action is not merely a matter of political expediency but is also a matter of shalom making. Since the purpose of covenant is shalom (a cosmic community of love), it cannot be achieved by evil means (such as retaliatory violence) but only by goodwill and moral means toward others. In other words, nonviolence is the exercise of power to achieve justice, motivated by love. Because love is the motivation, the practitioners of nonviolence in new covenant ethics are required to be nonviolent in both attitudes and actions.

Martin Luther King Jr., who attributes his method to Gandhi and its spirit to Jesus, is helpful for showing the connection between nonviolence and love. For King, although the immediate goal of nonviolence is to achieve justice, its ultimate goal is to build the beloved community. King believed that the struggle for justice and the task of building the beloved community could never be separate; the end and the means should cohere. King declared, "To meet hate with retaliatory hate would do nothing but intensify the existence of evil in the universe." The goal of nonviolence is "to win the friendship and understanding of the other."[34] King's idea of nonviolence, inspired by Jesus's Sermon, is consistent with a covenantal approach to nonviolence.

There is a close tie between nonviolence and just peacemaking. With shalom making as the ultimate goal, nonviolence pressures and invites opponents to come to the negotiating table to engage in the process of peaceful correction of injustices. While it uses a forceful measure to undo systemic injustice, its goal is to "bring opposed groups together around a negotiated vision of social coexistence and cooperation."[35]

33. Reinhold Niebuhr, *Moral Man and Immoral Society*, 34.

34. King, "An Experiment in Love," 17.

35. Cahill, *Blessed Are the Peacemakers*, 20.

Nonviolent action is closely associated with grassroots organizing, as mentioned above. Achieving justice is impossible without correcting injustices, which in turn requires a collective exercise of organized power. While community organizing concerns itself with accumulation of power, nonviolent action is the use (application) of the power. It takes strong political character and is enacted in the form of collective, direct actions such as marches, demonstrations, sit-ins, and civil disobedience if necessary. Since liberative justice is to correct social evils and set people free from oppression and exploitation, such correction is not possible without the mobilization of people and resources.

Summary

The four practices describe the rich, capacious, and dynamic nature of new covenant ethics. With shalom as the goal, new covenant ethics is praxiological in seeking just peace and in nonviolently organizing and mobilizing people at a grassroots level for positive social change. Despite their different emphases and strategies, these practices are all motivated by love, are equally committed to justice, and recognize the importance of power for social transformation.

New covenant ethics recognizes that injustice is a contributing factor to conflicts, and that peace is not possible without removing injustice. Its goal is to reorganize a society according to the principles of justice, and by doing so to reduce the causes of injustice, enmity, and alienation, and to achieve a more genuine peace that approximates shalom.

The four practices are interrelated and overlap, and some are complementary. Just peacemaking practice relies on communicative action for relationship building and conflict resolution (negotiation and reaching agreement). It also typically depends on grassroots community organizing and nonviolent action as a method that nurtures and expands and applies power (capability) of the people toward justice making because a dialogical approach and moral persuasion alone are limited in bringing the rich and powerful to the negotiating table. Just peacemaking practice would not be effectively sustainable, even if reconciliation is achieved, without the ongoing support of community organizing.

On the other hand, grassroots community organizing relies on communicative engagement in building trust and relationships, internally, and on coalitions with other organizations, externally. It resorts to nonviolent action for political change and just peacemaking as a means of democratic negotiations.

The four practices of new covenant ethics are applicable to both the internal life of the church and the public realm. As Gandhi and King demonstrated, nonviolent resistance is a practice that is shareable among people across diverse religious and cultural backgrounds. It presupposes that humans have the moral capacity both to love and to come to recognize this love and the good it represents. Likewise, new covenant ethics may use justice making and peacemaking in the public realm in restoring right relationships by correcting injustice and reconciliation. They are different employments and arrangements of the norms of love, justice, and power for the journey of people toward shalom. They integrate morality and action (discursive or collective), moral vision and praxis. These practices demonstrate that new covenant ethics is not idealistic, or merely speculative or moralistic, but is realistic in addressing the human problems of sin, collective egoism, and imbalances of power. It is concrete and practical in offering an alternative form of living together.

Together, these practices are important for bridging the gap between pacifism and political realism; they are morally consistent and politically effective. The four practices (communicative engagement, just peacemaking, community organizing, and nonviolence) are highly moral (consistent with the new covenant) and political (consistent with the covenantal drama of liberation-restoration) in their goal and processes. Together, they present a plausible and practical means of political transformation that dramatizes God's reign in a covenantal way. They are political alternatives to violence and acquiescence.

Conclusion

With distinctive features derived from the covenant of Jesus, new covenant ethics offers a plausible form of Christian ethic that serves as the basis of the Christian moral deliberation and witness in society.

New covenant ethics is Trinitarian and eschatological, involves just peacemaking, and is ecumenical, nonviolent, and eucharistic. It is the composite ethics of love, justice, and power, and it positions itself as the method of communicative engagement, just peacemaking, community organizing, and nonviolent action. New covenant ethics is an ecumenical ethics. Its relevance is not confined to a Christian community but extends to public engagement in the world. New covenant ethics equips Christians to faithfully and effectively follow and witness to Jesus Christ in every realm of a society to bring that society and its institutions closer to the vision of God's shalom.

In the context of the covenant of Jesus, the *goal* of Christian ethics is shalom (1 Cor. 10:31), achieved through the collaboration of God and humans; its *content* is Jesus Christ, the Son of God (1 Cor. 4:16–17; 11:1; Eph. 4:20), into whose form we are called to be transformed (Rom. 8:29); its *pattern* is the covenantal drama and its threefold dialectics; its *practices* are communicative, nonviolent, and just peacemaking; and its *power* is the Spirit, who works communicatively in and with us.[36]

In light of God's reconciliation and covenantal organizing in Jesus Christ, Christians are called to freely and openly engage with others to build a better and more just society.

36. Cf. Fee, *Paul, the Spirit, the People of God*, 106.

CHAPTER 5

The Strengths of New Covenant Ethics

The sociotheological idea of covenant is so rich with ethical content that it gives moral meaning to all it touches.

—Max L. Stackhouse, *Covenant and Commitments*

Christians find living in a secularizing society difficult. They often struggle to harmonize divine authority and human autonomy in order to determine how human freedom is compatible with God's omnipotent power. How worship life is related to their moral life, in a secularizing society where religion is relegated to the private realm, and individual autonomy and freedom are considered absolute and sacred, is not easy to address. Similarly, many Christians are unsure of how their Christian identity should manifest in their particular cultural contexts (race, gender, nationality) and how God's moral laws and God's commandments are related to their constantly changing situations. The failure to creatively adjudicate and balance these elements leads to identity confusion and moral legalism or relativism.

This chapter demonstrates the capaciousness and fertility of new covenant ethics by examining how it helps to clarify and reconstruct several binary (but often confusing or conflicting) ethical notions in Christian ethics: divine and human agency, norm and context, being and becoming (stability and change) of Christian identity, worship and ethics,[1] unity and diversity. This chapter approaches these binary notions by discussing the following questions: Why are these notions important in Christian ethics? How are they related to covenant? How does new covenant ethics

1. The worship-ethics pair is not necessarily binary, but in social practices it often operates in a binary way, as the prophets pointed out in the Bible.

help to reimagine and reconceptualize them in a way that is new, more coherent, and constructive than are their conventional understandings?

My objective is to demonstrate the constructive explanatory power of new covenant ethics in clarifying the nature and direction of the Christian moral life.

Divine Agency and Human Agency

A major problem of traditional scholastic theism is that it has been based more on speculative metaphysics than on biblical stories, and thus it fails to capture a distinctive biblical view of God and God's character. It postulates God's moral attributes from metaphysics without reference to the actual God who is revealed and communicated through covenant. The ideas of supernatural causality, God as the unmoved mover, divine immutability, and divine impassibility are some of the attributes thus affected. Thus traditional theism has faced difficulties in dealing with the idea of the freedom of human agency: How does God relate to the world, especially to humans who have free will and decision-making capacity? How can God's sovereignty and human freedom, God's omnipotence and the integrity of nature, be reconciled?

On the other hand, partly as a reaction to traditional scholastic theism, Enlightenment thinkers, especially, have moved the pendulum to the other extreme: human autonomy and self-sufficiency free from God. Assuming that God's sovereignty and human freedom are mutually exclusive, they have asserted freedom of human intellect and society from religion (and God) and have upheld science and reason as the alternative to divine revelation and the authority of the church. The word "enlightenment" means intellectual and moral awakening of humanity from the powers of religion. It means thinking for oneself without relying on any external authorities. It maintains that humans should use their own intellectual capacities (reason) in determining their thoughts and actions.

New covenant ethics offers a plausible theological perspective on the relationship between divine sovereignty and human freedom. By taking the integrity of both divine and human agency seriously, it overcomes two major problems with traditional scholastic theism in its view of divine agency: causalism and determinism. New covenant ethics also corrects the overblown, individualistic idea of human autonomy in Enlightenment philosophies.

Unlike the Enlightenment philosophical view that puts divine sovereignty in stark opposition to human autonomy, God's sovereignty and human freedom are not mutually exclusive in covenant. In covenant God does not efface or destroy human agency. Contrary to a popular perception of divine sovereignty, the God of the covenant is the God who respects and even validates the freedom of the human partner. Herman Bavinck notes, "[God] vouches for them but does so in such a way that they themselves, instructed and enabled by the Spirit, also consciously and voluntarily consent to this covenant."[2]

The covenant shows how God uses God's power for the true freedom and well-being of humanity. "Far from imposing, he invites and persuades. Far from demanding service from men in order to enhance himself, he gives his life in service to men for their enhancement."[3] From the beginning, God's will for humanity is their flourishing. The generosity and patience of God grant every creature necessary "space and time for the development of its own existence, thus conceding to this existence a reality side by side with His own, and fulfilling His will toward this other in such a way that He does not suspend and destroy it as this other but accompanies and sustains it and allows it to develop in freedom."[4] In particular, the new covenant of Jesus removes every ounce of doubt or suspicion about God's intention of domination or control over humans. God's suffering, steadfast love, and hope, demonstrated in the crucifixion and resurrection of Jesus, reveal how far God is willing to go in building friendship with humanity.

God's good intentions are also displayed in the transition of God's posture from God's unilateral love to God's invitation of humanity to a bilateral relationship. How, then, is human freedom possible in covenant? It is possible by virtue of God's free, kenotic decision and love toward humanity. *Kenōsis* is the sign not of God's weakness but of God's power and love. Through divine self-limitation, through *kenōsis*, God grants space for human freedom, agency, and moral growth. God is strong and compassionate enough to empty Godself in creating a bilateral relationship with humanity. God seeks a genuine fellowship with humans on the basis of freedom and love, and incarnation and the cross are the culmination of such a decision by God.

Covenant is the symbol of the authenticity of human freedom as well as God's good intention toward humanity. In covenant, humans are declared genuinely free moral (thus responsible) agents. Covenantal stipulations serve as a critical reminder of human freedom and agency because humans have freely agreed to abide by them. Covenant provides a safe space that protects humans from any fear of the arbitrary use of power by God. Although the covenant between God and humanity is asymmetrical, it is still "an agreement of the unequals upon just and equal terms."[5] Barth explains, "Precisely in this fellowship of [covenantal] encounter there is not merely

2. Bavinck, *Reformed Dogmatics*, 3:229.
3. McGill, *Suffering*, 82, cited in Timothy George, *God the Holy Trinity*, 126.
4. Barth, *Church Dogmatics* II/1, 409–10.
5. Perry Miller, *The New England Mind*, 376.

safeguarded the sovereignty of God, of Jesus Christ and of the Holy Spirit, but also the freedom of the human partner is preserved from dissolution."[6]

In covenant, God does not and cannot treat human partners arbitrarily, nor forfeit God's agreement with them. The very structure of covenant and stipulations protects partners from any arbitrariness and whims of the other because it is based on mutual agreement rather than unilateral dictation. Once covenant stipulations are established, God is equally bound by them. Covenant holds God to be consistent to God's promises; God cannot capriciously abolish them. Therefore, God binds Godself and places Godself under the yoke by entering a covenantal relationship with humanity.[7]

Then one may ask: Why is human freedom so important to God? We can think of a few theological reasons. Human beings, as created in the image of God, mirror God in themselves; the freedom of a human being mirrors the freedom of God. Without freedom, the idea of human moral agency itself becomes vacuous because one who is not free is not responsible for one's actions. Moral agency presupposes freedom. Without granting genuine freedom to humans, God cannot hold them morally accountable.

Furthermore, human freedom is indispensable for God's goal—fellowship (communion) with humanity (2 Chron. 20:7; James 2:23; Exod. 33:11; John 15:15).[8] As God wants friendship, friendship is achieved only when a human being interacts with God out of free will in response to the free grace of God.[9] In other words, the

6. Barth, *Church Dogmatics* IV/3, 540.

7. "He who creates is under no obligation to those whom he creates; God might slay His creatures, or torture them, or forget them, and none could call Him to account, but in the Covenant He has voluntarily tied His hands, willingly agreed to a set of terms . . . in place of an ontological relation, a connection determined by brute necessity and the ineluctable order of things, is substituted an equally certain but more honorable relation of assent. God forgoes what is His by right divine, preferring a spontaneous to an enforced service. His gesture is pure graciousness." Perry Miller, *The New England Mind*, 376.

8. 2 Chron. 20:7: "Did you not, O our God, drive out the inhabitants of this land before your people Israel, and give it forever to the descendants of your friend Abraham?" James 2:23: "Thus the scripture was fulfilled that says, 'Abraham believed God, and it was reckoned to him as righteousness,' and he was called the friend of God." Exod. 33:11: "Thus the LORD used to speak to Moses face to face, as one speaks to a friend. Then he would return to the camp; but his young assistant, Joshua son of Nun, would not leave the tent." John 15:15: "I do not call you servants any longer, because the servant does not know what the master is doing; but I have called you friends, because I have made known to you everything that I have heard from my Father."

9. Calvin also takes a similar position on human freedom in his explication of order. Perfect order indicates true harmony of relationship, and it is possible only on the basis of freedom and love. Any order based on coercion is not perfect. Coercion means that either God is not fully sovereign or human beings are not fully free and obedient. Their relationship with God is motivated by fear

very goal of covenant—fellowship and communion—requires the genuine freedom of the human partners. This explains why consent, which epitomizes the voluntary bilateral nature of relationship, is so important in covenant. In a sense, the unilateral love of God by itself is incomplete for achieving God's goal because genuine fellowship is possible only when God's initiating love is reciprocated by free and genuine human responses based on freedom, not on coercion. Various qualities of any good friendship—such as love, equality, mutuality, reciprocity, trust, and hope—are all implied in covenant.

The evidence of human freedom is also found in the fact that God's interaction with humans relies not on brute force but on communicative action. God does not compel but woos, does not coerce but persuades, does not overpower but empowers us.[10] The evidence of genuine human freedom is found in the fact that God's communicative action includes mutual reasoning—the exchange of claims, judgments, and ideas with humans. In communicating with humanity, God invites human partners "to attend to the proof, truth and goodness of the word announced."[11] God said through Isaiah: "Come now, let us argue it out" (Isa. 1:18).[12] Similarly, through the prophet Hosea, God calls Israel to repent and return to him from a crooked and rebellious way of life. Despite their status as God's creatures, human beings reasoned and argued with God. Scripture demonstrates many stories of communicative engagements between God and humans. Abraham engaged in communicative action with God regarding the judgment of Sodom and Gomorrah; Jacob wrestled with God for divine blessing; Job protested to God about the suffering of the innocent; and Habakkuk candidly questioned God's wisdom in governing the world. All these show that covenant empowers humans to engage with, even challenge, God in freedom when they perceive God to be failing to abide by covenantal stipulations.[13]

New covenant ethics responds to the critique of secular ethics that human freedom does not receive any genuine meaning in Christianity. Covenant clarifies the meaning of Christian obedience. Obedience in a covenantal relationship is not a

---

or constrained by coercion. Order is perfected through the voluntary obedience and submission of human beings to God's free will.

10. Pinnock, *Flame of Love*, 157.

11. Heppe, *Reformed Dogmatics*, 520, cited in Vanhoozer, *First Theology*, 120.

12. Isa. 54:13 reads: "All your children shall be taught by the LORD, / and great shall be the prosperity of your children." Jesus also said: "No one can come to me unless drawn by the Father who sent me; and I will raise that person up on the last day. It is written in the prophets, 'And they shall all be taught by God.' Everyone who has heard and learned from the Father comes to me" (John 6:44–45).

13. The communal-communicative dialectic does not alter the asymmetrical nature of their respective powers and statuses.

blind, slavish act coerced by fear, but a free, self-conscious moral act done out of gratitude, trust, and loyalty. It is rather a voluntary performance of the pledge that one has made when one enters a covenant.

Norm and Context

Every society requires certain shared moral norms, values, and ideals in maintaining a basic social order and in coordinating the various claims and interests of its members. However, changing historical and cultural situations call for the ongoing reinterpretation and adjustment of those norms, all the more so in a global society characterized by high mobility and fluidity. It is one thing to identify norms, but it is another thing to interpret and apply them in new social situations.

Christians likewise cannot avoid this dilemma. We preach that "Jesus Christ is the same yesterday and today and forever" (Heb. 13:8), but we must also ask, with Dietrich Bonhoeffer, "Who is Christ for us today?"[14] Discipleship does not mean blind obedience or mechanical repetition. Banal repetition is more an indication of a lack of imagination and creativity than a sign of fidelity, just as uncritical assimilation to culture is a sign of deficient identity and discerning spirit. Blind adherence to norms without a contextual consideration can lead to legalism, just as uncritical assimilation to cultural and technological changes can result in moral compromise and subjectivism.

New covenant ethics does not attempt to provide a detailed blueprint for our decisions in every new circumstance. "The covenant is not a static relationship but one that requires constant renewal and affirmation."[15] As signposts offering guidance for our decisions, covenant displays the organizing drama, patterns, and covenantal stipulations (God's commandments, Jesus's teachings, the apostles' moral admonitions). We need to interpret them in new social contexts. There is room for creative improvisation—practical wisdom. This contextual consideration does not necessarily mean moral compromise or moral relativism. Rather, it is a necessary attempt to live faithfully in a new social context. Interpretation in covenant is not arbitrary because covenant provides a coherent framework and directives where the norm is interpreted.

The biblical examples of covenant, especially the stories of covenant renewals, show how covenant can be adaptive to new and changing contexts without losing its integrity. The dialectics of covenant, especially the second and third dialectics, show that our relationship with God is neither static nor enclosed in the past but

14. Bonhoeffer, *Letters and Papers from Prison*, 362.

15. De Gruchy, *Reconciliation*, 187–88.

unfolds in history as we live in fellowship with God and others. Christian fidelity is neither static nor blind but dynamic and embodied. Obedience to the law in covenant is less a matter of servility to its letter than a matter of faithfulness to its spirit, which is to inquire and interrogate what a covenantal relationship actually demands in every context.

Covenant ethics embraces historical contingency as an intrinsic aspect of human existence, and this embrace has to do with the actional (performative) nature of the triune God and the contextual nature of God's communicative action. The God of Abraham, Isaac, and Jacob is a living God who always communicates with human partners in a fresh way in their personal situations. The image of the pillars of fire and cloud also aptly captures this dynamic aspect of God's presence and communication.

Contextual sensibility is central to the Bible. For example, starting with the four Gospels, various theologians and communities have developed diverse Christologies with different emphases and accents. This plurality partly reflects a desire among Christians to connect Jesus with their own social contexts in a personal and meaningful way. Critical issues of race, gender, class, and other social concerns cannot be separated from our christological imaginations. Contextual Christologies are not optional but integral to Christianity because, even today, we are asked by Jesus, "Who do you think I am?" This question can be answered only contextually, not abstractly.

With its foundation in the communicative action of the triune God and reliance on analogical imagination, new covenant ethics offers a sensible method to bridge the gap between norm and context. Of course, there is no single perfect congruence or unity between norm and context in history. There always exists the possibility of a variety of interpretations of both norm and context. As we discuss further in chapter 10, ethical reasoning is a process to bridge this gap between norm and context, between Jesus of the past and Jesus of the present, and to coordinate the differences.

Identity: Being and Becoming

New covenant ethics is equally helpful for theologically clarifying the dynamic and evolving nature of Christian identity. In a manner parallel to the dynamic relationship between norm and context, Christian identity also evolves in changing situations without losing its continuity. A number of psychological studies report that human identity is less a matter of the underlying substance (what one is) than a characteristic style of one's relationships with others (who one is).[16] A person's iden-

16. Vanhoozer, *Remythologizing Theology*, 333–34. The object relations theory affirms that identity is relationally constituted.

tity is not given in a predetermined form but gradually emerges as one interacts with one's significant others and one's environments. For example, a baby's early sense of self (identity) arises through interaction with the baby's parents or caregiver.

Covenant offers a relational, interactive view of human identity. Created in the image of God, one's Christian identity derives from one's covenantal relationship with God. In particular, the three dialectics have a great deal of power in explicating the formation, development, and growth of Christian identity. The following section discusses how the three dialectics are associated with the ideas of election, differentiation, and identity, respectively.

Unilateral-Bilateral

Covenant is the foundation of our Christian identity. Christian identity is constituted by God's election and call to covenant. The idea of election may raise some suspicion because of its abuses in recent history in the West to justify racism and ethnocentrism by Christians, but there is no necessary connection between election and its abuse. In fact, in the latter, humans corrupt the former by idolatrously assuming the role of God as elector. Entering a covenant with God is to belong to God; it is also a process to obtain a new identity as a child of God and to discover a new meaning and purpose of life.[17] A new identity discovered in God grants a person a sense of self-worth, integration, and purpose. In God's unconditional love revealed in Jesus, one finds that one is claimed and owned by God for God's purpose:[18] "you are my children," and "you are my people."

The idea of election describes the gifted nature of Christian identity because it claims that our relationship with God is not a matter of our choice first but of God's free grace. Election is constitutive of our identity because it gives us knowledge of our origin and destiny as God's children. Christian identity has a transcendent foundation. To be elected means to be known, accepted, and invited to fellowship by God regardless of one's own merits.

The unilateral-bilateral dialectic is helpful in clarifying the meaning and purpose of election. Election speaks more of God's steadfast love and firm commitment than of any person's or group's exclusive status, privilege, or special rights. It conveys the

17. Michael Horton says: "Nowhere in Scripture is the question of human identity asked or answered in the abstract, but only in terms of the covenantal—which is to say, ethical—commission that takes an explicitly narrative construction." Horton, "Image and Office," 198.

18. Personal identity is covenantally constituted in relation to God, other human beings, and nonhuman creatures. When these relationships (or the community where these relationships are embedded) lose a covenantal quality (whether broken or underdeveloped), the identity development of a person could be impaired or stalled.

unwavering depth of God's love and the assurance of God's commitment despite all the vicissitudes of life. Michael Walzer's observation about the psychological contribution of the idea of election is helpful: "Who would take the required risks, who would march into the wilderness or challenge the 'giants' of Canaan without some sense of an assured future? At the same time, the experience of making choices and accepting risks generates the very different ideas of commitment and consent."[19]

Election is an identity language, not a privilege claim. It assures a person's worth but does not give any license for privilege and power over others. It would be more accurate to say that election is more rhetorical and pastoral than ontological in communicating God's unconditional love, as it describes the depth and strength of God's love for each one of us.[20] By saying how God's love is unconditional, it intends to empower a person for sacrificial service for God and others. Election builds a bedrock foundation of identity and fidelity for a believer in God. Isaiah 54:10 reads:

> For the mountains may depart
> and the hills be removed,
> but my steadfast love shall not depart from you,
> and my covenant of peace shall not be removed,
> says the LORD, who has compassion on you.

Similarly, Romans 5:6–8 gives believers a strong sense of trust and security by proclaiming that God unconditionally offered his love and grace in Jesus Christ to us while we were still in our sins: "For while we were still weak, at the right time Christ died for the ungodly. Indeed, rarely will anyone die for a righteous person—though perhaps for a good person someone might actually dare to die. But God proves his love for us in that while we still were sinners Christ died for us."

The new covenant of Jesus, thanks to its inclusiveness, removes any misunderstanding associated with election. By expanding its membership (election) to the entirety of humanity, the new covenant of Jesus clearly repudiates any possible racial, ethnic, gender, or religious exclusivism based on election.[21]

19. Walzer, *Exodus and Revolution*, 81.

20. According to Terry Hargrave and Franz Pfitzer, love and trustworthiness constitute the deep and underlying structure of human identity and relationship. They are the rich soil from which a seed of a person's identity is rooted and grows to be capability-coherent with identity. See Hargrave and Pfitzer, *The New Contextual Therapy*, chap. 5.

21. Karl Barth made a significant contribution to theology by redefining election as God's free decision to love humanity in Jesus Christ from eternity. Jesus Christ is both the electing God and elected humanity simultaneously. God's election in Jesus Christ is the election of all humanity, not one racial or gender group, as he is the representative of both humanity and God.

Communal-Communicative

Christian identity first arises when a person enters a covenantal relationship with God and others, but it develops through communal-communicative fellowship with them. The second dialectic (communal-communicative) describes how the sense of alterity emerges out of an intersubjective, reciprocating relationship in the covenant. Miroslav Volf notes: "'Identity' includes connection, difference, and heterogeneity. The human self is formed not through a simple rejection of the other—through a binary logic of opposition and negation—but through a complex process of 'taking in' *and* 'keeping out.'"[22] The self exists in its relationship with the other, though it cannot be reduced to mere relationship. "To preserve both 'person' and 'relation' we must understand them in a reciprocal relationship: 'there are no persons without relations; but there are no relations without persons.' Persons are not relations; persons stand in relations that shape their identity."[23]

Human identity develops through identification (imitation) and differentiation.[24] For Christians, God is the most significant other for their development of faith identity. The God we encounter in covenant is omnipotent, trustworthy, and intimate as a mother is to her child. At the same time, however, God is the holy Other that humans cannot control or mess with. God is loving and friendly but inscrutable. In the mystery of the Trinity, God is simultaneously God over us (Father), God for us (Son), and God in us (Spirit). We are continuously unsettled and surprised by this God and attracted to him.[25]

God valorizes the human partner to be free, responsible, and compassionate. This fidelity and constancy of God have a transformative power—setting humans free from anxiety, fear, and carnal desires, and instilling in them the sense of trust and courage. Friendship is a suitable metaphor to describe the God-human relationship because it highlights the free, reciprocal, intimate nature of a covenantal relationship. Friendship is possible even between persons of different status, such as God and humans,[26] and this is what the communal-communicative dialectic describes.

22. Volf, *Exclusion and Embrace*, 66.

23. Volf, *Exclusion and Embrace*, 180.

24. Psychologists often call it the process of individuation.

25. Brueggemann, *The Covenanted Self*, chap. 1. Rudolf Otto's idea of the numinous shows a similar dynamic quality. A person's numinous experience includes both awe and attraction simultaneously, which Otto described as *mysterium tremendum et fascinans*.

26. Thomas Aquinas aptly noted: "Charity signifies not only the love of God, but also a certain friendship with Him; which implies, besides love, a certain mutual return of love, together with mutual communion. . . . Now this fellowship of man with God, which consists in a certain familiar colloquy with Him is begun, in this life, by grace, but will be perfected in the future life by glory.

Memory-Hope

Life is a journey, but humans do not journey without the guidance of values or without any sense of direction or vision. They do not approach the future *carte blanche*. Nor is their past a finished chapter; they constantly revisit it to reinterpret and seek new meanings or make sense out of life's contradictions, difficulties, and ambiguity. "We who live in time do not experience the past as something irretrievably lost and gone but as truly present, effectively shaping our identity and our destiny. . . . In this human time, the past is gathered up and preserved in our *memory*, and the future is anticipated and made real in our *imagination*."[27] Humans are capable of reflecting upon the past and imagining a different future.

The third dialectic of covenant captures effectively this dynamic, evolving nature of human identity. Human life is a journey from the past to the future, which the pilgrimage metaphor aptly describes. For Israelites, the journey was from Egypt to the promised land. Whereas Sinai was the birthplace of their identity, the wilderness was the furnace of identity growth (wrestling with the temptations of idolatry, doubt, and rebellion).

In a covenant relationship, Christian identity evolves in the tension between memory and hope, commitment and exploration.[28] The covenanted self is rooted but not self-enclosed, open but not relativistic, free but not self-sufficient. In a covenant fellowship, this God helps us to find and grow in a deep, unique, integrated, and differentiated identity. Many stories in the Bible (of patriarchs and matriarchs, David, Peter, Paul, Mary and Martha) show how God's constancy and faithfulness gradually transformed those individuals who lived in a long, enduring covenantal relationship with God.[29] One sees such examples in the Bible, with the name (identity) changes of Abram to Abraham, Jacob to Israel, and Simon to Peter. Covenantal identity is neither stuck in moratorium nor foreclosed, but remains dynamic, open, and growing in ongoing fellowship with God and others.[30] Covenantal identity is

---

Aquinas, *Summa Theologica* II-II.65.5, in *Summa Theologica, Volume II-Part II, First Section*, 865; see also II-II.23.1; Wadell, *Friendship and the Moral Life*.

27. Phan, "Betwixt and Between," 128–29.

28. James Marcia describes identity formation in terms of commitment and exploration, attachment and search, which is strikingly similar to the identity formation in the third dialectic of the covenant. According to him, a healthy identity integrates both dimensions in a dialectic manner. When this integration fails, a person undergoes moratorium, stall, foreclosure, and confusion of identity.

29. According to Charles Taylor, a dialogical relation with others is crucial for identity formation, and it cannot take place in isolation (Taylor, "The Politics of Recognition," 34).

30. Paul Ricoeur distinguishes two types of identity: *idem*- and *ipse*-identity. Unlike *idem*-identity that refers to immutable self-sameness (such as divine essence), *ipse*-identity describes

rooted in God's unconditional love, but it is also open to growth and changes in response to new and different surroundings. Empowered by God's electing grace and love (first dialectic), a Christian constantly grows to discover a deeper sense of self, vocation, and meaning in the world. This implies that in a covenant relationship, Christian identity experiences a creative tension and balance between being and becoming, sameness and otherness (second dialectic), and continuity and discontinuity (third dialectic).[31]

Particularity and Public Relevance

A consistent concern has been that the NT and Jesus's teachings are limited in offering sophisticated public ethics because the hard sayings of Jesus are difficult to apply to the general public. Conventionally, because of the radical nature of their moral demands, the Sermon on the Mount and Jesus's teachings have been treated as "in-house" ethics for the Christian community.[32] Because of this difficulty, Catholics and magisterial Protestant Christians have relied on natural law, reason, or moral laws or wisdom in the Bible for their public engagements.

Another dualistic approach is to assign Jesus's teachings and the Sermon on the Mount to personal ethics, while natural law and the Sinai covenant (and the OT) are for public (social) ethics. A similar attempt has been to assign love to Christians and justice to non-Christians (the public).

In fact, historically different interpretations and attributions of the significance of the Sermon on the Mount have divided Christians, most notably Anabaptists from mainline Protestant/Catholic Christians. The radical wing of the Reformation (historical peace churches of Mennonites and Anabaptists) has taken the Sermon on the Mount and Jesus's passion (crucifixion) as the foundation of their Christian ethics and has advocated a distinctive community of radical discipleship and theological identity, with nonviolence, pacifism, and civic nonengagement as the key practices and stance of Christians who follow Jesus. These churches have claimed that social justice is not the primary responsibility of Christians; to make the world

---

self-constancy of God or a person that is grounded in covenantal fidelity. A covenant identity is a form of *ipse*-identity. Ricoeur, *Oneself as Another*.

31. Cf. Appiah's model of rooted cosmopolitanism in *Cosmopolitanism*. Rom. 8:29 highlights God's initiative in outworking God's purpose in humanity.

32. The controversy between the two camps goes back to fathers of the early church, Tertullian and Justin Martyr, and it erupted fresh among Protestants during the Reformation, between Menno Simons and his followers and Lutherans and Calvinists. Even today, the controversy continues in these camps. Yoder and Hauerwas are the representatives of the former, while Max L. Stackhouse, James Gustafson, and David Hollenbach, among others, represent the latter.

turn out right is not their responsibility. This theological difference has separated pacifists from Catholics, realists, and just war theorists, with profound implications for the church-state relationship as well as Christian approaches to social justice and social transformation.

New covenant ethics does not accept a dichotomy between the ethics of the church and the ethics of society. It does not treat the Sermon on the Mount as "in-house" ethics. It does not separately assign different ethics for different audiences—love for Christians (church), justice for non-Christians (society).[33] Technically speaking, Christians live immediately under the binding authorities of the two covenants, the Noachian covenant and the covenant of Jesus. The two are distinct but not separate. The former has an immediate relevance for society while the latter is for the *ekklēsia*, but both apply to each other as justice and love apply to each other.[34]

At the same time, living under the binding power and authority of the covenant of Jesus, Christians are required to live out Jesus's commandments and moral teachings (as the Sermon on the Mount offers, for example) in their lives, including in the public realm and social institutions. Without disregarding justice, the covenant of Jesus is characterized by peacemaking, reconciliation, and love ethics. Peacemaking is proactive, not merely reactive. "It sees peace not as something to be achieved merely by refraining from war, but by taking peacemaking initiative. Peace, like war, must be waged. It must be waged courageously, persistently, creatively, with imagination, heart, and wisdom."[35]

The proactivity of peacemaking in the covenant of Jesus corresponds to God's own initiative in just peacemaking. In inviting humanity to a covenantal bond, God is proactive toward us. We are obligated to respond to God's proactive grace through our peacemaking initiative to others (the first dialectic).[36] It simultaneously rejects violence, withdrawal from society, and acquiescence or blind support of the government. It is active but peaceful, political but not partisan, militant but civic. This approach of just peacemaking is consistent with Jesus's commandment to be yeast, salt, light, and mustard seed—the metaphors of transformative nature at a grassroots level (not imperial, coercive, or hierarchical but local and spreading). In his life and teaching, Jesus embodied just peacemaking. Likewise, discipleship in the early church was characterized by righteousness and peacemaking.

33. New covenant ethics is different from the two-kingdom theory of Lutheran ethics that treats the government and other spheres as "not only de facto but even de jure void of grace." James K. A. Smith, "The Reformed (Transformationist) View," 92.

34. It treats the Sinai covenant as the enhancement and elaboration of the former in the life of Israelites, but renewed in the latter.

35. Stassen, *Just Peacemaking*, 18.

36. Cf. Stassen, *Just Peacemaking*, 19.

New covenant ethics claims that the integration between the NT and the OT in general, and the covenant of Jesus and the Noachian covenant (Jesus's ethics and public ethics) in particular, is possible because of the covenantal nature and ground of the Christian life. Both are part of God's single, ongoing covenantal drama toward shalom. They also share the same three dialectic patterns (unilateral-bilateral, communal-communicative, memory-hope). New covenant ethics offers a method that helps to organize not only the church but also a society and its institutions with the same final vision, principles, and logic. Finally, they have in common the triad of love, justice, and power as constitutive conceptual components, for they both enact the covenantal justice that rectifies injustices and restores right relationships. In short, while they are distinctive, there is continuity between them, despite the difference in their respective emphases, purposes, moral intensity, and demands. The new covenant of Jesus transcends, but neither denies nor contradicts, the Noachian covenant. One may say that the Noachian covenant and the covenant of Jesus are related as the penultimate and the ultimate.[37] If we borrow legal metaphors, one may claim that while the Noachian covenant (and the Decalogue to some extent) is protectionist,[38] the Sermon on the Mount communicates perfectionist intentions.

There is certainly a gap and tension between Jesus's ethics (the Sermon on the Mount) and the minimal order (justice) of the Noachian covenant, but the gap does not mean discontinuity or incompatibility. The triad of love, justice, and power and the four practices (communicative engagement, just peacemaking, community organizing, nonviolence) help to bridge the gap and ease the tension between the covenant of Jesus and the Noachian covenant. While justice and peacemaking are an integral aspect of every biblical covenant, peacemaking becomes far more explicit in the covenant of Jesus because of its clear and unrelenting commitment to peace, love, and nonviolence. With its emphasis on love, intimacy, and mutual sacrifice, the covenant of Jesus is communal, reciprocal, restorative, and nonviolent.

On the basis of Matthew 5:17, new covenant ethics does not choose between peace ethics (as Mennonites do) and justice (as Christian realists do) in addressing this gap but takes the just peacemaking approach. Specifically, while acknowledging the two different (but not dualistic) contexts, it bridges the gap by using various nonviolent means of just peacemaking to achieve both justice and love, such as communicative reasoning, moral persuasion, community organizing, and nonviolent action.

37. For the idea of penultimate addressing the necessity of common morality and justice for Christian witness and common well-being of a society, see Bonhoeffer, *Ethics*.

38. The Noachian covenant, often called the covenant of preservation, delineates God's commandments that intend to prevent creation from further moral deterioration after the Fall. The Sinai covenant is thicker than the Noachian covenant and thinner than the Beatitudes.

Christians are called to perform justice and peacemaking both in their communities and in their society. On the ground of the Noachian covenant, they demand social justice (equality, freedom, fair treatment, and respect for human rights); they are willing to work and invite others to promote justice in a society. Jeremiah 29:7 tells the exiled Jews to "seek the welfare of the city." Romans 13 teaches Christians to pray for their leaders (justice). On the other hand, Christians are called to pursue peacemaking. Although the fulfillment of the Noachian covenant (justice) is the most immediate and required task in the public realm, new covenant ethics does not stop there; it pursues the best approximation of shalom in light of the covenant of Jesus. Biblically speaking, God is still keeping Noah's covenant and moving it toward the covenant of Jesus. Again, Christopher Marshall makes a compelling point on the relevance of Jesus's ethics and the vision of shalom for Christian public engagement: "Yet Jesus is still serious about these demands; they are not impossible ideals but realistic goals to strive after. They are realistic insofar as they are empowered by the new reality of God's redeeming power that has broken into the world. So when Jesus summons his followers to perfection (Matt. 5:48), he counts genuine attainment to be possible, but not necessarily total attainment, for God's kingdom is not yet here in its fullness."[39]

One finds successful recent examples of such Christian witnesses in Martin Luther King Jr.'s civil rights movement and in Desmond Tutu's antiapartheid movement and the Truth and Reconciliation Commission. They were guided by the vision of Jesus's Sermon on the Mount while vigorously pursuing justice using various nonviolent means. Their movements, domestically and internationally, collaborated with other religious and cultural groups in fighting for the human rights of African persons and others, while fully committed to reconciliation with their oppressors. While fully aware of the sobering reality of sin and evil, they lived by the eschatological hope in reconciliation and restoration that Jesus has already wrought in his own covenant. They prove Marshall's point: "The peculiar problem for Christian ethics, then, lies not in articulating a 'creation ethic' that all people of goodwill can aspire to, but in deciding how the eschatological values of Christian existence are to be commended to, and worked out in the midst of, the wider fallen world."[40]

Fulfillment of the covenant of Jesus (more precisely, approximation to fulfillment) is uneven across social realms and levels. Certain realms and relationships, such as interpersonal relationships and family or church, could be relatively less challenging than the other realms and levels, such as societal realms or national or international levels.

39. Marshall, *Beyond Retribution*, 18.
40. Marshall, *Beyond Retribution*, 19.

Built upon Jesus's fulfillment of "the law and the prophets" and the other covenants, new covenant ethics offers a balanced and constructive approach that is faithful to the Bible as well as publicly relevant and practical in its social practices. Through the dialectic understanding of the two covenants, new covenant ethics creatively overcomes the conventional dichotomy between sectarian pacifism and Christian Realism. New covenant ethics is neither authoritarian (theocratic) nor sectarian (dualistic). Like the Mennonite ethics of John Howard Yoder, new covenant ethics centers on Jesus's moral teachings (and the Christ event); but like that of mainline Protestants and Catholics, it actively advocates for social justice in the public realm. Every social realm and every human authority is subjected to God's covenantal reign and the Lordship of Jesus. The world is fallen, but it is not completely deserted to Satan's control. Furthermore, God's work of restoration has already started in Jesus through his covenant.

In particular, the four practices of new covenant ethics are applicable to both the internal life of the church and the public realm. As Gandhi and King demonstrated, nonviolent resistance is shareable among people across diverse religious and cultural backgrounds. It presupposes that humans have the moral capacity both to love and to come to recognize this love and the good it represents. Likewise, new covenant ethics may use justice and peacemaking in the public realm in restoring right relationships by correcting injustice and pursuing reconciliation. They are different employments and arrangements of the norms of love, justice, and power for people's journey toward shalom. They integrate morality and action (discursive or collective), moral vision and praxis. These practices demonstrate that new covenant ethics is not idealistic, or merely speculative or moralistic, but realistic in addressing the human problems of sin, collective egoism, and imbalances of power. It is concrete and practical in offering an alternative form of living together.

Together, these practices are important for bridging the gap between pacifism and political realism; they are morally consistent and politically effective. The four practices (communicative engagement, just peacemaking, community organizing, and nonviolence) are highly moral (consistent with the new covenant) and political (consistent with the covenantal drama of liberation-restoration) in their goal and processes. Together, they present a plausible and practical means of a political transformation that dramatizes God's reign in a covenantal way. They are political alternatives to violence and acquiescence.

Worship and Ethics

In the Christian life, worship (and liturgy), like ethics, is covenantal in nature. In the OT, the establishment of a covenant is consummated by a ritual of animal cutting or a common meal. Major biblical rituals such as circumcision, sacrifices, shedding/sprinkling blood, a common meal, baptism, and the Eucharist are all covenantal rituals. Constituting the two pillars of the Christian life, worship and ethics operate under the same rubric of covenant. Worship (service to God) and ethics (service to people), *lex orandi* and *lex agendi*, are inseparable in covenant. They are the two different forms that our faith response takes to God's grace and commandments. To know and show gratitude to God is to acknowledge God in worship and to do his will in everyday life by serving others.[41]

We find the unity between worship and ethics in the two most exemplary covenants in the Bible: the Sinai covenant and the covenant of Jesus. As we discussed in chapter 1, the Ten Commandments are religious and ethical; they are inseparable. "Acknowledge today and take to heart that the LORD is God in heaven above and on the earth beneath; there is no other. Keep his statutes and his commandments, which I am commanding you today" (Deut. 4:39–40). Jesus also declares a new covenant and then gives a new commandment at the Last Supper to his disciples: "Love one another" (John 13:34). Paul also does not separate worship and ethics when he exhorts: "Present your bodies as a living sacrifice, holy and acceptable to God, which is your spiritual worship" (Rom. 12:1).

Surprisingly, the three dialectics of covenant help us to see how worship and ethics are integrated in the Christian life. Both worship and ethics have their source in God's initiating (unilateral) gracious act of deliverance (first dialectic); both are communicatively active, guided by the Spirit, in the covenantal relationship with God (second dialectic); and the Christian life proceeds in the axis of memory and hope through ongoing worship and ethical life (third dialectic).

Both worship and ethics have the same foundation: the triune God, who delivered us from the power of sin and death. They are indicative; they flow from a covenantal relationship in response to God's grace. As the triune God encounters us in worship, the same God invites us into a faithful moral life and leads us to the ministry of God's kingdom.[42] Specifically, both worship and ethics are also connected through God's holiness. God's holiness is the source of purification (worship) and sanctification (ethic), and, while distinctive, the two are intimately related in the

41. Their connection is found in the biblical text as well. "The Decalogue is bracketed by liturgical passages (Ex. 19:3–8, 24:3–8) in which the formation of community is anticipated and then solemnized in ceremony before God." Birch, *Let Justice Roll Down*, 175.

42. Nicholas Wolterstorff describes worship and ethics in relation to the idea of worth. Worship begins with the recognition of the worthiness of God—reverence of God as the creator, redeemer, and consummator, while ethics has to do with the recognition of the worthiness (intrinsic value) of humans and creatures. The worthiness of God cannot be separated from the worthiness of humans and creatures because of a covenantal structure of our existence. See his *Journey toward Justice*.

Bible and thus used in interchangeable ways. Cultic purity and moral sanctity are inseparable, as both are related to holiness. As God is holy, we are required to be holy. This means that in terms of purpose or effect, purification and sanctification are indistinguishable, just as goodness and godliness (piety) are. If worship offers humans the occasion to experience and purify themselves through God's holiness, then ethics offers them the occasion to live out (practice) this learned holiness of God in daily life.

Both worship and ethics are communicative. As we discussed, God's commandments and law (covenantal stipulations) are communicative in a covenant relationship. In worship, we bring and communicate our pain, suffering, and hope to God in our prayers, laments, supplications, and intercessions. Doxology, adoration, praise, and gratitude are integral parts of this communication. The Spirit has the power to convict, encourage, and forgive, thus turning our mourning into dancing and our cries into praise, thanksgiving, and adoration. Through worship people's spirits are animated, their minds are illumined, and their hearts are warmed.[43] Worship plays an important role in empowering and sustaining a covenantal bond between God and humans and strengthens fellowship and ministry of believers. This affectional and bonding power is primarily communicative and performative, more than the result of the socialization of worshipers in religious practices. While religious activities, music, the arts, and rhetoric certainly have emotional, evocative power to shape our affections, in covenantal ethics the change of affection and formation of Christian virtues are the work and fruits of the Spirit, not the product of religious socialization.

Worship is indispensable to the Christian moral life. It helps to consecrate God's people. Rituals have a cleansing, formative, and sanctifying power. "Gracious affections arise from the mind being enlightened, rightly and spiritually to understand or apprehend divine things."[44] That is, spiritually gifted emotion is based on a proper intellectual understanding of what is godly. Worship also calls for a human response. Cultic ceremony includes the pledge of obedience (loyalty) by Israelites, a solemn consecration as God's people (Exod. 24:9–11). Likewise, in the New Testament, we read, "Make every effort . . . to be holy; without holiness no one will see the Lord" (Heb. 12:14 NIV). The double focus of worship is "the glorification of God and the sanctification of human beings."[45] Worship as a process of purification offers the opportunity for self-examination and confession. Christians cannot be triumphant or arrogant because those who are covenanted with God are under God's judgment

43. May, *Testing the National Covenant*, 108.

44. Edwards, *A Treatise concerning Religious Affections*, 192.

45. Saliers, "Liturgy and Ethics," 28.

and grace. Once covenanted with God, their decisions and behaviors are subjected to the moral scrutiny of God. Worship offers opportunities for ongoing sanctification and growth through renewal, reorientation, and self-correction.

Worship is the occasion for us to participate in the mystery of God's life by experiencing the intimate, loving assurance of God (communion with God), while ethics is the opportunity for us to carry out and actualize God's vision and dream of the beloved community in history. Those who truly know the real God cannot but imitate his character and walk in his way. They are two different expressions of our gratitude to God's unconditional love and grace. Therefore, the rejection or suppression of one undermines the entire edifice of the covenant. When detached from ethics, worship and religious practices turn into magic; instead of promoting holiness, they mislead and corrupt people. The religious rituals of Israel faced severe criticism from the prophets when they were separated from ethics. Ethics was considered a crucial barometer that revealed the internal (spiritual) relationship of Israel with God. It was assumed that those who loved and worshiped God would live uprightly and justly in gratitude. John the Baptist warned the Pharisees and Sadducees not to boast of being Abraham's children, for God could turn the stones on the ground into Abraham's children (Matt. 3:9). Conversely, when detached from worship, ethics degenerates into abstract rules, heteronomous legalism, and joyless duty.

Worship and ethics are complementary; they strengthen one another. Worship informs and guides ethics (imparting the sense of holiness in its multifaceted aspects), and ethics fulfills worship by performing the demands of holiness in real, concrete forms in a daily moral life. True worshipers live a life that reflects God's holiness. Worship should bear fruit in ethics. The prophets were critical of worship and rituals detached from ethics. But without worship, ethics becomes abstract and dry, while without ethics rituals become magical. Worship precedes ethics, but it is incomplete without ethics. Because of its root in worship of the triune God, new covenantal ethics is never completely rational or cognitive but affectional and performative. Unlike secular liberal ethics (Kantianism and utilitarianism), new covenant ethics teaches and emphasizes the importance of embodied liturgical and spiritual practices, such as worship, prayer, hymn singing, and meditation. When properly conducted, these practices engender and invigorate the covenantal bond and fellowship through which faith, love, hope, and justice are nurtured and practiced.

As mentioned, in the OT cultic purification and sacrificial rituals are a part of God's atonement system through which God restores human partners from sin and iniquities. Through them, humans are brought back to a covenantal relationship. For Christians, Jesus's atoning work on the cross is the ground for the forgiveness of their sins and restoration with God and others. Hence, they are indispensable in maintaining a covenantal relationship with God. Purification and consecration are necessary for humans to fellowship with God. In the OT, humans could enter fellowship with God only when they were consecrated (sanctified) through various rituals of purification. A holy God wants God's human partners to be sanctified in every aspect of their lives by living a holy life, as salt and light, fully present in the world but not of the world.

However, there is a minor difference between the two. While worship highlights a more asymmetrical side of covenantal relationship (divine-human), ethics highlights a more symmetrical side (human-divine). If serving God is the center of worship, then serving others is the focus of ethics. While the worth of God as creator, redeemer, and sanctifier is the basis of worship, the worth of humans as God's image-bearers is the basis of ethics.

Unity and Diversity

A major intellectual challenge in philosophy since ancient times has been how to achieve unity out of the plurality of the universe.[46] This issue has become politically acute and pressing in the pluralistic society created by globalization and communication technologies. The tension between the demand for unity and the assertion of diversity is felt in all institutions of our society, as we see in conflicts between globalism (cosmopolitanism) and localism (nationalism, nativism), as well as in clashes between various identity claims and assertions (racial, ethnic, religious, sex, and gender).

New covenant ethics is able to address this concern in the Christian life. In fact, in a narrow, procedural sense, covenant is literally a mechanism that builds unity out of diversity through the consent of different parties in reaching the agreement. "It is significant that cutting (dividing) and binding, are the principal elements in terminology and early practice of covenant-making since a covenant both divides and binds, that is to say it clarifies and institutionalizes both the distinction between separate identities of the partners and their linkage. This is, of course, precisely what covenants are about. In other words, the covenant is . . . [like Martin] Buber's I-Thou relationship. . . . Though covenants, humans and their institutions are enabled to enter into dialogue while maintaining their respective integrities within a shared framework."[47]

Unity in covenant takes place in the context of the unity/communion of the triune God that covenant reflects. Shalom, the goal of covenant, describes the perfect unity of all creatures in their diversity. Our bond with God and others does not

46. Cf. Gunton, *The One, the Three, and the Many*.

47. Elazar, *Covenant and Polity in Biblical Israel*, 65.

eliminate our individuality and differences. God seeks fellowship and communion with human partners while respecting their particularities.

As the second dialectic indicates, the life in covenant is communally oriented and communicatively (dialogically) engaged to maintain and renew free, reciprocal, and equal relationship in a covenantal community. The unity built out of diversity forms the shape of a covenant community.[48] According to Elazar, "a covenant establishes a partnership linking diverse entities into a purposeful union of unlimited duration, but one in which the partners maintain their respective integrities throughout."[49]

Free, truthful communication is critical for achieving unity and solidarity among different parties. It is the assumption of covenant ethics that genuine unity is impossible without the free participation and commitment of each member. New covenant ethics takes diversity as a gift, not as a threat; as a given reality, not as a choice in building a just community. In covenant, differences among the members are constantly mediated and balanced through ongoing, dynamic, reciprocal communication between the partners. Only through communication and fellowship between the parties is covenant able to maintain this creative tension and balance between solidarity and freedom. Communication has the effect of differentiating and unifying the parties. On the one hand, it clarifies what the respective rights and responsibilities of each party are, and on the other hand, it has the effect of unifying the partners in deeper fellowship. In other words, good communication serves as a mediating mechanism that balances freedom and solidarity among the members.[50] Through communication, the life in covenant becomes a reciprocal and cooperative enterprise in which the partners constantly engage with each other.

Thanks to the communal-communicative mechanism of the covenant, freedom in covenant is "fettered freedom" or solidaric freedom, not autonomous, self-enclosed freedom, while solidarity is open, dialogical solidarity, not a suffocating, authoritarian one. Unity in the covenant is more historical and volitional than ontological, just as diversity is not individualistic and self-sufficient. In covenantal relationship, unity is not uniformity because it is not imposed or coerced by a powerful party, just as diversity is not chaos that rampages at the expense of solidarity. Thanks to its communicative aspect (together with protection of the basic rights and sanctity of each person), solidarity in covenant is not blindly undifferentiated but is highly differentiated and complex. Unity without due respect for particular-

48. Theorizing the relationship of the whole and parts, this principle has played an important role in the social imagination of Reformed Christian ethics, as well as in building a federal system for democratic societies, such as the United States.

49. Elazar, *Covenant and Polity in the Biblical Israel*, 70.

50. "Reciprocity is the glue that holds the relational polarities of uniqueness and unity together." Balswick, *The Reciprocating Self*, 35.

ity is totalitarian, oppressive, and uniformative, while particularity without unity is fragmented and chaotic, thus ultimately losing its distinctiveness.

Conclusion

Our discussion in this chapter has demonstrated that new covenant ethics (and its patterns of the covenantal drama and three dialectics) has compelling explanatory power to clarify often-confused or misunderstood moral notions in Christian ethics. New covenant ethics establishes the relationships of norm-context, being-becoming, worship-ethics, and unity-diversity in a proper balance and harmony, clarifying their dialectic tensions and boundaries. In the framework of new covenant ethics, these binary notions are complementary rather than conflicting. Their balance and harmony are important for living a faithful and fruitful Christian life in a covenantal relationship with God and others. Theological and moral distortions happen when Christians choose one side over the other, resulting in legalism (norm over context), spiritualism (worship over ethics), relativism (context over norm), moralism (ethics over worship), authoritarianism (unity over diversity), and fragmentation or tribalism (diversity over unity). Only through balance and creative tension are Christians able to engage in new situations with confidence, creativity, and openness without losing a sense of coherence and continuity.

CHAPTER 6

A Short Comparison with Other Christian Ethics

> Covenanting becomes a way to think about the nations and kingdoms of the earth, a way requiring risk, emotion, and solidarity. Covenanting . . . is the way all of society is intended to be with its markings of justice, freedom, abundance, and compassion. And the people . . . are to work toward that transformation and not give up on the world.
>
> —Walter Brueggemann,
> *A Social Reading of the Old Testament*

Having studied the distinctive nature and characteristics of new covenant ethics and its explanatory power, we now examine how new covenant ethics is different from other forms of Christian ethics: traditional Reformed covenant ethics, Reinhold Niebuhr's Christian Realism, John Howard Yoder's Mennonite ethics, Stanley Hauerwas's communitarian ethics, and liberation ethics.[1] My hope is that this comparison further clarifies the nature and distinctiveness of new covenant ethics and demonstrates its plausibility and strengths in addressing some difficult questions in the discipline of Christian ethics.

The focus of the comparison will be how new covenant ethics meets the criteria of a key metaphor: faithfulness, comprehensiveness, relevance, and motivation (or transforming power). As mentioned in the introduction, a good ethical metaphor is consistent in demonstrating faithfulness to the whole of Scripture, broad in encompassing the diverse literatures of Scripture, capacious for addressing relevant social issues coherently across diverse contexts, and practically efficacious for motivating human actions.

There is a caveat, however. Because of limited space, I must present these rich ethical traditions with broad strokes. Hence, the comparison is far from comprehen-

1. Cf. Hays, *Moral Vision*, chap. 12.

sive or detailed. I do not elaborate on the nuances and complexities of each ethical tradition (or representative) but rather highlight only the most tangible differences between the traditions (or representatives).

Traditional Covenant Ethics

Readers may be curious about how new covenant ethics differs from traditional covenant ethics, which is typically considered a kind of Reformed Christian ethics.[2] There are diverse ethical approaches that underscore "covenant" as a central motif of the Bible. It is true that new covenant ethics continues some key insights of traditional covenant ethics in its theological emphases: the sovereignty of God in history, a thorough critique of idolatry, the importance of the law and of a disciplined life (sanctification of both individuals and society), freedom, and the centrality of covenant in God's relationship with humanity.

However, new covenant ethics is distinguished from traditional covenant ethics in several areas. First, it brings conceptual clarity to the biblical idea of covenant and its ethical implications. For example, it clearly explicates the performative and communicative nature of covenant and develops a covenantally grounded theory of virtue and just peacemaking. It identifies covenant as the mechanism of God's organizing of a moral community with shalom as its telos. It also delves deeply into the constitutive structure of covenant by identifying love, justice, and power as its structural components. Its discussion of three dialectics adds explanatory power and a better understanding of the dynamics and operation of covenant.

Most distinctively, new covenant ethics explicitly takes the covenant of Jesus as its foundation and starting point. It approaches moral issues in the context of the new covenant of Jesus Christ, which, according to the biblical witness, is the most normative and immediately binding covenant over Christians. The new covenant of Jesus is the final and thus most authoritative covenant and has the final say. It fulfills the previous covenants; it simultaneously affirms, qualifies, and expands and elevates them.

This decision has huge implications for approaching Christian ethics. New covenant ethics reframes, rearranges, and revises the above theological themes and motifs in the context of the covenant of Jesus. In general, traditional covenant ethics has failed to fully develop the ethical implications of the covenant of Jesus on Christian ethics. While upholding the sole headship of Christ and salvation through faith in him, traditional covenant ethics does not unapologetically build the edifice of its eth-

2. There are other Christian ethicists who have published extensively on covenant outside the Reformed tradition. Among them are Methodists Paul Ramsey, William May, Joseph L. Allen.

ics on the new covenant of Jesus or take the Sermon on the Mount and the Gospels as the central moral teachings of the church. Instead, it builds Christian ethics on the basis of the structure and pattern of the biblical idea of covenant in general, and the Sinai covenant in particular. That is, it draws normative content and obligations from the structure of covenant (membership, importance of free agreement, divine initiative and law, vocation, federalism), notably natural law (the creation covenant), the Ten Commandments, and other divine commandments. To a considerable degree, this has to do with the misguided and dichotomous categorization between the unconditional and conditional covenants. Traditional covenant ethics regards the new covenant as the unconditional covenant (human moral responsibility is overshadowed by God's grace).

Consequently, if not intentionally, the new covenant of Jesus, together with the Sermon on the Mount, is marginalized from ethics. The tendency is that the Sinai covenant takes central priority in ethics while the new covenant is more concerned with soteriology. This disjointing creates theological tension, incoherence, contradictions, and moral problems in biblical hermeneutics and the Christian moral life. While it pays extensive attention to the OT, it does not see the overarching and intrinsic ethical connection between the OT and the NT; it does not see the Sermon on the Mount through the framework of the covenant renewal of Jesus. In this way, it has failed to resolve theologically a serious tension between the Mosaic law and the Sermon on the Mount—the emphasis on natural law, justice, law, order, and sanctification of a society, on the one hand, and the teachings of reconciliation, forgiveness, nonviolence, and love of enemy, on the other. New covenant ethics resolves this tension through its covenantal interpretation of the Sermon on the Mount, its proposal of the threefold dialectics, its exegesis of Matthew 5:17–18, and the intertestamental unity of covenant.

To no lesser extent, covenant ethics' focus on the Sinai covenant was partly a reflection of the sociopolitical location of its advocates. Covenant ethics grew in the soil of European Christendom and colonial America in order to address the demands of a social order during the Reformation and early modern eras, later incentivized by the European colonial project. Because of the magisterial status of mainstream Protestantism, its ethics naturally leaned toward active involvement in politics and social issues, the legitimacy of power, and the question of law and order, for which the Sinai covenant offered more detailed and extensive resources than the new covenant of Jesus. Out of its concern to establish a new divinely ordained society, it emphasized the importance of social justice and law and order but was reluctant to embrace nonviolence, virtue, and just peacemaking.

However, choosing the creation covenant (especially the idea of creation ordinances) and the Sinai covenant as the prima facie center of ethics has huge implications. For example, the identification of their unique social location with the Sinai covenant led Puritans to grievously misuse covenant to justify racism and colonialism. Identifying themselves as the new Israel, they racially reinterpreted the Sinai covenant and misappropriated the idea of election to justify colonialism and to build a racial hierarchy and ideology. Its tragic impact is still felt today.[3] The kinship identity of Israel was transposed to the racial category of whiteness. Completely reversing the intrinsic liberative message and purpose of the Sinai covenant, covenantal polity became a biological and racial category. The oppressive systems of slavery and segregation, and the corrupt ideologies of Manifest Destiny and apartheid, were the fruits of this misconceived interpretation of the creation covenant and the Sinai covenant.[4] Even today, some conservative American Christians use covenant for their "law and order" ideology, often justifying the punitive and exclusionary politics of the dominant group toward people of color and immigrants.[5]

Shifting the starting point and center of covenant ethics from Sinai to the new covenant is critical for freeing us from this racist misuse of covenant. New covenant ethics is inclusive and egalitarian. It expands the covenant membership to the entire humanity, explicitly correcting the hierarchy among humans. It embraces God, humanity, and other creatures, and it holds that all humans are to be free, equal, intimate, and mutually caring.[6] Because of its cosmic, inclusive, and egalitarian nature (Jews and gentiles, women and men, rich and poor), the new covenant is closer to the vision of shalom than the other covenants in the Bible. The Eucharist embodies this universal scope and moral nature.

Taking the covenant of Jesus as the ground of both Christian soteriology and ethics is long overdue. New covenant ethics brings theological coherence between soteriology and ethics, the OT and the NT. This coherence is possible through reception

3. John Leith identifies another shortcoming: "obscurantism when the will of God is prematurely identified with some human pattern of conduct." Leith, *An Introduction to the Reformed Tradition*, 80.

4. Some misused the creation covenant to justify racial hierarchy by asserting that it is intrinsic to the creation order that God had ordained. Slavery and apartheid developed on the basis of this racialization of the creation covenant. Racial, cultural, and linguistic diversities (Gen. 11), defined as the evidence of the creation order, were used to justify inequality among different races. In this framework, the idea of election (e.g., God's election of Afrikaners and Anglo-Saxons) placed whites at the top of the racial hierarchy.

5. Karl Barth is a theologian who has developed a coherent Christocentric theology of election on the basis of the covenant of Jesus, but with the effect of disregarding the ethical significance and meaning of the creation covenant and other covenants in the Bible. See Barth, *Church Dogmatics* II/2, 94–194. For the critique of Barth's view with the use of John Owen's pneumatology, see Suzanne McDonald's *Re-imaging Election*.

6. Schüssler Fiorenza, *In Memory of Her*, part 2.

history and the covenantal renewal of Jesus. The NT writers, broadly speaking, with analogical imagination, resorted to the pattern of the exodus story (paradigm) in interpreting the Christ event.

New covenant ethics revises some fallacies and limitations and expands the scope of the traditional Reformed idea of covenant and covenant ethics. It corrects the collusion of covenant theology with racism, colonialism, and white hegemony. By taking the covenant of Jesus as the foundation, new covenant ethics rectifies the theological misunderstandings of election, as well as the magisterial tendency (law and order) and legalism of traditional covenant ethics. Consistent with the new covenant of Jesus, it develops Christian ethics on the basis of just peacemaking.

Like traditional covenant ethics, new covenant ethics is faithful to the drama of the Bible. However, it is more comprehensive and relevant to the pluralistic cultural situation of our time.

Reinhold Niebuhr

Reinhold Niebuhr has been celebrated as America's theologian, and his Christian Realism in particular has been praised. Niebuhr's ideas of the love-justice dialectic and justice as the balance of power had huge impacts on Christian social ethics as well as American foreign policy during and after the Cold War (for instance, President Obama's policy in the Middle East and doctrine of pivot to East Asia; in fact, Niebuhr has been cited by Obama as one of his favorite philosophers).[7]

As a social ethicist, Niebuhr paid close attention to structural problems and issues and relied on political analysis in achieving social justice. Niebuhr's social ethics was shaped in the intersection between his theological anthropology and his ongoing social analysis. In fact, he continuously revised his political positions in response to unfolding human history and changing political-social realities.

Niebuhr's approach is based on theological anthropology and the religious meaning of the Christian gospel for human existence. He developed his social ethics with the sober recognition of the paradoxical nature of human reality caught between finiteness and freedom, limitation (e.g., illness and mortality) and vitality. In response to anxiety arising from the above tension, humans are willing to accumulate power by any means, even at the expense of others, using moral religious rhetoric and public policies to conceal their true intentions. Informed by theological anthropology (especially a robust doctrine of sin), the premise of Niebuhr's social ethics is this: "No human life is, in short, a simple construction of conscience or reason. All communities are more or less stable or precarious harmonies of vital capacities. They

7. Brooks, "Obama, Gospel and Verse."

are governed by power."[8] And groups are more arrogant, hypocritical, self-centered, and ruthless in pursuit of their ends than individuals are.[9]

Power itself is not evil, as it is an indication of human vitality. But because of human sinfulness, it always seeks inordinate self-interest at the sacrifice of others. This sinful nature is amplified in collective life. Because of the unavoidable nature of this human condition, love cannot be actualized in a collective life; only justice is a reasonable goal for human effort. Justice is possible through the balance of power: "Perfect love is sacrificial love, making no careful calculations between the interests of the self and the other."[10]

The heart of Niebuhr's social ethics is the dialectic of love and justice in response to a full recognition of sinful human nature and the nefarious operation of power in collective life. While Niebuhr eventually modified the form and expression of his ethics, the essential tenets of the dialectic of love and justice remained consistent, constituting the core of his Christian Realism. The dialectic of love and justice is his synthetic approach to address the paradoxical human condition between transcendence and history, ideal and real, utopianism and cynicism, what ought to be and what is.

Because of human sin in history, justice is only roughly achievable, while love is only eschatologically promised. Nevertheless, love serves as the lure toward higher and nobler moral aspirations. Thus, it is still ethically relevant as a critique of human moral hubris and utopianism as well as the antidote to cynicism.[11] The idea of justice mediates power and love; it is the beginning of love but is never perfect or complete because it is still self-interested. However, it is not sinful because it considers others' interests. It is a necessary compromise between transcendent love and sinful reality, freedom and coercion. The ultimate goal of ethics is love, but the practical goal is justice. Niebuhr was critical of any collective moral effort to achieve love in relationships between groups and nations because of its impossibility in history. He believed that justice is the best that humanity can attain in society, achieved through a balance of power.[12]

Niebuhr has been criticized for his overdependence on anthropological and social analysis rather than the biblical story and thick theological description. His

8. Reinhold Niebuhr, *The Nature and Destiny of Man*, 2:257.

9. Reinhold Niebuhr, *The Nature and Destiny of Man*, 2:208.

10. *Reinhold Niebuhr on Politics*, 157.

11. His dialectic of love and justice aims to avoid naïve moral idealism (e.g., the Social Gospel), liberal Christianity that only upholds love as an immediately binding norm, as well as the cold Machiavellianism of political realists who inordinately pursue power.

12. Niebuhr saw mutual love as a mediating notion (with some continuity as well as discontinuity) between love and justice.

ethics, under the influence of liberal theology, tends to abstract love and justice from the biblical drama. For example, he regarded Jesus as the ideal moral person of love. While praised for his excellent contribution to Christian public theology, Niebuhr did not hold God's person and action central in his ethics, and he did not consider the work of the Spirit and the church significant. Similarly, Niebuhr was criticized for his inattention to character formation and the cultivation of virtues because his emphasis on social justice led him to focus on power relations and social structures more than on moral agency. Theologically speaking, he had a higher view of sin and a lower view of sanctification (as well as Christology, pneumatology, and ecclesiology). Hence, his ethical remedy is institutional and pragmatic, that is, restraint of sin through checks and balances rather than transformation of society, even gradually and partially, through the diverse organizing of people, just peacemaking, moral persuasion, and habit and virtue formation.

Preoccupied with the sinful nature of humanity especially in collective life, treating sin as the human condition (original sin), Niebuhr tended to minimize or ignore the transformative possibility of human life in history. As we see in his misjudgment of and lack of commitment to the civil rights movement, Niebuhr underestimated the power of collective nonviolent resistance for social change and democratic renewal. King, on the other hand, showed that love is not an "impossible possibility" (a utopian ideal) but a form of power that is redemptive and benevolent in nature, exercised in nonviolence against injustice through forgiveness and peacemaking for repentant opponents.

New covenant ethics shares the same political insights of Niebuhr's interrelationship of love, justice, and power, in addition to his commitment to social justice, the balance of power, and the democratic principles of checks and balances.

However, unlike Niebuhr's theological thinness, new covenant ethics approaches love, justice, and power without compromising theological integrity and convictions. In particular, it identifies covenant as the constitutive relational structure of these three ideas. The ideas of love, justice, and power are covenantally informed and embedded because the new covenant offers a quintessentially relational and theological matrix of them. As discussed in the previous chapter, new covenant helps integrate the three in theological coherence and dialectic balance.

The covenantal matrix of love, justice, and power addresses some of the criticisms against Niebuhr. It particularly corrects Niebuhr's unbiblical notion of *agapē*, which was influenced by Anders Nygren. In new covenant ethics, love is not merely a negative norm—a mere critique of every achievement of justice—but is the commitment to and demonstration of a desirable moral community. It is defined more by shalom than *agapē*, mutuality than sacrifice, solidarity than heroic other-regarding, and communion than the crucifixion. As the first dialectic of unilateral-bilateral indicates, God's sacrifice and other-regarding service ultimately aim to build a community of shalom.

Similarly, Niebuhr's pragmatic idea of justice is theologically thin and morally quite reductionistic. By contrast, the thick covenantal ideas of *tsedaqah*, *mishpat*, and a fuller view of distributive justice offer better moral directives for addressing the complex social issues arising in the diverse social spheres of a highly pluralistic society. His mechanical view of love, justice, and power loses sight of the diverse forms and dynamics of civil society and alliances, including the church, and their transformative possibilities (e.g., protest, rebellion, experimentation).

New covenant ethics embodies love and justice in a relational, nonviolent, and reciprocal way. Thus, these two norms are far closer to each other than in Niebuhr. They also guide the use of power in a nonviolent and politically legitimate way under the stricture of constitution and the rule of law, which take the form of covenantal stipulations among citizens for embodying the principle of justice. And the practice of just peacemaking presents a necessary and important mediating structure between power and love. While conscious of the abusive possibility of power, new covenant ethics is open to the possibility of reform and mutual influence and learning within and among group relationships.

As the modern history of democracy demonstrates, covenant renders a plausible moral ground and direction for democracy. In a covenantal framework, democracy is the system of justice (checks and balances) that moves toward love (a more perfect union) through the fair distribution of power (influence, access, and resources). Covenant, especially its federal theology of unity-in-diversity, creates not only a system of checks and balances but also collaboration among various groups for the enhancement of the common good. By building the system of checks and balances as well as interdependence, covenantal federalization reduces the abuse of power and increases the possibility of mutual support.

New covenant ethics offers theological sociology in addition to theological anthropology. Its associational pluralism that imagines a society with multiple and federated organizations equips Christians with an appropriate vision and perspective for social engagements. While imperfect, public discourses and the rule of law have some moral and binding power. While the possibility of corruption and a manipulative use of communication always exists, there also exists a genuine desire for mutual understanding and agreement among people. The law can be misused as a moral or ideological cover for a dominant group in a society, but a good law can also restrain and hold them accountable.

The three dialectics of covenant help elucidate how love, justice, and power are interrelated. The first dialectic (unilateral-bilateral) explains where the motivation (a moral and psychological power in itself) for love and justice comes from; in other words, Christians are lured not just by an abstract ideal of *agapē* but also by the concrete experiential love of God in Jesus Christ. Their work for justice and peacemaking imitates God's love and justice.

The second dialectic sees how community is actually maintained and strengthened in love-justice relationships, which empower the participants and generate new power (social capital and organization); this is instrumental to grassroots organizing. The three dialectics explain how the unconditional love of God (*agapē* in Niebuhr's language) is related to mutual love (reciprocity and mutual respect) and justice (freedom and rights) among the members when expanded to a broader society.

Niebuhr does not offer any substantial definition of justice and a clear explication of its meaning other than the operating principle of the balance of power. While Niebuhr's insight is correct in claiming that a balance of power is crucial for achieving social justice, it is too narrow to address complex and diverse institutional realities and moral expectations. Compared to Niebuhr's abstract and thin moral imagination, covenant offers a more theologically informed, complex, and dynamic social imagination for social justice. A covenantal social imagination allows the pursuit of love, justice, and power—with shalom as their collective fulfillment—in diverse social realms while respecting distinctive functional requisites (called mandates; see chap. 11). The biblical idea of covenant as an organizing principle applies to the church, social institutions, government, and broader society (including the global community).

New covenant ethics offers politically realistic and effective options for social change that are consistent with the Christian faith and the new covenant of Jesus. Its practices of community organizing are far more effective than Christian Realism. Just peacemaking, community organizing, and nonviolence are important tools and strategies for social change and democracy that bridge the gap between love, justice, and power. New covenant ethics beseeches Christians to engage in radical organizing and the social transformation of values in every realm of society, starting with the institutions to which they belong. As a method of accumulating and exercising power, the practices of community organizing and nonviolent resistance are a creative way to fill the gap and bridge the tension between justice and love. The last century has shown the political effectiveness and moral consistency of major social transformation through the long-term organizing of people and movements of nonviolent resistance. Community organizing is indispensable for revitalizing and sustaining grassroots democracy. Democracy operates through daily organizing of ordinary people.

In short, new covenant ethics achieves Niebuhr's goal of social justice with better theological integrity and a refined social sensibility by offering covenant as an explicit and capacious theological foundation for love, justice, power, and actual political practices that approximate justice and love.

John Howard Yoder

In stark contrast to Reinhold Niebuhr's Christian Realism, John Howard Yoder attempted to build a Christian social ethic on the sole ground of Jesus.[13] Yoder was very critical of Niebuhr for his thin theology, especially Christology and ecclesiology: that is, Niebuhr's reduction of the rich teaching of Jesus and the cross into abstract principles of *agapē* love and his treatment of the Sermon on the Mount as a lofty but utopian moral ideal (the impossible possibility). Similarly, Yoder was critical of liberal/mainline Christians' treatment of Jesus as an ideal moral figure who is irrelevant for social ethics. For Yoder, Jesus is "not only relevant but also normative for a contemporary Christian social ethic."[14] His book *The Politics of Jesus*, now a classic in Christian ethics, presents a Jesus-centered social ethics, challenging the conventional liberal and mainline Christian approach to social ethics that marginalizes Jesus, the Sermon on the Mount, and the crucifixion. Yoder argued for the political and social-ethical significance of Jesus, in particular, the political nature of Jesus's ministry that revived the Jubilee tradition. The core characteristic of Jesus's social ethics was rejecting violence and retaliation, and choosing instead the path of love and suffering, which climaxed in the cross. The Sermon on the Mount and the gospel stories served as a cornerstone of his Jesus-centered Christian social ethics. Yoder presented the politics of Jesus as a radical alternative to liberal politics of democracy, liberationist insurrectionism, and evangelical quietism.

Yoder's social ethics was framed by a two-aeon messianic eschatology (the old order versus the new order), which sees Jesus and the church as countercultural, in diametric opposition to the powers; thus, any recourse to the state is not a viable option for Christians. He advocated "revolutionary subordination," which is "the

13. One should be aware of John Howard Yoder's sexual abuse of women, which was first disclosed in 1992. Given his towering status as one of the most influential Christian ethicists in the twentieth century, the scope and length of his abuse, along with the decades-long neglect by his denominational and academic supervisors, were a wake-up call for many Christians in dealing with sexual abuse within their communities. Yoder's scandal is especially disturbing and hurtful because his predatory behaviors were completely antithetical to his pacifist ethics, which upholds nonviolence, love, and self-sacrifice as the core requisites of Christian discipleship grounded in the cross of Jesus.

Given the astounding discrepancy between his ethics and actions, serious doubt has been raised about whether his work deserves any further scholarly attention and respect. While fully alive to the pain and anger of the victims of his abuse, this section critically engages Yoder's ethics with a focus on how new covenant ethics, with its deeper awareness of human brokenness, is more plausible and effective than Yoder's perfectionistic ethics in protecting the rights of women and in establishing a necessary moral mechanism of mutual accountability within a Christian community.

14. Yoder, *The Politics of Jesus*, 11.

act of voluntarily acceding to subordination [worldly systems (the powers)] in the power of Christ." For Yoder, the church does not expect the state to play any positive role: "The kind of faithfulness that is willing to accept evident defeat rather than complicity with evil is, by virtue of its conformity with what happens to God when he works among us, aligned with the ultimate triumph of the Lamb."[15] Hence, a proper Christian attitude is to just "accept the structures" of the world without joining them because "they are about to crumble away" anyway.[16]

Yoder's social ethics evolved, and his earlier highly sectarian and dualistic attitude was modified by his proposal of a tactical alliance. He proposed a "gradual eschatology" that softened his earlier dichotomous two-aeon eschatology. He allowed a selective engagement with the system by building coalitions and even seeking limited transformation. To the later Yoder, the social system and the state are not necessarily intrinsically evil or inimical to the church, but they are malleable. Churches sometimes need to cooperate with them for the common good (the well-being of humans and other creatures, including church members).

However, Yoder's eschatologies are incoherent; there is definitely a contradiction between the ideas of "revolutionary subordination" and tactical alliance. Janna Hunter-Bowman explains: "Yoder is mixing eschatologies, which are his social theories, and therefore is bequeathing us conceptually sloppy categories for thinking about agency and structural change." Because of this theological and conceptual confusion and unclarity, Yoder "fails to provide a fine-grained account of structural change, church-state relations in different temporal contexts, or interpersonal relationships."[17]

Like Yoder, new covenant ethics takes seriously the ministry, teachings, crucifixion, and resurrection of Jesus, and the Sermon on the Mount. But new covenant ethics reframes Jesus and the Sermon in a covenantal framework. Anabaptists (such as Yoder and his disciple Glen Stassen) fail to identify the covenantal renewal of the Sinai covenant as the context of Jesus's ministry and teaching. This covenantal vantage point has the effect of integrating the Anabaptist sensibility of the centrality of Jesus (the Sermon and nonviolence) with the Reformed, mainline Protestant, and Catholic emphasis on social justice and active political engagement.

Yoder did not see the deep intrinsic covenantal continuity between Jesus and the OT, although the covenantal drama is the key link in connecting the OT and the NT. The consequence is the unintended detachment of Jesus's story and politics from the rich covenantal stories and traditions of the OT (and failure to explore and draw

15. Yoder, *The Politics of Jesus*, 238.

16. Hunter-Bowman, "Constructive Agents under Duress," 155.

17. Hunter-Bowman, "Constructive Agents under Duress," 157.

the political and moral implications from the covenantal fabric of Jesus's ministry in the creative dialectic of continuity and discontinuity with the OT). By doing so, Yoder lost the realistic and pragmatic insights and motifs (institutional, legal, and public) rooted in his covenantal politics. His earlier apocalyptic eschatology overly emphasizes divine agency at the expense of human agency, peace (pacifism) over justice, and suffering ("subjection to the Powers whose sovereignty is broken already by Christ") over social participation. Consequently, he failed to see how God is working in history outside the church. Natural law, long-respected wisdom, and public norms are rejected because they compromise the distinctive Christian identity. His eschatology leads to suspicion of any meaningful dialogue with, collaboration with, and learning from non-Christians.

New covenant ethics addresses these difficulties by putting Jesus and his ethics in a dialectical relationship with the OT. It seeks the rich meaning and direct relevance of *Jesus* for social ethics through a covenantal interpretation of Jesus's ministry, teachings, and crucifixion. It is similar to Yoder in that Jesus organized people into God's community; this community is called to live out new covenant ethics. However, new covenant ethics, unlike Yoder, positively affirms Christian participation in and engagement with the state and other nonecclesial institutions under God's reign and the church's active social prophetic ministry in civil society. New covenant ethics addresses this concern by taking Jesus and his covenant as central, while not excluding non-Christians.

New covenant ethics is concerned not only with building up the church but also with building up society and its organizations, and with nurturing its citizens. A covenantal approach allows this because of its pertinence as an organizing principle. In fact, the church does not have to be the only new community that Christians are called to organize. As the Puritans demonstrated, various Christian organizations and social institutions, inspired by the new covenant, can be formed. Covenant serves as a coherent organizing mechanism for the church as well as for other institutions and democracy. Without being dualistic, some distinction is necessary for the sake of respect for and civility toward non-Christians.

New covenant ethics is applicable to personal, ecclesial, and public contexts, while mindful of the different dynamics of each context. New covenant ethics is not content with forming a countercultural community separated from society or consuming its energy in criticizing society and national and international policy makers. It actively participates in public discourses and social practices through community development and grassroots organizing.

The church can still be a model community for others by welcoming strangers and caring for the weak, the poor, and even the wicked, while prophetically and collaboratively engaging with others. Covenantal sociology allows and encourages such a distinction because each sphere is called to pursue a different mandate and service for God's kingdom. While interrelated, church and society are still governed by distinctive logics, criteria, and subject matter. That is to say, Christians can be formed and shaped by a particular narrative tradition while still being free to participate in other social spheres. Religious identity and social relevance, the tension between a particular narrative and public justice, need not be mutually exclusive, but rather can be complementary. Using the method of public theology, Christians "may actively engage in their professional contexts and the larger society out of their own particular beliefs and convictions while exercising sensitivity to a distinctive subject matter and the good of each sphere."[18]

Stanley Hauerwas

Stanley Hauerwas, deeply influenced by John Howard Yoder, explicitly develops his ethics in intellectually postmodern and culturally pluralistic contexts. Addressing the concern of fragmentation in a pluralistic society, Hauerwas's ethics takes a strong communitarian tone. Hauerwas argues that Christian ethics is inseparable from, and in fact utterly dependent on, the church. It makes sense only in the context of the church; outside the church, Christian ethics loses its meaning, intelligibility, and context.

He beseeches Christian churches to guard against the danger of uncritical assimilation to liberalism. Hauerwas is highly critical of a friendly relationship between mainline and Catholic Christians and Enlightenment ethics, along with modern ideologies and institutions (freedom, justice, human rights, and democracy). He holds that Christian ethics must find its own distinctive ground in its own story rather than in universal or public rules and norms. According to Hauerwas, in an attempt to be relevant (or public), Christian ethics abstracts Christian convictions into a few key principles, norms, and ideals shareable with everyone, while suppressing or marginalizing biblical narratives and rituals. The consequence is the uncritical assimilation to secular ideologies and the loss of its distinctive identity and narrative convictions.

Hauerwas presents a refreshing challenge and an attractive alternative to many Christians who are afflicted with fragmentation, anomie, and confusion in a global and pluralistic society. By restoring a clear sense of identity, Hauerwas's ethics imparts a strong sense of purpose and commitment for Christian churches. He emphasizes the critical role of the Christian community, narrative, and tradition for the formation of Christian identity, character, and agency.

However, Hauerwas tends to romanticize the church. He underestimates the dark or flawed side of community. A believer does gain strength and support from

18. Lee, "Public Theology," 60–61.

a Christian community. A community does play a crucial role for socialization of its members. However, socialization is not identical with moral formation; as the quality of moral formation depends on the moral quality of a community, its contribution could be healthy or detrimental for members. Some communities—even some Christian communities—are abusive, dehumanizing, and oppressive. Many young people today want to dissociate from the ills of a community ridden with parochialism, chauvinism, jingoism, and conformist pressure. They look for a more open and inclusive community.

This applies to the church as well. While church is a new community, it is still afflicted with the various flaws, limitations, and sinfulness of its members; it is still a broken social entity waiting for its final redemption. Moreover, the church is filled with members who belong to other institutions of society, such as hospitals, public schools, banks, multinational corporations, and the police. Members have been inevitably influenced by these institutions, and they carry such influence with them into the church, knowingly or unknowingly.

A covenantal approach does not deny the importance of a community for human social life, or the role of church tradition and practices in virtue formation. A human being desires belonging and relational security in a good community. Indeed, covenant is God's method of organizing a community, and the new covenant represents such a community.

However, while acknowledging the importance, indeed the indispensability, of community, new covenant ethics distances itself from a romantic or idealized view. In the Bible, a community is always under God's grace and judgment. Christians neither idealize nor demonize a community; rather, they are called to be aware of its fallen nature and its constructive potential. Communities, therefore, like individuals, are in need of God's forgiveness and continuous renewal (Rev. 2–3). They require ongoing communicative tests and the edification of their members. This insight applies to other institutions as well.

Created in the image of the triune God, a person is always culturally and socially situated, as communitarians point out, but a person is not absorbed by the community. In a covenantal community, a moral agent is far from being compliant and passive, but rather exercises an active, reflexive, critical ability. The covenanted self is able to distance self from community. Horton notes: "The human self is not merely situated in a hermeneutically sealed cultural-linguistic bubble; it is able to be drawn out of a purely mundane, chronological, and immanent context of self-identity to be written into a script that cuts across all times and places through the vertical 'intrusions' of the Spirit."[19]

19. Horton, "Image and Office," 202.

New covenant ethics imagines a liberative and restorative community where freedom and solidarity are balanced in friendship and trust. Through the communicative practices and mutual binding power of covenantal stipulations, covenant institutionalizes moral accountability among members while constantly striving toward deeper communion through truth telling, hospitality, and solidarity. That is, new covenant ethics is very conscious of the issues of justice and power in the life of a community. It institutionalizes the structure of accountability to prevent abuses and protect the basic rights of all members. Just peacemaking explicates the covenantal notion of community. It is organized among equal members according to the principles of justice striving for peace and love by redistributing power (resources) and responsibility.

With its goal of organizing a just and peaceful society, new covenant ethics emphasizes virtue formation as well as public policies, norms, and laws. Unlike Hauerwas, new covenant ethics seeks a critical but constructive alliance between Christianity and democracy and its institutions: constitutionalism, the rule of law, human rights, and civil society. Democracy, in my view, is a political system that more closely resonates with the biblical vision and norms of covenant than other systems. New covenant ethics does not hesitate to improve and expand democracy because it believes that public policy matters. Bad public policies affect personal choices and make a destructive impact on the formation of individual and institutional behaviors, characters, and relationships. Public policy can deter or incentivize human desires, behaviors, and institutional decisions, in either constructive or destructive directions.

While acknowledging the role of community for identity formation, new covenant ethics takes a different approach toward identity formation than Hauerwas does. While not denying the role of community, in new covenant ethics, the anchoring and sustaining power of one's identity come from a covenantal relationship with God and others. Sometimes the former transcends the boundary of a particular community. Our relationship with the triune God has a foundational, reorienting, and reconstituting power over one's identity and relationships.

Logically speaking, identity formation precedes character formation. That is to say, our Christian identity is constituted by God's unilateral election and call, while our moral character/virtue is formed through our moral responses to God's bilateral call in a covenantal relationship. Identity is given in our new relationship with God through adoption, and our character and virtue are built up through fellowship on the basis of this new identity.

New covenant ethics is indicative because it is grounded in Christian identity that the covenant creates in a believer. The indicative has a relational basis in the covenant. That is, a covenantal relationship grants a new identity and moral motivation to a person. This identity, grounded in the relationship with God, is not easily shaken because it has a transcendental basis, namely, God's election in Jesus Christ. In new covenant ethics, ethics is a natural expression of our identity. What we ought to do (imperative) flows from who we are in Jesus Christ (indicative).[20] "I am to do what I am."[21] Stephen Mott observes: "The authority which God's commands have over us, our understanding of their meaning, and even the ability to carry them out, all stem from the reality that it is our salvation in Christ which now defines our basic identity."[22]

According to Paul Ricoeur, "Character is truly the 'what' of the 'who.'"[23] When identity is underdeveloped, character formation is impossible. Similarly, when identity undergoes crisis, character (moral agency) also faces a challenge and is temporarily stalled.

The unilateral-bilateral dynamic helps to properly understand the relationship of identity, Christian moral formation, and moral actions. In new covenant ethics, our new identity as God's children is prior to our moral obligations. Moral decisions and actions are not only responses to a particular narrative (although its formative power is important) but also responses to God's communicative action—the exercise of one's covenantal accountability in relationship to God and others. That is to say, the immediate source of moral affections and desires is not so much biblical narratives and community traditions as it is the communicative love and grace of God. This relational communicative dynamic is more consistent with the biblical witness and explains the indicative nature of Christian ethics better than the postliberal communitarian approach of Hauerwas.

Covenant ethics' communicative model of rationality (ethical reasoning) is more sensible than Hauerwas's postliberal intratextual model of rationality. The process of intersubjective justification is indispensable for practical reasoning in a pluralistic society.[24] Hauerwas's understanding of rationality is too narrow not only for the task of public ethics but for Christian theology itself. In a postmodern society, Christian communities no longer maintain homogeneity, as the current disputes over

20. Nicholson says: "The covenant-theology represented at once an indicative and an imperative: the indicative, Israel's constitution as the people of Yahweh; the imperative, Israel's vocation to be the people of Yahweh." Nicholson, *God and His People*, 210. One finds the integration of the indicative and the imperative in the Ten Commandments, which begin with the preamble that recalls God's unconditional act of deliverance in Egypt. This covenantal narrative sets the tone and renders the indicative qualification for the following commandments.

21. Mott, *Biblical Ethics and Social Change*, 26.

22. Mott, *Biblical Ethics and Social Change*, 26.

23. Ricoeur, *Oneself as Another*, 122.

24. Cf. Harold I. Brown, *Rationality*.

gay marriage, abortion, immigration, and gun control indicate. A public life is not possible without rational discourse. One cannot but ask, "Which decision is more reasonable in this case?" "What principles are relevant here?" In response to these questions, a communicative model of rationality provides a plausible alternative between foundationalism and relativism. Such a claim makes it hard to avoid the charge of fideism because it makes Christian truth and moral claims self-referential. Rationality is concerned with questions of warrants, evidence, and justification presented in the process of exchanging validity claims.

Liberation Ethics

Unlike many traditional Western theologies, liberation ethics was born among scholars of color, activists, and women in the revolutionary (or politically equivalent) situations of radical social transformation. It carries a militant desire and unflinching passion to overcome centuries-long forms of oppression and subjugation (colonialism, racism, sexism, imperialism, etc.). It is a strong critique of institutional churches and the traditional ways of doing theology and ethics.

Accordingly, it is not a homogenous discipline. It has diverse theological and ethical perspectives, distinctive interests, and different histories, backgrounds, and cultural contexts. However, various liberation traditions do share common concerns, similar ethical methods, and related hermeneutical approaches. This section discusses Latin American and black liberation ethics as the primary interlocutors of liberation ethics.

I am aware that liberation ethicists are rightly suspicious of the idea of covenant because of its long history of misuse for racial exclusion and imperialism; covenant has been more a symbol of oppression than of transformation in their (and other intellectuals') perception. The word still connotes the conservatism of law and order and the white status quo rather than radical revolutionary politics. A similar practice of abusing covenant continues among conservative Zionists in Israel to justify the occupation of Palestine.

However, contrary to popular perception, the original ethos of the biblical covenant is liberative. The Puritans used covenant (specifically the exodus story and the Sinai covenant) to transform monarchy into democracy and assert popular sovereignty, human rights, and the rule of law. This liberative impulse was lost among white Christians. However, it was picked up afresh by African Americans to undergird their freedom struggles during the civil rights movement.

New covenant ethics is similar to liberation ethics in its emphasis on the liberative work of God in the exodus and Jesus's ministry. It agrees with several key theological commitments of liberation ethics: God's solidarity with and preferential option for the marginalized, the commitment to social justice, attention to social analysis, bottom-up organizing, and the importance of the moral agency of the oppressed. Like liberation ethics, it takes the work of justice as central to the gospel, neither optional nor ad hoc in the work of reconciliation or individual salvation. It claims that inequality, exploitation, and rigid stratification are antithetical to God's intention for a just and righteous community.

As the previous chapters have mentioned, new covenant ethics takes liberation as the first part of God's central work for humanity, the second part being rebuilding/restoring the shalom community. In the Bible, as Brueggemann holds, covenant describes a social relationship "not of control but of liberation."[25] It is the symbol that reveals the liberative moral nature of God. According to Brueggemann, "Yahweh is a God who forcefully, decisively, and willingly enters into solidarity with a group of helpless people. That solidarity is for the benefit of people who cannot act for themselves. That solidarity is an act of risk for Yahweh, for it puts Yahweh in conflict with other gods and with the awesome power of the empire. It is this act of enduring, risky solidarity that most decisively characterizes the God of the Bible. . . . Risky solidarity [is] *what we mean by covenant*."[26]

The biblical idea of covenant, as we see in the Sinai covenant and the covenant of Jesus, evokes and discharges a strong egalitarian and liberative vision and ethics. Like liberation ethics, new covenant ethics takes seriously political economy as the primary site of distributive justice, the location of power and political struggle. Attention to the political economy is reflected in Sabbath economics and Jubilee in Israel and the early church (cf. Jesus's mission statement in Luke 4:18—the declaration of Jubilee). Continuing God's liberative work, new covenant ethics teaches that Christians are called to practice solidarity with the poor and oppressed.

Despite their shared interests, concerns, and commitments, new covenant ethics differs from current liberationist ethics in several areas. Importantly, it takes covenant as the hermeneutical vantage point for understanding God's liberative work in the Bible. While important, liberation alone is not encompassing enough to properly understand God's work. New covenant ethics simultaneously emphasizes liberation and restoration, justice and love. Covenant bridges and mediates between liberation and restoration. God is a protagonist of liberation as well as a builder of a new city, and human beings are invited to be God's partners for this task through covenant. Liberative work is driven not only by God's justice but also by God's desire for fellowship. This means that the final actualization of liberation is predicated on covenant and shalom, and that the vision of a new, just community controls the nature

25. Brueggemann, *A Social Reading of the Old Testament*, 62.

26. Brueggemann, *A Social Reading of the Old Testament*, 56 (emphasis added).

and form that liberation takes. In covenant, liberation and restoration are inseparable.[27] God's liberation is necessary but not sufficient; it is the first step but not the final step, just as the exodus was only the first step to entering the promised land.

In moving from liberation to restoration, covenant calls for the redefinition and reworking of social relationships that include the transformation of values and unjust, unequal, and distorted institutional and social structures. In the exodus story, the Sinai covenant and the wilderness journey were as important as the judgment of Pharaoh (the plagues against Egypt and the drowning of his army in the Red Sea). Liberation is incomplete without life under Torah (instruction of God's way) and the cultivation of character through worship and ethics in every realm of social life. Liberation without any covenant (agreement) of people would be chaotic and authoritarian, while covenant without liberation would be the conservative condoning of the status quo. The success of liberation ultimately depends on how to build a righteous, just, and stable structure of social relationships among people. Covenant indicates such a structure. A covenantal rule-making process concretely channels and guides human energies and passion for liberation to construct a just order and social structure.

With its prophetic criticism and commitment to the transformation of an unjust system, liberation ethics has its theoretical strength in a revolutionary situation (or a situation of extreme injustice). But it is limited in offering necessary directives for a pluralistic society in nonrevolutionary situations, for example, the concrete demands of governance. Revolution and radical social changes cannot avoid the complex task of governance that includes maintaining basic social order, distributing power and resources, and adjudicating conflict. Without well-established procedures and a guiding moral framework, revolutions may engender chaos and end up creating another tyranny, as witnessed by numerous historical examples (e.g., the Soviet Union, China, Cuba). A just community does not automatically emerge after liberation; it requires a new kind of moral work and moral formation beyond the liberation struggles of protest and resistance. Because of its commitment to love, reconciliation, and moral formation, new covenant ethics rejects violence, while liberation ethics is open to violence on certain occasions. Instead, new covenant ethics presents community organizing and nonviolent direct action as political methods for effective social change.

New covenant ethics, with its critical awareness of this problem, offers "organizing" as a mechanism to mediate liberation and restoration through the building of

27. "The juxtaposition of exodus and Sinai-torah made explicit here indicates how the *event of liberation* and the *social practice of covenant* are fully teamed together. Israel will not have one without the other. Liberation is not an event without ongoing social implications." Brueggemann, *A Social Reading of the Old Testament*, 62.

a new, just society. A righteous community is one where the demands of liberation and restoration are partly actualized. It stresses the role of just law in the organizing process, with the belief that the work of liberation is not sustainable without being embodied in just laws. Sometimes the road to mature democracy is as difficult as the revolution itself. A just society requires publicly minded, virtuous citizens who are willing to organize themselves for meaningful change.

Liberation ethics has been criticized for its overreliance on Marxist social analysis and philosophical categories (use of violence, instrumental approach to power), which are not necessarily consistent with democratic principles of rule making, respect for civil-political rights, associational pluralism, and compromise and negotiation, let alone with the nonviolent way of Jesus. In other words, the relationship of liberation ethics with democratic institutions and values has often been ambiguous.

Like other religious disciplines, however, liberation ethics has evolved. Recent liberation ethicists are softening an earlier rigid Marxist social analysis and increasingly accommodating participatory democracy, civil society, the democratic process, the idea of human rights, and cultural pluralism. However, the relationship of liberation (Marxist philosophy) with democracy and its institutions (free speech, human rights, constitutionalism, rule making, civil society) still needs to be carefully sorted out as to which parts are compatible, which parts need to be revised or abandoned, and why. These changes, in my view, point toward a covenantal form of polity.[28]

Compared to liberation ethics, new covenant ethics offers a well-developed theological sociology and a more sophisticated theological ethics of democracy, human rights, and complex sociology that supports the democratic system of checks and balances, constitution, separation of powers, civil society, and the rule of law. When properly functioning, democracy continues the work of liberation in a quieter and more gradual way.

A challenge for liberation ethics is how to negotiate and coordinate diverse interests and competing political exertions for "liberation" in given social realities. One project of liberation does not necessarily cohere or coincide with the interests of another project of liberation. For example, the interests of the liberation of the poor and liberation of animals (ecology) do not always cohere.

28. One sees a similar possibility in theology as well. For example, while not identifying covenant as the organizing principle of *ecclesia*, Boff's criticism of the hierarchical and institutional church, along with his vision of ecclesio-genesis, extensively resonates with a covenantal vision of the church in its emphasis on grassroots democratic orientation, lay leadership, equality, and reciprocity in decision making. Likewise, the feminist/womanist ethical concerns of solidarity, justice, equality, care, and relationality resonate with the communal ethos and relational sensibility of new covenant ethics. Boff, *Ecclesiogenesis*.

A concern over the binary approach (the oppressors versus the oppressed) of liberation ethics has been raised even among liberationists because it is too narrow to understand the complex social reality and often perpetuates a system of marginalization against outsiders. In this context, liberationist philosophical claims (preferential option for the poor, hermeneutical privilege of the oppressed, the hermeneutics of suspicion), when essentialized and politicized, could have adverse effects and may impede the coalition-building process. They may create intellectual and cultural segregation. This is no longer a speculative question but a pressing pragmatic concern for addressing the complex realities of human oppression and liberation; hence, the growing academic interest in the intersectionality of various social oppressions is necessary and inevitable, especially in the time of global interconnectedness and interdependence.

Similarly, today in a pluralistic society, a democratic and communicative process is unavoidable for adjudicating diverse views and perspectives of social analysis and biblical hermeneutics, choosing strategies, and prioritizing political objectives. Without a clear democratic process in place (such as communicative action), the danger of the instrumental and utilitarian tendency looms large, justified by the passion for justice. The democratic process is necessary to resolve inevitable conflicts in the process of doing social analysis, developing strategies, and prioritizing political objectives.

Covenant offers a framework that respects diverse voices, mutual exchanges, and the negotiation of priorities and strategies. Its communicative method of adjudication and conflict resolution thus addresses concerns of plurality, diversity, and intersectionality. The covenant vision of shalom helps coordinate our conflicting interests and struggles for justice. A communicative approach of just peacemaking and coalition building is not only theologically faithful to the Bible but also politically more effective and realistic; for example, given the disparity of power in the United States, systematic racism cannot be dismantled by one party (people of color) alone but only through collaboration with white people.

New covenant ethics does not suppress the particularity of identity in its participants. In a covenantal community, each group celebrates a distinctive culture, history, and religious tradition but in coordination and collaboration with others under the principles of justice. By nature, covenant is built upon a clear interpersonal and intergroup egalitarian principle; each group and people find their own space, voice, claim, and seat at the table. The practice of grassroots organizing is designed to contribute to the project of liberation as well as coalition building.

Liberation theology emphasizes orthopraxis over orthodoxy, but more often than not, emotional and psychological burnout is a serious concern among revolutionaries when the intended revolution or transformation is delayed. The question is where one finds the ongoing infusion of motivation and hope for orthopraxis. Not only passion for justice and courage but also the virtues of patience, wisdom, gratitude, strong communal bond, and care are indispensable to sustain the zeal for transformation. Christian ministry in the context of new covenant ethics is restorative as well as liberative even for individual persons. Without this communal support system that covenant creates, liberation is not practically sustainable and liberation ethics may be populated by intellectual elites alone.

New covenant ethics gives sufficient attention to ethical motivation. Liberation in a covenantal framework is primarily God's effort in which human beings join as God's coworkers; the work of liberation is a response to God's ongoing work in history. The grace of God (experienced in deliverance) is an invigorating force for the work of justice and liberation. God's love and justice set the tone and direction for liberation and the organizing of a new community. In new covenant ethics, love is militant, justice is inclusive, and power is life affirming and transformative. New covenant ethics thus offers an integral social vision, a road map, and concrete practices for a liberation and restoration that empower and sustain people.

Conclusion

In a brief conversation with five different types of Christian ethics, this chapter has attempted to demonstrate the distinctive features and moral characteristics of new covenant ethics. In particular, new covenant ethics, taking the covenant of Jesus as its foundation, addresses the theological and moral limitations of traditional covenant ethics. Compared to traditional covenant ethics, it is thoroughly Jesus centered and is focused on just peacemaking and antiracism. Unlike Yoder and Hauerwas (representing Anabaptist/Mennonite ethics and postliberal theology), new covenant ethics takes seriously the binding power of norms and rules and the importance of diverse social institutions for human flourishing. Unlike Niebuhr, it offers a thick theological description of God's agency and initiative and a coherent theological framework for love, justice, and power. Finally, in contrast to liberation ethics, it emphasizes the importance of democratic processes and the goal of restoration.

I hope that this comparison highlights the fecundity and capaciousness of covenant as a key symbol of Christian ethics, interpreted in terms of the covenantal drama, three dialectics, triadic components (love, justice, power), and four practices. The new covenant is more capacious and dynamic than other key methodological motifs of Christian ethics, such as natural law, love/justice dialectic, crucifixion/resurrection event, narrative community of virtue, and liberation. Though not exhaustive, new covenant ethics embraces most of these motifs, and reinterprets and integrates them in a coherent framework: what they are and how they are interrelated. In short, new covenant is a rich, multilayered, and generative dynamic biblical symbol around which important theological and ethical motifs and themes cluster. It is a key link in Christian ethics for theological coherence, conceptual clarity, and practical feasibility.

Taking Jesus and his new covenant as the foundation (*pace* traditional covenant ethics), new covenant ethics is faithful to the biblical drama (*pace* Niebuhr), encompassing both the OT and the NT with a comprehensive scope in a coherent manner. Additionally, new covenant ethics is relevant for our current pluralistic cultural contexts of globalization by offering a complex and pluralistic vision of society and a method that adjudicates diverse voices and perspectives for building coalitions (*pace* Yoder and Hauerwas). New covenant ethics also presents a capacious moral framework that assists the complicated and difficult tasks of democratic institutional arrangement, rule making, and virtue formation that governance requires (*pace* liberation ethics). Finally, the four practices of new covenant ethics are both theologically informed and practically transformative under the guiding divine drama of liberation-restoration.

With these observations, we turn to the next chapter, which will present a further opportunity to explore the plausibility of new covenant ethics in harmonizing several conventionally challenging, binary categories in Christian ethics: indicative and imperative, divine agency and human agency, norm and context, particular and public, worship and ethics, and unity and diversity.

CHAPTER 7

Norms and Values

Only, live your life in a manner worthy of the gospel of Christ.

—Philippians 1:27

Therefore, my beloved, just as you have always obeyed me, not only in my presence, but much more now in my absence, work out your own salvation with fear and trembling; for it is God who is at work in you, enabling you both to will and to work for his good pleasure.

—Philippians 2:12–13

Our discussion of the covenantal drama and its dialectics has already shed some light on several key biblical moral norms/values, such as gratitude, love, justice, nonviolence, and peace. In addition to expanding observations on those norms, this chapter also studies several other salient moral norms/values of new covenant ethics: trust, truth telling, humility, freedom, solidarity, rights, and hope, while demonstrating how these norms/values are in essence "covenantal" norms/values.

Placing these values in covenant is important because covenant and its threefold dialectics offer a clear and proper theological framework to adequately understand and practice them. Bruce Birch notes: "Terms descriptive of God's character such as holiness, steadfast love, righteousness, justice, and compassion are not limited to covenantal texts but may best be understood in the context of the relationship which covenant implies."[1]

Most of these norms/values reflect God's moral character, as displayed in a covenantal relationship. They are descriptive of God's moral character because they are related to God's role in covenant relationship. They portray who God is, what God

1. Birch, *Let Justice Roll Down*, 147.

wants, and how God relates to humanity and achieves God's purpose. These covenantal values are instrumental in shaping the virtues of God's people[2] and building a just, righteous, and loving community. The Spirit germinates and nurtures these values in human partners. As mentioned in our discussion of motivational clauses in the Bible, the performative power of God in a covenant relationship motivates humans to practice them in response to God's grace.

These norms/values are predicated on the covenantal drama and the threefold dialectics of covenant, interrelated with each other.[3] The covenantal drama of liberation-restoration sets the overall tone and trajectory for the three dialectics. We may identify justice or ordering (as judgment against injustice, chaos, confusion) and reconciliation (or peace, love) as the two broad categories of values that reflect the themes of liberation and restoration. The drama is moving toward the actualization of shalom, which fulfills all these norms/values simultaneously. The norms/values can be categorized accordingly as follows:

Covenantal Drama
- a. Liberation: freedom, justice, courage, prophetic criticism
- b. Restoration: love, shalom, solidarity, peace, capability

1. Unilateral-Bilateral Dialectic
    - a. Unilateral: God's grace (unconditional love)
    - b. Bilateral: trust, gratitude, timely response (obedience), humility, generosity, hospitality
2. Communal-Communicative Dialectic
    - a. Communal: mutual love and respect, compassion, care, solidarity, collaboration
    - b. Communicative: freedom (self-assertion), equality, truthfulness, truth telling, justice, openness
3. Memory-Hope Dialectic
    - a. Memory: diligent and faithful remembrance (commemoration), storytelling; commitment, faithfulness
    - b. Hope: aspiration, joy, openness, creativity, perseverance

Under the rubric of the covenantal drama and its threefold dialectics, these norms/values are neither discrete nor abstract but rather are concrete, interrelated,

2. When internalized by members of a community through practices, they become virtues.

3. Terence E. Fretheim observes that "to know God is to be in a right relationship with him, with characteristics of love, trust, respect, and open communication." This observation reveals that core moral values such as love, trust, respect, and open communication derive from a covenantal relationship. Various biblical values cluster around the covenant. Fretheim, "אוד," 2:413.

and complementary.[4] Together with God's moral law, these values are indispensable to and normative for shaping our moral character and guiding our moral discernment. Across the Bible, these values are mentioned or implied in God's commandments and laws, as well as in wisdom literature, prophetic denunciations, Jesus's moral teachings, and the apostles' moral admonitions.

These norms/values are broader than the law and rules, but they do not replace them. These values inspire and guide the law.[5] Additionally, these values are not necessarily exclusive to Christians; they are found in other religions or secular moral philosophies, with different connotations and nuances, although the covenant offers a comprehensive and coherent framework for them to properly understand, balance, and complement each other. For example, in covenant, solidarity and freedom, humility and rights, love and justice complement one another.

The list of norms/values in this chapter is far from exhaustive. Certainly, there are other values, but I believe the values in this list are most representative; other, unmentioned ones are either correlated with or derived from these values.[6] Given limited space, the chapter will not discuss all the values listed above but only the central ones for each dialectic, with the focus on what each value means in covenant, how it is different from its secular counterpart, how it is related to other values, and what its importance is for the Christian life.

Gratitude

The Christian journey begins with experiencing God's unconditional love in Jesus. Gratitude is the most appropriate response to God's bountiful, unfailing love. Gifting is a consistent aspect of God's action toward humanity, from the very first covenant with creation/Adam to the new covenant of Jesus. God is a generous giver. In faith we recognize that creation and everything in it (rocks, water, air, trees, animals, etc.) are God's gifts for our responsible use. Redemption (remission of sin and healing) and the indwelling of the Spirit are also God's gifts. There is nothing that is completely our own. The apostle Paul declares: "What do you have that you did not receive? And if you received it, why do you boast as if it were not a gift?" (1 Cor. 4:7).

4. For example, Isa. 59:8 shows the inextricable tie between truth, justice, and equity.

5. Often termed norms or principles, these values are situated between basic Christian convictions and rules. These values are broader than rules and narrower than basic moral convictions. The rules reflect the values as their concrete moral behavioral applications. See chap. 10 for further discussion.

6. For example, the fruit of the Spirit (love, joy, peace, patience, kindness, generosity, faithfulness, gentleness, and self-control) in Gal. 5:22–23 significantly overlap with covenantal values of the three dialectics.

Hence, gratitude is a necessary and proper attitude to God's generous gifting. In the parallel to the unilateral-bilateral (gift-task), grace and gratitude go hand in hand.[7] Karl Barth puts it poetically: "grace and gratitude belong together like heaven and earth. Grace evokes gratitude like the voice an echo. Gratitude follows grace like thunder lightning."[8] In his letters to the Christians in Corinth, Paul repeatedly encourages them to express their thanksgiving in all things that they do because of God's grace. Gratitude constitutes one of the default modes of the Christian life. The entire Christian life (worship, psalm singing, justice work, community service, and hospitality) is driven by gratitude. We are not able to reciprocate God's generosity in any commensurate way. And God does not need our gifts (Ps. 50) but wants the life of thanksgiving, sharing, and caring for others that flows from our gratitude. To do so is regarded as the act of acknowledging the worth of God's gifting and Godself.

Gratitude plays a crucial role in our spiritual and moral formation. It sets the tone for our worship, ministry, and ethics. Metaphorically speaking, if grace is the root, then our moral life is the fruit, and the covenant is the vine through which God's grace flows.

God's grace is performative; it has the power to evoke a proper response to it and engenders gratitude in us, which results in the spiritual and moral fruits in response to God's grace. God's gifting sets off the chain reaction flow of giving and sharing, a positive feedback loop in the universe filling its every corner with God's regenerating and sanctifying love.

Many motivational clauses in Scripture remind us of our indebtedness to God and others by inducing appropriate attitudes and actions: patience, joy, thanksgiving, sharing, and works of justice, to name a few. Only when motivated by gratitude can Christians properly fulfill the covenantal obligations (worship and ethics). Henry Stob notes: "What drives the Christian to love and obedience is thankfulness. This gives to the moral life a characteristic note of joy. Appreciative of God's mercy, thankful for his unspeakable gift, happy in his gracious conferments, the Christian seeks with might and main to show forth [God's] praises and to do [God's] will."[9]

When thankfulness ceases, our spiritual life begins to dry up and moral life loses its anchor. If the drought continues, then the covenant relationship becomes dull and begins to crack, and its future looks uncertain. Gratitude is the soul of our worshipful heart that enables us to trace God's presence in our midst, and to sing the Lord's song despite the presence of difficulties in our lives. Christine Pohl declares:

7. Indeed, they share the same etymology in Greek: *charis* (grace) and *eucharistia* (gratitude).

8. Barth, *Church Dogmatics* IV/1, 41.

9. Stob, *Ethical Reflections*, 78.

"A posture of gratitude allows us to see beauty and to receive it, to recognize goodness and to take pleasure in it, even when circumstances are difficult."[10]

Interpreted in a covenantal context, gratitude has profound moral implications for the Christian life. It informs, generates, and fortifies other Christian values, such as stewardship, humility, hospitality, compassion, and mercy toward others.

A gifted nature of human existence defines every human being as a steward (caretaker) rather than an owner. In this sense, gratitude is an antidote to many ills of a neoliberal capitalist society. Gratitude disarms self-centeredness, pride, and self-preoccupation and helps us to be generous and compassionate. With trust in God's future provision in daily life, a grateful person is less anxious or complaining. Philippians 4:6 says: "Do not worry about anything, but in everything by prayer and supplication with thanksgiving let your requests be made known to God." It is an antidote to anxiety and greed. It helps us to focus on what matters in our lives and not to be anxious about, but rather hopeful for, the future ("God has been good and generous to me so God will continue to be so").

Gratitude naturally opens us to the lives of others. It helps us to be generous toward others without being arrogant or patronizing. Hospitality (generous sharing of food, shelter, and protection to a stranger) is a grateful expression of our experience of God's generosity toward us, we who are sinners, former enemies, and strangers to God. Christian hospitality receives its distinctive content from divine hospitality toward us. Motivated by divine self-giving, we can exercise genuine hospitality, finally to the extent of trying to do what Jesus said: "But love your enemies, do good, and lend, expecting nothing in return. Your reward will be great, and you will be children of the Most High; for he is kind to the ungrateful and the wicked. Be merciful, just as your Father is merciful" (Luke 6:35–36).

Gratitude evokes a sense of humility—acknowledging our indebtedness toward God and others and recognizing our creatureliness and limitations before God. Gratitude-centered work of charity and justice could save us from narcissism, self-righteousness, and despair. In this respect, one may say, gratitude has a leveling (egalitarian) effect. It contributes to removing the sense of moral superiority and moral righteousness in Christians in their generous actions toward others. That is, benefactors know that they are not intrinsically better than the poor and the debtors; they are all beneficiaries of God's grace. Showing mercy and compassion toward the poor, oppressed, and needy is simply a way to reciprocate what we freely received from God. We do it because, as Paul says, "God's grace compels me."

10. Pohl, *Living into Community*, 54.

Trust

Trust refers to "assured reliance on the character, ability, strength, or truth of someone or something."[11] Together with gratitude, trust characterizes one of the most foundational attitudes of a believer toward God.[12] Gratitude and trust are distinct but interrelated; God's grace is generative of trust and gratitude in humans. Technically speaking, while trust is the attitude toward God's person and future promises, gratitude is the response to what God has done (God's liberative work). Together they constitute the foundational rock of a covenantal relationship.

God's initiating love and liberative acts (the first dialectic) serve as the basis of our trust. God invites humans to an enduring relationship of mutual trust through the exchange of promises. Our trust in God and God's promise is based on God's demonstration of God's benevolence toward us. Such experience becomes a basis of trust in God's promise. By trusting God and God's promise, a believer remains in the covenant.[13]

Trust is central to covenant because covenant is a relationship built upon mutual trust. The covenant stands and falls with trust; a committed relationship is possible only on the basis of trust. As mentioned before, the centrality of trust in the covenant is found in the covenanting process; a covenant is formalized through the exchange of mutual pledges whose solemnity is symbolized by the covenant ritual of cutting an animal in half. The ritual implies that the rise and fall of covenant is based on the trustworthiness of each party's promise.

Trust is not merely the state of belief or cognitive consent. It is performative by nature. Trust indicates an active belief (action-producing) in the fulfillment of the promises that the other party makes. A person who makes a promise presents herself as a trustworthy person with her words. By making a promise, she holds herself accountable to her own words. Those who entrust are required to act according to it. To be trusted, a person has to prove her trustworthiness by fulfilling the promise; if she fails to keep the promise, the other person loses trust in her. Trust entails her acting accordingly; it entails the belief that she will live up to the promise. Promising is expressed through a person's actions. Trust always includes risk and vulnerability because we actually place ourselves or something we value in another's hands.[14]

11. Merriam-Webster Dictionary, s.v. "trust," http://www.merriam-webster.com/dictionary/trust. "Faith," "trust," and "fidelity" are cognates.

12. In a narrow sense, covenant can be called a trust-based, trust-building mechanism.

13. Trust determines how one party relates to the other in the future. When the idea is applied to a covenant relationship, we stay in the covenant only when we trust the other party. Pohl, *Living into Community*, 62.

14. Allen, *Love and Conflict*, 32.

Promise keeping is central to trust. While our initial trust in God (in entering a covenantal relationship) is motivated by God's benevolence, staying in the covenant requires both parties to be faithful to keep their promises. In the covenant relationship, covenantal stipulations (the law) serve as concrete criteria to test the sincerity of the parties. Sincerity leads to the deepening of trust between the covenantal parties.

If trust is an active inner disposition/attitude of a person toward others, then fidelity is a virtue of sincerity that is consistently manifested in a person's actions. Fidelity describes the faithfulness "demonstrated by continuing loyalty and support."[15] In a covenantal context, fidelity is broader than prescribed obligations in the written agreement. It includes performing what is expected in the covenant relationship beyond the letter of the stipulations. Fidelity typically includes the postures of compassion, benevolence, and care toward the partners in relationship. Fidelity encompasses both communal and communicative aspects, affectional (love) and just (fair) dimensions of a specific relationship. For example, the fidelity of a physician goes beyond medical treatment and includes care for a patient by acting "on behalf of the patient's best interest and well-being."[16]

The specific content of fidelity is intrinsic to a particular social relationship. It is relationally defined; the form that fidelity takes depends on relational and institutional contexts. For example, the content of a physician's fidelity is different from that of a financial adviser. Properly understanding the ethical nature and meaning of a particular social relationship is essential in grasping the nature of fidelity expected in a relationship.

One cannot emphasize enough the importance of trust for psychological formation and a social life. An infant first begins to learn the goodness or reliability of the world through the unconditional love and care of the mother or caregiver. Trust renders a sense of stability and security to an infant.

Trust is the glue and fabric of a society as it is indispensable for any sustained relationship. Trust becomes the basis of cooperation and solidarity.

Trust cannot be forced; it is free, voluntary, and ultimately mutual. Friendship is the most telling example of trust. Trust removes fear and anxiety in the relationship. There is no real freedom without trust. When trust is lost, the relationship breaks down and the institution suffers. A society of low trust is unstable, highly stressful, and prone to conflict and violence. Trust has a mobilizing power for energy, creativity, and goodness; it creates and expands breathing space for all involved.

15. *Oxford English and Spanish Dictionary, Thesaurus, and Spanish to English Translator*, s.v. "fidelity," https://www.lexico.com/en/definition/fidelity.

16. May, *The Physician's Covenant*, 149.

When trusted, people are relaxed, as their minds are set free from fear and anxiety; when trusted, people become unrestrained and self-expressive; when trusted, people take a risk and go out of their way for others. Therefore, trust is integral to personal fulfillment as well as social well-being. Life flourishes and shalom grows in trust.

Truth and Truth Telling

Another value or norm that is closely associated with trust is truth telling. Truth telling is highly emphasized in covenant because a covenantal relationship is sustained through trust, to which ongoing truthful communication is essential. Truth telling and trust are inseparable. Truth telling is indispensable to any trusted relationship. Truthfulness is a form of fidelity.

This intrinsic connection between truthfulness and trust is found in the Hebrew word *'emet,* which could mean truth as well as truthfulness (or faithfulness). *'Emet* connotes "the idea of stability and dependability," and *emuhan* "describes what is firm, unchangeable and trustworthy (from which we get 'Amen')."[17] This means that truth is a cognate of truthfulness, and it is also correlated with trust. Like trust or fidelity, truth is also performative because of its covenantal underpinning. *'Emet* has a factual dimension (locutionary), and this knowledge is always construed relationally (illocutionary), including the knowledge of the intentions of the parties and their particular contexts of the relationship. Truth in covenant is not only a matter of telling the truth but also of being true.[18] Truth is tested in terms of one's faithfulness to the promise, that is, sincerity in action. In covenant, truth is more a matter of truthfulness in one's intentions and actions, and thus should be warranted by sincerity. Truth telling pertains not only to the facticity of the content (which is absolutely important in this era of fake news) but also to the intention of the speaker. Truthfulness rests on being true to oneself and others in covenantal relationships.

A covenantal notion of truth is relational and performative rather than abstract and rationalistic. It is never separated from the good that the involved parties and a community pursue and envision, which is in a stark contrast with the Western account of knowledge as serving an instrumental role to the goals of control and mastery.

Since truth is performative, truth telling and trust go hand in hand. Speaking truth is the first step to building trust.[19] Trust is built upon a partner's sincerity and truthfulness. Oath taking is a ceremony to ensure the truthfulness of both parties

17. Christopher Wright, *An Eye for an Eye,* 135.

18. May, *The Physician's Covenant,* 151.

19. "A covenantal web, one might say, binds me together with the person to whom I am speaking. There can be no human community without the trust that follows from consistent truth-telling." Stassen and Gushee, *Kingdom Ethics,* 381.

in entering the covenant by upholding them and their accountability to the public. By violating the oath, one risks one's trustworthiness, and credibility or reputation in a society. Similarly, covenantal stipulations and the communicative nature of interactions in the covenant also encourage truth telling by binding each party to its words.

Lying distorts communication, erodes trust, and undermines community. Scripture allows no excuse for lying to God. The serpent in Genesis 3 lied to Adam and Eve, distorted their perception and judgment, and led them to destruction. In the Ten Commandments, God orders Israelites not to bear false witness against their neighbors. Lying derails relationships: it distorts our perception of reality and misleads us, resulting in distrust and conflict. Social trust can be maintained only through truth telling among a society's members.

God is the God of truth; the Word is identified as full of truth (John 1:14); likewise, the Spirit is called "the Spirit of truth" (John 14:17). Jesus called Satan "the father of lies" (John 8:44). Truth telling in new covenant ethics includes both factual and intentional aspects. Not only the veracity of information but also the state of the heart is included. Truth telling is an exercise of one's integrity. Every person owes truth telling to all other persons in God's community. Hence it constitutes a central piece of fidelity. Truth telling is the heart of a covenantal communication. Scripture, informed by a covenantal ethos, strongly condemns lies. In the new covenant of Jesus, both aspects are equally strengthened. Jesus said: "Let your word be 'Yes, Yes' or 'No, No'; anything more than this comes from the evil one" (Matt. 5:37). Truth telling applies not only to persons but also to empirical facts. A moral agent is responsible to be truthful in data gathering, analysis, evaluation, and judgment of empirical reality.

Truth telling is closely associated with social justice. The significance of truth telling was practiced in prophetic criticism in ancient Israel. Isaiah 59:8 indicates the inextricable ties between truth, justice, and equity. Justice is based on truth (what actually happened or is happening).[20] Unjust, oppressive regimes inevitably rely on and perpetuate lies because the regimes cannot be maintained when truth is publicly told.[21] Through truth telling, a society maintains its transparency, public accountability, and character, thus exercising a certain moral authority over people. When people no longer care about truth, common life suffers. The spread of rumors, disinformation, alternative facts, and conspiracy theories is severely damaging to the public trust and the common good. A social and psychological cost of distrust

20. "Only those who are in a state of truthfulness through the confession of their sin to Christ are not ashamed to tell the truth wherever it must be told." Bonhoeffer, *The Cost of Discipleship*, 100.

21. Stassen and Gushee, *Kingdom Ethics*, 386.

is high. Cynicism, distrust in public institutions, and withdrawal from civic participation grow, while public officials lose their moral authority. That is why oppressive regimes suppress the freedom of the press in fear of truth telling. They justify the status quo through manipulation of public opinion and the distortion of facts and history. They cannot withstand or even survive truth because truth telling takes away their moral authority.

Because of its respect of truth, covenant promotes a social relationship that is public and transparent in nature. A society that is committed to truth telling is also willing to hear truthful criticism shared in love.

Humility

Gratitude is closely associated with the virtue of humility. Humility is acknowledging our indebtedness toward God and others. We are not owners. Humans possess nothing as their own. To recognize that what we have is all from God and that we cannot possess anything permanently evokes humility in us. Our indebtedness to God and others leads us not to deceive/mislead ourselves with the idea of self-sufficiency or autonomy.

Humility includes both moral and intellectual dimensions. Humility is intellectually exercised in the form of a proper spiritual self-awareness. To be humble is to acknowledge God's right as the creator and our status as God's creatures. Humility begins with the acknowledgment of our origin as the creatures and our origin and proper (right) place in the universe. Made out of dust, we return to dust. "The virtue of humility will lead humans to acknowledge limits and repent of failures."[22] If pride has to do with overestimation of the self, humility puts the self in its right and proper moral place. That is to say, humility has a self-correcting power. It helps to remove the deceit, pretense, and aggrandized view of the self.

A humble person is open to different viewpoints and eager to learn from them. Humility is indispensable for communicative reasoning in new covenant ethics because it creates the epistemological openness to accept better arguments in discernment and deliberation. Intellectual humility is a way to overcome our epistemological limitations shaped by cultural conditioning. Our moral analysis and ethical evaluation are always limited and prejudiced by our personal and social experiences.

Humility is necessary for our spiritual and moral growth. We do not possess absolute knowledge of the world and society. In particular, openness is much more needed in dealing with an ambiguous and changing complex social reality. We need

22. Cahill, *Global Justice, Christology, and Christian Ethics*, 284.

others for our growth. While humility prompts moral imagination and the attitude of inquiry and dialogue, arrogance and pride stifle our listening ability and empathy.

Morally, humility is displayed in the form of respect for others and a willingness to collaborate with others for a common cause. Without humility, we cannot genuinely love others, nor can we exercise true solidarity with others.

Without it, we may lose track of God's movement in the world and miss the voice of the Spirit. As God did with Joseph and Mary, and Peter, God is revealed to us in very unpredictable ways and places, sometimes using complete strangers to communicate God's purpose. God challenges our narrow conventional assumptions. Only with humility are we ready to be open to this new surprising possibility—to be creative with God and others.

We need humility because we are still sinners and the world is still evolving; we do not live in a fully settled world. The possibility of progress as well as regress always exists with society and its institutions. Humility does not allow complacency with the status quo. A humble person consistently works for the betterment of herself and others rather than remaining content with the status quo.

Freedom

Covenant indicates a committed relationship, but it also presupposes the freedom of each party to enter and stay in it. This value derives from the liberative motif of the covenantal drama. Freedom is the characteristic of people living their life in the Spirit. Paul says: "Now the Lord is the Spirit, and where the Spirit of the Lord is, there is freedom" (2 Cor. 3:17). We love and fellowship with God and others, and we communicate our feelings and ideas out of freedom (second dialectic).

Covenant is impossible without assuming that humans are free to make and to keep promises. The covenantal agreement is not based on coercion but on free choice and decision. In making an agreement, a human partner is fully informed of what moral obligations (responsibility) ensue from it. As mentioned before, freedom is the necessary condition for moral agency. Without freedom, there is no moral accountability.[23]

The third dialectic (memory-hope) also assumes human freedom in exercising discernment and analogical imagination and interpreting the past redemptive event. A relationship based on freedom is not fixed or static but open to new challenges and opportunities. God wants us to be not only faithful servants but also creative partners. Freedom impels us to be adventurous in our journey with God. We grow

23. We have already discussed the idea of freedom in some details in the section on divine and human agency in chap. 5.

through trials and errors in life. We are called to be cocreators with God, and God is not afraid of this.

However, a covenantal idea of freedom is different from a secular liberal understanding. This freedom is neither individualistic nor self-enclosed but relational and intersubjective. Covenant does not undermine but strengthens freedom. Freedom is covenantally constituted; covenant offers its purpose, a proper structure, and a channel to exercise freedom. In particular, in light of its pluralistic social vision (chap. 11), covenant helps us to see what kinds of freedoms are appropriate in which social relationships. It prevents freedom from distraction and misuse. Human freedom in history is precarious and fragile; it carries in it the potential for chaos as well as creativity.

Freedom is not only passive (freedom from external control and interference) but also active; it refers to the capability to grow and flourish—to exercise and fulfill one's God-given dignity and gifts. Such freedom requires various social and communal supports such as trust, economic development, educational opportunities, and healing of traumas.[24] In a word, freedom grows in a trusted and caring relationship with others.

Even after we enter the covenant, our freedom and individuality do not disappear. Freedom becomes more active and expansive in the covenant because mutual trust and love in the covenant liberate a person from anxiety and fear, and energize the person toward its full actualization in a community. As Jürgen Moltmann nicely puts it, "trust is freedom's essential living space,"[25] and according to him, one finds in friendship such a mutually enhancing exercise of freedom.

> The person who is free is friendly, gracious, open and gives freely. He lets other people share in his life and is interested in the well-being of others. Intersubjective relationships are called free if they are marked by reciprocal recognition and mutual friendship. If I know that I am recognized and respected, I feel free and go out of myself and show myself as I am; if I feel disregarded, I withdraw into myself and defend myself. Recognition opens up a free space socially in which other people can develop freely. In a society like this the other person is not a restriction of my personal freedom; he complements it and enables it. The shared life develops out of the mutual participation in life. It is only a society of this kind that can be called a free society.[26]

24. Chap. 12 discusses justice as "capability" in detail.

25. Moltmann, *Ethics of Hope*, 210.

26. Moltmann, *Ethics of Hope*, 161. In German, "freedom" is a cognate of "friendship."

The kind of society Moltmann longs for is in fact what a covenant community is all about. Its moral qualities of graciousness, openness, sharing, care for others, intersubjectivity, reciprocity, and mutual enabling are covenantal in nature.

In covenant, freedom is not only a gift but also a task; it is not an escape from responsibility but a voluntary service for others. It is not for self-interest or fulfillment alone.[27] Calvin notes, "Nothing is plainer than this rule: that we should use our freedom if it results in the edification of our neighbor, but if it does not help our neighbor, then we should forgo it."[28] In covenant, freedom is a fettered freedom in our committed, accountable relationship with God and others. Personal ambitions, desires, and interests are disciplined by the love of God and others. True freedom comes only in the harmony of a person with God and others. Our use of freedom is guided by the purpose, meaning, and direction that God's covenantal drama provides: God's shalom and our friendship with others. One may say that outside of the covenant, freedom loses its anchor, direction, and intelligibility.

Solidarity

As balanced in a pair with freedom, solidarity is another aspect of covenant. Freedom and solidarity go hand in hand, just as grace and gratitude do. New covenant ethics declares that, having God as our sole creator and the planet as our only home, all lives are interdependent, along with their survival and well-being. The creation covenant (chap. 1) denotes the unity and solidarity of all lives in God. Wendell Berry notes, "The first principle of the Kingdom of God is that it includes everything," and another principle is that "everything in the kingdom is joined to it and to everything in it."[29] We find a similar observation of a covenantal bond in the apostle Paul's metaphor of the church as the body of Christ: the church is made up of many interconnected parts. When one part of the body suffers, the whole body suffers (1 Cor. 12:26). Humans are biologically, psychologically, and socially interdependent. Even empirically, for their survival, humans have to rely on other humans and creatures and collaborate with them. They are always in need of belonging, trusted relationships, giving and receiving affirmation and recognition, and connection and

27. In the covenant, "the blessings of liberty—most notably the freedoms of religion, speech, press, and peaceable assembly and the right of a trial by jury—are not private liberties but civil liberties. They do not simply carve out a little cave where each individual is on his or her own. They clear a space for the deliberations of the people as they freely debate, consider, and pursue questions of justice and the common good, as they affirm the community they are while pointing toward a community still in the making." May, *Testing the National Covenant*, 102.

28. Calvin, *Institutes of the Christian Religion*, 845.

29. Berry, *The Art of the Commonplace*, 219, 220.

affection with each other. To be covenanted means that we acknowledge our dependence on and indebtedness to God and others and use our freedom and resources responsibly for the common good.

The horizon of covenantal solidarity is planetary; it includes other creatures, the land, and future generations. Larry Rasmussen writes, "All that is, is kin and born to belonging. All is relational. Humankind and otherkind live into one another's lives and die into one another's deaths in relationships that either sustain or subvert creatures and the land. Nothing is, without the other. Such is the way of 'covenant' (the biblical term for relational living). Covenantal bonds—between God and Earth, between God and humankind, between humans and one another and the rest of life—establish, order, and sustain creation as we know it. The way of covenant, for better and worse, is the way things *are*."[30]

The goal of solidarity is the shalom community of all creatures for whose actualization Jesus died. All creatures belong to the same moral community, and each has a responsibility to respect and care for others "as beings who matter."[31] To be covenanted is to be solidaric, which means that everyone becomes a participant and partner in building the beloved community. We share the burdens and responsibilities, as well as the joys and delights, of cooperating with each other to promote the common good.

However, in covenant, solidarity is differentiated; it is maintained through free, constant communication and coordination among the members, while respecting the freedom and basic rights of each person. Together, freedom and solidarity—in their balance—form the structure of a responsible Christian life. Dietrich Bonhoeffer notes:

> The structure of responsible life is determined in a twofold manner, namely, by life's bond to human beings and to God, and by the freedom of one's own life. It is this bond of life to human beings and to God that constitutes the freedom of our own life. Without this bond and without this freedom there can be no responsibility. Only the life that, within this bond, has become selfless has the freedom of my very own life and action. The bond has the form of vicarious representative action and accordance with reality. Freedom exhibits itself in my accountability for my living and acting, and in the venture of concrete decision. This, then, is the framework within which we have to consider the structure of responsible life.[32]

30. Rasmussen, *Earth-Honoring Faith*, 17.
31. Allen, *Love and Conflict*, 32.
32. Bonhoeffer, *Ethics*, 257.

The excess of freedom could lead to antinomianism and anarchy, while the excess of solidarity could lead to tyranny and authoritarianism. Covenant avoids these two extremes. In the covenant, freedom is protected over against any form of tyranny, while it is ordered for its productivity and contribution for society's common good. Covenant mediates the two through the process of communal will formation where collaborative rule making (covenantal stipulation in mutual agreement) plays an important role. This agrees with Robert Dahl's claim that "one of the most fundamental of all human freedoms" is "the freedom to help determine, in cooperation with others, the laws and rules that one must obey."[33]

Love

This book has already discussed the triad of love, justice, and power as the composite elements of covenant. This section and the next will explicate love and justice in further detail, focusing on their individual moral qualities and attributes, in order to address the many confusions and misunderstandings that surround these two norms.

The Bible says that God is love (1 John 4:8). Love motivates God's action of deliverance. Love (*hesed*) in general describes generous and compassionate action toward a person or a people in relationship.[34] Like other notions, a proper understanding of love is possible only in a covenantal context.[35] In contrast to the abstract notion of *agapē* love (that is, disinterested, unconditional, sacrificial), covenantal love is concrete, personal, relational, passionate, and solidaric in nature. Love is the power God uses to deliver humanity, invite humanity, and bind humanity with God. In the Bible, God's love is mostly exercised either in the context of the existing covenantal relationship or in the anticipation of establishing a covenantal relationship. The covenantal nature of love is found in that *hesed* connotes "faithfulness," as it is translated as steadfast love; *hesed* describes "abiding loyalty to his covenant, his unshakable will to keep his gracious promise, commitment to God's purpose."[36] While God's love is unconditional, it is purposive.

33. Dahl, *A Preface to Economic Democracy*, 5.

34. Because of this relational as well as asymmetrical nature, *hesed* connotes simultaneously mercy, love, grace (asymmetrical), faithfulness, loyalty (relational), and is popularly translated as steadfast or unfailing love that captures both dimensions. As we see later, God's communal love is the overflow of the perichoretic life of the Trinity.

35. Nelson Glueck regards covenant as the appropriate context where *hesed* operates, as he upholds *hesed* as the heart of a covenantal relationship. Glueck, *Hesed in the Bible*.

36. Christopher Wright, *An Eye for an Eye*, 135.

Covenantal love presupposes bilaterality and solidarity.[37] The English translation of *hesed* as mercy or compassion misses this intrinsic relational and bilateral dimension,[38] rendering a false impression that *hesed* is a single, unidirectional love. God's love is demonstrated in relation to a particular person or people, often addressing the need of the other in relationship.[39] It seldom appears in contexts where no relationship has been established.[40] It includes both ethos and pathos, and hence it can express God's jealousy and righteous rage or protest toward a covenant partner that breaks a promise, as we see in God's treatment of Israel and Israel's lament toward God.

The covenantal drama and the three dialectics are helpful in understanding God's love. In a covenantal context, God's love is communal love that aims to build *koinōnia* and the shalom community. God's love is redemptively expressed in God's unconditional, unilateral grace toward humanity, but it is fulfilled in mutual love. God's love first takes a form of grace before entering the covenant, but it shifts to reciprocal friendship once covenant is established. While God has first loved us, God wants God's love to be replicated by human partners.

Martin Luther King Jr. accurately understood this covenantal nature of *agapē*: "Agape is love seeking to preserve and create community. It is insistence on community even when one seeks to break it. Agape is a willingness to go any length to restore community. . . . It is a willingness to forgive, not seven times, but seventy times to restore community."[41] God's love ultimately seeks communion—mutual self-giving love among the members in a manner analogous to God's own Trinitarian life.

Covenantal love describes generous and compassionate action toward a person or a people in relationship. The heart of love is not self-denial but stunning generosity and goodwill toward others, going beyond what is required. A "selfless" person cannot be a moral agent in its full-fledged sense.

In its agapeic, sacrificial quality, love means the surplus of goodwill toward others. It is willing to go beyond what is legally required and morally obligated; it disregards the merits of the recipient or the results of one's sacrifice. Love is the exercise of a sensitive heart and a generous spirit. It is not a mere reaction erupting only at the occasion of a crisis in another person. It is "an ever-present quality which will

37. Mott, *Biblical Ethics and Social Change*, 43.

38. This limitation applies to the Septuagint translation as well, which considered *eleos* (mercy) to be the closest analogue for the Hebrew word *hesed*.

39. Birch, *Let Justice Roll Down*, 152.

40. Freedman, *Anchor Bible Dictionary*, 378.

41. King, *Stride toward Freedom*, 87.

anticipate needs, understand other's limitations, search for solutions and initiate acts of benevolence, even when unstated or un-noticed by the recipient."[42]

Covenantal love is not exclusive but is expansive toward others. It is public, not ethnocentric. God's love has a transformative effect in a person. It can open a closed heart. Following God, humans are called to exercise and embody this love toward others (e.g., Ruth's love toward Naomi). To love is to open our arms toward others, as Jesus did on the cross, and embrace strangers, even enemies, as members of God's community.

The idea of love becomes abstract outside the covenant since it could be construed as interpersonal, emotional, or romantic. Because of its relational nature and intrinsic connection to justice and power, covenantal love is different from a typical Christian understanding of *agapē* love. The idea of *agapē* love—popularized by Swedish theologian Anders Nygren as self-denying, disinterested love—has been severely criticized by feminist and liberation theologians for its disregard and neglect of a legitimate concern for self-love and self-care because such concern is regarded as impure, self-focused, and self-interested.[43] The idea of *agapē* love has had a negative impact on the moral agency of women and the oppressed. In history, *agapē* love has been misused to maintain the unjust political status quo, including patriarchy. Women and the oppressed have been taught to exercise *agapē* love toward their oppressors—obey and love them regardless of their oppressive behaviors.

Love is not emotional but self-conscious and reflective in seeking the well-being of others and building fellowship. It is not blinded or shortsighted by passion but includes a deliberative posture and process. Covenantal love does not override but fulfills justice. It protects the boundary and the rights of each party, while simultaneously pursuing the boundlessness of friendship and *koinōnia*. Love is also a form of power, which is enduring and persistent benevolence toward others. As enduring benevolence, *agapē* love requires a great deal of capability on the part of a person.

Justice

Along with love, justice is one of the key norms of the Bible. God's reign is deeply associated with justice, and both liberation and restoration of the covenantal drama are essentially grounded in justice, while motivated by love. The covenantal drama

42. Gelman, "Tzedakah and Chesed."

43. Although Scripture tends to speak of love and justice together, a hellenized notion of *agapē* could pit it against justice; while *agapē* denies the calculation of self-interest, justice protects valid self-interests (including the rights of the poor and widows). *Agapē* love makes it hard to build the organic connection between love and justice.

carries two forms of justice: liberative in its critique and judgment of injustices, and restorative in reconciling and rehabilitating sinners in a just and righteous relationship with God and others.

Like *hesed*, righteousness and justice are God's attributes. It is the confession of ancient Israel and the early church that God is the God of righteousness and justice. For example, the psalmist praises: "Righteousness and justice are the foundation of your throne" (Ps. 89:14). Scripture repeatedly stresses that doing justice and righteousness is the way of God's people (Mic. 6:8), which they should pursue in all realms and levels of life.[44] In fact, Scripture teaches the importance of justice and righteousness by providing numerous teachings and examples of what righteousness and justice look like and how they can be performed in daily life (e.g., family, economy, criminal justice). The Ten Commandments and the 613 statutes and ordinances specify the demands of justice appropriate to various social relationships.

As with love, we cannot fully understand the biblical notion of justice and righteousness without their covenantal underpinnings. Together with *hesed*, righteousness and justice are relational in nature. In the OT, *tsedaqah* and *mishpat* are two representative Hebrew words, usually translated as righteousness and justice; they are often used as a couplet in the OT, disclosing their organic relationship.[45]

Tsedaqah

Tsedaqah has a multifaceted meaning and is used in a wide variety of ways in the Bible. In general, it means rightness or being right, straight, standard, as something ought to be, corresponding to a norm or standard. The word is used to describe an object, such as accurate weights and measures (Lev. 19:6; Deut. 25:15), or a person—a righteous person, God or human. However, in a more precise sense, *tsedaqah* describes what is morally right or expected in a specific social relationship or situation.[46] By implication, it refers to the intrinsic standards or expected normative behavior fitting to a particular social relationship.[47] Marshall writes: "The biblical notion of righteousness refers broadly to doing, being, declaring, or bringing about

44. Hollinger, *Choosing the Good*, 220.

45. Christopher Wright, *Old Testament Ethics*, 255. Like *hesed, tsedaqah* and *mishpat* have a range of meanings and connotations and nuances. The difference between "righteousness" and "justice" is not conclusive because the two words derive from the same linguistic stem. Marshall, *Beyond Retribution*, 36.

46. Christopher Wright, *Old Testament Ethics*, 256.

47. "Each relationship brings with it certain claims upon conduct, and the satisfaction of these claims, which issue from the relationships and in which alone the relationship can persist, is described by our term *sdq*." Rad, *Old Testament Theology*, 1:371.

what is right. Righteousness is a comprehensively relational reality. It is not a private moral attribute one has on one's own. It is something that inheres in our relationships as social beings. To be righteous is to be true to the demands of a relationship, whether that relationship is with God or with other persons."[48]

Hence, *tsedaqah* is relationally, covenantally discerned and applied. For example, righteousness or rightness in marriage is different from righteousness in business. In this sense, to be righteous means to live according to moral norms or standards intrinsic to a specific relationship, such as with a parent, spouse, friend, business partner, judge, or politician.[49] In the Bible, righteousness refers not only to external norms or standards but also to the moral integrity of a person. Mays comments: "[*Tsedaqah*] is the quality of life displayed by those who live up to the norms inherent in a given relationship and thereby do right by the other person or persons involved."[50]

Standards and norms of *tsedaqah* are usually delineated in the stipulations of a covenantal relationship, and they evaluate the fidelity of each party. The Ten Commandments are the charter of *tsedaqah* for Israel, showing how Israel is to relate to God, nature, and members of a community (in different relational contexts). The Covenant Code, Mosaic law, and other biblical teachings exhibit that *tsedaqah* is a covenantally informed concept; its standard is not abstract but defined according to the nature of the social relationship itself (Eph. 5:22–6:9; Col. 3:18–4:1).

Mishpat

While *tsedaqah* has to do with rightness in relationship, *mishpat* is concerned with a wide range of judicial activity in a society.[51] It refers to matters related to litigation—its process, verdict, and execution; or it concerns the action of a lawgiver, judge, or leader in the arbitration of a dispute, handing down of a judgment, or execution of a verdict. It can also mean a legal ordinance, especially case law (the Covenant Code) or one's legal right,[52] thus referring to a wider sense of justice.[53]

To do justice is to protect and restore the basic rights of persons when they are wronged or violated. The act of justice is usually concretized in the form of relief, release, and deliverance.[54] In the OT, it is frequently found in God's intervention

48. Marshall, "Divine Justice as Restorative Justice."

49. Christopher Wright, *Old Testament Ethics*, 256.

50. Mays, *Amos*, 92–93.

51. Christopher Wright, *An Eye for an Eye*, 134.

52. Some Bible versions translate justice (*mishpat*) as rights (e.g., Jer. 5:28).

53. Christopher Wright, *An Eye for an Eye*, 134.

54. Mott, *Biblical Ethics and Social Change*, 63.

to deliver the poor, widows, orphans, and strangers from the abuses of the rich and powerful, or Israel from the hands of her enemies. Imitating God's character, a commitment to *mishpat* is expressed in the biblical emphasis on the responsibility of a community to protect the weak and victims of injustices who are vulnerable to abuse and exploitation. The primary responsibility of a king or a judge is to protect their rights. Injustices against them are a sign of infidelity, a grave breach of the covenant, which the prophets passionately criticized.

As a couplet, righteousness and justice are complementary. "*Mishpat* is what needs to be done in a given situation if people and circumstances are to be restored to conformity with *tsedeq*/*tsedaqah*."[55] *Mishpat* and *tsedaqah* correspond to liberation and restoration of the covenantal drama. The former is protective and liberative, while the latter is normative (virtuous) and restorative, although they are sometimes used interchangeably. While *tsedaqah* describes what the relationship is originally meant to be and morally intended by God (the optimal moral relationship), *mishpat* has to do with the protection of rights of each party through a fair judicial system and the restoration of rights when they are violated. The relationship between *mishpat* and *tsedaqah* strikingly fits with the scheme of liberation-restoration in the covenantal drama.

This means that justice is central to the organizing work of covenant. God's righteousness and redemption, while distinctive, are not completely separate in the Bible. God's act of redemption is considered God's act of righteousness.[56] Out of God's righteousness, God saves God's people (Ps. 71:2, 15). This means that God's justice has a redemptive force and quality. God's righteousness is both ethical (liberative) and redemptive. God's righteousness is manifested in God's judgment against oppression, corruption, and evil, and such an act of judgment is redemptive because the oppressed or the enslaved will be saved as a result. However, God's righteousness is fulfilled in the restoration of those redeemed. Without restoration, redemption is not complete.

This pattern is also found in the NT. Marshall calls the gospel God's "eschatological justice initiative."[57] In particular, Paul's notion of the righteousness of God is both liberative and restorative. "For Paul . . . the justice of God is a dynamic, active power that breaks into situations of oppression and evil in order to bring liberation and restore freedom. Its basic concern is not to treat each person as each deserves but to do all that is necessary to make things right, even though it is totally undeserved

55. Christopher Wright, *Old Testament Ethics*, 257. Hence, one may say that *mishpat* pertains to the minimal requirement of justice, while *tsedaqah* is concerned with the optimal, normative form of social relationships.

56. Christopher Wright, *An Eye for an Eye*, 138.

57. Marshall, *Beyond Retribution*, 57.

and immensely costly. It is a restorative justice more than a retributive or distributive justice. It is God acting to end oppression and secure harmony and well-being [shalom], especially by meeting the needs of the disadvantaged and downtrodden."[58]

Hence, for Paul, justification is God's justice-making work. To justify means "to make right." The cross is God's work of justice for sinners and the oppressed, to liberate them from the power of sin (and law) and death, as they are unable to save themselves. The outcome of God's justice making in Christ is the restoration of shalom (Rom. 5:1).

In summary, God's justice is liberative and restorative justice, and covenant is the organizing framework and underlying paradigm that integrates them (see chap. 12). This evidences how covenant is central to the biblical vision and perspective of justice.

Rights

A right is a certain entitlement that a person has toward or from others. There are many interpretations of human rights: liberal ethics asserts that human rights are certain claims of entitlements granted to all humans simply because they are humans, while many theologians claim that human rights are grounded in the *imago Dei* (Gen. 1:26–27). From a covenantal perspective, right has to do with the status and standing of a human in relation to God as God's image-bearer. The *imago Dei* denotes the primordial, intrinsic relationship of humanity to God. The ground of rights is God's self-giving—God's unilateral act of creating humans as God's image-bearers and adopting them as God's children and covenantal partners. Contrary to a liberal theory of rights, in a covenantal context, "human rights are not claims against the sovereignty of God; rather respect for human rights is an implication of recognizing God's supremacy. For since human dignity is bestowed, based in God's love, the rights necessary concretely to protect and express that dignity are also bestowed. God is the provider and protector of human rights; we accept them as duties as we perceive God's love and acknowledge God's authority over us."[59]

Human rights are stipulated by the creation covenant, later reconfirmed by the Noachian covenant. The divine origin of human rights indicates that rights are a divine gift, not the result of human merit or accomplishment. Humans have a moral obligation before God to respect and care for other humans and creatures. Embedded in the covenant is the requirement that as much as we claim our own rights, we respect and uphold the rights of others. That is, rights are always balanced with duty or responsibility.

58. Marshall, *Beyond Retribution*, 67.
59. Mott, *Biblical Ethics and Social Change*, 52–53.

Since rights are based on the recognition of the intrinsic worth of humanity as God's creatures, every person is required to honor this worth by treating others with due respect and just treatment. Any form of discrimination or exclusion—by race, gender, age, nationality, etc.—undercuts people's God-given, basic rights in the creation community. This is an aspect of God's justice, to recognize God as the sovereign Creator and Lord and to recognize the worth of every person. Rights are indiscriminate and universal; there is no hierarchy within human dignity. The Bible includes the following rights: "The sanctity of life; the right not to be permanently deprived of land; equality in the means of livelihood and where this is not possible, equality of opportunity; the right to rest from work one day in seven; the right of a servant of God not to be the servant of anyone else; the right to be protected from the arbitrary exercise of power; equality before the law or equal subjection to the law of all classes."[60]

Because of their transcendental nature, no one can arbitrarily take them away. Rights are not created by human wisdom or choice; they exist whether socially recognized or not. Human rights are an integral aspect of justice. As justice is to give each person her or his due, then rights are the fundamental basic respect that we owe each person.

In a covenantal framework, rights are relational, because of the intrinsic relationship of humans with God and others. Rights are not absolute by themselves; they are embedded in a covenantal relationship to God and others. In covenant, rights are more protective than proactive—more concerned about abuse by the powerful than reconciling and restoring right relationships. In this sense, they are related to *mishpat*. Nicholas Wolterstorff notes: "Rights are God's charter for the weak and defenseless ones in society. A right is the legitimate claim for protection of those too weak to help themselves. . . . It is the claim of the little ones in society to restraint upon economic and political and physical forces that would otherwise be too strong for them to resist."[61]

A covenantal approach balances right and responsibility relationally—individual freedom and the common good. The immediate goal of rights is to protect the dignity of individuals, but the ultimate goal is the common flourishing of all God's creatures. Hence, with every claim of rights there is a corresponding responsibility. In a covenantal framework, rights and duty are not mutually exclusive. Rowan Williams says: "Central to this understanding of justice is the inseparability of justice from the restoring of 'communion'—the flow of life between agents in mutual support, anchored in the restoring of access to and intimacy with the creator."[62]

60. Mott, *Biblical Ethics and Social Change*, 52.

61. Wolterstorff, *Until Justice and Peace Embrace*, 84.

62. Rowan Williams, "Rights, Recognition, and the Body of Christ."

This covenantal understanding is corrective of a liberal concept of rights that is individualistic, isolated, self-sufficient, and monarchical. Lacking a thick hermeneutical framework and a vision of a good society, and because of its atomistic understanding of human life, the liberal concept of rights ends up reinforcing the image of individuals as free-floating entities detached from their communities. Individuals may have rights, but they are left solitary, lonely, and isolated.[63] Rights do not cultivate any respect for one another, solidarity with one another, or care for one another. Imprisoned within themselves, rights can become increasingly belligerent and desperate.

A covenantal idea of rights is more ecological, relational, and comprehensive than the liberal idea of rights. New covenant ethics is able to embrace the diverse generations of human rights. As human rights are grounded in human dignity, they include all basic claims that are necessary to protect dignity, not just civil and political rights but economic, social, and cultural rights as integral aspects of human rights. A covenantal approach to rights embraces the rights of God and other creatures. As the initiator and partner of the covenant, God has a certain "right" toward humans and nature. According to Nicholas Wolterstorff, the Old Testament writers assumed that "God has subjective rights—God can be wronged—and that those rights are not conferred but inherent, grounded in God's worth."[64] As the creator, God deserves human respect, affection, and love. Worship is the public act that acknowledges God's worth, and sanctified life is another way to give God God's due. Likewise, each creature has an intrinsic value and thus has certain rights, such as the right to subsistence—including habitat, space, access to resources, minimal protection and care, and support for its survival. Granted by God, these biotic rights are not nominal but substantial. Humans have a moral obligation to respect the rights of other creatures, and doing so is a way to recognize and honor God as the creator and generous giver.

Hope

As its third dialectic of memory-hope indicates, covenant is expectant. It is open and moves toward a new, fully restored future in the triune God. While rooted in God's

63. Hauerwas's critique is on target: "Contemporary political theory has tended to concentrate on the language of rights, not because we have a vision of the good community, but because we do not. As a result, we have tried to underwrite the view that a good society is one where everyone is to be left alone rather than one that tries to secure the kind of cooperation that gives one a sense of contributing to a worthy human enterprise." Hauerwas, "On the 'Right' to Be Tribal," 238–39, cited in Wolterstorff, *Justice*, 4.

64. Wolterstorff, *Justice*, 129.

initiating grace (unconditional love), covenant is pulled and energized by hope in God's promise of shalom. The entire covenantal drama and all biblical covenants would be meaningless without this realistic hope in the consummation of God's creation and the eternal communion of all lives.

Christian hope is intimately related to faith and love in the covenant. While faith is involved in the beginning of a covenant relationship (unilateral-bilateral), if love is the deepening of that relationship through fellowship (communal-communicative), then hope is the persistent striving toward the future in the expectant trust in God's promise despite various challenges and obstacles (memory-hope).

Hope and faith are closely tied. Both have to do with an invisible entity or being. In its relation to hope, Christian faith is expectant faith, and hope is the future shape of faith. Just as much as faith undergirds hope, hope sustains faith: "Now faith is the assurance of things hoped for, the conviction of things not seen" (Heb. 11:1).

Christian hope is eschatological. It is between the "already" and the "not yet" of God's reign in Jesus. It is rooted in God's reign already inaugurated in Jesus but not yet complete; hence hope takes a stance of actively waiting in expectation of its complete fulfillment. This hope is sustained in the Christian life of worship and fellowship through God's abiding presence in the life-giving Spirit.

In the covenant, as mentioned in chapter 3, hope is not only futuristic (blind fantasy or imaginary utopianism) but also recollective. It is always undergirded by the past memory of God's goodness and faithfulness. In the covenant of Jesus, our memory of God's love and mighty work in Jesus Christ (his death and resurrection) is the basis of our hope in God's future completion. Our memory of God's liberative work is our ever-renewing source of hope (Ps. 77). The content and object of Christian hope are God's shalom—the complete restoration and renewal of God's creation. Christians have a reason to hope because they have already received a "first installment" of God's promise in the Spirit (and God's love) poured into their hearts (Rom. 5:5; 2 Cor. 1:22).

Christian hope is different from the liberal idea of progress, an individualistic belief in self-fulfillment (personal dream), or the evangelical belief in individual salvation after death. With shalom as its goal, Christian hope is eschatological, cosmic, and communal. It is not only personal but also corporeal, just as God's incarnation takes seriously the material reality of every bit, ounce, and inch of creation (affirming the goodness of creation). It is not otherworldly but this-worldly. "Redemption does not leave the world behind but lifts creation to a higher level."[65] Hence a person of hope believes in God's promise and strives toward its fulfillment. In new covenant ethics, hope empowers our struggle for justice and peacemaking. Hope does not

65. Pinnock, *Flame of Love*, 54.

minimize or nullify human efforts in repairing the world (*tikkun olam*). In the framework of covenant, God's work and human efforts are collaborative, although the final fulfillment is God's gift.

In this time of deepening despair, cynicism, and helplessness—the death of soul, despite brilliant advancement of technology—Christians do not lose hope because of God's fidelity. Christian hope is based on God's faithfulness. It comes from trust in God's promise: since God is faithful, God will deliver God's promise. Fulfillment of the promise is beyond human efforts; rather, the future is in God's hands. God may tarry but will never be late. The good news of Easter is that death has been conquered, and God's commitment to the renewal and restoration of creation is firm. The Spirit is God's down payment for the authenticity of Christian hope. This is the bedrock of the Christian hope and comfort.

Hope is critical for the Christian journey, not only to sustain faith but also to be creative. It "summons to a decision and risk that stretches beyond the recognized patterns of recognition."[66] Hope also opens believers to see unrealized potential waiting in the future, as it awakens in us the courage to see new possibilities in God despite deepening suffering, impending destruction, and the spreading threat of death. "It is important that Jeremiah, most anguished of the prophets, speaks this hope, for only one in anguish could hope so deeply. It is equally important that he speaks this anticipation precisely at a time of historical brokenness when there seems no ground for hope. The new community he anticipates is not to be derived from the old shattered one. It depends only and singularly on a new move from God, a response to groans."[67]

Despite the growing threat of death and disintegration (de-creation) under neoliberal capitalism, covenantal hope sustains, enlivens, and energizes Christians to stand firm in truth, to give themselves fully to the work of justice and peace and love, and to seek new possibilities. By trusting God's faithfulness, Christians keep pressing on toward the future transformation because they know that God is already moving toward a new future in the world, and that their labor in the Lord is not in vain (1 Cor. 15:58).

Hope does not allow our complacency with the status quo; rather, it summons us "to a decision and risk that stretches beyond the recognized patterns of recognition."[68]

That is, hope demands that we critically examine our social relationships and institutions in light of God's righteousness and promised future and challenges us to press on toward their transformation.

66. O'Donovan, "Sanctification and Ethics," 156.

67. Brueggemann, *A Social Reading of the Old Testament*, 47.

68. O'Donovan, "Sanctification and Ethics," 156.

Conclusion

The objective of this chapter was to show how the covenantal drama and its threefold dialectics inform and shape several core norms/values of Christianity. While not comprehensive, our study has demonstrated that covenant offers a proper theological-ethical framework to interpret these values in their respective theological and moral meanings. Apart from the covenant, they may lose the interpretive context and moral balance and are thus likely to be abstract, distorted, or uncritically assimilated to other ideologies and moral philosophies (liberalism, Marxism, libertarianism, etc.).

The covenantal drama and its three dialectics help to clarify and qualify each value in its proper theological framework. New covenant ethics maintains a healthy balance between freedom and solidarity, love and justice, self-love and other-love, fairness and generosity, rights and responsibility, and attends to both the sinfulness and the redemptive possibility of humanity.[69] The composite of love, justice, power, and just peacemaking is an example of the synthesis that new covenant ethics accomplishes. In new covenant ethics, freedom is never individualistic nor self-sufficient but relational. Likewise, thanks to its emphasis on the protection of the basic rights and sanctity of each person, solidarity in the covenant is not blind and undifferentiated but rather a highly particular and complex solidarity. Our bond with God and others does not eliminate our individuality and our differences.

The balance and harmony between these values are important for a faithful and productive Christian life. Together, these values offer the antidotes against religious elitism and authoritarianism, shallow and thin contractualism and individualism, and various forms of privilege and power grounded in race, gender, and class. Covenantal values offer a practical and prudential guide in our ethical discernment and help us to see how to live concretely as God's covenant people. When these values are practiced in the context of the covenant of Jesus, Christians may develop virtues that embody these values: gratitude, trust, truth telling, humility, freedom, solidarity, love, justice, rights, and hope.

Together, these covenantal norms and values offer tough threads of spirituality and the fibers of sociality for Christians.[70] Combined, they serve as the moral

69. Similarly, Karl Barth pairs grace-holiness, mercy-righteousness, and patience-wisdom under the rubric of the perfections of divine love; unity-omnipresence, constancy-omnipotence, eternity and glory go under the rubric of the perfections of divine freedom.

70. Taken together, *hesed* and *'emet* portray God's character as steadfast, loyal, reliable, and truthful—all apt for describing God as "our Rock." Christopher Wright, *An Eye for an Eye*, 135. Likewise, based on these norms, the Christian life can be built upon the rock of Jesus Christ, who is the incarnation of loving, faithful, and truthful God.

threads to sustain a healthy covenantal relationship and build a strong Christian community. To practice them helps Christians to stay faithful in their relationship with God and to organize their personal and communal lives well in conformity to God's shalom. In his self-donating love, unswerving faithfulness, patience, long-suffering, hopefulness, and respect for and solidarity with others, Jesus himself modeled for us how to live as a covenanted person. Like Jesus, Christians may choose trust over distrust, forgiveness over grudges and hatred, and hope over pessimism and choose to respect the dignity of every person and resist every form of domination, enmity, and violence.

CHAPTER 8

The Three Ethical Motifs of Goal, Law, and Virtue

> Shalom is intertwined with justice. In shalom, each person enjoys justice, enjoys his or her rights. There is no shalom without justice. But shalom goes beyond justice. Shalom is the human being dwelling at peace in all his or her relationships: with God, with self, with fellows, with nature.
>
> —Nicholas Wolterstorff, *Hearing the Call*

Goal, law, and virtue are traditionally understood as the three major motifs of ethics. Historically, different types of ethics have developed around each of these motifs, and in ancient Greece they were called teleology, deontology, and aretology. Generally speaking, when ethical reflection takes place in relation to a goal, it is called teleology (*telos* = goal). The primary task of teleology is to identify desirable ends and goals. It attempts to answer this question: What goal or end ought to be sought? In teleology, what makes a decision or an action *moral* (typically framed in terms of good or bad) is how it contributes to the actualization of the designated goal.

When ethical reflection is assessed in conformity to universal rules and laws, it is called deontology (*deon* = duty). Deontology refers to an ethical approach that attends to the question: What is the law to be obeyed? This approach assumes that rules and laws provide a reliable ground for moral actions. Human decisions and actions are right or wrong according to their conformity to rules and laws. In general, in deontology, rules take on an unconditional character, without consideration of the context or the consequences of one's moral decisions.

Finally, when an ethical decision is guided by the character or virtues of a moral agent, it is called aretology (*aretē* = virtue). The primary question that virtue ethics asks is: What kind of people ought we to be? The focus is on the "being" rather than the "doing" of a person or a people, that is, the moral formation of a moral agent. Virtue ethics assumes that moral decisions and actions flow from one's character.

Although all three motifs of goal, law, and virtue are found in Scripture, various Christian ethical traditions have developed by focusing on one or two of these motifs. For example, the Social Gospel movement and liberation ethics are teleological in emphasis (Christianizing the social order and liberation from the hierarchies of gender, class, and race, respectively); divine command ethics tends to be deontological in its focus on God's commandments; Christian virtue ethics stresses the centrality of character formation through church life and practices. Despite their different conceptual categorizations, in actual life, the three motifs are not mutually exclusive but are interrelated in informing, guiding, and directing one's decisions and actions.[1]

New covenant ethics takes a different approach than these three motifs of ethics. Unlike other approaches, it refuses to prioritize one motif over the others as its starting point (or a priori orientation). Rather, it takes the God-human relationship, or the covenant, as its starting point, and exhibits how the three motifs (goal, law, and virtue) are all embedded and interrelated in the covenant in an organic and dynamic way.[2] Covenant does not displace these motifs but rather integrates them in a unique and organic way in its relational framework. Grounded in the deep mystery of the triune life, these motifs are covenantally mediated and harmonized. Covenant informs what each of these motifs means and how they are interrelated.

Goal: Shalom

First, as indicated by the covenantal drama of liberation-restoration, covenant has a strong teleological thrust. Indeed, the covenantal drama moves from creation and sin toward the full restoration of creation: shalom. Teleology (the goal we pursue) shapes our moral knowledge. Humans are typically able to see and act only within the scope of our envisioning. "To be human is to be oriented by some vision of the good life, some picture of what we think counts as 'flourishing.' And we *want* that. We crave it. We desire it. This is why our most fundamental mode of orientation to the world is love. We are oriented by our longings, directed by our desires. We adopt ways of life that are indexed to such visions of the good life, not usually be-

1. For example, while feminist ethics is teleological, it also upholds the sanctity (and rights) of a human, especially women. Another example is Catholic Thomistic ethics that integrates all three dimensions—teleological, deontological, and aretological.

2. This approach is different from a traditional Reformed covenantal approach that emphasizes divine command ethics over the other two motifs.

cause we 'think through' our options but rather because some picture captures our imagination."[3]

Shalom is the vision (goal) and content of God's reign, and it sets the horizon of our moral epistemology and the scope to imagine the future. All human aspirations and activities point toward shalom, where creatures flourish and live in right and peaceful relationships with one another. According to Cornelius Plantinga, "In the Bible, shalom means *universal flourishing, wholeness, and delight*—a rich state of affairs in which natural needs are satisfied and natural gifts fruitfully employed, a state of affairs that inspires joyful wonder as its Creator and Savior opens doors and welcomes the creatures in whom he delights."[4]

Commencing with the new covenant of Jesus, Revelation 22:1–5 describes a world of shalom as a gardened city—an earthy vision of life made good, right, and whole. This shalom is cosmic, earthly, and ecological, which is approximated as covenant organizing is expanded and deepened.

Shalom is a covenantally informed notion; it has a covenantal structure and content—diversity, accord, and harmony in unceasing communication among the members. The biblical notion of covenant is salvific in seeking the shalom of the persons, communities, nations, and creation of God in a comprehensive manner. It always displays the concern for "well-being and a healthy relationship characterized shalom."[5] Covenant helps to clarify what the nature and characteristics of shalom are. At the same time, covenant is a structured way to direct our lives toward this goal. God and humans work together toward a common vision of shalom, the historical fulfillment of God's very Trinitarian life.

Shalom describes the cosmic perfection of the covenant that God intended for creation. That is, it portrays the blissful and cosmic communion achieved in the covenant: the final actualization of the triune God's fellowship with humanity and other creatures. It indicates not merely the absence of enmity, alienation, or conflicts but the presence of active and energetic peace flowing from righteous and affectionate relationships—the endless feast and festival of all creatures in the cosmic dance of the triune God.[6]

3. James K. A. Smith, *You Are What You Love*, 11.

4. Plantinga, *Not the Way It's Supposed to Be*, 10. *Shalom* is a Hebrew work with multifarious meanings; it denotes wholeness, health, and fulfillment or sometimes simple absence of war and conflict.

5. Snyder, *The Protestant Ethic and the Spirit of Punishment*, 114.

6. Daniel Elazar explains, "The Hebrew terminology of the Jewish political tradition is especially rich in covenant-related terms, ranging from at least three terms for covenant in the Bible itself to the terminology of contemporary Israeli political life with its emphasis on 'compounding' (rather than forming) governments and polities; 'consenting' to the conclusions of meetings,

Reflecting the communion of the Trinitarian life, shalom describes the state where every creature flourishes in harmonious relationships. Shalom is characterized by mutual joy and enjoyment. Nicholas Wolterstorff muses: "Shalom at its highest is *enjoyment* in one's relationships. A nation may be at peace with all its neighbors and yet be miserable in its poverty. To dwell in shalom is to *enjoy* living before God, to *enjoy* living in one's physical surroundings, to *enjoy* living with one's fellows, to *enjoy* life with oneself."[7] Thus, shalom refers to the wholesome state where everything is perfectly reconciled. This reconciliation has begun in the covenant of Jesus but is now approximated through deepening of the *koinōnia* toward shalom. Shalom begins with reconciliation that restores alienated relationships. Covenant is the method to achieve both reconciliation and shalom. In history we approximate shalom through the deepening of covenant fellowship with God and others in Jesus. Enmity ends as all lives are reconciled with each other while fulfilling their potential. It is not static and immutable but a dynamic, active, and constantly engaging harmony among the members of creation.

Of the various covenants found in the Bible, the covenant of Jesus is the closest to home. The work of shalom through the covenant of Jesus commenced when God reconciled the entire creation in Jesus Christ, who is fully human and fully divine and is where God and humans encounter one another in completeness.[8] The covenant of Jesus most accurately describes what shalom looks like, for the breadth and depth of Christ's reconciliation, peace, and love point toward this vision of shalom. His Sermon on the Mount portrays the quality of shalom in explicit terms: righteousness, peace, nonviolence, forgiveness, love, and reconciliation.

Shalom and the Common Good

For Christians, shalom presents the most comprehensive idea of the common good. All other political and personal goals, including liberation, justice, self-fulfillment, and love, are subordinate to this ultimate goal. In general, the "common good" refers to the shared good of people. The common good encompasses the good of nations, groups, institutions, and individuals, claiming to benefit all members of a community.

However, the concept faces many challenges in a highly pluralistic world where people have very diverse views of the good. Many are hesitant to discuss the idea of

etc. Even words like *shalom* which have other manifest meanings have been demonstrated by philologists to contain strong covenantal connotations." Elazar, *Kinship and Consent*, 53.

7. Wolterstorff, *Until Justice and Peace Embrace*, 69–70.

8. Cf. Kapic, *Communion with God*, 233. In this sense, shalom is a sign of the messianic age (Isa. 9:6–7; cf. Isa. 26:1–3; 32:16–18; 52:7–10; 55:12–13).

one common good because it can be easily perceived as authoritarian or intolerant of differences. Nevertheless, the idea of the common good, even a provisional one, is important for the commonwealth of a global society that is in desperate need of coordinating the diverse interests and conflicting claims of individuals, groups, and nations. For its survival, a society needs some kind of a common vision and shared moral commitment among its members.[9] No community can survive without some minimal mutual commitment and sacrifice regarding what is right, good, and beautiful. Every community requires some binding commitment and loyalty toward a certain shared goal in order to coordinate its members beyond their immediate individual and group interests.

The common good ought to be public in nature, transcending the partial goods of a particular nation, race, class, or religion to be inclusive of all creatures, both human and nonhuman. Moreover, this requires the common participation and contribution of every single member. The common good is enhanced when the diverse goods of individuals and institutions of a society and a biotic community are promoted and harmonized.[10]

Without the guarantee of equal participation and inclusivity, the term "the common good" would be pretentious, functioning as a hegemonic ideology of a dominant group to protect its status quo. Therefore, the common good is "the good to be pursued in common."[11] This means that the integrity of the common good is decided through inclusiveness in membership along with respect for differences. Thus is met the procedural requirement in achieving the common good by stipulating respect for differences and equal participation in the decision-making process as the minimal requirements of the good.

A covenantal approach is effective in explaining how shalom can be approximated in a pluralistic society, that is, how shalom is related to the good of different societies and institutions. As indicated by its unity-in-diversity principle, covenant affirms a pluralistic arrangement of society with diverse social institutions and cultural groups. While all goods in our various spheres of life (marriage, work, school, medicine) point toward the grand cosmic shalom, each sphere has its own distinctive good and vision that its members aspire to achieve; for example, the good of

9. Some form of solidarity is indispensable for any community to exist and function as a community; common vision is required to be a people to form a republic. Hollenbach, *The Common Good and Christian Ethics*, 66.

10. Harmonizing the good of an individual, a society, and the global community is a major challenge. The spread of globalization has created a moral situation where the global common good (including the good of a biotic world) can no longer be disregarded, as we see in the escalating dangers of global warming and other ecological threats.

11. McCann, "The Good to Be Pursued in Common," 158–78.

marriage is erotic love, trust, and friendship between a wife and a husband. This vision is ultimately subject to God's grand vision, while still constituting a significant part of its fulfillment.

Furthermore, its communal-communicative dialectic balances and harmonizes unity and diversity (the collective good and the partial or individual good) as it pursues the common good. Communicative engagement is necessary to mediate and harmonize the good of a particular institution with others in the context of promoting the common good. Shalom refers to the good that is commonly and communicatively pursued, not imposed from above against one's will.[12] Shalom is the solidaric good that is sought through conversations and collaboration among the groups. A covenantal approach strikes a creative balance between individual freedom and social solidarity, the part and the whole. The embedded communicative, procedural requisites of the covenant (freedom, equality, and reciprocity) help to avoid the dangers of authoritarianism and the liberal ethic of atomistic individualism. Through communal-communicative engagement, the members of a society forge their overlapping interests and values toward a tentative good.

The inbreaking of God's shalom has already happened in the covenant of Jesus, and thus shalom is already partially realized by individuals and various social institutions. However, as an eschatological reality, the complete actualization of shalom is beyond human endeavor; it can be approximated in the present only analogously and collaboratively. Analogously, the good of each institution and individuals should correspond to shalom. This means that since covenant presents the best approximation of shalom in terms of structure and pattern, the life of institutions and individuals also needs to be covenantally structured and enacted. The good of a group or a nation is finite and incomplete. Therefore, covenant requires continuous critique, revision, and improvement in light of shalom. Collaboratively, all societies and their institutions should cooperate and contribute to the enhancement of the common good. No single institution can exclusively embody the common good of a society. The goods of each institution need to be harmonized and coordinated.

Some may raise a question: How can shalom be the common good for humanity, when it is a religious notion? While it is a theological concept rooted in Abrahamic religions, the vision of shalom is complex, dynamic, organic, and capacious enough to be the common good for all of humanity. It should not be imposed upon others but shared in a manner similar to how Martin Luther King Jr.'s vision of the beloved community was shared and embraced by many non-Christians.

12. "A common good . . . is an object of a shared longing that by finding certain virtues draws a number of persons to live together in mutually understood and practiced ways, that is some rule of law." Jenson, "The Triunity of Common Good," 333–34.

Law

The threefold pattern of covenant offers a theological framework for properly understanding the meaning and place of the law in Christian life. In covenant ethics, the law is not an abstract, heteronomous entity, which exists independently of history. First and foremost, the law designates the covenantal stipulations between God and humanity that concretize mutual expectations and obligations. The law is predicated on a covenant relationship; it is never prior to it. God's grace precedes and undergirds the law. The dialectic relationship of the indicative and the imperative (the unilateral-bilateral) in the covenant is critical for an accurate comprehension of the nature of the law. Since the covenant indicates a grace-based relationship, the law is in essence God's gift (unilateral) before it is a human obligation (bilateral). The law is given to people who have already been delivered from sin and have accepted God's invitation to the covenant. God's preceding grace and act of deliverance motivate human joyful obedience to the law.

In a covenantal relationship, the law is not heteronomous. It is the expression of God's benevolence for human beings, given with their best interest at heart. It indicates the terms by which humans voluntarily agree to abide when entering a covenant relationship with God.[13] Because of its relational nature, the law is not purely legalistic but also affectional.[14] Richard Mouw says, "We can perceive and participate fully in God's commands only when our minds and reason are regenerated by a living relationship with God."[15] Because of its covenantal nature, the law in Christian life encompasses affection, volition, and intellect. Inspired by God's love, learning and obeying the law are a delight and a joy, which Psalm 119 poetically and extensively articulates. Therefore, obedience to the law is not driven by fear of reprisal but by free human willingness to reciprocate God's love and faithfulness.

As norms and values describe God's character, the law is the concretization of the divine will in the form of commandments, rules, statutes, and ordinances. It serves as the criteria of self-regulation (test the intentions and actions) and mutual accountability of each party. The law guides choices and actions, assisting the parties to stay within the moral boundaries of the covenant.

The law, as covenantal stipulations, concretizes our moral expectations and responsibilities. The law gives specificity to God's call to love God and love neighbors. Stipulations specify concretely what mutual expectations and responsibilities are

13. The stipulations are not imposed upon humans alone but bind both God and humans.

14. Conversely, the idea of love in covenant ethics is neither purely emotional nor volitional. It is both affectional and legal; it is commanded by God as the norm summarizing the entire covenantal stipulations.

15. Mouw, *The God Who Commands*, 68–69.

in a relationship. In particular, the law specifies the requirements of righteousness and justice that are proper to a particular social relationship. It instructs and guides our conduct so that we stay in a faithful relationship with God. This is evident in the Hebrew word *torah*, which means "instruction." The law helps translate faith into concrete actions, specifying the concrete demands of righteousness and justice embedded in a covenant relationship.

In a covenantal relationship with God, the law is also indispensable in molding and shaping human character and virtue and in ordering individual and communal life. The law spells out the concrete ways to stay and grow in righteousness in covenant relationship with God and others. As concrete guidance for actions, the law helps people pattern their lives step-by-step toward God's character. The law, together with the narratives and wisdom of the Bible, offers insights on how to live faithfully in God.

The law is pedagogical prior to being deontological.[16] It serves as the signpost in our life journey as God's people. The law describes God's design for humanity, given for sanctification and flourishing.[17] Combining negative and positive rules, it sets the limits as well as guiding/inducing actions. "[Torah's] commands (halacha) are both specific enough to make the duties of Israel concrete (e.g., laws governing protection of the weak and showing hospitality to strangers) yet summary and comprehensive enough to require a fidelity beyond the details of a contract."[18] Communicative action theory is helpful in understanding the nature of the law in covenant ethics. The law is an aspect of God's communicative action, which is both informative and performative:

1. *Informative*: Delineating the demands of justice and righteousness, the law communicates God's expectation for God's people in a specific and concrete way. As in the case of the narrative, people learn about God's will from the law. The law is the constant, "clear and unified expression" of God's will.[19] Terence Fretheim notes: "Law parallels liturgy (rituals, songs, dance) in being the expression of God's good will and embedded in the narrative of God's

16. Calvin's idea of the third use of the law (à la Luther) captures this covenantal underpinning of the law. God's law is the signpost in our journey in navigating the historical terrains and complex social realities. Dumbrell also notes, "while Heb. torah does contain the concept of categorical imposition, this cannot be divorced, however, from the notion of guidance or instruction for life that the term also conveys." Dumbrell, *Covenant and Creation*, 91.

17. For Paul, it indicates "a way in which Christians are to walk." Deidun, *New Covenant Morality in Paul*, 24.

18. May, *Testing the National Covenant*, 94.

19. Eichrodt, *Theology of the Old Testament*, 242.

deliverance."[20] It instructs us on how to live out the meaning of covenant relationship in the various aspects of daily social life.

2. *Performative*: The authority of the law is based on its reasonableness, not on coercion—"brusque injunctions."[21] God persuades, never coercing, with the invitation to human beings to accept the law as their guide. This communicative nature is evident in the OT, where God's delineation of the law frequently includes the motivational clause attached to it.[22] The motivational clauses in Deuteronomy offer rationales on why the law should be obeyed. They take three different forms: teleological (telling the consequences of one's obedience or disobedience), aretological (encouraging imitation of God's past gracious acts), and empathetic (encouraging a show of mercy and fairness to others by remembering their miseries and sufferings in the past).

Among Christians, covenant, typically alluding to the Sinai covenant, is often understood as the set of God's laws agreed upon by the people. However, legalism and proceduralism are the dominant impression that emanates from this reference. In a covenantal context, these stipulations are not conditions required for admission to the covenant. Neither are they merits to accumulate. The law, ironically, is the sign of human freedom and not subjugation. For example, to Hebrews, the former slaves, the law indicated their freedom and dignity and their restoration as the image of God rather than a sign of suppression. Fretheim's comment is very helpful: "The law points up the fact that God has chosen not to do everything in this world by himself. . . . The law insists that there are important human initiatives and responsibilities to be undertaken. Human beings are given important tasks in furthering the cause of justice and good order in Israel and the larger creation."[23]

In the covenant, obedience to the law is the sign of fidelity and love. The Bible promises that obedience to the law leads to a fulfilling life. Stipulations are the symbol of freedom, mutual fidelity, and accountability before God. They serve as a moral plumb line that tests whether covenantal partners are being faithful to each other. Free obedience of people to the law is the sign of the changed heart of a believer. For those who do not have such a heart, the law becomes a burden and is experienced as condemnatory.

As they are freely agreed-upon terms of interaction of two parties, the stipulations play an important role in strengthening solidarity and community formation

20. Fretheim, *Exodus*, 203.

21. Patrick Miller, *Israelite Religion and Biblical Theology*, 499.

22. Patrick Miller, *Israelite Religion and Biblical Theology*, 499.

23. Fretheim, *Exodus*, 203–4.

while protecting the rights of each party. The stipulations we freely agree to hold us accountable to God and others in a concrete way. Covenantal stipulations serve as a stepping-stone for growth and for fellowship in community, as they are instrumental to our moral growth. They allow us to imitate God and deepen our relationship with God and others. As freely agreed-upon terms of interaction, they are also instrumental in strengthening solidarity while protecting the rights and freedoms of each party. Keeping the obligations of the covenant strengthens solidarity by enhancing the level of trust between the partners. Keeping the law also contributes to the strengthening of relationship, as it enhances the level of trust between the partners.

The law plays several crucial social and moral functions in the community. It helps to coordinate, adjust, and regulate mutual interactions in ongoing covenantal relationship (communal-communicative). In particular, because of its objective (regulative) nature, it is indispensable for arranging social life, personal and institutional relationships, and the global order. It is instrumental in organizing our collective life and building an orderly and just social life; the law brings structure to human life by offering principle, consistency, and reliability against moral confusion and disorder.[24] The law guides humanity toward shalom as a signpost toward the abundant and flourishing life.

The covenantal relationship is not only prior to the law, but it also always surpasses the law. Because of the intimate, graced nature of the covenant, the law does not exhaust or substitute for the covenant. May notes: "The covenant details duties that give specific content to the future, while enjoining a comprehensive fidelity that extends beyond particulars to unforeseen and unforeseeable contingencies."[25] Covenantal stipulations are "both specific enough to make the future duties of Israel concrete (e.g., the dietary laws and laws governing protection of the weak), yet summary enough (e.g., 'Love the Lord thy God with all thy heart . . .') to require a fidelity to the intent as well as the letter."[26]

Because of the communal nature of God's covenant, the law is more filial than judicial. In the covenant, the law is never intended to be an end by itself nor separate from God and others. That is, the law is a necessary aspect of a covenantal relationship, but it is never sufficient in itself. It is subjected to the covenant and always interpreted in the ongoing covenantal communication with God and others. Ancient Israel was conscious of this danger of legalism and checked against it by emphasizing the intimate and communal dimension of their covenantal relationship with God.

24. Fretheim, *Exodus*, 201. The law discloses God's will that extends into all aspects of human life that already experienced salvific will described in the narrative. The law is communicative, while the narrative is descriptive.

25. May, *The Physician's Covenant*, 113.

26. May, *The Physician's Covenant*, 115.

The double love commandments, as the summary of the law, are such a critical reminder and check against legalism. The goal of the covenant is love (communion), not legal regulation.[27]

Christians cannot ignore the moral law in their lives. Even after reconciliation with God in Jesus Christ, believers are obligated to obey and fulfill the law in their lives through the aid of the Spirit.[28] The moral law is also crucial for Christian public engagement in civil society, as it provides a common moral ground with others. Its abrogation would have a devastating social impact by removing the public standard of morality. To embrace it does not mean legalism. Together with the teachings and example of Jesus, the law helps us better manage and organize our lives.

The above explication shows a covenantal basis of the law. A covenantal approach avoids moral legalism without disregarding the law; it avoids moral relativism without disregarding particular cultural contexts of Christian life. It listens to culture without assimilating; it insists on its identity without being fundamentalist. It seeks justice (communicative, bilateral fairness) while being open to generosity and compassion (communal-community building). Outside the covenant, the meaning and purpose of the law would more than likely be distorted, degenerating into legalism.

Virtue

In a conventional understanding, virtues refer to excellent, praiseworthy, and prized moral traits that a community regards as canonical. The community's concept of the good and the good life is instrumental in shaping the imagination, affections, desires, and eventually the virtues of individuals. Virtues are not innate faculties but habits acquired over a long period of time as a person consistently pursues a certain cherished good.[29] Virtue formation occurs when a moral agent directs his desires toward a certain noble vision or good. Love of the good lures desires toward a virtuous development.[30]

27. Brevard S. Childs notes: "The ability of Deuteronomy to summarize the Law in terms of loving God with heart, soul and mind is a major check against all forms of legalism. According to Deuteronomy, the whole Mosaic law testifies to the living will of God whose eternal purpose for the life of his people provides the only grounds for life and salvation." Childs, *Old Testament Theology in a Canonical Context*, 56. John Barton similarly notes, "ethics is not so much a system of obligations as a way of communion with God." Barton, "Approaches to Ethics in the Old Testament," 130.

28. Paul's critique of the law (the Mosaic economy as understood by his contemporary Jews) was directed toward the salvific pretension of law keeping, not the ethical function of the law.

29. The idea of virtue is intimately associated with a telos. Gilbert Meilaender observes, "An ethic which focuses on virtue will tend to make vision central in the moral life." Meilaender, *The Theory and Practice of Virtue*, ix.

30. James K. A. Smith, *Desiring the Kingdom*.

Reformed covenant theology has seldom treated virtues as a focal point of Christian ethics, although the ideas of *imitatio Dei* and union with Christ have been studied with significant aretological implications. This underdevelopment has to do with the Reformed emphasis on divine grace and its corollary apprehension about works righteousness; that is, the emphasis on human virtues may inadvertently marginalize the importance of God's grace.

However, virtue formation is important in new covenant ethics.[31] Reflecting God's character, virtues describe excellent moral traits that God cultivates in a believer through a covenantal relationship. Virtues are necessary for a believer to live out covenant obligations faithfully. A covenantal relationship is sustained when the parties keep their promises, and keeping one's covenantal promises is not possible without necessary virtues. In short, staying in the covenant requires virtues.

In new covenant ethics, the covenantal drama (liberation-restoration) offers a narrative, dramatic context for virtue formation. The memory of God's delivering love and the hope of God's shalom push and pull human desires toward God and God's purpose. In addition, in the context of the covenant of Jesus, virtue formation has a Trinitarian character. It is a collaborative work of the triune God: the Father is the source and goal of Christian virtue formation, Jesus (the incarnate Logos) is the concrete moral exemplar (the new humanity) to imitate, and the Spirit is the power who instills the sense of new identity and molds Christian virtues in conformity to Jesus Christ. Christian virtue formation is eschatological in its horizon and scope, christological in its ethical content, and pneumatological in its formative and transformative logic and pattern.[32]

New covenant ethics, in its threefold dialectic, offers a plausible view of virtues. I contend that covenant constitutes the optimal condition for virtue formation for Christians. In what follows, I will show how the threefold dialectics of covenant are conducive to the development of virtues.

Unilateral-Bilateral

The idea of *imitatio Dei* is frequently mentioned as a central mechanism of virtue formation in a Christian context. Typically, it means that God's character sets the model for Christian virtue formation. Moral agents labor to imitate God's character in doing God's will. "The life of God models the moral life. God as experienced by

31. Another term that is interchangeable with "character" is the "mindset of Christ" that Paul admonishes in Philippians.

32. See Loder, *The Transformation Moment*; Loder, *The Logic of the Spirit*.

Israel and mediated to subsequent generations through the canon is to be imitated as moral agent, in both character and conduct."[33]

In the Bible, *imitatio Dei* is neither primarily deontological nor aretological, but covenantal in nature.[34] That is to say, a believer imitates God's character not only because it is God's demand but also because it is a proper way to respond to God's gracious action. In covenant ethics, the idea of *imitatio Dei* is primarily informed by the unilateral-bilateral dialectic. Far from being the self-motivated moral exertion of a moral agent, *imitatio Dei* is first and foremost a human response to God's gracious action; as is the case with the law, virtue is more indicative than imperative. As God has first acted justly, mercifully, and compassionately, the people who are covenanted with God are required to treat each other in the same manner. God famously commanded in Leviticus: "You shall be holy, for I the LORD your God am holy" (Lev. 19:2). We first experience and learn God's graciousness and righteous character through God's acts of deliverance or generous blessings. Imitation is primarily motivated not by a sense of duty or by the narrative power of a community; God's grace is the attraction and motivating power of virtue formation.

God's character and acts serve as the paradigmatic exemplar for Christian moral actions, just as God is the source of the image of God that humanity bears. *Imitatio Dei* is an endeavor and process to restore the *imago Dei* in humanity. By imitating God's character, humans grow into the likeness of God. Enamored of and amazed by God's grace, perfection, and beauty, humans are drawn toward God, and in the process their desires are transformed. This forms the impetus and sets the tone for our moral actions toward others. God's character constitutes the pattern or deep grammar of our actions. "We are to carry out to others the pattern of God's actions for us."[35] For example, *hesed* is not confined to God; it is one of the primary moral qualities that God requires of God's people (Hos. 6:6).

Covenant ethics has the merit of explaining where the motivation and energy for character formation come from and how it takes place. For Christians, God's love and grace serve as the motivating and formative force in our emulation of God's character. As we discussed in chapter 4, several motivational clauses in the Bible display the causal relationship between God's actions and human responsibility.

33. Birch, "Moral Agency, Community, and the Character of God in the Hebrew Bible," 31.

34. The idea of *imitatio Dei* is a broader and more inclusive moral category than the law. It underlies much of the content of the law and covenantal codes. For example, legal codes in the Book of the Covenant (Exod. 20:21–23:19) are inferred from God's character and God's historical acts. Hanson, *The People Called*, 44. The legal codes in the book urge Israel to act the way God has already acted toward them: "[God] executes justice for the orphan and the widow, and . . . loves the strangers, providing them with food and clothing. You shall also love the stranger, for you were strangers in the land of Egypt" (Deut. 10:18–19).

35. Mott, *Biblical Ethics and Social Change*, 28.

Christian virtues are indicative; they are first and foremost grounded in Christian identity. Identity is the ground of our virtue formation. Christian virtue is shaped on the basis of our new identity given in a covenantal relationship with God in Jesus Christ. Logically, in the covenant, our identity is prior to virtue formation, just as God's call is prior to our moral response. A new identity is given in our relationship with God (e.g., adoption), while virtues are built up through fellowship with God on the basis of this new identity.

Communal-Communicative

While the unilateral-bilateral dialectic shows the motivating source of Christian virtue formation, the communal-communicative dialectic describes how the process of virtue formation takes place. Virtue formation takes place through covenantal fellowship between the believer and God. Fellowship is a vehicle through which we learn to imitate God's character. *Imitatio Dei* is not a onetime event but an ongoing process. Thanks to God's living presence in our life, our communication with God is new and fresh every day. *Imitatio Dei* in the covenantal life is a process of believers' constant attunement to God; through ongoing fellowship, they attune their own disposition and conduct in conformity to God's character. To know and walk with God is to be attuned to God's disposition, character, and will—God's mind and heartbeat—which happens through communication.

Virtue formation gradually occurs as persons faithfully stay in the covenant in their trust in God's love and power. Fellowship and communication with God in Jesus Christ have transformative power in the Spirit. They lead to deeper intimacy and communion, gradually reorienting us by affecting our moral understanding and desires. As a child learns the character of a parent through enduring fellowship and exchange of life in a family, a person imitates God's character through living fellowship with God.

In the context of covenant, God's abiding presence and grace have the power to reorder and recenter our inner dispositions and desires as well as our external behaviors. The work of the Spirit is communicative and effectual in addressing an individual's particular concerns and situations. It has a regenerating, remolding, reordering power on our dispositions. It does not oppose or destroy all natural affections other than affection for God, but rather it reorders them in the comprehensive framework of the covenantal love of God, others, and nature, and it works to correct and perfect flawed, limited, partial, or distorted affections, toward more universal and wholesome ones.[36]

In God's fellowship with a believer, God constantly demonstrates God's fidelity and moral character and draws a believer closer to God. The believer, in turn, learns

36. Ottati, "The Reformed Tradition in Theological Ethics," 53.

God's character, values, and preferences. As fellowship continues, the believer experiences God's steadfastness and comes to a deeper understanding of God's character, intentions, and love, learning how to respond faithfully to God. Biblical figures (e.g., the patriarchs, Moses, David, Jesus's disciples, Mary) grew and matured in and through their long-standing, yet often tumultuous, covenantal relationships with God. Many of them were not all-noble, all-virtuous, or all-respected people at the beginning of their faith journeys; they were not highly regarded within their families; they were more often than not broken and flawed. For example, Jacob was not a person of outstanding character worthy of our imitation.

A key to fellowship is to stay faithfully in the covenant in single-hearted devotion and dedication.[37] Paul said, "We also boast in our sufferings, knowing that suffering produces endurance, and endurance produces character, and character produces hope" (Rom. 5:3–4). Our ongoing fellowship with God in the covenant gradually sanctifies us in conformity to Jesus Christ. God's self-donating communication opens, shakes, and loosens the self that is enclosed and *curved* inward (*incurvatus in se*). Through this fellowship, we partake in God's nature (2 Pet. 1:4) and are gradually transformed in the imitation of God. Through communication, human partners adopt God's goal as their own, God's law as their guidance, and Jesus as the moral exemplar to which to conform. This is what "putting on Christ" means. Jesus is the imprint of the *imago Dei* in us. "That is, God creates friendship with the justified by so transforming the human soul that it becomes, in some sense, connatural to God . . . and is united to God without intermediary. . . . In short, charity can be described as the friendship of women and men with God, because charity transforms its subjects into participants in the very mind and will of God."[38]

Moral growth happens to those who faithfully remain in the covenant through ongoing communication with God: "It informs and shapes us, it transforms and instructs us. We can grow into its truth as we can grow into Christ himself."[39] God gradually sets us free from our forms of bondage (pride, ignorance, idolatry, self-pity, narcissism, etc.) and restores us to become truly free persons. Continuously encountering the true and loving God in our fellowship with Jesus Christ, we open our hearts and take the risk of becoming vulnerable and truthful by giving ourselves to God in grateful response. "God completes or consummates the unfinished person-idea that is Abraham, Moses, David, etc. through an active dialogic penetration into the depth of their being. It is through the give and take of dialogue that a person—Bakhtin's 'voice-idea'—actualizes his or her potential, realizes his or her true self, and

37. The Shema calls for the loyalty, allegiance, and wholehearted devotion of a believer toward God, reciprocating God's own loyalty and devotion to the believer.

38. Porter, *The Recovery of Virtue*, 170.

39. Pinnock, *Flame of Love*, 227.

hence rings true or false. The nature, identity and character of a hero is inextricably connected to how that person addresses and answers others. One's inner man or soul is exhibited 'only by portraying his communion with another.'"[40] Walking with God describes a form of enduring communication with God, indicating fellowship and communion with God in everyday life. Enoch, Noah, and Abraham "walked with God" (Gen. 5:22, 24; 6:9; 15:6; 17:1), which means, in our context, that they lived in a living communication with God.

In the context of the covenant, not only narrative but also the law is instrumental in forming virtues. In order to walk with God, one needs guidance, directives, or signposts, and the law plays these roles. Walking with God, being righteous, and obeying God's law are interchangeable in Scripture. Walking with God means practicing righteousness and observing God's law.

Reflecting God's will and moral character, God's law offers concrete guidelines and directives for our desires and actions in imitating God. Like a vine branch that rises up through supporting poles and nets, the law helps to channel desires toward the noble direction that God has set. As discussed above, the law plays a pedagogical and instructional function for a believer's life. As God's words, the law is performative; it calls for a response from a hearer.[41] A covenantal relationship is maintained by the fidelity between God and believers. This fidelity is not ambiguous but is concretely tested by mutual accountability in reference to the agreed-upon stipulations. As a person matures in covenant relationship with God, the law is increasingly internalized and transfigured into virtuous dispositions and habits.

Memory-Hope

The covenant idea of virtue in new covenant ethics is contextual. Virtues may sound general, but in fact they are always contextually exercised. The practice of virtue requires practical wisdom. Virtue is not a fixed, mechanical, or perfunctory entity in a person but a creative (while stable) ability of a person to engage with new and different surroundings without losing continuity. Practical wisdom indicates the creative, adaptive ability of a moral agent to practice virtues in a faithful and contextual way.

Virtue is not self-enclosed or static but practical; it is exercised through practical wisdom in the changing context of life. Virtues are practiced in reference to one's role and identity embedded in specific social relationships. For example, a father who is

40. Vanhoozer, *Remythologizing Theology*, 332–33.

41. Knowing God's character is synonymous with knowing God's law. Knowing God meant obeying the covenant stipulations. Thus, Hosea rebuked the people for not knowing God (Hos. 4:1–2), and this lack of knowledge is synonymous with the lack of knowledge of the law (4:6).

generous toward others but carefree and negligent toward his children lacks character because he does not live up to his calling as a father. To be a responsible partner to God is to be faithful to the purpose of every particular covenant relationship.

This means that the formation and practice of virtue in new covenant ethics are analogical. Vanhoozer's model of imitation describes an analogical nature of our *imitatio Dei*: "Disciples are to imitate, but not replicate, Christ. To replicate is to make an exact copy, a duplicate. To imitate means to continue a pattern. . . . Imitation requires both fidelity and, in some cases, creativity if one is to continue the *same* pattern in a *different* situation."[42] New covenant ethics helps to develop virtue that is contextually relevant to various social relationships. To imitate is to live out the quality of moral life and moral conduct creatively in the various contexts of one's life. It is not just to blindly duplicate moral life and moral conduct but to joyfully embrace, internalize, and embody them in one's own moral agency. In this respect, the process of *imitatio Dei* also entails a moral agent's communicative self-reflection and engagement with others.

Finally, virtue formation in new covenant ethics is eschatological. There is no perfection of our virtues and character in this world. It is a long, patient, and arduous process that requires ongoing practices in God's grace.

Summary

A covenantal idea of virtue formation is different from communitarian and neo-Aristotelian approaches in terms of the source, impetus, and process of moral formation. A covenantal approach gives proper attention—in fact, a prior place—to the Spirit, the divine agent who works in collaboration with humans. In new covenant ethics, virtue formation is achieved in a covenantal relationship with God and others in the context of various communities and institutions. A covenantal approach directly focuses on God as the formative, inspirational, and pedagogical source of our character, rather than narrative or community (although they can assist in the process). Although the community, its narrative, and its various practices assist in this character formation, in the final analysis they are secondary to God's agency and God's covenantal relationship with a person. Virtues are gradually shaped when a believer responds to God's initiating grace and cooperates with God in obedience, faithfully staying in a covenantal relationship with God. This approach is consistent with the biblical description of virtues as the fruit of the Spirit (Gal. 5:22–23).

A covenantal approach attends to both the internal (desires, motivations, dispositions) and external (behavioral regulation and sanctions guided by the law)

42. Vanhoozer, *Faith Speaking Understanding*, 189.

dimensions of character/virtue formation. While the internal has to do with the transformation of inner dispositions, motivations, or desires, the external is concerned with the regulation of the behaviors by the law, commandments, and standards.[43] We cannot deny the importance of this deontological dimension in virtue formation. Internal desires (including the love of God and others) channel our dispositions and imaginations, while external covenantal stipulations (including the moral law and teachings of Jesus) regulate and guide our words and deeds toward the same goal.[44] We do not have to choose one over the other because both are interrelated in the covenant as we endeavor to live faithfully as God's children in the world.

Conclusion

New covenant ethics embraces the three motifs (goal, law, virtue) in an organic way, showing how they are interrelated in the covenant. In new covenant ethics, shalom—the goal of all human strivings and the fulfillment of creation (the flourishing of every life)—describes the eschatological perfection of God's covenant with creation and humanity. The law, meanwhile, indicates the minimum obligations to which covenantal partners are held accountable in order to stay in the covenant. Virtues are the noble and praiseworthy moral dispositions that believers learn as they partake in and imitate God's character through an ongoing fellowship with God in the covenant.

New covenant ethics recognizes the importance of goal, law, and virtue, as well as their contributions to the moral formation and ministry of God's people. Covenant serves as the fabric and scaffold of their unity-in-diversity; it is the "already" of shalom that a faith community experiences in relationship with God. Covenant is equally the constitutive context of a performative role of the law; it offers a pluralistic social vision that helps Christians to learn God's character (*imitatio Dei*) in diverse social relationships.

The three are complementary, and none of the three motifs is more important than the others. Because of shalom, relationships are never static but purposeful; because of the law, relationships are disciplined and free from slothfulness and decay;

43. Covenantal stipulations contain both teleological and deontological elements, that is, a promise on the future actions for the fulfillment of the agreement (together with a promise of the rewards for keeping the agreement) and binding obligations whose breach will invite negative sanctions. The unity of the internal and the external for virtue formation in the covenant takes place through the collaboration of the Trinitarian persons, the Word and the Spirit for the glory of the Father.

44. Righteousness is not just a norm but also a virtue in the Bible.

because of virtues, relationships are trusted and enjoyable. Together, they show the dynamic nature of covenant as the organizing method of God's reign.

Strictly speaking, the three motifs are subjected to the living relationship that God created with humans. Shalom is what the relationship intends to actualize; rules are what explicitly mediate, coordinate, and regulate the relationship; virtues are the inner sustaining power of the agent who faithfully remains in a covenantal relationship. Because of the covenantal matrix, the goal is not utilitarian, the law is not heteronomous, and the virtues are neither individualistic nor pietistic.

The three motifs are all theonomously and relationally understood and organized. God's presence and faithfulness are the empowering source of the human pursuit of shalom, obedience, and growth in virtuous maturity. Without a living relationship with God, these aspirations lose their impetus and orientation. The pursuit of shalom is not that of a utopian ideal; rather, shalom is already tasted and experienced in a living relationship. The law is neither abstract nor heteronomous because it is voluntary and instructive. And virtue formation finds a concrete exemplar in Jesus, who is close to each person in the Spirit.

CHAPTER 9

The Moral Authority of Scripture and Other Sources

> All scripture is inspired by God and is useful for teaching, for reproof, for correction, and for training in righteousness, so that everyone who belongs to God may be proficient, equipped for every good work.
>
> —2 Timothy 3:16–17

Protestant Christians hold up the Bible as the most important authority in their spiritual-moral life, as the Reformation principle of *sola Scriptura* implies.[1]

Many Christians appeal to the Bible for moral guidance and justification of their ethical decisions. In an unparalleled way, Scripture is understood as a unique, authoritative source of the Christian life because of its distinctiveness in providing the knowledge of who God is and what God does. Scripture is God's story: God is its protagonist, and it describes God's character and action, uniquely revealing God's intention and purpose for humanity and the world.

While there is a consensus that the Bible is authoritative for Christian ethics, there are substantial differences regarding the nature, character, and scope of its authority. Although all Christians take Scripture seriously in their moral life, they do not all necessarily approach Scripture in the same way. In fact, Christians differ substantially on how the Bible is authoritative, where its authority resides or derives from, and how the authority functions in the process of ethical reasoning.

1. There are certain serious misunderstandings regarding the Reformation idea of *sola Scriptura*. Protestants tend to think Scripture alone is enough in providing ready-made answers to all our moral issues; that Scripture has existed by itself; that it is an unmediated direct record/source of God's revelation, and therefore that our moral discussions should not go beyond the bounds of Scripture. This understanding of *sola Scriptura* ignores the necessary and creative role of the community in receiving and interpreting revelation in an ongoing manner. Indeed, moral understandings and practices are influenced by various interpretive traditions in history.

Different Christian groups take different moral teachings, events, or books (such as the exodus event, Ten Commandments, Sermon on the Mount, crucifixion and resurrection, Pauline epistles, or Synoptic Gospels) in Scripture as most authoritative or significant.[2]

This difficulty around biblical authority is aggravated because of hermeneutical differences in reading the Bible. "No matter how seriously the church may take the authority of the Bible, the slogan of sola Scriptura is both conceptually and practically untenable, because the interpretation of Scripture can never occur in a vacuum."[3] We interpret Scripture always through our own lenses under the influence of a particular tradition, channeled through our personal or social experience. This hermeneutical variation is especially acute when the biblical text is metaphoric or poetic in nature. In addition, a postmodern ethos of relativism and subjectivism (critiquing universality and metanarrative) tempts many Christians to read Scripture arbitrarily or treat every interpretation as equally valid.

The challenge is further complicated because there is a huge gap between biblical times and ours. Biblical writers and we are situated in very different cultures and historical contexts. The Bible is understandably silent on some complex issues that we face today, such as cloning, stem cell research, artificial intelligence, in vitro fertilization, abortion, pollution, and global warming.

These difficulties with the Bible and its authority pose major hermeneutical challenges to Christian ethics—how to address the diversity of theological-ethical perspectives within the Bible, how to discern God's will in our own personal and social life, and how to adjudicate conflicting interpretive claims within the community when each person believes he or she speaks on the basis of biblical authority. The stakes for these questions are extremely high, especially for Protestant Christians, because the question of biblical authority (e.g., the debate around inerrancy) has unfortunately been a cause of divisions, schisms, and conflicts among them. Although the misuse of a sacred canon is not confined to Christianity but can be found in every major religion, Christians have fought and even killed other Christians in the name of God while justifying their actions with passages from the Bible. In addition, slavery, genocide, sexism, colonialism, war, homophobia, and all other forms of discrimination have been endorsed by Christians appealing to the Bible.

This chapter studies how new covenant ethics addresses these challenges. It investigates the unique understanding and contributions of a covenantal approach for biblical authority. I claim that a covenantal approach offers a faithful, plausible understanding of the nature of the moral authority of Scripture because Scripture

2. Christians have unknowingly committed the fallacy of creating "the canon within the canon."

3. Hays, *Moral Vision*, 209.

is centered on God's dealing with humanity through covenants (chap. 1). In fact, Scripture is the covenantal document of God's covenantal community. The idea of communicative action and the second and third dialectics of covenant help to adjudicate the differences and tension. In addition to the moral authority of the Bible, this chapter examines the three other sources of moral authority in new covenant ethics—tradition, experience, and reason—and how new covenant ethics helps to clarify their respective roles and contributions to Christian ethics in close relation to each other and the Bible.

A Covenantal Approach: Scripture as Covenant Document of a Faith Community

New covenant ethics takes Scripture as the covenantal document of the diachronic faith community of Jews and Christians. Indeed, Christians call Scripture the Old and New Testaments, recognizing that the Greek word *diatheke* (testament) is a translation of the Hebrew word *berit* (covenant).[4] Some explanations for why it is a covenantal document are as follows.

First, the Bible contains the history, records, and terms of God's covenants with humanity. Scripture records the history of God's covenantal interactions with humanity and creation. Under its framework, major biblical events (creation, the Fall, Israel, exile, return, Jesus, and the church) find better coherence and unity. As chapter 1 exhibits, diverse genres of the Bible, such as narrative, worship materials (rituals, psalms), norms, values, laws, and wisdom literature, could be organized under the rubric of covenant. "The Bible is, to be sure, no science textbook, but neither is it restricted to serving only as a witness to Christ. Neither cosmo- nor Christocentric, the Scriptures are rather centered on God's covenant. The covenant involves the cosmos, and Christ is at the center, but covenantal efficacy is the more comprehensive term to cover all the things that God does with and in and through the Scriptures. What we have in the Scriptures is therefore everything that God deemed necessary and sufficient for the doctrinal, moral and spiritual welfare of his covenant people."[5] As an overarching story line and plot of the entire Scripture, covenant avoids the temptation of identifying a canon within the canon (thus attending to and bringing together diverse resources and genres).

Second, the Bible is a compiled work written by diverse people of God who lived in diverse contexts.[6] It presents their history, collective reflection, and wrestling on

4. Horton, *Covenant and Eschatology*, 129.

5. Vanhoozer, *First Theology*, 132.

6. Rabbinic Judaism, in its methodology of midrash (*hervruta*), understands that God's revela-

the meaning and nature of God's covenantal relationship with them. It was written and handed down to us in its current form by God's people who were covenanted with God.

Third, a covenantal approach to Scripture is more plausible than other theories (e.g., inerrancy) in explaining how its final canonical form was reached, and in understanding its nature and authority. God's communication (revelatory words and commandments) was initially preserved and passed down orally over a long period of time, then later documented. The documentation was necessary to keep the memory of a formative event, to accomplish pedagogical and liturgical purposes, to counter false claims and distortive interpretations, to defend the theological beliefs of the community against charges from the outside, and to help complement the practices of the faith community. This documentation process required the participation and decision of the faith community, and it was equivalent to a covenantal process because it included collective deliberation, communicative exchanges, and agreement of a community. The Bible, in its final canonical form, is the result of the agreement reached through a long process of communicative reflection within the Christian community in light of God's self-communication, which culminated in Jesus Christ. Its finalization required councils, in which representatives of the church gathered to deliberate on the sources. The final decision on the canon—which books should be included—was communicatively decided by a council.

Fourth, a covenantal approach is helpful in exhibiting how the faith community played a critical role in this canonical process. Scripture is the product of the faith community's long, cumulative processes of collective deliberations and communicative decision making. Biblical scholarship (in particular, various forms of criticism) shows that the Bible, contrary to a naïve claim of fundamentalists, was not written at once under direct divine revelation. Rather, the Bible has reached its current canonical form through a long process of compilation, correction, discernment, and criticism, which included internal debates. It is believed that some of the biblical stories were borrowed, added, and revised to provide better illustration of valid and plausible points about God in light of the framers' own faith experiences and theological reflections. This refining process was gradual and collaborative, consisting of compiling, editing, redacting, and rearranging texts to serve the purpose of authenticating God's communication with the faith community. In the process, numerous

tion continues through interpretive processes of a community. Judaism respects both the sanctity (normativity) of laws and the integrity of human freedom. The Torah originated from God; it is not of human invention. However, it is not fully efficacious without human acceptance. The law needs to be freely appropriated by humans. The Talmud dares to say that the Torah is from God, but its interpretation belongs to humanity, as summarized by "[Torah] is not in heaven" (Deut. 30:12). Hartman, *A Living Covenant*, 33.

theological minds and religious authorities, known and unknown, contributed to the shaping of the canon in its current final form. A mistaken understanding of *sola Scriptura* is that it ignores the inevitable and creative role of faith communities in receiving, recording, and interpreting God's revelation and the Christian moral understandings and practices that have been influenced by various interpretive traditions in history.

Unlike the claims of postliberal theologians, however, Scripture is more than a community's historical literary product. It is theonomous in its origin and communicative in its meaning and effect; it is not a purely human product. Its authority lies in the fact that it is the most reliable and authoritative resource and record of God's communications with humanity. Like John the Baptist, the Bible does not call attention to itself but testifies to the living triune God.[7] The Bible focuses on who God is and what God does to, for, and with God's people. In short, the Bible describes God's communicative action and participates in God's economy. Its authority is not reduced to the community's decision. Like covenantal stipulations do, the Bible as a covenant has a faith-communicative power. It has a normative, binding, and orienting authority over our knowledge of God's person and actions. This means that the Bible and the faith community are in a dialectical relationship. The Bible is not completely independent from a faith community; nor is it reduced to being in relationship with only one faith community.

What Is the Source of Scripture's Moral Authority?

Scripture has a unique status as the record of God's communication with Israel and the church. The Christ event was the pinnacle of God's self-communication, and only Scripture contains its witnesses. Scripture has the authority as the canon of Christianity—the collection of the most authoritative writings, documents, and records of the Christian community in history, especially as the description of the past actions of God. Scripture contains the most important content of God's communicative actions toward humanity and the world. One cannot have any knowledge of God's covenants without Scripture. Although God's communication also takes place beyond the bounds of Scripture, Scripture anchors God's speech acts in the tested and approved, namely, covenantal, documents.[8] Vanhoozer notes:

> YHWH's name and identity would be inaccessible without an anchoring divine speech act. To take the Scriptures as this anchoring speech act—as constitutive

7. Migliore, *Faith Seeking Understanding*, 53.
8. Vanhoozer, *Remythologizing Theology*, 214.

> of the covenant relationship—is also to view the prophetic and apostolic discourse as itself a mode of divinely authorized and commissioned communicative action. The covenant relation would not exist were it not for these texts—God's law and promises fixed in the writing—that constitute it. This is how the Law and Prophets present themselves: as part and parcel of communicative relation between God and his people, not as some independently observed record of alleged divine activity. Scripture is the means whereby God interacts socially (covenantally) through messages.[9]

Scripture is an anchor that also serves as the pointer in our communication with God. As the reliable device of God's revelation and communicative action, covenant offers the orienting framework for future interpretations. Scripture forms the foundational analogue to our understanding and interpretation of God and God's actions. We learn about God's redemptive will, plan, and methods through the Bible. Scripture as the record of God's communicative actions plays a critical role in understanding God's covenantal activities and communication today. In this respect, its authority is unparalleled. Technically, the canon is closed. Just as later generations of Israelites could not arbitrarily change the Ten Commandments, we cannot change the canon, even though fresh interpretations are always necessary. Such a unique status of the Bible calls for our sincere and thoughtful responses in dealing with its theological claims and moral teachings.[10]

However, the authority of Scripture is not confined to the past acts of God. Scripture is authoritative for us because it is the primary means of God's communication today as well. God still speaks to God's people through the Bible to lead and guide them and to fulfill God's promises for shalom in Jesus Christ. Specifically, the Spirit bridges the past and the present, the biblical world and our world, as the Spirit speaks to us in a way consistent with God's past utterances and actions. God still freshly speaks to us in our particular situations through Scripture. The illumination of the Spirit in our reading of Scripture may be invisible, but it is nevertheless real. In particular, the Spirit communicates God's revelation of Jesus (the Word of God) to each believer in a personal and contextual way.

The Bible attests to God's ongoing covenantal faithfulness in communicating with us. God speaks, commands, warns, convicts, and encourages God's people

9. Vanhoozer, *Remythologizing Theology*, 214, 215.

10. This unique authority of the Scripture is somewhat analogous to the first dialectic of the covenant itself: the Bible is the gift of the early Christian community for future generations. We are invited to respond to its claims.

through Scripture, so that we may believe and act accordingly. John declares: "But these are written so that you may come to believe" (John 20:31). Paul also confirms, "All scripture is inspired by God and is useful for teaching, for reproof, for correction, and for training in righteousness" (2 Tim. 3:16).

The Bible is a living document of communication through which the triune God speaks to us; we address God in our worship and moral life.[11] However, it is a mistake to reduce all of Scripture to God's communicative action. Scripture also has other materials beyond direct divine speeches, even though the latter are essential. "Scripture contains genres which cannot be assimilated to the model of divine communication to men."[12] It includes human communicative actions toward God and others, as well as people's own reflection on their covenantal relationship with God (including some successful cases, but predominantly human failures) and general moral lessons and wisdom gleaned from human experiences in light of God's providence in the world.[13] In other words, Scripture includes both divine communicative actions and human responses to them. Scripture in itself is the faithful witness to the failures, confusions, and searching questions of humans toward God. The purpose of Scripture is not to provide scientific information or historical records but to help God's people to live a faithful, righteous life. Reading and studying Scripture is a spiritual practice in our covenantal relationship with God and others. By reading Scripture, Christians learn to follow the way of God in a deeper and more faithful way. The goal is to constantly edify, nurture, and sustain the faith of the community and its members as God's covenantal partners in their life journeys. In this sense, it is infallible in "matters of salvation and practice of faith," namely, in guiding us in our knowledge and fellowship with God.

A covenantal approach, marked by the idea of divine communicative action in particular, helps to keep a healthy distinction between divine authority and scriptural authority, which is a source of confusion among many evangelical Christians. Without undermining the uniqueness of Scripture, a covenantal approach shows that scriptural authority is not identical to divine authority. The words of the Bible and the Word of God are not identical. Barth says that Scripture becomes the Word of God when it points to and witnesses the true, only Word of God, Jesus Christ.

11. The Psalms constitute a preeminent example.

12. Barton, *People of the Book*, 36. This is how a covenantal approach is different from that of Karl Barth.

13. "Scripture is neither simply the recital of the acts of God nor merely a book of inert propositions. Scripture is rather composed of divine-human speech acts that, through what they say, accomplish several authoritative cognitive, spiritual and social functions." Vanhoozer, *First Theology*, 131.

"The Bible is God's Word to the extent that God causes it to be His Word, to the extent that He speaks through it."[14] As the eternal Logos was hidden in human Jesus, the light of divine truth was refracted through the lenses of human writers. Hence, Scripture is never infinite, perfect, absolute, or infallible in itself. Scripture is the Word of God as it is continuously used and relied upon as a means of God's communicative action to us. Scripture is also informative; it explains what God did in specific moral situations, and why.

How Do We Read Scripture Covenantally?

If God still speaks to us in a real way through the Bible, then how should we read it? What does a covenantal approach teach us about it? The three dialectics shed some insight here. Since the Bible is the covenantal document of the people of God—a gift for us—we need to read it with the trust that God still speaks to us through it. This means that we attentively and humbly listen to it through careful study, just as we carefully treat a gift from our ancestors. We respect the covenantal authority of the Bible as the rule of faith and believe that God is still speaking to us through it. As both the early Christians and we are members of the same covenant community, we listen to their communicative actions through the Bible. We approach the Bible with a critical attitude that even odd, strange, weird, and completely irrelevant laws should not be hastily discarded.[15] Furthermore, we read Scripture communally, communicatively (second dialectic), and analogically (third dialectic).

Communally

We could think of reading the Bible "communally" in several aspects. We read Scripture not privately but in the life of a faith community under the guidance of the triune God. Reading communally means that we read the Bible collaboratively in a faith community with the goal of edifying our lives—to increase the love of God and others, seeking the shalom of creation.

To read it together is important because God could speak through our brothers and sisters when we interpret the Bible together. God's communicative action through the Bible and human interpretive works are not necessarily mutually exclusive. God's communication does not have to be always supernatural. God's

14. Barth, *Church Dogmatics* I/1, 109.

15. One such example is Ellen Davis's agricultural reading of the OT, especially of the book of Leviticus; she engages it using the insights of agriculture and is very effective in elucidating and retrieving its ecological meanings and significance. See Ellen F. Davis, *Scripture, Culture, and Agriculture,* chap. 5.

voice is mostly heard in the prayerful, collaborative, interpretive process of a faith community.

To read the Bible communally means to respect the entirety of the Bible and its diverse voices and genres. The Bible records the diverse voices and experiences of God's people together with multidimensional aspects of covenantal life. It is a misunderstanding to believe that Scripture is seamlessly and systematically arranged as a coherent treatise of Christian doctrines and ethics. It is rather a collection of writings that include diverse genres—historical, literary, poetic, theological, narrative, liturgical—written by multiple authors who engage with varied issues and concerns raised in different historical and social contexts. Scholarly findings (various kinds of biblical criticism such as historical, form, redaction, etc.) show that multiple hands and processes contributed to its final form.[16] In other words, the Bible is intentional in its design in respecting its own diversity of voices, while maintaining an overall theological unity.[17] The diversity of literary genres and forms is not necessarily detrimental to the Christian life because they offer numerous, complex, multifaceted aspects of the divine and human reality in a mutually complementary manner.[18] Rather, it is beneficial for us that the Bible is internally rich and resourceful in addressing diverse theological and ethical issues that humans experience in different cultural contexts. Such diversity enables Christians to have a fuller picture of God and God's relationship with the world in order to live faithfully in various and changing situations. Daniel Migliore says fittingly: "The church should not ignore or collapse this literary diversity into an artificial unity any more than it should anxiously try to harmonize the theological differences in the scriptural witnesses between the Old and the New Testaments, between Paul and James, or between John and the Synoptics."[19]

16. The Bible is not a single uniform work; rather, it is a collection of various different writings composed by a variety of authors to meet various needs and inquiries that have arisen in their particular contexts. Throughout the years, many authors have modified, refined, or augmented these writings from various theological perspectives in order to serve God's people better.

17. However, this does not mean Scripture lacks any meaningful unity. Regarding unity and diversity of Scripture, Vanhoozer writes: "The Bible is both a unified (one *mythos*) and many-voiced (i.e., polyphonic) discourse whose form is theologically significant. As opposed to monologic epics—comprehensive stories told by an omniscient narrator with a single set of concepts and categories—the Bible communicates its theodramatic story dialogically. To speak of *mythos* is to remember both that there is a unifying plot and that no one voice, perspective, or set of categories alone articulates it. Rather, the divine playwright employs a plurality of human voices to communicate what he was doing in Christ to reconcile the world to himself." Vanhoozer, *Remythologizing Theology*, 26.

18. Migliore, *Faith Seeking Understanding*, 53.

19. Migliore, *Faith Seeking Understanding*, 53.

The unity also means that despite diverse voices in it, it retains theological unity in witnessing to God and God's economy. As a covenantal document, Scripture maintains its unity-in-diversity. This communal unity emphasizes that we need to embrace the entirety of Scripture and its diverse voices rather than being selective, because God could speak to us in a million different ways through Scripture. To read Scripture in the unity-in-diversity means to interpret each passage and each book, each story and each parable, each proverb and each law, in the context of the entire canon.

Communicatively

It is a challenging task to discern the authentic messages of God among the diverse voices and interpretations usually written inextricably with the particular cultural perception, bias, self-interest, and ideology of that writer.

A communicative process is necessary to the discernment because of the polyphonic nature of Scripture. To read the Bible communicatively is to read critically and dialogically with the historical and literary sensitivity to diverse genres and forms of the Bible. To read communicatively is also to pay close attention to the historical, cultural, and social contexts where particular biblical literatures were written.

A covenantal approach welcomes diverse voices and creative imaginations in interpreting Scripture. Diverse voices can clarify and complement each other in offering a fuller picture of God and God's relationship with the world. By inviting diverse voices and interpretive visions, we may retrieve the forgotten or suppressed messages of Scripture and ascertain a deeper meaning and better articulation of the various texts of the Bible. Through communicative reading, the meanings of norms, values, and rules can be further clarified and discovered.

Reading the Bible communicatively means mutually testing and edifying one another when Christians interpret the Bible. Our biblical interpretation is never neutral. We use a hermeneutics both of trust and of suspicion, of yielding and of assertion, in the process of seeking a more proper, valid, and relevant meaning of the Bible. Each reader inevitably brings in a personal interest, experience, and assumptions to reading the Bible. There is a definite need for mutual discernment and testing through mutual listening and scrutiny among the members of a community in order to come to a better, deeper understanding of God's will for us.[20]

20. A communal-communicative reading is necessary because God's extrabiblical communication takes several different forms: direct, indirect, verbal, and nonverbal. Cf. Dulles, *Models of Revelation*. This approach also applies to our interpretation of Christian tradition.

At the same time, to read the Bible communicatively is to read with a sense of accountability. The meaning does not reside in the texts per se but arises out of the reader's communicative encounter with the triune God through the text. Meaning in Scripture is neither completely propositional, intratextual, nor subjective, but intersubjective and performative. This means that by reading the Bible we are held accountable to the message that we receive through it.

Analogically

It has been a challenging task for the church to apply the gospel to new ethical questions that the Bible does not address. Sometimes the incorporation of new members (e.g., gentiles) requires new theological work within a faith community; at other times new technological advancements, structural changes, and challenges of ideologies demand a response of that faith community. The first Jerusalem Council was such an example (Acts 15; Gal. 2).

Analogical imagination is necessary to bridge the gap between the biblical text and our particular cultural context.[21] Scripture does not provide Christians with all the rules and directives for the Christian life, although it is rich with narratives, norms, values, and wisdom. Even in a covenant relationship, all entailing or implied covenantal obligations cannot be completely specified in advance. Richard Hays's observation on NT ethics is helpful for understanding the necessity of analogical imagination in Christian moral reasoning: "We have here no system of commandments. The rules are exemplary not comprehensive, pointers to the kind of life expected in the community, but not a map of acceptable behavior. Still less does Matthew's Jesus state philosophical principles from which guidelines for behavior could be rationally derived. We are left with the puzzle that while Jesus plays the role of a conventional sage in Matthew, his teachings recorded here do not add up to an ethical system. It is not in such a program of teaching, apparently, that Matthew understands the will of God to be discovered."[22] Analogical imagination is central to the Bible, as its practice is found in many parts of the Bible. Scripture, specifically the four Gospels, discloses how different Christian communities in different histor-

21. For the detailed discussion of analogical imagination, see Spohn, *Go and Do Likewise*, chap. 3. The gap between the two worlds does not mean that they are completely alien to each other. Despite the gap, there can be some overlapping moral concerns, problems, and issues found across different historical times and contexts as believers attempt to live as God's people. Furthermore, humans throughout history remain human in this sense: they share certain identical or similar needs and desires despite different cultural manifestations, historical nuances, and hermeneutical practices in meeting and fulfilling these needs and desires.

22. Hays, *Moral Vision*, 98.

ical and cultural contexts differently appropriated the story of Jesus's life, ministry, death, and resurrection.

Biblical writers in many different places appeal to the analogical imagination of their readers, rather than giving their own direct answers; they invite the readers to reflect upon the events of the past in the context of the readers' own relationship with the covenantal God in anticipation of God's promised future, including what the event means for their covenantal relationship with God, and how they are to exercise their moral perceptions in the face of various dangers, temptations, and opportunities. Jesus also relied on analogical imagination for his covenantal renewal in bridging the gap between the OT (Sinai covenant) and his ministry. In preaching the parables, Jesus appeals to the analogical imagination of his audience. After telling the parable of the good Samaritan to the lawyer, Jesus told him, "Go and do likewise" (Luke 10:37).

To read the Bible using analogical imagination is to exercise "ruled creativity," that is, to read it both faithfully and contextually. To be faithful is to be truthful to the intention of the author. To read contextually is to be attentive to the circumstances or settings where Scripture was written and where it is interpreted today. That is, context includes both that of the biblical authors and our own. To exercise analogical imagination does not mean to blindly replicate the biblical authors' situations but to seek the analogical correlation between their worlds and ours through the appropriate study of the respective contexts in interpreting the biblical authors' words. That is, we study the authors' intentions in the Bible—what they attempt to do with their words (reports, witnesses, proclamations, storytelling, and moral claims) against their historical, cultural, and social contexts, and then explore what their words analogously mean for us today.

Covenant helps to elucidate the analogical nature of biblical hermeneutics. To read Scripture analogically is to interpret it today by using a covenantal imagination. As mentioned in chapter 3, covenant has a built-in analogical structure as the dialectic of memory-hope (promise-fulfillment) displays. The Bible is the book of memory and hope for the people of God; it is the record of God's past, dramatic acts of deliverance and the promise of their future fulfillment. While the canon is closed, the work of the triune God is not finished but continues through the Christian community in the power of the Spirit. God's past communicative action offers the anchor for our interpretation of Scripture, while God's future promises give us the vision and horizon for reading Scripture. The prime analogues in analogical imagination are the triune God, core biblical convictions, and norms/values embodied in the covenant of Jesus.

In the framework of new covenant ethics, analogical imagination is not individualistic, but the shared work of a community; the fruits of analogical imagination must be tested by a community. Furthermore, analogical imagination is not a purely human effort; in it, we read Scripture to listen to what God speaks to us today. The Spirit works through our analogical imagination by using the multifarious and multidimensional aspects of metaphors, parables, and stories in the Bible in communicating God's will to us today in a particular situation. Under the guidance of the Spirit, analogical imagination may lead us to find new and deeper meanings of the text and to retrieve Scripture's forgotten or suppressed messages.

Reading the Bible for Ethics: Suggestions

The discussion so far has been theological and theoretical, seeking a proper way to orient an interpretive posture on the covenantal basis and communicative nature of scriptural authority. How should we read the Bible practically for Christian ethics? When we read the Bible to deal with controversial moral issues, such as capital punishment or abortion, we may ask the following questions step-by-step.

1. Does the Bible in fact speak about the issue in question? Related to this question, does the Bible speak to the same identical issue that you are dealing with or is it actually a different issue?

As mentioned above, the Bible is sometimes completely silent on certain moral issues of our time. We need to be careful because, although the issue may look similar, it may not be the same as the issue we are dealing with today.[23] If the Bible is silent on the issue, then we need to rely on an analogical approach to bridge the gap between Scripture and our time.

2. What do different passages say about the issue?

One should study a moral issue in the full range of the biblical teachings, not selectively according to a preconceived agenda or under the influence of a group ideology or personal self-interest. When there are multiple passages related to an issue, we may ask to discriminate the weightiness among them.

3. Is a particular passage given for a particular audience (individuals or church), or for Christians in general? That is, is the passage time- and context-bound, or universally (transhistorically) applicable?

23. Hollinger, *Choosing the Good*, 156.

One needs to pay close attention to historical, cultural, and social contexts, where a particular biblical text was written and to whom it was addressed. As Scripture is the record and vehicle of God's communication, such communication is always situated and mediated through a particular culture and history. God's words in Scripture are addressed to a particular person or a people in a particular time and space, although some laws and rules are timelessly relevant across diverse cultures. The specific contexts of God's actions cannot be disregarded, because God speaks to particular persons or people (e.g., Israel, Egypt, Edom, Babylon) in particular contexts. Some biblical teachings may have been taken for granted in the eras and cultural settings when they were written (thus their authority remained unquestioned), but they were substantially renewed/revised later, specifically in the covenantal renewal of Jesus, and are thus now irrelevant, even unacceptable. For example, biblical teachings on slavery, wars, genocide, violence, patriarchy, and sexist views of women cannot be accepted by the church today because they are contrary to God's compassionate, redeeming love revealed in Jesus Christ.

4. What is the author's intention in a text of biblical literature?

A biblical author's intentions need to be carefully analyzed and discerned in terms of the audiences and circumstances. Like God's communication, a biblical author is also situated in a particular time and space, and the author's frailty and historical limitations affect moral teachings and the author's interpretations of God's communication. To find the author's intention is important because it offers a certain objective (realist) ground for our analogical thinking.

5. If there are multiple passages on the same issue (e.g., killing, same-sex relationships, women's leadership), are these passages coherent, ambiguous, or conflicting among themselves in addressing the issue?

Because of the diversity in voices, forms, and contexts, the Bible is not free from internal inconsistencies and gaps in some places. Some biblical passages are contradictory or inconsistent about the same event or issue; for example, we see the incongruence between Jesus's prohibition of divorce (Matt. 5:31–32; 19:9; Mark 10:11–12) and Paul's qualified allowance of it (1 Cor. 7:10–11, 12–16). One has to acknowledge that the adjudication of different and conflicting voices of the Bible is a challenging concern. We can rely on a few processes to remove or reduce mistakes and fallacies. Processes 2 and 3 above are helpful in the discernment of a more plausible direction. In addition, we could examine the concerned texts in light of the covenantal drama of God climaxed in the covenant of Jesus Christ. This means that, as we discuss in chapter 10, the four levels of moral discernment (particular judgment → rules → norms/values → worldviews) are useful for our hermeneutical decisions. That is, we need to examine a particular passage not only in its literary context but also in relation to tested norms/values and worldviews, in particular the covenantal drama of the Bible and the covenant of Jesus.

The covenant of Jesus offers a discriminating framework on diverse interpretations of the Bible, on human moral experiences that are brought in for communal testing. When there is conflict or ambiguity surrounding the texts among Christians, they need to be examined in light of the covenant of Jesus to see which are more coherent with it. That is, on the passages or teachings that are intratextually confused, contradictory, or silent, the covenant of Jesus has the adjudicatory power and final say. The covenant of Jesus deserves the "hermeneutical and normative priority"[24] because it is God's final covenant—the decisive event of God's self-communication. As aforementioned, all God's promises point toward this covenant and are fulfilled in it. However, centrality or finality does not mean exclusivity. As the idea of "fulfillment" (Matt. 5:17) indicates, apart from other stories in the Bible, the full significance, meaning, and implications of the covenant of Jesus cannot be fully comprehended.[25]

6. What are the directly relevant, most adequate, or most relevant biblical passages for the issue under discussion?

Some practices and teachings of the Bible look very foreign, troublesome, or even outrageous to our sentiment. But we should not rush to judgment. It is important to distinguish the authority of Scripture from the authorizations that it gives for particular moral judgments and decisions on a specific issue. Even if we may recognize the authority of Scripture for ethics, it is a different question whether it authorizes direct judgments on other subjects, for example, history and science.

The Bible cannot be taken lightly, but neither should all its passages be considered equally important or time-transcendent. Despite its authority as the canon, not every part of the Bible has equal moral authority or weight. Some of God's commandments and laws are universal, thus binding all of humanity, while others are time-bound and culturally limited as they were addressed to a particular person or a community, and thus are not repeatable. For example, the Decalogue, the Golden Rule, and the Sermon on the Mount have perennial normative authority and relevance, but other biblical commandments and injunctions are limited in time and

24. Cf. Hollinger, *Choosing the Good*, 172.

25. Cf. Bauckham, "Scripture and Authority," 8.

space. To distinguish them is the task of Christian ethics, and a covenantal approach offers a reasonable and reliable method to carry out this task.

For some readers, these hermeneutical questions may sound overly burdensome and complicated, but they are not new. Christian communities, including the early churches, have always wrestled with these questions because the stakes are too high for a hasty, careless interpretation. As the Bible is sacred canon, we need to interpret and use it with care, attentiveness, and openness. It becomes the living word through the Christian community's ongoing proclamation and practices wrought out of its covenantal commitment. Without ongoing communal readings, prayerful investigations, and new interpretations, the Bible fails to become a living document and cannot touch the actual lives of people.

Summary

The above discussion shows that the authority of the Bible (*sola Scriptura*) is far from a simple question, and that to properly read the Bible is not an easy task. Rather, it requires certain knowledge and hermeneutical skill. Scripture's authority is neither primarily propositional nor cultural-linguistic, but covenantal and communicative. Rather than treating the Bible as a rule book providing prooftexts for specific issues, a covenantal approach emphasizes the interpretive, communicative, and analogical nature of the Christian approach to the authority of the Bible. A covenantal approach offers some helpful clarifications on difficult questions around the authority of Scripture—the unity and diversity of Scripture, the gap between the text and the context, and priority among conflicting passages.

A covenantal approach avoids the pitfalls of narrow biblicism (which claims that Scripture represents a set of universal propositional truths that correspond to an unchanging state of affairs) and postmodern deconstructionism (which claims that scriptural meaning is any reader's free choice and personal interpretation). The reigning ethos of Scripture is neither literalism (biblicism) nor liberalism (social constructionism), neither objectivism nor subjectivism, but rather critical realism[26] that works through a communal, communicative, and analogical interpretation of the Bible. While biblicists confuse the authority of the Bible for the triune God,[27]

26. Critical realism is a form of epistemology that acknowledges referential values of the reality as well as historical and cultural conditioning of human knowledge. It relies on a communicative or an intersubjective notion of rationality to discern truth and morality.

27. The problem of a biblicist interpretation is that it treats the Bible as if once God spoke or acted in the past, then God retreated and resigned from history, leaving the Bible for us. This attitude verges on another form of deism or bibliolatry, as the Bible functionally replaces God.

and while postmodernists reduce the authority of the Bible to the custom and tradition of a religious community, a covenantal approach takes God's ongoing communicative action as objective reality (albeit one not completely transparent to our eyes) and communally and communicatively discerns it through intersubjective discernment within a Christian community.

Scripture and Other Normative Sources

Scripture has a unique, final authority, but it is not the only authority relevant for Christian ethics. It is foundational but not exhaustive in Christian ethics, just as the revelation of God in Jesus Christ is decisive and central for knowing who God is and what God does in history, without being exhaustive. Although Scripture is the unique and primary instrument of God's communication to humanity, God's communication is not limited to it either (Ps. 19). Nor has God's communication ceased with the completion of the canon; God has been continuously speaking to humanity using sources other than the Bible.

Scripture does not exhaust all the moral wisdom in the world. In addition, the desire to seek reliable and authentic moral truth and knowledge is found among non-Christians as well, by virtue of God's common grace operating in the world. That is, some form of natural law, wisdom, and common moral sentiments is found in every society, and Scripture itself affirms their roles and moral authority.[28]

Throughout church history, Christians have relied on sources other than the Bible, because the Bible does not speak of new social issues they have faced. To address the questions on which the Bible is silent or limited, Christian communities in the past have developed additional, supplementary guidance in dealing with challenging moral issues of their times. Even today, it is inevitable that we rely on additional moral authorities such as church tradition, reason, and experience, in conjunction with the Bible.

In the following section we study tradition, experience, and reason as the three auxiliary moral sources of Christian ethics. They too can be used as a means of the communicative power of the Spirit. They are necessary for Christian analogical imagination in discerning, affirming, and recontextualizing the truth of Scripture in new and changing contexts. Among them, reason and experience are important for building a common moral ground with non-Christians.

28. The relationship between the Bible and experience/reason is analogous to that of special revelation and general revelation (salvific grace and common grace), the covenant of Jesus and the creation covenant/Noachian covenant.

Tradition

Every major religion has a tradition developed and passed down over many generations in the form of shared words, documents, wisdom, and practices. In Christian history, tradition, along with the Bible, has served as an important moral source for Christians. Tradition literally means "what had been handed down to us." It is the product of a tradition-forming process in a Christian community. Tradition forming is indispensable for the Christian life; Christians have always found themselves compelled to seek God's will and read the Bible anew in different historical and cultural contexts. It should be noted that the gospel stories and the letters of the apostles had existed as "tradition" (the apostolic tradition) before the canonization of Scripture. The Bible itself includes multiple traditions (JEDP, Deuteronomic, wisdom, prophetic, apocalyptic, Pauline, Johannine, Petrine, etc.).

Tradition forming is a creative process. A Christian community does not mechanically repeat what has been passed down to it. Tradition develops in a process through which a Christian community adapts to new, changing situations, through the reinterpretation of the Bible and previous tradition and the incorporation of new elements (symbols, ideas, values, practices) from its environment. [29] For example, the influx of new members from different cultures (e.g., inclusion of the gentiles in the early church), new technological advancements, major societal changes such as modernization and globalization, and the rise of new philosophies and ideologies (e.g., Neoplatonism, Aristotelianism, existentialism, Marxism, postmodernism) call for a theological and moral response from a Christian community. The tradition-forming process typically includes retrieval of suppressed or forgotten symbols, creative reinterpretation of conventional ideas and concepts, or the introduction of new ideas.[30] Normative documents of Christianity (creeds and confessions) are the products of the churches' communal-communicative dialogue and analogical imagination in the face of changing cultural contexts and new ideological and material forces.

This means that tradition forming is a crucial part of the meaning-making process of a faith community in order to find new ways to make sense of their faith in a changing social situation. Successful tradition forming expands and deepens the moral imagination and authority of the church by generating new vitality and

29. According to Lesslie Newbigin, tradition develops sometimes by gradual adjustments, sometimes by radical changes, that is, through "paradigm shifts." Newbigin, *The Gospel in a Pluralist Society*, 46.

30. For example, black and Latin American liberation theologies appropriated Marxist ideas of social location and ideology, while process theology borrowed from Alfred North Whitehead's process philosophy.

renewal in a faith community. When a faith community neglects listening to its tradition, then the original teachings are reified or become irrelevant to new situations, thus compromising or losing their moral authority. Jaroslav Pelikan's comment captures the promise and risk of tradition forming: "Tradition is the living faith of the dead, while traditionalism is the dead faith of the living. Tradition lives in conversation with the past, while remembering where we are and when we are and that it is we who have to decide. Traditionalism supposes that nothing should ever be done for the first time, so all that is needed to solve any problem is to arrive at the supposedly unanimous testimony of this homogenized tradition."[31]

Tradition holds a moral authority over Christians because it is the deposit of a faith community's wisdom gleaned from a long deliberative process. After the completion of the canonization process, tradition usually means time-honored creeds, doctrines, and practices whose roots go back to the apostles and early churches. It includes both ecumenical and local forms—ancient ecumenical creeds that all Christians share (the church universal), the patristic and medieval literatures, the writings of the Reformers, and confessions and established practices of particular faith communities and denominations[32] (Catholic, Protestant, Anabaptist, liberationist, European, Native American, African American, Asian American, Latinx, feminist, etc.). These traditions represent diverse Christian communities' rich understandings and experiences of God in different life situations and social contexts. With distinctive theological and moral emphases and sets of values, beliefs, and moral practices, each tradition offers a distinctive interpretive lens for understanding God, the world, and the Bible. By setting the parameters in interpreting the Bible and prioritizing theological beliefs, moral values, and practices, each tradition deeply shapes the spiritual life, moral outlook, and interpretive lens of its members.

Tradition carries in it the record of previous generations' wrestling with the meaning and message of the gospel. From a covenantal perspective, it is the product of their attempts to live out covenantal fidelity in their own distinctive contexts. Tradition is part of a contextualized covenant. It shows how past generations of Christians have communicatively engaged with the gospel and their contexts in journeying from memory to hope. The transmission and reception of tradition always occur through human interpretations in particular cultural contexts. Hence, tradition needs to be contextually understood, just as we do with the Bible.

Because of the growing gap between the biblical era and our own time, tradition plays a more important role today in guiding Christians in their moral decisions and in enriching their moral knowledge of God. In an important way, tradition comple-

31. Pelikan, "Christianity as an Enfolding Circle," 57.

32. Hays, *Moral Vision*, 210.

ments Scripture and expands its applicative realms. Anchored in the Bible, tradition extends the moral universe and authority of the Bible to new times and contexts. As it is dependent on the Bible, its authority is not equal to that of the Bible. Nevertheless, it exercises a formative influence upon believers. Hence, it is accurate to say that while Scripture is *norma normans* ("the norming norm"), tradition is *norma normata* ("the normed norm").[33]

A covenantal approach is useful for analyzing and properly understanding the process of forming tradition. Christians attribute moral authority to tradition because they believe that tradition is part of the ongoing divine-human communication in Jesus Christ through the Spirit. Tradition is a product of the living covenantal relationship of past generations of Christians. The triune God, who was with Jesus and the apostles, was also present and communicating with the succeeding Christian communities throughout history.

In the Bible, covenant renewal frequently served as a community's crucial vehicle of tradition forming. We see examples of this in Deuteronomy, Joshua, the prophets, and in Jesus himself.[34] A covenant renewal was a collective work of a faith community to renew its covenantal pledges in a new, changing context. A successful covenantal renewal brought about the reinvigoration of a community's identity, deepening a shared sense of moral commitment and purpose.

The process of tradition forming is communicative and analogical. Tradition forming relies, implicitly or explicitly, upon processes similar or equivalent to covenanting. Its process is parallel to the way Scripture was formed, developed, and canonized. In early Christian history, the development of Christian traditions relied on various councils in addressing new theological questions and moral challenges. Protestant churches also issued confessions to speak to various contexts with fresh relevance. These councils and confessions used covenantal processes, relying on communicative actions and exchange of arguments in seeking agreements and decisions. Coming to an agreement, they obtained normative force.

As already mentioned, tradition forming is an integral part of a covenantal life. The third dialectic of the covenant describes how tradition forming occurs in a faith community. It takes place in the matrix of memory-hope as a faith community exercises collective analogical imagination in seeking ruled creativity.

New covenant ethics takes an open and critical posture toward inherited traditions. Through communicative examination of a Christian community, we need to discern what is vital and essential, and relevant from what is merely passed down, as

33. Hays, *Moral Vision*, 210.

34. One sees several examples of covenantal renewals recorded in Scripture (Josh. 24:25; 1 Sam. 12; 2 Kings 23:1–3). The renewal in Deut. 28–30 was made in the land of Moab, prior to the entry into the land, a covenant that seems to be a renewal of the former, and similar in character. See also the prayer in Neh. 9:6–10:39; Ps 78. McConville, "בְּרִית," 750.

well as distinguish what is consistent or incompatible with our covenantal relationship with God and others. In doing this we also participate in the tradition-forming process and contribute to the enrichment of our traditions. Like many previous generations of God's people, contemporary Christians are tasked with making our tradition a living tradition, further developing and refining it before we pass it on to the next generation. Through successful tradition forming, the gospel is freshly interpreted and the covenantal drama continues to expand in history. The normative power of a new tradition depends on how creative and faithful it is.

In our current context, each faith community needs to be self-aware and self-critical of its own tradition in relation to other traditions, remaining open to mutual learning for the enriching and refining of its own tradition. Each community could grow richer and more capacious through active mutual learning and conversations. Christian faith can be strengthened through encounters with the past faithful witnesses of diverse Christian communities. Traditions need to be learned and tested. Careful examination and communicative discernment are necessary.

Experience

Experience is the product of the sensed perception of the world. Sense perception is biological and social in nature. It is an indispensable aspect of the embodied nature of human life in history. Sense perception is an innately embodied process that takes place in a social context.[35] There is no pure social experience but only an interpreted one. A cultural tradition offers an interpretive lens for people to construct meaning out of their experiences of the world.

New covenant ethics does not disregard the role of experience in ethical reasoning. The Bible confirms the normative potential of human experience as both spiritual and sociological.[36] Spiritual experience is a powerful evidence of God's ongoing communicative action through the Word and the Spirit. The Bible records a wide variety of spiritual experiences, including the collective experience of the communicative power of the Spirit at Pentecost (Acts 2). Richard Hays says: "[Religious experience] serves not only to illuminate the meaning of the text but also to confirm the testimony of Scripture in the hearts and lives of the community. This is what the tradition calls '*testimonium internum Spiritus Sancti*.'"[37] Similarly, the apostle Peter's encounter with Cornelius (Acts 10), which was the result of God's communicative action, led to the reconstitution of membership within the Christian community. As we saw in the Azusa Street Revival in 1906, a strong religious experience could create a new

35. Morgan, *The Embodied Eye*, xvii.

36. Wesley's understanding of experience was more spiritual than sociological.

37. Hays, *Moral Vision*, 211.

religious tradition and restore egalitarianism among its participants. Spiritual experience, when authentic, gives immediacy to God's communicative action and support for the core moral teachings of the Bible. However, no matter what its supernatural origin may be, experience cannot claim direct normative status in the interpretation of the Bible until it is validated by the wider faith community[38] through rigorous communicative engagements. This is because not every spiritual experience is from God: "Beloved, do not believe every spirit, but test the spirits to see whether they are from God; for many false prophets have gone out into the world" (1 John 4:1).

As we see in the book of Proverbs, humans have some shared moral experiences and wisdom across diverse cultures and societies. A theological basis of such authority is God's creation covenant and the Noachian covenant. God's presence in history is beyond the walls of a faith community, as God still speaks and acts in history. God's common grace leads humans to find moral meanings and lessons through their experiences. However, as with spiritual experience, not all everyday moral experiences are normative. Experiences become normative when they are tested and validated by a wide faith community in light of the core theological convictions and norms of the Bible.

Today, collective social experiences by marginalized groups (race, ethnicity, gender) have become important sources for Christian ethics. Collective experiences of racism, sexism, and classism reveal certain discernible structural patterns of domination and marginalization. They offer reliable empirical data in understanding racism, sexism, and classism, which goes beyond personal experiences. On the basis of this pattern, feminists, womanists, and other liberation theologians claim that Scripture is not free from social privilege and biases of sex/gender, race, and class domination. Their research shows that the liberating message of the Bible was stifled or distorted by the power and privilege of a dominant group. To hear its liberating message, the Bible itself needs to be carefully studied in its historical context to be free from the pattern of patriarchy, racism, and other biases.

At the same time, normative claims of common experiences could also be very controversial, as we see in the debates around sexuality and gender justice: whether the experiences of sex/gender–marginalized groups (LGBTQ) should be a new norm in interpreting the Bible and Christian traditions, even when they appear not to be consistent with the coherent sexual ethics of the Bible. This is an extremely difficult challenge, which we will discuss in chapter 13 in detail.

New covenant ethics recognizes the normative potential of diverse social experiences; they can assist in finding new, deeper meanings of human moral life and retrieve forgotten or suppressed messages in Scripture. However, their normative claims should be redeemed through the deliberative process of communicative rea-

38. Hays, *Moral Vision*, 211.

soning in a faith community. Sociological patterns that good social scientific research provides can be valuable resources for the Christian task of communicative action, just peacemaking, community organizing, and nonviolent action. They also can help churches to freshly and liberatively understand the Bible and tradition, to discern and fight against the patterns of injustice and exploitation, and to move toward reconciliation and shalom.

Reason

Scripture encourages a good use of reason (e.g., wisdom literature) in discerning truth from lie, right from wrong, good from bad, fitting from unfitting. Reason may not transform our hearts, but it does help us to repudiate nonsense, fanaticism, fantasies, and deceptions. While limited, it is God's gift; it still can provide some insights for understanding moral life, as it does with physical and social realities. Humans obtain and organize knowledge and information by using reason. Reason helps to identify a certain tangible pattern arising from the observation of experiences and empirical realities. Its proper use provides clarity, comprehensibility, and coherence to our understanding. The advance of human civilization would not have been possible without use of reason. Physics, anthropology, psychology, and social sciences are the result of human use of reason. Using reason, humans have been able to discover the physical laws of the universe in a logical way.

Reason plays an important role in Christian moral assessment and in adjudication between conflicting or competing biblical interpretations and theological and moral claims. Christian theological reflection and ethical discernment are rational (reasoned) activities of Christians. Ethics as a moral science relies on reason in discerning right, good, and fittingness in our moral life. Reason helps to bring clarity and coherence to biblical interpretation, theological reflection, empirical analysis, and moral deliberation. By relying on reason, we weigh which interpretation or claim is more faithful to Scripture, which analysis is more relevant to a given issue, and which moral claim is more cogent than others. Without relying on reason, our moral discernment and discourse could be speculative (baseless) or arbitrary (incoherent).

Moral philosophy is a scientific discipline that studies the meaning and validity of various moral claims using rational analysis and reflection. It serves as a valuable source for our moral life by providing insights on human nature, our collective moral life, the nature of morality, and philosophical analysis of various moral notions (e.g., freedom, justice, good, right, desire, affection, rationality, etc.).

Moral philosophy has diverse intellectual traditions, each of which has its own distinctive coherent view of moral right and good. In the West, natural law, utilitarianism, Kantianism, libertarianism, social contract theory, Aristotelianism, and Marxism have achieved their status as influential moral traditions. With their appeal to human reason and experiences, these philosophies have had a profound impact on public policies as well as on Christian moral understandings.[39] Similarly, the moral philosophies of other religious traditions, such as Jewish, Islamic, Confucian, Hindu, and Buddhist traditions, are also important conversation partners and moral resources for Christians. Christian moral understanding is expanded and enriched through critical appropriation of moral philosophies, as it is with insightful social experiences.

New covenant ethics is willing to engage with various moral philosophies of the past and present and learn from their insights, analyses, and reflections on human moral experiences in diverse cultural contexts. However, it is critical of the claim of objectivity and universal authority that some moral philosophies make. Reason is far from neutral. It is part of a social process where humans interact with their environments. Its exercise is always influenced by a social location and a particular culture. In this sense, reason is never independent of experiences.

Instead of the Enlightenment's foundationalistic understanding of reason, new covenant ethics relies on a communicative theory of reason. Communicative reason is critical, intersubjective, and dialogical (second dialectic); it does not offer an unmediated, God's-eye view of moral realities. It calls into question the claim that reason has an intuitive or self-transcending power to immediately know the requirement of moral duty. Communicative reason also rejects the postmodern assertion that reduces human moral epistemology to historical contingency and social constructionism.

A communicative concept of rationality is neither foundationalistic nor relativistic, but critical-realistic. While it acknowledges the contextual nature of human moral reflection and knowledge, it does not assume that morality is completely socially constructive. Because of God's ongoing self-communication in history and the binding power of the Noachian covenant, a certain objective moral reality exists, even though no human has an immediate, direct access to or complete knowledge of it. New covenant ethics seeks a relatively reliable knowledge of morality through collective discernment by free, unrestrained mutual testing of moral claims and philosophies, to discern whether they are valid, justifiable, and congruent with the core norms/values and basic convictions of the Christian faith.

Conclusion: Relationship of the Four Sources

The four sources of Scripture, tradition, experience, and reason are not mutually exclusive but are interrelated in the practices of Christian ethical discernment and action. However, not all have equal authority. The Bible has the highest authority, followed by tradition, as these two sources offer more explicit knowledge of God's

39. Marshall, *Beyond Retribution*, 6.

intentions and commandments. Thus, they offer more direct moral guidance for Christians. Among the four sources, Scripture is the "norming norm" of Christian ethics. This does not mean we ought to overlook the other sources. Christians confess that God is the author of morality, whose moral demands are known through diverse sources. Scripture is central, but it is complemented by the other sources. All four sources are necessary for better discerning God's will in dealing with concrete moral issues and situations. Scripture itself acknowledges a possible constructive role of reason, experience, and the operation of tradition in human moral life. In terms of moral knowledge, we have to acknowledge that our tradition, reason, and experience already mediate our interpretation of Scripture.

A covenantal approach offers a constructive and plausible understanding of the authority of the Bible and its relationships with the other sources (tradition, experience, reason). It presents the respective authority of each source in a sensible and balanced way. Avoiding hermeneutical reductionism and individualism, new covenant ethics clarifies a distinctive but collaborative, complementary relationship among the four sources, with the Bible at the center. The moral sources are engaged, filtered, and transvalued in the context of God's covenant in Jesus Christ.

One of the reasons that Scripture and tradition are more authoritative than reason and experience is that they have already obtained their normative status through communicative tests and examinations in certain, if not all, faith communities. Social experience and moral philosophies do not offer explicit knowledge of God's intention for our moral life. However, they always have such a possibility through a covenantal ratification of a faith community. Through communicative screening in a Christian community, some of their claims may obtain normative status and be incorporated into a tradition. Therefore, the relationship of the four sources is dialectic and symbiotic. Covenant ethics allows the expansion of Scripture's moral imagination in conversation with the three other sources.

The four sources are not absolute in themselves. Only the triune God is the final authority. The four sources find their mutual testing and illumination in the covenant of Jesus. As the climax of God's covenantal drama, the covenant of Jesus is the peak of Scripture that brings these four sources together for the discernment of God's will for the rich and faithful Christian life, for justice, and for the shalom of creation. Through communicative reasoning and analogical imagination taking place in the context of the covenant of Jesus, Christians critically screen, engage, harmonize, and expand the moral horizon and relevance of these sources for a deeper knowledge of God and growth in faithful Christian witness.

CHAPTER 10

Ethical Reasoning

> I appeal to you therefore, brothers and sisters, by the mercies of God, to present your bodies as a living sacrifice, holy and acceptable to God, which is your spiritual worship. Do not be conformed to this world, but be transformed by the renewing of your minds, so that you may discern what is the will of God—what is good and acceptable and perfect.
>
> —Romans 12:1–2

One major dilemma in ethical decision making is how to bridge the gap between ethical constancy (moral ideals, norms, values, rules) and ethical contingency (particular situations and changing human conditions)—a tension between the "ought" and the "is."[1] Knowledge of ideals, norms, and values does not always lend immediate or automatic answers to moral situations. An epistemological gap does exist, so moral obligations should be discerned carefully in every particular context in reference to ideals, norms, values, and rules. Ethical reasoning, termed "practical wisdom" or "prudence" in common parlance, is the process that harmonizes ethical constancy and contingency. It describes a deliberative process that a person or a community relies on in reaching an ethical decision. Ethical reasoning is also unavoidable for Christians because the knowledge of God's will is not something given once and for all.[2]

1. Gustafson, *Theology and Ethics*, chap. 5.

2. Bonhoeffer asks, "With every new day, therefore, the question arises, how, today, here, in this situation, can I remain and be preserved within this new life with God, with Jesus Christ." Bonhoeffer, *Ethics*, 323.

Ethical reasoning deals with the question of how to discern God's will in our own personal and social life. It relies on a certain ethical method. An ethical method concerns the validity of ethical reasoning: how people morally "authorize" or justify their decisions, relying on certain normative sources and processes. The discussion of an ethical method typically includes the question of why people uphold certain resources (e.g., religious documents, traditions, ideologies, experience, reason), rather than others, as normative or authoritative, how they engage these resources with specific ethical issues and situations, and whether their use (or application) of the resources and analysis of ethical issues is apt and valid according to intellectual clarity, logical coherence, and relevance.

A particular ethical method of Christian ethics can be tested in terms of its undergirding theological convictions, choice of norms/values and rules, validity of empirical analyses, logical consistency of moral reasoning and justification, and effectiveness for social change. A good ethical method is indispensable for faithful Christian discipleship because it helps to increase the clarity, coherence, and efficiency in our moral decisions and actions, while reducing errors and mistakes.

This chapter studies covenantal reasoning as the method of new covenant ethics, which is dialectical, analogical, communal, and communicative. It explores the questions: What is covenantal reasoning? How is it related to the triune God and the new covenant, and how does it operate?

Our discussions in previous chapters offer a good foundation for our discussion in this chapter (the adjudication of levels). Our discussion of "norm and context" in chapter 5 is directly relevant to ethical reasoning in new covenant ethics; the discussion of the moral authority of Scripture in the previous chapter, summed up in the section "Reading the Bible for Ethics: Suggestions" (the unity and diversity of moral perspectives in Scripture, the gap between the biblical worlds and our times, adjudicating and prioritizing the conflicting biblical passages, assessing the relevance of a particular text for a contemporary moral issue), is also immediately relevant to the topic of this chapter.

Ethical hermeneutics of the Bible is germane to ethical reasoning because Christians take the Bible as the primary and highest authority in ethical reasoning among the moral sources. The suggestion that we read Scripture covenantally (that is, communally, communicatively, and analogically) generally applies to ethical reasoning as well. While ethical reasoning considerably overlaps with an ethical hermeneutic of Scripture, it is larger than the latter; ethical reasoning engages the three other moral sources (tradition, experience, reason) in a more extensive manner and scope. Empirical analysis is an indispensable process of ethical reasoning, just as theology plays a more prominent role in ethical reasoning as it informs and shapes the worldview and basic convictions of Christians.

The stakes of good ethical reasoning are very high today. Good ethical reasoning is necessary to avoid the moral reductionism (legalism), moral relativism, emotionalism, and sensationalism that are spreading in our society on the shoulders of reified identity politics, postmodernism, populism, and disinformation and alternative facts, which contribute to political polarization, social divisions, and cultural conflicts. It is crucial for Christians to serve as the peacemakers of God's kingdom and salt and light in a society rather than aggravating the polarization, divisions, and conflicts.

Covenantal Reasoning

New covenant ethics takes covenantal reasoning as a core process of ethical discernment. To reason covenantally means to seek God's will communally, dialectically, analogically, and communicatively through mutual scrutiny, testing, and collaboration. As we mentioned in chapter 5, new covenant ethics does not consider ethical contingency (particular situations and changing human conditions) undesirable, but rather regards it as an inevitable aspect of human life in history. "The covenant is not a static relationship but one that requires constant renewal and affirmation."[3] Moral requirements and obligations cannot be completely specified in advance but need to be continuously discerned in new and changing contexts.[4] The third dialectic of covenant exhibits that our relationship with God is neither static nor enclosed in the past, but constantly unfolds in history as we walk with God and others.

Covenantal reasoning is an indispensable process in our attempt to live faithfully as God's people in changing social contexts. The immediate goal of covenantal reasoning is to make a right, good, and fitting moral decision, but its long-term goal is to promote God's shalom.

Characteristics of Covenantal Reasoning

Covenantal reasoning has the following characteristics:

1. Covenantal reasoning is Trinitarian in nature: it seeks God's will revealed in Jesus Christ today through communicative engagement with the Spirit. The three persons of the Trinity are involved in the process of ethical discernment. The complete congruence between ethical constancy and ethical contingency is possible at the eschaton only through the work of the triune God. For the triune God, there is

3. De Gruchy, *Reconciliation*, 187–88.

4. This is consistent with the basic insight of communicative action theory, that is, the meaning of a specific speech act is comprehensible only in the particular context where the speech act occurs.

no gap between ethical constancy and ethical contingency. Specifically, the incarnation of the Logos, fully God and fully human, shows perfect harmony between ethical constancy and ethical contingency.

Theologically speaking, covenantal reasoning presupposes the ongoing self-communication of the triune God in history, which is addressed to a particular person in a particular context. Jesus promised, "For where two or three are gathered in my name, I am there among them" (Matt. 18:20). Covenantal reasoning is a response to God's self-communication that takes place in the new covenant. In the reasoning, we ask: What is going on here? What is God saying to this issue or this situation, and what should be our response to God? Through covenantal reasoning, we attempt to attune to the triune God's communicative action; in the final analysis, covenantal reasoning is the process through which we participate in the triune God's communicative action.

In the process of discernment, the Spirit plays an important role. Acts 15:28 ("For it has seemed good to the Holy Spirit and to us") shows how the early church engaged in collective discernment in communication with the Spirit. The members prayerfully listened to the Spirit and each other in the belief that the Spirit is active in the process of collective reasoning.

The Spirit is the bearer of divine truth, the testifier of the Word, and God's living presence in us today. The Word enters every particular moral situation of history through the Spirit. The Spirit enables the reality of the Word to be enfleshed in particular contexts, in a manner analogous to the incarnation of the Son.[5] The communicative action of the Spirit does not have to be supernatural because the Spirit could work in various means—written and preached words, conscience, wisdom, and assertions and arguments of the participants. The community needs to be open to the prompting and illumination of the Spirit in every present moment. The inclusion of and openness to diverse perspectives and ideas are crucial because we never know how the Spirit will speak through the participants.

At the same time, every claim of revelation from the Spirit should be tested by the members for its authenticity and validity: "Beloved, do not believe every spirit, but test the spirits to see whether they are from God; for many false prophets have gone out into the world" (1 John 4:1). The rigorous deliberative process of a community cannot be replaced by miraculous signs or by the personal charisma or authority of a leader.

2. Covenantal reasoning occurs in the context of the new covenant of Jesus Christ, the sign of God's reconciliation and *koinōnia*. Overcoming enmity and alienation,

5. Because of the pneumatological nature, covenantal reasoning is not just rational and procedural but also enspirited, affectional, and formative.

God has reconciled with humanity in Jesus Christ. Jesus Christ is God's decisive, if not sole, self-communication. The covenant of Jesus, and the reconciliation it has achieved, becomes the basis of the Christian life and moral discernment. It is in and through the new covenant of Jesus Christ that God speaks to us in a decisive and authoritative way.[6] We cannot fully hear God's voice outside of this new reconciled reality.[7] Jakób Jocz observes: "God meets man within time and space, exactly where man is to be found in the dimension of history. But such a supposition can only be justified on the basis of the covenant, for otherwise it is left to accident or caprice whether God wills to reveal Himself or not."[8]

Bonhoeffer was a Christian ethicist who took God's reconciliation with the world in Jesus Christ as the "methodological starting point" of his *Ethics* and as the basis of the Christian life. He declared, "Discerning the will of God is possible only on the basis of knowing the will of God in Jesus Christ."[9] In this covenant, Christians hear the call of God, discern God's will, and make decisions for discipleship and social witnesses.

3. In the process of ethical reasoning, new covenant ethics critically draws upon the four sources of Christian ethics—Scripture, tradition, experience, and reason. As mentioned in the previous chapter, all four sources, with different degrees of authority, are useful for assisting in the discernment of God's will. Although Scripture is the primary instrument of God's communication to humanity, it is not limited to it (Ps. 19:1–4). Nor does it provide all the information necessary for our moral judgment; acquired experiences, accumulated wisdom, and moral understanding are all valuable for Christian moral discernment as well, helping to expand and refine our moral understanding and imagination. New covenant ethics approaches each of these sources communicatively (i.e., critically and dialogically). No source, including Scripture, is exempt from communicative scrutiny and appreciation in the context of God's covenant in Jesus Christ.

6. One may say that Christian ethical reasoning is analogous to the incarnation of Jesus Christ, fully God and fully human, by seeking an option that is fully divine and fully worldly, fulfilling the reality of God's reconciliation in Jesus Christ.

7. To take the new covenant as the matrix of discernment means that our daily fellowship with God constitutes the existential-epistemological context of our discernment. Discernment is not something that Christians do abruptly; it is part of our ongoing fellowship (communication) with God. Humbly walking with God in our daily life is likely to make our discernment easier and more faithful. Ethical reasoning requires the special attention of a community when the natural flow and rhythm of life are disrupted because of the invention of a new technology, the development of new medicine, or the eruption of a new incident that causes a moral disagreement or confusion within the community.

8. Jocz, *The Covenant*, 255.

9. Bonhoeffer, *Ethics*, 323.

4. The decision reached through covenantal reasoning is provisional in nature. It is not final but is open to future revision. In history, Christians are still on a pilgrimage, always on the way toward deeper knowledge and fellowship with God. They are in constant need of repentance, empowerment, and growth in God's grace but are empowered by the hope for the final consummation. The Reformed maxim of *ecclesia reformata semper reformanda* describes the necessity of the church's ongoing discernment, revision, and correction as the community seeking God's will.

Method

Covenantal reasoning in new covenant ethics relies on dialectical, analogical, communal, and communicative reasoning.

Dialectical

"Dialectical thinking refers to the ability to view issues from multiple perspectives and to arrive at the most economical and reasonable reconciliation of seemingly contradictory information and postures." Dialectical thinking, as a form of analytical reasoning, pursues knowledge and truth assuming that "seemingly opposing views of reality can be reconciled into a meaning more reasonable than either of the seemingly contradictory positions."[10]

Dialectical reasoning describes a synthetic approach that seeks the creative tension, proper balance, and productive harmony between apparently competing or contradictory concepts, or opposing truths (e.g., divine-human agency, freedom-solidarity). It is used in an intellectual attempt to overcome rigid binary or dualistic thinking and to bring a creative resolution to divided, fragmented, or partial perceptions of the reality.

Dialectical reasoning helps to avoid or reduce unnecessary confusion, ambiguity, potential conflicts, and moral reductionism. When successful, dialectical reasoning adds epistemological expanse/capaciousness, nuances, and problem-solving power to ethical understanding, as it helps conceptually organize previously discrete elements in a more intelligible and holistic manner.

In Christian theology, dialectical thinking has been widely used to explain the mystery and economy of the triune God: the transcendence and immanence, hiddenness and revelation, threeness and oneness of God; the already and the not-yet, time and eternity, nature and grace, and so on. It is equally indispensable to properly understand God's organizing work in history: covenant. Since Jesus reconciled God

10. Manzo, "Dialectical Thinking."

with creation in his covenantal body, there is no strict separation between the church and the world. Any binary dualistic thinking goes against this reconciled reality of God in Jesus. Through God's covenantal organizing, God dialectically integrates unity-diversity, freedom-solidarity, love-justice-power. The organic, dialectic nature of God's covenant is the manifestation of the organic, dialectic nature of the triune life *ad extra*.

Dialectical thinking is crucial in demonstrating the capaciousness of a metaphor or a paradigm in explaining the complex reality with nuances and necessary attentiveness. This book has extensively discussed the dialectical nature of covenant and its various manifestations in chapters 3, 4, and 5: unilateral-bilateral, communal-communicative, memory-hope (promise-fulfillment); the composite of love, justice, and power; the relationships of indicative-imperative, norm-context, identity-change, particularity-relevance, worship-ethics, and unity-diversity; and the sinfulness and the redemptive possibility of humanity. Chapter 8 has demonstrated that covenant maintains a healthy balance and harmony between the binary categories of freedom and solidarity, love and justice, self-love and other-love, fairness and generosity, and rights and responsibility.

New covenant ethics displays a rich dialectical reasoning; it illuminates the complex, dynamic, mysterious nature of God's being and action, and creatively balances and integrates in tension important theological motifs and norms/values in Christian ethics, all of which contribute to the enhanced clarity, intelligibility, and capaciousness of Christian ethical reasoning.

Analogical

Analogical imagination is integral to covenantal reasoning in bridging the gap between ethical constancy and ethical contingency. As mentioned in chapters 3 and 9, analogical imagination plays a critical role in the creative form of the Christian journey and in the use of the Bible, and it does so with ethical reasoning in new covenant ethics as well. God's people are called to respond to God's unfolding covenantal drama in a fresh and faithful way, and analogical reasoning is the method they use to discern God's will in their changing contexts.

Analogical reasoning is a deliberative process by which we seek what God's will is for us today in light of God's actions in the past; it is necessary to live faithfully in history.[11] This process is congruent with N. T. Wright's idea of a five-act play:

11. Samuel Wells's idea of improvisation is congruent with my idea of analogical reasoning in the covenant. According to him, our ethical life faces moments of improvisation that call for creativity on our part. Wells explains that as the pivoting of our learned moral tradition, improvi-

"The Christian story is a five-act play—creation, Israel, Jesus, church and eschaton. We find ourselves in Act 4, and the most important events have already happened. Our role is to be faithful through Act 4, because God will do the rest in Act 5."[12]

Knowing how God redemptively dealt with God's people in the past helps us to gauge how God would do so today. "Improvisers use narrative competence to keep the full story in mind as they respond to new offers in order to move the story forward effectively. One key story-making skill is the ability to reincorporate earlier material in order to provide both continuity and closure. Reincorporation is about bringing back past elements of the story into the present scene in order to form a unified drama. Improvisers also need to be attentive to what is happening in the moment, for the future is formed out of the past and present."[13]

The Catholic scholar William Spohn builds Christian ethics on analogical reasoning, taking the parable of the Good Samaritan as the prime example. He argues, "The basic command that Jesus gives at the end of the Good Samaritan story invites Christians to think analogically: 'Go and do likewise.' The term 'likewise' implies that Christians should be faithful to the story of Jesus yet creative in applying it to their context."[14] When Jesus says, "The kingdom of God is like . . . ," he invites us into analogical thinking and corresponding action. The parables of Jesus are invaluable in showing us who God is and how God acts in the world. As much as the parables are descriptive of what God's reign is like, how God decides and acts, they also invite the audience to respond in a way that is appropriate to the reign that unfolds before their eyes in Jesus Christ.[15]

Preachers, including even biblicists who insist on literal interpretations, always exercise some form of analogical imagination when they preach, usually in the name of application. The application of the message of the Bible to our current contexts always relies on a certain form of analogical imagination. Vanhoozer notes, "The key thing to our faithful journey is to understand what God is doing in Christ so well

---

sation is the work of two crucial moments—formation and decision. Given its connotation and nuance, his idea of improvisation seems more appropriate to a personal moral decision than to a community's. Samuel Wells, "Improvising Leadership."

12. Samuel Wells, "Improvising Leadership." See also N. T. Wright, "How Can the Bible Be Authoritative?"; N. T. Wright, *The New Testament and the People of God*, 140.

13. Vanhoozer, *Faith Speaking Understanding*, 194.

14. Spohn, *Go and Do Likewise*, 4.

15. Spohn's idea of analogical imagination works better when the covenantal basis of Christian ethics, Jesus's moral teachings, is specified. Spohn's analysis of Jesus's moral pedagogy reveals the covenantal nature of Jesus's ministry and proclamation (which, unfortunately, Spohn and many others fail to identify).

that one can participate fittingly in the action even when the setting and scenery look completely different."[16]

Analogical imagination is a creative embodiment of the covenant drama in a new social context. It is "keeping with what went before."[17] Analogical imagination can be compared to the pivoting of a basketball player—one foot anchored in God's fidelity, the other searching for the right new path. We are constantly doing moral pivoting in a changing world.

One potential threat of analogical imagination is the possibility of arbitrariness (e.g., allegorical thinking), subjectivism in interpretation and reasoning. Analogical imagination in the new covenant is not arbitrary in covenant because covenant has a built-in analogical structure through its pattern of memory-hope, and because covenant stipulates that Christian moral actions be analogical to God's actions, just as our character imitates God's character. God's character and actions (revealed in Scripture and the traditions of the church) serve as the lead analogues of the Christian life.

In particular, the covenantal drama and the three dialectics assist the analogical imagination by offering theological and moral parameters. In our exercise of analogical imagination, God's liberation and merciful acts of deliverance (healing, exorcism, forgiveness, etc.) serve as "the prime analogate" that displays a certain moral pattern to follow in discerning God's will in concrete circumstances. In other words, various covenantal patterns and the memory of God's deliverance, the hope for God's fulfillment, and the covenantal stipulations comprise the constants in the imagining process.

This redemptive memory helps us to see the pattern or paradigm of God's communicative actions in our own contexts. Similarly, God's promises and future hope also guide our analogical imagination, as we pursue God's shalom and attempt to translate it into today's terms. The covenant renewals show how covenant can be adaptive to new and changing contexts without losing its integrity.

Communal

Covenantal reasoning, because of the very nature of covenant as collaborative, is reciprocal and cooperative in its disposition to seek God's will. It operates under the commonsense assumption that the wisdom of many is better than the wisdom of one; humble, collaborative efforts help avoid or reduce mistakes in our decision making. The reasoning process includes collaborative searching, speaking, listening, arguing, and discerning.

16. Vanhoozer, *Faith Speaking Understanding*, 191.
17. Vanhoozer, *Faith Speaking Understanding*, 194.

This collaborative aspect grows and intensifies in the new covenant. God's love and reconciliation with humanity in Jesus, the communal dynamic of the covenant (second dialectic), constitute the basis and moral ecology of covenantal deliberation. This communal foundation and ethos are crucial as they orient and channel the thoughts and deliberations of the participants toward shalom, the fulfillment of covenant. As the new covenant is disposed toward care and mutual sharing—the life of *koinōnia*—covenantal reasoning embodies the same ethos, sharing of wisdom, knowledge, and mutual judgment for the common good of the community. On the basis of mutual trust and respect for truth, the participants present their ideas and claims in sincerity and truthfulness.

In their search for truth, the participants listen, assert and adjust their views in light of the views of others, and implement their decisions together. Without the conscious recognition and commitment to this communal foundation and telos, there is no guarantee that covenantal reasoning will be protected from the threats of contentiousness and divisiveness that are widespread in our society.

The communal values of mutual love, respect, solidarity, and humility play an important role in creating and keeping a trusted atmosphere in the reasoning process.

Communicative

New covenant ethics relies on the method of communicative reasoning, which takes place through a community's discursive engagement and deliberation. With its emphasis on the free, equal, and reciprocal exchanges among all concerned parties, communicative reasoning rejects elitism or authoritarianism in the reasoning process.

Communicative reasoning consists of a prudent, dialogical process of mutual examination and assessment of empirical data and diverse moral claims presented to the participants. Mutual testing and examination are necessary for several reasons:

1. God's moral demands on a specific moral issue are not self-evident in every case; God's will is not always immediately and unambiguously available to us. God continues to communicate to us, but often in a mysterious and hidden way. The Word may come to us in disguised forms, as it has previously. The Spirit communicates with us in a myriad of ways, using diverse media, both verbal and nonverbal.
2. Human perception of God's demands is always bound by a particular culture and history. There is always a possibility for misunderstanding; the apostle Paul admonishes: "Examine yourselves to see whether you are living in the faith. Test yourselves. Do you not realize that Jesus Christ is in you?—unless, indeed, you fail to meet the test!" (2 Cor. 13:5).

3. Communicative examination is necessary because of human fallibility and the historical ambiguity of human existence. Unlike divine self-communication, human communication is always imperfect and limited, susceptible to mistakes, deception, and manipulation. Likewise, human sin distorts human moral understanding and communication. Our moral decisions are affected by multiple nonmoral factors, such as self-desires and ambitions, political ideology, vested interests, social customs and mores, knowingly and unknowingly. Cultural ethos, which is embedded in social scripts, is one of these factors.[18]
4. Moreover, decisions are made under the constraints of time, energy, and resources. Moral arguments can be influenced by social mores, ideologies, personal preferences, and vested political or monetary interests, especially when the result of the decision affects an individual's or a group's self-interest.[19] Mutual collaboration and scrutiny are necessary to mitigate these threats and limitations. In the process of honest, open, and reciprocal communication, hidden interests, hegemony, egoism, and inequality are revealed and brought into mutual scrutiny, while shared concerns and interests are discovered and realigned.

New covenant ethics encourages the participation of all concerned members and invites their wisdom and insights into the process of deliberation. In God's covenant, every person has equal membership and opportunity, so every person's dignity and rights should be respected. Decision making should not be the privilege

18. A social script informally defines what is "normal," and individuals try to find out and measure whether their decisions and actions are "normal" by the standards of a social script. A social script is a form of narrative that reflects the prevailing ethos of a society. It exercises a social constraint (in the form of implicit pressure) against individuals who do not accept or follow it. It is a human tendency to go along with a script—not to ruffle any feathers. Ethos, unless continuously scrutinized, could operate as peer pressure and social censure. For example, current practices of sexual ethics (sexual norms and activities) reflect the social script of sex—what is accepted and what is not accepted among one's peers and culture in general.

19. Hollinger, *Choosing the Good*, 180–85. On the necessity for communicative critique within a Christian community, Gregory Jones writes: "Institutional structures serve to facilitate and enhance the development of a variety of Christian practices. However, such institutional structures, because they are concerned with goods which are both coveted and scarce (e.g., power, status, wealth), also have tremendous potential for corrupting practices and malforming people. Hence local congregations, because of their ties to institutional structures, are those Christian communities most likely to have well-developed practices and also to have those practices (and consequently their people) to be accommodated to standards and realities antithetical to Christian convictions." Gregory Jones, *Transformed Judgment*, 131–32.

of a leader or a few elites alone, but rather it belongs to all concerned people. In the reality of human frailty and brokenness, covenant ethics values collective wisdom over any individual charismatic judgment. Diverse voices should be welcomed and heard; God's symphony is always polyphonic. Diversity should not be considered a cause of adversity but rather a blessing that brings rich ideas and perspectives for understanding God's will and the moral issues under discussion.

In covenantal reasoning, moral authority lies in neither force nor power but in the cogency of arguments through the participation and contributions of all concerned parties. The participants attentively hear each other's arguments in order to discern God's voice speaking through one another. Through the process of mutual discernment, various claims and ideas are assessed, then corrected and improved, if needed. Insufficient evidence, faulty logic, and incomplete explanations are respectfully challenged, corrected, supplemented, or, if indefensible in the communal spirit, discarded.[20]

Critical-Realist Epistemology

In assessing various moral claims, new covenant ethics relies on a critical-realist epistemology.[21] As it is communicative, covenantal reasoning is neither dogmatic nor relativistic but critical-realistic. In other words, new covenant ethics rejects both an objectivism that denies the historical embeddedness and contextuality of our ethical understandings and decisions, and a subjectivism that rejects any referential value in our moral knowledge. Unlike the rationalistic ethics of the Enlightenment, it does not claim any epistemological privilege of direct access, or exact correspondence, to reality; rather, it humbly acknowledges that our moral understanding is embedded in concrete historical and social contexts, and therefore is inevitably influenced by our experiences and particular cultural traditions. This does not mean, however, that every moral claim is equally authoritative. For Christians, new covenant ethics claims that God's constant moral character, moral principles and laws, and self-communication of the Spirit in Jesus Christ offer the reliable grounds and criteria for moral adjudication and discernment.

In a critical-realist view of morality, ethical decisions are based on rational justification rather than supernatural claims or foundationalism. If being rational means giving a good, coherent account or rationale of one's moral choice or decision, then

20. Van Gelder, *The Ministry of the Missional Church*, 115.

21. "Covenantal epistemology is simply the divinely enabled recognition of reality as divinely constructed and regulated in relationship. It is neither antirational nor even suprarational, but the right use of reason in covenantal obedience." Horton, *Covenant and Eschatology*, 140. For a detailed discussion of a critical-realist epistemology, see Huyssteen, *Theology and the Justification of Faith*.

the participants in covenantal reasoning seek to offer the best plausible account of their understanding of God's moral demands regarding a specific moral issue. At the same time, God's moral demands are real, but they are always construed through a particular historical and cultural lens and under the pressures and limitations of time and energy. Hence their decision is provisional, not absolute, and thus open to further revision and improvement when a better claim and moral justification is offered.

Summary and Observation

Ethical reasoning in new covenant ethics is dialectical in nature, communicative in process, analogical in application, and communal in its spirit and posture. This multifaceted aspect of covenantal reasoning helps Christians be faithful, relevant, and transformative; dialectical reasoning helps remove or reduce moral ambiguity and confusion, and brings clarity and intelligibility on a moral issue; a collaborative process may help nurture mutual understanding and trust, thus strengthening the bond among the participants; the process of analogical imagination and communicative engagement may evoke new moral imaginations and creativity that renew their faith and identity and refresh their commitments. Together, they contribute to the prudence (practical wisdom) of Christian decision making. Fittingness is the operative concept of covenantal reasoning. To be fitting is to respond rightly and appropriately to God's communication in our particular situations. It is the fruit of the skilled exercise of dialectical, analogical, communal, and communicative reasoning.

Some might question whether this form of complex thinking is possible. My answer is yes. Martin Luther King Jr.'s movement was effective partly because he relied on a similar kind of multifaceted reasoning in formulating his idea of nonviolent action. Nonviolence was dialectic in that it avoided the extremes of violence (retaliation) and resignation (cowardice). Influenced by Georg Wilhelm Friedrich Hegel, a German philosopher, King was well-known for his dialectic thinking in moral discernment. He was communicative in testing the best strategies and options of moral actions without contradicting his convictions. King was analogical in creatively applying Jesus's Sermon on the Mount ("love your enemy"; do not retaliate) to nonviolent resistance against social injustices. King also developed concrete rules of actions ("the Ten Commandments of nonviolence"). This was also the exercise of practical wisdom (improvising) that he inherited from the African American moral tradition. This multifaceted nature of covenantal reasoning is useful for Christian social ethics, which we will study in part 2.

In the new covenant of Jesus, ethical reasoning is not merely human intellectual activity. The triune God helps our reasoning through the communicative action of the Spirit, who empowers us to be faithful to memory, open to God's future, and skillful in attending to our social situations. It encourages collaboration and grants wisdom to see a broad, complex reality.

Covenantal reasoning embraces the possibility of disagreement in the process of reasoning as well. Despite the best efforts of the participants, a moral agreement is not always guaranteed. Nevertheless, it strongly emphasizes civility among the participants. As mentioned earlier, new covenant ethics prioritizes a nonviolent, discursive, collaborative approach in addressing common problems. Even if an agreement is not reached, civility and tolerance in respecting differences and willingness to continue conversations are important for the future of a community. Resentment, sabotage, or vilifying one's opponents is not consistent with the communal spirit of the new covenant. Different views on a moral issue should not lead to distrust, resentment, or hatred. While agreement may not be reached, a reasoning process may help clarify the complexity of issues and assist in narrowing the gap among different moral perspectives.

Process of Discernment

Ethical reasoning in new covenant ethics takes place through three steps: analytic-descriptive, normative-evaluative, and prescriptive-actional. In all stages, judgments and discernments are made through the exchange of prudent ideas, information, and truth claims or normative claims. Participants test the suitability of a participant's claim regarding a concern or issue in terms of truth (factual or empirical), rightness, goodness, and fittingness.

Analytic-Descriptive: Empirical Facts

The first stage has to do with the analysis and description of empirical reality, such as various social conditions, material forces, and cultural forces that affect moral issues. The objective is to understand what is actually going on. Many Christians often think that moral decisions are made by simply applying relevant biblical rules and norms and teachings to an issue. However, every ethical decision involves judgment on the factual, empirical aspects of the issue. As Alan Geyer states, "Ethics is not simply an argument about what ought to be; it is an almost uninterrupted argument about what is, what has been, and what will be . . . whose reading of history . . . which social analysis . . . which intelligence date shall we choose as being empirically sound."[22] Dennis Hollinger also notes: "Often differences in ethical decisions are due to differ-

22. Geyer, "Toward an Ecumenical Political Ethics," 135.

ing accounts of what is happening in a given situation. The particular way we portray the reality may well determine, at least in part, the ethical outcome."[23] Hence, an ethical decision emanating from a lack of empirical analysis is misconceived from the beginning and is thus likely to be flawed.

To understand the empirical aspects of a moral issue, we analyze the issue by relying on the work of social and natural sciences. Social science studies the pattern and regularity of human behaviors and various types of social conditionings in order to gauge their trajectory into the future. It seeks to grasp, as precisely as possible, the underlying structure and hidden causal relationships behind repeating patterns of human behavior.[24]

The participants in ethical reasoning collect and examine the historical data, social scientific studies, and other information on the issue; they test the validity and relevance of the collected information and data.

Normative-Evaluative: Rightness, Goodness, Fittingness

The second task in ethical reasoning is evaluation. This task focuses on the assessment of the rules, norms/values, and theological convictions related to the issue. New covenant ethics seeks to identify and articulate the normative standards and values pertaining to the issue. The question it asks is: What *ought* to go on? That is, "whether what is going on ought to go on."[25]

In the process of assessing various moral claims and options, new covenant ethics draws upon the four moral sources: Scripture, tradition, experience, and reason, by engaging with these sources dialectically, analogically, communally, and communicatively and assessing their relevance in the context of God's covenant in Jesus Christ. The participants discuss which rules are relevant in the case under consideration. What consequence (or result) is desired and should be pursued? They mutually test the fittingness (appropriateness) of proposed rules and norms/values, and the interpretations of Scripture and doctrines.

Typically, human ethical judgment is made in reference to personal judgments, rules, and norms that are grounded in sets of basic convictions (informed by a particular worldview). These normative categories exercise different degrees of moral authority and thus form a hierarchal structure—with a worldview on top and per-

23. Hollinger, *Choosing the Good*, 175.

24. Holland and Henriott, *Social Analysis*, 11.

25. Stackhouse, "The Tasks of Theological Ethics," 99.

sonal judgments at the bottom, while rules and norms/values are in the middle.[26] Together they contribute to a deductive form of a reasoning process.

A careful study of their respective authorities (normative levels) is necessary to see how particular ethical reasoning takes place and how the adjudication among these levels happens in one's reasoning process. The study is critical to make ethical reasoning as self-critical, self-reflective, and objective as possible, avoiding emotivism, sensationalism, selfish interests, and biases.

The Particular Judgment Level

A moral judgment at this level reflects an individual's unique personal situation or concern. No moral justification needs to be provided for the moral judgment, and ethical reflection (the process to critically think about and assess a moral issue and its social contexts) could be absent. Emotional reactions such as "That's wrong!" or "He's a jerk!" are also possible examples of judgment at this level. This judgment is seldom generalized to other situations or issues. The obvious danger of this approach is emotivism and subjectivism.

The Rules Level

Rules (e.g., "Thou shalt not murder"; "Do not lie") are useful for ethical decision making because they offer concrete (measurable) moral standards to guide and govern our decisions and actions; with specificity, rules stipulate what to do or not to do. They carry with them a certain tangible, objective, normative quality. Rules apply not just to one particular case but to all similar cases; it is more objective than particular and immediate judgments.

The potential danger of rules is legalism, which happens when they are absolutized or isolated from the moral categories of higher levels. The limitation is that a rule cannot be properly comprehended when it is detached from norms/values or taken out of the narrative context and worldview in which it is embedded.

The Norms/Values Level

Norms/values (e.g., justice, love, equality, freedom, solidarity, and compassion: "Love your neighbor as yourself") are more general and broader than rules in their

26. Beauchamp and Childress, *Principles of Biomedical Ethics*, 15–17; Stassen and Gushee, *Kingdom Ethics*, 100.

normative scope. They do not have the concrete measurability that rules have; they cannot tell us concretely what to do or not do. Norms/values get their interpretive guidance from specific rules. When properly identified and interpreted, norms/values are useful in informing, guiding, and qualifying rules.

Norms/values describe normative demands broader than rules. They do not have the specification of rules, but they expand the duty or normative expectation into a broader scope and are thus effective in addressing contingent moral situations that rules do not specify.[27] For example, the norms of rights, justice, solidarity, and compassion denote the duty to protect the weak and the vulnerable in the form of a more "comprehensive fidelity that exceeds specification of the rules."[28]

However, norms/values are not the highest moral category. Norms/values are more inclusive and general than rules but less inclusive than the basic conviction (the overarching narrative). They are embedded in a particular ideology or worldview and should be interpreted in light of a person's worldview and basic convictions. For Christians, norms/values should be consistent with the basic convictions of Christianity.

This means that different religions and moral philosophies may interpret the same norm/value, such as justice, with different emphases and nuances. Norms/values could come from different moral sources: religion, metaphysics, philosophy, cultural tradition, and social ethos and customs. As with rules, their adjudication is a challenge in a pluralistic society. The danger to ethics that relies on this level alone is abstract principlism.

The Worldview Level

A worldview, in general, describes the way one sees and approaches the world in its totality: its origin, destiny, and current moral state (what is wrong within it, and how to correct it).[29] Forming the deepest undercurrent of our thinking, a worldview informs and shapes ethics. Every ethics, either secular or religious, relies on a certain worldview—rough ideas on the ultimate (deity), humanity, and the natural world, and the relationships among them. Each worldview has a set of beliefs and convictions concerning truth, goodness, and beauty. A worldview constitutes the broadest epistemological matrix of ethical reasoning affecting the interpretation of norms/values, rules, and even immediate judgment. It informs our choice of rules, norms/values, even our interpretation of an ethical situation. A worldview typically

27. Cf. May, *The Physician's Covenant*, 114.
28. May, *The Physician's Covenant*, 114.
29. Hollinger, *Choosing the Good*, 61.

takes the form of theology, metaphysics, or political ideology (e.g., communism, libertarianism, fascism). For Christians, this level is closely associated with particular theological traditions. Theologies matter. Different Christian theologies give rise to different ecclesial and ethical traditions (e.g., Wesleyan, Reformed, Anabaptist, Catholic, white liberal, black, Pentecostal theology), and their basic convictions derive from their theologies. Basic convictions provide the motivation, energy, and theological rationale for moral decisions. Rules and norms/values render some directives to our decisions, but a worldview and its convictions grant a final vision and horizon of our moral imagination and thinking

Particular Judgment
|
Rules
|
Norms/Values
|
Worldviews

Summary/Observation

In this diagram, which spans from a particular moral judgment to a worldview, higher levels cover and warrant the lower levels. Lower levels must be justified by higher levels, with a worldview as the final authority. The higher a level goes up, the broader and more encompassing a normative scope becomes, while the lower it goes down, the more specific and narrow the scope becomes.

The adjudication of these levels is an important process of ethical reasoning. It is a grave mistake to make an ethical decision relying on a single level (or category in it) alone, whether personal intuition, a few rules (e.g., the Ten Commandments) or norms (e.g., the double love commandments, the Golden Rule), a single doctrine (e.g., Christology), or one narrative (e.g., crucifixion or resurrection). Such an approach is highly likely to produce a flawed or regrettable decision. An ongoing effort to critically examine and integrate all these levels in collaboration with other Christians is important to make a good moral judgment.

There is no guarantee that all the levels automatically cohere or harmonize, and a good ethical method and reasoning help reduce the tensions and conflicts between them. There is a growing tension between the levels of rules and norms/values and the worldview level in a pluralistic society because the latter tends to be metaphysical or religious (thus unique and distinctive), while the former are legalistic, abstract, and general. Tensions and disagreements among the levels are palpable in our public discourse in a pluralistic society because people choose not only different categories (levels) as their primary moral reference points, but also different worldviews. However, without some form of integration among the levels, ethics may become incoherent, arbitrary, confused, and self-contradictory because our decision may be based on one level at one time but on another level at other times. Every ethics seeks to bring some form of coherence and congruence among all these levels through its ethical method, but with different results.

Adjudication of the Levels

Scripture includes a variety of examples of these four levels in various combinations and intermixtures. For example, the section on the Covenant Code in Exodus is more rule oriented, while Paul's letters (before *paraenesis*) are filled with the explication of theological convictions.

Compared to the OT (especially the Noachian covenant and the Sinai covenant), the NT tends to focus more on narratives, theological claims, and norms/values than on specific rules. This misleads scholars into thinking that NT ethics is virtue ethics or that virtue is central. This is a mistake. Virtue ethics cannot capture the encompassing, complex, and relational nature of NT ethics, let alone its inextricable relationship with the OT.

Different scholars of Christian ethics may prioritize different levels or categories depending on their methods of ethics. Many Christians often prefer one particular level over against the others. For these reasons, a clear understanding of the levels and their relationships is important to avoid confusion, misunderstanding, and conflicts. Christians sometimes disagree because they unknowingly speak from different levels.[30] At other times, Christians may miscommunicate with and misunderstand each other without knowing why they disagree. This level analysis helps to avoid misunderstanding and reduce the danger of antagonism or conflicts by clarifying the areas of disagreement and consequently narrowing the gap of differences. For example, people may agree on the norms/values level and above but simply disagree on the rules level.

The level analysis and adjudication of the levels can help limit the dangers of ethical vagueness, moral reductionism, legalism, and principlism hidden in our reasoning process.[31] This method of adjudication among the levels, which is covenantal in

30. Stassen and Gushee, *Kingdom Ethics*, 99.

31. Joseph Fletcher's situational ethics made a reductionistic mistake by idealizing and absolutizing love as a single norm, while dismissing every law as legalism, thus opening itself to the charge of antinomianism. Fletcher, *Situation Ethics*.

nature, is not unusual in the ethical reasoning we find in Scripture. Both Testaments are rich with these multiple levels, mutually corroborating in ethical reasoning.

The Old Testament

In the OT, the multilevel adjudication is found in the relation among the double love norms, the Ten Commandments, and 613 statutes and ordinances. If the double love command refers to the core constitutive convictions of the covenantal relationship (i.e., love), then the Ten Commandments elaborate what the demands of the love of God and the love of the neighbor entail at the norms/values level, while the statutes and ordinances spell out in further detail what the requirements of the Ten Commandments look like in various social contexts. The 613 statutes and ordinances can be categorized in accordance with each of the Ten Commandments. Putting this relationship differently in a covenantal framework, one may say that if love is the ultimate goal, vision, and core value of the covenant relationship, then the Ten Commandments are the constitutional principles (the basic guidelines) of the relationship that are instrumental in reaching the goal, while the 613 statutes and ordinances (248 "positive" and 365 "negative" ones) are specific laws that touch nearly every aspect of life.

The double love commandment and the Ten Commandments are unalterable; even in a new situation, their binding authority is not lost, although their interpretations may vary in different contexts. In contrast, however, the 613 statutes and ordinances do not command the same degree of moral authority that the Ten Commandments do. They are culturally contingent, indicating the particular application of God's Ten Commandments to specific social and cultural situations.[32]

Some of these statutes and ordinances, especially moral ones such as the Jubilee law, are still valuable for our moral life and insights. They offer clues to Israel's jurisprudence and moral reasoning as the people of God: how Israel applied the demands and obligations of the covenant to their particular issues and problems. By carefully studying them in their cultural contexts, we may discern a deeper moral meaning behind them and glean moral wisdom and understanding for our own life.

The New Testament

We see a similar pattern of moral reasoning in Jesus Christ, particularly highlighted in his moral debates with the Pharisees. Jesus's ethical method in his Sermon on the

32. Dumbrell says that the Covenant Code (Exod. 21–23) is "contextual exposition based on the general social demands of the Decalogue." Dumbrell, *Covenant and Creation*, 93.

Mount and parables is congruent with the method of ethical reasoning in Deuteronomy, as we have just examined. He subjected various Mosaic rules (dietary, Sabbath, and cultic laws) to higher and broader moral values, such as righteousness, mercy, and faith, which are the core values of the covenant, in light of God's inbreaking reign. Jesus emphasized *fidelity to the intent and spirit, rather than the letter, of the law*, and by doing so he avoided the dangers of both legalism and antinomianism; he neither absolutized nor abolished the law but placed the law in a proper covenantal relationship with God.[33] Paul Hanson's analysis is worthy of citing at some length:

> At issue here was not the Torah, but how the Torah was being interpreted. The Torah was not to be construed as a long list of demands, but as a faithful guide to life in fellowship with God and other humans, a guide with a very distinctive heart. . . . The classical triad of justice and mercy and faith *were*! To be sensitive to these "weightier matters" meant to live from the center of the covenant relationship rather than on its periphery. That center was clear to Jesus because of his profound sense of God's presence, and the nearness of the Kingdom. By living in daily fellowship with God and by devoting himself utterly to God's Kingdom, Jesus was able to rediscover the essence of community in worship, righteousness, and compassion. And he gave expression to that essence in the form of the twin commandments that stand as the central pillars of the classical biblical faith.[34]

The Four Levels and New Covenant Ethics

This book has made a claim that covenant offers the most faithful and comprehensive description of a Christian worldview (the understanding of God and God's relationship with humans and nature). New covenant ethics identifies covenant as the key symbol of the Bible, and the covenantal drama of liberation-restoration as its story line. Covenant does not exhaust the entire Christian worldview and stories, but it is central to them; it renders a coherent structure and meaning to them. In particular, the covenantal drama and the three dialectics bring capaciousness, plausibility, and explanatory power to new covenant ethics, as demonstrated in chapters 4 and 5.

New covenant ethics offers a good method of ethical discernment and the adjudication of the levels. The new covenant of Jesus constitutes the framework by which all particular judgments, rules, and norms/values are assessed and evaluated.

33. Matthew graphically expresses the spirit of ethical reasoning in Jesus as follows: "And [Jesus] said to them, 'Therefore every scribe who has been trained for the kingdom of heaven is like the master of a household who brings out of his treasure what is new and what is old'" (Matt. 13:52).

34. Hanson, *The People Called*, 426.

New covenant ethics effectively attends to all levels; all levels (particular judgments, rules, norms/values, worldview) are inseparable in the covenantal matrix, just as law and gospel are inseparable. Covenant naturally embraces these four levels. All these normative categories are found in covenant. God's commandments to human covenantal partners come in the form of rules, laws, norms/values, as well as particular judgments. Rules and norms/values are necessary aspects of a covenantal relationship because they typically serve as covenantal stipulations in the Bible. Chapter 8 discussed how laws (rules) are integral to the covenant, while chapter 7 identified several salient moral norms/values (e.g., gratitude, trust, truth telling, humility, solidarity, justice, and love), while showing how they are in essence "covenantal," as they are embedded in the matrix of the covenantal drama and its threefold dialectics. In short, rules and norms/value find their narrative homes in covenant.

However, in new covenant ethics, none of these four levels is allowed to control the entire reasoning process. For example, rules and norms/values cannot exhaust a covenantal relationship and its demand of fidelity because a covenantal relationship is dynamic and open-ended and the demand for fidelity cannot be completely codified or fixed. If I may quote May again, "The covenant details duties that give specific content to the future, while enjoining a comprehensive fidelity that extends beyond particulars to unforeseen and unforeseeable contingencies."[35] In the covenantal matrix, rules and norms/values are never autonomous, nor ends by themselves, but are organically connected to the covenantal drama and the three dialectics (and to each other through the latter). Outside the new covenant, they lose their interpretive context and moral balance. Hence new covenant ethics, while recognizing the importance of rules and norms/values, does not slip to legalism or principlism.

While hierarchically arranged, all four levels are organically interrelated. Particular judgments, rules, and norms/values are all subjected to the Christian worldview (the covenantal drama and the three dialectics); conversely, basic convictions and worldview are never isolated from the other levels, like a head without a body. By its design, covenantal reasoning institutionalizes the evaluation of lower levels in light of higher levels, that is, particular judgments against rules, and rules against norms/values (embedded in the Ten Commandments, the double love commandments, the Sermon on the Mount), and norms/values against the covenantal drama culminated in the new covenant.

The four components of covenantal reasoning (communal, dialectical, analogical, communicative) are helpful for the adjudication of the level as well.

The adjudication is not an individual endeavor but the work of a community. It takes place communally in a community through collaboration among the

35. May, *The Physician's Covenant*, 113.

members. Such a collaborative approach is necessary to reduce errors, fallacies, and mistakes.

Dialectical reasoning clarifies mutual relationships and differences among rules, norms/ values, and theological categories. As chapter 7 explained, the Bible has multiple norms/values; these values are interrelated, and some are complementary. Dialectical thinking rejects any monistic idealization of a single norm, such as love, which is reductionistic and limited.[36] In the context of the covenantal drama, dialectical reasoning conceptually clarifies and reorganizes discrete rules, norms/ values, and theological ideas into proper and balanced interrelationships with distinctive boundaries and qualified meanings under a worldview. By doing so, it is able to address complicated moral cases where multiple, competing rules and norms/ values are involved. When different participants appeal to different rules and norms/ values, dialectical reasoning helps bring a balancing act and adjudication among competing categories.[37] In an important way, dialectical reasoning complements other reasonings, especially analogical reasoning, in the level analysis, which tends to be deductive.

Analogical reasoning plays a crucial role in the adjudication of the levels because it is designed to enhance the relevance of the rules, norms/values, and worldview to new, changing situations. Analogical reasoning helps reimagine and reinterpret the rules, norms/values, and specific theological convictions in a way that is not only consistent to the Christian worldview but also relevant to the contexts. Analogical reasoning also includes a creative task of driving new rules from norms/values, and new norms/values from the basic convictions of the worldview. The norm of religious freedom is a prominent example of such effort, which happened during the Reformation period.

Communicative reasoning is concerned with a critical, discriminatory, adjudicating process (weighing and judging available warrants and evidence) to select the most valid option among competing options. This approach applies to the level analysis and adjudication as well. When discrepancies and conflicts arise between or within the levels, communicative reasoning adjudicates the differences and bridges the gaps by weighing and assessing available warrants and pieces of evidence.

36. One finds such an example in situation ethics that upholds love as a single encompassing norm: "Love alone, because, as it were, it has a built-in moral compass enabling it to 'hone' intuitively upon the deepest need of the other, can allow itself to be directed completely by the situation. . . . It is able to embrace an ethic of radical responsibleness, meeting every situation on its own merits, with no prescriptive laws." Robinson, *Honest to God*, 115.

37. See Beauchamp and Childress, *Principles of Biomedical Ethics*, 16.

Prescriptive-Actional: Implementing the Ethical Reasoning

The third and final step in ethical reasoning in new covenant ethics is the prescriptive-actional stage. The participants seek to find specific guidelines for their actions, directives for what they ought to do in the given moral situation. Having finished the collaborative examination of empirical and normative claims, the participants now seek to identify fitting measures and action steps on the issue in light of their empirical and normative analysis.[38] They ask: What decisions and actions are fitting and appropriate given the particular social situation and in light of the normative evaluations? What resources are available, and what are sensible initial steps to implement the decision? In developing action plans, new covenant ethics takes seriously both the reality of God's grace and the reality of sin, and it seeks options that are contextually realistic while theologically faithful. The four practices (communicative engagements, just peacemaking, nonviolence, grassroots organizing) are employed in the process to achieve the action plans.

Conclusion

Grounded in the new covenant of Jesus, covenantal reasoning presents a plausible method of Christian ethics. Covenantal reasoning is dialectic, analogical, communal communicative, and collaborative. It offers a coherent, capacious model of Christian ethics that avoids moral legalism without disregarding the law and moral relativism without disregarding particular cultural contexts of the Christian life. Covenantal reasoning enables our moral life and discipleship to be self-reflective, sensible, collaborative, and creative. With its balanced emphasis on the consistency of basic convictions and the relevance of a moral situation, covenantal reasoning helps Christians make a fitting response to the triune God's communicative action. Rules and norms/values are critically evaluated and newly interpreted in the context of the new covenant of Jesus Christ in order to live faithfully as God's people in a new context. Covenantal reasoning even enables a creative endeavor to formulate new rules and norms/values in response to radically new cultural contexts as long as they are faithful to basic convictions. Accordingly, covenantal reasoning is capable of better addressing the complexities of the moral life today.

New covenant ethics defines reasoning as the task of the entire church, not just a few professional theologians or clergypersons. It is the activity of God's people,

38. In social ethics, each special covenant (e.g., family, school, corporation, hospital) serves the context of ethical reasoning by offering specific parameters for moral discernment.

who are transformed by the Spirit. As the apostle Paul admonishes in Romans 12:1–2, reasoning requires the transformation of our inner dispositions/desires (willingness to present our bodies as "a living sacrifice") and "the renewal of the mind" that comes from our deep affection for God and others. Ethical reasoning, called prudence or practical wisdom, is a virtuous skill that develops through numerous practices and training over time. Excellence in reasoning requires the training of skills and character formation. Hence, we should grow in our knowledge of God (theology) and God's moral character and demands (ethics). We also need to be trained in social analysis to better understand the pattern of the world for its transformation in God. In new covenant ethics, such ability is the result of a long, faithful covenantal relationship with God and others.

2

Social Ethics

A Critical Engagement with Social Issues of Our Time

CHAPTER 11

Covenantal Social Imagination

> Just as the single altar was reconstituted with the twelve stones, so has the one Israel been reconstituted anew now that the people have united afresh around their God.
>
> —Martin Buber, *Moses*

Part 1 of this book presented the Bible as a covenantal drama of God and defined covenant as God's communicative action to renew and reorganize creation. Taking the new covenant of Jesus as the pinnacle of this dramatic, organizing work of God, part 1 studied the three relational dialectics of covenant, its distinctive nature and characteristics, its four proactive social practices, its three ethical motifs (goal, rule, virtue), covenantal norms, and the method of ethical reasoning.

Part 2 proposes a model of covenantal social ethics by engaging various controversial social issues from the perspective of new covenant ethics. Its objective is to demonstrate the capaciousness and plausibility (problem-solving ability) of new covenant ethics by clarifying the complexity and moral nature of several controversial social issues and offering directives for dealing with them.

What Is Social Ethics?

In general, social ethics is an academic discipline that studies the normative grounds for organizing a society and arranging its diverse social institutions (such as government, economy, and criminal justice system) and communities. Normative grounds typically include a reigning vision of a society, ideas of justice, and the values and norms that guide and regulate institutional arrangements, decisions, and social practices. As mentioned in the introduction, ethics has to do with a normative organizing of human life. Organizing a society is a normative process of arranging various institutions and their relationships according to a particular vision and its related principles of justice and norms/values. These visions, ideals, and norms/values are usually inherited from the past in the form of cultural traditions, shared morality, and social mores. Among them, the prevailing vision of a society affects the overall tone and ethos of a moral life and informs and shapes the choice of norms, rules, and values.

Normative grounds are important because they offer legitimacy and moral authority in making and enforcing public laws and policies. Social ethics is widely practiced at various levels of a democratic society in which its members examine and evaluate the validity of government decisions, public policies, and laws in light of their shared normative grounds.

The concept of social justice is at the heart of social ethics because the organizing and arranging of social relationships and institutions, as well as the distribution of goods and resources, rely on the principles of justice. The principles of justice also play an important role in adjudicating and coordinating the conflicting claims of various sectors and groups of a society.

The discussion of social ethics does not take place in a cultural vacuum. It inevitably reflects the culture, historical experiences, and religious traditions of a particular society. Socialization is an important social process through which individuals internalize a society's norms, values, and ideals. Socialization takes place in early childhood but operates through various forms of prevailing social scripts as well. Since humans are social beings and their decisions are always influenced by their peers, colleagues, and family members, these scripts exercise society's power even on adult individuals, affecting their choices and interpretations of norms, values, and rules. Through the empirical study of the cultures, traditions, and institutions of a particular society, social ethics discovers what is the good (and human well-being) that this society envisions: which norms, ideals, and values are prioritized and institutionalized, and why, and how, they actually operate and evolve.

Social ethics cannot ignore the changing human conditions and cultural complexities created by radical economic and technological transformations. In our current social context, technology, globalization, the neoliberal market economy, and religious-cultural pluralism pose major challenges to common life. A major concern of contemporary social ethics in a pluralistic society is how to adjudicate substantially different visions of the good and the ideas of justice within a society. There is a growing possibility of tension between diverse groups as society becomes more heterogenous and pluralistic.[1] The need for rigorous and extensive social ethical discourses grows as our society gets more complex, divisive, and disruptive.

1. Because of its attention to justice, social ethics is intimately related to politics, as the imple-

Social ethics is a natural and necessary aspect of Christian life, ministry, and social witness. It is inevitable that Christians will engage social issues because all Christians are called to faithfully embody God's reign (to live out their fidelity to God and others) in every realm of a social life. That is, Christians are called to witness to God's justice, love, and peace, and work for the common flourishing of humanity as an indispensable aspect of their discipleship. Christians do not just passively live under law and civil authority (as the two-kingdom theory implies) but are called to constantly transform and enhance society using means consistent with Jesus's way, such as the vocational exercise of discipleship, public discourse, just peacemaking, community organizing, and social movements. Historically, Christians have actively engaged various political and social issues to address urgent challenges that humanity faces, such as economic inequality, human rights, fascism, genocide, ethno-racial conflicts, etc.

How is new covenant ethics related to social ethics? What are the unique features of its approach? New covenant ethics offers a theologically coherent and practically capacious moral framework for Christian social ethics. The covenantal drama of liberation-restoration, three dialectics, and covenantal values that we studied in part 1—as well as associational pluralism and the complex theories of justice we will study in this chapter and the next—provide rich resources and a plausible framework for a Christian social ethics capacious enough for addressing difficult social issues.

Covenantal Social Imagination: Associational Pluralism

As mentioned in the introduction, I claim that the capaciousness and plausibility of a key symbol depends on its capability to imagine and organize otherwise discrete, disjointed aspects of moral life into a more coherent and faithful vision than the alternatives, competently accounting for the ethical life of individuals, groups, and society. To avoid a socially reductionistic or simplistic view of social justice, a plausible, more holistic theory of social ethics requires an organic, complex, and coherent view of society and its diverse institutions. A social theory affects the underlying moral philosophical assumptions and ideas of justice of a particular social ethics.

New covenant ethics offers a rich social imagination that helps to discern how a society is constituted, how to order/organize it as a whole and among its various

mentation of justice is one of the primary responsibilities of politics. While politics is concerned with the security and well-being of a community through a just distribution of the resources and adjudication of conflicting interests, social ethics is concerned with a society's normative vision, rules, and processes. Social ethics is an integral part of politics, in general.

parts (how the parts are related to the whole, and vice versa). As the art of organizing, covenant imagines a society consisting of multiple spheres (and clusters of institutions in it), organically interrelated with other spheres while each sphere maintains its relative autonomy.[2] In ancient Israel, covenant was the source of their sociological imagination and organization. They imagined all social relationships (the structures and institutions of their society) in terms of the covenant. The plurality of social spheres is God's design from the beginning. God's rule is not monolithic but differentiated and accommodating to the needs of humanity. The Bible acknowledges and honors the validity/legitimate role of nonreligious authorities, offices, and vocations. The Mosaic laws discuss different social institutions; in his preaching, John the Baptist mentions soldiers and tax collectors; Jesus honors the Roman centurion's faith and acknowledges the practice of paying taxes to Caesar; Paul mentions the government.

Spheres and Institutions

The idea of social sphere is useful for social ethics because our social life takes place in social spheres and a moral assessment of a social issue cannot be separated from the purposes, rules, and practices of the particular social sphere to which it pertains. In fact, many moral issues that social ethics deals with are sphere based: politics, family, marriage, work, medicine, criminal justice, education, law, etc.

A sphere is "a cluster of practices and institutions" that works together to serve the common purpose in a "functional, ordered, and effective" manner.[3] Across all different cultures and times, Max Stackhouse identifies five spheres, which he calls "principalities."

- Economy—a system with the primary function of providing "the food, shelter, clothing, and opportunity for work and property for people to survive."
- Politics—refers to "a system of gaining, legitimating, and using coercive authorities to control violence within and beyond a society"[4] and to promote the common good through the adjudication of conflicting claims and coordination of diverse interests.

2. A covenantal social vision, while germane to the Bible, was further developed by early Reformed theorists, such as Johannes Althusius and the Puritans, and later refined by Abraham Kuyper and Herman Dooyeweerd. The late Max Stackhouse was a theological ethicist who elaborated on it in a globalizing social context by engaging social science and comparative religious ethics.

3. Stackhouse, "General Introduction," 36.

4. Stackhouse, "General Introduction," 37.

- Family—represents an institution that delineates a proper/moral use of human sexuality, birth and nurturing of children, fulfillment of emotional needs, and psychological growth through close-knit relationships.
- Media—refers to a structure of human communication that pertains to the exchange of information, imagination, thoughts, "feelings, aesthetic awareness, and conviction."
- Religion—a system of beliefs, moral codes, rituals identifying the ultimate being, principle, or meaning that "bonds people and the powers together."

Despite cultural and historical variations (and despite different ideological expressions and material-technological levels), these five spheres are found in every society. They meet the enduring needs of humanity: humans need to eat, procreate, organize their community lives in an orderly way, communicate their artifacts and emotions with each other for growth and collaboration, and seek an enduring meaning and purpose in all these activities. Each sphere performs a functional requisite. Theologically speaking, each sphere operates by a certain mandate (beyond productivity or profit) that describes a specific form of God's ordinance. That is, each sphere is a moral entity.

Each sphere has a cluster of institutions with "customary or legislated rules that assist, guide, or constrain social activities of institutions and their members." Each sphere and its institutions develop a method of fulfilling the sphere's goals and have respective standards measuring achievements and guiding and regulating activities.[5] With its own distinctive mandate (functional requirement), each sphere maintains a relative autonomy from the others with a different function, authority, boundary, and scope of influence. Its autonomy should be protected from intrusion from another sphere. At the same time, the spheres are interdependent and interconnected. Each sphere cannot survive by itself; it operates within the ecosystem of a society in constant interaction with other spheres—mutually influencing each other. While each sphere has its own purpose, function, and constituency, it can only achieve its goals in collaboration with others, especially in a complex, highly differentiated society such as ours.

Like a living organism, a society involves constantly occurring exchanges among relatively independent spheres in pursuing the common purpose. From a covenantal perspective, various social spheres are federally associated with each other, forming a social symbiosis in the context of the creation covenant. In other words, a society constitutes an ensemble of diverse spheres, checking and balancing, communicating and collaborating, for the common good.

5. Stackhouse, "General Introduction," 36.

In a democratic society, a government has mediated between diverse spheres and institutions using laws and public policies as guided by its constitution. Historically, in many cultures the church has provided moral vision and directives for society, various spheres, and their institutions. However, globalization has brought massive confusion, conflict, and dissonance among spheres. Today, protecting the autonomy of diverse spheres and coordinating their interrelationships is a massive challenge. The rise of the transnational global economy and global entertainment culture has disrupted the relatively stable system of spheres in a nation-state and severely blurred the boundaries between spheres and between nations. The ascendance of the economic sphere (especially corporations) and its encroachment into other spheres are now a major moral and political challenge for protecting the autonomy of other spheres (see chaps. 13–14).

When a sphere undergoes a major change, its shared rules, agreements, and expectations may need to be adjusted. But this does not mean that its mandate necessarily changes. Radical scientific and technological advances make existing laws and moral agreements outdated and irrelevant, as pluralism through demographic changes—the coexistence of diverse religious, racial, and ethnic groups and the rise of political polarization—makes a consensus on common moral standards and rules difficult to attain.

Spheres have moral significance in new covenant ethics because the common good is fulfilled through the contributions of and harmony among the spheres. Just as the body of Christ is built through the collaboration of various body parts, without the flourishing of individual spheres, the common good is not achievable and shalom is empty and abstract.[6]

A moral analysis of a particular social issue requires the study of its complex and intersectional (or interspheral) nature and scope because the issue is not isolated from but affected by different spheres and institutions. A moral decision in medicine, law, or education is never an isolated activity; it is affected by others. For example, abortion is not a purely personal sexual issue; it is an economic and a medical issue as well. Child rearing in families today is profoundly influenced by technology, entertainment (e.g., online gaming, pornography), and corporations. This is another example of how corporate power encroaches upon other spheres of life.

Without understanding intersphere relationships, it is difficult to properly identify the legitimate concerned parties on an issue (partners of a covenant). To identify concerned parties is not as simple as it may appear. For instance, in the current crim-

6. One could imagine the global society in a similar manner, that is, as an encompassing society with multiple global spheres.

inal justice system, the concerned parties are the offenders and the government. This arrangement usually comes at the expense of victims, which makes reconciliation between offenders and victims (and their families) insignificant or secondary. Similarly, in the economy, business decisions are made between big shareholders and business managers at the exclusion of employees and the environment.

Finally, social spheres are important because they are domains where Christian vocation and discipleship are exercised. Closely associated with the Protestant doctrine of vocation, each sphere (and institution) is a social locus where Christians live out God's calling. That is, through them, we work out the obligations of the new covenant of Jesus in relation to God and others.[7]

In addition, the spheres (and institutions) have formative power in shaping our moral character. Our sense of identity and moral responsibility is heavily and consciously shaped by our special covenants and their respective obligations.[8] While the life of faith is cultivated in the church, its actualization is in the spheres and institutions of society where individual Christians are called to serve.[9]

Institutions as Special Covenants

Each sphere has more than one institution; for example, family is a social sphere with marriage and family as its distinctive institutions. Within a sphere, institutions perform particular functions to help fulfill certain needs of the sphere. An institution is typically organized systematically with regulating rules, procedures, and agents to maintain predictability.

Institutions have their own respective, specified ends and means, and practices congruent with the purpose of a particular sphere. For example, an accounting firm has its own specific ends and means operating in accord with the purposes and rules of the larger economic sphere.

A major portion of modern human life is lived within various institutions. Institutions profoundly affect our moral life. Just like individuals, institutions and governments operate as moral agents. "It is not just that people are making choices about how they will behave in the economic system; the system is also making choices about who will remain viable in the system."[10]

The power and influence of certain institutions have declined in a global society, which is increasingly fluid and mobile. This is changing the nature of social relation-

7. Stackhouse, *Covenant and Commitments*, 142.
8. Allen, *Love and Conflict*, 41.
9. Stackhouse, *Covenant and Commitments*, 151.
10. Wink, *Engaging the Powers*, 79.

ships. Some institutions (such as marriage, family, and church) are getting shelled, and their functions are now carried out in informal, less structured ways (e.g., cohabitation, births out of wedlock, self-employment), while others (corporations such as Google and Amazon) have grown exponentially. However, although not as physically immediate as in the past, institutions still play a major role in society. While their controlling power over individuals may have declined, certain institutions still yield enormous influence.

For Christians, all major institutionalized social relationships could be considered covenantal in nature. They are based on certain enduring, socially structured forms of relationships with concerned parties binding with each other under a shared mission and shared rules. For example, marriage is based on the wife-husband relationship; school is based on the teacher-student relationship. Each institution is typically durable in its own unique mission, function, authority, and responsibility in society in relation to its members and other institutions.

No institution is exempt from the obligation of justice. Because of its publicly professed mission and its structured nature of relationships and social expectations, an institution is obligated to display moral qualities living up to norms inherent in given relationships and to respect the rights of various parties involved.

The structure and configuration of modern institutions have covenantal origins, marks, and qualities, which are still found in their mission statements and organizational structure (e.g., a board of trustees and its bylaws). Each institution has moral obligations to fulfill its mandate and promote justice and the common good, striving toward shalom. Joseph Allen calls these institutions special covenants, in contrast to the inclusive Covenant of Jesus.

As previously mentioned, while the new covenant of Jesus constitutes a universal covenant with all creatures as members, the members of a special covenant are limited to special interactions among a select group of people.[11] While there is one inclusive covenant, there are numerous special covenants.[12] Today, the moral obligation of the universal covenant is usually expressed in respecting the dignity and rights of humans and other creatures.

The rights pertaining to special covenants are special rights, "rights that arise out of some special interaction and belong only to the parties to that interaction. The corresponding responsibilities likewise belong to those parties and not to every human being as such. Relevant right and responsibility will differ from one kind of

11. Allen, *Love and Conflict*, 42.

12. While the boundary of the former never changes, it is not the case with the latter. New types of special covenants can be added as society differentiates further and new institutions and structures are formed. Conversely, as other special covenants become obsolete, they can be removed.

special covenant to another; therefore, special rights cannot contradict or override universal human rights."[13]

As human beings are simultaneously members of both the universal covenant and several special covenants (e.g., family, church, government, clubs), some tensions may arise. Detached from the universal covenant, a special covenant can be parochial, exclusive, and fragmented, inordinately asserting its own sovereignty at the expense of other covenants. Like individuals, institutions are morally ambiguous, tainted, and distorted by sin and the desire for power. Institutions are typically self-protective, egoistic, and even greedy. Some institutions are extremely powerful and domineering over others.[14] Hence, checks and balances within and among institutions are necessary.

The universal covenant is the basis, the default mode, of our existence. Even in their activities in various institutions, Christians live in awareness of the inclusive covenant; this awareness arises from their profession of God's sovereignty, the Lordship of Jesus, and solidarity with the entire creation. Even if our special relationships strain and break down, we cannot forfeit our obligations in the inclusive covenant—fidelity toward the estranged parties.[15] Even in our special relationships, we do not surrender our fidelity toward people outside these special relationships.

All institutions (e.g., marriage, hospitals, schools, corporation) carry in them God's purpose and moral demands.[16] In studying a special covenant, such as marriage, one asks what God requires in a given relationship. In the same vein as the biblical idea of *tsedaqah*, "what constitutes faithfulness depends in some respects upon the kind of covenant." "The kind of faithfulness that is appropriate is not the same for every special covenant, and yet what is appropriate is not simply whatever we choose to think."[17] While open to interpretation, the basic meaning and purpose of a special covenantal relationship are given by God. They should not be driven by individual expediency or self-interest, but rather they should attend to God's purpose. If a contract focuses merely on the agreement, a covenant attends to the relationship's intrinsic purpose as intended by God.

Like social spheres, the contours and relational dynamics of a special covenant evolve. The functional requisites and needs of its members change as it interacts with its social environments; hence, ongoing discernment is necessary. We need to ask carefully: What are the purpose, core values/norms, and mandates of a special cov-

13. Allen, *Love and Conflict*, 43.

14. Wink notes: "They [systems] are at once and the same time divinely ordained and acolytes of the kingdom of death." Wink, *Engaging the Powers*, 78.

15. Allen, *Love and Conflict*, 45.

16. Cf. Stackhouse, *Covenant and Commitments*, 142.

17. Allen, *Love and Conflict*, 44.

enant? Which rights belong to whom? How is a particular special covenant related to the universal covenant (the new covenant) and other covenants? For example, how is family related to work/economy, and how does the latter affect marriage, divorce, birthrate, and child care? What kind of justice-making and peacemaking work is needed? How can we approach it, and what are the first steps? Christians are the agents of liberation and restoration in each institution. They are called to constantly reform it toward a higher achievement of justice and peace in light of the universal Covenant of Jesus.

Summary

The organizing vision and principles of covenant apply to all aspects of human associational life. Because of this complex and capacious theological sociology, new covenant ethics offers a sophisticated form of Christian social ethics equipped with a plausible social vision and moral arrangements of spheres and institutions. Going beyond the confines of the church and individual evangelism, it helps Christians to approach all social spheres and their institutions as the loci of Christian discipleship, just peacemaking, and covenantal organizing. New covenant ethics takes every aspect of our social life—not only birth, marriage, burial, and Sunday worship but also entertainment, electing a leader, starting a school, the dedication of a public place, and an economic transaction—as somehow related to the holy.[18] In this respect, new covenant ethics is distinct from both liberal political theory that is based on abstract principles of justice and individual rights, and the sectarian ethics of Mennonites and Anabaptists, whose goal is the sanctification of the Christian community.

Christian Social Ethics and Public Engagement

In today's pluralistic society, Christian social ethics faces a growing gap or dissonance between the Christian worldview and secular liberalism, as well as other religious views. Many Christians are struggling to bridge the gap between their faith convictions and the current vision and arrangements of society. Unfortunately, tensions and conflicts are aggravating a deepening sense of polarization in the United States and elsewhere.

New covenant ethics faces the same difficulty. Living in a pluralistic society, Christians cannot impose their morality upon others. Humans are created as free beings in the image of God. If Christians are committed to religious liberty, then, by implication, they must accept their limited ability to legislate laws that fully reflect

18. Stackhouse, *Covenant and Commitments*, 157.

their values and convictions and seek a nonviolent and persuasive way to communicate their convictions.

This section studies how new covenant ethics addresses the epistemological gap or moral differences between its worldview and the current secular liberal worldview. I believe that new covenant ethics is uniquely resourced to address this concern.

Public Theology

In a pluralistic society, the claims of a particular religious group are not exempted from public reasoning and scrutiny.

> In a democratic and pluralistic society, legislation needs to be proposed and passed on the basis of a public ethic that can be affirmed by persons of various faiths and no faith. This public ethic can be an expression or translation of specific Christian faith, but that faith has to be expressed in terms that others can adopt as well, or it is an inappropriate establishment of religion. The legitimacy and enforcement of any law or public policy depends critically on the role of public consent. Christians are often quite impatient with these limits on making our values into public law; but such constraints are part of the genius of democracy; they protect our own liberty of conscience, and supporting them fits with biblical principles of justice and love.[19]

In their social engagement, Christians need to translate the moral vision, values, and demands of the covenant of Jesus into publicly accessible moral language through public theology. Public theology is not an attempt to dilute or water down Christian identity and convictions; rather, it attempts to demonstrate the validity and relevance of a particular religious belief to the public by interpreting specific religious convictions in ways that others can understand and possibly accept.[20] Public theology is necessary to bridge the epistemological gap between Christians and non-Christians.

This approach is similar to how Paul wanted to be like a Jew to Jews, a Greek to Greeks. Jeremiah told the Israelites to live actively in their place of exile and pray for the peace of the cities in Babylon. From a covenantal perspective, public theology engages non-Christians on the ground of the Noachian covenant in order to secure and promote social justice while always exerting love. There is a high possibility of overlap between covenantal values/norms and secular principles of justice, as we discuss in

19. Stassen and Gushee, *Kingdom Ethics*, 233.
20. Lee, "Public Theology," 50.

the next chapter. Therefore, equipped with public theology, Christians can effectively contribute to public discourse without sacrificing their theological convictions. Communicative exchanges of ideas, reflections, and critiques with other groups help to expand and refine the moral wisdom and imagination of the participants.

New Covenant Ethics and Public Engagement

As discussed in chapter 4, in their public engagement, Christians are bound by the Noachian covenant and the new covenant of Jesus. While most social ethics (including Christian ethics) take justice as the focal concern, new covenant ethics pursues justice and peace together (just peacemaking). Christian public engagement operates between the moral minimum of the Noachian covenant and the moral maximum of the covenant of Jesus Christ, between the *boundary* ethics of the Noachian covenant and the *boundless* ethics of Jesus, that is, justice making (*mishpat*) and peacemaking (shalom).

The two covenants are the crucial signposts of God's people called to be the salt and light of the world. Without being utopian or romantic, but with a realistic awareness of sin, the church attends to both boundary and boundless ethics. Christians work together with others both to establish a social arrangement based on justice (grounded in the Noachian covenant) and to move society toward shalom, which approximates the covenant of Jesus. Many different forms of institutional and social arrangements are possible in the spectrum between justice and shalom. To build justice and promote shalom, new covenant ethics critically incorporates various moral laws and teachings of the Bible and attends to other sources of ethics (tradition, experiences, reason). There is no society that perfectly embodies Jesus's ethics. Some societies more closely reflect the covenant of Jesus, while others, facing immediate challenges, may need to establish and implement the Noachian covenant's demands of justice in order to preserve the basic order.

There is potential tension in the process of transiting from justice to shalom. While justice is enforceable, shalom (especially its love dimension exercised in forgiveness and reconciliation) is not. Shalom is possible only when individuals and institutions voluntarily participate in it and practice it. When justice relies on coercion (enforcement) alone, then wholesome peace (shalom) cannot be reached. A healthy political community needs more than legislation and coercion; it needs goodwill and civic virtues (compassion, care, solidarity, and commitment to the common good). To achieve a more genuine and sustaining peace, love should be a motivating and guiding vision in demanding justice and exercising collective power.

With their commitment to nonviolence and trust building, the four practices of new covenant ethics (communicative engagements, just peacemaking, nonviolence, and grassroots organizing) help to mitigate the tension between the two.

The communicative engagement of new covenant ethics partly resolves this tension by helping parties accept the stipulations of justice on a voluntary basis. The enforceable dimension may not completely disappear in covenant, but it is definitely diminished. The process reaching a voluntary agreement is self-legislative, not heteronomous,[21] and accountability for justice arises from a free self-decision, not from coercion. Communicative engagement helps not only to establish the enforceable (the stipulations of justice) but also to build trust and mutual affection (the unenforceable) because its process is collaborative by nature.

In addition, bridging the gap between justice and shalom relies on various forms of civic education and practices in families, schools, religious groups, and other organizations. The implementation of justice and the approximation toward shalom depend on the moral capability, character, and desires of the members of a society. The crisis of contemporary liberal democratic society is that it increasingly depends on coercion and law. As mentioned above, these institutions play a vital role in pursuing the common good of a society. Hence, the empowerment of these institutions and their members is as important as public policies and laws for a good body politic. The four practices of new covenant ethics can help to strengthen these institutions and civil society with their emphasis on dialogue, nonviolence, reconciliation, grassroots networking, as well as justice.

Parameters of Assessment and Prescription

The covenantal drama—which involves the triad of love, justice, and power—is embodied in the three dialectics of covenantal values we studied in chapter 3. They offer Christian social ethics normative guidance for ethical analysis and discernment. Likewise, associational pluralism (multiple spheres and institutions) and special covenants offer conceptual categories and moral parameters to analyze and assess a particular social issue. They may not provide moral answers immediately, but they can clarify moral concerns and guide our deliberations.

Analysis at various levels is also important for properly understanding the moral complexities of any particular social issue. A social issue encompasses different levels simultaneously: individuals, institutions, spheres, society, and global society.[22] A certain social moral issue may appear individualistic or personal in nature but could be more affected by collective or structural forces; hence we must attend to diverse levels. The degree to which any level affects the issue cannot be predeter-

21. In covenant, there are other motivating factors that assist a voluntary decision, such as gratitude and future blessings.

22. A covenantal approach encompasses the vertical and horizontal aspects of social organizing. It encompasses different spheres horizontally (such as family, economy, politics, religion) and different levels vertically (such as personal, institutional, social, and global).

mined. Rather, the relative influence of a level should be discerned at a particular time in the context of a particular society. A difficult social issue, such as poverty, is typically a complex problem that encompasses multiple levels (individual, institutional, and societal) and often interlocks with other social spheres and institutions. Its solution takes comprehensive and dedicated actions over a long period of time. Without proper attention to interrelationships among the different levels, we may commit theoretical or moral reductionism, which reduces a complex social problem to merely individual responsibility or solely a structural issue.

Part 2 will engage eight different social issues. After briefly introducing a topic, each chapter will approach them in the following pattern:

1. *Analytic task*—discusses particular moral concerns and stakes (temptations, threats, and opportunities) for human well-being in general and Christians in particular.
2. *Evaluative task*—engages dominant moral approaches (mostly secular liberalism and conservative evangelicalism), which now form the polar extremes of politics in the United States, constantly clashing with one another across the political ideological spectrum,[23] and assesses their limitations and dangers. That is, part 2 will critically evaluate the theological assumptions and practices of conservative evangelical ethics and the reigning contractualism and principlism of liberal ethics in light of the covenantal drama of God, the three dialectics, and covenantal norms.[24] I engage with other Christian approaches (such as those of Anabaptists, liberationists, and Catholics) only when necessary and when relevant to the issue.
3. *Prescriptive task*—presents new covenant ethics as alternate understandings and practices to conservative evangelical ethics and secular liberal ethics.

23. Zauzmer, "'He Gets It.'"

24. In secular liberal ethics, principlism and contractualism serve as normative sources of social ethics and as the method for organizing society. Principlism represents the modernist desire to achieve a universal common morality based on common experience and rational analysis/reflection among people rather than religion or metaphysics. It has wide appeal today as the source of social ethics because it addresses the challenges of pluralism because of its apparent inclusiveness and generality. Secular liberal ethics claims that the principles have universal validity and transcultural appeal beyond a particular cultural entity or religion.

Similarly, contractualism has become the socially and economically dominant model of social interaction and arrangement in the United States and other industrialized societies. Contractualism is spread through the free-market ideology of freedom, mobility, individualism, and money, which results in the commodification of relationships. Individual rights and contractualism are closely associated. Contract is a primary way of entering a relationship with others in a liberal society: two autonomous individuals or groups agree to exchange goods to protect or promote their self-interests.

New covenant ethics challenges a narrow, truncated, theological ground of conservative evangelical ethics as well as the individualistic moral presuppositions and utilitarian beliefs and practices of liberal ethics, and invites the readers to engage in critical discernment in their personal and social lives.

In engaging several controversial social issues, my goal is not to offer any final answers but to help readers better understand the nature of their moral problems and assess complexities. In a pluralistic society, a gap between the Christian moral worldview and that of non-Christians, or even among those of different Christian groups, is inevitable in assessing moral problems and seeking solutions. This moral ambiguity is unavoidable because we are still living in the double bound of the covenant of Jesus and the Noachian covenant, between the penultimate and the ultimate. Because of this proleptic nature of the Christian life, proportionality is an important factor to consider in moral decisions—that is, to choose the best option among available ones instead of holding out for the absolute, idealistic one. Living between the boundary ethics of the Noachian covenant and the boundless ethics of the covenant of Jesus, Christians are called to constantly improve existing social structures, institutions, and social relationships. A careful social assessment is a precondition for a moral assessment. We ask:

1. Is there any undeniable pattern of oppression, discrimination, and inequality in a social relationship and an institution? Related to this question, we may ask: Does one sphere intrude on and unfairly control and undermine the integrity and moral decisions of other spheres? Is there a critical need for renewing a social compact to rearrange institutional relationships and structures?
2. Is the concern a matter of legislating the law or implementing government policies? Is a moral concern around a specific issue a matter of agency/capability; that is, is there a need to increase the capability of people through healing, empowerment, and character/virtue building?

With intellectual humility and an open mind, new covenant ethics patiently enacts communicative engagements with others in order to approximate God's shalom. It participates in the practices of just peacemaking, community organizing, and nonviolent action.

CHAPTER 12

Distributive Justice

You shall not render an unjust judgment; you shall not be partial to the poor or defer to the great: with justice you shall judge your neighbor.

—Leviticus 19:15

"The Spirit of the Lord is upon me,
  because he has anointed me
    to bring good news to the poor.
He has sent me to proclaim release to the captives
  and recovery of sight to the blind,
    to let the oppressed go free,
to proclaim the year of the Lord's favor."

—Luke 4:18–19

This book has mentioned that God's reign is deeply associated with justice displayed in the covenantal drama of liberation-restoration. The covenantal drama carries two forms of justice: liberative and restorative. The former is corrective justice[1] (*mishpat*) to rectify an unjust system, while the latter rehabilitates offenders.[2] Covenantal justice is committed to delivering victims from oppressors and restoring all people to new and just communities free of oppression and victimization. Covenantal justice is revolutionary in scope and nature, focusing on changing social structures and increasing the capability of people.

1. David Miller, "Justice."

2. Restoration in a theo-ethical sense and restorative justice are different in their scope and content, even as they are closely related. Restoration in the former sense concerns a communal and cosmic nature and scope, while the latter sense pertains narrowly to criminal justice.

Echoing the exodus and Jesus's movement, new covenant ethics recognizes that radical, liberative works of justice are necessary on certain occasions: when injustice is systematic, when human rights are being egregiously violated (e.g., apartheid, segregation, neoliberal oligarchy), when social mobility is blocked, and when human capabilities are being undermined. Liberative justice uses various nonviolent means of community organizing, nonviolent resistance, civil disobedience, and noncooperation to correct the unjust system.

However, the work of justice in new covenant ethics is not limited to disruptive actions and revolutionary measures that address systematic injustices. Even a relatively stable and just society requires the constant work of justice; this is distributive justice. While liberative justice focuses on changing a social system, distributive justice pertains to policies or legislative issues and pursues an ongoing implementation of justice and a gradual reform of democratic society. The two are not completely separate; an enduring or egregious failure of distributive justice is typically a sign that liberative justice is needed.

This chapter engages prominent secular principles of distributive justice from a covenantal perspective: equality (fairness), basic need, merit, capability, and liberation. This conversation is important because Christian social ethics cannot ignore secular theories of justice when dealing with a particular social issue. It asks: How is a covenantal approach to distributive justice different from other ethical approaches (notably liberal, libertarian, and Aristotelian)? What are its distinctive characteristics, and how does it contribute to debate on the topic?

Unlike secular theories of distributive justice, which prioritize one principle over the others, I claim that a covenantal approach embraces multiple principles in a coherent, clear, and harmonious theological and philosophical framework. At the same time, grounded in the biblical idea of *tsedaqah* (its relational view of justice) and associational pluralism, a covenantal approach offers a complex pluralistic view of distributive justice and attends to the complex nature and dynamics of diverse spheres and social relationships. That is to say, a complex theory of distributive justice corresponds to a complex and organic social imagination of new covenant ethics. The result is an encompassing, capacious view of distributive justice that respects and coordinates the plurality of distributive principles in a way that parallels the pluriformality of social life and contexts, and that more effectively mediates the tensions and conflicts among the principles.

Distributive Justice Defined

What, then, is distributive justice? A society is a large community of distribution; every day it distributes a variety of goods for numerous people in countless different ways. The government, various institutions, and individuals all function as agents of this distribution. A common life is sustained through the myriad of intricate networks of communication and distribution of goods. Without ongoing distribution, social life atrophies.

Society endlessly produces goods, not only material goods (e.g., food, shelter, other products) but also emotional and social goods (rights, responsibility, positions, membership, public recognitions, honor) that are distributed among its members. Social goods are treated with certain moral distinctions depending on kind and context.[3] That is to say, they are distributed for different reasons according to different principles. "Goods in the world have shared meanings because conception and creation are social processes. For the same reason, goods have different meanings in different societies."[4]

Distributive justice presupposes social cooperation and scarcity of resources. Distributive justice is an indispensable part of social ordination that properly shares benefits and burdens among the members. It assumes interdependence (a sense of a community) among the members. Humans are social animals; they cannot live outside society's distributive system. One person or family cannot produce everything they need. People belong to a society to benefit from this network. At the same time, people would not willingly sacrifice or accept others' burdens if they are not members of the same society.

"Distributive justice" is a multifaceted term with a wide range of meanings. But in the West, it is defined as "To each his own"—to give what one is owed or what one deserves. Different social philosophers differently interpret this definition and hence propose different standards of distribution that reflect different visions of society, justice, and human relationships.

Distributive justice assumes that social goods are low but demands and needs are high. Hypothetically, if resources are limitless, distributive justice is unnecessary because each person could get whatever the person wants. In scarcity, however, the sensitive concern is determining who receives which benefits by what standards. Distribution profoundly affects people's lives, and those who distribute benefits and burdens exercise enormous power. There have been constant attempts by respective groups, public or backroom, to intervene and influence these distributive processes to get favorable results (e.g., by lobbying, bribery, and contributing to political campaigns). Unfair distribution becomes the source of social strife and conflicts, sometimes creating revolutionary situations where people seek to overthrow the status quo and redefine the entire system of distribution. Many political revolutions and

3. Sandel, *Justice*, 97.
4. Walzer, *Spheres of Justice*, 7.

uprisings (e.g., the Arab Spring) have come from failed or unfair distribution. This exhibits the connectivity between distributive justice and liberative justice.

To prevent arbitrary corruption and monopoly in distribution, a society relies on certain principles of distributive justice that offer moral guidance. They are necessary to facilitate fair distribution and address conflicts of interest that arise in the process: who should pay and how much, who should receive what and how much. To resolve conflicts of interest, certain shared and agreed-upon principles are necessary.

Material principles of justice specify appropriate standards for regulating fair distribution; these typically include equality, need, merit, and capability. Material principles identify relevant properties that persons must possess to qualify for a particular distribution or benefit. For example, the principle of need declares that distribution based on need is just.

Every society has a certain idea of distributive justice that reflects that society's vision of the good and of human flourishing. Certain societies distribute social goods based on hierarchal power and ascriptive status (such as biological affiliations and traditions), other societies by individual achievements. For example, a libertarian view (with an atomistic view of individuals) claims that society works best when the government puts minimal burdens on individuals. In such a society, individuals are not obligated to society or other people. They are not burdened to share their resources to meet the needs of others. A communitarian society has a different view of the individual-society relationship. The members are responsible for the well-being of others, and the needs of other members are met by sharing burdens among the members.

Informed by a dominant religion or political ideology, every society has principles and a rationale for distributive justice: why social goods are shared differently among members and why such differences are acceptable.[5] The meaning of fairness, needs, merits, and capability is interpreted differently across a variety of historical circumstances, cultural traditions, and social *ethe*. Similarly, how to prioritize any specific principle over the others reflects the worldview—the ultimate, human nature, culture, and reigning ethos—of a particular society.

Identifying relevant properties and defining their meanings are not easy tasks. There are ongoing debates about what treating people equally means, what constitutes basic needs, and what merit and capability mean. Ambiguity exists over which properties are prior to anything else, and how they work in different contexts. Furthermore, the debates on distributive justice are intensified in a globalizing society because de-territorialization has made traditional borders porous; trade, migration,

5. Most arguments over distributive justice are about what kind of different treatments are appropriate. Allen, *Love and Conflict*, 158.

and exchanges make distribution a transnational matter, and a system of justice is no longer closed as it had been in the past. Accordingly, the distributive issue has become a hot controversy in the West. Different political parties offer starkly different visions of distributive justice; the visions prioritize different principles.

Principles of Distributive Justice

Discussions of distributive justice have encompassed four principles: (1) equality or fairness, (2) need, (3) merit, and (4) capability. In the following, we discuss these one at a time.

Equality (Fairness)

The equality principle requires that we treat people equally and fairly. It has two aspects—sanctity and treatment. All human beings, simply by being human, have equal dignity and worth, as prescribed in the idea of basic human rights. As the sanctity of life belongs to every person, it cannot be forfeited to any authority. It is protected in all circumstances. Equal treatment emphasizes "similar treatment for similar cases"; that is, all people who are in a similar situation should be treated equally. Thus, the equality principle means equality in worth, access, opportunity, treatment, and procedure, while not necessarily guaranteeing equality of outcome. "All people are ensured equal access to jobs, rights, housing, and pay. This does not mean that all people will get the jobs they want or entrance into the schools they desire, but no personal or external factors will prevent people from fairly competing for the rights and goods available in a given society."[6]

Justice as equality is a formality that is protected by constitutional law and decided by formal public criteria. Historically, it has taken much struggle for human rights movements (e.g., the civil rights movement, women's suffrage movement, First Nations' political movement, LGBTQ rights movement) to gain and implement equal justice.

John Rawls is one of the most well-known philosophers of this principle. He frames distributive justice under the rubric of fairness and proposes two general principles of justice. He proposes that all self-interested rational persons, behind the veil of ignorance, would choose these two principles in structuring a society of fair relationships:

- Principle of Equal Liberty: Each person has equal right to the most extensive liberties. This is compatible with similar liberties for all.

6. Hollinger, *Choosing the Good*, 229.

- Difference Principle: Social and economic inequalities should be arranged so that they are both (a) to the greatest benefit of the least advantaged persons, and (b) attached to offices and positions open to all under conditions of equality of opportunity.

The first principle guarantees the right of each person to have the most extensive basic liberties compatible with the liberty of others. It is egalitarian, since it distributes extensive liberties equally to all persons. The second principle states that social and economic positions are to be open to all with equal opportunity. If there is any inequality, it should be to everyone's advantage. In other words, inequality is acceptable to the extent that it benefits the least-advantaged persons.

New covenant ethics has a strong egalitarian emphasis. It claims that every person, created in God's image, is equal and has inalienable value before God. Every human being, simply by being created in the image of God, is sacred and deserves equal respect regardless of the merits the person possesses. From the beginning, God has bestowed equal dignity on every person. Basic rights, such as the sanctity of life, belong to every person and cannot be forfeited to any authority. For instance, God's commandment against murder given to Noah (Gen. 9:6) is universal and indiscriminately binding on every person. It is the duty of each person to respect the rights of others. In fact, respecting the rights of others is a way to respond to God's love.

From a covenantal perspective, the *imago Dei* indicates the intrinsic relationship of humanity with God. This principle pertains to the rights and membership of every person in the universal covenant of God, starting from the creation covenant, through the Noachian covenant, and culminating in the new covenant fulfilled by Jesus. By virtue of their membership in this community, humans have certain rights. Any exclusion or marginalization from the universal community and its basic rights violates and offends human dignity as well as covenantal bonding.

The equality principle rejects partial treatment based on ascriptive privilege and entitlement. In protecting equal treatment, Scripture speaks extensively of impartiality, especially on the part of judges and kings (Deut. 16:18–20). "You shall not render an unjust judgment; you shall not be partial to the poor or defer to the great: with justice you shall judge your neighbor" (Lev. 19:15). "For [God] makes his sun rise on the evil and on the good, and sends rain on the righteous and on the unrighteous" (Matt. 5:45). "For God shows no partiality" (Rom. 2:11).

The equality principle is difficult to implement because contextual factors such as past historical injustices or the special needs of people (e.g., the disabled) cannot be disregarded. It cannot be applied in any mechanical or blind way (contra Rawls's original position or veil of ignorance). If a social system has been or is unjust to a particular group (race, sex/gender, or class), equality can never be fully actualized without redressing the injustice. The impact or legacy of past injustices must be redressed in order to create more equitable conditions. Similarly, equality alone does not address the special needs of the disabled, who are unable to compete with the abled when both start from the same place. Basic rights are partaken by every human person, but special arrangements of authority and responsibility can be made. "The rule of equal treatment is not absolute, but it is perhaps the fundamental assumption we must make before considering rules for treating some people differently from others. The burden of proof always falls on those who treat persons unequally."[7]

Need

According to needs justice, society distributes resources to meet the basic needs of people regardless of their merits and contributions. According to this principle, people with the greatest needs should be provided more (or at least sufficient) resources.

Fortune or luck does not visit or treat humans equally. Some sow but do not reap; others do not sow but reap through the labor of others. That is why society needs a basic safety net for everyone. Economic security, income, and wealth have a lot to do with who owns the means of production, inherited financial assets, and social status because they determine how much one can reap and what access one has to opportunities. People with inherited assets, social status, and means of production have far better chances to gain the social goods that a society distributes. Unequal access to resources and opportunities inevitably leads to unequal distribution. Without meeting basic needs, equality and human dignity are not protected.

Meeting the needs of people has broad political implications. When their needs are not met, their participation is limited and our community is incomplete. When the poor are excluded from a community, injustices are reproduced and social relationships are further alienated. Relative social equality contributes to the cohesiveness and integration of society.

However, "need" is not unlimited. Given the scarcity of resources, how do we meet the need for everyone, and to what extent do we meet it? Different societies have different definitions of basic needs. For example, in the United States, health care is not considered by all to be a basic need or primary good, while in other countries, secondary education is not a primary good. Usually, however, primary goods in all societies include food, shelter, health, and safety (protection from danger and fear), which are met in the form of health care, unemployment subsidies, welfare payments, etc.

7. Smedes, *Mere Morality*, 38.

Like the equality principle, the criterion of need is supported by the Bible's firm mandate to care for the needy. It is the responsibility of God's people to protect and care for the needy among them because it is a way to reciprocate God's generous gift and care for them. Basic needs include a sense of safety and the removal of hunger, fear, and shame (Ezek. 34:25–30). Justice as need is emphasized in the Bible, as we see in its teachings on the Sabbath, Jubilee, and special care for the poor, widows, and orphans. God's care for the needy is regarded as an essential part of God's justice. Psalm 68:5–6 reads:

> Father of orphans and protector of widows
>   is God in his holy habitation.
> God gives the desolate a home to live in;
>   he leads out the prisoners to prosperity.

Psalm 113:7–9 testifies:

> He raises the poor from the dust,
>   and lifts the needy from the ash heap,
> to make them sit with princes,
>   with the princes of his people.
> He gives the barren woman a home,
>   making her the joyous mother of children.

The Bible emphasizes the need principle in two aspects, by and large: meeting the basic needs of people is crucial in protecting their dignity, which closely associates the need principle with the equality principle; and it is a way to express our solidarity with the needy in God. We are to care for people in need because they are our brothers and sisters in God. The need principle requires a corresponding compassion from society; it is fully achieved when it is upheld not only as the right of the needy but also as the responsibility of others in compassion. In addition, meeting basic needs is not sufficient if it does not address structural injustice. Charity offerings of free food and clothes or a stipend for utility bills or rent does not liberate people from poverty. Such relief typically helps people barely maintain minimal physical subsistence. This is far from overcoming poverty. More often than not, it ends up inculcating dependency. Typically, the poor have no savings or assets to build the economic capability of earning a sizable income or to protect them from emergencies.

Merit

Merit justice grants people what they earn—corresponding to their effort, abilities, and contributions. Merit is something an individual owns by nature or through effort, contributions, and achievement expended for a certain task. While equality and need (as basic rights) pertain equally to all members of humanity, merit is measured according to individual performance, contribution, ability, and expended effort.

Today, a merit approach is predominant in a neoliberal capitalist society under the auspices of its libertarian moral philosophy. People with more merit should be rewarded more than those with none. Merit (talent, skill, attractiveness, expertise, competence), in fact anything that is marketable, is determined by the market and is closely associated with individual freedom. Merit is what an individual owns, and freedom is ability to exercise it without societal intervention or hampering. In other words, we have "the right to do whatever we want with the things we own" insofar as the same rights of others are respected.[8]

Libertarians are ardent advocates of this principle of justice (freedom as right). Rewarding merit is the responsibility of a free society. Without rewarding merit, human freedom cannot be protected and humans cannot flourish, because creativity and a desire for productivity and work are curbed. The crux of libertarian philosophy is "the principle of self-ownership," and merit is what an individual owns. According to this principle, an individual is the most basic and (morally absolute) unit of morality and social life. An individual precedes a society (and its government); thus, the government should play a minimal role to protect individual freedom.

Individual freedom is actualized by ownership of one's self (body), skills, activities, and property. Merits are what individuals own from their effort or by nature's providence (luck, choice). Justice should protect individual freedom and its exercise. In a social life, merits are rewarded in a free market in the form of payment, a free exchange between a buyer and a seller. The role of merit is to create conditions that maximize individual freedom and protect free transactions. Proponents advocate an unregulated free market and a small government.

The merit principle has its place in the Bible. The Bible affirms and encourages the importance of individual responsibility, proper use of gift, and hard work; people should work hard to meet their basic needs. Scott Rae notes that in Scripture, poverty was sometimes considered a misfortune, but at other times it was understood as resulting from laziness—a lack of moral character (Prov. 6:6–11; 10:4–5; 24:30–34). In these situations, the sluggard is not entitled a share in any of society's goods. "It is assumed in both Testaments that if people are able to work to earn their share of society's goods, they are obligated to do so. If they are able and unwilling to work, they do not merit a share of society's goods (1 Thess. 5:12–14; 2 Thess. 3:6–10)."[9] While merit (hard work and its reward) is important, it is always pursued in the context of a community, in covenantal relationship with God, other people, and the land.

8. Sandel, *Justice*, 60.

9. Rae and Cox, *Bioethics*, 271.

Capability

Justice as capability is a relatively recent approach to justice compared to other theories. First suggested by Amartya Sen,[10] this approach has been significantly advanced through the scholarly works of Martha Nussbaum. The metric of capability as justice focuses on what individuals or groups can actually be and do rather than underscoring formal stipulations such as equality or right.[11] The capability approach seeks more than what distributive justice typically desires, namely, the distribution of goods or resources. The goal of capability is actual human flourishing. Its premise is that humans are agents, not passive objects or recipients. It treats persons as subjects rather than objects, protagonists rather than beneficiaries, who exercise their freedom in pursuing happiness, building meaningful relationships, and forming a just community. Protecting equality or meeting basic needs, although necessary, does not guarantee flourishing. In a society, typically, there always exists a gap between formal (*de jure*) freedom and equality and actual (*de facto*) freedom and equality. In a modern democratic society, every person is equal *de jure* but not *de facto*. The enduring existence of institutional racism, sexism, and classism is a glaring example of such a gap. Equality should be actualized rather than just legally pronounced, and its actualization is not possible without the enhancement of the capabilities of every person.

Similarly, capability and meeting basic needs are not necessarily identical. The scope of the former goes beyond the latter. Meeting the basic needs of people is not equivalent to their flourishing. The question is not only how to have sufficient resources to meet people's needs but also how to convert them into actual capabilities for people to achieve their flourishing.[12]

Instead of a formal or deductive method, the capability principle takes an empirical, contextual, and historical approach derived from awareness that various internal personal barriers and external social obstacles prevent the development of capability. Humans are born with some potential, but they are shaped in different ways in different social circumstances, typically under the regimented system of powers (race, gender, class, religion, colonialism). A capability approach pays attention to empirical, personal, and social realities where the demands of justice are measured for their actualization. It examines various personal, cultural, and social conditions that promote or impede the flourishing of individuals and groups. A capability approach supports various policies and measures that create opportunities, such as education and job training, in order to overcome the internal and external obstacles to human flourishing.

10. Sen, "Equality of What?"
11. Nussbaum, *Sex and Social Justice.*
12. Nussbaum, *Sex and Social Justice*, 34.

With its focus on the actual, functional side of justice, the capability approach fills in a missing aspect of formal theories of justice. It complements a formal theory of justice with its emphasis on empowering moral agency and creating the moral ecology and necessary conditions of flourishing. However, critics point out that the theory is overly subjective and contextual in nature (because it "considers people one by one"),[13] thus making it difficult to establish publicly accessible criteria for measurement and assessment. Which capabilities should be selected by what criteria, and to what extent should functioning and capability development be required? In general, the concept of justice is public, and its claims should be publicly assessed, tested, and adjudicated for stability in its implementation. Thus, it is not very effective as a reliable theory of justice. In addition, its implementation could be very expensive. But public criteria are not absolute in pursuing justice. As Martha Nussbaum's theory indicates, society can reach some provisional criteria of capability justice; that is, society can agree upon a minimum threshold of capability for everyone.

The idea of capability is not alien to new covenant ethics. Both capability theory and covenant ethics share human flourishing as the goal. Human flourishing cannot be achieved without growing the functional capabilities of people. In new covenant ethics, capability is related to the "power" aspect of the triad: power is indispensable for the survival and flourishing of every life. Likewise, the actualization of love and enactment of justice are impossible without the capability (power) of people.

The Bible teaches that God endows humans with innate capabilities (natural gifts and talents), nurtures God's creatures with God's generous care (Ps. 104), and creates the condition for flourishing. God's goal is shalom, and God works toward that end with human covenantal partners. Flourishing happens through the actualization of the gifts and talents of each person. Human flourishing is possible only in a just, righteous, and loving community. Covenant is a system that creates the condition for flourishing. God's people experience God's empowering and nurturing presence and work through covenant. By creating just and righteous relationships, covenant offers the optimal condition and the locus of growth in relationship with God and others. In the covenant, God uses various means of grace to empower humans. All members are both entitled to flourishing and called to diligently work toward it. At the same time, they have the responsibility to support and assist the flourishing of others.

To enhance the capability of people, new covenant ethics aims at personal transformation as well as structural change. New covenant ethics regards injustices as well as personal vices as major obstacles to flourishing because they suppress or deprive people of their capabilities. As aforementioned, grassroots organizing as a method increases social and political capability in new covenant ethics.

13. Nussbaum, *Sex and Social Justice*, 34.

Observations

Discerning how to distribute social goods to each person according to what the person is due is an ongoing deliberative process. In policy discussions and public debates, diverse theories of distributive justice differently interpret and prioritize these properties.

Each society, reflecting its culture, ideology, and tradition, sets different priorities among the principles of distributive justice.[14] While capitalism tends to prioritize merit over need, communism reverses these priorities. Justice as merit, advocated by libertarians, presupposes the liberal individualistic idea that humans are autonomous, while justice as need assumes that humans are deeply dependent on each other (solidaric) in fulfilling basic needs.[15] However, since the collapse of the Soviet Union, justice as merit has gained in importance worldwide through the spread of the neoliberal economy, to the extent that other principles of justice are threatened. Today, distributive justice is increasingly understood in terms of individual rights. That is, equality, merit, and basic needs are claimed as the rights of individuals. However, this tends to further remove distributive justice from community and relational contexts, curtailing a broad vision of the common good while increasing confusion and conflict.

One does not have to rely on only one principle. Distributive justice cannot be a single principle uniformly applied to all the spheres and relationships of a society. Diverse principles of justice are necessary to more adequately decide what is owed to whom. They are, in fact, complementary with each other in achieving a more holistic form of distributive justice in a society; for example, a certain principle may be more pertinent to a certain social sphere.

There is overlap between the principles. It is philosophically not easy to decide whether free access to health care fulfills needs justice or equal justice (or both) because health care is central to the protection of human dignity. Additionally, both need and equality are necessary to protect human dignity. Equal access to goods typically reiterates the meeting of needs, especially when the goods in question are food, shelter, and health care.

New covenant ethics offers a coherent conceptual framework to harmonize these competing principles.[16] We need such a framework because these principles do not

14. For example, in the United States, in the wake of the Great Recession in 2008, a reigning ethos is changing, which is more receptive to need, especially among millennials.

15. The two systems differ on whether fulfilling basic needs is a matter of basic human rights or not.

16. A Catholic approach takes the *imago Dei* as the foundation of distributive justice. David Hollenbach, a leading voice on the topic in the United States, defines equality, need, and merit as

automatically harmonize among themselves. Secular liberal ethics embraces these principles while suppressing any teleological framework because it intends to find a universal ground of the good among competing visions. But it has difficulty in coherently harmonizing these principles. Because of the lack of a common framework, people are confused and the principles clash with each other under the different ideologies held by different social groups. For example, this reductionism is seen in the current ideological conflict between meritocracy and economic rights. To a large extent, the political polarization in the United States has to do with the clashes over justice between those who absolutize individual merit (libertarians, neoliberals, conservative Christians) and those who uphold need-based justice (social democrats). A commonly shared, coherent moral framework of justice is lacking.

In new covenant ethics, these principles are not mutually exclusive but complementary. As discussed above, all four principles of justice (equality, need, merit, and capability) are found in the Bible clustered around covenant. From a covenantal perspective, all these principles are necessary to protect human dignity and promote human flourishing. No single principle alone can achieve the fulfillment of the complex and multifaceted nature of distributive justice. History tells us that coercive attempts to impose a single principle (equality, need, or merit) have caused more injustice and distortion and brought harm and suffering to many people. New covenant ethics affirms and celebrates these principles because they are necessary to achieve shalom. Shalom is better actualized when people's basic needs are met, equality is respected, and members are empowered to grow and fulfill their gifts and talents to serve the common good.

Just as love, justice, and power are inseparable in the new covenant of Jesus, need, equality, and capability are closely interrelated in new covenant ethics. The triad of love, justice, and power in new covenant ethics helps integrate these principles to some extent; love and power are correlated to the principles of need and capability, respectively. This implies that these principles are interrelated in covenant.

New covenant upholds the equality of all persons as God's image-bearers. At the same time, the covenant's intrinsic demand of love toward others (especially the poor and the marginalized) explains why the "need" principle is not optional but integral to distributive justice. Love is expressed in compassion toward the needy in recognition of solidarity. Likewise, because the new covenant recognizes the importance of power, the "capability" principle is indispensable in new covenant ethics:

---

the demands of human dignity. To respect the *imago Dei* is to recognize the equal worth of every person; similarly, refusal to meet the basic needs of the poor undermines their human dignity. Hollenbach, *Claims in Conflict*.

"without proper exercise of power, justice is not possible."[17] Love encourages and assists the growth of capability in each person in order to achieve a flourishing that fulfills shalom.

New covenantal ethics espouses a complex, pluralistic theory of distributive justice corresponding to its social vision of associational pluralism.[18] It understands and pursues distributive justice in contexts of different spheres and institutions (special covenants). Different spheres and institutions pursue different goals and distribute different social goods with different relational dynamics and moral norms and expectations.

A covenantal theory of distributive justice is more refined and sophisticated than the simple theory of justice in utilitarianism, libertarianism, and Marxism, which, respectively, uphold utility, merit, and equality as the single prevailing principle of justice. A single, simple theory of justice is limited, for it does not respect the diverse and complex nature of social relationships (spheres and institutions) and moral meanings of diverse goods; it does not make necessary distinctions in distributing goods and spheres. A simplistic theory of justice creates a sort of moral reductionism or totalitarianism; it causes injustice more than it fulfills justice.

New covenant ethics claims a correlation between a principle of justice and the goods circulating in a social sphere. Human experiences tell us that the meaning of distributive principles of justice and goods is sphere-specific. William Werpekowski notes, "Specification of justice requires specification of criteria appropriate to the nature of relationship in question."[19] For instance, fairness, need, and merit in the parent-child relationship are different from them in the employer-worker relationship. As we discussed before, justice (*tsedaqah*) is a covenantal notion in the Bible; to do justice means fitting a moral decision and action to the standards inherent to a specific social relationship.

Goods are distributed differently along different spheres according to different principles of justice. New covenant ethics notices that there is a certain correlation between social goods and social spheres. Although different societies may attribute different interpretations to specific social goods, the meanings of these goods are not completely relativistic. For example, there is general consensus that the primary good in marriage is affection and commitment, not money or status, although this was not always adequately actualized in history. The meaning of major social goods remains more or less stable, correlated to the social spheres and their mandates.

17. De Gruchy, *Reconciliation*, 202.

18. Cf. Walzer, *Spheres of Justice*.

19. Werpekowski, "Justice," 331, cited in Hollinger, *Choosing the Good*, 234.

Different goods are distributed for different reasons, and these differences result from the spheres to which these goods primarily belong. Social spheres and their mandates play an important role in defining the meaning and boundary of the principles, and the criteria, procedure, and agents of distribution. In distributing goods, each sphere follows the principles of justice most pertinent to it and the goods that it shares. Hence, the choice of a material principle of justice depends on the kinds of goods exchanged within a specific sphere (and among its institutions). For example, grades and diplomas are goods of the educational sphere, and merit is the appropriate principle of justice for grading the students' work. Roughly speaking, merit is the dominant principle in the economic sphere, equality is predominant in the political sphere, while need is predominant in health care. To properly understand a meaning of a good, we need to study not only a society's cultural tradition but also how that good is associated with a particular sphere and its institutions.

However, deciding which principle(s) of justice applies to which social relationships, or which social goods should be distributed to which people, is not as easy as it appears. Usually, more than one principle of distributive justice is involved in the distribution of a certain good. For example, organ transplantation in the United States is guided by the principles of need and equality. Moreover, there are ongoing public debates and social controversies, for example, in the area of college admissions: whether admission should be decided by merit alone or whether other factors (race, gender, heritage) should be considered, and if so, to what degree. The decision is a matter of broader society's ethical discernment about which principle of justice should be prioritized, for how long and to what extent (in relationship to other principles). The ongoing task of social ethics and public policy is to discern and establish reasonable criteria for distribution in applying the principles of justice. Careful distinctions are necessary to determine which material principles of justice are more appropriate for a specific social good.

To better construe the issue of fulfilling justice and to establish the standards of distribution, we must carefully examine each individual case and see which principles of justice apply to it, in what proportions, with which priorities, and why. Such discernment definitely requires a considerable degree of skill.

Through its complex, pluralistic theory, new covenant ethics helps reduce hermeneutical confusion and misunderstanding in applying the principles of justice. Thus, it secures reliability and a more objective possibility in ethical observations and deliberations. In studying a particular social issue, new covenant social ethics asks: What is a particular covenantal context and what does it mandate (or what is its intrinsic relational and moral requisite)? What kinds of goods are distributed? Which principles of justice are appropriate for this case? Are current, socially dominant principles of justice valid and relevant in light of the core convictions of the

Bible (refracted through the covenant of Jesus)? If a gap or a conflict exists between a secular (civic) choice principle and biblical convictions, what appropriate measure addresses it?

Conclusion

The above observation shows that new covenant ethics presents a coherent and plausible theory that integrates four principles of distributive justice. The four principles have their place in new covenant ethics, which brings them under the rubric of the divine drama of liberation-restoration. By virtue of its complex and pluralistic theological sociology (i.e., associational pluralism), distributive justice in new covenant ethics is different from a simplistic theory of justice. Within a covenantal framework, none of these principles are absolute or exclusive; rather, they complement each other in a balanced and harmonious way, contributing to the shalom community. Outside of this organic relational framework, the principles of justice are abstract, reified, and hegemonic, as seen in secular liberal ethics.

Furthermore, by showing the correlation between social goods and spheres, new covenant ethics offers a plausible moral explanation for why a particular distribution should happen according to a particular principle and not according to other principles. However, the work of distributive justice depends on the task of liberation-restoration. Without first setting structures and conditions to right, distributive justice serves only the status quo of unjust relationships, merely softening or mitigating its most devastating or destructive effects.

The task of justice is never completed in history. Despite God's ravishing love demonstrated in Jesus, brokenness, conflicts, and evils still persist. Discernment, deliberation, and nonviolent actions are indispensable aspects of a moral life for achieving relative justice in the context of human frailty and sin.

In the following chapters, we study how these principles of justice apply to various social issues; in the framework of new covenant ethics, we see whether justice is well served and what are current problems of justice in the United States. We offer alternatives in light of the vision, dynamics, and norms/values of new covenant ethics.

CHAPTER 13

Politics

> Man's capacity for justice makes democracy possible, but man's inclination to injustice makes democracy necessary.
>
> —Reinhold Niebuhr, *The Children of Light and the Children of Darkness*

> Every demon, according to the tradition, is a fallen angel; every hell on earth is a promise of paradise gone crazy and become self-absorbed. Each of these areas, and each segment of our diversified lives, can curve in on itself, begin to worship its own powers, deify its own potentialities, and conspire with others to monopolize its own benefits, as if it were self-sufficient. When that happens, evil possesses the individual life and wickedness begins to characterize culture. Civil society is deconstructed, politics become but an orgy of power, stupidity is celebrated, sickness besets many, businesses fail, the arts do not inspire, marriages fall apart, and prayer ceases.
>
> —Max Stackhouse, *Covenant and Commitments*

The collapse of the Soviet Union was a landmark historical event. More than just the end of the Cold War, it was the ideological victory of the United States over the Soviet Union, prompting the spread of liberal democracy and capitalism. It also opened up labor and commodity markets for corporations and heralded a brief period of US unipolar power.

However, starting in 2008, we saw the reversal of the democratic trend and the rise of illiberal and authoritarian political systems. This global political situation has to do with how the United States has misused its status as the unipolar superpower. US authority has been undermined, while in its place, Russia and China are emerging with assertive and authoritarian power. Countries that appeared to become liberal democracies in the 1990s—including Hungary, Poland, Thailand, and Turkey—have slid backward toward authoritarianism. The Arab Spring revolts of 2010–2011 disrupted dictatorships throughout the Middle East but yielded little in terms of democratization. In their wake, despotic regimes held on to power and civil wars racked Iraq, Libya, Syria (thanks to US military interference), and Yemen. But most surprising and perhaps most damaging has been the political success of nationalist populism in the United Kingdom and the United States, two of the world's most durable liberal democracies. In elections held in 2016, the voters of the United Kingdom chose to leave the European Union, and in the United States voters elected Donald Trump.

Today, liberal democracy is fraught with several major obstinate difficulties. The retreat of democracy has to do with the increasing internal contradictions of liberal democracy under new social-economic conditions. The converging forces of globalization, Internet technology, and neoliberalism have altered the social and cultural conditions of liberal democracy. These changes call for the restructuring of ideology, adaptability, public discourse, and the relationship between state and market.

We live in a deeply divided and fragmented society where civility and tolerance are frequent casualties. Politics is driven more and more by partisan power and control, private interests, and fulfilling the Nietzschean will to power. Ideological differences[1] and political interests clash around many critical issues—judicial appointments, the size and role of the government, taxes, abortion, budget deficits, the debt limit, same-sex marriage, and the list goes on.[2] These examples show that we are losing good democratic traditions of rule of law, constitutionalism, negotiation, compromise, public discourse, and the care of the commons.

This chapter begins by studying the crisis of liberal democracy in the West in light of rising illiberal democracy and authoritarianism. Then, it explores how the moral values and political insights of new covenant ethics could contribute to the renewal of democracy and civil society by examining its contributions to democracy

1. In the United States, the divisions between Republicans and Democrats increasingly reflect different political philosophies based on different views of human nature, society, and government.

2. Francis Fukuyama notes: "Our present world is simultaneously moving toward the opposing dystopias of hypercentralization and endless fragmentation. China, for instance, is building a massive dictatorship in which the government collects highly specific personal data on the daily transactions of every citizen. On the other hand, other parts of the world are seeing the breakdown of centralized institutions, the emergence of failed states, increasing polarization, and a growing lack of consensus over common ends. Social media and the Internet have facilitated the emergence of self-contained communities, walled off not by physical barriers but by shared identities." Fukuyama, "Against Identity Politics."

and democratic institutions such as human rights, constitutionalism, checks and balances, and unity-in-diversity. The current crisis, to a large extent, has to do with the decline of covenantalism in the West, in the United States in particular. I argue that the reconstruction of covenantal politics is necessary to revitalize domestic democracy and strengthen its viability in global civil society and the digital realm.

The State of Politics Today

Generally speaking, politics has to do with governance—the organizing or ordering of a society. It refers to various activities of governance: arranging institutions and legal procedures in order to distribute goods and adjudicating diverse claims and conflicting interests according to the principles of justice in light of a society's shared goal. In short, politics is the art of symbiosis.

Politics typically includes three dimensions: moral vision and values, power, and institutional structure.

1. *Morality*: Politics is guided by a certain moral vision of the good and values (right, good, and fitting): how institutions and people should behave and live under a particular polity.[3] Organizing a polity is a process of arranging and managing various institutions according to this vision and values. It includes the conception of justice that guides the authority and power to distribute goods and resources (including privileges, burdens, and responsibilities) by accepted procedures.
2. *Power*: Different from the moral dimension, this dimension concerns ways that people actually decide and behave, that is, the actual distribution of power: who has power, how much, and on what basis; who is influential and why. The power dimension encompasses class structure, ethnic composition, and type of economy.[4]
3. *Frame of government*: Politics always includes a certain form of governing structure and law that arranges various institutions and procedures. These structures regulate the behaviors of persons and groups in accordance with laws that reflect the society's moral vision and values.

Balance and harmony among the three are important to maintain a political order that is accepted as legitimate, efficient, and transparent. These dimensions are helpful for understanding several issues that are challenging the US political system

3. Elazar, *Covenant and Polity in Biblical Israel*, 29.
4. Elazar, *Covenant and Polity in Biblical Israel*, 29.

today: deepening political divisions, the rise of illiberal democracy, and distrust of the political system and its processes.

Threats to Liberal Democracy

Despite its super military power and rich resources, the United States is undergoing major political difficulties because of its dearth of shared moral vision and values/norms and its loss of legitimacy. Hence the rise of illiberal legitimacy and authoritarianism indicates a major threat to its democratic polity. A major threat to liberal democracy is its gradual loss of moral authority and political legitimacy, which creates cultural conditions auguring illiberal democracy and identity politics. Legitimacy means "the generalized perception that the actions of an entity are appropriate within some socially constructed systems of norms, values, and beliefs."[5]

The erosion of legitimacy reflects deepening economic inequality under neoliberalism. Over the past half century under neoliberalism, economic growth has become a major source of political legitimacy in the United States. However, stagnant or declining incomes and job losses/insecurity are no longer matters of the economic cycle (boom and recession) but have become a permanent structural reality of the system. Job insecurity and income inequality have become a source of collective angst and despair. When factories close down or move locations, the livelihoods of people are threatened, and local communities turn into ghost towns with the loss of income, security, and future hope. Economic insecurity and the decline of community contribute to the rise in divorce, depression, drug abuse, mental illness, and suicide.

When people do not experience any economic benefits, they lose trust in politics. The legitimacy of democracy, the government, and social institutions is challenged. Martin Fougère's observation is poignant: "Today our ways of governing become increasingly unpolitical as there are no institutions with the legitimacy—meaning, notably, both a political mandate and enough power—to organize the common good in today's globalized world."[6]

With the ascendance of neoliberalism, politics is more and more decided by corporate power. This has prompted the rise of populism in the United States and other places. The anger and frustration of people are prompted by a sense of injustice, exacerbated by the demise of their communities and the decline of their quality of life. Under corporate oligarchy, social mobility is stalled, equal opportunity sounds like a hollow slogan, and freedom is more nominal than actual, more formal than

5. Suchman, "Managing Legitimacy," 574.
6. Fougère, "Corporations as Political and Unpolitical Actors," 16.

substantial. While living in a globalizing society, more and more people feel lost, their voices muted on issues pertaining to their survival and future well-being.

What Is Liberal Democracy?

Liberal democracy is a political system characterized by constitutionalism (rule of law), respect for human rights, free elections, separation of powers among different branches, civil society, public discourse and civic virtue, and checks and balances. It upholds individual freedom and rights.[7] Democracy developed as a political system fighting against monarchy and aristocracy. Liberal democracy is "liberal" because it upholds the protection of individual freedom as one of its core creeds. It spread further as the majority world fought against external Western colonialism and internal military dictatorship and autocracy. "As of the end of 2017, 96 out of 167 countries with populations of at least 500,000 (57%) were democracies of some kind, and only 21 (13%) were autocracies. Nearly four dozen other countries—46, or 28%—exhibited elements of both democracy and autocracy."[8]

Liberal democracy relies on several mechanisms that prevent the concentration of power: the separation of powers, constitutionalism (and the rule of law), associational pluralism, and the idea of human rights. Most importantly, it declares that the sovereignty of the nation is with the people: it is the system "of the people, by the people, for the people," as President Abraham Lincoln has famously announced. People elect their representatives, and the government is open to periodic change through an election in which each citizen exercises the right to vote.

What Is Illiberal Democracy?

To the surprise of pundits and proponents of "the end of history," liberal democracy is now eroding in the United States and Europe—the birthplace of liberal democracy—and other parts of the world. Today, "illiberal democracy," or a similar tendency, is gaining ground. The election of Trump and other authoritarian leaders is a symptom of an undeniable trend sweeping the world, most notably affecting

7. Zakaria, "The Rise of Illiberal Democracy," 22–43. "Constitutional liberalism developed in Western Europe and the United States as a defense of the individual's right to life and property, and freedom of religion and speech. To secure these rights, it emphasized checks on the power of each branch of government, equality under the law, impartial courts and tribunals, and separation of church and state."

8. Desilver, "Despite Global Concerns about Democracy, More Than Half of Countries Are Democratic."

Russia, India, Turkey, Hungary, Poland, Peru, Sierra Leone, Slovakia, Pakistan, and the Philippines.

Illiberal democracy is pseudodemocracy. It retains a constitutional form of democracy—political leaders are elected through elections—but once elected, their power takes an authoritarian form that gradually dismantles the system of checks and balances, weakens the legislative and judicial branches, and curtails freedom of speech and the rule of law. It concentrates power into a single party or leader, amends the constitution using various extraconstitutional means, and employs the state media as a propaganda tool. Using its newly gained power, illiberal regimes further suppress free media outlets and opposition parties. It is "illiberal" because basic rights and freedoms (assembly, religion, media, and speech), democratic institutions, and free elections are not properly protected.

Illiberal democracy criticizes traditional liberal democracy as ineffective, secular, and alien.[9] This undermines national unity and identity grounded in a distinctive history, tradition, religion, and peoplehood. It is typically hostile to multiculturalism and emphasizes national identity, traditional values, "order, control of the press, family, religion, the cult of the homeland, and the 'mythification' of the past."[10] Illiberal democracy exploits popular discontent aroused by economic inequality, a longing for stability, and skepticism toward the current state of globalization. To gain and expand power, it exploits the fear, anxiety, and instability engendered by globalization and demographic changes. It labels globalism, multiculturalism, tolerance, diversity, and the rights of minorities as sheer elitist ideologies. Its political platform includes a strong military, control of the border, law and order, and an agenda that is markedly anti-immigration, anti-Islam, and antimulticultural. In the West, illiberal democracy takes a white nationalist or nativist form—a political expression of white identity politics. It scapegoats immigrants, refugees, and ethnic minorities, making them targets of the anger and frustration of white people who long for stability, power, and status. It does not hesitate to use disinformation, fake news, and violent rhetoric to achieve its political goals. The potential danger is that it may develop into a fascism where freedom of press, human rights, democratic checks and balances, and the rule of law become merely nominal or completely abolished under the control of one leader or a party.

The rise of illiberal democracy is structural. As mentioned before, it has to do with massive structural changes caused by several forces with their interlocking effects: globalization, economic inequality, moral relativism, and digitalization. The

9. Capitalizing on this crisis, Russia and China are aggressively seeking to expand their geopolitical influences by promoting their authoritarian framework of politics.

10. Dozier, "What Exactly Is 'Illiberal Democracy'?"

global economy along with the automation and outsourcing of jobs has destroyed the economic security of white blue-collar workers. Open borders and the influx of immigrants make them fearful of being replaced by people of color and, when combined with declining birthrates, of losing their status as the racial majority. Trump's campaign slogan, "Make America Great Again," touched the anxiety and nostalgia of whites and empowered them to reassert their cultural identity and hegemony against perceived threats from people of color. "During the 2016 campaign, the most potent political sentiment held that 'people like me' were not getting ahead because of 'people like them.' In the primary race, support for Trump among white Americans was weakly associated with whether people were worried about losing their jobs but strongly associated with whether people believed that employers were giving jobs to minorities instead of whites."[11] Unfortunately, the illiberal tendency will continue as long as key structural elements remain intact, regardless of the change of political parties. "Far from being a temporary or transitional stage, it appears that many countries are settling into a form of government that mixes a substantial degree of democracy with a substantial degree of illiberalism. Just as nations across the world have become comfortable with many variations of capitalism, they could well adopt and sustain varied forms of democracy."[12]

Identity Politics

Along with illiberal democracy, contemporary identity politics affects both the Right and the Left. Identity politics refers to political agendas and activities that are based on some aspect(s) of a person's identity: sexuality, gender, race, ethnicity, age, religion, disability, and so on. Examples include liberation movements of African Americans, feminists, womanists, Latinx, LGBTQ, Asian Americans, the Black Lives Matter movement, and the #MeToo movement.

While identity politics on the left focuses on equality and political recognition of various marginalized groups (ethno-racial and sexual minorities, women, and immigrants and refugees), the Right is passionate about the defense of traditional religious and cultural identity and heritage, symbolized by a national flag and border control, and white Protestant Christianity.

Not all members of a given group are involved in identity politics, but it gains its potency due to the pluralistic nature of society. Like the rise of illiberal democracy, identity politics results from the structural and demographic changes taking place in our society. The structural forces of globalization, migration, and the postmodern

11. Sides, Tesler, and Vavreck, "Five Myths about the 2016 Election."
12. Zakaria, "The Rise of Illiberal Democracy."

ideology of self-construction are conducive to the rise of identity politics—the rise of multiculturalism through hyperexchanges and movements of diverse ethno-racial peoples and cultural products in the same place.

Philosophically, postmodernism offers the philosophical foundation for identity politics, for identity politics is empowered by the postmodern sensibility toward particularity and multiculturalism. (1) Identity politics emphasizes the importance of distinctive lived experiences coming from different histories, cultures, and traditions. The postmodern epistemology of self-construction provides the intellectual justification of identity politics. (2) While emphasizing diversity, it minimizes the necessity of the national unity that has been coercive toward minority groups (via racism, sexism, and homophobia). Marginalized groups increasingly demand not only equal treatment under the law but also public recognition of their distinctiveness and differences. (3) Identity politics asserts its genuine equality against a dominant group and aspires to recover long-overdue justice for marginalized people. The proponents of identity politics see the inadequacies of current laws in addressing systematic injustices and discrimination. They challenge the dominant ways of thinking and living (lifestyle), and social mores and cultural expectations (white, male, heterosexual, Christian). Many of these new, assertive voices of identity are as necessary to protect basic human rights as they are politically overdue.[13] We need to give moral and emotional spaces for them to express their pain and suffering.

However, when confined to its echo chambers, a reified form of identity politics, which often borders on binary essentialism (oppressor-oppressed), may further fragment our democracy and create new forms of exclusionism toward outsiders. Rather than creating opportunities for dialogue, reified identity politics builds barriers between groups that operate within virtual intellectual enclaves and cultural bubbles.

Furthermore, a binary essentialism that operates by the logic of power may inadvertently cause another form of marginalization. "Just as dominant groups in the culture at large insist that the marginalized integrate by assimilating to dominant norms, so within some practices of identity politics dominant sub-groups may, in theory and practice, impose their vision of the group's identity onto all its members."[14] Instead of a binary logic that accrues hermeneutical privilege to the oppressed and a postmodern relativist approach, we need to take an inductive, communicative approach, examining each situation carefully in light of historical facts, evidence, and warrants.

13. For example, the Black Lives Matter movement is necessary to publicize and confront the police brutality against African Americans and other people of color.

14. Hayes, "Identity Politics."

A rigid form of identity politics, which operates with a binary logic or a monocategorical (siloed) approach, is unable to address the complexity of diverse cultural and racial relationships. Nor is it effective in building political coalitions that countervail the oligarchic power of corporations. A fractured form of identity politics that lacks respect for democratic procedures and the common goal is ultimately detrimental to the founding moral vision of identity politics. In a pluralistic society, we need a common vision to coordinate our conflicting interests and struggles as well as to legitimate the assertion of identity.

As we will soon discuss, a healthy form of identity politics need not rely on postmodernism and a binary logic. Rather, it could be incorporated into covenantal ethics, with its critical realist epistemology operating through communicative action.[15]

Summary

The liberal democratic order is facing a crisis as its institutions decay and its legitimacy is being challenged. Liberal democracy requires a major reinvention by adjusting to changing social conditions. While important, free elections alone do not create democracy. Democracy requires a democratic ecosystem (including cultural institutions such as free media, citizenship, and economic security/rights). Any successful democracy requires a vibrant democratic culture, a robust civil society, the support and commitment of the people (legitimacy), and a strong middle class (economic security).

It becomes clear that liberal democracy cannot survive unless current economic inequality and the concentration of wealth and power are corrected. Sensing the possibility of multiple system failures (e.g., global economic meltdown, the spread of the surveillance system and loss of privacy, and climate change), young people are eager to try a new system.[16] Repairing liberal democracy is not an easy task. "Democratic deficit"[17] is deep, and it could get worse if there is no major structural change, cultural renewal, and radical transformation of values.

On the other hand, fear, doubt, and angst about democracy are also felt within the conservative Christian community; suspicion, reservation, and criticism against liberal democracy are growing. Conservative Christians have been very critical of abstract liberal ethics, which is perceived to be oppressive to their particular moral convictions. They are willing to support illiberal democracy or authoritarianism

15. Francis Fukuyama is mistaken in claiming that multiculturalism has become an alternative vision of a society to liberal democracy because the former can be incorporated into the latter in a covenantal political framework.

16. Dembicki, "Naomi Klein."

17. Hollenbach, *The Common Good and Christian Ethics*, 212.

(Trumpism) to protect their political and social interests even at the expense of some democratic procedures and values, such as the human rights of religious, racial, and gender minorities. Communitarian and neoorthodox Christians call for a return to a primitive form of Christianity by abiding by a countercultural Christian narrative, tradition, and community life against a liberal society, while some advocate a neomonastic movement.

How can new covenant ethics address the challenges of democracy today? How can it empower and resuscitate civil society and its civic institutions?

The following section discusses the new covenant ethics approach to democracy. I claim that new covenant ethics is crucial to the renewal of democracy as its legitimacy is challenged and the foundations of democratic institutions and civil society are undermined by the rise of fake news, conspiracy theories, and the erosive power of money. This renewal is possible because there is a certain historical and moral affinity between democracy and covenant in modern Western history.[18] New covenant ethics offers a moral worldview, key organizing principles, core moral values, and practices that are indispensable to renew and expand democracy today. Revised in light of new covenant ethics, covenantal polity is a compelling alternative to hierarchal, contractual, organicist, and sectarian models of politics.

New Covenant Ethics

The rise of modern democracy and its institutions was a creative synthesis of Protestant Christianity (its Reformed and Anabaptist versions) and Enlightenment philosophy (notably social contractarians such as Thomas Hobbes, John Locke, and Jean-Jacques Rousseau).[19] Historians and political scientists acknowledge the distinctive contributions of covenant theology to modern democracy, constitutionalism, human rights, rule of law, associational pluralism, civil society, international law, lay educa-

18. I do not claim that democracy is a divinely ordained system for humanity. No political arrangement can fully meet the moral demands of God's reign because a political life is always characterized by moral ambiguity, sin, injustice, and conflicts. But certain political systems are relatively better than others when they are organized in a way that protects human dignity and justice and promotes human flourishing and the common good. Among various political systems practiced in human history, democracy best approximates the moral ideals that the covenant stands for. Its structural patterns, core values, and norms offer an organizational vision, a road map, and the directives for a better society.

19. Democracy (liberal, democratic socialist, participatory, representative) and Christianity have diverse forms and expressions in history. Not every form of Christianity was conducive to the development of democracy; in fact, some (the Roman Catholic Church before Vatican II and the Religious Right of the United States) have been reactionary or theocratic.

tion (literacy), and civic virtues.[20] Elazar observes that "the road to modern democracy began with the protestant Reformation in the sixteenth century, particularly among those exponents of Reformed Protestantism . . . who developed a theology and politics that set the Western world back on the road to popular self-government, emphasizing liberty and equality."[21] While far from perfect, without covenantalism the United States might have a very different form of democracy, or none at all.[22]

The biblical idea of covenant was rediscovered by Bullinger, Zwingli, Calvin, and other theologians during the Reformation. These early Reformed theologians identified covenant as consistent with how God deals with humanity, and they conceived the entirety of human history as covenantal history.[23] That is to say, covenant, based on a voluntary agreement under God, was viewed as a divinely ordained constitutive mechanism to arrange and order a society, with both theological coherence and practical applicability.

Refined through the Puritans of both England and New England, especially free church Calvinists and the radical wing of the Reformation (Anabaptists, Mennonites, and Quakers),[24] covenant provided a theologically grounded, politically effective paradigm for organizing both ecclesial and civic life. Democratic principles and values (such as constitutionalism, the rule of law, popular sovereignty, natural rights) advanced among free church Christians who took covenant as the constitutive model of their churches and society. Elazar observes: "Covenant provided reformers a voluntary compact rather than conquest, divine bequest, or organic evolution. Instead of regarding civil society as a private thing, a system of personalistic favoritism and clientelism, the new covenantalism construed civil society as a republic in the original sense of the Latin term *res publica,* meaning a public thing."[25]

In the following section, I engage new covenant ethics by discussing several core political principles of covenant that helped shape modern democracy and seeing how new covenant ethics invigorates, refines, and expands them.

20. H. Richard Niebuhr, "The Idea of Covenant and American Democracy," 126–35; Walzer, *The Revolution of the Saints;* May, *Testing the National Covenant,* but most extensively, Daniel J. Elazar's four-volume work in The Covenant Tradition in Politics Series: *Covenant and Polity in Biblical Israel; Covenant and Commonwealth; Covenant and Constitutionalism;* and *Covenant and Civil Society.*

21. Elazar, *Covenant and Commonwealth,* 312.

22. H. Richard Niebuhr, "The Idea of Covenant," 135.

23. Klempa, "The Concept of Covenant," 94.

24. Glen Stassen discusses the contribution of the Puritan idea of covenant for the rise of constitutional democracy, human rights, and science in Europe. He notes that the Puritan rage for order (and its early authoritarian tendency) was partly corrected with the more Christocentric voice of a radical wing of the Reformation: Baptists, Anabaptists, and Quakers. Stassen, *A Thicker Jesus,* 66.

25. Elazar, *Covenant and Commonwealth,* 154.

1. shalom
2. unity-in-diversity
3. public discourse
4. antidomination (checks and balances)
5. civil society and the subsidiarity principle
6. civic virtues and character formation
7. covenanting globalization

Shalom

Every society needs a common moral vision and certain shared norms that bind and guide individuals and institutions as the criteria of evaluation and adjudication. But a shared vision is challenging because of the radical diversity of religion and culture. Without it, however, politics becomes petty and partisan, as we are experiencing today; as a result, conflict and division grow and individuals lack motivation to participate in civic affairs and fulfill their civic responsibilities. Experts, bureaucrats, and political pundits may analyze numerous policies, but they fail to offer direction for the entire society. Some form of a common moral vision, other than economic prosperity, is indispensable, especially in a religiously and culturally pluralistic society like ours. The democratic system (constitutional principles, procedures) cannot be sustained without a viable democratic moral vision. John De Gruchy notes that democratic vision refers to "the hope for a society in which all people are truly equal and yet where difference is respected; a society where all people are really free, yet social responsibility rather than individual self-interest prevails; and a society which is truly just, and therefore one in which the vast gulf between the rich and the poor has been overcome."[26] This vision is consistent with covenant. As our current situation starkly illustrates, a democratic system without a democratic moral vision ends up as a heartless bureaucracy unable to inspire, move, and organize people for a larger cause or cope with major threats such as global warming.

New covenant ethics offers shalom as a democratic moral vision in a new cultural context. Shalom is not a parochial vision but a cosmic, cosmopolitan vision for building an ecological civilization in a globalizing world. It is an apt vision for a globalizing, pluralistic society because it is an ensemble of diverse creatures in a unity of love and harmony. It is inclusive and egalitarian and respects the basic

26. De Gruchy, *Christianity and Democracy*, 7. He says this vision originated in the prophetic vision of the OT, especially in the prophets' messianic hope for shalom, whereas the democratic system, its rudimentary form, developed in ancient Athens.

rights of every member, both human and nonhuman, while actualizing the common good.[27] Covenantally interpreted, shalom shows how the parts and whole are interrelated, balanced, and complementary toward one another. The core values and norms of new covenant ethics (see chap. 7) explain what shalom looks like and how it operates.

As a coherent moral vision, it helps overcome widening dissonance within liberal democracy—between right and responsibility, the individual and society, local and global, and justice and the common good. Shalom embodies human desires for freedom, justice, peace, and reciprocity (mutually caring community). It resists domination, concentration of power, and privilege, as well as antinomian, chaotic moral relativism. Shalom is broad enough to embrace new and diverse concerns of race, sex, gender, and class, while avoiding their reification into a parochial epistemology.

However, Christians should not impose this vision upon others, as the Religious Right has done. In the context of new covenant ethics, shalom can be translated into a public vision and language through publicly shared symbols, values, and ideals. Far from parochial, shalom resonates with the deep human desires for flourishing, peace, and security, even as Christians may differ on how to achieve these goals.

Unity-in-Diversity

New covenant ethics concretely embodies shalom in the institutional arrangements of society through the principle of unity-in-diversity. One major challenge facing democratic politics today is how to create meaningful unity (including a common purpose) out of diverse groups. In a pluralistic society, social integration is difficult; the nation is ideologically and politically divided. Through the global exchange of people, goods, and symbols, diverse cultures, beliefs, and ideologies coexist in one place. Furthermore, in response to centuries-long racism, sexism, and homophobia, and the influence of postmodernism, any claim of unity or integration is met with deep political and cultural suspicion. However, a democratic society—in fact, any society—cannot be built upon diversity alone. Ron Sider contends: "For without ideas in common, no common action would be possible, and without common action, men might exist but there could be no body social. For society to exist, and even more, for society to prosper, it is essential that all minds of the citizens should always be rallied and held together by some leading ideas."[28] Democracy,

27. Three blocks of text (Exod. 1–15; Gen. 47:13–26; and Deut. 12–25) show that the covenant intends "a just, egalitarian social order and process." Brueggemann, *A Social Reading of the Old Testament*, 59–60.

28. Sider, *The Scandal of Evangelical Politics*, 35.

for its long-term integrity and health, requires not only free self-assertion but also some shared rules and a sense of the common good to adjudicate diverse claims, coordinate exchanges, and distribute goods.[29] In fact, as society gets more complex and highly mobile, the necessity for coordination increases.

As we have discussed, covenant is the mechanism for organizing according to the principles of justice because it builds agreement among different parties. Covenant brings separate entities together to form a political body with a shared purpose without necessitating the sacrifice of their respective freedom, integrity, and identities. New covenant ethics upholds the idea of unity without suppressing the particularity of its participants (the second dialectic). In covenant, the communal dimension (love and unity) is as important as individual rights and self-assertion. "In sum, a covenant-based politics looks toward political arrangements established or more appropriately, compounded, through the linking of separate entities in such a way that each preserves its respective integrity while creating a common and continuing association to serve those purposes, broad or limited, for which it was called into being. These purposes range from keeping the peace through a permanent but very limited alliance of independent entities to the forging of a new polity through the union of previously separate entities to create a new whole."[30]

As a stepchild of covenant politics, liberal democracy also seeks to achieve unity among diverse groups on the basis of public reason and common interest. However, harmony in a pluralistic society is increasingly difficult to achieve because the moral commitment to the common good and respect for others have substantially eroded under the neoliberal culture of expressive individualism and utilitarianism. The ideas of human rights and the rule of law, detached from a deep moral vision and ground, are getting thinner and thinner. Also, the epistemological and experiential gaps among various cultural and age groups are quite large (due to a lack of openness to self-criticism or humility to yield to better, more cogent arguments made by others).

Today, the rise of authoritarian/illiberal democracy and deepening political polarization (along with divisive identity politics) are symptoms that a liberal approach to unity-in-diversity is failing. Unity and diversity seem increasingly incompatible ideas, either diverging toward monism (conformity) or factionalism (fragmentation).

29. Many community organizers in the post-Alinsky era are aware of this limitation of Alinsky's protest-based, populist orientation. Boyte observes: "IAF [Industrial Areas Foundation] groups believe that it is not sufficient to simply protest; to 'move into power' on a continuing basis in the modern world, citizens must also assume an important measure of responsibility for the basis public goods of their community." Boyte, *Commonwealth*, 82.

30. Elazar, *Covenant and Polity in Biblical Israel*, 44.

New covenant ethics rejects a traditional Eurocentric unity and social integration inherited from the colonial past. A genuine unity, though eschatological, is achieved through voluntary agreement based on justice. New covenant ethics nurtures particular group identities, but always in relation to justice in the context of the common good. New covenant ethics fully protects the rights of traditionally marginalized groups. Their diverse voices must be protected, and the long-ignored injustice and marginalization they have experienced must be corrected as soon as possible. In the conservative emphasis on national identity, unity and social integration typically entail assimilation to the status quo, which is unacceptable. It is disguised Eurocentrism (white normativity), not genuine and inclusive unity grounded in free, equal, and reciprocal agreement.

To a large extent, we acknowledge that current racial identity politics is a reaction to long-standing white identity politics that has dominated the political landscape and history. Public recognition and reparation of racial marginalization and exclusion (colonialism, genocide, slavery, and segregation) are overdue for racial minority groups.

At the same time, various identity groups must respect and abide by democratic rules and norms such as respecting civic rational discourses and public reasoning and the principles of justice. The particularity of identities and lived experiences cannot unreservedly override the necessity for reasoned deliberation and validity claims in the public square. Without a clear covenantal vision and shared guiding principles, identity politics will likely lead to the balkanization of the body politic. Strictly speaking, a parochial form of identity politics is not democratic but tribalistic and marginalizes those not belonging to the identity group. Francis Fukuyama observes:

> On the right, white nationalists would like to replace the creedal national identity with one based on race, ethnicity, and religion. On the left, the champions of identity politics have sought to undermine the legitimacy of the American national story by emphasizing victimization, insinuating in some cases that racism, gender discrimination, and other forms of systematic exclusion are in the country's DNA. Such flaws have been and continue to be features of American society, and they must be confronted. But progressives should also tell a different version of U.S. history, one focused on how an ever-broadening circle of people have overcome barriers to achieve recognition of their dignity.[31]

Our society needs to rebuild its national identity on the basis of a creedal identity that is informed by a shared vision, democratic values, and principles that encom-

31. Fukuyama, "Against Identity Politics."

pass diverse identity groups, and not on the basis of white normativity or postmodern self-construction.

Creedal identity is covenantally created on the basis of a shared moral vision, moral principles and values (freedom, equality, and rights), and past historical experiences that people have shared. Creedal identity is a collective identity—"something conceived or fabricated out of natures antecedently multiple."[32] It is a new collective identity built upon agreement among diverse groups. When society does not have such identity that people can trust or draw on, then they resort to their tribal identities that function as antecedent identities.

Creedal identity does not reject religious convictions, racial-ethnic traditions, or lived experiences. It translates and transvalues them into the creedal identity in the context of rising interdependence and solidarity.[33] Creedal identity is consistent with the spirit of the very opening of the US Constitution: "We the People." However, covenantal identity is neither fixed nor static. As the Constitution explains, it is "charged with the ongoing task of forming 'a more perfect Union.'" This means that "we are at once a community but also a community in the making. We are a reality, but also a project."[34] Its vision is congruent with the US motto, *E Pluribus Unum*, which underwrites America as a project of unity in diversity, diversity in unity—namely, a covenantal project.

Because the United States is different from European nations, creedal identity is urgently needed. While European national identity is natural (growing out of what already existed before modernity),[35] the national identity of the United States is artificial, made of immigrants with diverse racial, ethnic, and cultural identities from around the world. Such identity is necessary to educate younger generations and help immigrants assimilate into a society, though not in such a way that leaves their heritage behind.[36]

Through its practices of communicative action and just peacemaking, new covenant ethics finds and builds unity out of diversity and develops a creedal identity that embraces diverse cultural identities. The practice of communicative engagement invites people to public discourse in order to share ideas and mutual interests and build a new form of solidarity. Similarly, just peacemaking offers constructive ways to heal alienation and division among different racial, ethnic, and gender groups. Through these practices, different individuals and groups, once separated, alienated, and antagonized, may build among themselves a new form of social bonding.

32. May, *Testing the National Covenant*, 82.
33. Fukuyama, "Against Identity Politics."
34. May, *Testing the National Covenant*, 87.
35. May, *Testing the National Covenant*, 82.
36. Fukuyama, "Against Identity Politics."

Public Discourse

In democracy, public discourse plays a crucial role in clarifying concerns and issues and building consensus (or at least a majority view). In the process, it revitalizes democracy and civil society. A free, fair, and open rule-making procedure and public deliberation is crucial for democratic governance and its legitimacy. The law is the product of the sovereignty of the people in public discourse. When public discourse is distorted, democracy suffers. The demise of public discourse is a major concern. False information and manipulative communication are distorting our political life. The rise of fake news and alternative facts (including the dismissal of real news as fake) also threaten democracy. When trust is lost, relationships collapse and social interactions become costly. Name-calling, character assassination, and conspiracy theories in the corporate media are symptoms of the decaying public discourse.

Early liberal democracy grew through public discourse in Protestant churches and later in salons, restaurants, and other public spaces. Newspapers, magazines, radio, and TV broadcasts have historically played an important role in shaping public opinion. While they continue to function, they are losing influence as the digital realm becomes prominent. The most popular venues of information dissemination and news consumptions seem to be social networks and YouTube. People rely on them as their main sources of information and communication. A major challenge is how to covenantalize the digital realm and online communication and how to protect privacy, personal information, and transparency. The structure of regulation and screening is very weak. The danger of illiberal democracy and tyranny grows, to no lesser extent, with the distortion of public discourse in the digital realm. Strengthening transparency and accountability is necessary to protect the integrity of public discourse.

New covenant ethics assists the revitalization of public discourse. As Jürgen Habermas espouses, public discourse relies on communicative action among the members of a society. As its second dialectic indicates, new covenant ethics relies on discursive exchanges in forming a new collective will. Covenantal values of truthfulness, sincerity, and truth telling are critical in building trust and discerning what is right, good, and fitting. These values and habits counter the spread of disinformation, fake news, and "alternative facts." However, this does not mean that Christians attempt to impose their views; in its public engagement, new covenant ethics relies on public theology and public ethics to communicate its religious convictions and moral perspectives.

At the same time, however, if structural inequalities and power imbalances are not corrected, even fair, just deliberation (procedural democracy) is ineffective. Discourse ethics often overlooks the fact that the rule-making process is also political and is always influenced by structural inequality and power imbalance. "Widespread inequality and failures of reciprocity can justify nonpersuasive, even coercive, methods for the sake of deliberative goals."[37] Even before deliberation and public discourse start, some voices that challenge the status quo are marginalized, excluded, and silenced in deliberative processes.[38] Iris Marion Young notes:

> The deliberative democrat claims that parties to political conflict ought to deliberate with one another and through reasonable agreement try to come to an agreement on policy satisfactory to all. The activist is suspicious of exhortations to deliberate because he believes that in the real world of politics, where structural inequalities influence both procedures and outcomes, democratic processes that appear to conform to the norms of deliberation are usually biased toward more powerful agents. The activist thus recommends that those who care about promoting greater justice should engage primarily in critical oppositional activity, rather than attempt to come to agreement with those who support or benefit from existing power structures.[39]

This means that not only *de jure* freedom but also *de facto* freedom, that is, functional freedom and equality among the participants, is crucial for deliberative democracy. Deliberative democracy needs to be combined with grassroots politics and requires an independent judiciary and well-established laws.

Antidomination

As the neoliberal system is wreaking havoc on the planet and the majority of people, it creates conditions for breeding illiberal democracy in the West. The current status quo, when left alone, is likely to result in disastrous consequences for humanity and the planet alike. We must undo the oligarchic power of corporations, especially investment banks—often called too big to fail. Democracy is unable to survive under crushing inequality and unchecked, monopolized power. Governments and other institutions must properly regulate corporations. In particular, the renewal of democracy requires breaking the influence of money on politics.

As discussed, new covenant ethics is critical of domination, injustice, and the concentration of power. It relies on rule making, grassroots organizing, and nonviolent actions to create democratic culture and bring about necessary social changes.

37. Fung, "Deliberation before the Revolution," 399.
38. Santos, "Public Sphere and Epistemologies of the South," 43–67.
39. Young, "Activist Challenges to Deliberative Democracy," 670.

As is acknowledged in the Bible (Ps. 72; Ezek. 34:23), new covenant ethics affirms a positive role for government on economic life, while government must not be tyrannical or overly intrusive. Its mandate is to promote the common good, protect the boundaries between different spheres, and adjudicate their different claims. Even Adam Smith once declared: "Those exertions of the natural liberty of a few individuals, which might endanger the security of the whole society, are, and ought to be, restrained by the laws of all governments."[40] Even libertarians do not desire a completely unrestricted market; for example, some constrictions, such as the prohibition of slavery and child labor, were already in place before the rise of neoliberalism.

New covenant ethics utilizes communicative action and public discourse to make new rules to rein in the overblown power of corporations. It applies public pressure in the legislative process in order to promote the common good and strengthen the public obligation of corporations. Economic actors who act beyond the market undermine transparency and accountability, resulting in corruption.[41] It is necessary to build new fences around corporations,[42] to protect the autonomy and integrity of other spheres and institutions. Specifically, new covenant ethics seeks to remove corporate influence (money) in the democratic process. Such action will actually serve the long-term interests of the corporations, as well as the rest of society.

New covenant ethics encourages grassroots organizing of the poor, the marginalized, and ordinary citizens for political mobilization and social change. Grassroots organizing is useful to build collective power in order to correct injustices while affirming and building solidarity with and among the poor and the marginalized. Community organizing has two steps: de-organizing and reorganizing. Changing the current neoliberal system requires both dismantling and reconstructing. And this process is not possible without grassroots organization and the massive mobilization of people.

Democracy aims at peaceful reform through periodic elections. These elections adjust existing legal and institutional arrangements and patterns in response to new and changing situations and social needs. However, grassroots organizing and social movements are necessary to awaken, encourage, and mobilize people for democratic change. Grassroots democracy is necessary to revitalize democracy and make elections meaningful. The immediate political goal is to create more just and egalitarian social conditions where all are meaningfully included, information and resources are shared, and rights, including economic rights, are respected. Toward this end,

40. Adam Smith, *An Inquiry into the Nature and Causes of the Wealth of Nations*, 133.

41. One urgent area for change is to fully restore the Glass-Steagall Act or its equivalent (i.e., a law that separates investment and commercial banking and updates the laws that regulate finance and securities).

42. Finn, *The Moral Ecology of Markets*, 125.

new covenant ethics offers an inclusive vision and a plausible method of grassroots organizing and institutional organizing on multiple levels.

To regulate corporations and protect the weak, it is necessary to ratify economic rights as an intrinsic component of human rights. Given growing economic inequality, ratifying the economic rights of every person is necessary to protect human dignity and democracy. Civil-political rights and economic rights are inseparable. Political freedom needs a material basis (economic security). This idea did not originate with Karl Marx. It was a core idea of the seventeenth-century British political theorist James Harrington and his formulation of classical republicanism. One who does not own the means of production can never exercise political freedom, Harrington argued, because "the man that cannot live upon his own must be servant." Likewise, the man of immense wealth—whose fortune consigns great masses of men to servitude—is inevitably a kind of tyrant. After all, "where there is inequality of estates, there must be inequality of power, and where there is inequality of power, there can be no commonwealth."[43] The exercise of political liberty is impossible without the possession of some economic autonomy. Moreover, inequalities in wealth inevitably produce inequalities in political power. These truths were held fervently by America's first political theorists.

Civil Society and the Subsidiarity Principle

Civil society, consisting of a myriad of mediating communities and organizations (such as family, education, art, politics, medicine, religion, etc.), is critical for the health of democracy and the advance of the common good. As the government is limited in fulfilling the common good, the participation of all citizens through civil society is necessary. One of the best ways to enhance the common good is to strengthen individual organizations and coordinate their efforts toward a common purpose.

In addition, civil society and its various organizations serve as checks and balances against the state and corporations. Daniel Finn notes: "Without a vibrant civil society there is little hope that even a democratically structured government will be responsive to the moral convictions of its citizens."[44]

The vitality of civil society and its institutions is important for nurturing citizens and civic virtues. Since individuals are morally formed and nurtured in communities, the moral quality of these institutions makes a critical difference for character formation of individuals. In other words, moral conduct involves learned practices

43. Harrington, *The Commonwealth of Oceana*, 61.

44. Finn, *The Moral Ecology of Markets*, 143.

in a particular community; abstract principles of liberal ethics (e.g., Kantianism and utilitarianism) alone cannot achieve the moral formation of individuals.[45]

However, the neoliberal economic system and its monetary logic, and the cultural liturgy of material desires, are increasingly taking over civil society; social institutions are losing their moral underpinning. Habermas's theory of the "colonization of the lifeworld" refers to the subjugation of the lifeworld by the system—the utilitarian, monetary, impersonal-bureaucratic control of the state and economy over civil society. "Colonization" means the exercise of the inordinate power of the state and economy over other realms of society by breaking the covenantal, federal matrix of society. Michael Walzer's idea of "sphere injustice" also concerns this pathological, potentially tyrannical aspect of spheral relationships when the state or economic sphere intrudes and dominates other spheres of human associations.

New covenant ethics contributes to the revitalization of civil society through its social vision and its principles of unity-in-diversity (associational pluralism), subsidiarity, and vocation. It offers an adequate social imagination of civil society as a federalized, covenantal society of various organizations. Civil society and its organizations are interdependent as parts of the whole affecting one other. The restoration of civil society is associated with the vitality and vigor of individual institutions and civic organizations, and vice versa.

Institutions cannot operate by narrow instrumental purpose and technical efficiency alone. They require a guiding vision and values that serve the common good, care for their members, and collaborate with other institutions. Philip Selznick notes, "Institutions are established, not by decree alone, but as a result of being bound into the fabric of social life."[46] For example, economic activities, for their success, need a guiding moral vision and norms; they rely on noneconomic values rendered by the community. The economic sphere has its unique calling in society to behave responsibly toward its members and other institutions.

Through its unity-in-diversity principle, new covenant ethics protects the autonomy of individual organizations while encouraging collaboration among them. Individual institutions and civic organizations maintain autonomy but collaborate with each other to enhance the common good. The autonomy and health of each institution matter for democracy. When small organizations die, civil society also dies. New covenant ethics encourages and nurtures the bridging and bonding of relationships among different groups and organizations through engagement in public discourse, contesting of better claims, coalition building, dialogue, and negotiation.

45. See Stackhouse, *Covenant and Commitments*, 155–56.

46. Selznick, *Moral Commonwealth*, 232.

The subsidiarity principle is another covenant-informed principle that practices checks and balances against the centralized (imbalanced) power of the state and corporations; it is analogous to God's preferential option (special compassion) for the poor. In the subsidiarity principle, large organizations such as corporations or the government are called upon to protect smaller institutions such as the family. Protecting small institutions is important for democracy because they constitute the fabric of civil society; their vibrancy is crucial for checks and balances and the formation of citizenship and public virtues. John Dewey wrote, "Whatever the future may have in store, one thing is certain. Unless local communal life can be restored, the public cannot adequately resolve its more urgent problem, to find and identify itself."[47]

Civic Virtues and Character Formation

The rule of law and the protection of rights alone are not sufficient for constitutional democracy. Virtuous and responsible citizens committed to the public good (not just selfish interests or private pleasures) and participating in civic organizations and civic affairs are also necessary. Citizens with public virtues are indispensable for the function of democracy because democracy is meant to be by the people. A healthy democracy requires the morally informed political decisions and actions of its citizens. Neoliberalism has eroded public virtues and civic participation. Endless self-indulgence in entertainment, the pressure for survival, and the greed for excessive success deprive people of the opportunity to develop virtuous citizenship, social skills, and participation in civil responsibilities. Consequently, our public life is impoverished; public spirit and trust are thin, with people breaking agreement for self-interested purposes.

For example, meaningful public discourse is not possible without truth telling, mutual accountability, and the pursuit of the common good. When driven by self-interest alone, public discourse may be more manipulative than communicative. The demise of public virtue is reflected by the quality of democratic decisions and practices, such as public discourse and elections.

Likewise, the principles of majority rule and minority right are important for the actual function of liberal democracy, as they secure governance while protecting dissenting voices. However, this principle cannot function effectively if the members do not respect the majority's decision and are willing to abide by it. Today, this kind of commitment is increasingly rare; instead, endless self-assertion and attempts to win by any means occupy political processes, further fracturing our common life.

47. Dewey, *The Public and Its Problems*, 231.

New covenant ethics is not only institutional and legal but also praxiological and aretological. It emphasizes moral commitment beyond immediate self-interest and political expediency. It inculcates habits of generosity, patience, endurance, courage to stand for truth, tolerance to differences, negotiation, self-control, compassion, justice, and solidarity. It guides Christians to exercise their vocations in diverse social spheres and to live out discipleship and public virtues in correspondence to each sphere.

Covenanting Globalization

Not only the nation but also our global society must be reorganized. The United Nations and the Bretton Woods system were established at the end of World War II in order to avoid the pitfalls of the 1920s and 1930s. This new world order has been effective in promoting major democratic institutions (constitutionalism, human rights, civil society, associational pluralism) and, to some extent, has contributed to global peace. Far from being perfect, it has nonetheless been effective in making the world less violent and more conductive to international justice and stability compared to previous eras.

However, under the structural pressures of the interlocking forces of neoliberalism, globalization, digitization, and postmodern relativism, the post–World War II international framework is breaking down.[48] International institutions such as the International Monetary Fund, the World Bank, and the World Trade Organization (WTO) were created to address economic unification. However, they are under increasing attack because they lack transparency and accountability and are perceived as controlled by rich corporations and countries. For example, according to Jagdish Bhagwati, the corporate lobbies in pharmaceuticals have distorted and deformed the WTO, transforming it into "a royalty collection agency."[49]

A global society requires a global covenant (compact) that coordinates growing interdependence and exchanges. Organizing a global society is crucial because globalization, as it accelerates, creates growing interdependence and interconnectedness among various parts of the world. Globalization expands systems and activities of exchanges (trades of ideas, people, symbols, goods) and distribution beyond national boundaries. One nation or religious group cannot solve the growing human-made threats such as global warming, pollution, ozone degradation, acid

48. Thus losing the coordinating power and unity among politics, economic system, and civil society.

49. Bhagwati, *In Defense of Globalization*, 182.

rain, depletion of fish stocks, migrations and refugee problems, terrorism, and global pandemics (e.g., COVID-19).

Already, a failure to covenantalize the global order has created many problems. Our current political crisis arises from a gap between economic globalization and political-moral globalization. In the areas of the economy and popular culture, globalization has made substantial progress. However, the political and moral realm has lagged far behind. This status quo is unsustainable.

In the absence of a well-developed, binding global governance system, neoliberalism is taking advantage of this dissonance or vacuum and expanding its power and wealth. Politically powerful multinational corporations are creating favorable laws for themselves and exploiting poor countries for profit, resorting to child labor and sweatshops, often in complicity with dictators. Countless ordinary people, not seeing justice due to the deterioration of their life situations, are now rejecting globalization and liberal democracy and readily resorting to religious radicalism, ethnocentrism, nationalism, and authoritarianism. If globalization is to maintain legitimacy, it must expand democracy and justice to a global level. We must begin by regulating the global activities of multinational corporations.

Global covenanting builds global governance. Globalization without global governance is doomed to chaos and conflict. A global covenant should embody a deep desire for justice, peaceful coexistence, and fair order, through the delineation of structured accountability and boundaries under the law.

To create a global covenant means to federalize the international political community in a soft form by deepening the UN.[50] Federalization is useful in imagining the relationship between the local-local and the local-global. In a newly imagined global covenantal community, each community (with family, local organizations, civic groups) is internally organized as a self-governing unit while closely linked to others through covenantal relationships (maintained by communication and the rule of law). Each community is protected by self-governance even as it contributes toward the common good of a society.

Global governance inevitably includes a rule-making procedure. Like the international ratification of human rights, global society needs to establish legally binding international laws to regulate multinational corporations. Global governance cannot rest on voluntary compliance alone. When grounded in popular sovereignty, the rule of law creates political legitimacy. According to Johannes Althusius, "The rule of living, obeying, and administering is the will of God alone, which is the way of

50. Covenantal imagination offers the vision of *E Pluribus Unum* as the new order of the global community. See my *The Great World House*.

life, and the law of things to be done and to be omitted. . . . Therefore, this law alone prescribes not only the order of administering for the magistrate, but also the rule of living for all subjects."[51]

In new covenant ethics, law is not about private interest; law is not a transaction motivated by self-interest. Rather, it protects the public interest by reflecting the normative demands of justice.

Various forms of global exchanges (cultural and commercial) take place on certain "routines" specific to a field, domain, or good. While these routines are not static but open to a revision, they are nevertheless indispensable and could lay the foundation for global covenant. Major global institutions, starting with the UN, have been using the term "covenant" to envision a new, more deeply interconnected, more just and fair international community.

This compacting (covenanting) process is not utopian. There are already widely available moral resources and insights that derive from a covenant tradition. For example, average citizens (even non-Christians) of most countries today are familiar with the ideas of constitution, human rights, and rule of law. The Arab Spring, the Tiananmen Square uprising, and the Umbrella Movement protests in Hong Kong show the popular longing for democracy, human rights, freedom, transparency, government accountability to its people, and freedom of association (the products of covenantal moral imagination). Furthermore, a covenantally informed polity is broadly shared beyond the particular originating religious community—because it is not esoteric or gnostic but resonates with the deepest human yearnings for freedom, justice, relationships, and belonging.

In addition to rule making, we need to expand and vitalize global civil society and various global nongovernmental organizations (NGOs). Global covenanting should not expand American liberal democracy or hegemony or the American superpower. It should rather include international checks and balances and undo the inordinate powers of multinational corporations by establishing global democratic organizations. Powerful nations should not dominate and control. US citizens have moral and political responsibilities to rein in their nation and corporations and exercise leadership in covenantalizing the global community.

To covenantalize global society is not an easy task. However, we have no other options because globalization is impossible to undo, even if we wanted to. Even the Amish sell goods online.[52] The only way forward is to moralize global society. This boils down to organizing a globalizing world fairly at macro and local levels. Only constant, diligent, and fervent organizing work can approximate this grand covenantal vision.

51. Althusius, *Politica* 21.16–17.

52. "Buy Amish-Made Products," Amish America, http://amishamerica.com/store/.

New covenant ethics offers an encompassing political vision for global society and a framework of democratic governance—shalom, grassroots organizing for resistance to imperial power and tyranny of capital. It also offers a constructive governing framework for regulation by structuring communication, observing the rule of law, and building a global consociation. It remedies the deficit of democracy through communicative action (rule making), just peacemaking, and global grassroots organizing that interweave our life together through contributions from governments, corporations, NGOs, and religious groups.

Conclusion: Renewal of American Democracy

This chapter has shown the pertinence of covenant for democracy and how a renewed idea of covenant helps address the challenges facing democracy today. New covenant ethics offers a broader vision and a deeper moral ground, as well as the guiding norms and political practices necessary to empower democracy in a rapidly globalizing and digitalizing world.

Democracy is "an open-ended process in a constant need of broadening and deepening, and therefore of debate and clarification."[53] As we are living in a critical time, we require the expansion as well as the deepening of democracy. As the political arena (the overlapping or common interaction among people across national borders and clashes of political and economic interests) grows, democracy must expand accordingly. Deepening is required at every level—from grassroots organizing and campaign finance reform to the rule of law and the separation of powers—in order to confront the oligarchic power of corporations, address growing normless digital interactions, and fully embrace the suppressed rights of the marginalized.

The current political situation of the United States shows the demise of the covenantal tradition and the prevalence of contractualism. Covenant values and covenant ethos/practices, which once formed the social fabric of US society, have severely eroded, replaced by expressive individualism and expedient contractualism. The new generation has forgotten the covenant. Departing from the founding moral principles and values, the nation is now threatened by neoliberal oligarchy and authoritarianism. The United States is at a critical crossroads.

The future of the nation is inextricably tied to the revival of its covenantal tradition, in a new political context, through the expansion, self-correcting, and deepening of its vision and principles. Otherwise, the United States will be forced to choose between cultural-racial balkanization (fragmentation) and neoauthoritarianism. Without a firm moral foundation, liberal democracy is unsustainable in the United States.

53. De Gruchy, *Christianity and Democracy*, 7.

This means that major covenant renewal is overdue in the United States. Civil society and its organizations need renewal through the infusion of values and motivational energies beyond immediate institutional objectives and technical tasks. In his covenantal renewal of the small villages of Galilee, Jesus empowered marriage, family, and village life, strengthening the bonds that contributed to the long-term sustainability and solidarity of his community against exploitative forces. Martin Luther King Jr. was a religious moral leader who attempted the moral renewal of the republic. He appealed to the sacred democratic canons of the Declaration of Independence, the US Constitution, and the Bill of Rights—in particular, the covenantal vision and moral ideals embedded in them. The beloved community, King's social vision, was the public theological rephrase of the kingdom of God and shalom. His movement and its historical and global impact prove the political relevance and moral validity of covenantal ethics. King's example demonstrates that the racist taint of covenantalism can be overcome and located in a more genuinely inclusive and egalitarian ground.

The renewal of covenant today, however, cannot be pursued outside the ongoing debates on class, race, sexuality, and gender and the impact of digital communication and automation. These issues call for intense public discourse, collective deliberation, new rule making, and legal and institutional rearrangements.

Covenantal renewal is a necessary reconstructive effort of every nation. Its delay may result in deepening decay and growing social tension and conflict. Successful renewal and adaptation will bring necessary changes to social institutions. Doing so will yield new stability for a renewed moral foundation. Through the renewal of covenant, people will recommit themselves to the foundational values, principles, and credos of their society, while gaining awareness of new social contexts and a renewed sense of solidarity.

CHAPTER 14

Economic Ethics

> Now the whole group of those who believed were of one heart and soul, and no one claimed private ownership of any possessions, but everything they owned was held in common. With great power the apostles gave their testimony to the resurrection of the Lord Jesus, and great grace was upon them all. There was not a needy person among them, for as many as owned lands or houses sold them and brought the proceeds of what was sold.
>
> —Acts 4:32–34

The economy of human society has evolved from hunting and gathering to agricultural, then industrial, and now postindustrial forms. Since industrialization, humans have produced different forms of economic systems with different roles for the government in economic production and distribution: laissez-faire, mixed, socialist, and communist. The late twentieth century marked the triumph of capitalism over communism. Except for a handful of nations (China, Cuba, North Korea, Vietnam), humans today live under a capitalistic economic system. Today, among several different forms of capitalism (mercantile, classical, mixed [Keynesian], neoliberal), we see the global ascendance of neoliberalism.

The ascendance of the neoliberal economy is transforming human society, institutions, and social relationships. Its ascendance has to do with several factors both economic and noneconomic. At the political level, its rise corresponded to the collapse of the Soviet Union. As the slogan "There is no alternative" (TINA) indicates, proponents of neoliberal ideology portrayed a stark scenario in which the economic policies of the Soviet Union and communist countries led only to collapse and failure. Thus, the neoliberal model of freedom and free-market capitalism was proclaimed as the only viable and attractive option.

The global rise of neoliberalism is aided by impressive advances in technology and science and their increasing popular availability. In history, major structural changes are prompted by the growth of productive forces owing to technological development (e.g., domestication of animals, invention of the steam engine, fossil fuel engines, communication technology). Every transition has profoundly affected social relationships, institutions, and government systems beyond just economic relationships. Today communication and transportation technologies are overcoming geographical barriers and logistical difficulties in connecting different regions of the world; this allows corporations to expand business activities across the world. For instance, financial capital, not tied to any physical matter or particular location, is moved instantaneously according to market speculation.

This chapter studies a covenantal approach to economic justice as an alternative to the neoliberal economic system. In particular, I examine the heart of covenant economics, the Sabbath, and seek its meaning and implications for our society. The chapter examines how covenant economics differs from neoliberal economics and is an alternative to neoliberalism. I claim that neoliberalism is incompatible with new covenant ethics because it destroys the biotic world, erodes communities, is dangerous to democracy, and penalizes the poor. The current economic disparity calls for radical transformation through prophetic ministry and grassroots organizing of churches to undo neoliberalism's agenda and harmful effects.

Neoliberal Capitalism

What is neoliberalism? Neoliberalism is "a theory of political economic practices that proposes that human well-being can best be advanced by liberating individual entrepreneurial freedoms and skills within an institutional framework characterized by strong private property rights, free markets, and free trade."[1]

Neoliberalism is the revival of the nineteenth-century laissez-faire free-market capitalism that dominated Western economies until the Great Depression of the 1930s. Like classical capitalism, neoliberalism upholds the freedom of individuals and the market as well as the autonomy of corporations. It sees society as made up of autonomous individuals and sees free competition as fostering high productivity, efficiency, and human self-fulfillment. Therefore, neoliberals demand minimal governmental activity; that is, they limit it to the protection of private property, the provision of national security, and the oversight of the money supply. Neoliberal policies typically include the following: reversal of nationalization, dismantling of the welfare state, the privatization of common and collective lands and public enter-

1. David Harvey, *A Brief History of Neoliberalism*, 2.

prises (e.g., social housing, prison), and trickle-down economics that reduces taxes for the rich in order to "stimulate economic growth."

Ambitiously, neoliberalism envisions the world as a single free market with a free and unfettered flow of capital, labor, and goods. It claims that economic freedom in a globally open market spurs innovation and creativity, increases productivity, and offers greater consumer choices at lower prices. Neoliberals promise unfettered economic growth, rising living standards, flourishing democracy, and technological advances. They say that the free market will solve most problems.

Ever since the Soviet Union collapsed, neoliberals in the United States and United Kingdom, using their political and military hegemony, coerced nations into joining their global economy. In 1995, they created the World Trade Organization (WTO) to spur global trade by reducing tariffs, liberalizing trade rules, and instituting free trade agreements. Neoliberals forced nations to open their markets to Western investment by lowering tariffs, tax barriers, and environmental regulations. They used debt to coerce poorer nations into adopting neoliberal economic policies and eliminated traditional barriers and boundaries that had impeded the flow of capital, labor, and goods.[2] To compete economically or to abide by WTO rules, many countries cut social spending and subsidies for indigenous industries and lowered tariffs. This changed agriculture from a subsistence to a cash crop economy. In the process, labor and environmental regulations were relaxed. To force poor nations to adopt neoliberal policies, neoliberals exploited their economic vulnerabilities, such as debt insolvency, and radically imposed detrimental policies (e.g., structural adjustment programs, foreign direct investment).[3]

Results

While it has partly lowered extreme global poverty from 900 million people (12.8 percent of the global population) to 702 million (9.6 percent), neoliberalism has caused rising disparities between the rich and the poor. Since the mid-1980s, income inequality among most Organization for Economic Co-operation and Development (OECD) countries, especially the United States, has vastly increased.[4] Neoliberal economic globalization has sunk the majority of people into deeper despair, income decline, and alienation. Under neoliberalism, many middle-class or poor citizens have seen declines in actual income.

2. Cavanagh and Mander, *Alternative Economic Globalization*, 305.

3. For a detailed discussion, see Chang, *Bad Samaritans*.

4. Organization for Economic Co-operation and Development, *Growing Unequal?*, 27, 51; Reich, *Aftershock*, 18–25.

The mobility of capital, and even corporations, has seriously compromised the negotiating power of labor unions. Through "flexible" labor policies, workers work longer hours without secure contracts and benefits such as health insurance. Labor has little protection; in the social covenant of early industrialization, farmers-turned-workers were taken care of (or at least subsidized) by factories and companies through capital-labor relationships. Now, however, labor has lost its village and its agriculture (with its inborn safety net within the extended and intimate community) and is losing its jobs and wages. Labor's loss of community and reduction of jobs have led to economic and social homelessness. With no economic or job security, ordinary citizens are extremely vulnerable.

Despite ostensible GDP (gross domestic product) growth, employment rates and wages are significantly dropping; productivity has surged, but for most Americans, income and wages are stagnant. Those at the bottom are in hopeless situations. For the tens of millions in the middle class in the United States and other developed countries, neoliberal economic policy brings job insecurity, wage stagnation or decline, and the cutting of social safety nets. These all threaten basic human dignity. Desperate people work increasing hours without secure contracts and benefits such as health insurance. This threatens their health and family life.

The traditional social safety nets of family members, kin, churches, and neighbors, along with their emotional support, have gradually disappeared. Government is called on to fill this vacuum. But government programs are costly and are unable to fund the multitudes of unemployed, displaced, and dislocated people. Budget deficits and personal debt are increasingly a chronic problem while social unrest looms. Moreover, the local economy is destroyed; local businesses are forced to join the global market but are unable to compete with corporate hegemons. Communal networks and structures that protect local interests have been removed, and local authorities are increasingly dependent on large corporations.

Neoliberalism has removed social provisions for ordinary people, the community necessary for society's moral fabric, and social programs and welfare policies such as job safety, antitrust laws, environmental regulations, labor union laws, health care, and educational services for the poor. Neoliberal deregulation and labor flexibility destroy the poor and the weak.

The rich, on the other hand, do well. The middle class, however, loses economic independence. With debt, poor countries are permanently dependent on the West, and local communities lose their autonomy. People of color, women, and children are disproportionally hurt by economic inequality. Deregulation of finance laws, usury, and predatory lending practices are destroying weak and poor borrowers. Neoliberalism creates a stratified class system that impedes social mobility and suppresses equal opportunity.

Defenders of capitalism have claimed that it contributes to democracy and human rights by raising the middle class (whose interests align with the rule of law and political freedom), providing greater health education, and legally protecting private property and freedom of business activities. This is no longer the case.

Furthermore, the neoliberal economy destroys ecology. Neoliberalism fuels a global race toward the bottom, seeking cheaper and cheaper labor, natural resources, and toxic disposal sites. Its culture of endless production, reckless consumption, and commercial sprawl threatens the earth's carrying capacity.

Political Agenda

Why has neoliberalism been so effective? Because it is not just an economic system based on science and reason (market analysis, consumer choice); it is also a totalistic, even totalitarian, political economy and ideology.

Neoliberalism is also the metanarrative of global society (marked by the motto "there is no alternative"), positioning itself as an indispensable way of life. Not just driven by economic interest, it serves the political interests of the rich, who are determined to maintain their power and wealth. The neoliberal strategy is to present neoliberalism as inevitable, a natural or normal human condition.[5] Neoliberals utilize political and ideological tools to expand their class interests, not hesitating to employ various noneconomic tactics, such as political lobbying, economic policy manipulation, and media control to further their agenda. Deregulation of telecommunications laws, not scientific economic principles and logic, undergirds these tactics. They then use their political hegemony for economic benefit.

Another strategy is to burden ordinary taxpayers with funding corporations. According to David Harvey, in addition to the traditional method of capital accumulation by exploiting labor power, neoliberals practice "capital accumulation by dispossession."[6] They burden ordinary citizens with the social costs and liabilities of doing business, such as transportation, pollution, highways, harbors, communication, and education of workers.[7] Society, especially the poor, suffers high taxes, ecological degradation, deterioration of public health, poor quality of education, etc.

Another example of corporations and banks transferring their costs to taxpayers is government bailouts. The state continually intervenes to avert crises (e.g., the bailout of Chrysler in 1979, the Long-Term Capital Management hedge fund in 1998, the subprime mortgage crisis in 2008). Ordinary citizens, not corporations, bear the

5. Susan George, "A Short History of Neoliberalism."

6. David Harvey, *A Brief History of Neoliberalism*, 116, 162, 178.

7. David Harvey, *A Brief History of Neoliberalism*, 67.

burden. People see an increase in sales taxes and predatory practices of court fines, fees, and traffic-violation tickets. Moreover, while governments cut taxes for the rich, many states and localities make up lost revenue by penalizing the poor. "More than 7 million people nationwide may have had their driver's licenses suspended for failure to pay court or administrative debt." This system "perpetuates poverty by penalizing poverty."[8]

In the United States, neoliberalism has been particularly effective at hiding its deleterious consequences because its core values (individual freedom and property rights) closely resonate with the cultural values of the country (individuals are self-determining beings who shape their own destinies). In general, neoliberals use freedom for two purposes: First, individual creativity, competition, hard work, and individual desire for achievements and material comforts have been powerful incentives for capitalism; capitalism promises to reward successful people with material comfort. Neoliberalism, using marketing and advertising techniques and skills that appeal to consumer psychology, has normalized these desires into habits. Second, neoliberal freedom "subdue[s] and subvert[s]" by "'responsibilizing' every individual for the outcomes of the system."[9] Thus system benefits from individual hard work and contributions but eschews responsibility for its failures and the structural inequity it creates.

At least until the financial crisis of 2008, neoliberals were successful in elevating neoliberalism as the new global metanarrative (TINA), a worldview favored over any other economic system (socialism and Keynesianism).

However, in the wake of the 2008 financial crisis, neoliberalism has lost its moral credibility. Now, more and more people are aware of neoliberal capitalism's destructive consequences. Neoliberal capitalism, benefiting global corporations and the rich, is meeting an increasingly harsh backlash. People in the United States are crying for structural change. This is manifest in the Occupy Movement (the 99 percent versus the 1 percent), in massive millennial support for Bernie Sanders in the 2016 and 2020 presidential primaries, and even in the election of Donald Trump, a reality television star and businessman, in 2016.

Many mainline Protestants and Catholic bishops are critical of neoliberalism. Young people were enthusiastic about the progressive economic visions of several Democratic presidential candidates in 2020, such as Bernie Sanders, Elizabeth Warren, and Andrew Yang, whose platforms were explicitly against neoliberalism. Prompted by the Occupy Movement and the disillusionment and anger of blue-collar workers, they supported progressive agendas such as universal health care, free

8. "States across the Nation Are Criminalizing Poverty."

9. Kotsko, *Neoliberalism's Demons*, 140.

college education, and, in the case of Yang, universal basic income. These are serious attempts to decouple politics and economy from neoliberal ideology and control.

New Covenant Ethics

Transforming the neoliberal global economic system, which has consolidated its control over several decades, requires more than political resistance. The power and influence of neoliberalism are totalistic;[10] ideologically, it touches on anthropology (individualism) and sociology (contractualism), and appeals to human desire for pleasure, comfort, wealth, and self-fulfillment. Through careerism and consumerism, it already controls and disciplines human habits and practices. To counter it, a compelling alternative vision must be told. New covenant ethics criticizes neoliberalism and displays an alternative vision to it. Covenant economics is sharply contrasted in several aspects: it is not anthropocentric, but ecological, and it does not pit individual work ethic against government intervention but balances individual creativity with communal and governmental responsibility. Economic justice is essential to the covenant drama of the Bible. God's liberative and restorative work includes economic justice.

Sabbath Economics

Walter Brueggemann claims that "economics is the core preoccupation of the biblical tradition."[11] I claim that biblical economics is covenantal in nature, with Sabbath at its center.[12] Sabbath is found not only in the Torah, Nehemiah, and the prophetic literature but also in the Synoptic Gospels, the book of Acts, and the Pauline epistles.

Sabbath is not only a religious symbol (rest and worship) but also an economic one. It is more than ceasing work and activity. As the symbol of rest, wholeness, and restoration, the Sabbath communicates God's full intent for humanity. Sabbath is a symbol of restoration, wholeness (body, mind, spirit/soul), and joy. Sabbath and shalom are correlated to one another.

The Sabbath laws and practices were important in organizing Israel's life and community. Corresponding to the covenantal drama of liberation-restoration, Sab-

10. See Wolin, *Democracy Incorporated.* The corporate and business model of management and organizing has become pervasive, and careerism and financial reward have become the primary motivation for the elites and professionals.

11. Brueggemann, *Money and Possession,* xix.

12. The study of Sabbath economics in this chapter does not exhaust the biblical view of economic ethics because there are other symbols, teachings, and themes pertaining to economic ethics in the Bible.

bath embodies the heart of Israel's vision for a new society—the antidote to the predatory Pharaonic system of slavery and subjugation.

The Sabbath has rich theological and ethical meaning. Covenant and Sabbath are inseparable. Sabbath is the symbol of liberation, community, and shalom. It reveals God's intent for creation. Sabbath is eschatological. Covenant aims at Sabbath as the covenant people are called to live out and practice the Sabbath narrative and values. In the Bible, Sabbath is mentioned in key events such as creation (as the zenith of God's creation), the exodus story, and Jesus's ministry. It is identified as the symbol of the wholesome fulfillment of God's drama. That is, Sabbath touches the beginning, the middle (journey), and the end of human history, running through the entire divine drama. Hence, in its own way, the Sabbath represents the overarching covenantal plot of liberation-restoration in particular and the entire Bible in general. The following section will investigate the biblical theme of Sabbath in the OT and the NT with a focus on its relation to God's economy and the covenantal drama of liberation-restoration. It will demonstrate that Sabbath is at the center of God's economic organizing.

Creation

First and foremost, the Sabbath is inseparable from the creation story; it was instituted by God in Genesis. It materializes creational faith: the land and material goods belong to God and are God's gifts. Every Sabbath day is a reminder that the earth and everything in it belong not to humans but to God (first dialectic). The Sabbath is the climax of creation; the whole work of creation was performed for the sake of the Sabbath. It is the feast of the creation.[13]

The Sabbath is God's cosmic reorganizing. As God did at creation, in Sabbath, God reorganizes time and space. In a sense, the Sabbath temporarily repeats God's creation event. It puts a creative space between all competing/contesting parties (humans and land, farmers and domestic animals, masters and maids/servants). As a result, creation is reordered, reoriented, and renewed. Humans cease economic activities and focus on relationship renewal with God and with others. During Sabbath, all creatures reclaim their own space, breached boundaries are restored, and flourishing is experienced. The Sabbath refocuses our attention and energy on God, others, and our place in the universe. The Sabbath gives breathing room for all creatures, inanimate and animate alike, free from the compulsive rhythms and anxieties of performance and production.

Genuine rest comes from reorienting oneself in God's shalom, where everything is harmonious: rightly placed and rightly related, with a right functioning of giving and taking, flowing toward the flourishing of life. The Sabbath reminds us that God's moral community encompasses both humanity and other creatures. Every member

13. Moltmann, *God in Creation*, 277.

of God's *oikos* is equal on the Sabbath and takes the same Sabbath rest. From the beginning of creation, Sabbath implements God's care for human and nonhuman creatures. Every creature has the right to rest. On the Sabbath, the Spirit empowers each member to find its natural rhythm and pace, attuning to the flow, loops, and circulation of creation itself. The Sabbath restores and refreshes the agency and power of each creature. Every creature, especially the weak and the marginalized, reclaims its own space and boundary. This is what God designed and intended at creation. The Sabbath is the weekly foretaste of God's shalom.

Israel

In addition to being the climax of the creation story, the Sabbath is also the symbol of Israel's liberation from Egypt and its freedom as the people of God. The Sabbath is intimately associated with the exodus story—the beginning of Israel. The Israelites' collective experiences of slavery and God's redemption were brought together to build a covenant based on a just economic system. The Sabbath as a social and a legal institution was the fruit of a new social imagination of Israel as a free community.

For Israelites, the Sabbath was the symbol of liberation, equality, and righteousness. It remembered God's judgment of Pharaoh and his exploitative economic system to celebrate the annunciation of a free and egalitarian society where basic needs were met. "[Sabbath] is rather an icon for a socio-economic political arrangement of social power in a distinctive way that is critical of and an alternative to other social arrangements that are authorized by other gods."[14]

Through its covenantal system and Sabbath economics, Israel was intended to be an anti-Pharaoh society. The Sabbath was a radical turn way from a hierarchal economics to a covenant model—"a decentralized, egalitarian, tribal mode of life."[15] Israelites were called to practice an alternative economic system to Pharaoh's system of slavery. Sabbath constitutes a core identity marker for Israel. The Ten Commandments require every Israelite to practice the Sabbath. Every Sabbath observance remembers God's deliverance in the exodus event and beseeches Israelites to live up to their covenantal obligations. There are numerous stern warnings against its violation. Sabbath carries within it the memory of liberation: on every Sabbath, Israel reenacts the exodus event while remembering that the covenant God is the God who defends, advocates, and intervenes on behalf of the oppressed.

The exodus meant freedom not only from political oppression but also from economic exploitation. The Israelites learned that there is no genuine freedom without economic freedom. They realized that economic subsistence is critical for maintain-

14. Brueggemann, *Ice Axes for Frozen Seas*, 272.

15. Kinsler and Kinsler, *The Biblical Jubilee and the Struggle for Life*, 34.

ing their dignity and integrity as free people. Sabbath economics affirms the basic economic rights of every member of society.

The Bible's insight is that violating Sabbath leads to lack of care and compassion for the powerless, the poor, and other creatures, and ultimately sanctions social oppression. Alexia Salvatierra and Peter Heltzel note: "When sabbath is kept, oppression and exploitation can be ended, and there will be universal well-being throughout the whole community of creation."[16] In explicit terms, Deuteronomy 15:4 declares that when Sabbath economics is practiced, no one will be poor.

Sabbath economics also protects the subsistence of every family and clan. "The covenant required that each extended family have access to the basic resources for survival, particularly through the spirituality and practice of the Sabbath Day, the Sabbath Year, and the Jubilee."[17]

The Sabbath year (Lev. 25; Deut. 15:1–6) and Jubilee (every seventh year, every fiftieth year) served as the key mechanism of economic redistribution and restructuring: debts were canceled and slaves were released. The poor were freed from the decimating trap of the permanent insolvency of debts and restored to their inheritance land. By periodically correcting economic inequality, the Sabbath year and the Jubilee were the social performance of Israel's own exodus through communal care for the poor. "Jubilee is exodus spelled out in terms of social salvation."[18]

The Sabbath year and Jubilee restored all members of society to a level ground—dismantling incrementally built structural and systemic injustices through the inequality of wealth, power, and social influence. They aimed to avoid the concentration of power and regimentation of a hierarchical class system.

The relative equality achieved through the periodic redistribution of resources and power was crucial for protecting the family and its members, and ultimately for maintaining the community's unity as God's people. The Sabbath protected the economic viability of each family and clan. It was an early practice of the subsidiary principle.

> Extended families (*bet-abot*) formed the base, living in close proximity and reaching 50–100 people of various generations and relations. Access to the land was the primary basis for subsistence, identity, and self-determination. These extended families were gathered into associations or clans [*mishpachot*] for mutual support and protection at the level of villages or neighborhoods, insuring the survival of each family against military intrusion, providing wells and terraces and communal lands for grazing, offering loans without interest, organizing work teams, and celebrating festivals. These associations together formed tribes for mutual

16. Salvatierra and Heltzel, *Faith-Rooted Organizing*, 36.
17. Kinsler and Kinsler, *The Biblical Jubilee and the Struggle for Life*, 34.
18. Hoekendijk, "Mission—a Celebration of Freedom," 141, cited in Yoder, *The Politics of Jesus*, 38.

> defense and aid at yet another level as regional alliances to protect their independence and meeting internal crises, and they in turn formed the Israelite intertribal confederation or alliance.[19]

The result of Sabbath economics was community stability. Through the mutual support, care, and collaboration built through the tribe's covenant, they were able to overcome the ravages of droughts, insects, disease, and bandits. The Israelites did not have the typical burdens of city-states of the ancient Near East. Because of Sabbath economics, Israel's social system under the covenant was more egalitarian than that of surrounding nations. They were not exploited for tribute or forced to do labor for rulers of other city-states, although the gap between intention and practice was always part of its historical reality as well.

Pharaonic Neoliberalism	**Sabbath Economics**
Stratified (pyramidal)	Egalitarian
Surplus, storage, subjugation (competition)	Need-based, trust, subsistence, sustenance, sharing
Production, performance, exploitation	Rest, Sabbath (no exploitation and bondage)
Liberation from (reactive)	Liberation to (reshaped, reborn, responsive agency)

In the spirit of the exodus tradition, major covenant renewals in Scripture typically included the forgiveness of debts and the redistribution of resources among the members; Nehemiah canceled debts; Ezekiel prophesied the equitable redistribution of the land (Ezek. 48); Jesus taught cancellation of debt and forgiveness.

A strong message of economic justice rings throughout the Bible. In the teachings of the prophets and Jesus, economic justice takes a central place; they use many examples from the economic realm. In light of the memory of the exodus and the Torah's teachings on the Sabbath, the prophets critiqued various unjust exploitative practices of their society and called for fidelity to the covenant through true worship of God, caring for the poor, and practicing justice, compassion, and righteousness (Deut. 15:7–11; Amos 1–2).

Care for the Poor

God's covenant stipulation included care for the poor and marginalized. Israel's fidelity to God is evidenced by their care for the poor. Care for the poor concretely

19. Kinsler and Kinsler, *The Biblical Jubilee and the Struggle for Life*, 35.

reciprocates God's justice in the exodus. "Yahweh intends that Israel be a nation of sisters and brothers in which there will be no more poor (cf. Deut. 15:4). This in itself makes clear that, according to the Bible, the poor of Egypt are to become, through the Exodus, a kind of divinely-willed contrast-society."[20]

In the Bible, a litmus test of a people's covenantal fidelity is how they treat the poor and the voiceless. The poor need both love (because poverty is often the result of misfortunes) and justice (because their powerlessness is vulnerable to misuse and abuse by the powerful). The poor are the canary in the mine to indicate how God's people are abiding (or not abiding) by the covenantal requirements of love and justice.

God's new society does not allow poverty and exploitation. In a covenantal community, there should be no poor. The perpetuity of poverty and inequality was regarded as the sign of covenantal infidelity. Inequality forgets the gifted nature of existence; extreme inequality and rigid stratification undermine solidarity and directly go against God's plan. They are blatant evidence of apathy (instead of *hesed*) and injustice (instead of *tsedaqah* and *mishpat*). An unequal society is inevitably infested by injustice, exploitation, abuse, and violence.

Our discussion shows that Sabbath was central to God's organizing of a community. It is closely tied with the covenantal organizing of liberation-restoration. It served as the symbol of liberation and restoration. Through Moses, God used the Sabbath as a symbol of covenant in organizing a new and just community in which the religious and social and economic were inseparable. This implies that economics is central to God's own covenantal economy. One cannot think of covenant without Sabbath because it is the destiny of God's covenantal organizing.

Jesus and Sabbath Economics

Jesus inherited the Sabbath economics of the exodus tradition from his ancestors. At the heart of Jesus's kingdom message was the Jubilee declaration. Jesus's inauguration sermon (Luke 4:18–19) taught on the political economy of God's reign:

> "The Spirit of the Lord is upon me,
> because he has anointed me
> to bring good news to the poor.
> He has sent me to proclaim release to the captives
> and recovery of sight to the blind,
> to let the oppressed go free,
> to proclaim the year of the Lord's favor."

20. Norbert F. Lohfink, *Option for the Poor*, 45; Christopher Wright, *Old Testament Ethics*, 61.

The passage includes the two key motifs of the covenantal drama: liberation and restoration, seen in phrases such as "to let the oppressed go free" (liberation) and "to proclaim the year of the Lord's favor" (restoration), which portray God's full restoration of people from indebtedness and slavery in the Jubilee.

Slightly changing Isaiah 61, the manifesto shows that various forms of injustice are interrelated: political oppression, economic exploitation, criminal justice, and health-care impediment. The poor are usually the victims of multiple forms of injustice. The alternative is to restore the holistic covenantal community of God by liberating people from all these interlocking injustices. The passages affirm that Jubilee is the symbol of God's liberation and restoration.

Jesus's message and ministry of Jubilee were not only loyal to the Jewish tradition but also responsive to his particular historical and social context, the Jewish community living under the Roman Empire, as discussed in chapter 2. Rome was devastating the Jewish temple system, the local economy, and the Jewish people with heavy taxation and forced labor; debt and tax collectors added their own fees and unfair fraudulent charges. Jesus preached the reign of God as the new social vision and counteracted social disintegration by empowering family and local village communities. Jesus warned against the greed and the danger of ongoing accumulation of wealth: "No one can serve two masters; for a slave will either hate the one and love the other, or be devoted to the one and despise the other. You cannot serve God and wealth" (Matt. 6:24). He knew that accumulation discourages sharing, generosity, and care for others. Jesus's trust in God's provision is closely associated with his teachings on mutual sharing and cooperation.

The Lord's Prayer

Jesus taught his disciples to pray: "Forgive us our debts, as we also have forgiven our debtors" (Matt. 6:12). The Lord's Prayer reflects the desperate economic situation of the people in Jesus's time. Far from being a mere liturgical chant, the petition of daily bread and forgiveness of debts had real existential meaning and resonance with the people's desperately impoverished economic condition. "As in the jubilee, and as in the Lord's Prayer, *debt* is seen as the paradigmatic social evil."[21] The debt spoken of is genuinely a financial debt, and the Greek text "in its most materialistic sense"[22] indicates that Jesus's prayer is a Jubilee prayer. "The Lord's Prayer is a call to Sabbath-Jubilee spirituality as envisioned for the tribes of Yahweh in the Promised Land, a socioeconomic possibility that Israel abandoned under the monarchy so

21. Yoder, *The Politics of Jesus*, 34.
22. Yoder, *The Politics of Jesus*, 66.

that some could become rich and powerful and others would become poor and marginalized."[23]

In continuity with the Sabbath economics of Moses, Jesus taught his disciples to practice the Jubilee principle in their social relationships, including the forgiveness of debts. Daily bread in the Lord's Prayer harks back to God's faithful provision for the Israelites in the wilderness, while the petition for the forgiveness of debts suggests the design of Deuteronomy—the Sabbath economics of periodic releasing of slaves and forgiving of debts that was done to protect family units and the autonomy of tribal villages (Deut. 15:1–6; Exod. 21:1–7; Lev. 25). The pattern of motivation behind the commandment for forgiveness is typically covenantal when addressing economic concerns.

The Eucharist

Ritualizing Jesus's table fellowship (Mark 2:15; Luke 15:1–2), the Eucharist has profound economic meaning and implications. It embodies the spirit of the Jubilee with its message of mutual sharing and solidarity. In a richly symbolic way, the Eucharist performs the political economy of the new covenant community as Jesus did: politically, freedom and equality of all participants before God, and economically, the full and mutual sharing of their resources and lives.

The Eucharist advocates a new lifestyle that nurtures the communal spirit and reverses human sinful desires to possess, compete, monopolize, endlessly accumulate, and stratify people along power, privilege, and status. The eucharistic elements of grain and wine symbolize the sharing of economic resources among people. The three great OT money crops are grain, wine, and oil.[24] Partaking in the natural elements (bread and wine) of the Eucharist is "a symbolic recognition of the shared life and common destiny of humanity and nature. The natural order shares in God's work of giving life to human beings and of granting them new life. And conversely, human beings share in the care and cultivation of the earth and receive with thanksgiving its good gifts."[25]

First Corinthians 11 and 12 show the close connection between the Eucharist and the body of Christ in the distinctive social economic context of Corinth. The Eucharist is egalitarian in nature and is a divine practice of distributive justice. Migliore notes: "Christians cannot eat and drink at this table—where all are welcome and none goes hungry or thirsty—and continue to condone any form of discrim-

23. Kinsler and Kinsler, *The Biblical Jubilee and the Struggle for Life*, 101.

24. Brueggemann, *Money and Possession*, 2.

25. Migliore, *Faith Seeking Understanding*, 295.

ination or any social or economic policy that results in hunger or other forms of deprivation. . . . There is an intrinsic connection between responsible participation in the Lord's Supper and commitment to a fairer distribution of the goods of the earth to all its people."[26]

The Eucharist is not a magical emblem of personal salvation and spirituality. As the symbol of God's economy, it, along with the Sabbath, represents the complete antitype to the imperial political economy of Rome. All the commodities, resources, and materials are God's gifts given through his generous generativity of the earth.[27] That is, we owe our livelihood and economic activities to God and God's creation. God is the owner, and the earth is the primary producer, and humans are responsible to reciprocate their generosity.

When detached from the memory of Jesus's liberating ministry, this rite becomes an esoteric religious practice and loses its revolutionary message of political economy. Forgetting this memory "is closely linked to the practice of exploitative injustice."[28]

The Early Church

Early Christians continued Jesus's Sabbath economics through sharing and mutual aid in their communities. Consistent with the vision of the Eucharist, his community understood that sharing of resources was crucial for fulfilling God's covenant and was indispensable for building a free, egalitarian community intended by the new covenant.

The early Christians, like Jesus, militantly practiced their distinctive ethics and lifestyle grounded in Jubilee. According to N. T. Wright, "[Jesus] expected his followers to live by the jubilee principle among themselves. He expected, and taught, that they should forgive one another not only 'sins' but also debts. This may help to explain the remarkable practice within the early church whereby resources were pooled, in a fashion not unlike the Essene community of goods. Luke's description of this in Acts 4.34 echoes the description of the sabbatical year in Deuteronomy 15.4."[29] Jesus encouraged voluntary sharing, mutual aid, and deep compassion in the manner of God's love (*hesed*). Instead of obsessive possession or exploitation, the generous sharing of material goods to meet the needs of people was a major characteristic of Jesus's community.

26. Migliore, *Faith Seeking Understanding*, 294–95.
27. Brueggemann, *Money and Possession*, 2.
28. Cf. Brueggemann, *Money and Possession*, 5.
29. N. T. Wright, *Jesus and the Victory of God*, 278.

The early Christian community was a need-based and need-fulfilling community. The objective and criteria of its economy were to meet the need of all its members. The apostle Paul cites Exodus 16:18:

> "The one who had much did not have too much,
> and the one who had little did not have too little." (2 Cor. 8:15)

It was a community that sought "a fair balance between" the members with different resources and wealth. Paul emphasized "a fair balance" twice in 2 Corinthians 8:13–14. The message was that accumulating wealth when others suffer from poverty goes against God's will.

Christians pooled resources together and forgave debts to protect people from further disintegration, despair, and desperation. They exercised eucharistic hospitality toward all by sharing basic goods with members and strangers. Ron Sider notes: "Oneness in Christ for the earliest Christian community meant almost unlimited economic liability for, and sweeping economic availability to, the other members of Christ's body."[30] Without many rich or socially powerful members, they created a common fund to subsidize the poor, to pay for the burial of members, or to buy freedom for a member from slavery.[31]

By practicing Jubilee economics (Acts 2:44–45), Jesus's community provided a safety net for every member. They experienced God's generosity, mutual affection, and care among themselves, which in turn provided succor and energy to continue their lives under oppression. Internal cohesion, mutual aid, and collaboration helped protect the members against the erosive exploitations of the powerful. Forgiveness and reconciliation kept unity within a community, and the trust and love found in this new community set the oppressed people free from various self-defense mechanisms and released a new sense of spirit and energy. This assisted members in their communities.

The Christian practices of inclusivity, egalitarianism, and communal lifestyle granted the members a sense of comfort, security, and hope. This allowed them to gain the spiritual and moral high ground over their occupiers, no matter how much military power the oppressors had. The empire may rule and control people with the fear of death and threat of dispossession. However, for those who do not fear death and who have the safety net of community, an imperial rule loses its teeth. Through Jubilee economics, Jesus's movement was a silent and nonviolent but powerful social revolution from below.[32]

30. Sider, *Rich Christians in an Age of Hunger*, 90.

31. Horsley, *Covenant Economics*, 142–43.

32. For a more in-depth discussion, see Keesmaat and Walsh, *Romans Disarmed*.

Meanings and Implication

We have briefly reviewed Sabbath economics and its various practices and meanings in the Bible in order to find an alternative vision and alternative practices to neoliberalism. While the former leads to a community of solidarity, shalom, and sharing, the latter creates anxiety, division, competition, accumulation, and economic hierarchy.

Sabbath economics is neoliberalism thrown upside down. Sabbath economics is completely antithetical to the ideology and practices of neoliberalism: maximal profit, competition, consumerism, workaholism, possessive individualism, and rigid meritocracy. Like the Egyptian Pharaonic system, neoliberalism is "a regime of inordinate coveting"[33] that is brutal and boundless in instrumentalizing God's entire creation for endless profit gain. Neoliberalism morally justifies covetousness, greed, ruthless competition, and an economic caste system in order to stimulate insatiable consumerism and unlimited accumulation—which is the economic engine of neoliberalism. It increasingly resembles an extreme expression of fallen human nature that attempts to usurp God's place and authority (mirroring human rebellion with the tree of knowledge in Genesis 3 and the tower of Babel in Genesis 11).

To the contrary, Sabbath represents the economy of restoration (sharing, gratitude, and trust) in contrast to the economy of extraction that neoliberalism practices. "Sabbath is a refusal of the rat race of commodity acquisition; coveting is in contradiction to the alternative of Sabbath. Or better, Sabbath is the alternative to coveting."[34] The stark contrast between the two is the difference between God and mammon. One cannot serve both (Matt. 6:24). Sharing, rather than endless accumulation of wealth, is the covenantal way.

What does the Sabbath mean today? How can we translate the socioeconomic and ecological principles of the Sabbath into today's economic policies and practices? Is it an outdated system of the past, or does it have time-transcending messages for us today? We may gain several insights.

God's Gift

Sabbath speaks of the gifted nature of economy. It claims that the earth and everything (land, trees, wind, heat, energy) in it belong to God. In the final analysis, nothing is a private possession. But the neoliberal economy denies the gifted nature of economy and is thus anthropocentric, possessive, and predatory.

Our economic activities completely depend on God's provision and the biotic world. The current ecological crisis shows how much we are dependent on nature

33. Brueggemann, *Money and Possession*, 21.
34. Brueggemann, *Money and Possession*, 23.

and its proper ordering and functioning. In this vein, the Sabbath warns of the danger of human coveting, overproduction, overworking, and overconsumption. By setting limits against human greed and ambition (idolatry, coveting), it protects the rights of vulnerable humans and animals against exploitation. The lifestyle during the forty years in the wilderness emphasizes a need-based trust in God, not a greed- or anxiety-based economy.

The wilderness journey teaches God's faithful provision for the people through nature: quail, manna, and water. Manna speaks of God's faithfulness in the provision of daily bread in the wilderness. On the other hand, it is a carefully designed practice of God to undo coveting by liberating people from the instinctual desire to covet. Israelites learn how to trust God and God's timely provision, and they are liberated from psychological fear of destitution and scarcity. This practice trained the people to live by trust according to their needs and not by the greed of accumulation. Individuals are required to use their energies for creative purposes and the common good. Israel's wilderness experience of manna and the practice of Sabbath counters and rehabilitates human desires for materialistic possession. It does so by respecting the rights of others and the earth.

Solidaric

While neoliberalism is hyperindividualistic and denies the interdependent nature of human existence, Sabbath economics is socially minded. The biblical idea of covenant presupposes the solidarity of all lives in God. Humans are already inextricably embedded in nature and community from birth. No one survives by continuously violating the reality of primordial indebtedness and solidarity. Contrary to the assertions of neoliberals and some social contractarians (Thomas Hobbes), humans are first dependent upon others before being free and independent. Absolute independence or self-sufficiency is a delusion. Individual well-being is incomplete without social well-being, which is in turn inconceivable without justice and care for the poor. The sharing of material goods increases spiritual delight and satisfaction and deepens the covenantal bond among the members of a society.

Ecological

In Sabbath, any form of economy that ravages nature cannot be accepted as just. This is self-evident in the threat of global warming that we experience on a daily basis. Economy and ecology are interrelated. In God's economy (*oikonomia*), the entire creation is a household (*oikos*). The human economy relies on the great economy of God's creation. That is why any form of human economy cannot override the basic moral demands of creational economy. Economists must count the ecological costs of industries. The needs of nature and the damage inflicted upon nature must be registered by calculating what nature's economy requires for its own renewal. We must integrate ecological cost into economic decision making.[35]

Sabbath brings together ecological and social justice, the human economy and the creation economy, by respecting human rights and the rights of other creatures and the land. Ecologically, Sabbath economics reminds us that the human economy depends on the creation economy. The Sabbath is the goal of both economies. To practice the Sabbath is to subject the former to the latter and to protect creation and ourselves from our own greed through regular and periodic relief.

Protecting Family

As the basic unit of a society, a strong family is crucial for economic sustainability. According to studies, the absence of one or both parents is the single best predictor of poverty. The Sinai covenant had several economic measures that protected the family: the inalienable rights of family, land, and levirate marriage arrangement (Deut. 25:5–10); the ban against usury among Israelites (Lev. 25:35–38); the redemption of family lands, cancellation of debts, release from slavery on the Sabbath year, and the Jubilee. In addition, "the right of annual gleaning,"[36] triennial tithes as the social fund for the needy (Deut. 14:28–29), and "the availability of what grew of itself on the fallow land"[37] served as safety-net arrangements for families in need. These laws and statutes were established not just to care for the poor but also to protect the family.

Current practices of neoliberalism are very antifamily. Corporations value profit over the economic security of the family. Ongoing downsizing due to outsourcing and automation leads to worker insecurity and vulnerability to corporate abuse. Workers work more hours for the same pay. To survive, they sacrifice their health and their families. Secure jobs are critical for the stability of a family and a local community. As we see in many cities and towns in the US Midwest, when a factory shuts down, the entire local community suffers, and many families never recover. When companies leave, people disperse, following the jobs. The disintegration of white industrial towns is creating a toxic environment for the rise of white identity politics and nativism, not to mention depression, opioid addiction, and suicide.

35. Daly and Farley, *Ecological Economics*.

36. Christopher Wright, *Old Testament Ethics*, 173. Ruth 2 is a narrative example of this practice.

37. Christopher Wright, *Old Testament Ethics*, 173.

The entire society is responsible for protecting and strengthening the health and vitality of families. It can do so through a variety of social services such as: maternal and paternal leave, support for child care, paid leave for a sick child, flexible working hours, tax credit for home ownership, and passing legislation increasing minimum wage and forgiving student loans, and so on.

Entertainment businesses can assist families by regulating violent and sexual materials in the mass media and by producing more family-friendly advertising and programs.

Cancellation of Debt

Sabbath economics sees the forgiveness of debts as an integral part of the redistribution of resources. A covenantal renewal typically included cancellation of debt, implying that a new society is not possible without some kind of economic freedom and equality among members. Occasional corrections of systemic economic inequality (e.g., forgiveness of debt and land reform) are necessary to protect the socioeconomically powerless from exploitation. Cancellation of debts offers a fresh start for the indebted and helps them contribute to the common good as productive members of a society. Christians need to take leadership and advocate for the cancellation of debt. In our current context, this principle may especially apply to the cancellation of student loans.

Economic Rights

In God's covenant relationship with people, meeting the basic needs of the poor was a fundamental moral demand. A minimal level of subsistence must be guaranteed for every member of the community as a fundamental human right. A society has a moral responsibility to meet basic human needs for all citizens. Any society that fails to provide these things is unjust.

New covenant ethics envisions a society where the legitimate needs of the poor, downtrodden, and dispossessed are addressed and met, and these persons are given the same opportunities as other members of the community. Basic needs include health care, education, and goods and services essential to social participation such as utilities, transportation and communication services, safe drinking water, and good sanitation. Basic income and services are necessary to help members survive and to protect their moral agency.

Poverty is a threat to basic dignity and human community. Scripture strongly condemns any system that perpetuates poverty. Poverty is an invisible but real form of violence that causes the slow death of the poor (even without directly shedding any blood). Without economic rights, individuals are given formal freedom (*de jure*) but not actual freedom (*de facto*).

Economic rights are crucial to protect human dignity, the sense of self-esteem, and security. When a person's value is solely measured by marketable performance and merits, those unable to compete are socially expendable and disposable. The idea of economic rights was advocated by Martin Luther King Jr. and the Roman Catholic Church. For example, according to the US bishops, "All people have a right to economic initiative, to productive work, to just wages and benefits, to decent working conditions as well as to organize and join unions or other associations."[38]

In Sabbath economics, philanthropy cannot substitute for economic rights. Charity is helpful in meeting immediate needs, but it is not a fundamental solution. The poor should not be treated merely as the object of pity and sympathy but as equal members of a community. It is the duty of society to meet their basic needs; these cannot be left to individual acts of mercy.

Justice as Capability

If conservatives stress merit alone and secular socialists focus on basic need, new covenant ethics enhances the capability of people to "help individuals develop into the people they can be."[39] The capability approach attempts to convert resources (both endogamous and exogamous) into capabilities to achieve flourishing and well-being.

To eliminate poverty, in addition to meeting basic needs, it is necessary to enhance the capabilities of the poor. Meeting basic needs is not necessarily social and economic functioning. We require empowerment, for without it, meeting basic needs may inculcate permanent dependency. Ron Sider asserts that "neither economic changes by themselves nor behavioral changes in family life by themselves can solve contemporary poverty."[40] He suggests that a conventional approach to poverty be shifted away from financial subsidy to empowerment by increasing the ability of the poor and their communities.

Adequate access to productive resources and opportunities for self-development is one way to enhance capability. These include various social service programs, such as learning and skills development, job training, free education, health care, child care for parents, and the Head Start program. In addition to self-motivation and self-empowerment, communal support and the vitality of civil society are important

38. "A Catholic Framework for Economic Life."

39. Warren R. Copeland, *And the Poor Get Welfare*, 75.

40. Sider, *Just Generosity*, 125.

to fight poverty. The Sabbath increases communal capability. Sabbath is a communal, more specifically, a family-centered, day. Sabbath renews the relationship; it strengthens a social fabric and empowers the agency of people through rest and healing. Individual capability and work ethic grow as communal capability grows. Sider writes: "It is not only—or even primarily—a matter of unequal funding, although that is one problem. Lingering racism, unsafe drug-infested neighborhoods, dysfunctional families, malnutrition, oversized administrative bureaucracies, unresponsive teachers' unions, and peer pressure that mocks academic success all play a role."[41] This means that community organizing assists people in developing their capability.

The poor need jobs in order to flourish and live a life of dignity. Employment is essential to protect human dignity. Through work, humans participate and contribute, which enhances their feeling of self-worth and sense of meaning. Today, providing decent jobs is parallel to the inheritance of land in ancient Israel, which served as the enduring source of subsistence.

Covenant and Democratic Socialism

What does a covenantal economy mean for us today? How is it related to the modern economic system, and which economic system is closer to the spirit and vision of the covenantal economy?

Covenant envisions a radical democracy and an inclusive economy that is egalitarian, socially responsible, and public minded. Sabbath economics is need based, and subsistence and sustenance oriented, and seeks not affluence but adequacy. It provides social support for the fulfillment of personal potential and the enhancement of the common good. It balances and respects both freedom and the public good, both creativity and solidarity. It emphasizes socially responsible citizens and publicly minded economic policies. And it offers social support and cultivates personal motivation for fulfilling personal potential and enhancing the common good.[42]

Based on our brief study of ancient Israel and the early Christian community, it seems that among various economic systems, democratic socialism best approximates covenantal political economy. As a third way between capitalism and communism, democratic socialism upholds both civil-political and economic social rights.[43] That Scandinavian and northwestern European nations that practice democratic

41. Sider, *Just Generosity*, 198.

42. Martin Luther King Jr. said: "Good and just society is neither the thesis of capitalism nor the antithesis of communism, but a socially conscious democracy which reconciles the truths of individualism and collectivism." King, *Where Do We Go from Here*, 187.

43. See Sturm, "Martin Luther King, Jr., as Democratic Socialist," 79–105.

socialism enjoy a far better quality of social life and social harmony. Jewish communities in Israel after World War II also practiced democratic socialism through numerous local *kibbutzim*. As a third way between capitalism and communism, democratic socialism emphasizes government economic initiatives in distribution of economic benefits and technology and protects the basic economic and social needs of its members. Unlike neoliberalism, democratic socialism protects the basic economic rights of people and common space and lands; the government controls industries to bring about the common good of a society.

Democratic socialism emphasizes the active role of the government, which is necessary to protect the public good, human dignity, and economic rights. Economic injustices (a permanent underclass, extreme inequality, a skewed tax system that favors the rich) are signs that the greed and coveting of the elites and ruling class are rampant and in need of regulation. Coveting is "the endless propulsion of wanting and taking."[44] Coveting can be controlled only by setting clear boundaries and building walls around protected areas (community and commons). Democratic socialism claims that the government should oversee the market to protect the public good.

I acknowledge that there is a misplaced perception among evangelical Christians that democracy and capitalism are inseparable. Liberal democracy is often called democratic capitalism because of its intimate connection with capitalism.[45] Democratic capitalists believe that protecting individual freedom, competition, the free market, and limited government is most efficient in enhancing the public good, removing poverty, and increasing economic productivity.

While historically in the West, democracy and capitalism have developed in close connection, there is no necessary connection. Just as there are diverse forms of democracy, there are different forms of capitalism. Democracy requires more than the free market. It requires freedom of the press, the rule of law, the separation of powers, and free elections. As discussed above, the current form of capitalism (neoliberalism) actually undermines democracy. While the Bible values both individual freedom and communal well-being, the latter is ethically more important and foundational than the former because individual well-being is ultimately dependent on communal well-being.

Democratic socialism achieves a greater measure of equality among members of society by legislating various policies of income redistribution (progressive income taxation, food and housing subsidies, free college education). In the Bible, the ideal ruler, YHWH, takes responsibility for the needs of the people (Ezek. 34:23). The

44. Brueggemann, *Money and Possession*, 25.

45. Novak, *The Spirit of Democratic Capitalism*; Benne, *The Ethics of Democratic Capitalism*.

stipulations of the Mosaic law established legal mechanisms for protections the poor and vulnerable were entitled to guaranteed basic rights such as food (Lev. 19:9–10; Deut. 23:24; 24:19–22), clothing (Exod. 26–27), and just business dealings (Deut. 25:13–16). The law requires the community to provide a "safety net" for the poor and needy.

However, a covenantal form of democratic socialism is different from its secular counterpart, which relies heavily on the government for economic planning, social engineering, and redistribution. Rather, a covenantal approach has a strong communitarian tone and threads the balance of shared responsibility between individuals, the community, and the government. That is, it emphasizes self-help and self-responsibility nurtured in a myriad of civic organizations in civil society in addition to governmental initiatives and support. A covenantal model addresses not only the laws, structures, and policies of a society but also the character and virtue formation of its members, in addition to the role of the local community and organizations.

New covenant ethics places democratic socialism in a complex, pluralistic vision of a society. The belief that a society can be organized purely by state power (communism) or in terms of economic self-interest (neoliberal capitalism) is unrealistic. Civil society, sphere autonomy, and associational pluralism are critical. Unlike communism (Cuba, North Korea, China), democratic socialism encourages the democratic process of people directly electing their representatives and executives; the change of ruling party through democratic election is legally protected. Unlike the other two systems, it is not monistic (tyrannical power of money or state) but respects the plurality of social spheres and the creativity of individuals serving the common good. As we saw the seventy-year-long experiment of communism in the Soviet Union collapse, so we are also witnessing the unraveling and chaotic nature of neoliberalism in the United States.

Democratic socialism requires a corresponding social ethos that supports egalitarian law and a progressive tax system, and generous social welfare programs. We can learn from the Sinai covenant and Jesus: the wilderness journey, the manna from heaven, and the Sabbath teach us the limits of one's desires as well as the need to respect the boundaries and rights of the earth. Such practices, though countercultural, are necessary to build a communally oriented society—to learn how to live according to one's need in a symbiotic relationship with others and the earth. Such a society is achieved under a moral vision that is liberative, organic, encompassing, and ecological, just like the new covenant of Jesus.

A covenantal form of democratic socialism balances the common good with individual responsibility. New covenant ethics seeks both personal and structural transformation. It is concerned not only with distribution and protecting the poor but also with the individual pursuit of excellence in the context of community and care for creation. Everybody has the right and responsibility to participate in producing goods and services and sharing them among all members of humanity. Individual creativity, invention, production of wealth, and hard work in economic activities must be respected and encouraged. Covenant calls everyone to participate in and contribute to the common good. The poor also have obligations to society, but the rich should contribute more.

Economic Just Peacemaking

Economic development and security are important for just peacemaking. Without protecting the economic rights of the poor and the needy, social justice and harmonious social relationships are inconceivable. Symbolizing shalom, the Sabbath reminds us that genuine rest comes from just and righteous social relationships where everyone is in right and harmonious relationship attuned to God.

Covenant ethics recognizes that humans are social beings before they are individuals, and likewise, poverty is the result of relational and social failure, not necessarily the result of individual laziness. Bryant L. Myers notes: "Poverty is a result of relationships that do not work, that are not just, that are not for life, that are not harmonious or enjoyable. Poverty is the absence of shalom in all its meanings. It is interesting to note that this view is consistent with the Hebraic worldview, in which relationships are the highest good, while alienation is the lowest. All five poverty frameworks provide explanations that rest on the idea of relationships, that are fragmented, dysfunctional, or oppressive."[46]

Christopher Wright says that, in the Old Testament, "the primary cause [of poverty] is the exploitation of others by those whose own selfish interests are served by keeping others poor."[47] Poverty is not purely economic or quantifiable but is deeply ingrained in the imbalance of power in a community that leads to exploitation of the poor.[48] The greed of the rich perpetuates poverty (Mic. 2:1–2); hence, curbing excessive economic inequality is necessary. In the OT, poverty is understood more as powerlessness than as impoverishment. "The most common word for poverty in the OT (*ani* and *anaw*) implies vulnerability to oppression more than material destitution."[49] The poor are not only economically powerless but also politically and socially vulnerable. It is the profound insight of the Bible that poverty results in political and social disempowerment.

46. Myers, *Walking with the Poor*, 143.
47. Christopher Wright, *Old Testament Ethics*, 170.
48. Sider, *Just Generosity*, 82.
49. Bretherton, "Exorcizing Democracy," 15.

An unequal and stratified society is unstable and violent. Neoliberalism rewards the winner with wealth, pleasure, social status, political influence, and reputation, while relegating "losers" to the expendable category. "Inequality is dangerous for liberal democracy. And the dangers are self-perpetuating: disparities of wealth make it difficult to organize countervailing powers, and the absence of countervailing powers makes for increasingly radical disparities. The long-term effect of this process, the characteristic product of radical inequality, is tyranny in everyday life: the arrogance of the wealthy, the humbling of the poor."[50] Relative equality among members is necessary to maintain the trust and high moral spirit of a community. Inequality undermines trust and unity, breeds social cynicism, and results in high crime rates. This compromises the quality of life for both the poor and the rich.[51]

More equal societies have fewer teenage mothers, lower homicide rates, less violence, less obesity, lower prison inmate rates, less use of illegal drugs, less mental illness, and lower infant mortality rates. These societies have more social mobility, a high level of social cohesiveness and mutual trust, and longer life expectancies. Inequality drives competition and fuels consumerism, which makes it harder to reduce global warming. Equal societies perform better on the Global Peace Index as well as the World Happiness Index.[52] More equal societies spend a higher proportion of their income on overseas aid. In short, a more egalitarian society is more stable and offers a better quality of life. These societies are conducive to human flourishing.

Practices: Intentional Communities

Neoliberalism, globalization, and digitization have substantially changed the nature and meaning of work. Work is more than a means of making money; it is vital for human self-actualization (thriving). Work is a part of the "natural condition" of human beings. Work is integral to who we are; Adam was a gardener. Through work, we continue God's creative work and contribute to the common good of society. The lack or loss of work wounds human dignity and self-esteem at its core. As seen in the Rust Belt of the United States, when work disappears, communities disappear and profound psychological problems (depression, suicide, addiction) adhere to

50. Walzer, "Gulf Crisis," 25.

51. Richard Wilkinson and Kate Pickett explain that economic inequality not only undermines social trust (i.e., covenants) but also tends to increase physical and mental illness among both the poor and the rich. Their book demonstrates how the basic moral insights of Sabbath are true and relevant today (Wilkinson and Pickett, *The Spirit Level*).

52. "Mental Health."

individuals and their families. How can we preserve meaningful jobs in a society that has become more and more automated (computers, AI, robotics)? This is not only for economic security but for human self-development and emotional well-being. A major rationale behind basic universal income is economic security. But it does not address the question of vocation, self-fulfillment, and economic security. Balancing self-fulfillment and economic security is a critical social issue.

A radical social vision and creative moral imagination are necessary to address the challenges to work. I suggest that Christians seriously consider various forms of faith-rooted intentional communities in local contexts. To do so creatively implements the Sabbath economy in a local community as an alternative to greedy, competitive, and dehumanizing neoliberalism. Jesus's answer to the excruciating social situation was neither competition nor exploitation of the weaker members for self-gain nor self-protection. He promoted sharing, care, and generosity and the building up of unity in trusting in God. Practicing Jubilee economics, Jesus's community, with few rich or socially powerful members, provided a safety net for every member. They experienced God's generous reign, mutual love, and affection among themselves.

Jesus's followers treated each other as a surrogate family. Such an approach was an integral part of Jesus's covenantal organizing. It had the effect of increasing the power of the people, raising self-esteem, and creating internal unity. Although Jesus did not apply this accumulated power to direct protest or confrontation against Roman imperial rule, the insight is important. Through the organizing work of Jesus, people were freed from isolation, competition, desperation, and hopelessness in order to build their own community where they could find dignity, support, and hope. These new ethical and community-organizing practices gave Jesus's followers the spiritual and moral high ground over the occupiers.

Today, Jesus's model has applicability in the form of intentional community. Intentional communities should be ecological, economic, and emotionally empowering. Through a creative combination of governmental subsidy, economic cooperation, and sharing of labor, an intentional community is created that practices covenant among members. It is encouraging to see that intentional communities are growing all over the world to address loneliness and ecological and economic need. Restoring local practices of agriculture, gardening, shared labor, and communal life helps cope with the onslaught of technology, globalization, and neoliberal oligarchy. This does not mean sectarian withdrawal (contra the Benedict Option). Rather, it secures a viable communal ground to fight against the erosive power of neoliberalism. There is no reason why we cannot both build a local community through intentional communities and publicly promote justice and the common good.

Conclusion

Sabbath economics offers an alternative to the structural injustice and exploitation of neoliberal economics. Neoliberalism and the current practices of multinational corporations are anticovenantal and anti-Jubilee. For too long the churches of the United States have sanctified this neoliberalism as a God-sanctioned moral economy while demonizing Soviet communism. Rather than looking for a better, more equitable system, they compare neoliberalism with a failed economic system. It is time to engage in prophetic ministry in order to break the vicious cycle of consumption, obsession with possessions and wealth, and accumulation of power to the rich alone.

God's new covenant challenges our patterns of greed and consumption and teaches an ecologically oriented lifestyle. Without sharing, there is no community. The covenant protects the poor, the biosphere, and creatures to build a free, egalitarian, and reciprocal community. It is a restorative economy for the body and soul (Sabbath rest) that is free of debt (Sabbath year) but includes property and land (Jubilee).

New covenant ethics offers a necessary antidote to neoliberal capitalism. The Sabbath principles of universal mandatory rest on the Sabbath, periodic cancellation of debt, protection of economic rights and the family, and the empowerment of the poor are contrary to capitalistic principles of individual consumption, individual greed, private property, and "possessive individualism." Having served as the symbol of a counterimperial political economy against Rome, the Eucharist represents the complete antitype of the political economy of neoliberalism.

CHAPTER 15

Creation Care

The more I wonder, the more I love.

—Alice Walker, *The Color Purple*

Shatter, my God, through the daring of your revelation the childishly timid outlook that can conceive of nothing greater or more vital in the world than the pitiable perfection of our human organism.

—Pierre Teilhard de Chardin, *Hymn of the Universe*

This is the law pertaining to land animal and bird and every living creature that moves through the waters and every creature that swarms upon the earth, to make a distinction between the unclean and the clean, and between the living creature that may be eaten and the living creature that may not be eaten.

—Leviticus 11:46–47

We are living in critical times. We face an ecological crisis of almost unimaginable scope and magnitude. Disaster is no longer a future prediction but an everyday reality—drought, famine, flooding, rising sea levels, and desertification. Cumulative human consumption is destroying the planet in fundamental and unprecedented ways; the facts and figures are undeniable. The planet is suffering from human overuse and exploitation of resources. Human-made disasters have already displaced millions of people and are a major cause of migration and the refugee crisis.[1]

The ecological crisis poses an existential threat to human existence because ecological sustainability constitutes the foundation of human survival. Nature is striking

1. Chan, "Paris Accord Considers Climate Change as a Factor in Mass Migration."

back in order to regain the equilibrium of the ecological system. It seems that the revenge of Mother Nature is against human greed, infidelity, and violence.

Among the growing list of ecological problems (e.g., water shortages and contamination, urban sprawl, air pollution, ocean acidification, declines of plant and animal populations endangering species, overuse of plastics, depletion of natural resources, and soil erosion), global warming poses the most serious, extensive, and immediate threat. Global warming refers to a gradual rise of the earth's overall atmospheric temperature through the greenhouse effect caused by CO_2, chlorofluorocarbons, methane, and other greenhouse gases (GHGs). The level of CO_2 produced by fossil fuels and other GHGs is now surpassing the planet's capability to absorb it, now hitting 405 parts per million (ppm) through its natural cycle (photosynthesis) and ordinary feedback system (oceanic sinking of CO_2). The year 2019 was the second-warmest year in the 140 years of official record keeping. Global land and ocean temperatures were 0.95°C (1.71°F) above average. This value is only 0.04°C (0.07°F) less than the record high value of 0.99°C (1.78°F) above average set in 2016. If these trends hold, by the end of the century, CO_2 levels may surpass 800 ppm. Correspondingly, global temperature could reach about 4° C (10° F) higher than it is now.[2]

Global warming has dire consequences for nature: melting glaciers, extreme weather patterns (frequent storms, flooding, wildfires, heat waves, droughts, freezing winters, hurricanes), rising sea levels, and the thawing of the permafrost. The warming of seawater is starving the plankton population and destroying the bottom of the oceanic food chain. Rising sea levels will cause extensive loss of coastal and island habitats and depletion of significant freshwater sources and agricultural areas, prompting an immigration and refugee crisis. Shortages of water, food, and natural resources will multiply. Also, similar to the COVID-19 pandemic, more and more epidemics will break out if global warming worsens through the thawing of the permafrost and if humans continue to encroach upon the habitats of other creatures. On a political level, global warming could lead to military conflicts as superpowers and nation-states escalate competition in order to secure water, food, and natural resources. The proliferation of refugees and migration is already an international political and social crisis. In the West, this has elicited the rise of white nationalism and authoritarian governments. The poor and marginalized will suffer first and most.

Global warming is accelerating far faster than scholars projected. Global warming, left unaddressed, is a game changer for humanity and other species. The window of opportunity to address global warming is closing more every day. If the issue is

2. National Centers for Environmental Information (NOAA), "Global Climate Report—Annual 2019"; Houghton, *Global Warming*, 140–45.

not addressed, the consequence will be catastrophic. The planet will survive, but humanity will never be the same. "If humanity wishes to preserve a planet similar to that on which civilization developed and to which life on Earth is adapted, paleoclimate evidence and ongoing climate change suggest that CO_2 will need to be reduced from [current levels] to at most 350 ppm."[3]

This chapter studies a covenantal ground of ecological ethics, while recognizing that, historically, Christianity's anthropocentric theology and practices have contributed to the degradation and abuse of nature. Still, today, many churches are egregiously failing in the teaching of ecological ethics.

What Are the Causes of This Crisis?

There are many material causes for the current crisis: inordinate use of fossil fuels, consumption of resources, urbanization, deforestation, and consumer lifestyles. But the current ecological crisis in general, and global warming in particular, has to do with the distinctive mindset, values, and patterns of modernity and the economic system created by industrialization—the very foundation of current Western civilization. Industrialization, which transformed agricultural-based economies into manufacturing-based ones, massively influenced nature because it used fossil fuels (coal, oil, and natural gas) as major sources of energy. First used in trains and steamships, these fuels were later used for motor vehicles, airplanes, and electric power for homes and factories. Industrialization was revolutionary in its productive power, but it uprooted humanity from its agricultural and ecological foundations and placed it in urban contexts. Currently 55 percent of the global population lives in cities, but that number is expected to increase to 68 percent by 2050.[4]

Industrialization was based on a distinctive philosophical movement called modernity. Emerging especially during the Enlightenment, modernity was a comprehensive worldview and way of life that transformed the West from a feudal to an industrial society. But the modernistic mindset turned out to be extremely harmful to nature because of its anthropocentricity; it placed humanity at the center of the universe and gave humans a sense of entitlement to control and dominate nature and other species. This mindset was intellectually supported by science and the discovery of new physical laws that helped people to understand the previously unknown operations of nature.

This modernistic mindset is powerfully enfleshed in capitalism and technology that uses science to bend the physical world to serve human desires. As a new civ-

3. Hansen, "Target Atmospheric CO_2."

4. "68% of the World Population Projected to Live in Urban Areas by 2050, Says UN."

ilizational paradigm that replaced feudal society, modernity has decisively altered people's relationship with nature and community, and it has decoupled the tie between people and their places. Modernity's other core assumptions and implications include the following:

- Nature has a virtually limitless storehouse of resources for human use.
- Nature is malleable and can be reconfigured for human ends.
- Humanity has the commission to use and control nature.
- Humanity has the right to use nature's resources for ongoing improvement in the material standard of living.
- Ongoing economic growth is the most effective way to promote the continuing elevation of material standards of living.
- The quality of life itself is furthered by an economic system directed to ever-expanding material abundance.
- Human problems can be solved through effective use of reason, education, and science and technology.[5]

In modernity, the human attitude toward nature is control and mastery. Nature is completely objectified for human use and consumption. While modernity proposes science and technology as rational and morally neutral enterprises, they are in fact empowered by capitalism and used for control and mastery. Capitalism creates a seductive environment in which science and technology are used for commercial gain and to encourage money, pleasure, and comfort.

This instrumentalist mindset was central to Western colonialism. Greedy for endless material extraction and capital accumulation, the West used its advanced science and technology to colonize the rest of the world. This tendency continues even today. The rest of the world is forced to adopt modernity, bending to the power of the Western empire, for their survival, to compete in the global economy. Numerous human tribes, religions, cultures, and traditions have been destroyed; meanwhile, China, India, and others have found survival impossible without adopting the Western system (industrialization, capitalism, and science/technology). The colonial experiences of humiliation and subjugation are huge motivators to compete with the West on Western terms,[6] that is, placing the national focus on economic growth, science, and technology; expending much effort on economic development; and expanding productive forces and the market. Consequently, rising consumption levels correlate with the increasing use of natural resources and fossil fuels.

5. This list is from Rasmussen, *Earth Community, Earth Ethics*, 61.

6. Cf. Zakaria, *Post-American World*.

The growth-driven economy of developing countries relies on cheap wage workers and a consumer class that prompts urbanization. This shift from agriculture to capitalism (either state directed or neoliberal) and urbanization, modeled by the US style of consumption, has devastated the environment. Almost every nation is now competing for natural resources. Moreover, globalization has further exacerbated this situation by accelerating international trade, travel, and deregulation of environmental laws. In addition, thanks to improving human health and living conditions (made possible by industrialization), the human population has grown rapidly. And population increase means more consumption, in principle, unless consumption per capita radically decreases (e.g., by making technologies more efficient and energy conserving).[7]

One can easily imagine the devastating impact the modernist worldview has had on nature. The current ecological crisis is the inevitable consequence of the modern anthropocentric worldview. Industrialization that drives the capitalistic system's ethos of maximum profit has come at the expense of the earth and other species.

Unfortunately, this mindset is partly consistent with the Protestant Christian worldview. Medieval historian Lynn White Jr. points out that "Christianity bears a huge burden of guilt for the present situation"[8] because of its unique role in the development of modern science and technology. "Viewed historically, modern technology is an extrapolation of natural theology and . . . is at least partly to be explained as an Occidental, voluntarist realization of the Christian dogma of man's transcendence of, and rightful mastery over, nature."[9] The charge is that Christianity is the source of Western anthropocentrism: nature lacks intrinsic moral value, hence, humans have no ethical obligation toward it. This anthropocentric view has opened the door for the plundering of nature.

Sadly, many conservative Christians still uphold the dominion principle as a defining theological ground for human relationship with nature. For them, the idea of the *imago Dei* grants humans higher status and privilege over nature. For them, stewardship ironically means extending human control over nature and the efficient use of natural resources through diligent labor and technological-economic development for human prosperity and happiness.[10]

7. $I = P \times A \times T$. This equation was first proposed by Paul Ehrlich and John Holdren to estimate the overall impact of human economic activities on the environment: Environmental Impact (I) equals Population (P) times Affluence (A) times Technology (T), where A is essentially consumption per capita and T is a measure of overall technological efficiency. The environmental impact of an increase in population could actually go down if A and T are ecologically energy friendly.

8. White, "The Historical Roots of Our Ecologic Crisis," 12.

9. White, "The Historical Roots of Our Ecologic Crisis," 12.

10. Beisner, *Prosperity and Poverty*, xii.

There is a strong political reaction from the left to the anthropocentrism within Protestant Christianity. Ecologically conscious atheists, paganists, ecofeminists, and indigenous people are highly critical of Christianity in general, and Protestant Christianity in particular. They attempt to radically redefine human relationship with nature by rejecting the Christian monotheistic worldview of body-soul dualism and androcentrism. They see these as a major theological cause of the current disaster. The traditional theological paradigm undergirds ethics and lifestyles that denigrate other species and religiously sanction their misuse and exploitation. Monotheism describes God as the remote, transcendental, and superior being over nature. The cultural mandate of dominion/domination has definitely shaped the Christian and Western view of nature; that is, God and humanity are superior to and transcendent to nature, which turns into a mere object of consumption and control. This attitude is displayed in the dualism of soul and body, spirit and matter, that treats the latter as inferior or intrinsically evil.[11]

Without addressing the ecological complaint against it, Christianity will lose its credibility and moral authority.

New Covenant Ethics

These complaints and criticisms are valid. Christians must humbly acknowledge that their theologies and anthropocentric practices have indeed contributed to the current despoliation of the earth. As Max Weber demonstrated in his book *The Protestant Ethic and the Spirit of Capitalism*, religious beliefs have economic implications. Human attitudes toward nature have ecological effects. Theology matters to nature.

How can we reset our relationship with nature while respecting just and rightful claims of nature and other creatures? What kind of theology and ethics can help us overcome dualism and anthropocentrism? New covenant ethics provides a faithful and coherent Christian approach to nature in a way that is distinctively biblical and ecological. In a fresh way, covenant respects the proper place of humanity and nature in God and offers a moral way to relate to nature without anthropocentrism or idealism. It overcomes the modern dualistic and instrumentalist view of the human-nature relationship.

In the following paragraphs, we examine the covenantal relationship of God, humanity, and nature by briefly reviewing the major covenants in Scripture.

11. This dualism is found in several distorted forms of Christian theology, not only anthropology but also soteriology and eschatology.

Trinity

Theologically, the doctrine of the Trinity helps address the charge of monism and helps overcome a series of binary understandings: reason/emotion, mind/body, man/woman, human/nature, objectivity/subjectivity, transcendence/immanence, freedom/solidarity, individual/society.

The rediscovery of the doctrine of the Trinity has had a revolutionary impact on Christian theology and ethics. It reimagines the God of causality in classical theology as the God of relationship found in the Bible. In fact, congruent to the covenantal drama, the Trinity means that God is not a remote, distant, and alien deity but a relational and communicative one. The three-in-one, one-in-three, the Trinity is a theological ground of relational ontology that has replaced the substance ontology in traditional scholastic theology. Reflecting this God, being-in-relation is the nature of things. Everything is connected to everything else.

The triune God is not only transcendent but also immanent. A Trinitarian-covenantal approach to ecology reenchants our nature. God is not separate from nature. God reveals Godself not only through historical events and human messengers but also through nature. Scripture and nature are the two books of God. Jesus Christ is not only our personal savior but also the redeemer of creation by reconciling creation through his incarnation, crucifixion, and resurrection. The Spirit is not only the personal sanctifier but also the planter and germinator of creation. God's Spirit rests on every life and moves it toward flourishing and shalom.

Covenant and the Land

The ecological nature of covenant ethics is evident in that all major covenants treat the earth as an integral partner of the human covenant with God:

- the creation covenant: God–Adam/Eve–the garden (Eden)
- the Noachian covenant: God–Noah–the earth (postdiluvian world)
- the Sinai covenant: God–Israel–the land (Canaan)
- the new covenant: God–humanity–the new creation (new heaven and new earth)

The first human beings and Eden, Noah and the earth, Israel and Canaan, humanity and the new creation are inextricably bound together. This means that the land is a covenantal entity and the earth is an integral part of God's covenant. The Bible understands the land as a covenant partner with humanity in God. Our relationship with the land is the mode of our covenantal life with God. Humans belong to God through the earth. Human existence is earthbound and earth tethered. There is no direct belonging to God without the earth's mediation. In this light, soul-body dualism is heresy. Moltmann notes: "The modern split into soul and body, subject and object, person and thing, does justice neither to the totality of human beings, nor to their natural living community with the earth. If the modern fissure is rigorously pushed through, human bodiliness is destroyed and the natural community of life is ruined. Modern anthropocentrism is deadly for human beings to themselves."[12]

Throughout the Bible, the land is the barometer of human covenantal fidelity to God and others. That is, the land serves as God's agent. God uses land to bless as well as punish humans (Lev. 26:3–4, 14–20). When injustices, oppression, and exploitations abound, the land becomes uninhabitable (covered by the flood in the judgment), vomiting out its residents.[13] In the context of new covenant ethics, social justice and environmental justice are inseparable. Abuse of the land is typically the sign of social injustices, and vice versa. Human greed and violence always lead to the exploitation of the land. Sin has negative effects, ecological as well as social; it breaks down not only the human-God and human-human relationships but also the human-nature relationship. As creation is an integral moral system, the toxic power of sin affects all members, including humans, other species, and nature.

Creation Covenant

The Christian association with ecological degradation has to do with a narrow, distorted understanding of the doctrine of creation, in particular the cultural mandate (Gen. 1:26): "Let them have dominion over the fish of the sea, and over the birds of the air, and over the cattle, and over all the wild animals of the earth, and over every creeping thing that creeps upon the earth." This passage, combined with (or as a natural inference of) the *imago Dei* (Gen. 1:27),[14] has been widely used to justify the violent, abusive, and rapacious treatment of nature. Taken out of its biblical and covenantal context, the cultural mandate has been twisted into the ideology of conquest and mastery.[15] It has provided a theological rationale for anthropocentrism and an ontological hierarchy to place humanity above nature, creating a hierarchical order

12. Moltmann, *Ethics of Hope*, 222.

13. Rasmussen also points out that links exist among "injustice, unpeace, creation's disintegration." *Earth Community, Earth Ethics*, 12.

14. Dominion is the natural implication of the *imago Dei*; a human is God's representative.

15. Migliore, *Faith Seeking Understanding*, 98. This narrative of mastery was further justified in the context of God's declaration after the first couple's disobedience (Gen 3:17–19), namely, the perceived hostility of nature toward humans.

of God-humans-nature. This view was propagated by eminent theologians of the past (such as Aquinas) and is still widely spread among conservative Christians.

Covenant offers a broader context and a more accurate reading of the Genesis story and the cultural mandate. We must begin by looking at the cultural mandate in its biblical context. The opening two chapters of Genesis say that humans belong to the earth; the earth is a source of their identity. The story leading to God's creation of human beings is not a mere "stage prop" but rather reveals their origin and their intrinsic connectivity to the earth. Genesis 2:7 describes humans as earthlings (*adam*). Made from the earth (*adamah*), they will return to it again. They are eternally tethered to the earth.

Other creatures were not created for human consumption. God's blessing (be fruitful and multiply) was given first to animals and then to humans. Of course, this does not mean that humans are made of dust alone. We are also God's image-bearers created by God's breath. Humans have a double origin: earth and God. This double origin is what characterizes humanity and is the source of endless tension and anxiety—fragile but curious, instinctual but creative, physical and spiritual, ceaselessly searching for mystery, purpose, meaning, and eternity while facing persistent physical, biological, and emotional needs. Humans are bonded to both God and earth. Separated from either of these two sources, humans are unable to be fully human; they are disoriented and displaced in the infinitely vast and mysterious universe. We languish from the moment we forget our intrinsic relationship with God and the earth.[16]

Then how should we interpret the cultural mandate (Gen. 1:26–28) in the context of the creation covenant? A traditional, hierarchal view of domination is incompatible with the covenant premise of the creation story. The passages cannot be viewed apart from a broad literary context and the covenantal underpinning of creation in the chapter. Human dominion is subjected to a covenantal relationship between human beings and the earth. To be covenanted is to exercise fidelity and accountability to God and others—committed to and caring for the well-being of others. In a covenantal context, dominion is not the justification of control, mastery, and exploitation but the calling of responsibility, serving, caring, and observing. It cannot violate the rightness of other creatures' space and boundaries.

The Hebrew word for dominion (Gen. 1:26–28) is *radah*, which means to "tread down," to "dominate," and to "subjugate." This word, in the context of the Hebrew Bible, describes the relationship between a king and his people. One cannot think of Israel's kingship outside a covenantal relationship of God and the people. Dominion is not domination. Dominion in the Bible does not mean mastery or control but care

16. Cf. Rasmussen, *Earth-Honoring Faith*, 19.

and execution of justice, particularly for the poor and marginalized (Ps. 72).[17] Rulers should embody righteousness in their actions and use power to approximate shalom. This means that our dominion over nature is not ontological but, as God's stewards, functional. A covenantal relationship defines the nature and content of dominion and sets limits to human exercises of it. Just as a king's authority is subjected to God and to the king's people, human dominion is defined by covenantal accountability rather than sheer autocracy and mastery.

A more explicit covenantal understanding of dominion (as service and responsibility) is clearly found in Genesis 2:15 ("The LORD God took the man and put him in the garden of Eden to till it and keep it"). The word for "till" in Hebrew is *abad*, which means to serve with reverence. The word for "keep" is *shamar*, which means to guard, to watch, and to protect. In other words, God's commandment *abad* emphasizes that the earth is worthy of our service, while *shamar* calls for human attention to and care of the earth. They are commandments for humanity to care for the earth with reverence and watchfulness, recognizing the primacy and needs of the earth.[18] To treat the gift with care is to respect God, the giver.[19] Such an attitude is consistent with the covenantal underpinning of the creation story.

God's commandments to "subdue" and rule (Gen. 1:28) and to "till" and "keep" (Gen. 2:15) complement and balance each other; while the former describes the commissioned power of humanity, the latter describes human responsibility for the earth as servant. This means that humans are charged to treat the earth covenantally—with knowledge and attentiveness, while respecting the boundaries and limits of their actions and claims.[20] This is, in fact, no different from their treatment of other humans.

The ethical meaning and significance of the creation covenant are that the Genesis story is more than cosmogony (the birth of the world); it defines creation as a moral community and refuses to relegate the earth as merely the environment of human economic life.

Noachian Covenant

Noah's story (Gen. 6:11–9:19) tells of the fate of humanity when the covenant with God and nature is broken and when humans forget their responsibility toward

17. Butkus, "The Stewardship of Creation."

18. Ellen F. Davis, *Scripture, Culture, and Agriculture*, 32.

19. Humans are ordained to serve the land (till and keep it) in the manner that priests serve the temple. The Bible associates the land (Eden, Canaan, the earth) with the temple—a sacred place, a sanctuary where God rests and communes with humans and other creatures.

20. Ellen F. Davis, *Scripture, Culture, and Agriculture*, 30.

others. The result is God's punishment through an ecological disaster. "There is an integrity to creation that depends on humans seeing themselves as properly placed within a network of creation and God. The drama shows us that neither God nor the creation itself can tolerate violence, manipulation, or shame. Instead of the hubris that characterized Adam and his descendants, Noah stands out as a beacon of the humbled *adam* who is faithful to the needs of *adamah*."[21] The flood is the negative communicative action of the earth against disloyal humanity.

As mentioned in chapter 1, the Noachian covenant is an ecological covenant. Covenantal care, solidarity, and responsibility are found in God's commandment to invite other creatures into the ark. After the flood, Noah fulfilled the role of Adam in caring for the earth. The Noachian covenant explicitly discusses the ecological ground for God's relationship with humanity by specifying the earth (Gen. 9:13) and other creatures as covenantal partners. Specifically, the Noachian covenant mentions "every living creature" (*kol-nepes haaya*) five times as the covenantal partner (9:10, 12, 15, 16, 17).

The implication of the Noachian covenant is tremendous. Covenant defines membership—who has a right and responsibility to whom. Since membership in covenant defines the boundaries and scope of care, protection, respect, and rights, every living being, as a partner of the Noachian covenant, is entitled to such care, protection, respect, and rights. God's reign is not for humans alone but for the entire creation—planets, birds, fish, plants, which are wonderfully joined together. God's care and fidelity to other creatures are described in many parts of the Bible.[22] Furthermore, the Noachian covenant is "an everlasting covenant (*berit olam*). It is not a temporary agreement or provisional pledge but a covenant in perpetuity."[23] Since it is an everlasting covenant, it binds all of humanity, even after the new covenant of Jesus. Given the fallenness and violent disposition of humanity, the membership of every creature and the perpetuity of the Noachian covenant remind humans of their responsibilities and obligations toward other creatures. It reaffirms the boundary and limit of human power.

Sinai Covenant

This ecological concern continues in the life of Israel. As we discussed in the previous chapter, the Sabbath, Sabbath year, and Jubilee capture how central ecology is to

21. Wirzba, *The Paradise of God*, 34.

22. Psalm 147:7–9 reads, "Sing to the LORD with thanksgiving; / make music to our God on the lyre. / He covers the heavens with clouds, / prepares rain for the earth, / makes grass grow on the hills. / He gives to the animals their food, / and to the young ravens when they cry."

23. Bouma-Prediger, *For the Beauty of the Earth*, 93.

the Sinai covenant. Sabbath is a temporal tie between God and Israel, and between the great economy and the human economy. It has binding power by demanding that periodic rest be given to all creatures for rejuvenation.

Since we have already discussed Sabbath economics, this section focuses on the book of Leviticus. Leviticus continues the covenantal vision and message that the earth should not be viewed as something created for humanity's rule and domination. Rather, the earth is to be seen as part of the holy created order, through which humanity is made holy. Humans are intricately tied to the integrity and future of the earth.

Ellen Davis's agrarian reading of Leviticus is refreshing and insightful in its understanding of the covenantal vision (shalom) and memory (Genesis) of biblical ecology. Belonging to the Priestly writings of the Bible, Leviticus's literary style is liturgical, embodied, and symbolic. This helps convey the deep covenantal structure of God's creation and the dynamic and interdependent relationships among God's creatures.[24] According to Davis, Leviticus envisions a fully enchanted, complex, and organic creation where nature, cult, economy, eating, family, dressing, politics, and ethics are all interrelated in an organic, complex, and dynamic way.

In particular, the book teaches about specific rituals that treat nature with care and respect. Leviticus is in a sense a practical theology of "tilling and keeping" (Gen. 2:15). People need to learn and obtain a caring and serving mindset through these habitual practices. These practices engender and stir an embodied imagination of fidelity, care, and gratitude. Ritual practices assist in the character formation of God's people by making the covenantal vision and values inform and penetrate every aspect of human life such as food, sex, governance, production, distribution, parenting, caring, punishing, and living responsibly as members of God's creation community.

Holiness is the goal of those practices. The Holiness Code teaches humans how to live fittingly, harmoniously, and justly with the natural order of creation. Holiness is the source of healthy life, and it is only possible when the integrity and complex interlocking relationships of all creatures are affirmed and celebrated. Covenant is maintained when partners learn and exercise fidelity to one another through repeated practices. Ritual practices form and cultivate particular moral dispositions and attitudes.

Davis's fresh and insightful reading of Leviticus affirms how a covenantal vision is an ecological vision and how deeply it has saturated the entire life of the Israelites. It compellingly shows that ecology (treatment of other creatures and the land) is an integral part of a moral life. It reinscribes the Genesis, especially Noachian, vision of covenantal fidelity for them: that there is an inviolable, sacred bond between a

24. Ellen F. Davis, *Scripture, Culture, and Agriculture*, 87.

human world and a natural world. Humans need to treat nature with a worshipful (serving) attitude. Worship cannot be separated from our dealings with other creatures and the land.

New Covenant

The new covenant of Jesus continues the vision of the creation, Noachian, and Sinai covenants. New covenant encompasses all creatures as restoration and reconciliation take place at the cosmic level (Col. 1:16–17). Ecological lessons may not be immediate or explicit, but the incarnation of Jesus Christ has profound ecological significance, meaning, and implication. Jesus became flesh (not just human flesh but the flesh of nature). Flesh pertains to all creatures. The creating power of God has become flesh. This recapitulates the creation story. The new covenant of Jesus Christ is cosmic and eschatological. God in Jesus restores creation and sets it once again toward shalom, its original eschatological destiny.

In light of Bonhoeffer's ethics, Larry Rasmussen distinguishes "*Menschwerdung* [becoming human] and *Inkarnation* [incarnation]," which terms in his view are not interchangeable. *Inkarnation* is far broader, more far ranging than *Menschwerdung*, while the latter is one instance of *Inkarnation*. The domain of *Inkarnation* is creation, or cosmos, while that of *Menschwerdung* is human society only.

> *Inkarnation* necessarily includes the human story but its cosmic reach encompasses far more, and Bonhoeffer was deliberate in his choice of words.
>
> Put it this way: When "incarnation" is used christologically, the proper reference is Christ Jesus as the one in whom "all things in heaven and on earth were created" and in whom "all things hold together," "the firstborn of all creation" and "the firstborn of the dead." In this one all "the fullness of God was pleased to dwell," and "through him God was pleased to reconcile to himself all things, whether on earth or in heaven . . ." (i.e., all creation). "All things"—*ta panta*—is a drumbeat in this Colossians hymn [Col. 1:15–20], repeated five times in five verses.
>
> Or consider the Prologue to John's Gospel. The creating Word (Wisdom) was with God, was God, and is the one through whom all things came into being and without whom "not one thing came into being." This same one also pitched his tent among us [John 1:1–3, 14]. In short, when incarnation announces God in Christ, it is the Cosmic Christ as the living presence in all that is, was, and will be.[25]

25. Rasmussen, "Friendly Amendment," 13–14.

Incarnation discloses the depth of God's care and solidarity with the earth and all creatures. Rasmussen adds: "It starts in heaven with God as Word/Wisdom creating the world and then, with a downward arc, covenants with 'all flesh' (Gen. 9:16–17). This is YHWH, 'the God *of all flesh*' (Jer. 32:27) who 'will pour out my spirit on *all flesh*' (Joel 2:28). This one, sometimes named *Sophia* (Wisdom), sometimes *Logos* (Word) also chooses to become *sarx* (flesh) as a person and dwell among people, 'full of grace and truth.'"[26] In short, there is no salvation outside the flesh; that is why God became flesh. The incarnation is not only for the redemption of humanity but also for the redemption of all creation and its creatures. This insight is consistent with the scope and content of the creation covenant, the Noachian covenant, and the new covenant of Jesus. It delineates the scope and depth of God's redemptive will.[27]

In summary, through the incarnation of Jesus and his new covenant, the creation covenant is restored to its original wholeness and integrity. It is elevated into the covenant of peace (shalom) in which God, the earth, and all creatures exist in symbiotic unity and harmony. The incarnation of the Logos in Jesus not only recapitulates the creation story but is also consistent with the fundamentals of covenantal drama and logic: God is faithful to God's creation, thus God never abandons it. The incarnation is God's repairing work of broken creation (*tikkun olam*). As Paul declared, Jesus Christ is "the New Adam by whose death and resurrection all things are put right."[28]

Meaning of Salvation

The Christian redemption is cosmic in its nature and scope and includes not only humans but also other creatures and the planet. As Colossians, among many biblical texts, makes clear, Christ's redemptive work is as wide as creation itself. Human salvation is incomplete until creation is free from its futility; humanity is in intrinsic solidarity with the rest of creation. Our life is not isolated from other species of animals and plants. We are part of an ecosystem that is covenantally interconnected under God's covenantal reign.[29] Scott Hoezee puts it well: "The redemption that God has in store catches up not just human beings but also trees, shrubs, rivers, lions, lambs,

26. Rasmussen, "Friendly Amendment," 14–15.

27. In a similar vein, Bonhoeffer states, "The subject matter of a Christian ethic is God's reality revealed in Christ becoming real [*Wirklichwerden*] among God's creatures." Bonhoeffer, *Ethics*, 49.

28. Bouma-Prediger, *For the Beauty of the Earth*, 116.

29. Our diet (which is central to our health) is inseparable from a biotic world. Modern medicine, with its curative rather than preventive focus, loses this perspective.

and snakes. Indeed, if Jesus did not die for white-tailed deer, redheaded woodpeckers, blue whales, and green Belizean rain forests, then he did not die for you and me."[30]

The cosmic scope and redemptive will of God are also found in the Lord's Prayer when we pray that "[God's] will be done on earth as it is in heaven" and in the Apostles' Creed when we confess that we believe in "the resurrection of the body and life everlasting." The resurrection of Jesus involves not only humans but also other creatures and the entire earth. It renews and restores the goodness of creation, transforming the old creation into a new one.

This cosmic, ecological meaning of God's redemption has profound implications for Christian eschatology. In particular, it corrects a distorted understanding of eschatology (for example, that popularized by *Left Behind*) that has had such a destructive influence on Christian ecological understanding because it treats the earth as temporary or ultimately disposable.[31] Some evangelical Christians believe that our eternal home is an otherworldly heaven and that this world will be completely destroyed at the moment of the rapture.

Creation is not a waystation until the eschaton comes. Rather, it is our eternal home. Christian eschatological hope is the restoration of the fully covenanted creation. The new heaven and earth are *renewed*,[32] not replaced. God's future is earthly. Heaven will come to earth just as God came to us in Jesus Christ and dwelt among us. God will dwell with us and other creatures as prefigured by God's presence in the temple. The separation between heaven and earth will be overcome when heaven is fully incarnate on earth.

Revelation 21:1–6, 22 sees a world of shalom, the fully covenanted creation in which each creature has its own place and dignity. The treasure that humanity finds in heaven turns out to be the treasures and wealth of the nations; "the best they have known and loved on earth redeemed of all imperfections and transfigured by the radiance of God."[33] This is the vision of an ecological civilization (a wonderful combination of rural and urban—thus a gardened city), not a return to the Stone

30. Bouma-Prediger, *For the Beauty of the Earth*, 116.

31. An egregious misinterpretation of 2 Pet. 3:10 has played a destructive role in widely propagating this bad eschatology among Christians, for example, when it is translated: "and the earth and the works that are upon it will be burned up" (RSV). However, the NRSV offers a more accurate translation of this verse: "and the earth and everything that is done on it will be disclosed." Similarly, the NIV states: "and the earth and everything done in it will be laid bare." Thus, these translations rightly underlie the essential continuity, not discontinuity, of this world with the eschaton. Bouma-Prediger, *For the Beauty of the Earth*, 68.

32. Cf. 2 Cor. 5:4.

33. Caird, *The Revelation of St. John*, 279–80.

Age. Evil and its minions are no more. In this completely sanctified city, there is no temple, for God is the temple. Heaven is the actualization of God's shalom. Nothing is excluded.

Lessons and Implications

God's covenant with other creatures and the earth has several moral lessons. What does it ethically mean that we are in a covenantal relationship with the earth? We can draw several lessons and implications from the preceding discussion on covenant and ecology in the Bible.

Creation is God's *oikos*—the default moral community that is prior to any human society, ethnic community, or institution. God welcomes all creatures (birds, trees, fish, insects, flowers, animals, even bacteria) as members of this community. New covenant ethics envisions the planet as God's green kinship community where all lives are "caught in an inescapable network of mutuality, tied in a single garment of destiny."[34] All creatures, both human and nonhuman, are radically bound together, in difference from and interdependence with each other. In the covenantal logic of creation, the flourishing of a species depends on others; a change in one place or species affects others.[35] Shalom is not possible without mutual flourishing because in the deep covenantal fabric of creation, "existence is co-existence" and being is always "being with."[36]

All creatures have moral standing in the universe in relation to God and other creatures. They have intrinsic value, thus deserving our respect. They are not mere objects of human consumption but indispensable members of the earth community; their loss is a genuine tragedy to God and to us. We share the planet and our common destiny with other creatures. There is no exit. We have a shared destiny. There is no border in the air we breathe or the sunlight we enjoy. We are all members of the earth. There will be no peace for humans without peace for other creatures. If nature perishes, we all perish.

God is covenantally committed to creation and all members—their sanctity and perfection in vitality and diversity. Creation as a whole, and its members, big and small, human and nonhuman, animate and inanimate, have integrity and intrinsic value. God cares for nonhuman species. To be covenanted is to take the earth as God's gift for all creatures. While nature's ecosystem has an amazing self-renewing power, it is finite and vulnerable to harm and violence. Earth's treasures are a onetime

34. King, "Letter from Birmingham City Jail," 290.
35. Küng, *A Global Ethic for Global Politics and Economics*, 26.
36. Rasmussen, *Earth Community, Earth Ethics*, 106.

endowment.[37] Sun, oceans, skies, forests, rivers, and mountains cannot be created by humankind, just as no human power can resurrect an extinct species.[38]

Thus, we should respect the integrity of creation. There exists a marvelously fine-tuned equilibrium, delicate interlocking symbiosis, and dynamic communication in creation. We should not mess with this. The first principle of ecological ethics is to be "mindful of limits that are built into the created order as both inescapable and fitting,"[39] and accommodate our activities to nature, not the other way around. We must be careful with what we do to the planet and other creatures. What we leave here stays here, and what we do here has enduring impact.

Humans belong to the earth community. The earth is the precondition of our biological existence, and our life utterly depends on it. While we cannot do without other creatures, they can do without us.[40] Without a fertile land, blue sea, clean water, fresh air, and balanced temperatures, there is no healthy and vibrant human life. Culture (all human activity) presupposes nature. Culture is rooted in the tilling of the land (agriculture). Thus, culture is in fact "second nature" to humanity. Nature is not what is around us, but it is the reason we are alive at all. "It is nature-culture, culture as our rendition of nature."[41] Our economic decisions must account for the ecosphere and other creatures. Hence, when we care for the earth, we in fact care for ourselves.

Global Green Covenant

Our covenantal organizing of the shalom community includes the well-being of other kinds of creatures and the earth in our moral imagination, affection, and action. A new global covenant is green and completely earthbound and grounded when promoting the shalom of every creature. Specifically, there is urgent need for a global covenant on global warming. It is critical to reduce CO_2 and other GHG emissions before it is too late. The Paris Agreement must be expanded and strengthened into a binding covenant that establishes and enforces global environmental and labor standards.

We need an immediate change of environmental policies by strengthening international agreements and treaties by establishing legally binding limits on greenhouse gases. I support the idea of a "Green Fund"—a promising international campaign in which developed countries help fund developing countries in adapting to and

37. Rasmussen, *Earth Community, Earth Ethics*, 102.
38. Rasmussen, *Earth Community, Earth Ethics*, 102.
39. Ellen F. Davis, *Scripture, Culture, and Agriculture*, 31.
40. Rasmussen, *Earth Community, Earth Ethics*, 36–37.
41. Rasmussen, *Earth-Honoring Faith*, 45.

mitigating climate change. Our national priority should be to advance and popularize "green energy" (renewables)—wind, solar, tidal, geothermal, and hydroelectric—and to improve the energy efficiency of motor vehicles, buildings, etc. It is also necessary to implement carbon taxes on rich countries in order to raise funds. A binding and enforceable green covenant is not possible without the massive grassroots mobilization of people to countervail the strong lobbies of fossil fuel (oil and coal) companies to which our politicians are beholden.

Covenantal Values

The covenantal values/norms (from chap. 7) of gratitude, justice, love, humility, hospitality, truth telling, and solidarity apply to our relationships with other creatures.[42] Covenantal values are ecological values that are necessary to carry out our responsibilities as caretakers of creation. For example, love describes life-affirming, life-nourishing, and life-fulfilling power. Similarly, holiness denotes how to live harmoniously and justly with other creatures, respecting their intrinsic values and rights. We humans must learn how to live faithfully with other creatures with respect and care.

The new covenant affirms the intrinsic value and worth of all living creatures. All creatures have a right to exist and are entitled to the space and resources necessary for their survival and thriving. To do justice to them is to respect their rights and to treat them as genuine members of God's community—"differentiated others" in God's covenant.[43] For example, as much as God protects the rights of humans, God also cares for the rights of the land. Leviticus 26:34 reads: "Then the land shall enjoy its sabbath years as long as it lies desolate, while you are in the land of your enemies; then the land shall rest, and enjoy its sabbath years."

Stewardship is based on the humble recognition of our limitations in knowing nature. The best way is to understand how nature works and minimize our interruptions of nature. We need to be humble and cautious when applying our technology to nature by accepting the limitations of our knowledge. Our attitude to nature should be that of the Hebrew word *yada*—deep intimacy and friendship that attend to its particularity, not instrumental reason (abstract, utilitarian, controlling, dominating, consumptive). Our relationship with the earth requires intimate knowledge and attentiveness to its changes so that we can adapt in a harmonious way. We should relate to the earth symbiotically and communally, not unilaterally or instrumentally.

42. My list is somewhat different from that of Bouma-Prediger, but there are overlaps.

43. Rasmussen, *Earth Community, Earth Ethics*, 106.

Green Spirituality and Practices

Local communities may organize community gardens, green community development, and farmers' markets (to purchase and consume local foods seasonally). They may use local products and experiment with intentional communities. Churches may take active leadership roles in city farming and community gardens (food self-sufficiency), in promoting slow food, and in reducing consumption of meat and dairy products. Churches may set a vegetarian day and practice it.

The ministry of Christian just peacemaking should include other creatures; in fact, we humans need to repent and ask forgiveness for our abuse and misuses. This can be done through poetry and rituals. Similarly, sanctification means establishing right relations not only with humans but also with other creatures and the earth. We should treat other creatures justly.[44] One way to practice justice for other creatures is to keep the Sabbath so that creatures may have much-needed and rightful rest for full restoration. Sabbath is also the right of other creatures and the earth.

The current ecological crisis calls for comprehensive reform (transformation) of our thinking, acting, social relations, and policies. The new covenant of Jesus sees the horizon of our moral thinking as the planet, not just humanity. Our discipleship, ideas of holiness, and sanctification need to be green, and they need to fully incorporate our dependence on the earth and other creatures. We are covenantally interrelated not just to God but also to trees, land, and animals.

Churches must assist their members to enhance their ecological literacy through preaching and Bible study. Just as every good, enduring, covenantal, and enriching relationship requires knowledge, our relationship with the land requires knowledge based on good observations. This knowledge is particular, local, and intimate in nature.

Churches must develop ecologically grounded earth liturgies; they should write new psalms and hymns, develop communal practices that nurture the vision and values of the new covenant, and recapitulate the vision of Leviticus. Consistent with the agrarian vision of Leviticus, churches may help their members develop green virtues informed by the covenantal values/norms discussed above. Rituals that use natural symbols are excellent mediums of communication. To make our spiritual life green, worship needs to invite the earth and other creatures as partners and members.[45]

At a personal level, changes in our lifestyle and consumption patterns are neces-

44. "Ecological justice names the disposition to act fairly when faced with the competing claims of creatures human and nonhuman, of endangered species and damaged ecosystems." Bouma-Prediger, *For the Beauty of the Earth*, 152.

45. "Blessing of the Animals. World Animal Day at Saint John the Divine, New York, 7 Oct. 2012," YouTube, October 9, 2012, https://www.youtube.com/watch?v=6vy8UozvNYo; "St. Fran-

sary. Rather than consumerism, competition, greed, and control and domination, we must encourage and model the simple life and frugality. Concretely, a changing lifestyle includes expanding the use of green energy and stopping or reducing the use of fossil fuels. We must distance ourselves from using wasteful products, such as powerboats, gasoline-powered yard equipment, fireplaces and wood stoves, recreational off-road vehicles, pesticides, fertilizers, hazardous cleaners and paints, etc. It is a good idea to periodically assess dietary habits, individual and family carbon footprints, and various practices of community that affect the ecology. To do so is a matter of justice as well as stewardship. Sustainability is integral to new covenant ethics. All resources should be equitably distributed and sustainably used in order to contribute to the well-being of all God's creatures, both human and nonhuman.

Nonviolent practice is also relevant in relating to other creatures. Nonviolence is a green virtue. Nonviolence negatively means nondomination and nonmalfeasance, while positively it pursues love, care, and compassion for others. As Martin Luther King Jr. declared, "The aftermath of nonviolence is reconciliation and the creation of the beloved community."[46] The heart of nonviolence is a reverence for life, which at its center is life ethics, a core creed of ecological ethics. Nonviolence is based on respect for all life.

Nonviolence is consistent with God's original intention, and it represents the spirit of the new covenant. God prescribed a vegetarian way of life for humanity. Human responsibility and care for other creatures are demonstrated in humanity's original vegetarianism. Despite God letting humans eat animals after the flood, this was not God's original preference. Even when humans would eat meat, they were still to be morally responsible to animals in their husbandry, butchery, and conservation. This implies that God was concerned with humans forgetting the rights of other creatures and abusing other creatures if they were carnivorous. The emphasis is particularly important to counter violent human disposition after the Fall. This is an indirect reminder that the well-being of human life is interdependent with that of other creatures.

Nonviolence is indispensable for sustainability because it promotes an ecologically sensitive lifestyle that avoids both external and internal violence. For example, inordinate greed, materialism, and the desire for domination—all contribute to ecological degradation. New covenant ethics condemns pollution, reckless consumption, and exploitation of nature as the violent acts of humans.

---

cis Day 2009 at the Cathedral Church of St. John the Divine, NYC," YouTube, October 17, 2009, https://www.youtube.com/watch?v=L6zEqa89qgk.

46. King, "The Power of Nonviolence," 12.

Conclusion

This chapter showed that the Bible is not anthropocentric. From the beginning, covenantal fidelity and commitment extend to the earth and other creatures. Anthropocentrism is sinful because it puts ourselves at the center of the universe and displaces God. It also exploits other creatures and the earth. Anthropocentrism is the site of the first rebellion.

Modern Western civilization, in the interlocked system of modernist ideology, industrialization, capitalism, science and technology, is wrecking the planet. Repeating the deadly mistakes of the tree of knowledge (Gen. 3) and the tower of Babel (Gen. 11), humans try to usurp God's place by forfeiting their covenantal responsibility to God and other creatures. As a result, it seems humanity has been exiled from our earth home.

In this grim situation, I believe that new covenant ethics offers an alternative and contrasting worldview and way of life. New covenant ethics undermines traditional anthropocentrism and the instrumental attitude of conservative Christian ethics. It challenges a modernistic worldview by including other creatures and the earth as integral members of God's covenant community. It rejects the dualism of mind and body and cultivates a proper ethic of care, peace, and solidarity among all creatures. It reaffirms covenantal fidelity as the default posture of humanity toward the earth and other creatures. New covenant ethics is ecological ethics. It reenchants our ravaged world as the sacred community by providing a theological basis for restoring unity and solidarity between humanity and other creatures in God as part of a moral community. This corrects the misguided beliefs that God cares only for humans and that other creatures exist only for human use and benefit.

It is high time to work together to address the impending ecological crisis. Facing the enormity of the threats, there is a temptation to despair and hopelessness. But let us trust in God's promise and pray for God's wisdom and blessing. Let us remember the rainbow that came after the flood, the symbol of God's faithfulness.

CHAPTER 16

Criminal Justice

> The prison has become a black hole in which the detritus of contemporary capitalism is deposited. Mass imprisonment generates profits as it devours social wealth, and thus it tends to reproduce the very conditions that lead people to prison.
>
> —Angela Y. Davis, *Are Prisons Obsolete?*

The blissful story of Eden ends in human sin and divine punishment (Gen. 3). Ever since, the human story has been an ongoing alternation between human sin, God's reluctant but inevitable punishment, and God's gracious restoration. We find this recurring cycle (sin → punishment → restoration → sin) pointedly in the book of Judges.

For Christians, the question of punishment is not so simple, partly because of the sinful nature of all humanity and the availability of God's redeeming grace. While punishment of crime is inevitable this side of heaven, it raises a series of theological, ethical, and practical questions: How is punishment against another person justified? Who should be punished, and what is a fair and appropriate form of punishment? What kind of justice do we seek in punishment? Why do we punish, and what do we want to achieve through punishment? Who has the legitimate authority to carry out punishment? Punishing other humans cannot be taken lightly. False accusations could ruin other persons' reputations and futures, even kill them; it is necessary to exercise justice, but it is a painful process.

This chapter studies a covenantal approach to criminal justice. It begins with a brief survey of three different approaches to criminal justice and then examines the unique punitive culture of the United States (its high incarceration rate and capital punishment) and how it colludes with racism and neoliberal capitalism to create the industrial prison system. Then, the chapter proposes new covenant ethics as a creative model that balances retributive and restorative justice.

Approaches to Criminal Justice

In human history, several different theories have been discussed to justify the moral validity of punishment: retribution, deterrence, and rehabilitation.

Retribution

In general, retribution means the infliction of punishment against the wrongs committed by a person or a group. Retribution as a form of justice is necessary to vindicate wrongs done by offenders. This theory is based on a deontological (duty-oriented) approach to punishment: punishment of an offender is inherently just and right because crime is inherently wrong. Punishment is morally justified to address the wrong done to a victim. This theory is based on the assumption that it is the duty of a society to punish an offender in order to rectify the wrong. Without punishment, injustice is done to a victim. As free, responsible moral agents, offenders deserve punishment for the wrongs they have done, which have violated the rights of a victim. As offenders are accountable for their actions, they are treated as moral agents. They deserve negative goods (demerits), such as fines or incarceration, in proportion to their offenses.

Retributive justice is universally practiced. Every society has a certain principle of retributive justice; for example, the Golden Rule is a principle of justice that includes retributive justice. The Bible upholds the Golden Rule (Matt. 7:12; Luke 6:31).

Retributive theory is limited in that it does not prevent further crime; its objective is to achieve justice through fair punishment, not the rehabilitation or reform of offenders in order to bring them back to society as productive members. Technically speaking, there is no guarantee that an offender may not commit the same crime again. Similarly, there is no attention to reconciliation between offenders and victims. While retributive justice may mete justice (by addressing the rights of victims), it is questionable how much healing and closure it brings to a victim.

Deterrence

Together with retribution, deterrence is one of the oldest penal philosophies. The advocates of this position claim that punishment has a positive effect on a society; it deters future offenders and crimes. This view is based on a realistic assessment of human nature that believes unpunished crimes would incur further offenses or encourage similar offenses. The other side of this preventive purpose is the desire to protect a basic social order and the safety of people. Punishment represents the collective will of people against the antisocial crimes of offenders. Punishment is a warning to offenders that they will pay the price for their antisocial actions. Relying on this assumption, traditional societies took various extreme measures to amplify their deterring effects, using extremely brutal and cruel means of punishment (public torture and execution).[1] This theory has its own limitations: more often than not, the deterring effect is exaggerated, and the punishment loses fairness and justice (it is not proportionate to the crime) in order to maximize its preventive effects. Often, offenders are scapegoated to mollify the fear, anxiety, and anger of people. Punishment may deter future crimes, but it does not change offenders.

Rehabilitation

This theory is relatively modern in its inception and development compared to the theories of retribution and deterrence. It approaches punishment from a medical perspective. That is, since crimes and antisocial behaviors are kinds of diseases offenders are suffering from, punishment should be a process of treatment. The goal is the healing of offenders, not punishment per se. Reform offers a better, more fundamental solution to crimes than retribution and deterrence. That is, punishment should be used as an opportunity to inculcate positive change in offenders' criminal propensities or antisocial behaviors. It regards retribution and deterrence as inhumane, as they tend to be vengeful. The focus is an offender's correction and healing, using various treatment and therapeutic methods. Retribution and deterrence are incomplete and ineffective in preventing crimes because they fail to recognize the similarities between the motives of offenders and nonoffenders. The theory finds the well-being of a society in the well-being of an offender. However, it does not pay the necessary and proper care and attention to victims and their sense of justice. As in deterrence theory, a victim's pain and suffering are secondary to the rehabilitation of an offender.

Comparison of the Approaches to Criminal Justice

While retribution is deontological and retrospective (in response to the crime that has already happened), deterrence and rehabilitation are teleological and thus prospective approaches; they focus on the positive consequences of punishment. They understand punishment as a means to achieve a certain goal.

All three theories are still widely used in accounting for and justifying the purpose and necessity of punishment. Each theory has its own merits, and the config-

1. Public punishment, especially the death penalty, played a collective psychological function as a form of pseudoreligious ritual for collective catharsis and expiation of guilt, the mechanism of scapegoating that René Girard brilliantly describes. The lynching of African Americans performed a similar psychological function in the Jim/Jane Crow era.

uration of the criminal justice system and penological practices are shaped by the particular history, culture, and ethos of society. As the ethos changes, the system and practices also change. For example, northern European countries rely on rehabilitation theory based on their humanitarian and social democratic tradition, while the United States resorts more to the retribution and deterrence theory because of its distinctive punitive culture associated with racism and classism.[2]

How a society punishes offenders is very revealing of its deep collective psychology and cultural tradition. Crimes evoke intense emotions, and punishment is shaped by emotions to no lesser extent. In general, the criminal justice system, like other social practices, reflects cultural assumptions and biases (e.g., a social script of punishment). If a culture is punitive toward offenders (or biased against particular racial or ethnic groups), then this punitive culture and bias are reflected in punishment. Punishment could be easily prompted by the feeling of vengeance or fear. People are vulnerable to demagogic manipulation of politicians who take advantage of popular emotions and sentiments. Accordingly, one may carefully examine the narrative and social ethos around criminal justice and how they affect the social perception and treatment of offenders and their punishment. Harsh treatment reflects the deep, underlying emotions and sentiments of a society and the whims of a majority group. This is because offenders, once found guilty, become socially powerless to protect themselves; they lose their rights and are socially stigmatized throughout their entire lives.

Typically, social bias and inequality are reflected in the definition and categorization of crime and punishment; the poor tend to receive harsher punishment for the same crimes that the rich commit. The penal system is also influenced by inequality of power. The rich and powerful in authoritarian regimes of the past and the present use the penal system for their political purpose to punish those (political opponents and social critics) who are critical of the current status quo.

The Bible is deeply aware that the criminal system can operate unjustly toward the poor and the marginalized. Early Christians, as a social minority, had a special sympathy toward prisoners. Not only did the teachings of their nonviolent faith starkly contrast with Rome's brutal, inhumane treatment of prisoners, but they spoke against a skewed criminal justice against the poor, minorities, and powerless. In its origin, Christianity had a special memory of the unjust criminal justice system. Overshadowed by soteriology, we do not pay enough attention to Jesus's encounter with the unfair criminal justice system. Jesus was falsely convicted, tortured, and

2. The harshness or leniency of punishment is negatively correlated with the level of social capital (trust, intimacy, neighborliness) among the members of a society. A society of low trust tends to be more punitive than those with a high trust level among the members.

put to death by a foreign imperial power in response to the accusation of the leaders of his own people. He was imprisoned, tortured, and sentenced to death. The resurrected Jesus still carries the marks of his torture and death. This was the most difficult time in his earthly life: his disciples, friends, and followers abandoned and denied him; he was isolated from his mother and friends; he was publicly ridiculed; once a hero, he became a nobody.

Punitive Culture of the United States

Any moral discussion of criminal justice in the United States must include mention of the country's distinctively punitive culture. Currently, it incarcerates more people than any other country in the world. Prison populations in the United States and the world have increased 10 percent over the past decade.[3] But even after considering that upward trend, the scale and punitiveness of the US penal system are unparalleled.[4] The following statistics reveal the depth of its cruelty and inhumane nature:

- In 2017, the US state and federal prison population was 1,439,808.[5] The number of people serving life sentences increased from 34,000 in 1984 to 161,957 in 2016.[6] In 2019, there were about 63,000 youth in confinement, with many being held for offenses that are not considered crimes, such as violating probation or being a refugee waiting for placement with family or friends.[7]
- Twenty-five percent of people arrested and in the criminal justice system have serious mental illnesses; a person with mental illness stays four to eight times longer in jail than someone without a mental illness for the exact same charge; 40 percent of people with serious mental illness will be involved in the criminal justice system at some point in their lives. In 2017, incarcerating people with serious mental illness cost the US government $80 billion and the states $71 billion.[8]
- The majority of women prisoners are incarcerated for nonviolent crimes such as prostitution, fraud, and drug offenses.[9] Only 36 percent of arrested women are arrested for violent offenses. Women account for only 8 percent of the

3. "Global Prison Trends 2017."
4. Cf. Wagner and Sawyer, "Mass Incarceration."
5. "Criminal Justice Facts."
6. "Criminal Justice Facts."
7. Wagner and Sawyer, "Mass Incarceration."
8. Zezima, "Incarcerated with Mental Illness."
9. Though cf. Niall McCarthy, "No Country Incarcerates More Women Than the US."

> convicted violent felons.[10] "Approximately 62 percent of women in prison have children under the age of 18."[11]

The punishment continues even after the offenders have paid the price for their offenses. Stigma follows them: criminal records impede job opportunities, social life, and the exercise of voting rights. There is some truth in the slogan "orange is the new black." They are socially ostracized and treated as second-class citizens. This reality is far worse for people of color.

Where has this punitive culture come from? Several converging factors contribute to it: the criminal justice system in the United States is highly racialized (thus discriminatory), capitalized (thus exploitative), and politicized (thus expedient). The combined cultural forces of its long-standing racism, which has criminalized people of color and the poor; the political expedience of using "law and order" for electoral gain; and the neoliberal rush for profit making have created a society of mass incarceration. Of course, undergirding these forces are an individualistic culture and the Protestant ethic of punishment that assigns all responsibility to the offender without considering structural factors such as poverty, racism, and lack of economic opportunities.[12] In the following, we will examine a few distinctive features of the dominant social narrative (a social script) around punishment in the United States today.

"Law and Order"

In the United States and other countries, "law and order" is an expression that has been frequently used by politicians for harsh punishment of offenders because of its political expediency. Politicians, both liberal and conservative, have used the fear of crime to gain votes. The rhetoric of law and order is typically associated with the age-old theory of deterrence. Its assumption is that harsh punishment will deter crimes. Nelson Rockefeller of New York introduced the mandatory sentencing law, "get tough, punish the offender." It is designed to punish repeat offenders more harshly. It appeals to the basic desire of every person to live in a safe community. The propaganda of law and order takes advantage of this fear for political gain, which typically leads to harsh punishment of offenders. The mandatory sentencing law, the

10. "Words from Prison—Did You Know . . . ?"

11. Camhi, "Women's Experience behind Bars."

12. Chuck Colson's viewpoint exemplifies this perspective: "Crime is not caused by environment or poverty or deprivation. It is caused by individuals making wrong moral choices. . . . The answer to crime therefore is the conversion of the wrongdoer to a more responsible lifestyle." Schulz, "From the White House to the Jailhouse to the Pulpit."

"three strikes" statute,[13] and longer sentencing laws in the United States are products of this propaganda. Because of its appealing power, politicians have been eager to propose and pass "tough-on-crime" legislation and claim it as their achievement.

This political tactic proved effective in the United States because it resonated with the Protestant individualistic ethic (that entirely blames offenders for their actions), which is still pervasive in American culture. The rhetoric also carries a strong racist undertone that appeals to subtle but deep-seated antiblack and antibrown sentiments among whites. Demonizing offenders is a way for white politicians to exploit the emotional vulnerabilities and racial prejudices of whites for political gain. White politicians exploit the fear, anxiety, and vulnerabilities of white citizens; racism and criminal justice amplify each other. Historically, whites have used the criminal law to punish people of color to maintain the racial hierarchy. White racism holds negative stereotypes of other races to protect its power and privilege. One such stereotype concerns the criminality of black and brown people, attributing their crimes to genetic characteristics. Law-and-order rhetoric is coded to justify the harsh treatment of people of color (racial profiling, excessive use of force, harsh sentencing and treatment). White politicians, both liberals and conservatives, have repeatedly used law-and-order rhetoric to appeal for white votes. A textbook strategy was "war on drugs," which has been widely used by white politicians for their electoral victories, without hesitating to criminalize African Americans.

During the last four decades, the number of Americans arrested and incarcerated for drug-related offenses has been steeply increasing; those incarcerated in 2017 numbered 452,964, while it was 40,900 in 1980.[14] As of 2017, more people were behind bars for drug offenses than were in prison or jail for any crime in 1980.[15]

Another problem with the war on drugs is the cost of incarcerating people charged with drug-related offenses. Since 1971, the United States has spent an estimated $1 trillion to incarcerate people for drug-related charges. In 2015, the federal government spent over $3.3 billion, and state governments an additional $7 billion, to incarcerate drug offenders.[16] However, data show the enforcement of strict drug laws is not cost-effective in comparison to marijuana legalization. These research

13. According to the "three strikes" statute in the Violent Control and Law Enforcement Act (1994), life imprisonment is mandated for a convicted felon who has been convicted of a serious violent felony by a federal court and has two or more previous convictions—at least one of which is a serious violent felony—in either a federal or state court.

14. "Criminal Justice Facts."

15. "Criminal Justice Facts."

16. See Bureau of Prisons, *Annual Determination of Average Cost of Incarceration*, 81 Fed. Reg. 46957 (US Department of Justice, 2016), 46957, document 2016-17040; Wagner and Rabuy, "Mass Incarceration."

findings push for justice in drug sentencing and a more effective approach to drug-related offenses.

Recent trends are still discouraging. The danger to recycle law and order for a racist political agenda is growing in a time like ours, where white people feel anxious, insecure, and displaced. As we see in President Trump's use of this tactic and ongoing anti-immigration and antiblack rhetoric, the law-and-order rhetoric capitalizes on white populist anger and fear, manipulating emotions of white people for political gain.

Racism and Criminal Justice

As mentioned, the US criminal justice system is deeply affected by racism and nativism. It operates by removing and controlling "otherness"—nonwhites. Phobias are a typical response to otherness. Because of xenophobia, otherness engenders "anxiety and insecurity" among people, prompting negative reactions toward the smallest suspicious behaviors and unusual actions.

This fear, amplified by racism, is reflected in every aspect of the penal system—arrest, prosecution, sentencing, imprisonment, service, and postrelease and parole. Michelle Alexander observes: "Whiteness mitigates crime, whereas blackness defines the criminal."[17] As a result, racial minority groups, especially African Americans and Latinx, are overrepresented in the criminal justice system. People of color make up 37 percent of the US population but 67 percent of the prison population.[18]

Harsh punishments in the United States get even harsher for people of color and the poor. For example, the implementation of the half-century-long War on Drugs has resulted in the mass incarceration of African Americans and has had a devastating effect on African American families and communities in addition to those who are convicted. While the rate of drug usage is similar across all races, poor people of color in urban areas are excessively targeted for searches, arrests, and convictions.

Vast numbers of people are swept into the criminal justice system by the police, who conduct drug operations primarily in poor communities of color. They are rewarded in cash—through drug forfeiture laws and federal grant programs—for rounding up as many people as possible.[19]

The half-century-long War on Drugs has resulted in lopsided racial geography of mass incarceration.[20] Racial bias is particularly stark for African Americans, who,

17. Alexander, *The New Jim Crow*, 199.
18. "Criminal Justice Facts."
19. Alexander, *The New Jim Crow*, 185.
20. Wagner and Kopf, "The Racial Geography of Mass Incarceration."

despite representing only 12.5 percent of all substance users, constitute nearly 30 percent of all arrests for drug law violations.[21] While African Americans and whites have similar substance usage rates, the imprisonment rate of African Americans for drug-related offenses is almost six times that of whites.[22] This bias is seen at both the federal and the state level: minorities constitute almost 80 percent of federal and 60 percent of state drug-related imprisonments. People of color receive longer sentences than white defendants charged with the same drug offense, and prosecutors use the mandatory minimum sentence more often for people of color.[23]

Michelle Alexander's book *The New Jim Crow* compiles evidence for the systemic intersection between racism and criminal justice in the United States. Alexander calls the prison complex a new Jim Crow system and sees many parallels between contemporary mass incarceration and legalized racial segregation in the United States. It is a system designed to socially control and exploit blacks. The current criminal justice system continues the white collective agenda of black enslavement and exploitation in a different institutional guise. She notes: "Mass incarceration in the United States had, in fact, emerged as a stunningly comprehensive and well-disguised system of racialized social control that functions in a manner strikingly similar to Jim Crow."[24]

Classism: Criminalization of the Poor

In addition to race and xenophobia, classism has gravely skewed criminal justice against the poor. As money intrudes every sphere, neoliberalism has a distortive effect on the criminal justice system. We live in a society where millions of people feel that they are becoming disposable in this rat-race world run by global capitalism. A neoliberal society is apathetic to the poor, the disabled, and the least among us. Among them, former convicts and those with criminal records feel more intensely their sense of exclusion and marginalization.

It is common sense that an adequate legal defense makes a substantial difference in conviction and sentencing, but in the United States, the poor and people of color do not get an adequate defense in court. In our penal system, meaningful legal representation is generally denied to defendants who are poor. Reports the *New York Times*: "Roughly four out of five criminal defendants are too poor to hire a lawyer and use public defenders or court-appointed lawyers." The poor are pressured to

21. "Criminal Justice Fact Sheet."
22. "Criminal Justice Fact Sheet."
23. "Race and the Drug War."
24. Alexander, *The New Jim Crow*, 4.

plead guilty even if they are innocent. "When threatened with lengthy sentences, they opt for a plea bargain and a lighter punishment—even when innocent."

The public defender system is deeply flawed with inadequate compensation and overloaded cases. "The sheer size of caseloads makes it impossible for them to provide what the Constitution requires: a reasonably effective defense." Arrestees sometimes agree to plea deals without any legal advice from public defenders. According to the studies, "public defenders have two to almost five times as many cases as they should."[25] While private lawyers give full attention to their clients, public defenders are only able to provide mediocre care to their clients. The glaring injustice shows the systemic bias against those who cannot afford an expensive defense lawyer.

The poor are criminalized for the financial gain of the prison industry and the revenue increases of municipalities. Under the neoliberal system (in particular its policy of exploitation by deprivation as discussed in chapter 14), there is every incentive for municipalities to charge and convict every violation, even minor infractions and misdemeanors, in order meet their budgets through jail costs, traffic tickets, and other fees. Those poor who are charged for minor infractions (e.g., traffic violations) cannot afford to pay bail and are incarcerated in municipal detainment centers and local jails while awaiting trial; "the longer they remain in jail, the more they are assessed fines and fees and then further incarcerated for their inability to pay."[26]

Our punitive culture is grievously taken advantage of by corporations under neoliberal ethos and policies. The private prison complex is another example of privatization of the public realm under neoliberalism, which hands over the management of the prison system to private industry.

The convergence of multiple social forces (political-economic interests) has contributed to the development and spread of the prison-industrial complex: the law and order of populist politics, job creation for rural areas, and the neoliberal ideology of privatization. It is a distinctively American phenomenon, feeding on the confluence of racism, punitive ethos, and neoliberal capitalist interests that are now almost unstoppable, with a life of their own. The United States is now incarcerating more people while fewer people are committing crimes![27]

Private prisons are a lucrative multibillion-dollar industry, so there is every incentive to increase the inmate population rather than solving the very social conditions (poverty, racism, educational opportunity) that engender crimes. The primary and central motif is profit, not rehabilitation. Under the current arrangement of private

25. Oppel and Patel, "One Lawyer, 194 Felony Cases, and No Time."

26. Beckett, "Mass Incarceration," 221.

27. "The incarceration rate rose independent of crime—but not of criminal-justice policy." Coates, "The Black Family in the Age of Mass Incarceration."

prisons, there is a huge financial incentive to have more prisoners, more convictions, harsher sentences, longer prison terms, and more money for prison business.[28] Steven R. Donziger comments that "if crime is going up, then we need to build more prisons; and if crime is going down, it's because we built more prisons—and building even more prisons will therefore drive crime down even lower."[29] Like other corporations, private prisons attempt to squeeze out maximal surplus value through labor exploitation and preying on the vulnerability and desperation of poor inmates through overcharging for necessary goods.

The poor are not only overcriminalized but also ruthlessly exploited when they are incarcerated. The prison phone system is a $1.2 billion-a-year business market controlled by a few private companies. These phone companies pay "hundreds of millions of dollars in concession fees, known as commissions," "to state and local prison systems in exchange for exclusive contracts."[30] "Prison payphone service providers often charge high per minute rates for inmate calling from prisons or jails, as well as high per call rates or connection fees for each collect prison call made."[31] Abusing their position, phone companies price-gouge families by adding numerous ancillary fees and charges when they provide inmate calling services.[32] The Federal Communications Commission (FCC) tried to set rate caps in August 2016, but the telephone companies contested this in court. For now, only interim rate caps are in effect, which "apply only to interstate long-distance calls, but not to in-state long distance, local, or international calls."[33]

New Covenant Ethics

New covenant ethics offers a coherent and balanced moral framework that constructively connects retributive justice and restorative justice. Covenant refers to a method of just peacemaking. Justice and reconciliation are equally the content of covenant.

The biblical idea of justice is basically covenantal, as is its view of retributive and restorative justice. Unlike deontological and teleological approaches that rely on abstract principles (retribution, deterrence), covenant ethics takes a relational approach. Offenses are understood relationally, as the hurt and breach of a relationship.

28. Schlosser, "The Prison-Industrial Complex."

29. Steven R. Donziger is a young attorney who headed the National Criminal Justice Commission in 1996.

30. Timothy Williams, "The High Cost of Calling the Imprisoned."

31. "Inmate Calling Rates."

32. "Inmate Calling Rates."

33. "Telephone Service for Incarcerated Individuals."

Even in God's punitive actions (e.g., expulsion of Adam and Eve from Eden, Cain's exile from community, and the Babylonian captivity of Israel), God consistently demonstrates mercy and generosity, never failing to give the hope of restoration.

Hence, in a covenantal framework, retributive justice is enacted only for the restoration of an offender and the repair of a breached relationship. A covenantal approach helps to clarify the meaning, purpose, and place of retributive justice in relation to restorative justice.

Retributive Justice

Covenantal ethics embraces retributive justice as it takes seriously the moral accountability of each member to live under God's moral law and to pledge to accept recompense when the law is breached. The biblical idea of retribution is based on the idea of certain rules and laws that all members must keep in order to protect the rights of members and social well-being; they delineate the minimal conditions of human flourishing. Breach of the law undermines social trust and communal bond and threatens the vital condition of mutual flourishing. Christopher Marshall points out that there is even "a kind of inbuilt law of recompense in the universe that means people 'reap whatever they sow' (Galatians 6:7, cf. Ecclesiastes 10:8; Proverbs 1:32; 26:27; Psalm 7:15–16). In addition, the basic retributive concepts of guilt, desert, proportionality, and atonement are widely attested in the Old Testament legal and cultic system, and undergird moral and theological teaching in the New Testament as well."[34]

Like other forms of justice, the biblical idea of retributive justice is closely associated with covenant. Starting with the expulsion of the first couple from Eden, and including the exile of Israel, God has punished the violators of covenants. In fact, many biblical covenants—it is most detailed in the Sinai covenant—include negative stipulations: God's warning of punishment against those who break them, along with blessings and rewards for those who keep them. God's punishment is the execution of the covenantal stipulations.

This means that covenant does not gloss over crimes and offenses. To do so goes against the covenant because crimes are a breach of the covenantal relationship.

Marshall describes the covenantal nature of retributive justice in the Bible:

> Biblical justice is retributive justice insofar as it turns on the principles of moral culpability, measured recompense, and the rule of law. It would be a mistake to conclude, however, that biblical teaching on justice is wholly or solely controlled

34. Marshall, "Divine Justice as Restorative Justice," 13–14.

> by some impersonal metaphysical principle of measure for measure. Instead it has a distinctively personal and relational character. Justice in ancient Israel involved doing all that was needed to create, sustain, and restore healthy relationships within the covenant community. Criminal offending was considered wrong, first because it breaches the relational commitments that hold society together and, second, because the wrongful deeds themselves unleash a disordering power in the community that threatens to trigger a chain-reaction of ruin and disaster unless it is arrested.[35]

In new covenant ethics, retribution is also grounded in the assumption that humans are free and responsible moral agents and therefore are accountable for their actions. Retribution is a way of respecting each person (offender) as a rightful/responsible member of a society.

The *lex talionis* (Gen. 9:5–6; Lev. 24:17; Exod. 21:12, 24; Num. 35:31; Deut. 19:11–12) represents the biblical principle of retributive justice. For example, Exodus 21:24 reads: "eye for eye, tooth for tooth, hand for hand, foot for foot." To modern sentiment, the *lex talionis* sounds harsh and inhumane because it demands the bodily punishment of the offender by the wronged in exact correspondence to the wrongs inflicted. However, its focus is not corporal retaliation but parity in punishment. The intent of God's command is to restrict vengeance in punishment. In short, the punishment should not exceed the crime. This fulfills justice in retribution. Similarly, in Genesis 9:6 and Leviticus 24:19–20, which are frequently misinterpreted as biblical sources that sanctify capital punishment, the thrust is to underscore the sanctity of human life, not to support its destruction.[36]

The Bible strengthens this check against vengeance. Having received authority from God to execute retributive justice, the government and judges are required to administer it in a fair and just way. I do not believe that Jesus completely forfeited *lex talionis* (any form of retributive justice), but he did point out its limitations—sinful misuse and misapplication that are driven or motivated by revenge rather than fitting retribution. He sternly warns about the spirit of vengeance that the *lex talionis* typically entails. However, punishment does not aim at personal vindictiveness or revenge. "On the contrary, its function is to prevent persons from anaesthetizing themselves against grace. Excommunication is the form under which the church continues to make grace available to the impenitent."[37] In the context of the new covenant, one may say that punishment is the communicative action of a society

35. Marshall, "Divine Justice as Restorative Justice," 14.
36. Beckett, "Mass Incarceration," 232.
37. Jeschke, *Discipling the Brother*, 105.

to offenders by condemning wrongful acts. It communicates that crimes are not acceptable. In covenant, punishment is pedagogical rather than punitive. Covenant ethics does not exclude the deterring effect of punishment, but "its overriding purpose is to promote repentance, reformation, and restoration of offenders."[38] While condemning criminal acts, it does not condemn the offender. New covenant ethics seeks the healing of an offender as well as the relationship broken or damaged by the offender's wrongful act.

Restorative Justice

Under the covenantal drama of liberation-restoration, new covenant ethics is committed to restorative justice. The impetus and trajectory of God's covenant are restorative. As we saw in the first two chapters, covenant indicates God's constant effort to restore a wholesome relationship with humanity. The motif of restoration is intrinsic to the covenant, as the covenantal drama of liberation-restoration indicates. Divine justice in the OT is restorative in essence (Deut. 30:3; Pss. 85:10; 103:8–10; 130:3–4; Isa. 32:17; Ezek. 33:11; Mic. 7:18). Even the Sinai covenant teaches that vengeance belongs to God (Deut. 32:35). This standpoint is not lost but invigorated in the New Testament (Rom. 12:17–21; Gal. 6:1; 1 Pet. 3:9).

Jesus's response to John the Baptist's inquiry on evidence of his messiahship was characterized by the theme of restoration. "Go and tell John what you hear and see: the blind receive their sight, the lame walk, the lepers are cleansed, the deaf hear, the dead are raised, and the poor have good news brought to them. And blessed is anyone who takes no offense at me" (Matt. 11:4–6). Luke 4:18 includes the release of prisoners as an aspect of Jesus's restorative mission. He showed his care for and solidarity with prisoners by putting them alongside the hungry, the stranger, and the sick (Matt. 25:34–45).

God's new covenant is restorative as it makes all things right, "reversing the effects of sin and death."[39] Through the covenant, "others" and "strangers" are reconciled and become mutual friends, and sinners are restored into a community again. The guiding spirit of the new covenant is not revenge but restoration. The Sermon on the Mount shows that when we are unfairly offended or harmed, our attitude is not retaliation or vengeance but overcoming evil with good. In several places in the gospel, Jesus calls for forgiveness of offenders (Matt. 18:21–35), most notably in the Lord's Prayer and when he talks about love of enemies (Matt. 5:38–48; Luke 6:27–36). New covenant underscores nonretaliation, nonvengeance, nonviolence, and reconciliation.

38. Marshall, *Beyond Retribution*, 197.

39. Gentry and Wellum, *Kingdom through Covenant*, 595.

The motif of restoration is corroborated by the doctrines of justification, reconciliation, and atonement. It is evident that God's justification of sinners (*dikaiosyne*) is the exercise of God's restorative justice. The apostle Paul's epistle to the Galatians makes clear that the goal is "to restore the erring fellow member to his former condition and mend the injured relationships."[40] Paul is consistent with the primary aim of covenant—to repair and build relationship on the basis of justice and love of God. Discipline cannot diverge from its primary intent.

Restoration cannot take place without reconciliation between the alienated parties. Reconciliation denotes "the restoration of relationships that wrongs have ruptured with the aims of realizing a condition of right relationship."[41] Paul compares reconciliation to demolishing the wall of enmity between alienated parties. He declares: "For he is our peace; in his flesh he has made both groups into one and has broken down the dividing wall, that is, the hostility between us" (Eph. 2:14). Reconciliation cannot be abstract. If Christians are called to be ministers of reconciliation, then restorative justice is definitely a way of practicing it.

Atonement System

We briefly mentioned in chapter 1 that the atonement system is integral to God's covenant with humans. Through the atonement system, God offers human offenders the opportunity to repair a broken or violated relationship. To commit a crime is to break a covenant between the parties, and atonement is needed to repair the relationship to bring back an offender to a community. Since God knows human frailty, the atonement system is indispensable in maintaining a covenantal relationship and achieving God's goal. Atonement typically happens through communicative action between offenders and God: repentance, confession, and sacrifice on the human's part, and pardon on God's part. Atonement is a peacemaking work of God. Marshall notes: "The atonement is an all-encompassing act of justice-making that overthrows oppressive powers (cf. Rom. 8:38–39; 1 Cor. 15:24–26), forgives all those guilty of collaboration with the enemy ([Rom.] 5:6–10), and restores to full covenant-relationship all who believe, Gentiles as well as Jews."[42]

Restorative justice continues the spirit of the atonement system of the Bible. Just as atonement is made available by God for humans in the divine-human covenant, so it should be available for offenders so that they can be fully restored into a society.

40. Dunn, *The Epistle to the Galatians*, 320–21.

41. Philpott, *Just and Unjust Peace*, 54.

42. Marshall, *Beyond Retribution*, 58–59.

In particular, covenanted people are called to reciprocate God's compassion and love toward them through their care of the poor, the oppressed, and the vulnerable. A truer and higher form of justice in criminal justice is actualized when offenders are fully rehabilitated.

Summary

Criminal justice in new covenant ethics is not just punitive but restorative, correcting and repairing broken relationships. The interconnection between retribution and restoration is congruent to the covenantal drama of liberation and restoration, just peacemaking, and the triad of love, justice, and power. Retribution is the exercise of justice against crimes, while restoration is performance of love to offenders. This implies that retribution cannot be vengeful but must be fair (which *lex talionis* demands), and thus should be oriented toward restoration. A society should use the power of its justice system for this objective.

Just as retributive justice cannot be taken lightly by Christians, so also restorative justice is not merely optional for Christians. New covenant ethics institutionalizes both retribution (when the covenantal agreement is violated) and restoration through its intrinsic atonement system. Retribution and restoration go hand in hand in covenant—the former to hold the offender accountable for personal action ("just deserts of wrongdoings")[43] and the latter to invite the offender back to the relationship by providing a redemptive path from the past wrongs. Both are necessary to maintain the relational integrity of the covenant and to fulfill its purpose.[44]

The relationship is consistent with just peacemaking; just peacemaking in criminal justice respects both justice (retribution of offense) and peace (reconciliation between offenders and offended), retributive justice and restorative justice. The covenantal aphorism fits well with these two dimensions of criminal justice: "Punishment alone can never put things right." It cannot repair the relationship, and we need reconciliation. "Restorative justice places emphasis on the moral and spiritual obligations that come with crime to respond in a way that endeavors to make things right."[45] In new covenant ethics, retribution cannot be thought of apart from restoration; it is part of repairing and should serve the purpose of restoration, just as justice is inseparable from love and peacemaking.

43. Cf. Marshall, *Beyond Retribution*, 141.

44. Advocates of retributive justice often claim that the OT presentation of God is wrathful, and that OT justice is retributive. However, the central biblical ideas of redemption (forgiveness), shalom, Jubilee, and Sabbath point toward restoration.

45. Marshall, *Beyond Retribution*, 141.

Practices of Restorative Justice

One practical question is how to translate the biblical view of restorative justice into practices and a structural change of a penal system. New covenant ethics offers some insights. In new covenant ethics, restoration includes the process of reconciliation, and when applied to criminal justice, it means reconciliation between an offender, a victim, a victim's family, and communities that contribute to the repair of broken and offended relationships. Reconciliation is a process of just peacemaking. The state is not the only player of the criminal justice system, and it is not interested in reconciliation; therefore, it is necessary to transfer power from the state to a community in order to attend to the interest of immediately concerned parties. This will seek healing and restoration and will carefully attend to the damage done to victims and communities.

Following is a discussion of how restorative justice can be practiced at the three different levels: interpersonal, institutional, and societal.

1. *Interpersonal level.* There is no restoration of an offender without repairing the relationship with a victim; the initiative should first come from an offender. Both an offender and a victim have a responsibility for reconciliation. Reciprocity is key to repairing relationships at this level. From a biblical perspective, reconciliation does not refer to a passive absence of enmity but to the active presence of fellowship and friendship.

However, reconciliation should not be hurried, nor should it be done in a trite or shallow way. Empowering victims is the first major step. It is crucial for a Christian community to create the atmosphere of reconciliation and offer the support for it. A safe environment and sufficient time should be given for victims to express their hurts and pain and share the effects of the crime. When the atmosphere is ready, an offender is given the opportunity to genuinely express repentance and seek forgiveness from the victim and remedy the effects of the crime. The victim, in turn, is to show willingness to forgive and desire a new, commonly shared future.

2. *Institutional level.* In addition to their reconciliation with the victims, offenders should be brought back to a community. Without their restoration, God's just peacemaking is unfinished and a community is not complete. In practicing restorative justice, Christians need to be reminded of God's acceptance of sinners in Jesus Christ, of God's patience and resilient grace. "Bear one another's burdens, and in this way you will fulfill the law of Christ" (Gal. 6:2). Jesus's new covenant community welcomed all people and provided shelter, food, and care for them. Similarly, 2 Corinthians 2 discloses Paul's remarkable concern for the well-being of an offender in the church in Corinth.

Christians could practice restorative justice in their community by mediating reconciliation and offering a welcoming community of hospitality. One way is to address the immediate needs of families. The families of those incarcerated also suffer enormously,[46] due to the loss of personal contact and material support from loved ones, as prisons are usually built in rural areas that require families to travel long distances. Churches need to provide a meaningful community for them.

The social, economic, and psychological tolls of incarceration are overwhelming; marriages break down and children grow up without a father or a mother. Criminal records take away any hope to live as a meaningful member of society. Criminalization destroys an offender almost permanently. Even after release, offenders experience various legal barriers to employment, public benefits, housing, and voting. The financial burden of families continues. In a word, there is no hope even after discharge from a prison, for released convicts need communities and jobs.

3. *Societal level.* First and foremost, we need to fix the broken structure of the criminal justice system in the United States. The current justice system is highly unfair and skewed; it overcriminalizes the poor and people of color. Comprehensive structural reform is necessary. The system is structured to socially punish people of color, exploit their cheap labor for corporate wealth accumulation, and perpetuate the cultural racial hierarchy and ideology of white normativity.

Fortunately, there is a growing bipartisan effort to reduce the overcrowded population of the federal and state prisons in the United States. This shift is affected by several factors: the sharp decline of crimes since the early 1990s[47] as well as "conservative concerns about careening financial costs, libertarian unease with government overreach, and progressive outrage at civil and human rights abuses."[48]

However, from a covenantal perspective, the reform of the criminal justice system should go further. To reduce recidivism, society needs to offer various rehabilitation programs for offenders to empower their capabilities during their prison time and afterward. Instead of a preoccupation with punishment, the penal system should focus on restoration by enacting and implementing concrete programs that have been proven effective. The justice system needs to actively find alternatives to incarceration such as earned rehabilitation incentive programs, community service, parole, etc., which will help lessen the burden of the inmates' families. Christians should join in reforming the criminal justice system. It is time to organize boycotts and divest from the private prison-industrial complex and the companies that exploit the labor of inmates.

The abolition of capital punishment is another area for reform in light of restorative justice. The United States is the only country in the West where capital

46. DeVuono-Powell et al., "Who Pays?"

47. Ford, "Can Bipartisanship End Mass Incarceration?"

48. Beckett, "Mass Incarceration," 221–22.

punishment is still legal. The criminal justice system relies heavily on retributive and deterrence theories over rehabilitation and restorative justice. Advocates for retributive justice argue that punishment should fit the crime—that is, it should be proportionate to the crime committed. Capital punishment is necessary to fulfill retributive justice. As the Bible says, an eye for an eye, a life for a life; thus, a murderer should be punished with the death penalty. The abolition of capital punishment goes against the *lex talionis* of the Bible and the principle of justice. It is less than what an offender deserves. Capital punishment respects the sanctity of the life of victims.

However, the question concerning exact retribution is whether perfect fulfillment of *lex talionis* is even impossible. For example, as we see with rape and torture, we use the principle of proportionality instead. Even in the case of homicide, many killers are not executed, except in cases of premeditated first-degree murder.

Furthermore, given the flaws of the current penal system, one should consider another rule: the innocent should never be punished, let alone be executed. Execution has been unfairly applied to the poor, people of color, and other marginalized groups. The abolition of capital punishment is not the sign of "weakness," as conservative politicians assert. Rather, capital punishment is a cruel and unusual measure and a violation of the Eighth Amendment.

As for deterrence, the deterring effect of capital punishment is inconclusive. The same deterring effect against murder can be achieved by life imprisonment, and, given the skewed nature of the criminal justice system in the United States, this change is necessary to prevent innocent (falsely accused) people from being executed. This injustice can never be fully corrected.

Capital punishment is antithetical to the new covenant. As mentioned, Jesus's way in the Sermon on the Mount is thoroughly nonviolent. Nonviolence must not be confused with nonresistance or resignation. It refers to active resistance without using violence. It is not submission to evil but overcoming it with goodness. We can achieve the goal of deterrence and protection of safety through "life without parole" even in the most heinous crimes. However, we must achieve the goal without sanctioning capital punishment. Life without parole could achieve the same goal of retribution without perpetuating violence.

As stated before, new covenant is the creative composite of love, justice, and power. Capital punishment has punishment (justice), but it does not have restoration (love). It destroys a human life and eliminates the opportunity for reconciliation with victims and restoration of offenders. It is a sign of weakness—that society cannot rehabilitate one of its deranged, broken, and failed members. This is the logical consequence of a state-oriented, punitive-based penal system that marginalizes victims and communities with a goal not of reconciliation and restoration. Capital punishment takes away any opportunity for rehabilitation and restoration. To abolish capital punishment is a necessary step in moving toward restorative justice.

Dismantling Punitive Culture

Churches should exercise leadership in undoing an excessively punitive culture and dismantling the system of mass incarceration. They should correct a dominant cultural narrative that scapegoats and demonizes offenders. Toward this end, several covenantal values help us change the extremely punitive culture and rewrite the social script around criminal justice. Covenantal values should help undo this and offer an alternative vision.

The rhetoric of law and order relies on the sensational vilification of criminals in order to manipulate collective psychology. Offenders and former convicts are often treated as subhuman, even demonic figures who are completely different from normal people (thus averting the need for compassion). A number of TV series about prison inmates propagate the stereotype of offenders as wretched "others" to fear and to avoid. This is a dangerous practice because they are treated as irredeemable and not deserving of a second chance. Rather than seeing offenses as behaviors that constitute only a part of their lives, these stereotypes essentialize the totality of these persons as criminals.[49]

Human Dignity

Because of this highly punitive culture, even "civil rights advocates have long been reluctant to [advocate] on behalf of criminals."[50] Michelle Alexander writes, "Criminals, it turns out, are the one social group in America we have permission to hate. In 'colorblind' America, criminals are the new whipping boys. They are entitled to no respect and little moral concern."[51] The social stigma of criminal conviction is seared into their social identity. Even after their release, their criminal records follow them. The debt to society is paid, but punishment continues. Their dignity and worth are permanently compromised in the process. "They will be discriminated against, legally, for the rest of their lives—denied employment, housing, education, and public benefits. Unable to surmount these obstacles, most will eventually return to prison and then be released again, caught in a closed circuit of perpetual marginality."[52]

49. Snyder notes that the doctrine of total depravity has contributed to racialization of crime and the spread of punitive culture (Snyder, *The Protestant Ethic and the Spirit of Punishment*, 33–54).

50. Alexander, *The New Jim Crow*, 226.

51. Alexander, *The New Jim Crow*, 141.

52. Alexander, *The New Jim Crow*, 186–87.

We treat them as totally depraved, dangers and threats to civilization; we justify the deprivation of their civil rights and the application of lifelong discrimination. We refuse to see and affirm their humanity—God's image-bearers—and we label them as threats to be removed. However, treating offenders as such is not only a violation of human dignity but also counterproductive; it is human emotional nature that antisocial attitudes and criminal behaviors grow when a person feels completely abandoned by a society and has no stake in it.

Affirming the dignity and basic humanity of all offenders is a step toward cleansing the punitive culture. Noah's covenant, which binds all of humanity, shows that despite human sin, God still protects and cares for the dignity of every person and creature. God still preserves and watches over humanity to protect it from further destruction. He maintains basic justice. The value and worth of every creature are reaffirmed by God's covenantal commitment. The human condition has changed because of sin, but humans have not completely fallen out of God's grace. The Fall does not mean the ceasing of God's grace, God's sovereignty, or God's redeeming goodwill toward humanity. As we saw in chapter 1, far from giving up, God rather initiates redemptive work through a series of covenants. "Even a criminal has the right to claim his or her dignity and worth before God and others in the context of [covenantal] reciprocity. The dynamic of the covenant is that we are in relationship with God and with each other, and we have the right to make claims, assert our needs and present our desires, just as others have toward us."[53]

Nothing could alter this most fundamental moral status of all human beings. They are God's image-bearers and the members of God's family, the universal community of the covenant.

Humility

We need to exercise humility before God in our treatment of offenders. A sober awareness of one's own vulnerability is called on before judging others. *We live in God's forgiving grace. We are all sinners, and we all live with the possibility to falter and offend others.* We all have sinned and fallen short of the glory of God. We recognize our solidarity in brokenness and God's grace: "For as all die in Adam, so all will be made alive in Christ" (1 Cor. 15:22). Paul admonishes: "My friends, if anyone is detected in a transgression, you who have received the Spirit should restore such a one in a spirit of gentleness. Take care that you yourselves are not tempted. Bear one another's burdens, and in this way you will fulfill the law of Christ" (Gal. 6:1–2). But because of God's unmerited grace, we all are given a new opportunity. If God had

53. Snyder, *The Protestant Ethic and the Spirit of Punishment*, 116.

not exercised restorative justice, we would be destined to eternal separation from God. Hence, in response to God's forgiveness, we need to live with humility, share burdens with each other, and show compassion and hospitality toward everyone, including offenders.

Solidarity

The current US penal system operates by the accountability principle (retribution), which is solely placed on the offender. The failure of society is never adequately accounted for. Poverty, racism, sexism, poor public education, and high housing prices are positively correlated with crime rates. In other words, while crimes are committed by individuals, they are not purely individual incidents but social phenomena. They significantly reflect various social conditions such as broken families, structural injustices (race and class), and unresolved historical traumas and pains, etc. While offenders cannot be free from responsibility, society cannot be completely free from guilt, either. Scapegoating offenders is a convenient mechanism of avoiding collective guilt.[54] Some crimes are committed out of desperation, as in the case of Jean Valjean in Victor Hugo's novel *Les Misérables*. We need to transform the built-in injustices and social conditions that systemically violate the dignity of people, frustrate their flourishing, and push them toward antisocial actions.

However, in the United States, individualism and its ideology of freedom are blinding people to these social conditions of stratification. This serves as an ideology for the harsh treatment and economic exploitation of prisoners. Historically, one cannot deny that a Protestant individualistic theology of sin and redemption has contributed to the shaping of such cultural ethos. The new covenant challenges this approach. It teaches that we are our brother's and sister's keepers. We are joined in mutual accountability. When one harms others, it affects everybody. When one suffers, all suffer. An offender's rehabilitation matters for the well-being of the entire community. The Bible exhorts: "Remember those who are in prison, as though you were in prison with them" (Heb. 13:3).

Conclusion

This chapter began with a brief survey of three theories of punishment: retribution, deterrence, and rehabilitation. Imprisonment is a necessary evil. "From Jeremiah's cistern to Micaiah's starvation rations, and from the psalmists' despairing cries to the Romans' vigorous beatings, the Bible always associates prisons with darkness and

54. Girard, *Violence and the Sacred*; Girard, *The Scapegoat*.

misery."[55] However, punishment raises moral concerns because it relies on violence, even the killing of other human beings in capital punishment. It requires extreme care and caution because it can easily corrupt us. I think the punitive culture of the United States is such a sign of corruption.

With its fair, balanced, and sensible relationship between retributive and restorative justice, new covenant ethics offers a coherent moral framework to approach criminal justice. Through punishment, it achieves retributive justice. But its goal is always to return offenders back to a community. To counter the punitive spirit, new covenant ethics focuses on the restoration of offenders. In the final analysis, God's justice is salvific, not retributive. Punishment alone never achieves shalom. Cruel, harsh punishment without any effort to restore offenders is not compatible with the spirit of the new covenant. As high rates of recidivism indicate, it is also ineffective. Retributive justice apart from restorative justice is not biblical.

55. Beckett, "Mass Incarceration," 227, drawing from Marshall, "Prison, Prisoners and the Bible," 5–6.

CHAPTER 17

Race

> Racism is particularly alive and well in America. It is America's original sin and as it is institutionalized at all levels of society, it is its most persistent and intractable evil. Though racism inflicts massive suffering, few American theologians have even bothered to address white supremacy as a moral evil and as a radical contradiction of our humanity and religious identities.
>
> —James H. Cone, "Theology's Great Sin"

> Oppressed people cannot remain oppressed forever. The yearning for freedom eventually manifests itself. The Bible tells the thrilling story of how Moses stood in Pharaoh's court centuries ago and cried, "Let my people go." This was an opening chapter in a continuing story. The present struggle in the United States is a later chapter in the same story.
>
> —Martin Luther King Jr.,
> "Where Do We Go from Here?"

In many parts of the West, the demon of racism is once again rearing its ugly head in the form of xenophobia and nativism. Racial relationships are deteriorating in the face of demographic and other changes, including economic difficulties and the influx of immigrants from the global South.[1] White nationalists declare that affirmative action is reverse discrimination. Billboards in the South read "multiculturalism is white genocide." After a brief elated moment of optimism with the election of Barack Obama to the US presidency, racial tensions, conflicts, and inflammatory

1. A majority of Americans across all racial groups say that race relations are bad. Anna Brown, "Key Findings on Americans' Views of Race in 2019."

rhetoric are growing with the election of Donald Trump. Racial reconciliation seems even more remote today. The election of Trump dissipated the euphoria of the postracial society engendered by the election of Obama.

In the United States, why is the race issue so difficult to solve? Why are Christians unable to address this even among themselves? Why do many white Christians repeatedly stand on the wrong side of this issue? How do we dismantle racism? How do we identify and name the patterns of white normativity and disrupt white supremacy and normativity to reach a new social compact on race relationships?

This chapter studies racism. I claim that uprooting racism is difficult because racism is tied to white racial identity and protects white power and privilege. After discussing key concepts related to racism, this chapter explores a covenantal approach as a constructive alternative to postracial or colorblind approaches such as "multiculturalism," the black-white binary, and rigid identity politics.

Patterns of Racism

Racism is deeply engrained in Western society. It is the product of whites, a major part of the modern European worldview and its colonialist project. Whites have created various institutional organizational structures (political, legal, military, educational, economic) based on racial hierarchy with whites on top. Our current society is not free from this legacy. Racism has never died off but has always remained a part of the undercurrent of the United States—always simmering and festering under the surface but erupting time and time again when whites feel threatened or see opportunities for political and economic gain. Affirmative action may have opened a door of entry for people of color, but the institutional ethos, policy, and informal power structure are white oriented and advantaged ("the invisible knapsack of white privilege").[2] Despite some progress, the pattern of discrimination and unfair treatment is still found in every realm of US society. Here are some examples:

Criminal justice. People of color, especially African Americans and Latinx, get longer sentences than white people for the same crimes. Although African Americans and Latinx compose 29 percent of the US population, they make up 57 percent of the US prison population.[3] The US Sentencing Commission found that African Americans get 19.1 percent longer sentences than whites for the same crime. "All else held equal, black arrestees were 75 percent more likely to face a charge with a mandatory minimum sentence than white arrestees."[4] African American and Latinx

2. This phrase was coined in the 1980s by the feminist scholar Peggy McIntosh.

3. US Bureau of Justice Statistics, *Prisoners in 2016*; Rastogi et al., "2010 Census Brief."

4. Lopez, "Report."

adults are, respectively, 5.9 times and 3.1 times more likely to be incarcerated than whites.[5] On average, when the victim is white, African American defendants are three times as likely to receive the death penalty relative to white defendants.[6]

Environment. Residential areas where people of color live are far more likely to be used as dumping places of toxins, pollutants, and hazardous materials than suburban or largely white neighborhoods. Three in five African Americans live in communities with abandoned toxic-waste sites.[7] Residents of these areas also have higher exposure rates to air pollution and carcinogens than non-Hispanic white people. Perhaps most tragic is that low-income areas and communities of color across the nation are susceptible to water contamination.[8]

Wealth inequality. In 2013, the net worth of white households was $144,200, roughly thirteen times that of black households; 72 percent of white householders owned their own home, compared with 43 percent of black householders. In 2013, the wealth of white households was thirteen times the median wealth of black households; in 2010 the disparity was eight times.[9]

Life expectancy. By 2011, the life expectancy for white men was 76.6 years; for black men it was 72.2 years; for white women it was 81.1 years, and for black women 78.2 years.[10]

Authority. In her research, Robin DiAngelo found fifteen major institutions, including the presidency, the teaching profession, and professional football teams, disproportionately controlled by whites in 2016–2017.[11]

Original Sin of the United States and the Modern West

In the United States, the root of racism is deep because it is tied with white identity. There is compelling evidence to suggest that racism is the original sin of the United States (and the modern West).[12] Racism was an integral part of the Euro-

5. US Bureau of Justice Statistics, *Prisoners in 2016*, 8, table 6.

6. "Facts about the Death Penalty"; "Death Penalty and Race."

7. Rasmussen, *Earth Community, Earth Ethics*, 74–75.

8. Bell, "5 Things to Know about Communities of Color and Environmental Justice."

9. "On Views of Race and Inequality, Blacks and Whites Are Worlds Apart." Kochhar and Fry, "Wealth Inequality Has Widened along Racial, Ethnic Lines Since End of Great Recession."

10. National Center for Health Statistics of the Centers for Disease Control and Prevention, "United States Life Expectancy (a) at Birth (in Years) by Race and Gender and (b) Relative Difference (%) Overall and by Gender: 1900–2011," cited in Bond and Herman, "Lagging Life Expectancy for Black Men."

11. DiAngelo, "No, I Won't Stop Saying 'White Supremacy.'"

12. In addition to James Cone's quotation on racism as America's original sin in this chapter's epigraph, see Wallis, *America's Original Sin*, especially "The Original Sin and Its Legacy," 33–56.

pean colonial project—in expropriating the land and exploiting people of color for capital accumulation. The United States of America was established "as a white society, founded upon a genocide of another race, and then the enslavement of yet another."[13] Consequently, every modern institution, which was founded by whites, was affected by racism—its culture, policy, and power structure.[14] This is one of the reasons why uprooting racism has been so difficult.[15]

Racial Hierarchy, Racialization, White Normativity, White Fragility

In discussing racism, the clarification of key sociological concepts is necessary because whites and people of color have very different perceptions and experiences of racism. For whites, racism typically describes individual racial prejudice commonly found in every society. When they see or hear about an incident of racial discrimination, they dismiss it as an isolated case of an individual's mistake. They believe that racism can be fixed with more education; it will disappear with the passage of time.

However, racism is not simply a personal or cultural bias against other racial groups. Researchers point out that racism is rooted in intergroup conflict over resources, ways of life, and defense of group position.[16] "[Racism] results from the transformation of race prejudice and/or ethnocentrism through the exercise of power against a racial group defined as inferior, by individuals and institutions with the intentional or unintentional support of the entire culture."[17]

This means that racism is a group power dynamic that operates through social structures, institutions, and culture creating that materially and ideologically justifies and defends the power and privilege of a dominant race.[18] Racism inevitably produces unequal treatment and different social outcomes for different races as measurable by wage, housing, promotion, and employment figures.

To assure their domination and hegemony over people of color, whites developed a comprehensive theory of race using pseudoscience and heretical religion,

13. Wallis, *God's Politics*, 308.

14. See Barndt, *Dismantling Racism*, 75–100.

15. Critical race theory helps to understand this historical, distinctively Western origin of racism.

16. Emerson and Smith, *Divided by Faith*, 74.

17. J. M. Jones, "The Concept of Racism and Its Changing Reality," 28. Jane Elliot's famous experimentation shows how discrimination is socially constructed. It proves the validity of this definition: even arbitrarily selected physical features could be used to create the hierarchy within a group when supported/reinforced by power.

18. This definition of racism as bias plus power was first proposed by Patricia A. Bidol in *Developing New Perspectives on Race*.

notably the Göttingen school's tripartite taxonomy of Caucasoid, Mongoloid, and Negroid. The category "white" was created in distinction from other "inferior races" to perpetuate the pattern and structure of racial hierarchy, which was then implemented legally and socially (slavery, segregation, and South African apartheid). The project was effective, and its impact was totalistic. White dominance in the modern world was achieved with military power, advanced technology, and science. Most of the world adopted the system and organization of white civilization in the name of modernization. This was Westernization in which whiteness was upheld (and adored) as the symbol of prestige, power, goodness, and beauty.

Whites have developed a racial hierarchy in terms of status, power, and privilege, with whites on top, blacks at the bottom, and Latinx and Asian Americans in the middle, on the basis of their genocide of Native Americans. Each race group is "scientifically" categorized according to its physical features (assigning different merits, legal values, and moral properties to each group) and cognitive superiority or intellectual inferiority. All the desirable characteristics are attributed to the top category, and all the undesirable features to the bottom—white versus black symbolism. Hierarchy entails membership, rights, privilege, and entitlement. Its goal is to protect white privilege and power.

Whites have also created racial stereotypes by ascribing certain negative moral attributes and characteristics (stereotypes) to each racial group (e.g., "yellow" is cunning, docile, and obedient, while "black" equals lewd, lazy, and violent). Racial stereotypes essentialize certain cultural traits and biological features, without plausible grounds, as a fixed, immutable property of each group. Whiteness is also a racial stereotype; however, this stereotype is assigned a positive essence.

Enforced by law, force, and religious-cultural indoctrination, stereotypes have justified slavery, segregation, and racial discrimination.[19] Anyone, either white or person of color, who violates this hierarchy is severely punished. The goal of this racial hierarchy is to perpetuate white supremacy. White supremacy guarantees white privilege and power materialized in better opportunities and resources in every aspect of social life: jobs, promotion, wealth, education, housing, safety, etc.

19. This approach does not explain how Asian Americans are consistently treated as aliens and outsiders while blacks are inferior. A racial geometry approach that utilizes two sets of variables—insider-outsider and superior-inferior—is helpful to understand racism against Asian Americans. A different trajectory approach takes racialization as "an open-ended, variable process that has played out differently for each subordinate group." Kim, "The Racial Triangulation of Asian Americans," 105. However, this approach fails to describe the complex and multifarious dimensions of interracial interactions as well as the strategies of control, domination, and hegemony by whites. Racialization of a particular group never happens in a vacuum in isolation from other racial groups. There is no autonomy in racialization; it is mutually constitutive.

Peggy McIntosh observes: "I have come to see white privilege as an invisible package of unearned assets which I can count on cashing in each day, but about which I was 'meant' to remain oblivious. White privilege is like an invisible weightless backpack of special provisions, maps, passports, codebooks, visas, clothes, tools and blank checks."[20]

Racialization

Racialization refers to a particular aspect of the socialization process that reproduces racial hierarchy and stereotypes. It is essential in maintaining racial hierarchy by forcing members to internalize the racial worldview of whites. The racialization process is overseen by whites through their control of social cultural institutions: the media, literature, education, and arts.

A central aspect of racialization is the formation of racial identity and identification; that is, every member of a society is identified first and foremost by skin color. Racial identity serves as the primer of one's social identity. The force of race and racialization is found in that racial identification and racial hierarchy supersede other kinds of social stratification, such as class, education, professional skills and merits, gender, and religion. For example, a poor, uneducated white is sometimes treated socially higher than a rich, educated person of color. Disregarding "higher-order traits, such as personality, intelligence, and moral behavior," "society frequently chooses to ignore these scientific truths, creates races and endows them with pseudo-permanent characteristics."[21] Institutional rigidity of racial hierarchy and racialization have mitigated considerably since the civil rights movement. But their centuries-long legacy still continues in the form of whiteness and white normativity.

People raised in Western societies are socially conditioned to racialization and racial stereotypes to various degrees. Even those raised outside the West are receptive to stereotypes because of the influence of colonialism and the global power of Hollywood movies and the Western media.

Whiteness/White Normativity

Whiteness and white normativity are notions useful to comprehend more invisible, informal, cultural, and noninstitutional, but still disciplinary, forces of racialization. It is the symbol that indicates superiority, normativity, privilege, and the power of

20. McIntosh, "White Privilege."
21. Delgado and Stefancic, *Critical Race Theory*, 8–9.

white people. Taking whites as the standard of humanity, whiteness is associated with all positive traits of humanity, while nonwhites are associated with negative, inferior, and deviant traits. Whiteness is less a physiological term than a social notion, a particular cultural gaze—a way of seeing the world. Whiteness disguises a "natural" way of life. Willie Jennings states, "Whiteness is a way of imagining the world moving around you, flowing around your body with you being at the center. Whiteness is a way of imagining the true, the good, and the beautiful configured around white bodies."[22]

As a symbolic force representing truth, morality, and beauty in the West, white normativity is reproduced through the multitudes of symbolic images, metaphors, ideologies, ideas, and practices that affirm and reinforce negative stereotypes of people of color. For example, until very recently, all the heroes/heroines in popular culture (e.g., Superman, Spider-Man, Wonder Woman, Iron Man) were white, as were political and social leaders and educators.

The cultural pervasiveness of whiteness implies the thoroughness and maturation of the racialization process as embedded in the makeup of society itself. Whiteness symbolizes a world where white culture is the defining character and normative frame of reference and civilizational achievement for humanity. Through the racialization process, whiteness takes the tone and pretense of natural, normal, and civilized. Whiteness has a naming and disciplinary power. A white gaze operates as a navel gaze for humanity and civilization; those who do not adopt this gaze are marginalized, isolated, and treated as uncivilized or unsophisticated. In society, whiteness functions as a criterion that delineates the accepted range of conduct and characteristics. People of color must learn and conform to the white way of life for their survival.

Unlike white supremacy that typically takes an overt discriminatory or violent form, whiteness operates more subtly and sometimes even unconsciously. It operates in nonjudicial ways, through various social practices and networks, cultural ethos, and religious symbols. Using informal cultural and institutional forces, whiteness maintains racial hierarchy and its structural pattern in order to protect white interests. The law and policies may no longer be blatantly discriminatory, but white control of a society continues by holding on to upper-echelon positions of power and influencing every realm of society. Whiteness has been constantly adapting to changing environments in order to maintain white hegemony and racial hierarchy, if necessary, by co-opting people of color socialized by whiteness. The border between whiteness and white supremacy is thin. Whiteness could easily turn into white supremacy when whites feel threatened.

22. Jennings, "To Be a Christian Intellectual."

White Fragility

Whiteness is central to white racial and cultural identity. Racialization and white culture are intermeshed; for whites to change whiteness is tantamount to compromising on normativity itself—the ideal form of human life and civility of human existence. Hence, any challenge evokes white emotional reaction. "White fragility," a term coined by Robin DiAngelo,[23] refers to defensive emotional and psychological mechanisms experienced by whites when confronted with discussions about race and racism. White fragility is the other, more psychological, side of white normativity and superiority. It is an emotional reaction (e.g., anger, fear, frustration, guilt, and tears) when white power and privilege are uncovered, disrupted, or threatened. "White fragility is a state in which even a minimum amount of racial stress in one's habits becomes intolerable, triggering a range of defensive moves. These moves include the outward display of emotions such as anger, fear, and guilt and behaviors such as argumentation, silence, and leaving the stress-inducing situation. These behaviors, in turn, reinstate white racial equilibrium. Racial stress results from an interruption to what is racially familiar."[24]

White fragility results from cultural and psychological sources. First, it is an outcome of the racialization of whites in white supremacy/normativity. In general, whites feel uncomfortable about or unsettled by discussing race issues because many of them are raised or live in racially and culturally homogeneous communities. Because of their upbringing, whites are comfortable with the current pattern of racial arrangement that benefits them. But more immediately, white fragility is a psychological reaction out of fear of being called a racist (or perhaps out of defense of the myth of white innocence), and of losing privilege and power.

Being a racist goes against a white's self-identity as a good moral person. In addition, there is a deep psychological fear within whites of the loss of white privilege and power in particular and the de-racializing of white normativity in general through demographic changes induced by globalization and migration. Most white Americans agree that slavery, segregation, and racial discrimination are wrong, but they are not willing to accept that they are beneficiaries of unequal power relations due to whiteness. They credit their current superior positions and privilege to their merits. To those enjoying the privilege and power, it is utterly discomforting and upsetting to be challenged about it, let alone lose the privileges. In order to not lose these benefits, whites employ various psychological excuses and evasive techniques to avoid confronting racism head-on.

23. See DiAngelo, *White Fragility*.
24. DiAngelo, *White Fragility*, 103.

Hence, white fragility is not a sign of white weakness or a sign of receptivity to the suffering of people of color. It is rather a tool to keep and reproduce white supremacy/normativity as a defensive mechanism when challenged. DiAngelo considers it "a form of bullying; I am going to make it so miserable for you to confront me—no matter how diplomatically you try to do so—that you will simply back off, give up, and never raise the issue again."[25]

White fragility is found across ideological differences, among liberals, moderates, and conservatives. Liberals and moderates may have abandoned a crude and violent form of white supremacy, but they still hold on to white normativity, privilege, and power. White fragility could easily develop into white supremacy through reassertion of white power. The rise of white nationalism and the overwhelming white support for Trump in 2016 can be seen as white exercise of white supremacy out of white fragility.

White Nationalism

Together with white fragility, the spread of white nationalism discloses how deeply racism is embedded in the fabric of the United States. White supremacy has a long history in the United States, and its current nationalist assertion has to do with perceived shifts in racial power relationships with changing demographics and the political advances of people of color.

Racial hierarchy and white supremacy have been challenged through various anticolonial, antiracist movements such as the civil rights movement. White nationalism is a reactionary political expression of whites who want to keep white hegemony intact in every social realm. It is motivated by fear about the ascendance of people of color in various realms of society (including Barack Obama's presidency) and a demographic change that numerically threatens the majority status of whites (which could be translated into voting power). This shift of power (or its perception) threatens white identity built upon white privilege and power and shakes whites' racialized moral world: whites are superior to other races; modern civilization and its institutions and achievements are their brilliant works that have benefited all of humanity. The slogan "Take America back" is a code that reasserts white supremacy against the perceived threat and loss of white, Christian, and American power.

Borrowing from other groups' identity politics, white nationalists identify themselves as victims of government policies, globalization, and liberal media that favor people of color over whites; they claim that whites are reversely discriminated against, and that their rights need to be protected. White conservatives greatly ex-

25. DiAngelo, *White Fragility*, 112.

aggerate the extent to which minority groups receive advantages. However, the idea of white victimhood is preposterous because whites in the United States still control the power and resources in almost all major institutions. The reality for many marginalized groups remains unchanged: African Americans continue to be subjected to police violence, Asian Americans continue to be treated as aliens, and Latinx continue to be conceived as illegal immigrants.

Individualism and White Insulation

White normativity and fragility (and a colorblind approach to race) are supported by a prevailing individualism in a neoliberal society. Under the ideological cover of individualism, whites claim that as individuals they have nothing to do with racism—neither contributing to nor benefiting from it. They typically reduce racism to personal bias and often dismiss various evidences of racism as isolated incidents caused by some bad whites or exaggerated victim plays by people of color. These incidents, they say, are overblown by the left-wing media. Viewing racism in terms of individual accountability, whites are blind to structural or institutional racial injustices.[26] Individualizing racism is a convenient way to cover up the existing racial hierarchy and its ongoing institutional benefits and privilege.

Culturally, white racism is reproduced partly through white social insulation from people of color.[27] White insulation occurs primarily through residential segregation and geographical distance. Residential areas, schools, and churches are still segregated by race. Whites protect their segregated spaces from the others.

White segregated spaces create white social belonging via a subculture that reinforces whiteness (white social norms, expectations, and identity) and racial stereotypes. Racial slurs and stereotypical views are frequently spoken unchallenged. We see a similar pattern in white fraternities, social clubs, and corporate boardrooms.

One also sees a high level of racial bias among whites living in rural areas of the South who have little opportunity to interact with and know people of color and are therefore unaware of how racism affects people of color. For example, for them a social movement like Black Lives Matter is ridiculous or exaggerated. They ask: Why black lives alone? All lives matter! They have never experienced discrimination and brutality in their personal encounter with the police.

White self-insulation is found in numerous studies. Robert P. Jones of the Public Religion Research Institute has found that the social networks of whites are 91 per-

26. Emerson and Smith, *Divided by Faith*, 91.

27. See Kelly Brown Douglas, *Stand Your Ground*, especially chap. 1, on the relationship between white racism (Anglo-Saxon exceptionalism) and the stand-your-ground law.

cent white, and three-quarters of whites have *entirely* white social networks.[28] Many whites grow uncomfortable if the black proportion of their neighborhoods reaches 8 percent, the "tipping point" around which "white flight" begins.[29] White insulation is a major source of white fragility because an insulated environment renders racial comfort to whites and deprives them of the opportunity to know different cultures and befriend people of color. This lowers their ability to bear racial stress.[30]

The pattern of white insulation and racialization continues today, instilling a sense of racial superiority into white children. For example, the CNN-Kids' test, based on a test of 133 five-year-old white and black girls in the greater Atlanta area,[31] shows that white children still have an overwhelming racial bias against African Americans because white parents do not talk to their children about race. Consequently, children imbibe and continue various racial stereotypes they receive from their parents and neighbors.[32]

This is another example of white privilege and power that promote white flourishing in many areas of social life without interracial cultural knowledge or relationship with people of color; whites do not have to teach the race issue because it does not affect the academic and professional success of their children.

White Christianity and Racism

Unfortunately, there has been a deep historical collusion between white Christianity and white racism. White racism would not have survived this long without the support of white Christianity. From the beginning of colonial history, white Christianity actively aligned itself with Western colonialism, genocide, and slavery, offering religious justification and assistance through sermons, teachings, rituals, and the arts. For example, it justified colonialism and slavery as God's providence and as a necessary tool to save barbarians from idolatry, savagery, and darkness.

In particular, whites misused covenant theology to create white exceptionalism: whites are the chosen race, just as ancient Israel was. For example, Puritans in New England misappropriated the exodus narrative to justify their colonial conquest of "the new land" and the genocide of Native Americans and enslavement of blacks. It is not difficult to see the connection between white exceptionalism

28. Robert P. Jones, "Self-Segregation."

29. Hacker, *Two Nations*, 36.

30. DiAngelo, "White Fragility," 54.

31. "Study: White and Black Children Biased toward Lighter Skin."

32. A 2007 study in the *Journal of Marriage and Family* found that 75 percent of white families with kindergartners never talk about race. In contrast, the CNN study exhibits that about 75 percent of African American parents discuss race with their children.

and the ideology of Manifest Destiny and the redeemer nation: whites are elected by God to civilize the rest of the world. America has a special place for this task in God's providence. Even today white supremacy and white nationalism are fueled by white exceptionalism.

Many conservative evangelicals are still sticking to this racist mythology, as it serves their core cultural and religious identity. In the white conservative Christian mindset, whiteness, Christianity, and the USA (white Christian America) are amalgamated; they cannot think of one without the other two.

Many white conservative evangelicals cannot imagine "an America that is not also pre-eminently white and Christian," likewise a "Christianity that is not also white and '100-percent American.'"[33] This racist theology is espoused in many different forms in popular culture through mass media (e.g., Fox News and Breitbart), bumper stickers, cartoons, talk shows, reality shows (*Duck Dynasty*), fine art products, and songs ("God Bless America"), revealing how closely tied these nationalist, racist, religious sentiments are.[34]

Although not in the same violent and radical form as white nationalism or white identity groups, white Christianity indirectly supports or condones racial hierarchy. The images of God, Jesus, angels, Mary, and the disciples are predominantly white. Many Christians still practice their faith without any critical questions on how their religious practices and liturgies perpetuate racial hierarchy, whiteness, and white normativity. This collusion is clearer in white evangelicals in the United States: the vast majority of them voted for Trump in 2016, and a majority have consistently been his most reliable political base, despite his many racist remarks and support for white nationalist sentiments.

New Covenant Ethics

What does new covenant ethics say about current racial relationships, and what does it mean in this context? Can it dismantle centuries-old racial privilege and power and undo racial superiority and inferiority that have been internalized like a pervasive toxic radiation? How do we dismantle racial hierarchy and create a new, inclusive, egalitarian community? How can we overcome racism? New covenant ethics and its four practices offer a proper vision and necessary practices to achieve this goal.

As racism and colonialism have been systematic and totalizing, true transformation must not be superficial; it must be comprehensive. Therefore, to dismantle racial hierarchy, a multipronged approach is necessary to reorganize racial relations

33. Clark, "Christian Nationalism and White Nationalism."

34. Cf. Kelly J. Baker, "The Artifacts of White Supremacy."

in new ways on inclusive, egalitarian, and reciprocal grounds. New covenant ethics offers wonderful insights about deconstructing racism and reconstructing a racially just society.

As described above, whites used covenant theology to justify racism, completely reversing the intrinsic liberative message and purpose of the covenant. Theological critique and reconstruction are important in dismantling racism because the answer to bad religion is not atheism but good religion. Likewise, the correction of bad covenant theology is good covenant theology.

A theological and hermeneutical flaw played an important role in the Puritan reading of the exodus story. I would say that the Puritan misuse of covenant theology was the combined result of a hermeneutical failure and the Puritan greed for domination and wealth. The Puritans in England and New England extensively borrowed from the exodus story in theologically interpreting their political and social situations. But they gravely failed in their analogical imagination by racially identifying themselves as the new Israel and then transposing the kinship identity of the Israelites to a racial one.

Specifically, they failed to see that for Christians, the new covenant of Jesus is the final covenant. Thus, this covenant is the most authoritative and binding, and has the final say over the other covenants, including the Sinai covenant. In the new covenant, Jesus shattered all kinds of artificial boundaries that excluded people and created a new community of God. In the new covenant, the march of God's people toward the promised land is—as Jesus's was—through the cross, a complete renunciation of violence, not through conquering and genocide.

The Puritan racist legacy has been challenged and partly corrected over the past centuries through the abolitionist movement, the civil rights movement, and the human rights movements of Native Americans, Latinx, and Asian Americans. However, a more thorough theological work is necessary to undo its mistaken mythology and harmful legacy. For this correction, we need an alternative theological framework to Puritan covenant theology. A shift in the theological anchor from the Sinai covenant to the new covenant is critical. Since racial hierarchy is not compatible with God's design in creation and the new covenant, we need to de-organize the hierarchy and reorganize our racial relationships on a completely new foundation. The covenantal drama of liberation and restoration is directly relevant here; it reveals that white supremacy and white normativity are incompatible with God's being and action.

The evil and demonic nature of racism becomes evident when evaluated in light of the new covenant of Jesus and covenantal norms and values (chap. 7). Racism goes against the heart of the new covenant—its vision, values, norms, and ethos. Racism is exclusionary in its vision, hierarchal in its structure, and violent in nature. Racial hierarchy goes against the covenantal principle of free, egalitarian, and reciprocal relationship that covenant embodies. Racism is incompatible with the vision of the shalom community that new covenant ethics intends. New covenant ethics is based on the inclusive vision of God for humanity as a free, egalitarian, intimate, and mutually caring community. A true covenantal community is inclusive, egalitarian, reciprocal, and solidaric. Any Christian claim of a racial-ethnic covenant is not only outdated and destructive but also heretical; it goes against the new covenant of Jesus that encompasses the entire creation. Jesus is a new Adam, and the new covenant indicates the forming of a new inclusive community in him. Jesus's new covenant, with the Eucharist as its emblem, directly addresses the division between Jews and gentiles, women and men, and the rich and the poor. "The open table embodied egalitarianism, disrupted the 'pleasure of hierarchy' and domination, and abolished the etiquette of empire. The open table embodied the desire for and the design of the reign of God. All are welcome."[35]

Racism perpetuates racial hierarchy among different racial groups in every realm of life. But the God of Jesus Christ affirms the dignity and equality of all human beings regardless of their skin color. Their basic rights ensue from their membership in God's family. Racism denies the dignity of each person for whom Jesus died.

Racism is violence against other human beings. It harms and hampers the flourishing of a person. In particular, racism has a destructive impact on the psyche and mental health of people of color. In a racialized society, the people of color always feel dissonance between their true selves and the world imposed by white normativity. They are subjected to ongoing racial micro-aggressions, and verbal and behavioral violence that denigrates them. When they accumulate, these aggressions become traumatic.

Racism goes against the principles of justice. It denies the equality of all people and does not give fair opportunity to people of color. It excludes or marginalizes people of color from full participation in the community. Racism undermines the community that God intends for humanity, the beloved community that God intends to create. New covenant ethics stipulates the arrangement of *a just and right relationship* among members; this applies to racial relationships as well. A just and right relationship presumes equal rights of the participants. As mentioned, the Eucharist embodies the community of inclusivity, equality, and diversity. "If my sister or brother is not at the table, we are not the flesh of Christ. If my sister's mark of sexuality must be obscured, if my brother's mark of race must be disguised, if my sister's mark of culture must be repressed, then we are not the flesh of Christ. For, it is through and in Christ's own flesh that the 'other' is my sister, is my brother; indeed, the 'other' is me."[36]

35. M. Shawn Copeland, *Enfleshing Freedom*, 56–57.

36. M. Shawn Copeland, *Enfleshing Freedom*, 82.

Racism excludes and marginalizes people of color. It militates against the equality and unity (interdependence) of every human being in God. By dividing and stratifying people, it blocks genuine communication and undermines the reconciling work of God in Jesus by creating divisions and conflicts. Racism denies God's desire for the shalom community. It frustrates God's desire for common flourishing. Jesus came to give life abundantly, but racism suffocates it. It impedes people of color from actualizing their full potential to fully participate in social life and contribute to the common good.

In short, racism is antijustice, antishalom, and anticovenant. Racism is the evidence of alienation, brokenness, sin, and domination. It impedes the development of friendship.

Racial Justice and Peacemaking

Many white evangelicals typically take a colorblind approach to race: they treat racism as solely the problem of interpersonal bias, not as a structural or institutional issue.[37] Therefore, the responsibility of white Christians toward other races is only to show courtesy and fairness. As a consequence, the racial hierarchy and racialization process itself are left unchallenged. This postracial attitude is theologically assisted by the idea of personal salvation, personal relationship with God, and an emphasis on evangelism. "Don't dissipate any of your energies fighting race issues. Focus everything on evangelism." They focus on reconciliation over justice. Since we are all believers, our cultural differences should not matter; to be an authentic Christian is to disregard and overcome cultural and racial differences and celebrate unity in Jesus Christ.

However, just peacemaking helps to set the priority correctly: racial justice precedes racial reconciliation. In the covenantal drama (judgment and restoration), reconciliation begins with God's liberating work (justice), with shalom (the cosmic beloved community) as its goal.

The covenantal drama of liberation-restoration and just peacemaking in new covenant ethics clarifies the relationship and sequence between racial reconciliation and racial justice. This is often confusing and controversial among Christians. While both are equally important values of Christian faith, new covenant ethics specifies that putting things right or organizing a new relationship begins with justice and then moves to peacemaking.

Christians adopting a colorblind approach are typically committed to racial reconciliation over racial justice. They assert racial reconciliation as the priority of racial relationships. Evangelicals think forgiveness alone is sufficient in achieving reconcil-

37. Emerson and Smith, *Divided by Faith*, 89.

iation because that is what God did in Jesus Christ. That is, reconciliation is central to what Jesus achieved through his atoning death on the cross and is hence the heart of the gospel. Their focus is often interpersonal peace, harmony, and love rather than justice, reparation of wrongs, and equality. Some even think that demanding justice is detrimental to racial reconciliation; however, this is tantamount to glossing over past harms and ongoing suffering without reparation.

The fallacy of conservative evangelicals is that they do not attend to the existing racial hierarchy or attempt to correct it. They uphold love and peace but are not committed to repairing past wrongs, sharing power, or giving up their privilege. However, more often than not, the message of racial reconciliation by white Christians is more an expression of white fragility than a genuine concern for the biblical notion of reconciliation. Glen Stassen and David Gushee are correct in saying: "The problem is that when white evangelicals speak of forgiveness and reconciliation they normally do not do so out of the experience of solidarity with blacks in suffering for justice but instead as a substitute for that work of justice."[38]

In a covenantal framework, justice is integral to reconciliation. Reconciliation without justice is cheap or fake reconciliation. Miroslav Volf warns: "Forgiveness is not a substitute for justice."[39] In the covenant, a right relationship (righteousness) includes both justice and relational restoration (reconciliation).

Reconciliation is not a wishy-washy, feel-good relationship. Reconciliation from a biblical perspective refers not to passive absence of enmity but to an active presence of fellowship and friendship. Genuine reconciliation is impossible without the restoration of "trust," and trust is rooted in truth telling, the acknowledgment and confession of past wrongs, and reparations.[40]

Reparations

Given the racial history of the United States and its predatory nature evidenced in slavery, genocide, and segregation, racial just peacemaking requires more than publicly denouncing racism or apologizing for past wrongs. It requires reparations. As mentioned, to make racial relationship right requires repairing past wrongs and reconciling with the victims.[41] Some progressive whites think that affirmative ac-

38. Stassen and Gushee, *Kingdom Ethics*, 407.

39. Volf, *Exclusion and Embrace*, 123.

40. Truth telling was a core principle of the Truth and Reconciliation Commission in South Africa. For further information and a theological basis of the Commission, see Tutu, *No Future without Forgiveness*.

41. Jennifer Harvey's book *Dear White Christians* offers the critique of the inadequacy of a reconciliation model and compelling argument for reparation.

tion is sufficient to compensate past wrongs, even while nearly two-thirds of whites oppose it.[42]

However, this policy is not enough to repair or amend historical injustices. We need meaningful reparations for African Americans and First Nations people. Without reparations, genuine racial reconciliation is unlikely. A refusal to redress the historical will further deteriorate racial relationships. Randy Woodley firmly clarifies the responsibility of offenders for reconciliation: "Reparation . . . is the enduring effort to *make compensation* for what has been taken. Acts of reparation are unambiguous and should have a direct relationship to the offense . . . if land has been stolen, then *land plus other compensation should be given to the offended party in order to compensate for the loss of capital in the land.* . . . The weight of making reparations is on the offender. The choice of how to use the restitution is up to the offended."[43] Through reparations, a broken relationship is repaired and moves toward full restoration. Racial reconciliation without reparations is a cheap reconciliation. Reparations are consistent with the spirit of Jesus's gospel and the new covenant. We see this in Jesus's interaction with Zacchaeus (Luke 19:1–10).

There have been consistent requests for reparations. John Conyers, a late congressman from Detroit, introduced the bill HR 40 in 1989 and every year thereafter until he resigned from Congress in 2017. He named the bill HR 40 to suggest the "40 acres and a mule" that the US government had promised former slaves after the Civil War.[44]

According to Ta-Nehisi Coates, America's prosperity is tied to its history of slavery and racism.[45] Slaves were the largest property asset in the United States and helped found the American economy. Whites systemically exploited and plundered African Americans and Native Americans for their profits. The effects of slavery and segregation continue today. Racism has shaped the policies of all states in the United States, in the areas of employment, education, and housing. The laws and structures of cities are not accidental. These are premediated designs to keep African Americans out or to exploit them. Coates claims: "The legacy of slavery extends in the policy of the American government, in the policy of the states in the deep South, in the policies even of cities and states in the north long past slavery, for 100 years after. And the effects are there. And the people who suffered those effects are the people who were redlined, the people who suffered job discrimination, the people who suffered from educational discrimination are very much alive and still with us."[46]

42. Byrd, "Most White Americans Will Never Be Affected by Affirmative Action."

43. Woodley, "Reparations," 266–67.

44. Currently, Representative Jim Clyburn has proposed a similar bill called 10-20-30.

45. Coates, "The Case for Reparations."

46. Cornish, "'The Atlantic's' Ta-Nehisi Coates Builds 'A Case for Reparations.'"

Opponents point out serious logistical difficulties in determining which individuals are qualified for reparations (e.g., do people of mixed-race heritage qualify?). However, reparations do not have to be direct monetary payments to individual descendants of slaves. They can take the form of more funding for schools where minorities are in the majority, or of offering programs that empower the capability of African Americans or improve African American communities.

Reparations are necessary to move toward a liberated and reconciled future together. Churches, Christian colleges, and organizations need to be proactive on this long-overdue correction of injustice. It is encouraging that some schools are moving toward this direction.[47]

Challenges in Uprooting Racism

Both whites and people of color must work together to deconstruct the racial hierarchy and confront whiteness in critical self-reflection and moral persuasion (truth telling and collective action) in order to reconstruct our identities in the covenantal unity-in-diversity.

In racial just peacemaking, it is important to bridge a profound perception gap between whites and people of color on the reality of racism. As mentioned above, most whites typically tend to regard racism as a thing of the long-ago past, thus denying the reality of subtle and indirect forms of racism in society (especially white normativity and supremacy). They do not see the pressing need for any major reorganization of racial relationships. Whites typically believe that we are now living in a postracial (or a colorblind) society and advocate a racial melting pot as an ideal vision of society. They point out the inclusion of minority members in their institutions and the success of African American athletes and celebrities. Whites think the call of racism is an exaggerated victim play of many people of color who cannot compete with whites. They also claim that they should not be held accountable for the past wrongs of slavery and segregation done by their ancestors. Consequently, many whites consider race questions irrelevant to their lives.

Accordingly, the white threshold for racism is very high. They refuse to acknowledge that racism exists in subtle and indirect forms. Whites conceptualize racism in binary terms (racist versus nonracist) and define racism in individualistic behavioral terms. Whites think of themselves as nonracists with no further action or change required because they have not used any racist words or committed racist acts against people of color. Therefore, they endorse the idea of a postracial society.

Many whites assume that they are not racists either because they have persons of color as friends or in-laws or because they have never been involved in any racial

47. For examples, see Harris, "Higher Education's Reckoning with Slavery."

incident with people of color. However, when people of color around them never personally talk about race issues, this is a sure sign of caution for whites. As a person of color, I completely agree with DiAngelo's warning: "If racism is not a topic of discussion between a white person and a person of color who are friends, this absence of conversation may indicate a lack of cross-racial trust."[48]

Uprooting racism is difficult because racism is tied up with white racial identity. Whites need a radical reconstruction of their racial identity. Unless whites develop a new, healthy, relativized, and contextualized racial identity, they are vulnerable to white fragility and white normativity. In turn, it is difficult to dismantle white identity because it is grounded in a sense of superiority that serves as a source of self-esteem. That is, white identity is tied with human primeval emotions of security, pride, fear, anxiety, desire for recognition, and domination/superiority. Most whites refuse to abandon the white gaze and white normativity because, for them, they are evidence of their superiority. When whites lose their sense of superiority, they are psychologically vulnerable to populist demagoguery and xenophobia.

Also, fallen human nature tends to protect its own self-interest, even using unjust means unless challenged or confronted. Reinhold Niebuhr's book *Moral Man and Immoral Society* insightfully identifies the selfish human tendency to benefit from unjust social arrangements and moral self-deception—to hide the gap between individual racial bias and structural racism. Comfortable with standing at the top of the racial hierarchy, whites have no incentive to change the system that benefits them. Current existing racial hierarchy and white normativity protect and advance the self-interest of whites, hence there is little or no incentive to eradicate them.[49] Whites typically overlook or tolerate subtle racist sentiments and views for their own emotional comfort or to protect self-interest and the racial status quo.

What Can Whites Do?

Among the various actions available to whites to undo institutional racism are purposively forming interracial relationships and undertaking grassroots organizing in their communities.

Communicative Action

If whites truly want racial reconciliation and care about racial justice, they need to break white insulation and white apathy, and initiate genuine friendship with people

48. DiAngelo, *White Fragility*, 81.
49. Delgado and Stefancic, *Critical Race Theory*, 8.

of color and build solidarity with them. Interracial fellowship could help change conventional white identity based on racial superiority.

One evidence of white privilege is that whites do not have to know the histories and cultures of other races. Thus whites need to be proactive in deepening their knowledge of the history and culture of people of color.

Whites need to accept that no white institution is free from racism; even if legal segregation is abolished and racial discrimination is prohibited, informal racial hierarchy still remains and social ethos and practices are still beneficial toward whites. Through the help and leadership of people of color, whites may scrutinize themselves, their institutions, and how racism plagues and mutates the society. They need to acknowledge that they are in fact responsible for eradicating it because white racism is a white product. Truthful confession and genuine acknowledgment of past sins/guilt must occur prior to reconciliation. Specifically, antiracism workshops are very helpful to enlighten knowledge of racial history, racialization, white normativity, micro-aggressions, and white fragility.

Given past history and current privilege, it is not wise for white Christians to preach and speak of racial reconciliation and forgiveness. To do so would invite deeper suspicion because the rhetoric has been profusely used to justify racial hierarchy and pacify rightful resistance. It is ethically more appropriate for whites to advocate racial justice and show solidarity with people of color. Meanwhile, people of color can speak of the beloved community, forgiveness, and the hope of reconciliation. "In short, while black [and Native American, Latinx, and Asian American] Christians are morally entitled to emphasize the ultimate aim of reconciliation, white Christians are generally not thus entitled. Our calling is to join in the struggle for justice; only within that context can we then, later, speak credibly of reconciliation."[50]

Practicing inclusiveness and equal treatment, sharing power with people of color, and demonstrating solidarity with people of color in confronting institutional racism are critical to build trust and repair alienated relationships.

But in dismantling racism, the leadership should come from the people of color. Whites need to empty their power and empower leadership of people of color. In his parable, Jesus's depiction of a Samaritan as a moral hero was intentional. The parable describes a Samaritan as a moral hero, a benefactor, and a loving and merciful person who impeccably fulfills the demands of the second love commandment. The parable had the effect of breaking a Jewish cultural stereotype that vilified Samaritans but elevated Jews, especially priests and Levites, as the elected, moral exemplars of God. The parable was Jesus's rhetorical affirmative action that counterbalanced a skewed social perception and symbolic representation of Samaritans.

50. Stassen and Gushee, *Kingdom Ethics*, 407.

To repair a broken relationship and move toward friendship, each party needs to go an extra mile beyond what the law requires. Reconciliation requires the courage to be vulnerable (a victim forgoing individual rights through forgiveness as well as a perpetrator confronting his shame through truthful confession). The road to reconciliation leads toward Golgotha—denying oneself and carrying one's cross, as Jesus did. And it is only possible through God's grace.

Community Organizing and Nonviolence

Despite some progress, many spheres and institutions of Western society are still thoroughly tainted by racism. While they may legally and ideologically reject it, racial hierarchy is still entrenched in their social fabric. Racism, like other forms of social injustice, will not automatically or voluntarily be removed as time progresses because it is sinful human nature not to give up power and hegemony. Given the fact that whiteness has saturated Western society over the centuries, undoing it will take persistent efforts of deconstruction and reconstruction. Frederick Douglass noted that the oppressors do not voluntarily give up their power and privilege without countervailing power. Sociologist David Wellman found that "the essential feature of racism is not hostility or misperception, but rather the defense of a system from which advantage is derived on the basis of race."[51]

Racial justice is a matter not only of legislation and education but also of implementation. There is a profound gap between policies of racial justice and their implementation. The three constitutional amendments passed after the Civil War (the Thirteenth, Fourteenth, and Fifteenth Amendments) were never fully implemented until the civil rights movement had prompted massive grassroots organizing and assertion for equality. Even today, while no mainstream institution or leader would not condemn racism and would not stand for racial diversity in public, the undoing of racial hierarchy seems overly sluggish and slow. In a white hegemonic society, implementation of racial equality at the institutional and societal level is a separate task.

Diverse strategies are necessary to dismantle racism, such as introducing explicitly antiracist policies for the inclusion and equality of people of color, antiracism workshops, seminars, and cultural sensitivity training. Grassroots organizing within an institution and society is necessary to undo institutional racism. Through organizing, people of color and white people of goodwill may request the full inclusion and equality of people of color. They may request an institution to become inclusive and antiracist and to share power through the amendment of institutional policies,

51. Wellman, *Portraits of White Racism*, 210.

community standards, and laws. To do so, they may study how policies are practiced, where power is located, and what access people of color have to it. Without intentional collective efforts, white normativity and fragility do not change.

Coalition building is a concrete way to facilitate and actualize the covenantal principle of unity-in-diversity. Community organizing, especially coalition building, helps bridge the isolated divides among different racial groups and communities. Coalition helps build mutual understanding and solidarity among the participants. Without coalition building (covenanting) among people of color (victims of racism) and conscientious whites, racial justice is difficult to achieve because of the superiority of white power and its institutional controls and its divide-and-conquer tactics.

Covenant Vision for Racial Relations: Unity-in-Diversity

In working for racial justice and harmony, we need a vision and a road map. The question is, what is a relevant vision in dismantling whiteness and achieving racial justice and reconciliation? How can we build a meaningfully inclusive and egalitarian community that respects the distinctive cultural identity and racial histories of each group?

The ideas of a melting pot (a colorblind society), "multiculturalism," black-white binary, and rigid identity politics are not helpful because each leaves whiteness in place, fragmenting and potentially dividing people of color.

1. A colorblind society claims that American society is now equal and inclusive, in which everyone can freely participate. Although a colorblind society might be an ideal for a racially just society, to declare it is premature. In the current context, the idea functions more as a disguise for white normativity than as a reality. Although many people no longer use the metaphor of a melting pot, the idea of a colorblind society is not different from it. The "pot" is nothing other than "white normativity" that melts and absorbs all racial differences and particularities into whiteness, and by so doing sustains a racial hierarchy.

A covenantal approach rejects any white-centered unity or integration because this actually means the assimilation into white normativity. As an alternative to white normativity (whiteness), we need a genuinely inclusive, egalitarian, and solidaric vision of a human community.

2. The idea of multiculturalism is also limited. In the United States, cultural diversity and racial diversity are incongruent. People of color experience cognitive dissonance, for many whites affirm and celebrate cultural diversity (especially food, music, art, customs, rituals) while keeping racial hierarchy. They appropriate, utilize,

and commercialize cultural assets and heritage without permission. This affirmation of cultural diversity occurs under the rubric of multiculturalism (which in turn is prompted by globalization and corporate interest in commodifying what is "new" and unfamiliar) while not addressing racial inequality.

3. A rigid form of identity politics is ultimately detrimental to the cause of full liberation and reconciliation. It may fall under the divide-and-conquer strategy of whites. In fighting against white racism, a reified form of identity politics that is narrow in its racial self-interest is to be rejected. An essentialized form of identity politics is counterproductive in overcoming racism because of its tendency toward fragmentation, division, and enmity. The danger of identity politics is that it may lead to the balkanization of the republic. More importantly, it is necessary to bring together diverse racial groups into a new form of solidarity because one group alone can never achieve racial justice and equality. All groups, while advocating for their distinctive concerns, work together under a shared democratic framework and values in seeking the vision of common flourishing.

4. A black-white binary is also limited because it excludes other races and their suffering, histories, and experiences. For example, Asian American experiences of racism are different from those of African Americans. The binary is too narrow to address complex racial dynamics and the torturous history of racialization in the United States. The binary could triangulate racial relationships and further white strategies of divide-and-conquer, resulting in reductionism and distortion. Racism and colonial history did not stop with one group of people of color. A dichotomous black-white approach to racism is no longer relevant in a radically pluralistic society. It inevitably creates a barrier for others to enter into meaningful conversations and actions on race. It perpetuates the narrative of the forever foreignness of Asian Americans and the marginalization of Latinx. This binary approach turns Asian Americans into the middleman minority and inadvertently plays into the model minority myth. It turns Latinx into invaders. When the binary is insisted upon, it may tempt Asian Americans to "be like whites," aspiring to their status, power, and privilege. It is not merely a matter of attention, recognition, or severity of victimization.

New covenant ethics offers a plausible framework in conceiving and imagining a constructive relationship among different racial and ethnic (and religious) groups. New covenant ethics finds in Jesus's shalom community a rich, diverse, and rainbow community that respects diversity of cultures in the solidarity of humanity in God. Paul's ecclesial vision and Martin Luther King Jr.'s idea of the beloved community (later rephrased as the "great world house") embody this vision of an inclusive human community where diversity is celebrated and solidarity is affirmed. "Rather than uplifting one race and ethnicity as the ultimate image of God, we must establish churches that honor the breadth of God's image found in a range of cultural expressions."[52]

The covenantal principle of unity-in-diversity addresses these questions. Covenant pertains to organizing mutually committed relationships among different individuals and groups according to the principles of justice and peace in God. Covenant offers a way to recognize the cultural and racial particularities of each group without disregarding our solidarity and unity. The interracial relationships can be thought of as interracial covenant relationships. While celebrating a distinctive culture, history, and experience, they seek the common good and unity among diverse groups through communicative engagements.

To relate to people of other races covenantally is to recognize the distinctive history and culture of each group and to legitimate their concerns rather than treating them as secondary suffering. One group's justice cannot be achieved at the expense of another. Simultaneously, the ignored past wrongs and ongoing suffering of a particular race group (e.g., criminalization of black and brown bodies, police brutality, exclusion of Asian Americans) should be communally addressed by all groups.

Covenanting is a way to affirm solidarity and particularity among different racial groups. Practically, this means that every racial group enters a covenantal relationship with others by engaging with them "communally" and "communicatively." As mentioned, each racial group acknowledges the intrinsic unity, solidarity, and interdependence of its group with others, and their commitment to the common good. Through communicative engagements, each group enters into a democratic, equal, and reciprocal relationship with each other. In a covenant framework, their relationships are interracial and intercultural, not paternal, hierarchal, multicultural, or binary. Each group keeps a distinctiveness.

King's perspective on interracial relationships is congruent with the new covenantal ethics that I lay out here. King believed that the destiny of African Americans was tied to other racial groups and humanity itself. In his coalition-building work during the civil rights movement, King regarded different racial and cultural groups as "partners in power."[53] He said: "A true alliance is based upon some self-interest of each component group and a common interest into which they merge."[54]

By listening to the voices and perspectives of others, we correct our narrow tribalistic or stereotypical perspectives of them. Through communicative interactions, our racial identities are transfigured and transvalued into a creedal identity and discovery of others. To be covenantal is to make space for others by imitating God, who made

52. Rah, *The Next Evangelicalism*, 85.

53. King, *Where Do We Go from Here*, 55.

54. King, *Where Do We Go from Here*, 159.

space for us in Jesus. Volf notes: "The faith in Jesus Christ, who made our cause his cause, frees us from pursuing our interests only, and creates in us the space for the interests of others."[55] Communication may not immediately lead to agreement, but it reduces bias and misunderstandings and expands the space for self and others. This tills the ground for deeper bonding and entering into "enlarged thinking."[56]

Conclusion

The new covenant embodies a new vision of humanity in the context of God's creation (it is thus not anthropocentric), which is egalitarian (thus not hierarchal), reciprocal (thus not individualistic), and pluralistic (thus not monopolizing or binary). As the new covenant indicates, this restructuring is ecological (thus restoring the bond between humanity and the land) and eschatological (thus not utopian, romantic, or moralistic but futuristic and empirical). It prioritizes sharing over domination, care over control, reciprocity over autonomy, and solidarity over self-sufficiency. It radically directs a conversion from the whiteness and neoliberal capitalism that still epitomize instrumental and predatory attitudes toward the land and other people.

US society is still a racialized society, and racism still manifests at every level of our social life: personal, cultural, institutional, and societal. Racism is a white habit. A habit does not easily go away. Racial relationships are constantly contested, negotiated, and aligned for recognition and privilege among different groups.

Because of the deep-seated nature of racial hierarchy and racialization, racism exists by mutating and adapting to changing power relationships and social situations. Only consistently and intentionally antiracist commitment and solidaric action will overcome racism. The racial hierarchy that glorifies whiteness is the dark principality that divides us and impedes reconciliation. Like transforming a long-established dietary habit, dismantling racial hierarchy takes time. But a simple passage of time does not lead to dismantling. It requires a constant work of vigilance, interracial exchanges, prophetic criticism, and collective action. Christians of all races/ethnicities should work together to undo racial hierarchy and build in its place the structures of justice, equality, and community of friendship.

White churches need to show leadership in dismantling racism in society rather than being cesspools of racial bias. The close tie between Christianity and racism discredits the authenticity of Christian claims and undermines the integrity of the gospel. This is one of the reasons for the silent exodus of young people from the

55. Volf, *Exclusion and Embrace*, 215.

56. Cf. Volf, *Exclusion and Embrace*, 212–13.

church. New covenant ethics is antiracist in its justice orientation; it is for reconciliation in its peacemaking; it is inclusive and egalitarian, and it affirms diverse voices. It encourages sharing power and empowers the marginalized.

Racial just peacemaking is a long, treacherous journey filled with anger, guilt, suspicion, doubt, and despair. While remembering the painful past of slavery, segregation, and discrimination, we should never lose hope for a new and just community. It is encouraging that there is growing awareness among young people about the necessity of reparations, friendship, and courageous acts of solidarity in order to achieve meaningful reconciliation and racial justice.

CHAPTER 18

Sex and Marriage

"Have you not read that the one who made them at the beginning 'made them male and female,' and said, 'For this reason a man shall leave his father and mother and be joined to his wife, and the two shall become one flesh'? So they are no longer two, but one flesh. Therefore what God has joined together, let no one separate. . . .

"For there are eunuchs who have been so from birth, and there are eunuchs who have been made eunuchs by others, and there are eunuchs who have made themselves eunuchs for the sake of the kingdom of heaven. Let anyone accept this who can."

—Matthew 19:4–6, 12

Individual intentions and interests, desires and feelings are not essentially private but tied to language and culture and thus inherently susceptible of interpretation, discussion, and change.

—Thomas McCarthy, "Translator's Introduction"

Humans are passionate, and sex constitutes a crucial part of human passion. While sex does not define or determine all that a human is, it is nonetheless an undisputable aspect of human life. Along with hunger and desire for safety, sex is the most powerful human passion. It attracts, enriches, energizes, and destroys humans.

However, the meaning and ethics of sex are socially constructed, and the cultural and personal meaning of sex is radically changing, reflecting the post-Christian era of the United States. The pervasiveness of premarital sex, the increase in cohabitation, and the wide use of pornography among young people, including Christians, indicate that much of the culture has moved away from traditional sexual ethics grounded in a biblical perspective.

The crisis of Christian sexual ethics comes from an altered cultural milieu and social conditions, assumptions, and expectations. Our understanding and practice of sex are now shaped by individualistic moral ethos stemming from the sexual revolution of the 1960s. Ongoing advances in medical technologies (contraception, abortion) have granted people greater control over their sex lives, freeing them from the possibility of pregnancy. Sex has been decoupled from procreation. On the other hand, Hollywood and social media have effectively changed the social scripts around sex.[1] They have mystified the power of sex and rendered romantic sexual relationships as therapeutic, fulfilling, and redemptive.

The new social-economic reality under neoliberalism also affects sexual morality. Delayed marriages and a long period of adult single life also encourage premarital sexual activities; marriage is postponed or avoided altogether. People increasingly believe that a single life without sex (celibacy) is unrealistic in a society where sexual stimulation is relentlessly ubiquitous. There is growing reluctance about marriage among young people even while they long for stability, because of the burden of binding obligations and the fear of complicated divorce.

Thus, more and more people are living as singles but not without sex. This is the result of both individual choice and social conditioning. The contemporary demise of community, fragmentation, and utilitarian transactional relationships create the conditions for many to live as singles. However, while enjoying the benefits and freedom of being single, they are also isolated. Living without sex is emotionally difficult.

The current social scripts on sex are highly individualistic, contractual, and pleasure seeking. These scripts are widely circulated and reinforced among friends and peers. Sex is treated as a private individual possession. Thus, how to use it is a personal decision. Fulfilling sexual desire is integral to an individual's personal (emotional and psychological) fulfillment. Enjoying sexual pleasure is a human entitlement; that is, everyone has a right to have sex. As long as it does not harm others, sexual ethics is a private matter, not the business of society or church.

Expressive individualism, supported by neoliberalism, sanctifies and glorifies personal desires; indeed, the "expressive" part primarily pertains to desires. Expressive individualism protects the unhampered expression of individual desires as long as it does not harm others or impede others' expressions. In our cultural liturgy of desire, where self-fulfillment is a cultural slogan, to suppress and frustrate "natural"

1. Caroline J. Simon's book *Bringing Sex into Focus* is helpful in identifying six "lenses" through which to understand sex and sexuality: covenantal, procreative, expressive, romantic, power, and plain sex.

sexual desires is regarded as oppressive or harmful to oneself[2]—self-unfulfillment at best, and the source of mental illness at worst.

Among young singles, premarital sexual interactions are acceptable when done consensually and safely. Casual sex and experimental sex are no longer a major concern if sex partners are consensual. Free from any commitment and obligations, sex is increasingly casual and practiced for mutual pleasure and self-release. Many young adults have sex without any intention of a long-term relationship. As many as 90 to 95 percent of Americans have had premarital sex.[3] Empirical studies show that more people today are willing to experiment with open marriage, open sexual relationships, and sex with multiple partners (polyamory), while longing for a stable, trusted relationship is a still noticeable undercurrent.

Sex is also commodified for mass consumption. Neoliberal consumerism capitalizes on expressive individualism and pleasure seeking. Among human desires, sexual desire (which can be intense, powerful, almost unceasing) is an easy target for business for profit gain. Sexual stimuli are ubiquitous online and off-line, and sexual attraction/appeal is transformed into a consumer product. Our perception of sex and sexual desire is "disciplined" by neoliberal consumerism: twenty-four-hour free online pornography, prostitution, strip bars, sex toys, sex robots, etc.

Sex in the Church

The massive cultural shift of sex ethics is greatly affecting churches. The high view of sexual freedom in popular culture radically clashes with the traditional moral teachings of Christianity. This cultural trend undermines and threatens traditional Christian sex ethics. What is truly troubling is that traditional sexual ethics has lost its authority and appeal among young Christians. Biblical teachings and norms (the virtue of chastity, the practice of celibacy, and the prohibition of premarital sex, cohabitation, same-sex marriage, and extramarital relationships) are being rejected and replaced by the secular sexual ethics of personal pleasure, relational satisfaction, and covenant bonding between same-sex couples. The sexual scandals and abuses of both Catholic priests and Protestant clergymen (pedophile priests and predatory megachurch pastors) further discredit Christian sexual ethics and its last hanging threads of moral authority.

Believing that a cultural shift is irreversible and that traditional sexual ethics is overly restrictive, some liberal Christians call for a radical revision of Christian sexual ethics

2. Cf. Michel Foucault's critique of the "repressive hypothesis" in *A History of Sexuality*, 1:15–50.
3. Regnerus and Uecker, *Premarital Sex in America*, 59.

(making them more open, permissive, and realistic), while more conservative Christians double down on biblical teachings (treating compromising traditional sexual ethics as tantamount to moral apostasy). It should be acknowledged that many churches have utterly failed in engaging with the cultural shift and secular sex ethics by insisting on a narrow legalistic message that lacks cultural nuances and complexities.

Facing the cultural shift of sex ethics, many feel powerless. Thus, many remain silent and afraid to upset people. Many young pastors are frustrated, for teaching a traditional form of sexual ethics is like barking at a tree. Afraid of being called "outdated," young Christians have abandoned the church's teachings on sex and have adopted secular sexual ethics, which teaches that safe, consensual sex between adult singles is acceptable.

It is very clear that churches cannot avoid this issue; it is too important and too powerful to avoid open conversations. It is time for churches to revisit and renew their sexual ethics. They cannot behave like ostriches burying their heads in the sand. The cultural trends and secular cultural view of sex raise several unavoidable questions: When increasing numbers of adults in the United States remain lifelong singles, what does it mean that sex belongs to marriage? Should sex be tied (restricted) to marriage? What is the role and contribution of marriage for human flourishing and the common good?

This chapter studies covenantal sexual ethics. The Bible explicitly denotes covenant as the foundational framework for sex and marriage. A covenantal metaphor of marriage is indelible in the Bible. Indeed, sex and marriage serve as key metaphors of a covenantal relationship with God in the Bible (between Yahweh and Israel, between Christ and the church). In particular, this chapter examines premarital sex, divorce, and same-sex marriage from a covenantal perspective, exploring how to bridge the gap between popular culture and biblical teachings of sexual ethics. This chapter asks: What is a covenantal model of sex and marriage? How is it different from a secular liberal model, the contractual model of a nuclear family, and the Catholic sacramental model? What does sex mean in a covenantal relationship? How does covenant yield a better or deeper understanding of sex? What does Scripture show and tell about the purposes of sex? What is the end goal that defines what it is? What constitutes marriage? With a deeper understanding of human desire around sex and the sexual relationship, I claim that new covenant ethics is a third way that goes beyond legalism and sexual libertarianism.

A Cultural View of Sex

Our view and practice of sex is not neutral; it is socially and culturally defined. "Current sexual ethics" is not completely objective. It is more the product of expressive individualism and a hedonistic culture that prioritizes individual desires and self-gratification.[4] Neoliberalism overpromises the satisfaction of desires, and sex is one such promise. Using its logic of demonization (self-blaming and other blaming), it encourages a person to keep trying until one finds the right person rather than focusing on virtue formation and maturity of the self. It is a serious distortion of human moral reality.

Consensual Sex

Secular ethics takes a strong contractual form. Consent is its only relevant ethical criterion. Yet while consent is a necessary criterion in a Christian perspective, consent alone is too narrow to serve as a moral framework for sex. Its ascendance as the dominant criterion reflects a contractual approach to sex. In this framework, consensual sex is permitted for the self-gratification of each person without any commitment or relationship. The scope of consensual sex and its contractual nature could easily expand to sexual activities involving more than two people.

In addition, a sexual partner could give consent for the wrong reasons. Consent may be given "in a context of rivalry, fear of not being accepted, manipulation for self-satisfaction and eventual abandonment."[5] Sometimes consent is something one buys quid pro quo, as in prostitution. Without the guarantee of true equality and reciprocity, free consent in sex could be something psychologically coerced or given out of desperation.

Viewed in the framework of love, justice, and power, consent is the requisite in order for justice to be met in a sexual act. However, it is not sufficient. In addition, sex could be a power act in order to entice and achieve one's nonsexual goals. True sex should fulfill justice (consent), love (union), and power (equality).

As a form of human relationship, sex is more than an individual decision; it is social, economic, and not completely free from power dynamics. As we are social beings influenced by and influential in a web of relationships, no decision is made in a vacuum.

Men and women approach and experience sex differently. For women, the primary objective of sex is not always sexual pleasure. Men tend to engage in sex to gratify their sexual desires, while women have sex to acquire desired resources (e.g., status, attention, self-esteem) or emotional connection with their partner.[6] Sexual

4. One's attitudes and decisions on sexual relationships are not completely free from economic considerations. For example, in Greco-Roman society, arranged marriages were a tool of political and economic power. Consider also the roles of slavery and temple prostitution in the sexual economy!

5. Stassen and Gushee, *Kingdom Ethics*, 292.

6. Regnerus and Uecker, *Premarital Sex in America*, 53.

double standards still remain strong in society. Women are still more vulnerable in sexual relationships than men. Compared to men, the sexual standard is still unfavorable to them. Sexual acts, despite their consent, inevitably involve more risk for them. That is why women play the role of gatekeepers in sexual relationships.[7]

Casual Sex

Sex cannot be conducted in a cavalier manner. Sex could result either in deeper intimacy and affection or hurt and alienation. The idea of casual sex (no strings attached) flies against basic psychological experience and knowledge. Sexual acts cannot be separated from a person's sense of self. "To attempt to separate the sex act from the personhood of the participant, then, is doomed to failure. Instead, the participants must engage in the act cognizant of what its specific act of sex is intended to declare."[8]

Casual sex in a hookup culture is not beneficial because it intentionally brackets commitment and trust for the pursuit of a momentary transaction; devoid of trust and commitment, sex could be manipulative and emotionally deceptive even if done consensually. Sex can be done to meet other emotional needs and desires, for example, as a desperate way to seek approval from another party, as a way to control the other party, or as a vehicle to find what we are missing in life by impressing others.

The norm of consent is tenuous. The rule of consent and the desire for self-gratification do not always easily cohere. Under the powerful force of self-gratification, consent could easily be nominal in certain cases or manipulated, as seen on college campuses. As sex is highly intense and intimate, it can harm the involved parties, especially weaker ones.

Similarly, the widespread presence of pornography and the use of sex robots reveal the tenuous nature of sexual relationships: even consensual sex does not satisfy deep human relational needs. Today, ironically, many people across generations are increasingly seeking sexual gratification through pornography. The cultural prevalence of pornography is the confluence of two major cultural forces around sex: expressive individualism and consumerism. It is self-reclusive, narcissistic, and hedonistic. It is evidence of the fetishization (thingification) of the self and the instrumentalization (commodification) of women. The thriving of the porn industry colludes with a neoliberal society just as sex trafficking, prostitution, and pedophilia victimize poor young women and children.

Self-centered, self-indulging sex could ultimately be self-draining, shaming, and alienating. Promiscuous, irresponsible sex can result in hurt, shame, and the lower-

7. Regnerus and Uecker, *Premarital Sex in America*, 57.

8. Grenz, *Sexual Ethics*, 81.

ing of self-esteem. Sex pursued in the current social scripts of self-gratification and contractualism is more likely to lead to self-alienation and other-objectification, fetishization rather than flourishing. The drama of Adam and Eve in Genesis 3 tells us something profound about ourselves: in our selfish love and ambition, we are wounded, exiled, and alienated persons driven to find reconciliation, a faithful community, and mutual affirmation that can overcome our alienation and isolation.

Sex cannot be a solution to individual emotional problems, even if it gives momentary distraction. Self-oriented sex could gravely hurt the partner and engender distrust. The recent movie *Don Jon* shows that good sex is more than a momentary, instant experience of self-gratification; it requires commitment and trust. The popular culture, under the influence of neoliberal commodification of sex, still tends to idealize sex rather than honestly confronting the consequences of bad sex, which leaves behind shame, self-immolation, and distrust, sometimes betrayal.

Consensual sex *is not bad, but it is not good enough*. Sex should be consensual at minimum, but not all consensual sex contributes (even with immediate physical gratification) to human flourishing.[9] There is a deep hunger for good sex. But good sex is not just about sexual satisfaction. Love and sexual gratification are two different entities; even when gratified, participants could be still thirsty for love. Sexual desire is often completely self-centered and self-enclosed (curved toward the self), while love is other-regarding.

New Covenant Ethics

The Bible, in general, defines a covenant relationship as the appropriate moral framework for sex.[10] A covenantal relationship helps to properly channel sexual desires toward human flourishing as God intended. Covenantal sex is relational and reciprocal, neither individualistic nor utilitarian. Sexual intercourse indicates the union of two differentiated persons. It is the most visible and physically explicit display of unity-in-diversity. Covenant offers a much deeper understanding of sex. From a covenantal perspective, sexual ecstasy is not the final end but a conduit for entering into a deeper chamber of mutual encounter and love. The three dialectics of covenant help to clarify the nature of sex from a covenantal perspective.

1. *Unilateral-bilateral*. Like all other Christian actions, sex should be guided by God's self-giving love toward us. Sex is God's unique gift; hence, our use of it should

9. Sprinkle, "What Is a Christian Sexual Ethic?"

10. While it is true that noncovenantal forms of sex, for example, polygamy and concubinage, were practiced by patriarchs and kings in the OT, Gen. 1–2 and the NT define marriage as a covenantal union between a wife and a husband.

be responsive (responsible) to God's grace, to our partner, and to our community. The body belongs to God, together with its desires. Our body is not merely the mass of various desires but the temple of the Spirit.

> Do you not know that whoever is united to a prostitute becomes one body with her? For it is said, "The two shall be one flesh." But anyone united to the Lord becomes one spirit with him. Shun fornication! Every sin that a person commits is outside the body; but the fornicator sins against the body itself. Or do you not know that your body is a temple of the Holy Spirit within you, which you have from God, and that you are not your own? For you were bought with a price; therefore glorify God in your body. (1 Cor. 6:16–20)

Paul's message is that our body is not our own but "bought with a price." Indeed, the body and spirit are inextricable; the one who is joined to the Lord becomes one spirit with him, just as the one who is joined to a prostitute becomes one body with her. Our body and the Spirit are now in solidarity. The body belongs to the Spirit. Sexual immorality that misuses our body offends the Spirit. To sanctify our body, the Spirit affirms, convicts, nudges, guides, and ennobles our desires. Sexual relationship or our use of sex should be attuned with God's covenantal design for humans and its gift character.

2. *Communal-communicative.* Sex is communal and communicative. God's declaration of "one flesh" of the first couple in the creation covenant points toward the principle of unity-in-diversity. It describes the sexual union that fulfills both individuality and solidarity, communicative freedom and communal bond. Covenantal sex is more than exchange based on temporary consent. The distinction cannot be clearer. Covenantal sex is not for self-gratification but for union through mutual giving. In unity-in-diversity (sexual differentiation), two persons become one body when actualized by sex. A mysterious emotional/psychic bonding occurs in sex, and it can be blissful and life renewing.

The ecstasy and joy that sexual union brings in marriage are far more than sensual gratification, release, or scintillation. For Christians, covenantal sex in God is a feast of *koinōnia*; it elevates both parties to a different level of mutual knowledge, friendship, and union. Free self-giving and other-receiving take place in sexual intercourse. The union encompasses every dimension of our existence: body, mind, emotion, and spirit.

3. *Memory-hope.* Finally, to enter sexual union is not only to share life fellowship but also to commit to a shared journey toward the future. It is neither completely biological, nor is its purpose entirely private to the two persons. It seeks shalom

of each person and a community. It is eschatological; the partners grow together toward deeper union in mutual trust, respect, and care, and work to expand God's shalom through their shared life that is a blessing to others.

Theological Meaning of Sex

Sex has a profound theological meaning in the Bible. As sex brings about the unity of bodies and emotions between two persons, sexual union is a sacrament of communion that covenant seeks to fulfill. Covenantal sex is a sacrament that points toward divine love and shalom. It was later taken up by Paul to describe a profound union between Jesus Christ and the church.

In the Bible, sex (and marriage) was one of the primary metaphors used to describe a covenantal relationship between God and God's people. Covenant fidelity between God and humans was frequently compared to a marital relationship (exclusive sexual relationship) between a husband and a wife. Breaking fidelity with God through idolatry is compared to adultery in the Bible (Jer. 3:8–9; 5:7; 23:14; Ezek. 16:32; 23:37; Hos. 1:2; 2:2; James 4:4).

The ecstasy of full bodily communion is the emblem of the mystery of Trinitarian *perichōrēsis*. In its full inclusion of the physical dimension, sexual union is the apex of human communion. Humans can partake in the mystery of divine *perichōrēsis* and foretaste the joy and blissfulness of divine-human communion that the covenant promises. Paul sees that our marital unions and our union with Christ are inseparable (Eph. 5:22–33). "Sexual intimacy in marriage gives us something like a momentary glimpse of our future ecstasy. It is a fleeting and shadowy foretaste of the social intimacy we will experience in the age to come, even though sex itself will pass away. . . . This new emphasis in the New Testament relativizes the importance of marriage and sexual intimacy because our future destiny so completely overwhelms all of our present sexual longing."[11]

Sexual desire is intense and sexual intercourse offers a powerful experience, but it is a shadow of the deeper mystery of the communion of the triune God. Sarah Coakley claims that sex is one of several human desires.[12] Divine desire is more fundamental than sex; the Spirit both stokes and constrains desire! "Our experience of romantic love, sexual desire, and all forms of beauty . . . is testimony to our ultimate desire for God."[13]

11. Jonathan Grant, *Divine Sex*, 147.

12. Coakley, *God, Sexuality, and the Self*; Coakley, *The New Asceticism*.

13. Jonathan Grant, *Divine Sex*, 153.

Sex and Virtue Formation

Sex cannot be cavalierly treated as a momentary activity for emotional release or fun; sex has profound impact, changing us. Our treatment of the other party in sex shapes our character. Sex as a social practice of desire inevitably shapes our disposition, virtue, and character powerfully. Sex is a form of exchange—a communication and communion of bodies. The insights of depth psychology and moral experiences tell us that "how we relate our inner selves to other persons is what shapes us as well as defiles us (Mark 7:21), and sex surely does relate our inner selves to other persons: this is the realistic biblical-Hebraic understanding of one-flesh union (1 Cor 6:12–20; Gen 2:24). We become who we are in the way we relate to others in our practices, and this is true at depths we cannot control in our sexual relating."[14]

When a person uses sex only for self-gratification, it reinforces selfish and egoistic dispositions and will likely inflict emotional hurt on the partner. Sex is never mere sex. Every intentional act influences an actor, but sex is more so because sex is a unique communicative act involving the body, emotions, and will. Even casual sex communicates our deepest selves; consensual, nonmonetary sex has a bonding effect between partners because our deepest selves are exchanged.

Good sex, as the union of two persons, involves an emotional and personal commitment and mutual trust. From a covenantal perspective, there is no bodily union without emotional and spiritual union. Good sex requires maturity—not only physical maturity but also emotional and moral maturity—for sex is not merely physical; it is emotional, psychological, and spiritual. Maturity means the ability to understand the purpose of sex, to respect and care for the other party, and to behave responsibly toward oneself and the other. Only mature people can have a mature sexual relationship. Sanctified sex involves a long moral process.

Criteria of Covenantal Sex

New covenant ethics offers certain criteria of covenantal sex. In addition to consent and relational knowledge between the two partners, sex should be done with equality and respect of the other. It should involve integrity such as truth telling, transparency, love, faithfulness, and enduring loyalty. Covenant relationship does not guarantee that every sex act is good and perfect. But these criteria are conducive to good sex,[15] and they overlap with covenantal values (chap. 7). The criteria are

14. Stassen and Gushee, *Kingdom Ethics*, 292.

15. Christian ethicists have developed the criteria for a desirable form of sex. For example, Margaret Farley proposes seven principles: do no unjust harm, free consent, mutuality, equality,

necessary to protect the partners because sex entails vulnerability, as one gives the most intimate self to the other. Casual sex, typically devoid of these qualities, cannot fully achieve the purpose of sex.

One may claim that premarital sex in some instances could meet the requirement of covenant. Consensual sex is often confused with covenantal sex. However, the two are very different, just as contract and covenant are different. Covenant sex always includes moral criteria (norms) that exceed mere consent between parties. These norms are not of human origin (though they are always interpreted in particular cultural contexts) but begin with God's will. For example, consensual sex is possible with three or four adults. Covenantal sex involves more than just a romantic feeling.

There is premarital sex that may lead to cohabitation, which then leads to marriage on the basis of an enduring commitment and deepening bond. Similarly, some cohabitation may have all three components (justice-consent, reciprocity, and love), or be moving in that direction, but it is not sufficient to be fully covenantal. It still hinges on individualistic consent and not the public good. Covenantal sex is both personal and public; it is based on intimacy and personal knowledge, but it is also organized into an institution that is committed to exclusive relationships. Covenant becomes the foundation for marriage and family through institutionalization. Because of the public nature of covenant, sex must protect a socially weaker party (often women) from the abuse/misuse of a stronger party (typically men).

As the communion of two persons, sex requires full commitment and vulnerability. These are ultimately protected by exclusive loyalty to one another. Without exclusive loyalty, complete vulnerability and commitment are not possible. Without the protection of marriage, the bond is not stable, and any kind of relational breach deeply hurts both parties. As a public institution, marriage provides each party the stability and predictability of relationship. Marriage, as a covenantal ritual, publicly declares a lifelong companionship and the ecstasy of sexual union. It institutionalizes the exchange of deepest emotions, thoughts, ideas, material goods, and bodies.

Marriage has public implications. God declared: "Therefore a man leaves his father and his mother and clings to his wife, and they become one flesh" (Gen. 2:24). New covenant ethics rejects the private/public dichotomy that treats sex and marriage as purely private. Rather, it approaches sex and marriage in the context of God's shalom. Sexual union is the height of a covenantal bonding experience between humans, and covenant bonding in sex constitutes the most basic fabric of the community: family.

---

commitment, fruitfulness, and social justice. Farley, *Just Love*. These are all relational rather than biological, thus pointing toward the covenantal nature of sexual union.

It is a shared truth that the stability of sex and marriage is crucial for the moral and psychological formation of children. "Children conceived outside of marriage are at risk of abandonment, neglect or violent death, and the emotions/moral development of children caught in a home characterized by marital infidelity is likely to be hindered."[16] The government, the church, and other institutions cannot replace a good family. No amount of money can achieve what a stable family alone can do. No matter how much the cultural view of sex and sexual ethics changes, this remains true.[17]

A loving family is a great refuge and comfort in a fluid world, just as good friendships are for individuals in a lonely society. Marriage does not solve all human problems, but a stable marriage is indispensable for the flourishing of children. While the desire of singles and same-sex couples to have their own biological children is understandable, the decision should not be based solely on their individual wishes or desires. Rather, the well-being of children should be the priority.[18]

Discipleship and Sexual Ethics: Condemn or Condone?

How can we uphold biblical sexual ethics against secular sexual ethics that condones casual sex, pornography, and other practices without being legalistic? How can we communicate the validity of covenantal sex with sufficient sensibility to the generations who have already adopted secular sexual ethics? How can we help teens and young adults understand and practice covenantal sex ethics in this utilitarian and hedonistic culture?

First and foremost, churches must engage in a major perspectival and attitudinal change when approaching sex ethics. Rather than judging, churches may look at sex in a broad social context that includes human brokenness, economic strain, and deep desires for relationship. As we see in the cohabitation of young people today, living together is not merely a matter of sexual desire, but financial considerations and emotional stability are also involved.

Currently, there is a glaring gap between "what is" and "what ought to be" regarding sexual ethics, and it cannot be easily bridged. It seems that only open, patient, and genuine communicative engagement and care can help bridge the gap. Rather than treating sex as a danger or a taboo, or leaving the issue completely to private decisions, churches need to actively engage with this topic by creating an open and

16. Stassen and Gushee, *Kingdom Ethics*, 295.

17. See Dawn, *Sexual Character*, part 2.

18. This concern is valid, particularly given the spreading practice of surrogacy. However, the role of single adults and same-sex couples in adoption and fostering should also be considered in providing nurture and protection for many children in need of a home. Song, *Covenant and Calling*.

safe environment for conversations among young members. Through this, young members may develop mature ideas and perspectives on sex. Churches should offer or strongly encourage families to get sex education.

Churches may acknowledge that sexual sins are not special or distinctive from other kinds of sins. However, instead of insisting on narrow and legalistic sexual ethics that even their own members fail to live out, churches need to demonstrate the mystery and beauty of sexual union based on covenantal bonding. They should offer good examples of the beauty and blessing of covenant sex in a committed spousal relationship. This task is not as difficult as it may sound. After all, people's ideas of ideal sexual relationships are congruent with a covenantal vision of sex and marriage. People look for trust, reciprocity, genuine transparency, and complete commitment in a romantic relationship. Human nature is relational and interdependent, seeking trusted bonds and relationships of mutual care and loyalty. Church may help people find covenantal values that strengthen marriage: gratitude, truthfulness, compassion, justice, and solidarity.

This means that churches take a pastoral-pedagogical approach and focus on the moral formation of their members. Churches can be pastoral without compromising their core biblical convictions on sex, that is, neither condemning nor condoning it. In particular, as churches today are losing their moral authority over their members' sexual ethics, their ministry will be more effective through inductive and dialogical care than through a judgmental approach. They should see sexual ethics as more a matter of maturity and growth—sanctification—than of deontological legalism.

A covenantal view of sex requires a higher standard from church members than does the view of society. However, we should always approach sex pastorally without losing compassionate hearts and moral convictions. Sex is covenantal, neither casual nor merely consensual. It belongs to a lifelong monogamous covenantal relationship. But we cannot achieve this maturity immediately. Just as a human's covenantal relationship with God goes through many ups and downs to reach maturity, covenantal sex is not automatically actualized by the institution of marriage. Virtue/character formation and maturity are needed for self-control. The goal is restoration, not condemnation. Christian sanctification is guided by the law, but the law alone cannot achieve it. Individuals should voluntarily accept the law. The development of identity and the growth of virtues are necessary. To be a spiritually and morally mature Christian takes time, but this course is far from a straight line. In the current cultural milieu, patience is necessary even through the relapses, mistakes, and trials of some young members.

This pastoral-pedagogical posture was at the heart of Jesus's approach toward the marginalized and the outcasts of his time. Jesus's relationship with outcasts, sinners, tax collectors, and prostitutes offers good insights on understanding the nature of pastoral care and accommodation. Just as God acted for broken humanity (the first dialectic), Jesus approached them with a deep sense of compassion rather than an attitude of vindictive moralism. Rather than judging them, Jesus communally and communicatively engaged them (e.g., the Samaritan woman, Zacchaeus). Jesus approached them more as a friend than as a moral teacher, built a trusted relationship with them, and helped them to see a better, deeper, and nobler truth and life promised in God.

Jesus's interaction with the Samaritan woman (John 4:7–26) exhibits such an attitude. While already knowing the woman's tortuous history of marriage and sexual life, Jesus neither condemned her nor condoned her behavior; through patient and engaging conversation, he pointed her to a better way of life that he himself embodies and satisfied her deeper thirst.

Likewise, Jesus's table fellowship with outcasts beseeches us to take a patient pastoral heart toward others' brokenness. Jesus helped people grow and mature in their faith journeys. We need to take the humble attitude of "growing or journeying together" rather than legalistic judgment because the goal is restoration and shalom. Fully and compassionately attending to human brokenness, a pedagogical approach is futuristic but not antinomian, empowering but not condoning immorality. It focuses on people's moral capabilities. Such an attitude is pulled by hope (the third dialectic) and remembers God's own patience toward us in delivering us—waiting for our growth.

Such a posture requires "patience" and perseverance in our relationships. It demonstrates grace and love without completely surrendering personal responsibility or the task and communicative dimensions. We need to be liberated from culture's seductive powers and overpromises on sex and be restored to the mysterious union and fullness of sex that God has promised. As God has given sex as a gift, God can restore it in Jesus.

The vision of covenantal sex still holds; God's forgiveness cannot be abused or reduced to "cheap grace." It is always a costly forgiveness, and it is for our well-being. God's unconditional love is not purposeless, but purpose-driven and oriented toward our ongoing spiritual and moral growth in conformity to Jesus.

Divorce

Matthew 5:31–32 and Matthew 19:3–9 disclose that Jesus has a very high view of marriage and a stringent bar for divorce. Divorce is not allowed except in cases of infidelity. In a society where more than half of all marriages end up in divorce, his teaching may look irrelevant. "It was also said, 'Whoever divorces his wife, let him give her a certificate of divorce.' But I say to you that anyone who divorces his wife, except on the ground of unchastity, causes her to commit adultery; and whoever marries a divorced woman commits adultery" (Matt. 5:31–32).

However, this is not the whole picture. Jesus's teaching on divorce should be interpreted in the context of a particular cultural context and his covenant renewal (the new covenant). In Jesus's time, a Jewish man had the privilege of unilaterally divorcing his wife without her consent. Jesus's purpose in the passage was to make it harder for a husband to divorce his wife. Prior to the Mosaic law, a man simply had to send his wife away and declare that she was no longer his wife.

Jesus's view of marriage is liberative and restorative. It is liberative in its emphasis on freedom, equal rights, and reciprocity between the spouses, and it is restorative in its aim to restore a just, fair, and loving relationship in marriage. In his covenantal renewal, Jesus restores God's original intention for marriage.

In light of Jesus's covenantal renewal, Deuteronomy 24:1 is solely androcentric; it violates the spirit of reciprocity in marriage intended by God in Genesis. Divorce was equivalent to social death for women. Divorce not only traumatized women but also put women whose parents were not financially rich in a position of financial and emotional vulnerability; some of them were sold into prostitution. This still happens in some poor countries today.

Jewish husbands were misusing and abusing Moses's teaching on divorce and subjugating women. Divorce certificates became a mere nominal procedure that lacked moral substance. Jesus's high standard of divorce rejects this prevailing patriarchal practice of abuse and restores the true purpose of marriage as the covenant. It corrects the inequality between a man and a woman in marriage and invigorates women's rights.

Jesus's teaching was consistent with the Jubilee tradition—liberating the socially weak and restoring them to a new, just relationship. It has the effect of protecting married women from abuse of power and women in general from economic destitution. This also refurbished stability to the family and children. Jesus's prohibition of divorce "protected women from the Jewish man's unilateral right to dismiss his wife, and from the Roman man's tendency to use wife and female relatives as pawns in a game of political and economic power."[19]

Jesus reemphasizes the sanctity of marriage and family by reminding us that marriage is more than a contract between two individuals.[20] The Bible upholds the

19. Cahill, *Sex, Gender, and Christian Ethics*, 156. Cahill elaborates a covenantal nature of marriage in the NT: "The primary kinds of sexual conduct that are excluded by New Testament teaching are status-marking, boundary-erecting, other-dominating, and self-promoting actions and practices, especially when they deprive others of what they require to survive and to 'flourish' as human beings" (157).

20. Jesus also *relativizes* the importance of marriage and the family in the kingdom when he

norm of lifetime marriage. A selfish or casual divorce (for male power and privilege) goes against God's will. A strong marriage makes the entire family strong emotionally, socially, and financially, while a failed marriage leaves a permanent scar on the spouses and especially their children.

Our time is different from that of Jesus. Though not fully realized yet, women's rights in marriage have greatly improved. Just as with casual sex, marriage has become contractualized in neoliberal society. The bond and tie of many marriages are weakened or under duress. No-fault divorce laws indicate that a contractual view of marriage is prevailing. Half of all marriages in the United States end up in divorce. How should we understand divorce when no-fault divorce is increasingly the standard?

Divorce is tragic, never desirable. It cannot be taken lightly. Divorce is discouraged because of the covenantal and communal nature of marriage. However, it is difficult to idealize marriage; it is still a relationship between two sinful, broken persons, and marriages can break down for a variety of reasons, including and beyond adultery. In certain marriages, the union can break and its mandate can remain fulfilled. Jesus is transforming marriage, restoring it to its original unitive vision under the dawning reign of God. Marriage should not exclusively be thought in terms of love and sacrifice; the norm of justice also applies to marriage. Divorce can be considered when the dignity (basic rights) of one party is severely harmed and compromised. In particular, ongoing physical and emotional abuse, extramarital affairs, or abandonment goes against the norm of justice. The purpose of marriage is not fulfilled because the marriage covenant is violated.

A difficult question is the case of no-fault divorce. There are many "virtual" divorces (marked by distrust and the ceasing of an intimate relationship). Here, marriage has turned into a shell of its former self, or even worse, distrust and accumulated wounds create a toxic environment for spouses and children. When covenant is broken to the extent it is irrecoverable, then its termination can be considered. In light of the Bible and the divine-human covenant, covenant can be voided when the stipulations are violated to the harm of one party.

However, the couple must make an effort to mend and restore marriage because divorce and remarriage take away any chance of reconciliation. The practices of communicative action and just peacemaking are also applicable to marriage relationships. When the couple undergoes strain, they may seek reconciliation through marital counseling, family intervention, and temporary separation for spiritual and emotional renewal. Friends and family can play an important role as emotional

---

says, "Whoever does the will of God is my brother and sister and mother" (Mark 3:35). See Beckett, "Desire in Singleness," 193–212.

supporters of the couple as prayer partners. Reconciliation could help reduce poisonous, antagonistic sentiments and further alienation. Such an effort is necessary not only for the couple but also for children who are emotionally and morally disoriented and distraught, and even feel abandoned. Early childhood memories of alienated parental marriage traumatize children's view of marriage. It is far from being a contract between two private individuals. The well-being of children must be accounted for in the decision.

Churches may support young people with premarital preparation and counseling for marriage building and divorce prevention. Many failed marriages result from immaturity and impulsive decisions. Counseling may remind couples that marriage is more than just sexual union; it includes emotional, spiritual, and moral union. A good marriage requires two mature persons with a clear understanding of what is at stake.

Same-Sex Marriage

The issue of same-sex marriage is probably one of the most explosive issues for churches. Christians are deeply divided, and passions run very high on both sides of the issue. For liberal Christians, same-sex marriage is settled, no longer a controversial matter; they assert that Christians should repent of their past mistakes and fully embrace LGBTQ issues. On the other hand, conservative Christians more strongly stick to a traditional heterosexual view of marriage and cisgender identity. The issue is so politicized that meaningful dialogue is difficult. Like abortion, it is used as a litmus test in deciding friends, allies, and enemies. Both sides hold entrenched attitudes and are willing to utilize legal and political means to enforce and impose them upon others.

Same-sex marriage is increasingly accepted as a social norm. Especially in the United States, there has been a dramatic shift. In 1989 (the year Denmark became the first country to grant legal status to gay couples), 69 percent of the population opposed same-sex marriage.[21] By 2012 it had gained majority approval, becoming the law of the land in 2015. Following the *Obergefell v. Hodges* ruling, the United States is now one of the twenty-six countries that authorize same-sex marriage. At the time of this chapter's writing, the Pew Research Center indicates that 60 percent of the US population sees gay marriage favorably, with millennial support reaching 74 percent.[22]

We can roughly think of three different ethical positions on same-sex marriage among Christians: conservative traditionalists, revisionists, and moderate tradition-

21. Frizell, "This Is How Much More Popular Same-Sex Marriage Is Today Than in 1989."
22. "Attitudes on Same-Sex Marriage."

alists. Each group is not theologically homogeneous but holds to different theological emphases and complexities. The three groups differ in their views of (1) the authority of the Bible (including the texts that offer prima facie prohibition of same-sex erotic behavior) and (2) "nature" or "natural" in terms of same-sex attraction and orientation, and identity.

Conservative Traditionalist View

Traditionalists hold that same-sex marriage is not normative because it goes against God's creative designs for humanity: God ordained marriage to be a union between a man and a woman. The Nashville Statement claims: "We deny that adopting a homosexual or transgender self-conception is consistent with God's holy purposes in creation and redemption."[23] Traditionalists' view of same-sex marriage is grounded in the prohibition passages on same-sex relations in the Bible (Lev. 18:22; 20:13; Rom. 1:26–27; 1 Cor. 6:9–11; and 1 Tim. 1:10).

Traditionalists claim that despite Jesus's revision of some Old Testament rules in his covenantal renewal, the early church was consistent in retaining its teaching on sexual morality. This includes homosexual acts, which are mentioned in lists of behaviors deemed unacceptable to God. They point out that the Bible denounces all kinds of same-sex relations. The prohibition texts are concerned not about particular types of homosexual activities but about homosexual acts in general. Traditionalists are deeply concerned that same-sex marriages will undermine the sanctity of the family and the psychological and moral formation of children by revising the definition of family, gender roles, and identities. They point out that same-sex relationships are not procreative; thus, it is emotionally detrimental for a child not to be raised by its biological mother and father. In this respect, traditionalists claim, traditional marriage relationships are not a matter of discriminating against same-sex couples but are about serving the public interest.

Traditionalists in general do not accept that same-sex attraction and orientation are inborn, and thus incorrigible. They see homosexuality as a choice of an immoral lifestyle or the effect of early childhood upbringing, or both; in short, it is a learned behavior. Hence, they are worried that legalization of same-sex marriage will encourage and normalize homosexual behavior among youths.

Christians with a traditional view of marriage tend to take a binary view of sexual roles and gender identity. They treat the ideas of sexual identity and sexual orientation as recent cultural phenomena; Christians should not use or adopt such categories or languages because they are not based on biblical anthropology but on

23. *Nashville Statement*, article 7.

secular, anti-Christian anthropologies. For example, Rosaria Butterfield, a former lesbian, stresses the need for Christians to "reject any identity that Christ has not prepared" for the believer.[24]

Progressive Revisionist View

Revisionist views are diverse but generally built upon some or all of the following core claims as they attempt to set aside or relativize the prohibition passages.[25]

1. The prohibition passages are not concerned with covenantal same-sex relationships, but rather concern the abuse of sex in human trafficking, temple prostitution, pedophilia, economic exploitation, and promiscuity. Paul condemns only predatory and promiscuous homosexual acts by heterosexual persons who have "exchanged natural intercourse for unnatural." Paul's negative judgment, so the argument goes, is not on persons who are "naturally" homosexual. Furthermore, these prohibitions relate to the Old Testament's ritual "purity rules" and are therefore morally irrelevant today. The Old Testament contains many prohibitions, regarding such things as circumcision and dietary practices, which were abolished by Jesus and the early Christians. In the same manner, the prohibition texts on same-sex relationship should be abolished today, as they are obsolete.[26]
2. The effective ministry and experiential witnesses of LBGTQ Christians demonstrate that the Holy Spirit is no less working among them than among heterosexual Christians. Such fresh and enduring experiences challenge the traditional definition of marriage and the interpretation of prohibition codes in the Bible; in light of new experiential evidence, prohibition codes should be revised.
3. Like people of color and women, LGBTQ people have been historically oppressed and victimized by homophobia, exclusion, and violence. Today their basic rights, including the right of marriage, should be fully restored. Revisionists point out the high rates of suicide and depression among the LGBTQ population as validating this concern.
4. The biblical view of sexuality is very limited in understanding complex human sexuality, such as sexual orientation and gender identity. The prohibition codes in the NT are irrelevant to the sexual behaviors of people with

24. Butterfield, *Openness Unhindered*, 4.
25. Sprinkle, "Conclusion," 218.
26. See Countryman, *Dirt, Greed, and Sex*.

> same-sex orientation because the prohibition codes pertain to narrow acts of *porneia* only. Revisionists claim that because of its cultural confinement, same-sex orientation is something that the biblical authors, including Paul, never properly discovered; thus, prohibition texts, while consistent, are culturally limited and no longer relevant for the moral experiences of LGBTQ people. They claim that Paul condemns only predatory and promiscuous homosexual acts by heterosexual persons who have "exchanged natural intercourse for unnatural." Hence the prohibition is completely irrelevant in this aspect. Revisionists call for the supplementation of the prohibition texts with modern experiences.

These claims are not necessarily mutually exclusive but overlapping. Revisionists mix some or all of the above claims in their advocacy for same-sex marriage.

The problem with (1) is that Jesus in fact did not abolish or redefine but reaffirmed creational marriage (heterosexual) in his otherwise radical covenantal renewal. As for (2), collective human experiences could serve as important moral sources, as mentioned in chapter 9, but not to the extent that they override the consistent moral teaching on marriage in the Bible, as the norming norm. The concern about marginalization raised in (3) is completely valid, and Christians of all stripes need to repent and protect the civil-political rights of LGBTQ people; however, the Christian definition of marriage, as in other world religions of Middle Eastern origin, does not belong to the civic authority. One can fully protect the civil-political rights of LGBTQ people while respecting religious definitions and practices of marriage that have continued for several millennia.

Among these claims, (4) is most forceful in that it does not deny the consistency and noncompromising position of the Bible in prohibiting same-sex erotic practices and that same-sex desires arising from sexual orientation are "natural." There is a truth in the revisionist claims based on empirical observation. According to Mark Yarhouse, while the vast majority of people have opposite-sex attractions, some experience attraction to the same sex (6 percent of men and 4.5 percent of women). Among those with same-sex attraction, about 2 percent of men and about 1 percent of women have same-sex orientation, that is, the attraction is strong and persistent enough for them to feel that they are oriented toward the same sex.[27]

The revisionists follow a secular script of LGBTQ identity; they rely on the discovery metaphor by emphasizing that same-sex attractions signal who a person really is.[28] Sexual identity is something that is discovered. As natural feelings, sex

27. Yarhouse, *Homosexuality and the Christian*, 42.
28. Yarhouse, *Homosexuality and the Christian*, 55.

attractions are at the core of who you really are as a person, as "intended by God." There is no gap between sex attraction, sexual behavior, and sexual identity. Same-sex behavior is a natural manifestation of that core identity. Same-sex behavior is crucial for individual self-fulfillment; nothing is wrong with a behavior that matches who you "really are."[29] This is a powerful and appealing social script of sex, especially in the culture of expressive individualism.

In other words, it is claimed that same-sex orientation (or bisexual orientation) is natural and beyond the control of an individual; it reveals who a person truly is—it is the core aspect of one's personal identity. In an individualistic, highly sexualized society, no gap exists between sexual attraction/orientation and sexual identity. Sexual identity is grounded in sexual orientation. As "natural" sexual orientation, it is believed to be intended by God. Same-sex behavior is an expression of that orientation and crucial for one's self-fulfillment as a sexual being that God has intended at creation.[30] To suppress this desire is cruel and inhumane. Doesn't Paul's admonition in 1 Corinthians 7:2, 8–9, apply to gays and lesbians who are struggling with burning passion? "A primary reason so many people have changed their mind on gay marriage is that it now seems almost unthinkably cruel to condemn someone to a life of lonely singleness, to deny them the chance to experience what all those songs and movies and sermons tell us is one of the most essential human experiences: falling in love and building a life with someone."[31]

Revisionists claim that same-sex marriage, like heterosexual marriage, can fulfill the covenantal ideal—the consensual and lifelong monogamous commitment.

Moderate Traditionalist View

Moderate traditionalists offer a different approach. They affirm the existence of same-sex attraction/orientation. Moderates believe that conservative Christians have failed by defining LGBTQ sexuality purely as a matter of lifestyle and personal choice without paying close attention to the biological basis of same-sex attraction and disregarding the psychological and social marginalization of LGBTQ persons. It is unreasonable to expect LGBTQ people to change their orientations if they are innate.

But moderates are critical of revisionists as well. While sexual orientation is biologically and psychologically grounded, the question of sexual identity is not solely biologically determined but is also culturally constructed. There is no seamless, air-

29. Yarhouse, *Homosexuality and the Christian*, 49.
30. Yarhouse, *Homosexuality and the Christian*, 49.
31. Matthew Jones, "Homosexuality and Sexual Identity," 152.

tight continuity between sexual orientation and sexual identity. While revisionists derive sexual identity directly from biological determinism, Yarhouse and other moderate traditionalists distinguish attraction and orientation from homosexual behavior and faith identity. Identity is a complex and multidimensional issue. Sexual identity is only one of many identities we embrace.

Furthermore, same-sex orientation is not the defining element of Christian identity. Sexual identity is concerned with what persons intend to do or actually do with their homosexual attraction and orientation, that is, how persons attribute or make meaning out of their homosexual attraction and orientation. To a large extent, it depends on which script one chooses to apply to one's experiences of same-sex attraction and behavior. One's religion or worldview plays an important role in the process of meaning making and sexual identity attribution and synthesis. It is significantly affected by one's beliefs about sex and sexual behavior and the value one places on them.[32] What do gay and lesbian Christians do in relation to Christian identity? There are two different scripts to sexual identity among Christians (with multiple variations within each): a secular script and a biblical script centering on Christ.[33]

Moderates say revisionists are operating with a simplistic anthropology that assumes that whatever is must be good: they have a theology of creation but no theology of sin and redemption. Furthermore, they have a realized eschatology that equates personal fulfillment with sexual fulfillment that expects sexual "salvation" now.

For moderates, the most crucial text concerning homosexuality is probably Romans 1, because this passage condemns homosexual behavior in the most explicitly theological terms.[34] According to Richard Hays, Paul specifies homosexual intercourse, with a vivid graphic image, to explain how human fallenness distorts God's creation order. For Paul, all homosexual activity is "prima facie evidence of humanity's tragic confusion and alienation from God the Creator."[35] God made man and woman biologically complement each other in marriage, to fulfill God's blessing for humanity: "Be fruitful and multiply." However, when human beings engage in homosexual practices, they are exchanging the truth of God's created roles for a lie.[36]

For moderates, eschatology (God's abiding presence with us in the Spirit and the promise of the full redemption of the body) theologically matters in addressing the issue; Paul portrays human beings as fallen creatures in bondage to sin but set free

32. Yarhouse, *Homosexuality and the Christian*, 39.

33. Yarhouse, *Homosexuality and the Christian*, 51.

34. Hays, *Moral Vision*, 383.

35. Hays, *Moral Vision*, 389.

36. Hays, *Moral Vision*, 388.

in Christ through the obedience of faith. He also looks to the future resurrection as the locus of bodily fulfillment.

In the current cultural situation, a revisionist position is culturally dominant, especially among young people, as it looks more humane and culturally relevant, while rectifying the past wrongs against the LGBTQ people. The argument for a revisionist approach to same-sex relations has limitations, however. Same-sex behaviors are not solely biologically predetermined; choice and cultural habits also shape it, no matter how meager they may be. This is what distinguishes this issue from, for example, racial discrimination. It would not be an exaggeration to say that same-sex marriage has gained popular support partly because of expressive individualism. In our current cultural milieu of expressive individualism and idealization of romantic love, one cannot deny that an individual person's sexual orientation and desire tend to trump all other concerns and considerations. They strongly resonate with the core values of a secular sexual ethic: be true to yourself; make sure it's consensual; seek pleasure, avoid suffering; and don't hurt anyone else.

Nature: Biological Determinism or Complex Ambiguity?

It is an open question whether sexual orientation is primarily inborn or socially developed (in early childhood); empirical studies show that both are possible causes, making this moral quandary even more complicated and controversial. Humans are not born with a clear-cut (dichotomous) sexual orientation. As with other natural attractions and orientations, homosexual attraction and orientation are not immoral in and of themselves, especially when they are caused by biological factors. However, not every attraction, including a sexual one, is as it is supposed to be.

A critical aspect of the Christian debates on same-sex marriage turns on the notion of "nature." Except for conservatives, most Christian scholars agree that both same-sex attraction and orientation actually exist. But they differ on how to interpret them and what to do with them. A key difference is whether same-sex attraction and orientation are normative or an aspect of fallenness. For revisionists, same-sex attraction and orientation are God-given and should thus be respected by all means. For moderate traditionalists, they are real but part of fallen nature, not what God originally intended. They question how we should understand same-sex desire and sexual orientation. Are they sinful or natural? One sign of human fallenness and brokenness or a valid natural desire that stems from God's creation covenant (as natural as heterosexual desires)?

Humans are embedded in nature, physical organisms living in interaction with the biotic world. We cannot reject the idea of nature outright because it offers moral parameters of our life as God's creature. Our bodies are the source of desires, joy, and satisfaction but are also beset by limitations and finitudes. God's incarnation in Jesus Christ affirms the goodness of the creation and bodily life.[37]

The natural refers to the goodness of physical creation.[38] Unnatural are the fallen/distortive aspects of creation that are now part of human biological and social life (e.g., idolatry, sexual immorality). Creation now is both good and fallen. It is not that some aspects of creation are fallen and others are still good, but that goodness and fallenness together permeate creation. Because of sin, not everything that happens in nature is "natural." For humans, both sinful and nonsinful nature can be felt as "natural." Our perception or understanding of natural is partly culture- and time-dependent. What is natural in one society may not be natural in another. As a society changes, what people believe is natural today may be regarded as unnatural tomorrow, depending on how broadly it is accepted by a society. For example, among young people today, premarital sex and cohabitation are more or less accepted as "natural."[39]

How do we know which aspects of human life and experiences are natural (thus to be preserved) and which are fallen? The creation covenant and the new covenant of Jesus offer the criteria for distinguishing the natural from the unnatural. While we cannot disregard enduring sexual attractions that individuals feel, we cannot easily dismiss the biological ground of marriage: procreation and sexual differentiation. The creation covenant and the new covenant equally uphold this differentiation as the basis of marriage.

In the biblical narrative, God's good creation is structured by natural law, and sexual differentiation between man and woman is one of the laws. The creation narrative in Genesis 1:27 and 2:24 is important for covenantal sexual ethics because it denotes the normative form of sexual relationship. As part of the creation narrative, the passages attribute moral significance to procreation ("be fruitful and multiply") and describe a complementary communion between male and female. The gender complementarity in the text is consistent with the references to other complementarities and differentiations that God's covenantal organizing embeds in the fabric of creation. In other words, gender complementarity refers to sex difference and is an integral part of God's covenant.

Male-female sexual difference is normative in the Bible, especially in the Genesis story, and was reaffirmed by Jesus in his covenantal renewal. This difference has a covenantal significance; it sets the pattern for sexual relationship.[40] The difference

37. See Rowan Williams, "The Body's Grace."

38. Bonhoeffer, *Ethics*, 174.

39. Bonhoeffer, *Ethics*, 173. Bonhoeffer's distinction is helpful: what is natural is fallen creation that is formed in Christ (the penultimate), what is unnatural is fallen creation that not formed in Christ and thus sinful.

40. For the theological significance of sexual differentiation, see Roberts, *Covenant and Creation*.

is the culmination of God's creation, which is covenantally structured and organized—a clear and definite form of differentiation that is necessary for the holistic union between male and female in all aspects of their communication and fellowship. Furthermore, in the Genesis story, procreation, no matter how it has become insignificant for our time, is an intrinsic part of this union.

Marriage is a covenant that God ordained between man and woman at God's creation. Scripture is consistent on this matter. Given this clarity and consistency, as far as the Bible is concerned, it would be difficult to accept same-sex marriage as theologically normative (though its potential as a civic accommodation is another matter). Same-sex marriage does not fully fulfill God's creational intent.

Even in his covenantal renewal, Jesus did not abolish marriage; rather he restored marriage as delineated at the creation covenant and strengthened it. Jesus's statement in Matthew 19:4–5 ("Have you not read that the one who made them at the beginning 'made them male and female,' and said, 'For this reason a man shall leave his father and mother and be joined to his wife, and the two shall become one flesh'?")[41] is important, as it reminds us of the original intention and meaning of the marriage covenant. That is, it puts marriage in the transformative context of the new covenant. Jesus's covenantal renewal fully restored the original creational intention of marriage in God—to redeem humanity from the powers of sin, evil, and death, and to restore them to God's original plan.

Same-Sex Covenant?

Can covenantal marriage be applicable to same-sex relationships? All Christians accept covenant as a central biblical term that defines marriage. The advocates of same-sex marriage propose monogamous covenantal partnerships as an ideal and normative requirement. For them, same-sex marriage fulfills the covenantal demand of marriage no less than does a heterosexual marriage because it stipulates that the two persons enter an exclusive and lifelong monogamous relationship with each other. That is, the moral ideal of covenantal marriage can be achieved in the same-sex relationship.

In light of the covenantal renewal of the Bible, in particular Jesus's, one may say, a revisionist's definition of same-sex marriage as covenant is tantamount to calling for a major "covenantal renewal" on Christian sexual ethics.[42] On the other hand,

41. By referring to the Genesis story, Jesus restores the sanctity of the marriage covenant. His statement has the effect of undoing a sinful pattern and practices of a society—a patriarchal, male power/privilege in marriage.

42. For the support of the same-sex covenantal relationship, see Keen, *Scripture, Ethics, and the Possibility of Same-Sex Relationships*; Song, *Covenant and Calling*; Coakley, *The New Asceticism*.

traditionalists believe that a traditional definition of marriage is not something to be subjected to revision at all.

This difference leads us to ask, What counts as "covenant" in marriage? Does it mean a committed mutual agreement between any two persons or only between a man and a woman? How much does sexual difference matter? These have become divisive theological questions for Christians today.

Same-sex marriage fulfills some important demands of marriage: personal fulfillment and public (legal) recognition. However, the biblical idea of marriage covenant is more than the legal contractual arrangement of passion, commitment, and intimacy between two persons. What distinguishes covenant from legal contract is its God-given normativity (creational intention that God's incarnation in Jesus reaffirmed). The above components (the moral quality of sexual relationship) are necessary but not sufficient, even in an exclusive relationship, unless they cohere with God's creational and redemptive will. Such an understanding is in fact contractual rather than covenantal.

Marriage as covenant has a theonomous basis. By repeating "Therefore what God has joined together, let no one separate," Jesus declares a strong, theonomous basis of marriage grounded in the creation covenant. Jesus's citation of Genesis 1:27 and 2:24 is important because he reaffirms the creational basis for marriage under the new covenant. The apostle Paul also reiterates this truth in Ephesians 5:31–32: marriage includes the union at all levels: emotional, social, legal, spiritual, and biological. The whole of Scripture testifies that God's designing of marriage is for the lifelong exclusive union of a man and a woman. Scripture is consistent in this affirmation. New covenant does not render the creation covenant obsolete or insignificant, but rather builds upon it and expands and intensifies it.

> Jesus thus suggests a basis for interpreting Scripture: we are to evaluate scriptural perspectives according to the way they reflect God s vision in creation, along with the possible provision for human hardness of heart. . . . Indeed, one might then see Jesus' entire teaching as expounding what it means to be a real human being who lives according to the vision of the Creator, as he makes explicit in his comment reported by the evangelist on loving enemies (Matt. 5:44). The Torah does not begin with the concrete commands in Exodus to Deuteronomy that make allowance for human willfulness. It begins with the vision in Genesis 1–2, and Jesus fulfills the Torah partly by reaffirming its vision, indicating its implications, and challenging his disciples to live by this vision.[43]

43. Goldingay et al., "Same-Sex Marriage and Anglican Theology," 19.

Gender difference is integral to God's creation of humanity (the first covenant), in a manner consistent with God's preceding covenantal organizing work of differentiating and uniting in the first five days. It is critical to understand that Jesus's covenantal renewal is to restore and recapitulate God's purpose and vision in creation. In other words, creation and redemption are not contradictory. This hermeneutical principle helped the early church overcome the temptations and threats of Gnosticism and all sorts of overblown spiritualism that denied the body and Christian responsibility in the world, on the one hand, and hedonistic overindulgence and promiscuity in the body and its desires, on the other. Covenantal marriage avoids the two extremes.

A biological differentiation, beyond emotional/affective differentiation, is crucial for the moral constitution of marriage. Cahill writes: "Contemporary Christian ethicists debating sex and gender rightly hold up equality, intimacy, and fulfillment as moral criteria. But they often fail to ask whether these values are any less relative or more objective than the sexual systems they are eager to dismantle."[44] The covenant of Jesus fulfills the creation covenant by strengthening marriage ethics, with biological differentiation as its constitutive normative aspect.

Similarly, the biblical idea of covenantal marriage presupposes procreation. Procreation is an aspect of the marriage mandate, even though it is not exhaustive of marriage itself. Some heterosexual marriages do not include procreation (e.g., infertile and elderly couples), but their mode of sexual complementarity is still open and oriented to it, in terms of genus and typology. Although not all sex leads to reproduction, openness to new life is a theological premise of marriage as designed by God in the creation covenant, and it cannot be lightly dismissed.

Celibacy and Community

Celibacy has been a consistent request of traditionalists (Catholics and evangelicals) for LGBTQ people. However, it has lost its persuasive power after the sexual revolution and the social situation of fluidity, mobility, and expressive individualism. Now, even the building and keeping of friendships are increasingly difficult so that a committed romantic partner seems to be the only viable relational option.

There is strong cultural resistance because the very idea of celibacy has become alien to the popular culture. Revisionists strongly reject the idea because it seems not only legalistic but also inhumane. Revisionists have a different moral position on celibacy from traditionalists and moderates; the question boils down to whether celibacy should be a free choice or an obligation. Loader claims that celibacy should

44. Cahill, *Sex, Gender, and Christian Ethics*, 11.

never be an obligation; it is unjust and inhumane to take away the opportunity for gays and lesbians to express their natural sexual desires.[45] On the other hand, Wesley Hill argues that celibacy is not purely free choice because it is a noble calling for LGBTQ people, required by their distinctive circumstances; it does not have to be inhumane.[46]

It is undeniable that sex is a strong enduring human drive. Sex is important theologically because it is the sacrament of covenantal communion. But sex is not indispensable; neither is marriage permanent or absolute. The current cultural view of sex, its glorification and indispensability, is not what the Bible teaches, just as the suppression of sex is not acceptable.

While never losing its genuine compassion toward the difficulty of celibacy, the church should not be afraid to teach the rich tradition of celibacy in Christianity to heterosexuals as well as LGBTQ persons. Celibacy is not an impossible option for both heterosexual Christians and LGBTQ Christians. Celibacy is the courageous practice of Christians who, through their discipleship, point toward life in Jesus Christ. It is definitely "a difficult, costly obedience." Hays writes, "Anyone who does not recognize this as a description of authentic Christian existence has never struggled seriously with the imperatives of the gospel, which challenge and frustrate our 'natural' impulses in countless ways."[47]

Jesus, Paul, and many other Christians, especially in the Catholic tradition, show that one could live a meaningful life without sexual relationships. They demonstrate how to show their Christian identity over other forms of identity. In the Bible, while faithful monogamy is the only legitimate expression of human sexuality, celibacy and singleness are equally legitimate; neither one is the superior way.[48]

More importantly and urgently, churches need to develop a theology of singlehood and expand and intensify ministry for all types of singles: unmarried, separated, divorced, and widowed. Marriage should not be mandatory for leadership. "Singles should not be 'singled out' for second-class Christian status."[49] The Bible offers stories of people who are in a wide variety of life situations and callings.

Both caring for the unmarried and offering a meaningful community for them are of equal concern for churches. Every person needs a close-knit and trusting community even for the person's basic mental health. It has become emotionally challenging for people to remain celibate today because genuine friendship and nonsexual intimacy are increasingly rare in a hypermobile, fluid, and transactional

45. Loader, "Homosexuality and the Bible."

46. Hill, "Christ, Scripture, and Spiritual Friendship," 144–47.

47. Hays, *Moral Vision*, 402.

48. Grenz, *Sexual Ethics*, chap. 9.

49. Stassen and Gushee, *Kingdom Ethics*, 303.

society. Even friendship seems transitory and insufficient to meet emotional need, intimacy, and full acceptance.

Only the kind of radically inclusive, generous, caring, and intimate community that the new covenant envisions can meaningfully sustain the standard of celibacy. Churches cannot demand celibacy from people without providing community for them. To do so is overly cruel and unpractical. The practice of celibacy was possible for the early Christians and the Catholic Church (though far from being perfect) because there was a strong community of belonging, sharing, and support for celibates.

As in the case of abortion and physician-assisted suicide, the faith decisions of many gay and lesbian Christians depend on what kind of community they find around them, and what form of communal support and care is available for them. In response to God's call to share God's blessings with a wider world, Christians need to fully embrace celibate LGBTQ persons as members of their families, and this is part of the covenantal task and expression of our gratitude to God through our love of our brothers and sisters. In a neoliberal capitalist society, the nuclear family, just like atomic individuals, has become autonomous and self-enclosed. God's covenantal family is personal and public, not private and individualistic. Covenantal love is a communal love—the love that builds a community and overflows toward others. This love is expressed in the form of hospitality, care, and sharing. The story of Ruth is an excellent example because it displays the familial solidarity and loyalty that go beyond a biological and conjugal connection. Ruth and Naomi, two destitute women, find a community and mutual support in each other. We remember that the early Christians operated more like an extended family in God, sharing their care, love, and resources. Jesus and the new covenant redefine the family. The Epistles also say that we are of the same household of God, and one body in Christ. This redefinition is not to abolish the biological family but to relocate it in a broader, more inclusive community of God's family.

Without first offering a strong covenantal bond, friendship, and ongoing *koinōnia*, churches will continue to be on the losing side on this issue. Without living out more fully, energetically, and passionately the covenant virtues of trust, solidarity, and care of LGBTQ people, the church's traditional sexual ethics will miserably fail.

Just Peacemaking between Traditionalists and Revisionists

Just peacemaking between conservative traditionalists and revisionists seems increasingly necessary given the growing misunderstanding and antagonism in the current toxic and polarizing political situation. Without it, both sides of this issue are likely to entrench their views further, and this issue may become a single moral litmus test for all other issues, thus further dividing, distorting, and poisoning public discourse and civil society. Given the highly religious nature and history of the United States, conservative Christians are not likely to change their views on same-sex marriage, while the overwhelming majority of young people already support it. Therefore, a pragmatic decision in the public realm (rather than personal conscience) is necessary for the common interests of US society. Below are a few suggestions for just peacemaking.

Homophobia and heterosexual exclusivism do not have a place in the Christian community. There are passages in the Bible that welcome sexual outliers and those who had been stigmatized in the community.[50]

> As for the eunuchs who keep my sabbaths,
> who choose the things that please me
> and hold fast to my covenant,
> I will give them, in my house and within my walls,
> a monument and a name
> better than sons or daughters;
> I will give them an everlasting name
> that shall not be cut off. (Isa. 56:4–5)

The civil-political rights and dignity of LGBTQ people must be respected. Marriage is a special covenant, and it cannot override the universal covenant of God in Jesus; therefore, the issue of sexual identity cannot overrule the demands and concerns of the universal covenant (the creation covenant, the Noachian covenant). Evangelical Christians need genuinely and publicly to repent of our mistreatment of LGBTQ people and the violation of their rights (especially through marginalization and violence), for LGBTQ people have equal rights as members of God's universal covenant community.

Traditionalists and revisionists should not attempt to solve the issue of same-sex marriage with political power or legislation alone. They should seek mutual understanding and even compromise. Rather than vilifying and condemning the other party, it is necessary to tone down militant, vitriolic language and show tolerance toward others; both groups may enter some form of civic compromise (contract), although it may not be perfect for either party.

Revisionists and traditionalists object to the position of the other party out of deep moral convictions ("objectionable differences") that neither side wants to yield. Increasingly, the sentiment and passion around the issue are historically similar to those

50. Zimmerman, "Isaiah for Our Time."

of religious conflicts, and the ongoing clash of convictions may lead to furthering of enmity and even violence. Hence, given the intensity of passion around this issue, both may simply agree to disagree and accommodate each other's position in a peaceful agreement, as we do with other religious groups in interreligious dialogue.

Civility toward the other group, and mutual pastoral accommodation and reasonable compromise, is necessary: while nonaffirming Christians may support the legalization of same-sex marriage with all the civil and political benefits it entails, they may claim religious freedom in refraining from sacralizing same-sex marriages in churches. While traditionalists may not theologically accept same-sex marriage as a biblical option, they may still politically support the full civil rights of LGBTQ persons, including civil marriage, and work together to reduce and remove social stigma, eliminate marginalization, and increase their legal protections. In a democratic society, all citizens need to respect the majority rule while they protect the minority rights. Christians may legally support civil marriage, which is not the same as ecclesial marriage. And in return, they may request religious freedom on this issue. Christians should not be discouraged from attending their LBGTQ friends' weddings. Traditionalists need to heed Jeremiah's teaching for the exiles: pray for the peace of the city.

In addition, some form of pastoral accommodation of LGBTQ members in churches is worth considering, in order to ensure for them space in the life of the church, such as membership and leadership. Pastoral accommodation means "making space [in the church] for imperfect patterns of life whilst maintaining a clear witness to perfection."[51] In Christian history, out of sheer pastoral concern, churches have continuously made accommodation (formal and informal) for members who live less than ideal lives as disciples of Jesus. For example, even conservative churches, at least informally, accommodate people on divorce and remarriage, just as the Roman Catholic Church does on contraception. Likewise, evangelical missionaries and African churches have accommodated polygamous converts. To exercise pastoral accommodation is to attend carefully and compassionately to the reality of human pain, suffering, limitation, and brokenness without compromising the biblical moral standards and convictions.

Some might criticize such a move as condoning sin or allowing a dangerous moral compromise. These concerns are legitimate because a pastoral accommodation could be easily misused on other moral issues as well. We should be careful not to confuse pastoral accommodation with forfeiting the moral standards themselves, such that the standards become *de facto* meaningless. However, the need for pastoral accommodation in sexual ethics is real for young people in particular, and churches need to engage it with a clear purpose and carefully defined boundaries.

51. Holmes, "Listening to the Past and Reflecting on the Present," 191.

On the other hand, the revisionists should accept and respect the religious freedom and moral conscience of Christians with a traditional view, and accommodate their request that churches, parochial schools, and religious organizations fully enjoy their religious freedom. Advocates for same-sex marriage should understand that the refusal of many traditionalists to sanctify same-sex behavior emanates from deep religious conviction rather than bigotry. Both sides may not get everything they want, but they can live peacefully.

For LGBTQ persons, compromise may appear to be less than a full acceptance of their identities and their long-overdue civil political rights, while for traditionalists it is a severe compromise of their sacred religious convictions. However, in this case, tolerance seems to be a matter of the virtue of wisdom rather than a matter of selling out their convictions or being complicit with injustice. When both groups sharply disagree on a certain issue out of conviction, the only option (while living together) is to agree to avoid verbal and physical violence, find an arrangement that accommodates both sides, and prohibit discrimination of the others based on their convictions.[52]

Tolerance is an expression of civility, generosity, and humility. It is different from forbearance; it accepts differences without resentment, vilification, and depersonalizing of the other. To be tolerant is to accept the other despite differences. When differences are irresolvable, because of indeterminacy or the plurality of goods that people love and pursue, tolerance is a way to give each side its due. That is, tolerance is an appropriate response to our social situation where the convictions of both sides cannot be compromised. In this case, tolerance is a form of justice and love. It accepts the other party in choosing and pursuing what the other party loves. It enables both sides to achieve peace and give to each other what each is due. Tolerance is a passive way of just peacemaking.

> There is indeterminacy to the human good and a diversity of possible loves and goods that humans pursue. A concern with justice arises out of this indeterminacy and this diversity: we want to give each other what each is due. Sometimes, what another is due is patient endurance of her choices and the pursuit of her loves. Tolerance is the virtue of reacting with patient endurance in the right sorts of circumstances. Tolerance is thus a part of justice. It is a perfection of our responses to the differences of others, and more particularly, to objectionable differences. It enables us to achieve peace and give to each other what each is due. The tolerant respond with patient endurance without either resentment or desire to express their outrage.[53]

52. Goodstein, "Utah Passes Antidiscrimination Bill Backed by Mormon Leaders."
53. Fileva, review of *Tolerance among the Virtues*.

Conclusion

Sex is ubiquitous in a neoliberal society that capitalizes every human desire. As one of the most powerful human drives, it is simultaneously glorified and commodified in popular culture. Conservative Christians and secular people overvalue sex, either as a danger or as a reward; on the other hand, traditional ascetics undervalue it.[54] Sexual ethics and marriage in the Bible are covenantal in nature. Covenant sex ethics neither overvalues nor undervalues sex.

New covenant offers the telos, ethos, spirit, and parameters of a good sexual relationship. It rejects a consumeristic, fetishized view that seeks sex for momentary self-gratification and a contractual approach that treats sexual relationship as completely transactional for mutual gratification.

It is not an easy task to bridge a growing gap between biblical sexual ethics and a cultural trend that has converted many young Christians. New covenant ethics may not immediately address the challenges that churches face today. However, churches should not be afraid of offering moral teachings on the beauty and promise of covenantal sex ethics. It may not be easy, but those who find it are like a merchant who finds a precious pearl.

Sex is covenantal and belongs to a lifelong monogamous covenantal relationship. Monogamous, egalitarian, and committed marriage was one of the "deepest transformations of Christian thinking about marriage."[55] Through his covenantal renewal, Jesus restored and reinvented the original liberative, egalitarian, reciprocal meaning of marriage and human life intended by God. Moral standards of his community were consistent with the foundational convictions of the Bible, with a sense of renewed vitality and relevance in God. The sexual conduct of early Christians was characterized by the values of equality, respect, and love, while ever striving to achieve holiness. Early Christians were minorities in their practices of sex in Greco-Roman society; their covenantal view of sex and sexual discipline was countercultural, but it gradually transformed a patriarchal and promiscuous culture into a more egalitarian and committed one.

54. Some contemporary authors (including Wesley Hill and Sarah Coakley) have attempted to reclaim and reconfigure the ascetic vision from its historical excesses and problems.

55. Cahill, *Sex, Gender, and Christian Ethics*, 184.

CHAPTER 19

Medical Ethics

And the dust returns to the earth as it was, and the breath returns to God who gave it.

—Ecclesiastes 12:7

"He will wipe every tear from their eyes.
Death will be no more;
mourning and crying and pain will be no more,
for the first things have passed away."

—Revelation 21:4

Medical ethics[1] studies the values that guide the practice of medicine and scientific research. No discussion of health and medical ethics today can occur without proper attention given to the impressive advances in medical technology and their profound impact on human life—prolonging human life expectancy, curing many diseases, and the promise of enhanced human capability (transhumanism). At the same time, technological advances pose new moral quandaries, especially regarding the boundary between life and death, and the beginning and end of human life.

As we see in the modern debates on abortion, IVF (in vitro fertilization), PAS (physician-assisted suicide), cloning, genetic enhancement, stem cell therapy, etc., the advance of medical technology poses a huge moral challenge; either it opens

1. Medical ethics and bioethics are often distinguished; the former focuses on the specific moral obligations of health-care providers when caring for patients while the latter focuses on the investigation of broader systematic and philosophical issues involved biomedical practices and research. In general, medical ethics is seen as a subfield of bioethics.

up completely unknown realms of ethical conundrums (e.g., cloning) or it confounds traditional moral boundaries and ethical norms and categories in medical ethics (such as sanctity of life, informed consent, human rights, and quality of life). Technology is incredibly beneficial and has achieved great goods, but it can also be oppressive to the poor and detrimental to the common good.

At the same time, finding shared moral grounds has become increasingly difficult in our pluralistic social contexts. Medicine as a social practice is always informed by a certain worldview or vision of health, body, and vocation of physicians. Today, the worldview and moral assumptions behind medical technology are very much instrumental and individualistic (sometimes envisioning technopia), driven by the neoliberal capitalist agenda and ethos of maximal profit and desire for control.[2] The practice of medicine is tied to market logic and cutthroat competition, which discourage a broad and equitable sharing of the benefits of medical technology for all.

This chapter studies the plausibility and relevance of covenant ethics for medical ethics. The chapter asks: What is a covenantal understanding of medicine and medical practices, and how is it different from a contractual (liberal humanist) approach? How do its insights illuminate controversial issues of our time, such as abortion, euthanasia, and health care? Covenant ethics offers a proper vision and a sensible account of core norms (principles such as autonomy, beneficence, nonmaleficence, and justice), vocational understanding, and practices.

The historical tradition of medicine in the West carries rich covenantal values and assumptions going back to the Hippocratic oath and the millennia-long work of Christians in the medical field. Until recently, medical ethics carried within it more of a covenantal ethos and grounding than other realms.[3] However, this tradition is now receding as utilitarian contractualism, as in other social spheres, is becoming dominant. One may say that the current controversies are the tensions between the remaining covenantal presuppositions and the intrusion of contractual and consumerist ethos and practices.

A Modernistic View of Medicine: Norms/Values

Contemporary practices of medicine increasingly reflect a secular modernist view of humanity. That is, they are marked by science and a market logic that emphasizes in-

2. Bishop, *The Anticipatory Corpse*.

3. The fruitfulness of the metaphor of covenant for medical ethics is found in the works of two major medical ethicists, Paul Ramsey and William May. See Ramsey, *The Patient as Person*. Ramsey's book is structured entirely around covenant. May also has made substantial contributions to medical ethics by identifying covenant as a key metaphor of medical practices in comparison to other metaphors such as paternalism, utility, and contract.

dividual autonomy, rationality, power over nature (disease), unlocking mystery, optimism of human progress, expansion of choices, and convenience/comfort. Under the influence of secularization and the pressures of pluralism, bioethical discourses over the past few decades have relied on general (transcultural) moral principles and rules for moral analysis and decision making: the principles of dignity, individual autonomy, choice, rights, norms of nonmaleficence, and distributive justice.

Human Dignity

Human dignity is the foundational norm in medical ethics. It means that every person is born with inherent value. Thus, all are equally valuable and deserve equal respect despite illness or disability. This principle is important because humans are vulnerable to sickness, abuse, discrimination, and in some extreme cases, uninformed experimentation. People with disability and persons of color are especially vulnerable.

The respect for human dignity is practiced through equal treatment: all persons deserve equal access to medical treatment and should not be harmed in the process. Persons may lose social utility because of illness but must not lose a job or their sacredness because of it. Patients may have differences in social status, race, education, job, and rank, but at least in medicine, in matters of their life and health, they should be treated equally by a physician. The principle of human dignity serves as a moral foundation for the principles of autonomy, beneficence (doing good), and nonmaleficence (doing no harm).

Autonomy/Informed Decision

The principle of autonomy emphasizes the ethical importance of free choice in the decisions that patients make on matters pertaining to their health.[4] Informed consent is necessary to protect human dignity, as it gives a patient the power to set limits on a physician's actions. Autonomy is the basis of informed consent, just as freedom is the precondition for any moral decision. This principle stipulates that a patient has autonomy of thought, intention, and action in making decisions regarding matters of personal health.

4. According to Tom Beauchamp and James Childress, genuine autonomy should be intentional, competent in understanding information, and sufficiently free from both internal and external pressures (Beauchamp and Childress, *Principles of Biomedical Ethics*, 123). In *Practical Decision Making in Health Care Ethics*, R. J. Devetterre identifies reasoning, understanding, and evaluation as the three constitutive elements of autonomy. Surrogate decision making in medical ethics is an extension of the principle of autonomy.

Therefore, the decision-making process should be free of coercion or deception and fully informed by a physician. For a patient to make a fully informed decision, the patient must understand all the risks and benefits of the procedure and the likelihood of success. A physician has the duty to share all necessary information. Autonomy includes the right to refuse treatment, even if a specific medical procedure may benefit a patient. Since some medical decisions are highly technical or may involve high emotions, it is difficult to expect a patient to be operating under fully informed consent. That is why a physician's competence and fidelity (truthfulness, beneficence, nonmaleficence) are morally and professionally important.

Beneficence

The principle of beneficence means that the intention and practice of medical professionals are to benefit a patient and contribute to the patient's well-being, both emotional and physical. The action of the good Samaritan in the parable of Jesus is an excellent example of beneficence. Some philosophers claim beneficence is optional—more a virtue of a physician than an obligation. Hence, even a physician who fails to exhibit is not morally deficient.

Beneficence comes in both general and specific obligatory forms. However, it is very difficult to point out what the obligations of beneficence are. Different health-care providers exercise different degrees of beneficence. It does not have to be observed impartially.[5] Legal punishment is rarely applied for failing to follow the rules of beneficence. However, from a Christian perspective, beneficence is still an important principle because it is necessary to serve the moral purpose of medicine: health.

Nonmaleficence

Nonmaleficence means that a physician has the obligation not to injure or inflict evil. It is coined in the popular maxim *primum non nocere* (first, do no harm). It is the most essential obligation in the practice of medicine. Typically codified in the form of specific legal prohibitions, the principle should be obeyed without exception and punished when violated.[6] The obligations of nonmaleficence are far more stringent than those of beneficence; when the two clash, nonmaleficence overrides beneficence.[7]

5. Beauchamp and Childress, *Principles of Biomedical Ethics*, 262.
6. Beauchamp and Childress, *Principles of Biomedical Ethics*, 262.
7. However, it is not always clear where nonmaleficence ends and where beneficence begins

In medical practices, harm usually happens in the form of negligence or incompetence that does not fulfill the duty toward a patient. Medical practitioners are required to acquire professional competence (obtained through medical education and training) and to exercise due diligence in caring for patients.[8]

Conflict between Autonomy and Beneficence

A potential conflict exists between a physician's act (beneficence or nonmaleficence) and a patient's autonomy. Autonomy can come into conflict with beneficence when a patient disagrees with a physician's recommendation of what serves the patient's best interest. In this case, it is a moral question whether a physician can override a patient's autonomy. Paternalism refers to "actions taken toward another person without their consent, or a refusal to accept that person's own choices, desires, or actions, intended solely for the benefit of that person."[9] Paternalistic intervention is justified in certain conditions, for example, when a patient does not want treatment because of religious or cultural views (e.g., Jehovah's Witnesses' rejection of blood transfusion), or when a patient wants unnecessary treatment (e.g., cosmetic surgery) or to prolong a futile treatment. While many societies prioritize beneficence over autonomy, Western societies tend to respect the autonomy of patients even in cases where the physician believes patients are not acting in their own best interest.

Distributive Justice

Medical treatment incurs several costs. It is necessary to weigh the benefits and burdens of treatment. As we discussed, distributive justice is concerned with the fair distribution of goods, services, and burdens among persons in conditions of insufficiency (scarcity and competition).[10] Distributive justice in medicine involves allocating health-care goods and services that are scarce and insufficient to address all human illness and pain. This gives rise to competing priorities and obligations, especially when the treatment is scarce (e.g., organ transplant). Today, prolonged life expectancy and the rise of medical expenses have significantly raised medical costs. Despite available cures, the poor cannot afford the rising costs in the United States and other parts of the world.

---

because removing harmful conditions is a form of beneficence that requires positive actions for the patient.

8. If they fail to acquire competence or to provide due diligence, then this principle does not matter (because they are incompetent and patients are immediately exposed to harms).

9. Tubbs, *A Handbook of Bioethics Terms*, 122.

10. Beauchamp and Childress, *Principles of Biomedical Ethics*, 327.

Physicians must balance the specific personal need of patients with the overall public need of the health-care system. Physicians need to carefully decide on the best use of resources for their patients rather than narrowly focusing on each individual patient. They need to discern which treatments are obligatory (essential) and which are optional. A reasonable decision is finding which option benefits a patient most after weighing and assessing the medical condition and financial resources of the patient. Unnecessary treatments (e.g., cosmetic surgery) and a futile prolonging of life go against distributive justice. "Letting die" is prudent stewardship of limited resources. However, the distinction between obligatory and optional treatments will likely be further blurred and contested as human desire for bodily perfection grows, enhancement technologies become available, and the rich want to benefit from them. Good stewardship of resources is necessary to do justice to the basic needs of people and serve the common good of health care.

The Quality of Life

The principle of quality of life is gaining attention in medical ethics today, especially in medical issues such as the treatment of dying persons, fetuses, and newborns with severe medical problems. We need to look at the quality of life claim in this cultural context. The quality of life principle is informed by individualism and the principle of utility. Just as human dignity is interpreted through the lens of individual autonomy and rights, the quality of life standard is interpreted through utilitarian (cost-benefit) terms. The quality of life principle is frequently appealed to when a patient wants to avoid or reduce suffering. Norman Geisler argues that quality of life is a "thinly veiled form of utilitarianism."[11]

The idea of quality of life has merit because it illustrates the capability and particular personal situation of a patient. "When quality of life is sufficiently low and an intervention produces more harm than benefit for the patient, caregivers may justifiably withhold or withdraw treatment."[12] Interpreted under a utilitarian social script, however, it faces serious moral concerns. In general, utilitarianism treats suffering and pain as futile and meaningless (they go against individual self-interest/quality of life). That is, every unconquerable pain/suffering is considered useless. Utilitarianism relies heavily on a cost-benefit analysis that determines the utility of intervention in terms of reduction of pain/suffering and increase of pleasure.[13]

11. Geisler, *Christian Ethics*, 183.

12. Beauchamp and Childress, *Principles of Biomedical Ethics*, 215.

13. The Quality Adjusted Life Year (QALY) is a metric that measures the burden of disease—both the quality and the quantity of a patient's lived life.

The principle of the quality of life frequently conflicts with the norm of the sanctity of life. That is, when interpreted in a utilitarian way, the quality of life principle may relativize the inalienable worth of a person. Since it heavily depends on individual self-assessment, it is ambiguous and difficult to measure; it could easily be confused with personal preference and calculation. In particular, the principle can potentially be misused and abused, which may work against the free decision of a patient when medical care is seen or felt to be too burdensome. A medical community or a family may use the quality of life principle for a quick solution in order to ease financial and psychological burdens. The principle may end up morally justifying the removal of nonproductive members or patients who incur great costs to families or a society (the poor, the disabled, the mentally ill, and old patients). What operates under the slogan of "quality of life" may actually be social Darwinism and eugenics in disguise.

Therefore, a medical community needs to develop well-defined criteria in applying this principle in order to avoid arbitrary decisions, personal preferences, and utilitarianism (purely financial considerations). The quality of life principle is misleading. "Quality of life for the patient should also not be confused with the quality or the value of life for others, and proxies should not refuse treatment against the incompetent patient's interests to avoid burdens to the family or costs to society. The incompetent patient's best medical interests generally should be the decisive criterion for a proxy, even if these interests conflict with familial interests."[14]

Hence, the quality of life should not be defined by utility alone. In covenant ethics, love, justice, and power are more foundational values that define the quality of life. We may not completely disregard the quality of life principle from a pastoral perspective, if not a moral perspective. The case of "letting die" accepts this principle to a certain extent. However, medical decision making encompasses more than just utility or quality of life.

Medical Futility

Medical futility is another norm that physicians attend to in treating patients. It is associated with the distributive principle and the quality of life principle. Futility in medicine refers to "a situation in which patients who are irreversibly dying have reached a point at which further treatment provides no physiological benefit or is hopeless and becomes optional."[15] That is, any treatment is "highly unlikely to be efficacious" and rather becomes "more burdensome than beneficial."[16] In this

14. Beauchamp and Childress, *Principles of Biomedical Ethics*, 216.
15. Beauchamp and Childress, *Principles of Biomedical Ethics*, 212.
16. Beauchamp and Childress, *Principles of Biomedical Ethics*, 212–13.

situation, a physician makes a realistic assessment of treatment in light of medical condition and available material resources. Futility is an important factor that affects distributive justice in medicine.

The decision on futility is highly controversial because religious traditions and secular utilitarian values have diverging views on human sanctity. Today, in particular, the advancement of medical technology and enhancement technologies are changing views on health and expectations of human frailty and death. Thus, ideas about medical futility itself are changing. We are living in a society where "youth and strength are idealized, aging is transformed into a disease, and any form of dependence is eschewed as contrary to the dignity of the human person," and sickness is considered evil.[17] Medical practitioners are emerging as technocrats and liberators of humanity from disease.[18]

With cure or the unlimited prolonging of human life as its only goal (telos), medical technology increasingly performs a soteriological function in a secular context. That is, medicine is perceived as a utopian project that eliminates disease, suffering, pain, and death, and gives infinite freedom and choices for individuals. Technology projects an overly optimistic view of autonomy; to purchase technology is to enhance one's autonomy (in choosing one's physical shape, ability, and offspring) and is a completely acceptable idea in the culture of individualism and commercialism. Today, we see this ideology in medical technologies for human enhancement, IVF, and other reproductive technologies.

Transhumanism is a movement that combines medicine, technology, and capitalism. Inspired by modern beliefs in endless progress and science, transhumanism aims to increase individual autonomy and freedom by building a sovereign body that overcomes illness, old age, and infertility, and enhances physical shape, strength, mental ability, and the family gene pool. Many transhumanists perceive death, physical suffering, and bodily limitation or immobility as fundamental problems to which enhancement technology offers a solution. However, in the long term, we do not know whether this will lead to utopia or dystopia. It could rather complicate distributive justice because of the obvious gap between patients' high hopes for cures through technology and the actual reality of human frailty and limited resources.

Norms and Medical Worldviews

The reliance on principlism (norms/principles) tends to grow in a pluralistic society because moral principles are broader than rules and acceptable by different religious

17. Khushf, "Illness, the Problem of Evil, and the Analogical Structure of Healing," 23.

18. Interestingly, underneath it is a secularized message of the exodus—the liberation from disease and mortality and the hope for permanent youth, cure, and immortality.

and cultural groups because of their generality. However, these principles are not interpreted neutrally. Depending on the framework, the meaning and implications of norms can be interpreted in very different ways.

In a pluralistic society, the adjudication of these principles is increasingly difficult. Different individuals and groups interpret and prioritize differently depending on their moral frameworks. For example, a pro-life camp in the abortion debate emphasizes nonmaleficence over other norms, while the pro-choice position upholds beneficence for women, at least implicitly.

For instance, nonmaleficence is interpreted very differently in the treatment of a terminally ill patient. For some people, life-sustaining technologies such as artificial hydration, respiration, and nutrition are discouraged as they only prolong the patient's suffering and harm the patient in that manner. Others, however, would argue that removing such technologies amounts to abandoning the patient, thus harming the patient by directly, or indirectly, causing the patient's death.

Today, as in other domains of social life, contractualism deeply shapes medical ethics—the interpretation of the ideas of human dignity, informed decision, autonomy, justice, and nonmaleficence. Contractualism upholds the idea that a medical decision should be the agreement between a physician and a patient. In a contractual framework, these norms are approached as values decided contractually between a physician (or a hospital) and a patient. These norms are changing or losing their normative meaning (contents) under a widespread contractualism in medical practice. It is difficult to couch and practice the norms of generosity, commitment, and empathy in a contractual model. The principle of beneficence becomes nominal,[19] as the value of care is eroded. Care is something to purchase rather than receive; thus, one gets better care when one pays more. Or when death is imminent, care becomes completely futile. Consequently, the idea of informed consent is potent in this framework. On the contrary, the idea of human dignity, a cornerstone of liberal medical ethics, actually becomes weaker or even compromised. A contractual model narrows the moral perspective to immediate self-interest and profit. Consequently, the sense of public responsibility or a long-term perspective on medical decision making is severely underemphasized.

These norms are always interpreted in a particular social historical context, influenced by a dominant ideology or cultural ethos such as expressive individualism and utilitarianism. Today, a contractual model is closely tied to neoliberal capitalism, individualism, and utilitarianism. Individuals approach the relationship from the perspective of self-interest and autonomy, while medical practitioners approach it from their own self-interest, which is closely tied to corporate interests.

19. Rusthoven and Bartholomew, *Covenantal Biomedical Ethics for Contemporary Medicine.*

The corporatization of medicine for financial interest shapes medical decisions. We see this in the use of medical technologies for human enhancement, IVF, and other reproductive technologies. To purchase technology in order to enhance one's autonomy or to produce future offspring is accepted in the culture of individualism and utilitarianism. Commercialized medicine appeals to this ethos by offering more choices regarding one's physical shape, ability, and offspring in order to strengthen social competitiveness and family gene pool.

For example, today IVF and other reproductive technologies are quickly advancing because they are highly profitable but only lightly regulated. From sex selection to surrogates, IVF clinics in the United States provide rich clients with services outlawed elsewhere due to a host of ethical questions and dilemmas. They are commodifying human life, and children, and surrogate women, who tend to be poor; sperm and egg donors are exposed to their abuse and exploitation.[20] This does not mean all reproductive technologies and treatments are dangerous. Rather, we need to carefully examine their application and subject them to the commonly accepted norms of medicine. For example, physicians and technicians cannot solely serve the immediate interest of a patient (future parent) without considering the well-being of a child. Every parent, biological and nonbiological, and society have a covenantal responsibility toward a child.

The ascending contractual model is increasingly distorting medical practices and relationships between physicians and patients; the physicians' sense of fidelity is being eroded by neoliberalism. Troubling incidents are arising in which physicians, using their immense power over patients, do not fully disclose information about treatment. Under the pressure of corporate capitalism, medicine tends to see patients as consumers; the welfare of corporations, hospitals, and physicians often takes precedence over individual patients. Patients are manipulated, and the public bears unnecessary financial burdens for frivolous but expensive medical tests, as well as for prescriptions that result in addiction in some cases (e.g., painkillers).

The physician-patient relationship has also undergone changes. As we see rising litigation about medical practices, physicians get defensive in their practices (by demanding more screenings and tests). Many victims of opioid death and addictions are filing lawsuits against physicians, pharmacists, and pharmaceutical companies.

However, a contractual view of medicine is truncated; it is prone to be distortive. Ultimately, it cannot fulfill the mandate of medicine. It loses a holistic perspective of health that encompasses the spiritual-psychosomatic constitution of our existence. In addition, we know that not every contract is ethically right. Medical ethics cannot avoid the question of care that goes beyond monetary purchase. If everything is con-

20. Cha, "From Sex Selection to Surrogates."

tractual (grounded in self-interest), then there is not much room for care. If medicine loses the quality of care even when a cure is not possible, it betrays its mission.

To take individual autonomy or right as the only normative basis of a medical decision is limited and potentially distortive because it is detached from community, social cultural contexts and forces, and various concerned parties. It is also quite unilateral in disregarding responsibility toward others. Considering persons independent, fully autonomous entities is an example of very Western, modernistic thinking. No matter how potent this ideology is today, it is not true psychologically, developmentally, or socially.

The idea of rights does not offer much-needed insights into the complex social conditions and relational dynamics that patients experience. An individualist concept of rights makes it difficult to connect informed consent with the other two principles. For example, controversial medical issues, such as abortion and physician-assisted suicide, cannot be adequately understood apart from difficult human conditions. "There are unusually few criteria for determining when the term [human right] is used correctly and when incorrectly."[21]

New Covenant Ethics

How does new covenant ethics understand these norms and practices? Even with a quick glance, one can see in the principles previously discussed that a covenantal agreement is reached through the informed consent of the parties; the principle of beneficence is associated with the covenantal values of love and compassion, whereas nonmaleficence is associated with nonviolence. New covenant ethics also upholds the principles of human dignity and distributive justice. In fact, as these norms have developed under the influence of Protestant Christianity, they can be incorporated into a covenantal framework of new covenant ethics. From a covenantal perspective, these principles describe what kind of fidelity is required for a physician in treating a patient, with accountability also to a patient's family and a broader society.

Under the overarching vision of shalom, new covenant offers a capacious moral framework for these principles and practices. Medicine pursues health, which is not confined to physical healing but involves the entire person. Shalom and health are cognates; they seek the wholeness (body, emotion, and spirit) of each person and the entire community. The preamble of the World Health Organization constitution declares health to be "a state of complete physical, mental and social well-being and not merely the absence of disease or infirmity."[22] For Christians, pursuing health is

21. Griffin, *On Human Rights*, 15.

22. Grad, "The Constitution of the World Health Organization," 984.

part of shalom seeking because health is essential for human flourishing. The story of God's salvation includes the story of health that ultimately aims at shalom—the health of God's entire creation. In new covenant ethics, health is holistic. It involves not only smooth bodily functioning but also emotional, mental, and relational health. Hence, it is inevitably concerned with the nature and quality of relationship with God, others, and creation.

Although medical technology has contributed to the reduction of physical pain, the extension of life expectancy, and the control of diseases, human suffering in general has not abated in the neoliberal system. While the area of physical health may have progressed through scientific-technological advancements, mental health is seriously deteriorating. This is seen in the epidemic of anxiety disorders, depression, and other mental illness in all age and income groups.[23] "Pain comes in many shapes and sizes and it is never possible to separate the psychological aspects of pain from the organic."[24] The rise of mental illness is directly associated with the deterioration of social relationships and life quality. Covenant attempts to build and invigorate this deficiency. A strong covenantal relationship that cultivates trusted, truthful, and caring interactions is conducive to mental health. With its distinctive relational sensibility, new covenant ethics helps to embed the principles of medical ethics in a coherent and plausible moral framework; these norms are not abstract but relational and mutually interrelated.[25]

New covenant ethics affirms the invaluable worth of every person, for God is the creator of life, and every life is God's gift. To respect others is the responsibility of every person (first dialectic). As life is a gift, it does not belong to us; we need to use it in a responsible way. Life should be protected, nurtured, and celebrated.

However, the dignity of human life is neither absolute nor unlimited; it is mortal. In new covenant ethics, the dignity of human life does not mean its absolutization or sovereignty. The right to life is more about protection against harm than it is totalistic. Our destiny is from dust to dust; as earthlings, we are part of nature and subjected to its law, like other creatures.

Unlike a modern secular approach, new covenant ethics takes health in the context of a broader view of human origin and destiny as God's creature. That is, it takes finitude, vulnerability, and mortality as integral parts of general human experience and medical practices. Our body is not immortal; as a biological organism, it is on a journey from its beginning to its end. Medicine may cure many diseases and tech-

23. Asian spirituality, medicine, and spiritual practices (including martial arts, yoga, and meditation) show this inextricable and organic connection between mind and body.

24. Hauerwas, "Salvation and Health," 48.

25. William May's book *The Physician's Covenant* is helpful in exhibiting their interconnections.

nology may extend our life, but these cannot overcome mortality or suffering. The goal of human bodily existence is not immortality but shalom. The acceptance of this finitude is the wisdom that brings peace to us and helps us manage our life and resources in a more productive and meaningful way. Peaceful acceptance of mortality sets patients free from obsession with futile treatments, anguish, and anxiety.

From a covenantal perspective, autonomy does not mean self-sufficiency. Respect for autonomy does not have the final say. Futility should be a factor in treatment. Hence, the exercise of one's freedom should be moral and communal; the specific content of free decision is tested in relation to other norms. Freedom to choose is respected, but it is exercised responsibly (in an informed manner) for the common good. New covenant ethics ties medical decisions to the common good—how they contribute to God's shalom. One's obligations go beyond the immediate boundaries of contractual parties.

A covenantal approach takes both care and cure in balance. Paul Ramsey notes, "The patient has entered a covenant with the physician for his complete care, not for continuing useless efforts to cure."[26] In the NT, the word "heal" (*therapeuō*) has the double meaning of cure and care. Care is more important than cure for the church, as the former is the basis and ground of the latter. Care as the exercise of love (*hesed*) is a key sign of discipleship. The physician is obliged more toward care than toward the cure of a patient. Medical competence is important, but it does not exhaust all the responsibilities of a physician. Healing is eschatological. "Becoming whole does not mean being perfect, but being completed. It does not necessarily mean happiness but growth. It is often painful, but, fortunately, it is never boring. It is not getting out of life what we think we want, but it is the development and purification of the soul."[27] A covenantal responsibility of physicians and health-care practitioners is to journey together with patients in their pain and suffering regardless of the consequences. In the early Christian community under Jesus's new covenant, the sick and the old found support and care, and the hope that transcends this life even when cure was futile.

Covenant takes both cure and care as the constitutive elements of medical practice. In treating a patient, a physician has a caring responsibility that goes beyond the letter of the contract. This means that a physician's fidelity to a patient applies not only to the treatment and medical conditions of a patient but also to the conditions that cause illness. A physician may not cure the illness but can still provide care and alleviate the burden of a patient. The physician can still contribute to the wholeness of a patient.

26. Ramsey, *The Patient as Person*, 134.

27. Sanford, *Healing and Wholeness*, 20.

A physician is not only a specialist but also a steward who is called to embody virtues and values. Fidelity is required regardless of the ability to cure. Because of its communal and solidaric nature, beneficence is more prominent. The obligation to others in the covenant comprehensively extends beyond any narrow specification in legal stipulations or moral codes. The participants are called to show compassion and obligation beyond the letter of the law. In a covenantal context, beneficence is expressed through compassion and goodwill toward patients and their families.

In a covenantal framework, patients should also exercise fidelity toward physicians, their families, and society. They are partners in healing. Covenant ethics is reciprocal. Rights and duties are not unilateral; both a physician and a patient are responsible. Healing is collaborative. Mutual trust and clear communication of medical symptoms and options are important to achieve goals. In our culture and modern medical ethics, the virtue of a patient has been severely ignored and overshadowed by rights language. Along with rights, the responsibility of patients should be equally emphasized. Virtues such as fortitude, patience, self-observance, and care are helpful for patients to improve their health and maximize the effect of medical treatment.

With this general observation as background, we now discuss two major issues of medical ethics: abortion and physician-assisted suicide (PAS).

Abortion

Abortion has been a politically charged and divisive issue for several decades. The passion on both sides refuses to abate. Both sides are ideologically entrenched, and it becomes a hot-button issue in every presidential election because the president has the power to appoint a Supreme Court justice who could influence future decisions (or reverse past ones). Christians are not exempt from this division. In fact, conservative evangelicals have been the most vocally pro-life, antiabortion group.

What Is Abortion?

Abortion describes the termination of a pregnancy and typically has two forms: (1) natural abortion (or miscarriage) and (2) induced abortion using medical means to terminate a pregnancy. Since its nationwide legalization in 1973, induced abortion has become one of the most common surgical procedures in the United States. According to a survey by the Guttmacher Institute, the abortion rates steadily declined between 2011 and 2017, mostly due to the improvement and increase in contraceptive use, the decline in sexual activity, and increase in self-managed abortion using medication, that is, abortion performed without clinical supervision; there were

1,058,000 abortions in 2011, but 862,000 abortions in 2017 due to the decreases of births and pregnancies.[28] Public opinion in the United States on legalized abortion has remained relatively stable over the years; as of 2019, 61 percent of Americans approve of the legalization of abortion, while 38 percent think it should be illegal in all or most cases; however, 77 percent of white evangelicals in the United States hold that abortion should be illegal in all or most cases.[29]

Two foundational US Supreme Court cases on abortion—*Roe v. Wade* (1973) and *Planned Parenthood v. Casey* (1992)—set the tone and context for current debates on abortion. Both decisions have served as bulwarks to protect abortion rights.

While acknowledging women's constitutional right to receive an abortion (protected by the due process clause of the Fourteenth Amendment), *Roe v. Wade* attempted to balance the protection of a woman's health and the protection of a potential human life. It showed limited respect toward potential human life by permitting the state to regulate women's access to abortion in the second and third trimesters when fetal viability becomes stronger.

In *Planned Parenthood v. Casey*, the Court declared, "An undue burden exists and therefore a provision of law is invalid if its purpose or effect is to place substantial obstacles in the path of a woman seeking an abortion before the fetus attains viability." An "undue burden" is "an obstacle that is intentionally and unfairly put in the way of a party that is seeking to exercise a constitutional right." By replacing *Roe*'s trimester framework with the "undue burden" standard, the case had the effect of strengthening a woman's right to procure an abortion while weakening the state's protection of potential life.[30]

What Does Scripture Say about Abortion?

In general, the Bible is committed to the preservation, protection, and sanctity of life. For example, Kira Schlesinger reminds us that the "whole of the biblical witness is an expansive pro-life statement, from the creation of the cosmos to the second coming of Christ."[31] While rendering some legal protection to the fetus, Scripture and tradition do not clearly stipulate the full personhood of the fetus.

There is no direct and explicit reference to the status of the unborn child in the rest of the New Testament. There is no explicit mention for or against abortion in the Old or New Testament. Exodus 21:22–25 includes a reference to miscarriage

28. Nash and Dreweke, "The US Abortion Rate Continues to Drop."
29. "Public Opinion on Abortion."
30. Dunlap, "Three Constitutional Basics Every Abortion Rights Supporter Should Know."
31. Schlesinger, *Pro-Choice and Christian*, 92–93.

resulting from unintentional injury but does not talk about intentional abortion. In this instance, the crime is treated as part of property law in the broad context of the *lex talionis*. Punishment is required for the offender whose action results in the loss of a fetus, but it is not a quid pro quo, a life for a life. Rather, the husband of the woman receives monetary reparation for the potential loss of progeny. This passage does not explicitly address abortion. However, the mother and the fetus are qualitatively distinct. Only the mother is declared to be a legal person to whom the *lex talionis* applies.[32]

The Septuagint interpretation of Exodus 21:22–25 shares the same moral assumption. A determining factor for liability in miscarriage is how far the pregnancy is advanced at the time of miscarriage (that is, whether the miscarried fetus is formed or not). It renders some legal status to the already formed fetus, but the deformed or not-yet-formed fetus is not given the legal status of personhood.

On the other hand, early Christians in the Greco-Roman world rejected abortion and infanticide. The Didache, a very early handbook of ethics, teaches: "You shall not murder a child by abortion nor shall you kill one who has been born" (2:2).

Personhood

Since Scripture does not provide a clear and well-defined moral guideline about abortion, scholars have explored the issue by relying on core norms/values and basic convictions of the Bible. Today national debates on abortion in the United States turn on the definition of personhood and rights language.

The advocates of both pro-choice and pro-life positions agree that a person has certain rights (e.g., the right to life) and that one's personhood is not based on performance or capability but on something inherent and sacred in the person. Simply by virtue of the fact that one is a person, rights are conferred. Regardless of social status, religion, national origin, race, or any other social categories, the fundamental dignity and rights of a person are transcendentally endowed and inalienable.[33] However, the sides divide sharply over the definition of personhood and the moral and legal status of the fetus: When does a human life begin? Who/what is the fetus? Is it merely bodily tissue, or does it constitute a full person? Does the fetus have full-fledged rights?

There are divergent views on when a human life begins (or, more precisely, when an embryo or fetus attains personhood) in pregnancy: conception, implantation, "quick-

32. Hays, *Moral Vision*, 447.

33. Personhood is a highly contested notion, historically loaded and politically charged because the history of slavery and genocide and eugenics has revolved around these questions.

ening," viability, or birth. Conflicts are inevitable when the theological or philosophical definition of a person differs from the legal definition. These conflicts are increasingly inevitable in a religiously pluralistic society. The questions of when life begins and when the fetus becomes a human being do not exactly coincide. The different answers to these two questions should be attended to. Some may believe that life begins with conception, but this does not necessarily mean that a zygote has full legal rights as a person.

This question on personhood and the beginning of human life recurs in the debates on embryonic stem cell research: Is it acceptable to use human embryos for therapeutic research for healing certain diseases? What do we do with the leftover embryos from infertility treatments? Can embryos be created for research purposes? The answers to these questions, as in the case of abortion, depend on how one thinks of the personhood of the zygote and the beginning of human life. If one believes that a zygote is a full person whose life has begun from the moment of conception, then any destruction of a stem cell is equivalent to destroying a human life.

The majority of Christian ethicists oppose creating embryonic stem cells for research because it not only destroys nascent life but also commodifies the procreative process so that women's bodies can be exploited for profit. These concerns are more acute today because embryonic stem cell research and therapeutic cloning are closely tied with commercial interests.

Pro-Life Perspective

A pro-life position claims that human personhood is endowed from the moment of conception. The fetus is a full person and has the right to life simply by being a member of a human species rather than by having the ability to perform certain functions.[34] Once it is defined/declared that personhood begins at conception, the fetus has an inalienable right to life and abortion becomes the intentional killing (tantamount to murder) of a human person. Hence it cannot be legally permitted; every human being has the moral duty to protect an innocent person.[35]

Within pro-life positions, several divergent perspectives exist. For those who follow the principle that life begins at conception, even coerced or highly undesirable acts, such as rape and incest, do not justify abortion. Even if conception is the

34. Clark and Rakestraw, *Readings in Christian Ethics*, 2:527.

35. Kaczor claims that a human embryo "is a whole, complete organism, a living individual human being whose cells work together in a coordinated effort of self-development towards maturity." Kaczor, *The Ethics of Abortion*, 113. However, despite his high view of personhood, Kaczor notes that indirect abortions are ethically permissible in the case of maternal-fetal conflict as long as the abortion is performed compliant with the principles of double effect. Indirect abortion refers to a form of abortion whose primary effect is a medical treatment of a pregnant woman, while the death of fetus (abortion) is only a secondary effect in operation.

consequence of rape or incest, which is morally outrageous and despicable, it does not alter the moral status of the fetus as a person.[36] A woman who is impregnated by rape or incest is still morally obligated to protect and preserve the life of the fetus.

This essentialist view faces difficulties when the right to life of the fetus is in conflict with the life of the mother. That is, the life of the mother can sometimes be threatened by her pregnancy. This view cannot offer a coherent moral principle that adjudicates the conflicting claims of rights and obligations. Pro-life proponents tend to choose a mother's right over the fetus's right, but the position is not consistent.

Pro-Choice Perspective

While Catholics and evangelicals mostly follow the pro-life perspective, many mainline Christians and secular feminists and liberals uphold a pro-choice position. In contrast to an essentialist perspective of the pro-life position, the pro-choice perspective generally follows functionalism: "an organism is a human person by virtue of its ability to function personally; a human organism is a human person if it can or will act personally, that is, if it acts as a moral, intellectual, spiritual agent."[37] Pro-choice advocates make a moral and legal distinction between a fetus and a person. That is, the fetus is a biological form of life but does not have moral agency; consequently, it has no right to life. Acting personally indicates the ability to think, feel, and communicate in an entity that has rough human features.[38] One traditional criterion similar to this is the principle of viability—the ability to breathe by oneself from the moment of birth. For example, Kevin Wildes notes, "while the early human embryo is worthy of respect, it ought not to be given personal moral status until there has been sufficient development of the embryo."[39]

There are divergent positions within the pro-choice perspective. A Christian pro-choice position claims that the fetus is in the process of becoming a human but is not yet a full member of the human community. It has certain moral rights but not full legal rights. Just as a child and an adult have different statuses and rights in society, the fetus has different legal protections. It should be protected, but not at the expense of the life of the mother.

For secular pro-choice advocates, the personhood of the fetus is nonexistent, or ambiguous at best. They cannot attribute personhood to a zygote (a fertilized egg) because a huge biological transformation is required for a zygote to grow into a child.[40] Hence, when the difficult moral decision of abortion is faced, it is the

36. Kaczor, *The Ethics of Abortion*, 196.

37. Clark and Rakestraw, *Readings in Christian Ethics*, 2:528.

38. See Fletcher, "Indicators of Humanhood," 1–4.

39. Wildes, "The Stem Cell Report," 14.

40. Schlesinger, *Pro-Choice and Christian*, 85.

pregnant woman who has moral authority to make the decision because only she has full indisputable personhood.[41]

Politically, the pro-choice position is closely associated with the overall goals of the feminist movement. Feminists claim that pregnancy has been an impediment to women's freedom and self-fulfillment; pregnancy ties women to the biological process and the household. Feminists focus on the negative impact of pregnancy on women's agency and freedom. Women control their own bodies and fertility. Legal abortion as women's constitutional right is crucial to secure and expand their agency and autonomy, and thus their equality. Women should use reproductive technologies, such as abortion, contraception, and sterilization techniques, that offer liberating options for women. In this ideological framework, the current secular pro-choice feminist perspective treats abortion as a purely surgical issue.

New Covenant Ethics

What is the approach of new covenant ethics to abortion? Who is the fetus in God's covenantal community? Its relational approach is more adequate in addressing the moral concerns pertaining to abortion.

New covenant ethics is critical of the current individualistic and rights-centered approaches of both sides in the abortion debate. The language of rights (right to life of an unborn child versus right of a woman to her body and fertility) is dominant in these debates, but it is not helpful in addressing the moral issues around induced abortion. Despite its legitimate place in a legal system, rights language has become overly individualistic in the current secular cultural context. Contemporary rights-based ethics relies solely on justice as entitlement (equality) at the expense of other principles (justice as need and capability). Rights language is not helpful because it abstracts the decision from women's stories and particular relationships. Indeed, it fails to attend to women's stories and their agonies in pregnancy; their stories are suppressed or hidden out of shame, regret, guilt, or fear of ostracization. From a covenantal perspective, rights language is not relational but reductive. To frame abortion as the conflict a between woman's right and a fetus's right is tragic and unhelpful because both women and fetuses are marginalized and powerless.[42]

Because of their individualistic ethics, conservative Christians tend to believe that abortion rates can be lowered through moral education on sex (abstinence)[43] and

41. Schlesinger, *Pro-Choice and Christian*, 87.

42. Part of the reason why this issue is difficult is because it is built upon the narratives of historical/social and ontological victimhood. Victimhood (or defense of victims) makes the issue highly emotional and uncompromising.

43. Traditionally, sexual illegitimacy (premarital sex, sex outside of marriage) was frequently

tougher antiabortion laws. Their strategy is to expand state-level restrictions on abortion and ultimately reverse *Roe v. Wade*. Over the past few decades, in fact, many states controlled by the Republicans have dramatically expanded restrictions on abortion. For example, Nebraska outlaws abortion twenty weeks into pregnancy based on the understanding that fetuses can feel pain after that point. Charmaine Yoest, president of Americans United for Life, explains, "We know that it makes a difference what the law says in any particular state." "You can see dramatic decreases in abortion."[44] However, the pro-life approach of conservative Christians is limited, and potentially distortive, in guiding churches on this issue of abortion. Their perspective neglects the socioeconomic realities surrounding abortion. Because of their individualistic ethics, they refuse to consider the social cultural contexts, economic concerns, and family situations a woman faces in making the difficult decision on abortion. For example, Elizabeth Nash, a Guttmacher public policy associate, notes that restrictive state laws tend to have little impact on affluent and middle-class women: "What they end up doing is targeting the most vulnerable women—the ones without resources to go other places."[45]

Likewise, the secular pro-choice position fails to seriously attend to the social and relational matrix of women's decision on abortion, as well as the psychological weight and agony of abortion. Abortion affects the psychological health of women, even women fully committed to a pro-choice position. New covenant ethics disagrees with the secular pro-choice perspective that dismisses the embryo and fetus as mere human tissue and declines to respect it as a form of human life. New covenant ethics sees this as the instrumentalization of human life. A society that does not respect the lives of the vulnerable (both human and nonhuman) is a cruel one.

Although a secular feminist revolt against the received sexist norms of patriarchy is justified, secular feminism's view of women's agency and bodily freedom is shaped by a modernistic individualism rather than the relational, solidaric, and care ethic that feminism claims to pursue. Jean Bethke Elshtain notes: "The irony of the moment may well be that women, caught in the grip of the rationalist world view, wind up endorsing the image of freedom from nature that, historically, has invited the most insidious forms of domination—of women and of whole ways of life. It is a technocratic prejudice, not a liberating or democratic ideal, that we are somehow most 'human' when we are in absolute control."[46]

From a covenantal perspective, we are stewards of lives regarded as gifts to a human community. In the Bible, God is the God of life. God is for life, and God's

---

the impetus for abortion. However, this concern is mitigated because of the wide availability of measures of contraception.

44. Associated Press, "US Abortion Rate Up Slightly after Years of Decline."

45. Associated Press, "US Abortion Rate Up Slightly after Years of Decline."

46. Elshtain, "Reflections on Abortion, Values and the Family," 67.

purpose is the flourishing of all lives. The story of Jesus consummates in the resurrection—the symbol of God's triumph over death. Christians are called to protect innocent lives and practice expansive life ethics. Life is a gift from God because our body is the temple of the Spirit. Our bodies are not our own. Covenant assumes and recognizes the gift dimension of human life. Human life is not an isolated event. Human life is not purely individualistic. Human life is possible through the contribution of many known and unknown hands who make possible the continuation of human life. Humans are indebted to others. This implies that the fetus cannot be treated as a mere body or a malignant tumor. It is a form of life in the process of developing into a full human being. The fetus is a prospective member of God's covenantal community. Though not a full person yet, it still is a person in process. It is in a relationship with God (cf. Noah's covenant—God's covenant with all lives); it is also under the promise and blessing of the atoning work of Jesus Christ. Jürgen Moltmann claims: "God has a relationship to every embryo, every severely handicapped person, and every person suffering from one of the diseases of old age, and he is honored and glorified in them when their dignity is respected."[47] Therefore, abortion induced in any form, whether warranted or not, is, in principle, an undesirable violent action. Abortion is never a purely utilitarian nor pragmatic medical procedure, but is always a moral decision. The Spirit grieves whenever there is an abortion.

All members of a community are responsible in welcoming, nurturing, and educating a child. Every abortion should be done in grief rather than relief or celebration. It convicts the community of its moral limitations and unfaithfulness toward each other. Abortion saddens us because it indicates the loss not only of life but also of a potential particular person—the mystery, gift, and character of this potential person are lost.

From a covenantal perspective, every form of abortion, in principle, is undesirable, because every life is a gift. In light of God's shalom in which every life flourishes, abortion is tragic. Intentional abortion, in the final analysis, goes against this telos of God. It becomes clear in the context of the new covenant that every life should be welcomed, nourished, and protected.

Why Do Women Have Abortions?

New covenant ethics avoids the danger of moral reductionism and abstractionism found in rights language. It attends to various moral complexities around abortion that are complicated, even tragic, social realities and moral dilemmas.

One common claim among poor women resorting to abortion is that they have no other choice. Personal accounts of women disclose that their actual decisions are

47. Moltmann, *God for a Secular Society*, 84.

informed less by the idea of women's rights than by their personal situation, capability (relational complexity), and family conditions. They measure their medical decision concerning the consequences of pregnancy against their circumstances. Abortion is neither purely a medical nor a personal moral issue, but mostly social and economic in nature. Various social and cultural factors (such as limited financial resources and social biases against single parenthood, and individual factors such as desires for self-fulfillment and job arrangements) also impinge on the decision. Like other human activities, medical decisions, such as abortion, are embodied decisions. Despite basic biological similarities, each decision to end a pregnancy is different, just as each individual pregnancy is different from another. An abortion is the sum decision consisting of a particular woman with a particular man in a particular social context. Therefore, a woman's choice toward abortion is not purely individualistic but inevitably relational, social, and economic in nature, influenced by her surroundings.

Pregnancy and childbirth are highly burdensome and difficult, and potentially life changing.[48] They have a long-term effect on a woman's social status, future marriage, education, and professional career, and affect the lives of other children in the case of a poor family. Women's decisions on abortion are affected by multiple factors, but finances, access to high-quality contraceptives, and individual self-fulfillment play a major role in them.[49] According to the "fact sheet" of the Guttmacher Institute, in the year 2014:

- about 60 percent of US women having an abortion were in their twenties, about 11 percent were teenagers
- racially, white, black, and Latinx patients accounted for 39 percent, 28 percent, and 25 percent of abortions in 2014, respectively, while other races and ethnicities accounted for 9 percent
- about 75 percent of abortion patients in the United States are poor or low income
- 59 percent of the patients already have had at least one birth
- 62 percent are religiously affiliated (Catholic, 24 percent; mainline Protestant, 17 percent; evangelical Protestant, 13 percent; other religions, 8 percent).[50]

The abortion rate fluctuates according to economic cycles: abortions decrease when the economy is doing well, but they increase when the economy is struggling.

48. Cf. Alexander, "My Rapist Apologized."
49. Alan Guttmacher Institute, "US Abortion Patients."
50. Alan Guttmacher Institute, "Induced Abortion in the United States."

This shows just how much abortion is influenced by a woman's economic situation. Furthermore, while permitting legal abortion (virtually in any stage), US society is awfully limited in its support for pregnant women, mothers, children, families, and especially the poor and people of color.[51] Expensive health-care costs, lack of a child-care support system, and a highly competitive job market are major contributing factors in women's decisions for abortion.

The contractual nature of many sexual relationships also influences women's abortion decisions. The current (individualistic, utilitarian, and contractual) social script on sex has made pregnancy a woman's responsibility. Given the available medical technology to terminate pregnancy, continuing the pregnancy against the will of a male partner seems personally irresponsible and culturally outdated. A woman is more likely to resort to abortion when her male partner is financially and emotionally unsupportive about the pregnancy and raising the child. This is because society still holds the single mother responsible for unwanted or unsupported pregnancy and expects her to raise the child. A woman might choose abortion fearing that the child might scare away potential male partners or a husband. When relational and financial supports are unavailable, abortion may be the easiest and simplest, the most practical measure to clean up a potential relationship mess.

Christine Pohl's observation is poignant: "Policies, and the absence of them, no health care, family, maternity and paternity leave, and mother/child nutrition are deeply connected to whether or not abortion will seem reasonable and responsible."[52] Many women seem to be conditioned to choose abortion. "Claiming no choice is a wounded, despairing response to a situation that allowed few good options."[53]

With its relational approach, new covenant ethics changes the moral rhetoric and framework around abortion. It sees the fetus and a mother in the context of human interdependence and mutual accountability. That is, every baby is conceived and born into the nexus of social relationships and certain social conditions. In this regard, every abortion indicates the failure of our fidelity (not just that of a pregnant woman but also her partner, family, church, and society) to a developing life-form.

New Covenant Ethics

The debate on when a fetus becomes a person is not likely to be resolved anytime soon. Hence, new covenantal ethics proposes an incremental approach that I believe

51. Pohl, "Abortion," 221.
52. Pohl, "Abortion," 221.
53. Pohl, "Abortion," 216.

is more effective in the long run than the black-and-white approach of either a full ban or complete freedom from restrictions on abortion. From a covenantal perspective, important questions are: What can we do to promote the culture that respects life and enhances women's capability? Practically, how can we reduce abortion? The focus should be to nurture a pro-life culture that reveres every life and enhances women's capability instead of fighting about whose rights should be protected. The Christian community and the broader society must do their best to remove or reduce the contributing factors to abortion by taking an incremental approach focusing on reducing abortion rates.

Unless the social capability of women (jobs, education, child care, economic subsistence) is addressed—in particular, for women of color, poor women, and less educated women—the number of abortions is not likely to decline. Hence, prevention requires the provision of various kinds of support systems: financial, emotional or relational, and medical. Although preventive measures, such as sex education, can help reduce the number of abortions, the reduction of the abortion rate requires more than the moral determinations of pregnant women. A pro-life vision is more likely to be actualized through the pro-life conditioning of a society that respects and protects life in general. In this respect, pro-life Christians must practice consistent life ethics that values life in every form, not just in abortion. Life ethics should expand to the issues of war, the death penalty, a living wage, health care, creation care, and care for the marginalized.

Any decision on abortion is a tragic one; nevertheless, it is inevitable in certain cases in a broken world. Abortion is morally permissible in cases of rape and incest. A woman should not be forced to carry a pregnancy against her will in cases of rape and incest, for conception is against her will, and thus fidelity has already been violated by another. To force her to carry a pregnancy is to further traumatize her victimization.

Abortion should be legally available for women in those tragic cases.[54] From a practical point of view, the complete ban of abortion is not feasible. Like prostitution, it faces the problem of enforceability. When abortion is banned, it typically mushrooms in unregulated "back-alley" abortion clinics that harm and undermine women's health and even their lives.[55]

However, it is equally wise to apply specific criteria to different phases of pregnancy, degrees of protection based on the developmental stage of the fetus. If abortion is inevitable, then it should occur within the first trimester. We should also at-

54. For a philosophical analysis of this position, see Spiegel, "Can a Christian Be Morally Pro-Life and Politically Pro-Choice?," 107–15.

55. Stassen and Gushee, *Kingdom Ethics*, 234.

tend to the pain inflicted upon the fetus. While freedom of women over their bodies should be respected, these freedoms need to be balanced with other factors—the culture respecting life. From the perspective of just peacemaking (and given our covenantal responsibility to the fetus), it makes sense to discourage late-term abortions unless the mother faces a medical emergency. I am not opposed to measures that discourage or restrict abortion such as requiring parental consent for a minor's abortion, imposing a twenty-four-hour waiting period, and offering information on crisis pregnancy services. For example, it is theologically reasonable and politically practicable to ban third-trimester abortions or partial-birth abortions except when a woman's physical health is seriously in danger.

In fact, public opinion on abortion in the United States is closely associated with the permissible time of abortion. Sixty-one percent of US adults believe abortion should be allowed in the first trimester of a pregnancy; opposition to abortion rises to 64 percent in the second trimester of a pregnancy, with support dropping to 27 percent. The level of opposition increases further in the third trimester, with 80 percent opposing abortion and only 14 percent supporting it.[56]

Euthanasia

Euthanasia, originating from Greek, means "good death." It refers to an intentional act to end the life of "an individual in a (relatively) peaceful or painless manner to prevent extended suffering or a prolonged dying process for that individual."[57]

Euthanasia is divided into active and passive forms, depending on the way it is conducted. Described as "mercy killing," active euthanasia directly takes the life of a patient by using a toxin or other lethal means to cause death. Passive euthanasia is an indirect act that causes the death of a patient by intentionally withholding or withdrawing a treatment that is necessary to sustain life. One may characterize the distinction as the difference between commission (committing killing) and omission (refraining treatment). In passive euthanasia, it is not a direct act of killing but a disease that causes death; but death is still intentional.

Euthanasia is also categorized as voluntary and involuntary, depending on "the degree of that person's voluntary request [or informed consent] for it."[58] Voluntary euthanasia occurs when a fully competent patient makes the free, informed request for euthanasia. That is, a patient volunteers to end his or her life and asks for assis-

56. "Abortion."

57. Tubbs, *A Handbook of Bioethics Terms*, 54.

58. Tubbs, *A Handbook of Bioethics Terms*, 55.

tance from others in so doing. Physician-assisted suicide (PAS) is currently legalized in some parts of the United States[59] and in several other countries, including Canada, the Netherlands, Belgium, Switzerland, and Colombia. It has a wider appeal in the cultural milieu of expressive individualism.

Nonvoluntary euthanasia occurs when a patient is unable to make an informed request or consent because the patient is unable (as in the case of an infant, a very small child, or one who is mentally incompetent such as someone in a persistent vegetative state or coma) to understand his or her medical condition and make an informed request or consent. Finally, involuntary euthanasia describes a kind of euthanasia that happens either without a patient's informed consent or contrary to a patient's expressed wishes. No matter the motivation, it is tantamount to killing a patient who does not have any desire to die.

Letting Die

Any discussion of euthanasia must take up the distinction between passive euthanasia and letting die. Letting die is similar to passive euthanasia in that the underlying disease or injury is the direct cause of death. But it is different in terms of intention. Unlike passive euthanasia, letting die never intends to bring about the death of a patient, although a physician knows that a patient will die soon. The critical difference is whether death is something foreseen or something intentional. Letting die simply lets nature (via disease or injury) take its own course. Guided by the principle of medical futility, letting die is a decision based on foresight; the death does not result from intention. Recognizing the futility of further treatment, it changes the focus from cure to care, such as pain management and emotional and spiritual support in order to help patients approach death. Letting die still involves commitment to life. It does not withhold life-prolonging or life-sustaining technologies if they can potentially save one's life.[60] In letting die, commitment and emphasis move from cure to care of a patient in the dying process. There seems to be no difference when viewed from the outside, but from the perspective of the new covenant, the distinction between intention and foresight is important. The intention of killing (ending a life) someone is never justifiable, but futile treatment is also not good and responsible stewardship. In light of God's sacrificial love in Jesus Christ (memory) and in the hope of resurrection, letting die is a reasonable, unproblematic option for Christians.

59. Physician-assisted suicide is permitted, with the stipulation that the patient must administer the lethal dosage of medication herself or himself without the assistance of a medical professional.

60. Clark and Rakestraw, *Readings in Christian Ethics*, 2:96.

Substituted Judgment

Substituted judgment plays an important role in medical decisions. When a patient is incompetent, temporarily or permanently, to give informed consent on medical treatment, medical professionals rely on advance directives and living wills as a substitute for informed consent. When advance directives and living wills are not available, the decision-making authority is handed over to a surrogate decision-maker who decides in place of the patient. Usually next of kin (parent, spouse, or other family member) or a person designated as a durable power of attorney can exercise surrogate judgment. The surrogate should have "sufficient knowledge of the beliefs, values, fears, and aspirations of that individual to confidently predict what he would choose if he were currently competent and able to choose. In other words, the surrogate should be able to answer the question, 'What would this patient want in this situation?'"[61] To avoid unnecessary conflicts among family members at the time of a medical crisis, preparing a living will in advance is necessary.[62]

Physician-Assisted Suicide (PAS)

Assisted suicide has been practiced throughout human history. PAS is a form of voluntary euthanasia conducted with the assistance of a physician.

The moral norms of medical ethics are involved in the debate on the morality of PAS. Advocates of PAS appeal to the principle of autonomy. They claim that euthanasia is a way to exercise final control and power over one's body. Advocates of PAS assert that it does not harm any other person, but only the patient. To voluntarily take one's life is one's free choice; PAS respects the autonomy (right) of a dying person. Medical professionals thus have the responsibility (beneficence) to assist it.

There is controversy whether PAS is an expression of care (a beneficent act of a physician) or the violation of the norm of nonmaleficence. Its defenders say it is an exercise of compassion to relieve the pain and suffering of a patient. However, critics assert that in light of the sanctity of life, it is a harm to life. In addition to autonomy, advocates also appeal to the principle of the quality of life; instead of going through a prolonged period of pain and other suffering related to illness (e.g., financial burden), PAS is a better option to keep a patient's quality of life.

As in the abortion issue, to frame the debate in terms of right to life (and right to die) alone misses what is going on. PAS cannot solely be discussed in terms

61. Tubbs, *A Handbook of Bioethics Terms*, 160–61.

62. Substituted judgment is different from the best interest judgment. Both are made by the surrogate, but the former attempts to reconstruct a patient's own judgment while the latter decides what would be good for a patient, thus a surrogate's own judgment.

of individual rights or autonomy. Richard A. McCormick offers four factors that contribute to the cultural acceptance of PAS: (1) the absolutization of autonomy, (2) the secularization of medicine, (3) the inadequate management of pain, and (4) the financial pressure of health care.[63]

PAS is another form of medical practice that embodies an individualistic view of human life and medical decision making. Idealized in the form of a courageous individual decision—the final heroic exercise of agency—PAS gives the facade of death as something one chooses and controls.

PAS is a product of contractual utilitarian thinking (the greatest good for the greatest number), for a patient is released from suffering and the patient's family and the state are relieved of the financial burden of care. However, underneath PAS is a deep fear, anxiety, and sense of isolation.

The cultural acceptance of PAS reflects the changed cultural perception of death, which is another sign of the declining Christian influence. Over the past few decades, the cultural perception of death has dramatically changed in a post-Christian culture. This affects people's decisions about death. To a considerable degree, PAS is driven by the fear of pain and loneliness. This fear gets stronger as humans lose narratives and a meaning system that address the question of death. A God-less culture has lost the horizon of perspective to see life and death in a non-zero-sum relationship. In a naturalist worldview that dismisses God and eternity, people lack resources to cope with the threat of death. Lacking symbols and rituals, they are afraid to confront the naked reality of death alone.

For those who believe death is the ultimate end of life, "the alternatives are health or death," as Bonhoeffer said. "The value of suffering as the forming of life through the threat of death is disregarded, even ridiculed."[64] In this cultural milieu, physicians are under pressure from increasing numbers of patients who, with an unrealistic expectation of technology, are demanding cure at whatever cost. If a cure is not available, they request PAS.

The individual capability of a patient and the availability of communal support are other factors in decision making about PAS. Pain management could enhance the capability of a patient in the last stage of life. The inadequate management of pain and the insufficiency of palliative care make a huge difference. Most people who receive palliative care are cancer patients, but only a small number of cancer patients have access to palliative care. Most people who die from euthanasia or PAS in the Netherlands are cancer patients. This shows that palliative care makes a difference for patients when deciding their fate.[65]

63. McCormick, "Physician-Assisted Suicide," 1132–34.

64. Bonhoeffer, *Ethics*, 129.

65. Materstvedt et al., "Euthanasia and Physician Assisted Suicide," 97.

New Covenant Ethics

The Bible does not offer specific guidance on PAS or letting die. New covenant ethics opposes PAS for several reasons. PAS is not an exercise of human autonomy but a tragic and desperate effort to cope with insurmountable pain, fear, and loneliness that individuals face. From a covenantal perspective, enhancing pain management and communal care could substantially reduce the attraction of PAS because unmanaged pain and financial burdens are major contributing factors for seeking PAS.

New covenant ethics believes that, in principle, PAS goes against the sanctity of life that God has granted. Autonomy or informed consent alone cannot triumph over the norm of dignity. Human sanctity is a universal standard. It is not solely up to an individual's whims and decisions. After all, we do not recognize consent to adult slavery (selling oneself as a slave) for a similar reason. "We should not confuse respect for a person and his dignity with a readiness to permit or assist him to do whatever he chooses."[66]

PAS may appear to affirm and expand individual choice and autonomy. But our exercise of autonomy is not abstract; it is always socially embedded. Once legally available, there is the danger of coercion of a patient who refuses PAS. "The decision and plea to be killed is hardly an unforced decision if the terms and conditions under which we deliver care for the dying is already woefully mistargeted, inadequate, or downright neglectful."[67] In a patient's decision on life and death, the patient may be coerced to choose death (from pressure from family members, caregivers, or government) rather than being allowed to exercise his or her autonomy. This is a slippery slope for other persons whose lives are judged by society as lacking "quality." As a result, human dignity and reverence for life will further shrink.

Furthermore, legalizing PAS will dangerously reinforce the contractual social ethos so that "the role of caregivers shifts from simple solidarity with the patient to that of managers of an event that the patient has not fully owned."[68] Additionally, family members will approach a patient from the perspective of management rather than solidarity and companionship in pain; thus, life can be extinguished when it loses its "quality." Hence, in our society, where suicide and depression rates are going up, PAS is likely to have more social traction. Without supportive measures that enhance the capability of patients, that PAS becomes an accepted practice of medicine is probable.

A patient on her or his deathbed is in desperate need of communal fidelity in the form of presence, care, aid, support, and sharing. A Christian community needs to

66. May, *Testing the Medical Covenant*, 26.
67. May, *Testing the Medical Covenant*, 26.
68. May, *Testing the Medical Covenant*, 27.

show solidarity with people in pain/suffering and become a patient's companion in weathering the last stage of life on Earth. The church, historically, has played an important role in care for the ill. Through its communal love and generous support, a Christian community may demonstrate, physically and emotionally, God's abiding grace in times of suffering and pain (exemplifying the vision of 1 Corinthians 12—solidarity in suffering); that is, the patient is not abandoned in a dark dungeon of loneliness and despair.

The story of God's incarnation and suffering in Jesus equips Christianity to deal with the fear of suffering and death. The story of death is central to the Christian narrative and its rituals. Both baptism and the Eucharist have to do with death—the former, the death of our old selves; the latter, the death of our Lord. "Death and resurrection are inevitably and necessarily woven together in the Christian imagination."[69] From a covenantal perspective, death is part of the spiritual journey.

When recovery is unlikely, it is reasonable not to prolong life in futility. For Christians, a good death is not a painless death but one well prepared for and consonant with a patient's identity in the hope of resurrection. It is a death that one faces not in isolation but in community. Even when facing death (seemingly meaningless pain), we are not lost from God's sight, care, and goodness. Life does not end with death. Our covenantal relationship with God is not only confined to our body and history but is also promised and continued to eternity; relationship with God is the unity of body and soul. It does not terminate at the moment of death.

A dying person often desperately looks for assurance, promise, and comfort. The presence of the family and community is the most empowering experience for the dying. For Christians, faith is a blessing and the gospel is hope. The fear of being isolated and abandoned (physically, emotionally, and historically forgotten) is countered by God's promise of abiding presence, love, and compassion.

Health-Care System

In the United States, the health-care system is market driven and profit motivated. Health is treated more as an individual good than as a public good. Except for the poor (Medicaid) and the elderly (Medicare), health care is distributed (in fact purchased) according to the financial contributions of people. The US health-care system is defined by individual merit rather than basic need and equality. The system is designed to offer more choices for individuals rather than to meet basic needs. Consequently, tens of millions are suffering from a lack of adequate care, while only a limited number of rich individuals can afford both care and meaning-

69. Guroian, "Learning How to Die Well," 1077.

ful choice. The uninsured live with fear, anxiety, and a growing sense of despair. As William May laments, "they suffer a triple deprivation—the pain of illness, the desperation of little or no treatment, and cruel proof that they do not really belong to the community."[70]

Simultaneously, under prevailing neoliberal capitalism, we see the blatant commodification of health care for corporate profit. Like other corporations, insurance and pharmaceutical companies lobby to set high prices for their products and seek tax benefits. Driven by financial gain, many doctors pursue specialist tracks in their career choices. May critiques: "We tend to be acute care gluttons and preventive care anemics."[71] Consequently, citizens are woefully underprovided for in preventive and primary care and mental health coverage, although as of 2017, health-care spending accounted for 18 percent of the US GDP, reaching $3.5 trillion, or $10,739 per capita.[72]

From a covenantal perspective, health care is a social good.[73] It is a necessity of life. Every person instinctively seeks out health.[74] Along with food, clothing, and shelter, health care is a basic human good that everybody needs for their dignity and flourishing. Every person has the right to health care regardless of individual abilities, wealth, and racial/gender background. Since it is indispensable, it is immoral when health care is guided by profit motive and the principle of utility rather than directed toward the common good of society. When driven by profit, the dignity of individuals is undermined. "When we do not give access to care, we also diminish the vigor of our common life. Sick people cannot work productively. In relieving individual, private distress, a nation enables its people to contribute more fully to public life and to economic well-being. Thereby the nation serves its own public flourishing, not only instrumentally but also morally and psychologically to the degree that it signals by its care the strength of its covenant with its own."[75]

Medicine is a bellwether of a community's empathy toward human dignity. The most visible indicator of whether a person is cared for is how a community treats her when she is ill. Together with basic income, health care is one of the key indices of social solidarity and fidelity—how "communal" and caring a particular society is. As observed in the COVID-19 crisis in 2020, catching a disease is not necessarily individualistic but involves vulnerability to transmission from others. Most people are not responsible for the diseases they get. This indicates that health cannot be a

70. May, *The Physician's Covenant*, 211.
71. May, *The Physician's Covenant*, 211.
72. Centers for Medicare & Medicaid Services, "National Health Expenditures 2017 Highlights."
73. For a Catholic view of health care as social good, see Craig, *Health Care as a Social Good.*
74. May, *The Physician's Covenant*, 229.
75. May, *The Physician's Covenant*, 211.

purely individual concern but is also a social one, and therefore ultimately a matter of public interest. If one uninsured person gets sick, many others could also become infected.

Health care should be distributed according to the principles of equality and need rather than according to merit and individual freedom. Health-care equity should be guaranteed for every person, and costs should be distributed based on ability to pay. As far as health care is concerned, individual freedom should sometimes be restricted to protect others' human dignity and to promote the common good (such as controlling disease and health-care costs). Accessibility and the cost of health care profoundly affect medical decisions. Current health-care costs are soaring to the extent that the system is unsustainable. Revamping the health-care system will have a direct impact on the decisions of millions of people on abortion, end-of-life care, and addiction treatment, such as in the opioid crisis.

Christians should take heed and recognize the similarity of Jesus's healing ministry to modern-day universal health care, which also, theoretically, provides health care for the poor. Jesus's preaching and teaching ministry was predominately for the poor and the sick. For those who lacked adequate resources, he performed a wide variety of healing miracles, holistically encompassing mental, relational, and physical illnesses—and *free of charge*. However, Christians should also note the covenantal vision of the kingdom of God that informed and empowered Jesus's healing ministry. These miracles were not just physical but also liberative and restorative, as the sick were also empowered as God's children to be active members of a community. Many of the sick were marginalized at two levels—by the sickness itself and by a society either cautious of contagious diseases (e.g., lepers) or lacking resources. Jesus healed them holistically.[76]

Conclusion

This chapter contrasted a secular approach of medical ethics with new covenant ethics in examining several core norms of medical ethics (dignity, autonomy, beneficence, nonmaleficence, distributive justice, quality of life, and medial futility); it then discussed two controversial issues in medical ethics—abortion and euthanasia—before briefly surveying the health-care system. The chapter exhibited how

76. The question of distributive justice is even worse when we consider poor countries. For example, to a great extent, the HIV/AIDS pandemic persists due to unavailability of appropriate medication. For example, Atripla is sold for $1,800 per month, which is an unbelievable price for persons living on less than $2 a day. Given that big pharmaceutical companies earn hundreds of billions of dollars a year, they have the moral responsibility to provide medication at a feasible *de facto pro bono* rate to these countries. Lemberg, "Distributive Justice—Bioethics in Medical Practice."

a social script around medical norms, in particular human dignity, has substantially changed and how a utilitarian and contractual model is increasingly dominating medical decisions and practices under the heavy influence of neoliberal individualism and corporate interests.

New covenant ethics offers a counter to secular medical ethics, a more holistic understanding of health and a coherent moral framework of medical ethics. Its vision of health (shalom) and relational values of mutual responsibility, solidarity, and human dignity offers an alternative to the current individualistic view of medical ethics that sees the physician and the patient as merely contractual partners.

Care for the sick, the stranger, and the poor is a bellwether of a community's moral character. Christianity has a consistently proud history of this through the building of hospitals and various kinds of mission work in poor areas and the majority world. Churches need to continue this work of care, but at the same time they need to speak out and profess that health care is not a choice or a privilege but a right. A costly lesson of COVID-19 is that in a globalizing, interdependent world where pandemics are probable, a utilitarian and contractual approach is myopic and truncated. New covenant ethics reminds us that we are interdependent in our health; only by caring for others can we care for ourselves.

CHAPTER 20

War, Peace, and Just Peacemaking

For out of Zion shall go forth instruction,
and the word of the Lord from Jerusalem.
He shall judge between the nations,
and shall arbitrate for many peoples;
they shall beat their swords into plowshares,
and their spears into pruning hooks;
nation shall not lift up sword against nation,
neither shall they learn war anymore.

—Isaiah 2:3–4

War, that dread force that leaves men physically handicapped and psychologically upset. War, that leaves our nations with orphans and widows. War, that piles our national debts higher than mountains of gold. War, that causes our moral standards to disintegrate.

—Martin Luther King Jr., "False Gods We Worship."

For more than two millennia the use of violence has been a contentious problem for Christians; pacifists and realists have been debating the issue throughout Christian history. Pacifists claim that the use of violence contradicts the Christian confession of Jesus as the Prince of Peace and his uncompromising teachings on nonviolence and love. We must practice peace demonstrated by Christ's willing acceptance of the cross.

To realists, on the other hand, even after the coming of the Prince of Peace and his victory over evil and sin, and despite persistent longing for peace, the possibility of peace in history is still precarious.

In spite of their differences, both groups agree that nonviolence is not directly applicable to public life, which is still ridden with sin and evil. Pacifists tend to choose the route of noninvolvement in political life, opting for the politics of God. Realists advocate the active work for justice even if the transformation is only incremental and never perfect.

That said, pacifists choose nonviolence as a consistent lifestyle. This is the heart of their calling as disciples of Jesus; they even risk persecution if necessary. Realists, on the other hand, regard the government use of violence as inevitable in domestic and international matters to maintain basic order (peace and justice) in a sinful world. The differences of the two groups reflect their respective views on the moral demands of Jesus's teachings and discipleship, and the transformative power of God's reign in the Spirit.

This chapter studies the ethics of war, peace, and just peacemaking from a covenantal perspective. It presents covenant ethics as a plausible theory of just peacemaking that takes seriously both the ideal of peace and the reality of power and conflict. The close ties between covenant, just peacemaking, and rule making have already been demonstrated; hence, the practical and international dimensions of just peacemaking will be discussed here, with a focus on covenanting as a just peacemaking mechanism, while addressing the concerns of just war theory and pacifism.

Covenant has contributed to the rise of modern democracy, human rights, the rule of law, civil society, and global civil society. Despite the strong affinity and allure of peacemaking to the covenantal or quasi-covenantal structure of the post–World War II arrangements, covenant has not been systematically studied as a resource or paradigm of just peacemaking. Just peacemaking theory has been engaged by the late progressive Baptist Glen Stassen and recently by Catholic theologians. This chapter discusses various assumptions, norms, and practices of peacemaking that are embedded in new covenant ethics: that is, how covenant is associated with peacemaking in terms of protecting and respecting human rights, resolving conflict nonviolently through negotiation, rule setting and agreement to prevent conflicts, and mediating idealism and realism.

A covenantal theory of just peacemaking thus contributes to the reduction of war and conflict. The chapter begins with a brief introduction of just war theory and pacifism, before moving on to the just peacemaking theory of Glen Stassen in order to offer a covenantal theory of just peacemaking. The chapter shows the affinity and similarity between the two and claims that covenantal ethics offers a more coherent theory of just peacemaking.

Just War Theory

War is an organized, systematic, state-sponsored activity of violence against another nation or people. The goal of war is winning. War is the greatest evil because it is the worst form of violence. War is destructive and devastating. Civilians are driven from their homes, towns, and villages, which are bombed or burned. War brings ecological damage, as large areas of land become uninhabitable, poisoned by dangerous chemicals and littered with unexploded weapons that go on killing for years to come. War takes away even a minimal sense of dignity, norms, and respect from the people involved. War breeds enmity, suspicion, and anger among the peoples. War leaves a permanent scar on people, continuing across generations as violence begets violence. War only destroys, it never builds. While World War I killed 39 million people (with 30 million civilian casualties), World War II killed 51 million, including 34 million civilians.[1]

At first glance, the idea of just war seems like an oxymoron. If war is all destructive and violent, with winning as its utmost goal, how is it ever just? The history of just war theory goes back to ancient Greece, Rome, and China. The theory is the result of rational reflection on the cruelty and destructiveness of war, which ruthlessly destroys innocent lives and property. This led to the claim that some wars are more morally justifiable than others. The theory grew out of the attempt to approximate justice (that is, to reduce evil) even in waging and conducting war and to develop the criteria of justifiable violence in war. Military violence, even if unavoidable, could be limited in war, reducing unnecessary sacrifice of human lives and damage of property. Just as there is justifiable use of violence by the government, so there is in war.

Historically, the support of just war theory is associated with the political status and influence of Christians in a society. Just war theory was adopted in Christendom (through Ambrose and Augustine, and later Aquinas) where Christians were an integral part of the political elite who wielded power, including military decisions and actions.[2]

Traditionally, Christians have accepted the validity of just war theory on the basis of two accounts: the reality of sin and the political and moral responsibility of the state. That is, sin and evil still exist in the world, and war and violence are part of this reality. War is sometimes inevitable for the state to defend life, property of people, and the security and order of a society. The advocates share the conviction of Augustine that "redemption in Jesus Christ has very limited practical effect on the political order, but the political realm is inhabited mostly by people whose loves are disordered and whose idea of peace is distorted by vice."[3]

The advocates of just war theory find justification in biblical and philosophical sources. Biblically, as Romans 13:1–7 and 1 Peter 2:13–14 indicate, just war theorists

1. Clark and Rakestraw, *Readings in Christian Ethics*, 2:489.

2. Cahill, *Blessed Are the Peacemakers*, 8.

3. Cahill, *Blessed Are the Peacemakers*, 25.

claim that the primary responsibility of the state is the security of its people from external and internal threats. God has commissioned civil authorities to maintain justice for their citizens ("punish those who do wrong and praise those who do right"). They bear and use "the sword" to accomplish justice, which is inevitable given the sinful nature of humanity after the Fall. In this biblical understanding, it is not a stretch to view just war as using "the sword" to defend basic order and establish justice.

Philosophically, just war theory is based on natural law theory and the principle of justice. "It makes the logical point that in order to justify the killing that occurs in war, there must be a reason so important that it overrides the truth that killing people is wrong. War can be justified only by the necessity to vindicate justice and to protect the innocent against unjust aggressors."[4] That is, a war for self-defense and protection of innocent citizens is morally justifiable in light of reason and experience.

However, it should be noted that the advocates of just war theory are not warmongers. Rather, they attempt to reconcile three conflicting moral claims: (1) killing other human beings is wrong; (2) it is the duty of the state to protect innocent civilians and defend important moral principles; and (3) the use of force for self-defense is justified. Hence, war can be justly waged as self-defense to protect innocent citizens and moral principles, although it is tragic and should be avoided as much as possible.

It was through Hugo Grotius that just war theory made its impact in modern international law; it is now widely adopted and taught in military manuals for training in the armed service. Just war theory offers moral criteria for the international community to judge and assess the rationales in initiating and conducting war. Even if war is inevitable, war should be initiated and conducted according to the principles of justice, not arbitrarily. It should be declared for a just cause by a just authority as the last resort. Its conduct should be subjected to the principles of justice and the rule of law (both domestic and international).

The theory has two main parts, *jus ad bellum* and *jus in bello*: the former is concerned with justice in going to war, the latter with justice in conducting war.

jus ad bellum—just cause, just authority, clear public announcement, last resort, just intention, probability of success, proportionality of cost

jus in bello—just means of warfare, discrimination between combatants and noncombatants, proportionality of harm, fair treatment of prisoners and neutral parties

However, just war theory has faced major criticism for its limitations and misuses/abuses in history. The heart of the criticism is that it is overly optimistic in

4. Stassen and Gushee, *Kingdom Ethics*, 158.

anticipating that war will be just. Specifically, the standards for just war theory have rarely been observed in actual military conflicts; they are usually sacrificed for victory by any means. Despite its rational and prudential objectives in constraining the use of military force, it has failed to restrain war and violations.

Going to war is frequently decided by national interests rather than just cause, driven by the collective emotion of nationalism to punish or get even with other nations. Political leaders have abused just war theory to justify military aggression and pursue their political ambition and self-interest. Through propaganda, they dramatize and exaggerate the threat posed by the enemy (e.g., "to stop the Communist invasion," "extensive weapons of mass destruction," "connections with Al Qaeda"). Even when a war is unjust, a government justifies its actions (even to the point of manufacturing specious evidence) in order to appeal to the public. Therefore, the majority usually end up supporting their country's wars.[5] For example, Americans initially supported every war in the twentieth century, even the Vietnam War, which ultimately was viewed as a mistake by 80 percent of Americans. In the twenty-first century, 56 percent initially supported the Iraq War. Many Christians tend to support war in practice out of national loyalty, fear, or simply care for military servicemen and servicewomen. Moreover, the extensive use of military drones and the novel doctrine of preemptive strikes severely weaken the core principles of the theory to the extent that it threatens to void the entire theory itself.

To correct its limitations, just war tradition has been moving forward a position that favors peace and stricter interpretation and application of just war criteria,[6] in particular, the principles of just authority and last resort. To strengthen the standards, scholars have added two new principles in its interpretation and application.

The first is *jus ante bellum*, that is, the ethics of preparation for war. A particular decision/act of war cannot be morally judged in isolation. Military action often hides the underlying causes of historical grievances and current injustices behind terrorist acts. A diachronic study of the historical and social factors that affect and underlie the relationship of the two warring collective parties is necessary. War is more often a collective emotional act (stemming from nationalism and ethnocentrism). We need to examine the underlying political-economic and cultural dynamics that trigger violent conflicts and generate grievance and anger. Imperialism and unrestrained arms competition, unresolved past political grievances, and economic inequality tend to encourage war and violent conflicts. This principle could be viewed as a variation or elaboration of the principle of right intention.

5. Clark and Rakestraw, *Readings in Christian Ethics*, 2:490.

6. See Christiansen et al., "Must Just Peace and Just War Be Mutually Exclusive?," 105–27.

The other is *jus post bellum*, that is, the just resolution of a military conflict. The study of the immediate and long-term impact of war on the warring nations and surrounding nations includes social infrastructure (e.g., health, education). In particular, in our world of exchanges and interdependence, war creates refugees and ecological harms. Even after the victory of military intervention, a country should not seek punishment or shaming but restoration. *Jus post bellum* aims at the restoration of justice, the rule of law, and assured self-government through democratic elections.[7] This principle is not brand-new; it could be viewed as a variation or elaboration of the principles of proportionality and noncombatant immunity.

Recognizing the limitations of just war theory in the post–Cold War era, there is also a movement to bring just war theory closer to just peacemaking. Obviously the two additional criteria of just war theory (*jus ante bellum* and *jus post bellum*), just discussed, reflect such a change of direction. The Catholic Nonviolence Initiative appealed to Pope Francis to write an encyclical on "nonviolence and just peace." In response to this appeal, some Catholic scholars, such as Drew Christiansen, Tobias Winright, Laurie Johnston, and Mark J. Allman, have endeavored to integrate the traditional idea of just war theory with just peacemaking theory. They call this new stance "just-war peacemaking"—a position that advocates stricter interpretation and application of just war criteria. [8] The following statement of Winright concisely sums up the changing ethos among Catholic just war theorists: "the pivot foot could be nonviolence, but the other foot still allows for the possibility of armed force in accordance with just war reasoning and principles, with both feet being used towards the goal of just peace."[9]

Despite its limitation, just war theory is still morally and politically useful because it provides the global community with the shared criteria to assess an individual nation's use of military force. For example, when the criteria are violated or deemed insufficient, just war theory helps to mobilize global public opinion and put pressure on the aggressor's decisions and practices. Similarly, the criteria offer a moral ground to forbid preemptive strikes and nuclear attacks. "An honest appraisal of war through the lens of just war criteria would forbid any consideration of nuclear strikes and would rule out virtually all forms of large-scale, unilateral military intervention. It would leave only self-defense and limited, legally constrained uses of multilateral force to protect civilians to restore conditions of justice."[10]

7. Cahill, *Blessed Are the Peacemakers*, 12.

8. Christiansen et al., "Must Just Peace and Just War Be Mutually Exclusive?," 106.

9. Winright, "Why I Shall Continue to Use and Teach Just War Theory," 142.

10. Cortright, *Peace*, 16.

Pacifism

Christian pacifism stands in complete opposition to the just war theory regarding Christian involvement in war.[11] In contrast to just war theory's reliance on a general theory of justice, Christian pacifism is explicitly based on the NT ideal of love, peace, and forgiveness taught and embodied by Jesus. Pacifists claim that nonviolence is a way of discipleship to Jesus Christ.[12] As the Prince of Peace, he has inaugurated the reign of peace. Pacifists claim that pacifism is the moral obligation of Christians as they follow Jesus: never make war nor be violent. Christian life and violence are incompatible.

Pacifism has its biblical basis in Matthew 5:38–48, Luke 6:27–36, and 1 Peter 2:18–23. In the Sermon on the Mount, Jesus teaches his disciples not to "resist [or set themselves against] an evildoer," but rather to love their enemies and pray for those who persecute them (Matt. 5:39, 44). The renunciation of violence is the consistent teaching and action of Jesus in the gospel stories. Jesus lived nonviolently even when he had every reason to rely on violence to defend himself. He loved and died for his enemies and taught his followers to love their enemies without retaliating against them. The crucifixion demonstrates that suffering rather than violence (including in self-defense) is the way of God's kingdom. Rather than inflicting harm on others, Christians should choose self-sacrificing love for their enemies, as Jesus taught.

This pacifist claim is compelling because, inspired by the Sermon on the Mount, the early Christians rejected military service and participation in war. "Whenever the issue of military service and warfare was discussed, Christians were prohibited from participating. Nowhere in the written record in the first three hundred years of Christianity is killing ever justified. Not even for soldiers."[13] Historically, Mennonites, Anabaptists, and Quakers have been pioneers in peace studies and antiwar movements, abolition of slavery, conflict resolution, and conciliation programs.

Christian pacifists uphold nonviolence more as a way of life than as a theory about war. Christian pacifists typically see nonviolence as achievable in the Christian community but not in society, at least not until Jesus returns. The calling of the church in the world is to be a contrasting (alternative) community of peace in a violence-ridden world. Peace and justice outside the church become an irrelevant concern for pacifists. In a sense, their worldview is dualistic, and their ethics

11. Pacifism in Christianity takes diverse forms, from strict (absolute) to pragmatic. The discussion in this section is confined to pacifists who stand in Christian peace traditions (Mennonites, Anabaptists, and Quakers).

12. Stassen and Gushee, *Kingdom Ethics*, 166.

13. Cortright, *Peace*, 196–97.

sectarian. The way of Jesus is viewed as radically opposed to the way of the world. The church's ministry to society is evangelical witness, not social transformation. Christians are called not to fix the world but to be a moral example for the world, a city on a hill (Matt. 5:14). John Howard Yoder claims that Christians do not have a duty to transform society. It is God's work.[14] Rather than be relevant in society or try to fix an unjust social system,[15] Christians should eagerly accept suffering in their "revolutionary subordination," even persecution, in following Jesus.

Critique

Pacifism has been criticized for its moral idealism. The absolute prohibition of any use of force seems unrealistic and flies against common sense. Absolute pacifism that forbids the use of violence even for self-defense goes against the basic human instinct of self-protection. Given the broken reality of the world and the existence of evil, its high moral standard seems to be only for a select few. And social justice or international order and peace is only a secondary concern. While its ideal is noble and lofty, it turns out to be more effective in criticism of violence and war than in preventing war and armed conflicts. Pacifism is limited in bringing peace outside a Christian community. Pacifism often fails to teach Christians what is required to achieve peace in the national or international realm. It is powerless when an armed conflict breaks out.

Its absolute, staunch commitment to peace sometimes sounds legalistic and lacks wisdom and practicality. It may absolutize the value of peace in separation from other values. It faces the difficulty of constructively conceiving God's presence in the world (outside the church) and imagining the moral relationship between church and the world—both places where Christians live. It is limited in offering any concrete moral guidance for Christians living in complex situations.

It is dubitable whether passive acceptance of suffering when facing evildoers is the entirety of Jesus's teaching. It is doubtful whether this is an accurate interpretation of Matthew 5:39. It is equally questionable whether Jesus's life and death should be imitated in a literal way or interpreted in an analogical way when following him. One can argue that Jesus's clearing of the temple was contrary to the pacifists' claim; in fact, it was not a passive acceptance of suffering nor a practice of nonresistance. It was a violent and righteous confrontation with the exploitative temple system and its leaders, who were collaborating with Rome.

14. Clark and Rakestraw, *Readings in Christian Ethics*, 2:492.

15. In a similar vein, Stanley Hauerwas dismisses social justice work as futile attempts to be approved by a society.

Pacifism fails to see the centrality of justice in the Bible. It is a constitutive element of God's reign and the covenantal drama. A major problem of pacifism is that it dismisses the concern for justice as a secondary or marginal issue in understanding Jesus, God, and the Christian life. Nonretaliation and nonviolent resistance should be carefully distinguished; otherwise, nonresistance is construed as acquiescence to evil. Other than nonretaliation and patient suffering, pacifism often fails to offer any constructive option to overcome social evil.

New Covenant Ethics

What does new covenant ethics offer to just war theory and pacifism? How is new covenant ethics different from them? The purpose of new covenant ethics is peace (shalom), and it condemns war as a moral evil. The new covenant is the "covenant of peace," fulfilling the prophecies of Ezekiel (37:26; 34:25) and Isaiah (54:10). The Eucharist is an *agapē* peace meal.

New covenant ethics agrees with several key claims of pacifism, especially leaving vengeance to God as it belongs to God; vengeance creates more evils and violence. Jesus was adamant in advocating nonviolence. Violence definitely belongs to the sinful pattern of the world, not God's kingdom. Jesus preached shalom in a consistent manner. The dawning/unfolding reign of God has delivered us from the power and slavery of sin and invites us into the way of shalom. Christians are called to be peacemakers doing the ministry of reconciliation. Peacemaking is the requisite of believers who have experienced God's initiating grace, and it is a way to actively participate in God's reign. New covenant ethics disagrees with just war theory when the latter treats Jesus's teachings of peace and the love of enemy as merely a matter of intention, rather than action.

New covenant ethics shares the same premise of pacifism: violence is morally undesirable. It never morally justifies war because war is evil. War is not compatible with God's intention for the shalom community in the covenant of Jesus. It destroys life, property, and nature; women, the elderly, children, and the socially weak are the greatest victims of war; it dehumanizes others and leaves permanent scars. The use of military force excludes any option of peaceful resolution of the conflict. Military competition is wasteful. The countries of the world spend exorbitant amounts of money for their military forces, about $1.6 trillion per year. The United States spends "$740 billion for its military while 12.5 million children in the United States are living in food-insecure homes."[16]

In its proactive peacemaking work, however, new covenant ethics is different from pacifism, which focuses on the passive side of peace, renunciation of violence,

16. Williamson, "America Doesn't Just Have a Gun Crisis."

and patient suffering. The premise of new covenant ethics is that in the situation of human brokenness and sin, peace is not something that is given but something to be achieved by constant collaborative efforts among people by removing enmities, resolving conflicts, and building friendship.

New covenant ethics never separates peace from justice; it stresses that justice is central to peacemaking. It challenges a core theological premise of pacifism: the passive acceptance of suffering while facing evildoers. Christians are called to put things right, to repair the word (*tikkun olam*, as Judaism teaches)—to do justice and peacemaking, not peacemaking alone. Taking the Sermon on the Mount and Jesus's covenant as the foundation of Christian ethics, it is committed to nonviolent peacemaking. New covenant ethics seeks the congruence of the moral end (shalom) and the means. If the goal is peace, then the means should cohere with it. The Lordship of Christ is righteous, nonviolent, and restorative in principle.

Unlike pacifism, new covenant ethics does not take a sectarian posture to the world and the issues of social justice. In general, new covenant ethics is aligned with pragmatic or realistic pacifism rather than absolute pacifism.[17] While acknowledging the inevitability of coercion (such as the presence of police) in our collective life, it labors to reduce it. New covenant ethics distances itself from pacifists who do not positively appreciate the constructive role of the government and its mandate of keeping basic order, maintaining justice, and protecting people's lives and ensuring their safety. Rejecting a sectarian approach as well as Luther's two-kingdom theory, new covenant ethics claims the state can play an important role for justice and peacebuilding. As discussed in chapter 11, God's covenantal reign (restorative power) is now working in every domain and sphere of human life. Just peacemaking should be pursued not only in the church but also in every level and domain of society—family, neighborhood, workplace, nation, and global society. The responsibility of Christians is to collaborate with all people of goodwill and members of other religions to build, sustain, and expand a just peace in every domain and at every level of human life.

While the foundation of new covenant ethics is peace, new covenant ethics overlaps with just war theory in some areas. Just war theory carries in it a covenantal ethos; by delineating the criteria, just war theory serves as an international agreement in regulating the entering and conducting of war with agreed-upon criteria and procedures. From a covenantal perspective, just war theory could be justifiable on the basis of the Noachian covenant. It is necessary to prevent humanity from further deteriorating into conflicts, violence, and evil. Just war preserves a minimal justice even in the immoral situation of engaging war. However, as noted above, a

17. My approach is similar to David Cortright's idea of "realistic pacifism."

major problem of traditional just war theory is that the justification of war is easily subordinated to the selfish interests of political leaders or individual nations. Hence the concern has been how to strengthen and enforce the just war criteria thoroughly and rigorously.

New covenant ethics can help strengthen the criteria and practices of just war theory with the covenantal principles of institutional checks and balances, the rule of law, and a pluralistic social vision (associational pluralism). For example, the criterion of just authority can be strengthened by making constitutional processes rigorous when war is declared by the government. In other words, the declaration of war should go through a democratic process rather than being entrusted to a single leader or a party.[18] Additionally, government accountability, transparency, and freedom of the press must be secured so that people can assess war-related political situations accurately.

In addition, by creating and strengthening the covenant of global governance, new covenant ethics minimizes the necessity of war among individual nations. In the spirit of communicative engagement and just peacemaking of new covenant ethics, every means of conflict resolution and prevention must be exhausted before resorting to war. Engaging war should require the consensus of an international community. Consultation with other nations and the approval of the global political body (the United Nations) should be mandatory given the high-level interdependence of the world and the overwhelming destructiveness of war today. For example, the environmental damages, refugee needs, and economic costs will be borne by other nations as well as the warring parties.

However, the new covenant, despite its overwhelming emphasis on peace, nonviolence, and love, is still an eschatological covenant. It has not yet completely done away with the tragic dimensions of human history such as division, conflicts, and war. The Prince of Peace has not yet returned. As just war advocates point out, new covenant ethics acknowledges that, this side of heaven, we cannot completely remove evil, and the complete abolition of coercion in our collective life is impossible in history. Paul did not oppose the use of force by the government (Rom. 13:4), even as he was fully committed to the nonviolent way of Jesus. The use of force, tragic though it may be, cannot be avoided in justifiable self-defense and protection of innocent people. This is a case of "just policing," not just war.[19]

When an international community achieves a certain level of democratic governance through covenantal organizing, just policing could operate like the profes-

18. The US Constitution clearly specifies that declaring war is the responsibility of Congress. However, presidents often do not respect this process and constitutional requirement.

19. Winright, "Just Cause and Preemptive Strikes in the War on Terrorism," 157–81.

sional police work of the state, and international peacekeeping could be far more effective in addressing regional conflicts rather than leaving them to conflicting or warring parties. In the same spirit, the global ratification of the International Criminal Court is crucial to reduce wars and military conflicts and mitigate global warming. If political leaders are internationally held accountable for their decisions to enter into and conduct war, they would have second thoughts before committing violations.

Similarly, it is more appropriate to treat terrorism as a matter of international crime than as a belligerent act of war against a nation. It avoids the temptation for politicians to declare their side righteous, engage in unilateral and indiscriminate acts of war, and use terrorism as an excuse to invade another nation. This will also deny the hero status of terrorists among their constituencies.[20] The use of war and military means in Iraq and Afghanistan has dramatically increased international resentment against the United States.

There is an eschatological tension between peace/love ("already") and conflict/power ("not yet"), which calls for rigorous and faithful ethical discernment. This often involves painful decisions within a Christian community. While Christians pray and dream of shalom, the demand for justice is felt as urgent and acute in the growing inequality and spread of social evils today.

New covenant ethics strives toward peace but does not exclude exceptional situations that allow for justifiable and prudential use of military force. This requires a global community to collectively deliberate on issues such as the protection of the vulnerable and the innocent and the prevention of genocide.[21] If the use of military force is considered, it should only be a last resort, solely as a defensive act that uses just means and morally legitimate methods. By subjecting the use of military force to stringent moral and legal constraints, military operations in the twenty-first century will take more the character of police power than a traditional military campaign driven by the uncanny or predatory ambition of an individual nation. Just policing is the middle ground between just war theory and pacifism, and it is applied to cases such as R2P ("the responsibility to protect") in promoting international peace and justice. In 2005, the General Assembly of the UN adopted the resolution on R2P that defines humanitarian intervention to protect human rights as the obligation of the international community, especially to prevent four types of mass atrocities: "genocide, ethnic cleansing, war crimes and crimes against humanity."[22] The use of just policing and R2P should be subjected to the rule of law; its legitimacy is

20. Stassen, *Just Peacemaking*, 7.

21. "It is impossible to defend, yet difficult to exclude, any and all potential uses of armed force." Cahill, *Blessed Are the Peacemakers*, 324.

22. United Nations, "Responsibility to Protect"; see paragraph 139 of the 2005 World Summit Outcome Document.

earned through just procedures and authority. It should also protect the right of conscientious objectors who disagree with the very idea of war and all the evils ensuing from it.

New covenant ethics actively supports UN peacekeeping (R2P) in its effort to prevent (or stop) violent military attacks. It is based on the notion that, hypothetically speaking, even if war is abolished, policing (coercive use of power) is still necessary.

International Peacemaking

The practice of just peacemaking is central to new covenant ethics, which is applicable to international relationships. Today, expanding and strengthening fair global governance are a key to international peace and justice. Without such a major reorganizing of the global society, democracy is threatened and the global liberal world order is vulnerable to the reigning power of neoliberalism. As mentioned in chapter 13, new covenant ethics advocates the global covenant in various spheres (climate change, human rights, politics, economic regulation), including the strengthening of the UN. The practices of new covenant ethics (communicative action, just peacemaking, community organizing, nonviolent actions) are equally relevant in international realms.

Informed by the covenantal vision of shalom, the Bible is deeply concerned about international just peacemaking, as portrayed by the messianic peace treaty in Isaiah 2 (and Mic. 4). It is international in scope; voluntary and reciprocal in nature, based on shared morality; and informed by God's Word. The text does not explain what made the radical conversion of the nations toward disarmament possible; however, in quite some detail, the passage shows what enduring peace looks like: nations stop teaching and practicing war, but instead participate in peaceful resolution of conflicts through negotiation and compromise. Rather than being used for building armaments, military expenditures are instead used for economic security and human development.[23] People are finally free from the fear of war and poverty. The passage implies that the messianic era is the time when the covenant of peace is finally fulfilled at an international level. What is notable is that the core moral emphases and underlying assumptions are covenantal in nature.

The international relevance of covenant for just peacemaking is demonstrated in the frequent references to the word "covenant" in the reconstructive work of the post–World War II and postapartheid South Africa eras. In fact, a long period of relative peace without another global scale of war after World War II was possible

23. Kimelman, "Judaism, War, and Weapons of Mass Destruction," 379–80.

thanks to the partial covenantalizing of the global community (e.g., the UN, the Universal Declaration of Human Rights, the Bretton Woods system), along with other factors such as nuclear deterrence.

New covenant ethics offers a mechanism of international rule making, fair arrangement, and collaboration to build the structures of global democratic governance according to the principles of justice. The first step toward covenantalizing global society is to expand a mutually agreed-upon democratic framework, such as the UN, and to strengthen the rule of law in the international realm. Both are crucial aspects of global governance. Rule making is the procedure to create and implement standards of behavior with global reach.[24] Covenant, once established, has a binding power. One of the concrete ways to prevent war is for all nations to enter a mutually binding agreement (e.g., the Universal Declaration of Human Rights) and create a neutral mediating/policing body that enforces the agreement. Through the invigoration of global civil society and international collaboration, the global community needs to demonstrate that any rogue nation that goes to war without the approval of the UN and global public opinion will pay dearly for its action. In this era of global media and the rising global civil society, this is not impossible. George W. Bush's war on Iraq (under the false premise of Iraq's possession of weapons of mass destruction) and his policy of preemptive strike are a recent example of a nation, even a superpower, violating an international covenant (which skirted UN approval and the completion of full weapons inspection), alienating the international community, and inviting more hostile actions (terrorism).

As mentioned in chapter 13, new covenant ethics endeavors to turn the interstate relationship into a covenantal one and to bring undemocratized (unorganized) aspects of international relationships into a global covenantal framework. The more that peace, justice, and harmony are achieved through politics, the less violence that will occur; this axiom applies to every level of political life, including the international one. Strengthening democracy and a covenantal form of international order and the UN would help reduce the possibility of war and military conflicts. Democratic nations rarely go to war with one another, and the international sharing of power and accountability is crucial for preventing war. Societies that achieve better gender equality are also less likely to use military force in resolving conflicts.[25] Authoritarian, self-righteous, and vindictive nations are prone to military aggression. For example, the Axis alliance of World War II (Germany, Italy, and Japan) consisted of authoritarian regimes that disregarded the sovereignty of people, rule of law, and human rights; they relied rather on the whims and charisma of their dictatorial leaders.

24. Scherer and Palazzo, "The New Political Role of Business in a Globalized World," 909.
25. Cortright, *Peace*, 335.

In modern history, there has been an ongoing attempt at global covenanting through rule making. President Woodrow Wilson's Fourteen Points were covenantal in nature; the proposal included further economic empowering of the downtrodden and the construction of a collective international body to mediate conflicts.[26] His idea was picked up again only after another devastating world war. In the aftermath of the devastating carnage of two world wars, people saw the suffering and mass destruction and, in particular, the futility of war in the era of nuclear weapons. The historical development of just peacemaking theory and its incentives after World War II coincide with the postwar rise of the covenantal structures of the international community. In other words, the peacemaking approach to international conflict and the covenantal understanding of international relationships are correlated. The formation of the UN, motivated by the devastating experiences of destruction of World War II and genocide, took a form of covenant among the nations. Indeed, the UN called one of its important declarations a "covenant." This shows the resilience and practical feasibility of the covenantal idea for global just peacemaking.

Strengthening global civil society, in addition to international law and multilateral institutions, could help covenantalize the global society. International bodies and global civil society can provide checks and balances against aggressive actions by nations and political groups to prevent or reduce military conflicts and war. Global civil society and transnational nongovernmental organizations (NGOs) could play a crucial mediating role in promoting mutual understanding and trust among people of different nations and mobilizing global public opinion against the misuse of power and rogue actions of a superpower. They could be instrumental in international cooperation and trust.[27] Global NGOs are less partisan and nationalistic than nations in defending one ideology, religion, or nation-state against another. They typically have a long-term view of reality. They could be counterforces against the unjust system. A rich covenantal potential (a new binding relationship) exists among them for the common good. They could bond people together as a new, third creative force of peacemaking across the nations.

These groups have been at the forefront of positive developments toward democracy in the past century: the rise of peace movements, the spread of nonviolence, and the covenantal form of global structure and institutional bodies. Nonviolent resistance has made significant contributions to social change. It is now upheld as a

26. "President Woodrow Wilson's 14 Points (1918)."

27. The so-called Kantian triad—democracy, economic interdependence, and mutual participation in international organizations—fosters peace and trust among nations by strengthening global civil society.

viable alternative to armed resistance or war. While far from guaranteeing success, its historical report card is impressive in the past century.

In the following section, I want to briefly compare new covenant ethics with the just peacemaking theory (JPT) initiated by Glen Stassen. JPT is similar to new covenant ethics in its attempt to integrate just war theory and pacifism. The two approaches operate from different theological/theoretical assumptions, however. New covenant ethics has more theological substance, stronger coherence, and wider applicability than just peacemaking theory. I claim that Stassen's JPT can be theologically and practically strengthened when placed in an explicitly covenantal framework. Throughout the comparison, I show the strengths and plausibility of new covenant ethics.

Comparison: New Covenant Ethics and Glen Stassen's Just Peacemaking Theory (JPT)

Just peacemaking theory attempts to go beyond just war theory and pacifism by addressing the demands of both justice and peace together. While pacifists choose peace over justice, just war theorists put justice over peace. Conversely, just peacemaking simultaneously embraces both justice and peace rather than choosing one over the other.

Let us examine the historical background of its rise:

1. The theory was developed in the wake of the collapse of the Soviet Union to address complex national and social relationships in the post–Cold War era. The threat of superpower military conflicts receded, but human rights abuses, local military skirmishes, genocides (e.g., Yugoslavia, Rwanda), the spread of terrorism, ethno-racial conflicts, and civil wars are not abating. This indicates the rising need for international collaboration for peace and justice in a globalizing world. JPT was developed out of the awareness that these problems could be solved politically rather than militarily. "Peacebuilding is a practical response to conditions of violence that aims to alleviate the existential situations of those affected by war; and to do so in cooperation with other advocates and activists, on a spectrum from grassroots to midlevel to national and international governments and civil society organizations."[28] To do so, it is crucial to create the social conditions and cultural milieu that reduce war and violent conflicts and promote peace and trust.

2. The devastating power of weapons of mass destruction (WMD) exceeds the moral imagination and conventional boundaries of just war theory. Nuclear weapons can never be used as instruments of justice and utterly fail to meet the just war crite-

28. Cahill, *Blessed Are the Peacemakers*, 19.

ria. The just war criteria are irrelevant in the era of the WMD. Therefore, the use of such weapons is to be avoided through international diplomacy and negotiations.

3. The theory was also inspired by many success stories of nonviolent resistance (e.g., boycotts, practices of civil disobedience, sanctions) in the past century—Indian independence, the civil rights movement, the democracy movements of South Korea and the Philippines, etc. It is an effective approach in a shrinking, interdependent world. Just peacemaking was prompted by the awareness that war and military conflicts are costly and destructive. Nonviolent means and conflict resolutions could achieve a political goal with less harm and a more lasting peace.

As a third option between just war theory and pacifism, just peacemaking theory has gained prominence among Christians and grassroots/nongovernmental activists. Rather than replacing just war and pacifist theory, Stassen claims, JPT attempts to complement them, as a third option.[29]

Unlike pacifism, JPT understands peace as something that must be waged. "It sees peace not as something to be achieved merely by refraining from war, but by peacemaking initiatives."[30] Jesus encouraged his disciples to be proactive in peacemaking (Matt. 5:9). JPT is "proactive ethics" for peacemaking that explores which practices of war prevention and peacemaking are productive and relevant in the post–Cold War world. It seeks to build a long-term peace between conflicting parties (such as religious, ethno-racial, or civil groups) and creates a sustainable social condition for peace by addressing the root causes of conflicts, such as poverty, structural injustices, and the wounds/trauma of past oppression.

By and large, its goal is the resolution of conflict and the promotion of peace and justice. John Paul Lederach defines just peace as "an orientation toward conflict transformation characterized by approaches that reduce violence and destructive cycles of social interaction and at the same time increase justice in any human relationship."[31] Just peacemaking involves more than merely ending violent conflict; it also actively nurtures the sustainable conditions of peace and justice through economic empowerment, good democratic governance, and interreligious dialogue.

JPT intends to be a paradigm of ethics that prevents violence with a wide range of application. This includes conflict resolution and international cooperation that builds peace by reducing violence/war and elaborating the necessary measures/steps for international peacemaking. JPT creates an alternative to violence—preventing or resolving conflicts through various strategies and methods of conflict resolution.

29. Stassen, *Just Peacemaking*, 2.

30. Stassen, *Just Peacemaking*, 18.

31. Lederach, *The Moral Imagination*, 182.

Glen Stassen: Ten Practices of Just Peacemaking

Glen Stassen's ten practices aptly embody the contents of just peacemaking. Stassen arranges the ten practices under three subheadings: peacemaking initiatives, justice, and love and community. In other words, just peacemaking is proactive in nature and grounded in justice, and it seeks love and community with others. Rather than developing a comprehensive theory based on a single religious belief or political ideology, Stassen focuses on ten peacemaking practices for a pragmatic purpose—for wide applicability across different religious, cultural communities and nations. He believes that practices can be shared by and accommodated to different theoretical and theological metaphysical and philosophical frameworks. The ten practices follow:

1. Support nonviolent direct action.
2. Take independent initiatives to reduce threat.
3. Use cooperative conflict resolution.
4. Acknowledge responsibility for conflict and injustice and seek repentance and forgiveness.
5. Advance democracy, human rights, and religious liberty.
6. Foster just and sustainable economic development.
7. Work with emerging cooperative forces in the international system.
8. Strengthen the United Nations and international efforts for cooperation and human rights.
9. Reduce offensive weapons and weapons trade.
10. Encourage grassroots peacemaking groups and voluntary associations.[32]

Pacifists and just war theorists have had different responses to JPT. Pacifists tend to receive Stassen's just peacemaking more favorably, given that Stassen's theory is inspired by the Sermon on the Mount with its emphasis on nonviolence. Stassen crafted ten practices of "biblically informed" peacemaking practices based on Jesus's transforming initiatives. However, just war theorists are more skeptical because "the underlying philosophy of just peacemaking does not seem persuasive enough to guide and limit the policy of the solitary super-power."[33]

JPT and New Covenant Ethics

We will take up both similarities and differences between the two ethical approaches before exploring the connection between just peacemaking and communicative en-

32. Stassen and Gushee, *Kingdom Ethics*, 169–73.
33. Stone, "Realist Criticism of Just Peacemaking Theory," 256.

gagement, after which we will engage other elements of Stassen's ten practices in relation to new covenant ethics.

Similarities

One sees a great deal of similarity between JPT and new covenant ethics in terms of goal, ethos, and emphases. The aim of just peacemaking coincides with that of covenant: to avoid violence/enmity and build peace/mutual understanding on the basis of justice. Neither seeks passive pacifism nor an unjust peace imposed by the powerful, but both seek an active peace with the presence of justice and the elimination of structural injustice and violence.

Both emphasize peacemaking (cooperation and negotiation, conflict resolution) as a way to avoid or reduce wars and build international peace and justice. For both theories, peace is not merely the absence of conflict but is also the effort to establish just, trusting relationships. Both want to create and empower the ecology of peace: mutual understanding, trust building, forgiveness by removing enmity, reducing the fear of retaliation, and proactively seeking reconciliation. Finally, both reject the sectarian posture of some pacifists and take seriously social justice as the primary contributing factor that prevents war and promotes peace and trust in international relationships.

JPT shares several core norms, values, and practices with covenant ethics. Some core values of new covenant ethics are presupposed or upheld in JPT's ten practices: justice, rights, truth telling, solidarity, commitment to democracy, religious freedom, civic participation, nonviolent resistance, and support of international cooperation through the work of the UN and other international bodies, as discussed in chapters 13 and 14. One can also see the affinity between the grassroots community organizing of new covenant ethics and the tenth practice: "Encourage grassroots peacemaking groups and voluntary associations." In fact, new covenant ethics identifies just peacemaking as one of its core moral practices. In this respect, it has no major difficulty in adopting Stassen's ten practices as its own.

Differences

However, the two approaches exhibit considerable differences in theological assumptions, theoretical coherence, and ethical nuances. Other than peacemaking, JPT does not propose any explicit social vision. Nor does it explain how its key practices (such as nonviolent resistance, democracy, human rights, and internationalism) are interrelated. Stassen intentionally presents JPT as a practice-oriented paradigm of ethics and refuses to offer any coherent theory that integrates the ten practices. Such an approach has its own strengths and limitations.

Its merit is that JPT can be embraced by diverse religious and civil groups despite their theological and philosophical differences. The ten practices serve more or less as the middle axiom (a compact) among them. However, JPT has been criticized for its inadequate notions of justice and peace: "its normative account of justice and peace are too thin and therefore offer inadequate guidance in complex empirical cases."[34]

Just peacemaking requires an appropriate theoretical framework that connects vision, norms, strategies, and practices. Without it, practices may lose conceptual clarity, orientation, and moral direction. Practices cannot be completely free from certain theoretical (either theological or metaphysical) assumptions. Theoretical questions are inevitably raised when a society undergoes major social, economic, and cultural changes. In such a situation, it is inevitable to ask and decide afresh what each practice means in a newly changed context. In my view, Stassen's ten practices of JPT now require such a readjustment.

Stassen claims that JPT derives these practices from the Sermon on the Mount. However, he removes explicit theological language and symbols to make his ten practices function as public ethics of justice peacemaking in a global society. The Sermon on the Mount, interpreted as character ethics by Stassen, is not capacious enough to embrace all ten practices of JPT. For example, the practices of democracy, global order, NGOs, and civil society cannot be directly derived from the Sermon. Rather, these practices are Stassen's extrapolation of his Anabaptist theology. He needs a more expansive biblical-theological framework. Because of this loose theological connection between the ten practices and the Sermon, his theory is unable to fully motivate Christians. Moreover, it assimilates Christian convictions to secular political ideologies—ironically, the very danger he strongly warned against in his final book, *A Thicker Jesus*.

New covenant offers an inclusive theoretical framework to embrace the ten practices of JPT. When its covenantal underpinning is recognized, the rich, inclusive vision of the Sermon on the Mount's message of justice and peace comes fully alive, along with its political efficacy based on nonviolent action. When detached from its covenantal grounding, the Sermon may sound one-sidedly pacifist while losing its realistic emphasis on justice; its teachings can easily be discarded as utopian moral idealism or as framed solely in idealistic, pacifist terms. Absolute pacifism does not adequately reflect Jesus's ethics.

In distinction from JPT's practice-oriented paradigm, new covenant ethics offers a coherent moral framework for just peacemaking without compromising political practicality. Stassen's JPT is better conceptualized and practiced in a cov-

34. Lambelet, "Just Peacemaking," 1.

enantal framework.[35] New covenant ethics can strengthen Stassen's practices in several areas.

As explained in chapter 4, new covenant ethics is an expansive theory of just peacemaking guided by the divine drama of liberation-restoration. Covenant is more than an agreement between two parties; it is an organizing method that addresses hostility and estrangement in order to bring about reconciliation. As God's method of putting things right, justice and peace are intrinsic to covenant; covenant restores a just relationship (through the correction of injustices) and reaches peace (reconciliation). Covenant is a unique biblical idea that exhibits an intrinsic connection between justice and peace. New covenant and the triad of love, justice, and power are helpful in theologically elaborating just peacemaking with moral clarity and conceptual coherence. That is, new covenant, as the organic composite of love, justice, and power, intends to build peaceful relationships on the basis of justice and trust through the restructuring of power relations.

New covenant ethics offers a spiritual and moral motivation for just peacemaking: Christians taking independent initiatives for peace replicate God's own initiative in making peace with humanity in Jesus Christ (first dialectic). The motivating force for these proactive decisions is God's grace. As God has achieved justice (justification) and peace (reconciliation) with humanity in Jesus, Christians are called to be proactive peacemakers (second practice: take independent initiatives to reduce threat). They are given the ministry of reconciliation, and God's Spirit draws us toward this direction.

Through its ideas of the covenantal drama of liberation-restoration, the triad of love, justice, and power, and the three dialectics, new covenant ethics offers a more elaborate theory on just peacemaking. It makes a theoretically compelling case on how justice and peace are interrelated, why justice is critical for peacemaking, and how it is achieved. For example, covenant offers a theological framework for making, sustaining, and expanding peace.

New covenant ethics upholds the ideas of shalom, basic rights of every person, and social justice, and the importance of trust building, dialogue, conflict resolution, and collaboration, which are all important for just peacemaking. Also, new covenant ethics' complex theory of distributive justice (equality, need, merit, and capability) plays an important role in promoting justice, peacemaking, and democracy by clarifying the complicated moral issues related to the distribution of goods and the reduction of social conflicts around it.

35. This claim is based on the observation that Stassen's JPT is inspired by the Sermon on the Mount. Just as the Sermon could be understood as a covenant for a better understanding of Jesus's teachings, just peacemaking could theoretically be better framed by covenant.

As discussed in chapter 4, the practices of new covenant ethics (communicative engagement, just peacemaking, community organizing, and nonviolent direct action) are instrumental in repairing broken relationships, transforming unjust systems, and building a new, just community. They promote dialogue and local collaboration, the establishment of the structures of justice, checks and balances, and mutual accountability and cooperation. In a far more explicit and realistic way, the four practices of new covenant ethics address the questions of power, inequality, injustice, and agency, which are crucial for just peacemaking.

Communicative Action

There is an intimate connection between just peacemaking and communicative engagement, in particular, conflict resolution and new rule making. New covenant ethics believes that dialogue is the primary method of conflict resolution and collaboration building. The process of just peacemaking includes truth telling, confession, repentance, reparation, and forgiveness, which, when properly enacted, are helpful for healing the past, building trust, and building the common future (reconciliation). As we have seen in the Truth and Reconciliation Commission of South Africa, this concerns "not merely restoring rights but also redressing the wide set of wounds that political injustices have inflicted on persons and relationships."[36] Confession of guilt and hearing the stories of victims are important for just peacemaking.

Confession is a part of the reconciliation process. When covenant fidelity is broken or a pledge is violated, the confession of sins and mistakes is necessary for the healing and restoration of relationship.[37] "Therefore confess your sins to one another, and pray for one another, so that you may be healed" (James 5:16). The fourth practice of JPT ("Acknowledge responsibility for conflict and injustice and seek repentance and forgiveness") is a rephrasing of "confession" of sins in the process of reconciliation in new covenant ethics.

Democracy

Stassen points out that just peacemaking is positively correlated with democracy. This observation is correct. There is an overlap between democracy and just peacemaking in their rejection of violence and in their resolution of differences and con-

36. Philpott, *Just and Unjust Peace*, 55.

37. The importance of confession as a major spiritual practice of the Christian life (the sacrament of penance for the Roman Catholics) attests that a genuine and truthful admission of one's wrongs has a healing and restorative effect.

flicts (in favor of negotiation and compromise). Democracy is a political system that reduces violence and institutionalizes a system of nonviolent transition of power. Intrinsic to democracy, the rule of law, and human rights, a civil society is equally important for just peacemaking (fifth practice of JPT). Various institutions and the political structure of democracy are conducive to just peacemaking, in that institutional checks and balances against the monopoly of power are created. In general, these democratic infrastructures and mechanisms are deeply conducive to justice and peace building. Likewise, empowering civil society is important for just peacemaking.

The idea of covenant is intimately related to democracy. Historically, covenant has made a direct contribution to the rise of the rule of law, democratic participation, grassroots organizing, coalition building among NGOs, and civic organizations, as elaborated in chapter 13. The democratic ideas of a constitution, the rule of law, checks and balances, human rights, agreement, and collaboration were informed by covenantal theology. A close historical tie between covenant and democracy thus exhibits new covenant ethics' contributive potential and efficacy for just peacemaking. New covenant ethics is an ethical framework that promotes both democracy and just peacemaking. It strengthens and expands negotiation, agreement, and compromise in solving problems. It also emphasizes citizen participation, vibrancy of local organizations, civil society, and collaboration in peaceful conflict resolution.

Democratic Rule Making

Peace has internal and external dimensions. The removal of internal and external violence is one of the major features of God's peace. Inner peace is achieved through virtue development, while external peace is improved through justice (which is achieved through the dismantling of an unjust social system, democratic rule making, and the separation of powers).

JPT is based more in virtues and practices than in rules. As mentioned in chapter 8, new covenant ethics attends to virtue formation (compassion, generosity, peace, and nonviolence) as well as to the rule making necessary for justice and peace, and employs the method of organizing strategies for just peacemaking.[38] Unlike Stassen's model, new covenant ethics puts great emphasis on building the structures of justice (a constitution, the rule of law, checks and balances) and establishing new organizations, domestic and international, to prevent wars and promote peace. It also offers a theoretical framework to achieve them and a concrete method for their creation. Rule making relies on communicative action of the participants.

38. Cf. McCarthy and O'Neill, *Becoming Nonviolent Peacemakers*, 2.

Stassen's theory can be strengthened by adopting the democratic rule making of new covenant ethics that relies on communicative engagement. A communicative approach to rule making is covenantal: it creates binding stipulations and the structure of accountability, which specifies retribution against violators, when entering the binding relationship of mutual agreement. True peace is possible on the basis of mutual trust, and its sustenance requires the robust rule of law, domestic and international, based on the agreement and mutual trust of the participants.

The rule of law is integral to democracy. In the modern history of democracy, the rule of law has been critical to prevent tyranny, just as the separation of powers has been critical to prevent the concentration of power. The rule of law was developed out of the radical covenantal politics of the Puritans in Europe. It contributed to reining in the tyrannical power of monarchs and dictators. The new structure includes legal forms (such as the Human Rights Council and the Gender Equality Commission) that protect the achievement of the democratic struggle and implement the values of justice (basic human rights) in a realistic way with binding political power.

Grassroots Community Organizing

New covenant ethics is politically realistic. It is concerned with the question of power in just peacemaking (correcting the unjust status quo) and the enforcement of the agreed-upon rules in international relationships. This concern is more explicitly addressed in its close tie with community organizing and nonviolent action. Just peacemaking in new covenant ethics does not rely on negotiation alone; it begins with justice making. This is not possible without the positive accumulation and constructive use of power of nonviolent resistance and liberative movement for justice and equality. These create the conditions for negotiation and conflict resolution. New covenant ethics is not afraid of using pressure, moral and political, to bring recalcitrant parties to the negotiation table.

Grassroots organizing is indispensable for the self-empowerment of people and democracy. Genuine democracy is sustained by civic grassroots participation and organizing of people. When people are bound together and collaborate to solve local problems in light of the principles of justice, democracy expands and deepens and the possibility of violence abates.

As discussed in chapter 4, grassroots organizing complements just peacemaking. The empowerment of the poor and the oppressed is crucial for achieving and implementing justice; similarly, nonviolent resistance is necessary for correcting social injustices and restoring justice in social and international relationships. When power is unequally distributed and concentrated in a few rich corporations and individuals, peacemaking must start by de-organizing their power.

Grassroots organizing is necessary to put pressure on perpetrators to take responsibility for criminal (unlawful) actions and undo an unjust social system. New covenant ethics' grassroots community organizing offers a method of building and accumulating power. The question of power is central to the task of just peacemaking. Any attempt at reconciliation that does not address the question of power is flawed. Any theory of just peacemaking that is not capable of elaborating the relationship between justice, peace, and power is limited. Injustice and violence are the consequences of the abuse of power, resulting from the imbalance of power. The powerful do not voluntarily give up their power and privilege. According to realists, this is what pacifism and just peacemaking theory often underestimate or ignore. New covenant ethics emphasizes that restructuring unjust power relations is necessary for just peacemaking.

Economic Justice

Glen Stassen's ten practices were crafted in the context of the post–Cold War liberal world order dominated by the United States. In fact, JPT's view of a rising global order is quite optimistic, as we see in the seventh practice. However, this is no longer the case. He did not foresee the rise of protectionism, the spread of illiberal democracy and authoritarian regimes, deepening economic inequality, life-threatening ecological degradation, and the demise of the welfare state, which are all tied to global capitalism. JPT does not explain how globalized neoliberalism is undermining democracy, engendering class conflicts, and impeding economic development. Nor does it see how corporations frequently violate basic human rights (or collude with authoritarian regimes) for profit. New covenant ethics' view of economic justice is far more radical and effective in a neoliberal context. Embodying the ethos of biblical economics, new covenant ethics advocates democratic socialism that balances civil-political rights as well as economic rights, which is more conducive to just peacemaking than either neoliberal democracy or communism.

Although neoliberal corporate elites present globalization as a benign force of peacemaking, this is false. It has exacerbated the tension and conflict along diverse identity lines and loyalties, as we have seen in Brexit, the election of Trump, and the rise of illiberal democracy. Just peacemaking cannot be selective; it should apply to every sphere of a global society. There is no peacemaking without justice making in economic globalization. The failure of justice making in this realm undermines its alleged peacemaking because of global economic integration and interdependence. Without genuine just peacemaking in the economic realm, the work of globalization is likely to fail, resulting in increasing racial conflicts, even foreboding another major war.

Ecology

Glen Stassen's theory is still anthropocentric; it fails to address the ecological aspects of peacemaking. There is no reference to just peacemaking with other species and the planet, despite the pressing urgency and impact of global warming on refugees and migration, international competition, and racial/ethnic conflicts. In this era of global warming, ecological peacemaking is a pressing and unavoidable concern. Today, as the COVID-19 crisis has demonstrated, there is no peace for humanity without a just relationship with other creatures. Ruthless human intrusion into their living spaces, driven by unbridled human greed, has resulted in a devastating consequence on human health and common life. Ecological sustainability is the foundation of our economic sustainability and political stability, even biological survival itself. Just peacemaking must include the protection not only of human rights but also of the rights of other species—their habitats and subsistence. Christians should take responsible action (*Stellvertretung*) for just peacemaking, not only on behalf of people under the threat of genocide but also to protect the habitats and basic rights of animals. The new covenant offers a comprehensive framework for peacemaking that embraces an ecological dimension. The scope of covenantal just peacemaking is cosmic. Colossians 1:19–20 describes the universal scope of the new covenant and its accomplishment of peace. The reconciliation effected by the blood of the cross of Jesus is not individualistic or anthropocentric (as evangelicals preach), but cosmic and ecological—"all things."

This discussion demonstrates that new covenant ethics can accommodate crucial points and major moral values and practices of JPT, but with theoretical coherence and integration. It offers a capacious theoretical framework because the ten practices of just peacemaking need to be revised in response to the erosive power of communication technology, globalization, predatory corporations, oligarchic legislation, neoliberal corporatocracy and economic inequality, and massive immigration—the forces and conditions that engender conflicts, authoritarian regimes, and illiberal democracy.

Conclusion

New covenant ethics creatively combines the peace tradition with the just war tradition in the organic triad of love, justice, and power. By integrating morality and political effectiveness, it presents a meaningful answer to the use of military force by nations and the helplessness of pacifism in confronting egregious human rights abuse and genocide.

Like just peacemaking theory, new covenant ethics mediates between the moral minimalism of just war theory and the moral maximalism of pacifism. It is more realistic than pacifism but more idealistic than just war theory. A covenantal theory of just peacemaking avoids the frequent opportunism of a just war theory and the utopian idealism of pacifism by focusing its moral energy and effort on justice and peace building—conflict resolution and reconciliation (and their processes and practices) that nurture trust to avoid war and violent conflicts.

Like JPT, new covenant ethics takes a third position between just war theory and pacifism. But because of its explicit covenantal foundation, it addresses the tension between the two theories more adequately and effectively. Also, it better resolves the tension between the confessional and public dimensions of just peacemaking than does Stassen's model. New covenant ethics offers Christians a coherent theological framework for just peacemaking with conceptual clarity on its purpose (shalom), procedure (communicative engagements), and method (nonviolence and community organizing) in various levels and spheres of society (interpersonal, local, national, regional, and global).

Through the repairing of relationships, trust building, truth telling (confession), and correction of past wrongs, it inserts a new fabric of mutual understanding, trust, and solidarity. Its practices of community organizing and nonviolence add a realistic and practical dimension to just peacemaking, while its tie with democratic imagination and institutions (human rights, rule of law, and civil society in domestic and global realms) confirms its plausibility as a theory of just peacemaking.

Just peacemaking is far from a smooth process. Human sinfulness poses a threat to every step (e.g., confession could be considered forced, thus only partial, even untruthful). Forgiveness is more often than not difficult because of the charged emotions of vengefulness and the trauma of victimization. Additionally, perpetrators are not willing to give up their privilege, power, and status, thus desiring reconciliation without reparations; habituated to the pattern and comfort of privilege and power, they react strongly to any attempt to take away their privilege. They want to keep reconciliation at a purely emotional or spiritual level without introducing meaningful new legislation that undoes power and privilege. Covenant ethics also recognizes that agreements and promises can easily be broken, distorted by self-interest and political expediency.

Achieving just peacemaking in history is a complicated, challenging, tricky, tortuous, and laborious process (third dialectic: process-journeying). There is no easy and quick fix in reconciliation and peace building. The existence of evil and the use of lethal force are the perennial moral dilemmas of history.[39] We cannot be overly

39. Cahill, *Blessed Are the Peacemakers*, 34.

optimistic or pessimistic. Our incremental progress cannot lose a sense of hope inspired by memories of past achievements. It is an ongoing work of healing, trust building, renewal, and rediscovery. One lives covenantally in just peacemaking by being watchful of ourselves and others. Required are "constant renewal and affirmation" of our minds, hearts, and collective actions.[40]

Just peacemaking begins with the humble acknowledgment that we are all broken but are also already invited to God's redemption in Jesus Christ. Here, solidarity includes both positives and negatives, a shared future (redemption) and shared brokenness. "An understanding of our solidarity in sin (the proper meaning of 'original sin') is a necessary step along the road to reconciliation."[41] The ongoing work of peacemaking through confession and forgiveness is necessary. Hence, without love and solidarity, peace and justice are incomplete.

The demand for just peacemaking is growing in a globalizing world that is financially integrated. More and more people sense our interdependence and interconnectivity through the Internet, popular culture, market exchanges of goods and products, and movements of people. Equipped with the vision and practice of new covenant ethics, the historical prospects of justice and peace may be challenging, but progress is not impossible.

40. De Gruchy, *Reconciliation*, 188.

41. De Gruchy, *Reconciliation*, 191.

Conclusion

For he looked forward to the city that has foundations, whose architect and builder is God.

—Hebrews 11:10

If life severs itself from this form, if it tries to assert itself in freedom from this form, if it will not allow itself to be served by the form of the natural, then it destroys itself down to its roots. Life that makes itself absolute, that makes itself its own goal, destroys itself.

—Dietrich Bonhoeffer, *Ethics*

The journey of this book began with the story of *Friends*, a popular sitcom. The show is about a group of friends seeking a trusted community grounded in "friendship." In a world where more and more families break down, it seems that only a pack of trusted friends is a meaningful option to meet our social and relational needs. Characterized by trust, freedom, and reciprocity, friendship is the social oxygen for humans, who are relational animals. To love others is to be friends with them. Friendship does not override kinship, but it is ethically higher than it; sometimes it can even be thicker than kinship.

Primary institutions (family, church, schools, neighborhood) that lack the quality of friendship are being shelled. Today, the neoliberal system is the stealthy enemy of friendship. It liquefies anything solid, including social relationships; it turns all relationships, including spousal ones, into a calculated monetary transaction of self-interest.

The story of the Bible is the story of God's friendship. Jesus is the friend of sinners; in him, God befriends humanity, inviting them to a new true home of Trinitarian fellowship (John 14:20). The Father wants to expand God's filial friendship to the entire creation—including humanity and the earth itself—through Jesus in the Spirit. This massive project of befriending is called "covenant" in the Bible. Divine covenant is the metaphor of divine friendship in the Bible. Open and generous friendship is the sign of maturity, and shalom is its ultimate reward. Shalom is the quality that divine friendship seeks and embodies. God often called persons and people who were covenanted with God (Abraham, Moses, Israel) "friend." Jesus did the same with his disciples.

Using a typological method, this book has presented the Bible as God's drama of liberation-restoration achieved through covenant. In the Bible, shalom shares qualities with good friendship: love, justice, trust, peace, and reciprocity, where everyone flourishes in open communion of life. Since the breach of the first friendship in Eden, the effort to restore friendship and shalom is always initiated by the loving God, who liberates disarrayed and lost humans from the shackles of sin (self-destruction, self-hatred, oppression, alienation, exploitation). God restores them to a new relationship with God and others; this friendship is called covenant. God condemns sin and injustices (e.g., racism, classism, sexism, homophobia, ageism, ableism) because they block friendship among people. Liberation is God's act of justice for the oppressed as judgment against the oppressing powers, while restoration is God's act of reconciliation with enemies (chap. 3). Liberation is justice making, while restoration is peacemaking; together they constitute just peacemaking. Sabbath and Jubilee are both biblical symbols of shalom and practices of just peacemaking. The new covenant of Jesus is the climax of this covenantal drama, and just peacemaking is the ongoing work of God that fulfills all the previous covenants in a cosmic, inclusive, egalitarian, nonviolent, and eschatological framework (chap. 4). On the basis of this covenant, God wants Christians to reciprocate God's act of grace to others who have not yet personally experienced God's love.

New covenant ethics is constructed upon the above theological premises. It is a nonviolent method of just peacemaking and organizing that rebuilds friendship with God and others. The ultimate goal of friendship and just peacemaking is the shalom community of reconciliation and justice.

Among the rich potential and promises of the biblical idea of covenant, I would like to highlight two distinctive merits that this work has explored: one is the covenant in general, and the other is the new covenant in particular. Covenant helps us to understand God's intention, the deep structures of God's creation and moral relationships among creatures.[1] Covenant in general, and the new covenant in particular, offers a comprehensive framework for organizing human moral life in relation to God and others. That is, covenant indicates God's way of managing God's

1. Ellen F. Davis, *Scripture, Culture, and Agriculture*, 87.

household at every level (interpersonal, institutional, societal, and global). In the Bible, ethics takes covenantal form because it is understood as the art of organizing our life together (symbiosis) in God. The triune God is the master architect of this organizing.

In a rich and compelling way, covenant describes who humanity is, in its dependence on God and the earth and other creatures as *adama* and *imago Dei*, and what they are supposed to be. Specifically, the covenantal drama and the three patterns of covenant (unilateral-bilateral, communal-communicative, memory-hope) are crucial for understanding the distinctive nature, characteristics, dynamics, and parameters of Christian ethics. They offer a concrete description of ways to organize the Christian moral life: (1) New covenant ethics is indicative before being imperative. It is gratitude driven (unilateral-bilateral), grounded in the identity derived from our covenantal relationship with God and others. It is always empowered and motivated by God's grace to reciprocate it toward others. (2) New covenant ethics is communicative. Life in covenant is lived out in ongoing communicative action, the fellowship of love and justice, as members communally and communicatively deliberate on concerned moral issues and discern God's will. (3) New covenant ethics is analogical and eschatological. God's moral demands are newly discerned and interpreted in new, changing contexts, faithful to Scripture and tradition but creative and embodied in a particular context. Finally, it is eschatological: the work of justice, peacemaking, and personal sanctification is never complete in history; brokenness and injustices still exist along with the possibility of reform and progress. Hence, Christians are neither overly pessimistic nor overly optimistic, but they strive for the betterment of the world in the memory of God's redemption and in the hope of God's consummation.

I believe that Matthew 5:17–18 is critical for properly understanding the moral meaning and nature of the Sermon on the Mount through the relationship of Jesus with the law and the prophets (by extension, the NT and the OT). This passage affirms the eschatological nature of Christian moral life, which has profound implications in understanding the very nature and scope of Christian ethics, especially in formulating the church's relationship with society and the church's public ministry.

That is, the eschatological reservation of the new covenant—the already and the not-yet, fulfilling but not abolishing—allows new covenant ethics to not lose its public scope and relevance (not yet) as well as to maintain its particular spiritual and moral convictions (already).

Taking the Noachian covenant as a specific common covenantal framework for humanity and other creatures (Gen. 9:1–17), new covenant ethics embraces natural law and the mandates of diverse social spheres to appreciate common moral experiences and the wisdom of age-old religious cultural traditions. The Noachian covenant is the common ground but not the goal itself. The new covenant constantly nudges, compels, and sublimates it toward shalom through the ongoing practices of communicative engagement, just peacemaking, grassroots organizing, and nonviolent action in order to build a more just and peaceful society that approximates shalom. This means that, in their public engagements, Christians are bound by the Noachian covenant (justice) but are always enhanced and nudged by the new covenant of Jesus. The new covenant does not abolish but fulfills the Noachian and other covenants. Just peacemaking plays an important role in bridging the two covenants in the public realm.

The eschatological understanding of the passage helps to overcome the longstanding division and conflict between the sectarian pacifist ethics of the Anabaptists and the natural law, the public ethics of Roman Catholic, and mainline Protestant churches, while assigning a full moral significance and commitment to Jesus's ethics in the Sermon on the Mount and the Gospels. New covenant ethics is uncompromisingly Jesus centered but equally publicly relevant. Through its dialectic understanding of the Noachian covenant and the new covenant of Jesus (the latter as fulfillment of the former), new covenant ethics is applicable to the church as well as the public realm.

So, then, how is the new covenant relevant for today?

In a sense, every ethic is a response to a particular context, while it seeks an ultimate vision, reliable norms and rules, and trusted values to guide our decisions and actions. Christian ethics is no different. It inquires how Christians can live faithfully as God's people, following Jesus. But this inquiry always happens in a particular context, wrestling with particular issues of a particular time, anticipating God's living guidance in our deliberation aided by biblical vision, norms, values, and examples.

New covenant ethics is relevant to our current social situation, which is overwhelmed by globalization, digitization, and neoliberalism. This becomes increasingly clear as we face the painful and costly experience of the global COVID-19 crisis. Humanity is not able to address its common challenges without a capacious and complex moral framework that offers a plausible inspiring vision, a fair and reciprocal method of rule making, and concrete practices that correct inequalities and injustices.

Modern Western civilization has lost its broader moral vision and framework that inspire people with new moral imagination, motivate good citizenship and responsibility, correctly inform one's sense of duty, and prompt the humility to be open-minded to critiques and different ideas. Despite impressive achievements of medical and communication technologies, the quality of life of ordinary people—

the middle-class and the poor—is worse today than in the past. What we are witnessing today is the demonic reign of Mammon (money), Mars (military power), and Venus (sex). While created good, these things are dislodged from a necessary moral framework and have become demons. Unruly, self-gratifying, irresponsible, never-quenched desires are justified and glorified in the name of individual identity, self-expression, and self-fulfillment; corporations and the rich have turned democracy into plutocracy. Society is increasingly chaotic, seen in ideological moral relativism, identity politics, claims of autocracy, and illiberal democracy.

The exasperating fractures, conflicts, and divisions indicate that expressive individualism, competition, and the pursuit of self-fulfillment can rip our society apart and fail all of us. We need a moral framework where individual pursuit and fulfillment are coordinated and conflicts are adjudicated. Intense competition for survival and rabid ambition for success characterize our *modus vivendi*. In order to be "productive" and "relevant" in a globalizing world, we no longer have time to build friendships. To handle stress, distress, and depression, more people rely on the self-medication of pornography, binge drinking, drugs, entertainment, sports, etc. But these are distractive, not restorative. There is no rest.

Rising rates of suicide, addiction, and drug overdose reveal how much our society is losing the covenantal quality of care, aid, support, and sharing. Groanings are rising, suffering and pain spread, and despair and hopelessness are deepening. By the standards of both the Bible and human history, this kind of civilization is unsustainable. It will collapse from within.

The countries in the majority world do not necessarily fare better. Under pressure from the global neoliberal system, they increasingly adopt contractual forms of relationships modeled after the market relationship. There is a growing, acute tension between a contractual model (based on atomistic individualism) and a traditional collectivist (organicist) model.

The world seems at a crossroads; it either rebuilds and expands an expansive system of trust, rules, and solidarity among nations and cultures, or it degenerates into endless competition, fragmentation, violence, floating individualism, and parochial tribalism. Living in a radically changed social condition of globalization and digitization, we need a major recovenanting and renewal as the church, the nation, and the global community. Our current crisis is an opportunity to re-create and expand our mutual trust, commitment, and friendship (covenant) rather than falling into endless confusion and deadly chaos.

Covenanting is the apt response of people to current social situations that urgently require reliable, trustworthy communication, coordination, and collaboration. A covenant model is a third model between individualism and collectivism. Covenant has to do with the just binding and bonding of people. It is a mechanism of organizing—a control mechanism of conflict by nurturing trust, opening the channel of communication, negotiating different claims, and resolving conflicts. When it works well, covenant contributes to reducing distrust and ameliorating destructive conflicts. May writes: "A covenant exists . . . between all the citizens of a democracy when they all feel themselves subject to the same weakness and the same dangers; their interests as well as their compassion makes it a rule with them to lend one another assistance when required."[2]

Every sustained meaningful relationship or organization in society has some explicit or implicit form of covenant—certain goals, rules, and expectations that the participants or members share. Relationships and organizations alike operate by covenant, as there is a tacit expectation that the participants will continue to operate and abide by shared expectations, goals, and agreed-upon rules. When such expectations are severely unmet, or when rules are consistently violated, relationships break and organizations gradually collapse. Division, suspicion, unhelpful conflicts, and rancor are typical signs of this brokenness. Unless the relationship and the organization are restored and renewed through the renewal or revision of covenant, they may deteriorate and reach the point of no return: dissolution.

To avoid conflict and achieve better coordination and collaboration, the global community needs a structure of coordination and collaboration—a shared system with rules and accountability that reaches across the member nations of the global society. This agreed-upon structure may take the form of a covenant (a compact, technically) based on cogent arguments and claims presented through free, fair, and transparent communication among the members.

The interdependent reality of a global society, the threat of neoliberalism, and impending global crises reaffirm the importance and value of a covenantal approach to ethics.

To save ourselves and the planet from impending global warming, to prepare for and prevent another global pandemic like COVID-19, to avoid the waste of resources due to military buildup and competition, we have no other option than to establish the global covenant among different cultures, civilizations, countries, and contexts.

With this shalom vision of a cosmic scope, ecological sensibility, democratic rule making, and communicative framework, new covenant ethics presents a compelling vision and ethical paradigm for the global community. New covenant ethics is thoroughly ecological, as it seeks to build the shalom community, the cosmic beloved community of God, where every creature finds its living space, subsistence, and flourishing. New covenant, as the fulfillment of the creation covenant, reminds us

2. May, *The Physician's Covenant*, 223.

that humans belong to the earth and are utterly dependent on other creatures. The earth and other creatures are the members of God's covenantal community, and human economic activities cannot be separated from this ecological foundation and covenantal commitment. New covenant teaches that "the beauty and dignity of human life depends upon living within certain limits that are necessary and therefore becoming."[3] God's "economy" (*oikonomia*) concerns itself with the entire creation as it cares for not only humans but all life-forms. Hence, stewardship (*oikonomos*) is a life-caring attitude of service and responsibility guided by God's rules of limitation and freedom for common flourishing.

New covenant ethics is ecumenical, based on its inclusiveness, egalitarianism, solidarity, and respect of the basic rights of all members of God's new covenant community. Max Stackhouse affirms that covenant is a "biblically based and theologically rooted, but broadly ecumenical social ethic, one intentionally open to interfaith influences and able to give guidance in and to the emerging global civilization."[4]

While informed by Jesus's ethics, new covenant ethics and its practices (communicative engagement, just peacemaking, rule making, and nonviolence) have public relevance to global civil society and democracy. Through communicative engagement, it listens to and shares ideas to find common interests; just peacemaking offers a method of conflict resolution and reconciliation on the basis of justice; community organizing, with its ultimate goal of organizing of the shalom community, builds trust and a power base; nonviolent action mobilizes the people of goodwill for a peaceful social change.

Its inclusive, ecological, ecumenical, dialogical, and democratic method offers a plausible moral framework for participation, deliberation, and common action as its just peacemaking, community organizing, and nonviolence present shareable practical methods of trust building and coalition building. These result in social change across diverse cultures and social contexts.

While grounded in the new covenant of Jesus, new covenant ethics is not imposing but invitational. Proposing new covenant ethics, however, does not mean that Christians are somehow morally superior or better than non-Christians. While constantly failing in their justice and peacemaking—in fact, more so these days—Christians are restored by God's grace again and again. However, they are different from non-Christians in that they have a vision and a road map, and the promise of God's forgiving and empowering presence in their midst. As Stackhouse noted, "the issue is not whether believers are more righteous than nonbelievers, a very difficult

3. Ellen F. Davis, *Scripture, Culture, and Agriculture*, 80.

4. Stackhouse, "The Fifth Social Gospel and the Global Mission of the Church," 185.

case to make, but whether believers have a better account of why we all are as we are in moral and spiritual matters, and why we need not despair."[5]

There is another reason why new covenant ethics is relevant. New covenant ethics gives necessary attention to the continuity and change (discontinuity) between the past and the present of modern civilization (third dialectic). With its origin in the Near East (Judaism and Christianity), it embodies a unique vision that balances the passion for freedom and justice with community and peace. Covenant has significantly informed and shaped modern Western civilization through the rule of law, constitutionalism, human rights, democracy, the free market, freedom, associational pluralism, civil society, etc. When this metasymbol of organizing (liberation-restoration) is lost, the civilizational edifice of modernity is threatened, vulnerable to either collapse or revert to chaos and authoritarianism. Despite its misuses and abuses, modern democracy, human rights, associational pluralism, and other modern values come from a particular biblical moral vision—covenantalism.

This book has repeatedly shown how Western society is moving away from a covenantal worldview and organizing structure to a highly individualistic contractual society. Today, covenant has almost faded away from culture, and its marks are no longer tangible in contract. Even contract seems no longer fair and has lost legitimacy. The two seem very similar, but they are very different. "Contracts govern economies; covenants permeate lives. Contracts include provisions for expedient discharge; covenants nourish rather than limit and terminate relationships. Contracts end in files; covenants become part of one's history and shape, in unexpected ways, self-perception and perhaps destiny."[6] Secular liberal ethics that relies on Enlightenment humanism alone, with its emphases on "individual will, freedom, rationality, and optimistic faith in human agency,"[7] cannot build thick relationships, reliable moral accountability, and commitment to the common good.

New covenant ethics offers a sensible and compelling alternative to conservative evangelicalism and secular liberal ethics. In the United States, conservative evangelicalism and secular liberal ethics are competitors, polarizing our politics and public life; Trump has escalated the division and polarity further. The divisive effects are alarming. Both continue Puritan covenant ethics to some extent but in completely different moral frameworks. While conservative evangelicalism still holds on to the narrow and misguided tribal authoritarian form of covenant, secular liberal ethics relies on contract that originates in Puritan covenant (via the social contract theory of John Locke) of a secularized polity detached from the original humanist moral

5. Stackhouse, "The Tasks of Theological Ethics," 100.
6. May, "Moral Leadership in the Corporate Setting," 190.
7. Thweatt-Bates, *Cyborg Selves*, 47.

script of covenant, its Christian root. Enlightenment values are now almost completely rescripted under the neoliberal and utilitarian worldview. Consequently, it seems, with the exception of rich corporations, society is unraveling, institutions are being shelled, communities are dissolving, and the social fabric is eroding.

In this atmosphere, the idea of human dignity, a cornerstone of liberal ethics, is getting weaker and emptier because it is detached from its theistic root and moral tradition that offer clear and definitive moral content. Michael Spezio asserts, "Any view of the human that marginalizes or denigrates relationality risks being itself marginalized as pure fiction or as denying that which belongs to the core of human strength and maturity."[8] What we are witnessing today is the moral collapse of the Enlightenment project. We need to listen to Bonhoeffer's prophetic words: "the loss of this ultimate will sooner or later lead to the collapse of the penultimate, if we do not succeed in claiming these penultimate things once again for the ultimate."[9]

> One is born of a covenant and into a covenant, and wherever one moves in life, one makes a covenant or acts on the basis of the already existing covenant. If everything that comes under the term of covenant were dissolved, existence would fall to pieces, because no soul can live an isolated life. It not only means that it cannot get along without the assistance of others; it is in direct conflict with its essence to be something apart. It can only exist as a link of a whole, and it cannot work and act without working in connection with other souls and through them. Therefore the annihilation of the covenant would not be the ruin of society, but the dissolution of each individual soul.[10]

Covenant should not be dismissed as a thing of the past, an outdated idea, or a racist ideology: it offers the scaffold of a common life and a compelling option in today's pluralistic and global era. It embodies a plausible way of organizing social relationships and institutions on the basis of freedom, justice, and reciprocity, with attention to institutional diversity and unity of society.

What are the implications of new covenant ethics for Christian social witness and discipleship? Living under the binding authority and empowerment of the new covenant of Jesus, Christians are called to live out Jesus's commandments and moral teachings (e.g., the Sermon on the Mount) in their lives, and in every domain of their activities, both personal and public. Christians are called to fulfill "the law and the prophets" in Jesus Christ. In their personal lives and in the Christian community,

8. Spezio, "Human or Vulcan?," 151.
9. Bonhoeffer, *Ethics*, 169.
10. Pedersen, *Israel*, 1:308.

Christians should be guided by the covenant of Jesus, which provides clear and explicit knowledge in God's will and purpose. Christian discipleship and witness in society become "an ethical outworking" of the covenant of Jesus.[11] God challenges us to reciprocate God's love and justice, using power in every realm of our life, based on and already experienced in God's love and justice, expressed in the power of the incarnation, earthly ministry, crucifixion, and resurrection of Jesus. New covenant is a centrifugal hub from which God's moral vision shines out to every domain of society and creation. Therefore, Christians are called to live out our faiths in every realm of a society with commitment, care, and a sense of responsibility, namely, giving our bodies as a living sacrifice (Rom. 12:1).

11. Cf. Stackhouse, *Covenant and Commitments*, 142.

Discussion Questions

Introduction

1. What is ethics, and why is it indispensable for human life?
2. What is a key metaphor, and why is it important for Christian ethics? Share some examples of key metaphors for Christian ethics. Which one do you think is closest to the ethics of your own community?
3. In what sense is covenant a key metaphor of the Bible and the Christian life? How does covenant help you to better understand who God is and what God does (God's reign) in the world?

Part 1
New Covenant Ethics: Biblical Foundation, Features, and Method

Chapter 1. Brief Overview of the Old Testament Covenants

1. What are the major covenants in the OT? How are they similar to or different from each other in terms of purpose, scope, and partners?
2. Is God's covenantal relationship in the OT confined to Israel only or open to other people and species? Name the covenants that are universal in their nature and scope.
3. In what sense is creation covenantal? Explain using Genesis 1–2.
4. Discuss the meaning and significance of the creation covenant and the Noachian covenant for ecology and Christian public engagement today.
5. Read Exodus 19–20 and identify the covenantal motifs in those chapters. What does it mean that the Ten Commandments are covenantal? How does the reading help you to understand the Ten Commandments better? How does it change your perception of the Ten Commandments?

Chapter 2. The New Covenant of Jesus Christ

1. In what sense does the NT continue the covenantal drama of the OT? Why is this continuity important for Christian spiritual and moral life today? What danger do you see when Christians fail to see the continuity between the two testaments?
2. How does the idea of covenant help you to better understand Jesus's life, ministry, death, and resurrection? In particular, how are Jesus's preaching and ministry related to his covenantal renewal? Give some concrete pieces of evidence.
3. In what sense is the Sermon on the Mount covenantal? How is the Sermon the reworking of the Sinai covenant in a new social-cultural context? What was its role and function within Jesus's covenant and community?
4. Why did Jesus call his covenant the new covenant? How does the new covenant of Jesus relate to and fulfill all previous covenants?
5. If covenant helps to properly understand the depth of God's ethos and pathos (in particular, in God's relationship with God's people), how does it help you to interpret your own spiritual journey and your relationship with God? Consider some crises or difficult moments in your spiritual relationship with God, if they exist. How does the idea of covenant help you to understand God's faithfulness in those moments?

Chapter 3. Covenantal Drama and Threefold Dialectics

1. In what sense is covenant God's organizing mechanism of God's people and community (creation, Israel, and the church)? How does God organize a moral community using covenant?
2. The author claims that covenant is far more than free agreement (like a contract). What does he mean by that? Can you explain it in terms of the threefold dialectic? (One way of approaching this could involve unpacking the following statement: "the covenant is a grace-based, dialogical and performative, and hope-driven event" [p. 74].) What does covenant mean to you now, and how is it different from your previous understanding?
3. Discuss the triad of love, justice, and power. Many Christians are still struggling to properly define the relationships among love and justice and power. In fact, they are divided politically in terms of prioritizing one value over the others; for example, while conservatives tend to put love over justice, progressives sometimes prioritize justice over love. How are they related to each other in covenant? How does covenant mediate and reorganize their

relationship? How does the discussion of the triad in this chapter clarify the confusion and misunderstanding among Christians on these ideas?

4. How do the communal-communicative and memory-hope dialectics help you gain a better understanding of the Christian practices of praise, prayer, and lament? How could your study of the threefold dialectics help you to clarify or strengthen your spiritual life or your church's worship life?
5. Motivating individuals and institutions to do ethical actions is a major challenge in ethics because knowing what is ethical does not always lead to doing what is right. How does new covenant ethics and its threefold dialectics address this concern? Where do Christians find the motivation to live ethically?

Chapter 4. The Distinctive Nature, Characteristics, and Practices of New Covenant Ethics

1. Discuss what new covenant ethics is—its biblical foundation, scope, and distinctive features. How does it continue Jesus's ministry and the spirit of the Sermon on the Mount?
2. Name a few distinctive characteristics of new covenant ethics. For example, in what sense is new covenant ethics Trinitarian or eschatological?
3. Informed by Jesus and his ministry, new covenant ethics is just peacemaking. Discuss what this means. How does new covenant ethics combine justice and peacemaking?
4. Interpret the Eucharist from a covenantal perspective. How does new covenant ethics offer a more inclusive and organic understanding of the Eucharist? What theological and moral meanings do different names for the Eucharist have for the Christian spiritual-moral life?
5. Name four different practices of new covenant ethics. How are they related to Jesus's ministry? What do they mean for your own local ministry and social engagements?

Chapter 5. The Strengths of New Covenant Ethics

1. Discuss how new covenant ethics is able to reconcile some potentially confusing or binary theological or ethical categories in the Christian life. For example, how does new covenant ethics harmonize God's sovereign power and human freedom? What does this mean for your spiritual life?
2. How does new covenant ethics harmonize norm and context?
3. How does new covenant ethics harmonize the particularity and public engagement of the church?

4. How does new covenant ethics constructively conceive the relationship between worship and ethics in the Christian life? How are worship and ethics interrelated?
5. Why is the harmony and balance between these binary notions so important for Christian ministry and discipleship? What dangers or distortions do we experience when Christians choose one side or aspect of the binary over the other? Give examples from your own personal or church life about the difficulty that arises when the balance is broken (e.g., unity-diversity, worship, and ethics).

Chapter 6. A Short Comparison with Other Christian Ethics

1. Discuss the merits of new covenant ethics in comparison to other paradigms of ethics.
2. How is new covenant ethics different from traditional covenantal ethics? How does it overcome major limitations of the latter, such as misuse of covenant for ethnocentrism and racism?
3. How is new covenant ethics similar to and different from the Christian Realism of Reinhold Niebuhr? Liberation ethics? John Howard Yoder's Mennonite ethics?

Chapter 7. Norms and Values

1. Discuss how norms and values can be organized in terms of the covenantal drama and threefold dialectics: How does a covenantal approach offer a better understanding of key norms and values of the Bible and their interdependent relationship?
2. Identify several key norms and values of the Bible and describe how they are related to covenant in general and to the new covenant of Jesus in particular.
3. Discuss how they are interrelated in terms of the covenantal drama and threefold dialectics.
4. Discuss the importance of gratitude in a covenantal framework. What is it, and what is its source or initiator? How is it related to the unilateral-bilateral dialectic? Why do you think it is central to the Christian life? How does it inform other norms and values?
5. Discuss the importance of truth/truth telling for our social life from a covenantal perspective. How is truth telling related to trust? In what sense is it covenantal? How do misinformation and fake news harm mutual trust and undermine democracy?

6. Among the norms and values in the chapter, which norms and values do you or your church have difficulty keeping or practicing, and why? Are there any theological or practical reasons for this? How does your study of new covenant ethics help with its correction or improvement?

Chapter 8. The Three Ethical Motifs of Goal, Law, and Virtue

1. What are teleology, deontology, and aretology? What roles do goal, rule, and virtue play, and how do they shape our moral life?
2. What is a covenantal approach to goal? Why does the author name shalom as the goal of the Christian life? What is shalom from a covenantal perspective? Do you think it could serve as the common good for humanity?
3. What is a covenantal approach to the law, and how is it different from typical deontology? In what sense is it informative and performative?
4. How does new covenant ethics understand virtue formation and growth of Christians? How does virtue formation take place in a covenant relationship? Explain this in terms of the threefold dialectics. How is this different from the virtue ethics of Stanley Hauerwas?
5. How are the three motifs of goal, rule, and virtue interrelated around covenant? How does new covenant ethics offer a more biblical, holistic, and organic understanding of the three motifs and the Christian moral life?

Chapter 9. The Moral Authority of Scripture and Other Sources

1. Discuss a covenantal understanding of Scripture and its authority. What does it mean that Scripture is the covenantal document of a faith community? How does new covenant ethics define the authority of Scripture? What about the canonicity of the Bible, especially its overall unity and coherence, despite its diverse literary genres, authors, and historical contexts of composition?
2. What do we mean when we say Scripture is the norming norm? How does this conceive the relationship of Scripture with the other sources of Christian ethics (tradition, experience, and reason)?
3. What does it mean when the author says that we should read Scripture communally, communicatively, and analogically? Discuss how analogical imagination is involved in our reading of Scripture. Likewise, how does a covenantal approach lead to a better understanding of the Christian tradition and its moral authority? In particular, how does the idea of covenantal renewal help with understanding tradition?
4. Discuss the relative authority of experience and reason compared to that of Scripture and tradition from a covenantal perspective. Why do you think

Christians should (or should not) use experience and reason in their ethical reasoning? Are experience and reason antithetical to Scripture? What is their proper authority, and how do we properly discern it?

5. The conflicts that Christians experience among themselves frequently have to do with their different prioritizing and understanding of the sources of authority (Scripture, tradition, experience, reason). Identify one divisive social issue in your community (e.g., abortion, immigration, critical race theory) and examine how it is affected by different views of the sources of authority.

Chapter 10. Ethical Reasoning

1. What is ethical reasoning, and why is it important for the Christian life? How is ethical reasoning different from supernatural religious experience (e.g., a dream, a vision)? What happens when Christians fail to grow in ethical reasoning?
2. Unpack and explain the following characteristics of covenantal reasoning: "Ethical reasoning in new covenant ethics is dialectical in nature, communicative in process, analogical in application, and communal in its spirit and posture" (p. 228).
3. Discuss why Christians' ethical reasoning should be communal, communicative, and covenantal. What limitations or dangers do we face when ethical reasoning fails to be communal and communicative?
4. Discuss the role of analogical imagination for ethical reasoning. What is analogical imagination, and how is it inevitably involved in the process of Christian ethical reasoning?
5. Name the four levels of ethical reasoning and how they are interrelated. What problems could Christians face if they use only one level to the exclusion of the others? For example, what problem could arise when Christians rely on only the rule level or the particular judgment level?

Part 2
Social Ethics:
A Critical Engagement with Social Issues of Our Time

Chapter 11. Covenantal Social Imagination

1. What is social ethics? How is it related to theological ethics, and how is it different from personal ethics? What is its role in our society? Discuss in terms of subject matter, scope, and purpose.

2. Why is social ethics important for Christian life and witness? What happens when churches fail to develop and teach faithful and capacious social ethics? Share some recent examples.
3. What is associational pluralism, and how is it similar to the unity-in-diversity principle of covenant? How does it imagine a society and its different social spheres and institutions and their relationships? How is it related to covenant? Share some examples of associational pluralism in the Bible. How does covenant inform them?
4. What is the subsidiarity principle? How is it related to the autonomy of social spheres?
5. Why is the autonomy of social spheres (e.g., the free press) important for justice to protect peoples' basic rights and maintain a minimal degree of social justice? How does totalitarianism, fascism, or authoritarianism typically violate the autonomy of social spheres? Consider recent historical and contemporary examples, such as Nazi Germany, Soviet communism, Islamic theocracy, or others.

Chapter 12. Distributive Justice

1. What is distributive justice? What is its role in a society, and why does it matter for people? What happens when people feel distributive justice is violated? Discuss recent examples (e.g., immigration, affirmative action, the bailout of the Wall Street banks in 2008).
2. Discuss different material principles of distributive justice (equality, need, merit, and capability) and how they are different and interrelated. Which principle do you feel is central to you or your community, and why?
3. Why do you think a complex theory of distributive justice is more important than a simple theory?
4. How would you describe a covenantal approach to distributive justice? How is it different from conventional approaches? How does it allow for a complex view of distributive justice?

Chapter 13. Politics

1. Reinhold Niebuhr famously said: "[Human] capacity for justice makes democracy possible, but [human] inclination to injustice makes democracy necessary." What does he mean by this statement? How is it related to human sin and human potential for justice? How does the biblical idea of covenant (its drama; its triad of love, justice, and power; and its threefold dialectics)

help us to understand the delicate and ambivalent nature of humanity and democracy?

2. Is democracy more congruent with Christianity than with other political systems? Or is it simply a liberal bias? How does the idea of covenant help us to see some intrinsic connection between Christian faith and democracy?
3. Discuss the covenantal basis of modern democracy. How did covenantalism inform democracy and its institutions—for example, rule of law?
4. What is illiberal democracy, and how is it different from liberal democracy? How is the rise of illiberal democracy and identity politics in the West related to the erosion of covenantalism in its political and civic life?
5. In your view, how could new covenant ethics help to renew, empower, and expand democracy? Answer in the context of your own community.

Chapter 14. Economic Ethics

1. What is neoliberalism, and how is it different from other forms of economic systems, such as the mixed economy of Keynesianism?
2. Discuss the key features of neoliberalism and its impact on politics, culture, and social institutions, including churches. How can the churches be free from its temptations and seductions?
3. Discuss the economic meanings and significance of the Sabbath. What is Sabbath economics, and how is it different from neoliberalism? Share three or four major differences between them. What are some ways that churches and Christians can practice Sabbath economics today, even as an experimental form?
4. Why do you think millennials and Generation Z in the United States are far more receptive to democratic socialism than baby boomers? How is new covenantal ethics similar to and different from democratic socialism?
5. What is the importance of jobs for human well-being, both financial and emotional? How could Christians respond to the harsh economic reality that jobs are disappearing due to globalization, advancing technologies, and various neoliberal policies?
6. In this context, do you think a faith-rooted, intentional community is a viable option for Christians to cope with the challenges?
7. As a Christian, how do you understand the idea of universal basic income? Would you consider this a viable moral response or a shortcut to moral irresponsibility?

Chapter 15. Creation Care

1. Share your experiences of global warming, using recent examples of ecological incidents (e.g., heat waves, floods, fires, hurricanes, droughts). How does global warming pose threats to you and your community?
2. What are the causes of global warming? How are they related to a particular worldview and mind-set of modernity? How is Christianity, covenant ethics in particular, different from this worldview? In response to the threats of global warming, name a few things that you can do to mitigate global warming in your personal life and community.
3. What does it mean for humans to be in a covenantal relationship with nature? If we are covenanted with nature, how does it change our perception of other species and the planet? What covenantal obligations do we have toward them according to Scripture? Name two or three concrete obligations.
4. In light of the creation covenant, what is a proper theological meaning of the cultural mandate (Gen. 1:28)? In particular, what does dominion mean in a covenant context?
5. What theological and ethical resources does Jesus offer for creation care? What is the importance of the incarnation of Jesus and his new covenant for ecological ethics? In light of the fact that the new covenant is the fulfillment of the creation covenant, what does salvation mean for you?

Chapter 16. Criminal Justice

1. Consider retribution, deterrence, and rehabilitation. How do these three understandings and justifications of criminal punishment differ?
2. Discuss the intersectionality between race, class, and the criminal justice system. For example, how does racism and/or poverty currently criminalize the poor and the marginalized?
3. Describe the punitive culture prevailing in the United States, using recent statistics or sharing a few examples. What are its causes, and why is it problematic? How is it related to the prison-industrial complex and corruptions in the criminal justice system? Assess its (im)moral nature and validity (or lack thereof) in the context of new covenant ethics.
4. What is restorative justice, and how is it different from retributive justice? In what sense is restorative justice covenantal? How is it related to just peacemaking? How can you practice restorative justice in your own community?
5. How does new covenant ethics help to constructively embrace and balance the validity and importance of both retributive and restorative justice?

Chapter 17. Race

1. The author states, "There is compelling evidence to suggest that racism is the original sin of the United States (and the modern West)" (p. 375). What does this statement mean? Do you agree or disagree with this statement? Why?
2. Critical race theory has been a focal point of national controversy in the United States. Discuss this theory's merits and limitations. How can a covenantal approach clarify some of the controversies pertaining to critical race theory?
3. Discuss the relationship between racial reconciliation and racial justice. Which should be prior for Christians, and why? Engage this topic from a covenantal perspective.
4. What does it mean that interracial relationships can be conceived as covenantal? What merits and limitations do you see in this approach? What would its actual practices look like in your own cultural context?

Chapter 18. Sex and Marriage

1. Discuss the differences between covenant and contract in a sexual relationship. How does a contractual view shape the cultural understanding of sex, such as casual or consensual sex? What does it mean to say that a biblical view of marriage is covenantal? How is it different from contract?
2. Discuss the erosion of marriage (and even sex) today. How does individualism and/or pornography affect sexual desire and sexual relationship? What could be its long-term effects on the emotional and psychological well-being of individuals and society?
3. Discuss three different ethical approaches to same-sex marriage. How does each approach justify its moral validity in terms of the four sources of Christian ethics (Scripture, tradition, experience, and reason)?
4. Advocates of same-sex marriage claim it is equally covenantal to marriage between a woman and a man. What do they mean by this? In your view, can same-sex marriage be equally covenantal?
5. Same-sex marriage has been a divisive issue in churches today, making it a major source of political polarization in many countries, and there seems no possibility of resolution in the foreseeable future. How can Christians maintain civility among themselves despite deep theological differences? How can a covenantal approach help to build and promote civility, tolerance, and mutual respect?

Chapter 19. Medical Ethics

1. Discuss positive (beneficial) and negative (detrimental) influences of the Enlightenment worldview and (modern) individualism on medical choices and practices, such as abortion or physician-assisted suicide (PAS).
2. Discuss the personhood of a fetus. Why is it important, and how does it divide the current discussions of abortion? What is a covenantal approach to abortion?
3. Examine the reasons why women resort to abortion. What did you learn from your study, and can you think of some measures that could help to reduce abortion?
4. Discuss the view of death in popular culture today. How should Christians respond to it? What is a covenantal view of death, and how is it different from that in popular culture?

Chapter 20. War, Peace, and Just Peacemaking

1. Discuss just war theory, pacifism, and just peacemaking. What are their respective views on the use of violence against another nation, their biblical foundations, and their theological justifications? What are their limitations and strengths?
2. Discuss various modern attempts to correct or improve just war theory. Can you identify one or two of them?
3. How is just peacemaking different from pacifism? Was Jesus a pacifist or a just peacemaker?
4. Is self-defense acceptable in just peacemaking or not? If so, why? If not, why not?
5. Describe a covenantal approach to just peacemaking. How is it similar to and different from Glen Stassen's just peacemaking theory (JPT)?

Bibliography

"Abortion." Gallup. Accessed January 8, 2021. http://news.gallup.com/poll/1576/abortion.aspx.

Alan Guttmacher Institute. "Induced Abortion in the United States." September 2019. https://www.guttmacher.org/fact-sheet/induced-abortion-united-states#.

———. *Perspective on Sexual & Reproductive Health*. September 2005.

———. "US Abortion Patients." May 9, 2016. https://www.guttmacher.org/infographic/2016/us-abortion-patients.

Alexander, Michelle. "My Rapist Apologized: I Still Needed an Abortion." *New York Times*, May 23, 2019. https://www.nytimes.com/2019/05/23/opinion/abortion-legislation-rape.html?eType=EmailBlastContent&eId=b19eb556-e1e2-41d4-be2b-84b297235775.

———. *The New Jim Crow: Mass Incarceration in the Age of Colorblindness*. New York: New Press, 2012.

Allan, Pierre, and Alexis Keller, eds. *What Is a Just Peace?* New York: Oxford University Press, 2008.

Allen, Joseph L. *Love and Conflict: A Covenantal Model of Christian Ethics*. Lanham, MD: University Press of America, 1995.

Allison, Dale. *The Sermon on the Mount: Inspiring the Moral Imagination*. New York: Crossroad, 1999.

Althusius, Johannes. *Politica: An Abridged Translation of Politics Methodically Set Forth and Illustrated with Sacred and Profane Examples*. Edited and translated by Frederick S. Carney. Indianapolis: Liberty Fund, 1995.

Appiah, Kwame Anthony. *Cosmopolitanism: Ethics in a World of Strangers*. New York: Norton, 2006.

Aquinas, Thomas. *Summa Theologica, Volume II–Part II, First Section*. 1912. Reprint, New York: Cosimo Classics, 2007.

Associated Press. "US Abortion Rate Up Slightly after Years of Decline." Last updated October 25, 2015. https://www.foxnews.com/health/u-s-abortion-rate-up-slightly-after-years-of-decline.

"Attitudes on Same-Sex Marriage." Pew Research Center, May 14, 2019. https://www.pewforum.org/fact-sheet/changing-attitudes-on-gay-marriage.

Baker, Christopher. *Covenant and Liberation: Giving New Heart to God's Endangered Family*. New York: Lang, 1991.

Baker, Kelly J. "The Artifacts of White Supremacy." Religion & Culture Forum, June 14, 2017. http://voices.uchicago.edu/religionculture/2017/06/14/813/.

Balswick, Jack O., et al. *The Reciprocating Self: Human Development in Theological Perspective*. Downers Grove, IL: IVP Academic, 2016.

Barndt, Joseph R. *Dismantling Racism: The Continuing Challenge to White America*. Minneapolis: Augsburg, 1991.

Barth, Karl. *Church Dogmatics*. 13 vols. Edinburgh: T&T Clark, 1957–1975.

Barton, John. "Approaches to Ethics in the Old Testament." In *Beginning Old Testament Study*, edited by John Rogerson, 113–30. Philadelphia: Westminster, 1982.

———. *People of the Book: The Authority of the Bible in Christianity*. New York: SPCK, 1988.

Bauckham, Richard. "Scripture and Authority." *Transformation* 15, no. 2 (April 1998): 5–11.

Bavinck, Herman. *Reformed Dogmatics*. Vol. 3, *Sin and Salvation in Christ*. Grand Rapids: Baker Academic, 2006.

Beale, G. K. *Handbook on the New Testament Use of the Old Testament: Exegesis and Interpretation*. Grand Rapids: Baker Academic, 2012.

Beauchamp, Tom L., and James F. Childress. *Principle of Biomedical Ethics*. 4th ed. New York: Oxford University Press, 1994.

Beckett, Joshua. "Desire in Singleness: Ascetics and Eternity (or, Why Christians Don't Need to Get Married)." In Kutter Calloway, *Breaking the Marriage Idol: Reconstructing Our Cultural and Spiritual Norms*, 193–212. Downers Grove, IL: IVP, 2018.

———. "Mass Incarceration." In *Discerning Ethics: Diverse Christian Responses to Divisive Moral Issues*, edited by Hak Joon Lee and Tim Dearborn, 218–35. Downers Grove, IL: IVP Academic, 2020.

Beisner, E. Calvin. *Prosperity and Poverty: The Compassionate Use of Resources in a World of Scarcity*. 1988. Reprint, Eugene, OR: Wipf & Stock, 2001.

Bell, Jasmine. "5 Things to Know about Communities of Color and Environmental Justice." Center for American Progress, April 25, 2016. https://www.americanprogress.org/issues/race/news/2016/04/25/136361/5-things-to-know-about-communities-of-color-and-environmental-justice/.

Benne, Robert. *The Ethics of Democratic Capitalism: A Moral Reassessment*. Philadelphia: Fortress, 1981.

Berry, Wendell. *The Art of the Commonplace: The Agrarian Essays of Wendell Berry*. Washington, DC: Counterpoint, 2002.

Bhagwati, Jagdish. *In Defense of Globalization*. New York: Oxford University Press, 2004.

Bidol, Patricia A. *Developing New Perspectives on Race: An Innovative Multi-Media Social Studies Curriculum in Racism Awareness for the Secondary Level.* Detroit: New Perspectives on Race, 1972.

Birch, Bruce. *Let Justice Roll Down: The Old Testament, Ethics, and Christian Life.* Louisville: Westminster John Knox, 1991.

———. "Moral Agency, Community, and the Character of God in the Hebrew Bible." *Semeia* 66 (1994): 23–41.

Birmingham Theological Seminary. "Kingdom, Covenants and Canon of the Old Testament." 2012. http://btsfreeccm.org/local/lmp/lessons.php?lesson=KOT3text.

Bishop, Jeffery P. *The Anticipatory Corpse: Medicine, Power, and the Care of the Dying.* Notre Dame: University of Notre Dame Press, 2011.

Boff, Leonardo. *Ecclesiogenesis: The Base Communities Reinvent the Church.* Maryknoll, NY: Orbis, 1986.

Bond, Jermaine, and Allen A. Herman. "Lagging Life Expectancy for Black Men: A Public Health Imperative." *American Journal of Public Health* 106, no. 7 (2016): 1167–69.

Bonhoeffer, Dietrich. *The Cost of Discipleship.* New York: Macmillan, 1963.

———. *Ethics.* Edited by Clifford J. Green. Translated by Reinhard Krauss, Douglas W. Stott, and Charles C. West. Dietrich Bonhoeffer Works, vol. 6. Minneapolis: Fortress, 2009.

———. *Letters and Papers from Prison.* Edited by John W. de Gruchy. Translated by Isabel Best, Lisa E. Dahill, Reinhard Krauss, and Nancy Lukens. Dietrich Bonhoeffer Works, vol. 8. Minneapolis: Fortress, 2010.

Boulaga, Fabian Eboussi. *Christianity without Fetishes: An African Critique and Recapture of Christianity.* Maryknoll, NY: Orbis, 1984.

Bouma-Prediger, Steven. *For the Beauty of the Earth: A Christian Vision for Creation Care.* 2nd ed. Grand Rapids: Baker Academic, 2010.

Boyte, Harry. *Commonwealth: A Return to Citizen Politics.* New York: Free Press, 1990.

Braaten, Carl. *No Other Gospel! Christianity among the World's Religions.* Minneapolis: Fortress, 1992.

Bradley, James E. *Religion, Revolution, and English Radicalism: Non-Conformity in Eighteenth Century Politics and Society.* Cambridge: Cambridge University Press, 1990.

Bretherton, Luke. "Exorcizing Democracy: The Theopolitical Challenge of Black Power." *Journal of the Society of Christian Ethics* 38, no. 1 (2018): 3–24.

Brooks, David. "Obama, Gospel and Verse." *New York Times*, April 26, 2007. https://www.nytimes.com/2007/04/26/opinion/26brooks.html.

Brown, Anna. "Key Findings on Americans' Views of Race in 2019." Pew Research Center, April 9, 2019. https://www.pewresearch.org/fact-tank/2019/04/09/key-findings-on-americans-views-of-race-in-2019/.

Brown, Harold I. *Rationality.* New York: Routledge, 1990.

Brown, Raymond E. *The Gospel according to John 13–22*. New York: Anchor Bible Doubleday, 1970.

Brueggemann, Walter. *The Covenanted Self: Explorations in Law and Covenant*. Minneapolis: Fortress, 1999.

———. *Ice Axes for Frozen Seas: A Biblical Theology of Provocation*. Waco, TX: Baylor University Press, 2014.

———. *Money and Possession*. Louisville: Westminster John Knox, 2016.

———. *A Social Reading of the Old Testament: Prophetic Approaches to Israel's Communal Life*. Minneapolis: Fortress, 1994.

Buber, Martin. *Moses*. Oxford: East and West Library, 1946.

Butkus, Russell A. "The Stewardship of Creation." Center for Christian Ethics at Baylor University, 2002. https://www.baylor.edu/ifl/christianreflection/CreationarticleButkus.pdf.

Butterfield, Rosaria Champagne. *Openness Unhindered: Further Thoughts of an Unlikely Convert*. Pittsburgh: Crown & Covenant Publications, 2015.

Byrd, W. Carson. "Most White Americans Will Never Be Affected by Affirmative Action. So Why Do They Hate It So Much?" *Washington Post*, October 18, 2018. https://www.washingtonpost.com/nation/2018/10/19/most-white-americans-will-never-experience-affirmative-action-so-why-do-they-hate-it-so-much/.

Cahill, Lisa Sowle. *Blessed Are the Peacemakers: Pacifism, Just War, and Peacemaking*. Minneapolis: Fortress, 2019.

———. *Global Justice, Christology, and Christian Ethics*. Cambridge: Cambridge University Press, 2013.

———. *Sex, Gender, and Christian Ethics*. New York: Cambridge University Press, 1996.

Caird, G. B. *The Revelation of St. John*. New York: Harper & Row, 1966.

Calvin, John. *Institutes of the Christian Religion*. Edited by John T. McNeil. Philadelphia: Westminster, 1960.

Camhi, Natasha. "Women's Experience behind Bars." Brennan Center for Justice, August 24, 2018. https://www.brennancenter.org/our-work/analysis-opinion/womens-experience-behind-bars.

Camosy, Charles. *Beyond the Abortion Wars: A Way Forward for a New Generation*. Grand Rapids: Eerdmans, 2015.

Carter, J. Kameron. *Race: A Theological Account*. New York: Oxford University Press, 2008.

Carter, Warren. *Matthew and the Margins: A Sociopolitical and Religious Reading*. Maryknoll, NY: Orbis, 2001.

"A Catholic Framework for Economic Life." Statement of the US Bishops. Catholic Research Economists Discussion Organization, November 1996. https://credo-economists.org/2014/04/catholic-framework-economic-life/.

Cavanagh, John, and Jerry Mander, eds. *Alternative Economic Globalization: A Better World Is Possible.* 2nd ed. San Francisco: Berrett-Koehler, 2004.

Centers for Medicare & Medicaid Services. "National Health Expenditures 2017 Highlights." December 6, 2018. https://www.cms.gov/Research-Statistics-Data-and-Systems/Statistics-Trends-and-Reports/NationalHealthExpendData/Downloads/highlights.pdf.

Cha, Ariana Eunjung. "From Sex Selection to Surrogates, American IVF Clinics Provide Services Outlawed Elsewhere." *Washington Post,* December 30, 2018. https://www.washingtonpost.com/national/health-science/from-sex-selection-to-surrogates-american-ivf-clinics-provide-services-outlawed-elsewhere/2018/12/29/0b596668-03c0-11e9-9122-82e98f91ee6f_story.html?utm_term=.5c33c3e213f3.

Chan, Sewell. "Paris Accord Considers Climate Change as a Factor in Mass Migration." *New York Times,* December 12, 2015. http://www.nytimes.com/2015/12/13/world/europe/paris-accord-considers-climate-change-as-a-factor-in-mass-migration.html?emc=eta1.

Chang, Ha-Joon. *Bad Samaritans: The Myth of Free Trade and the Secret History of Capitalism.* New York: Bloomsbury, 2008.

Childs, Brevard. *Old Testament Theology in a Canonical Context.* Philadelphia: Fortress, 1985.

Christiansen, Drew, Tobias Winright, Laurie Johnston, and Mark H. Allman. "Must Just Peace and Just War Be Mutually Exclusive?" *Horizons* 45, no. 1 (2018): 105–8.

Clark, David K., and Robert V. Rakestraw, eds. *Readings in Christian Ethics.* Vol. 2, *Issues and Applications.* Grand Rapids: Baker Books, 1996.

Clark, Fred. "Christian Nationalism and White Nationalism." *Patheos,* June 27, 2017. http://www.patheos.com/blogs/slacktivist/2017/06/27/christian-nationalism-white-nationalism/#JBzzCUYSrwbW4wZQ.99.

Coakley, Sarah. *God, Sexuality, and the Self: An Essay "On the Trinity."* New York: Cambridge University Press, 2013.

———. *The New Asceticism: Sexuality, Gender, and Quest for God.* New York: Bloomsbury Continuum, 2015.

Coates, Ta-Nehisi. "The Black Family in the Age of Mass Incarceration." *Atlantic,* October 2015. https://www.theatlantic.com/magazine/archive/2015/10/the-black-family-in-the-age-of-mass-incarceration/403246/.

———. "The Case for Reparations." *Atlantic,* June 2014. https://www.theatlantic.com/magazine/archive/2014/06/the-case-for-reparations/361631/.

Cone, James H. "Theology's Great Sin: Silence in the Face of White Supremacy." In *Theology in Global Context: Essays in Honor of Robert C. Neville,* edited by Amos Yong and Peter Goodwin Heltzel. New York: T&T Clark International, 2004.

Copeland, M. Shawn. *Enfleshing Freedom: Body, Race, and Being*. Minneapolis: Fortress, 2010.

Copeland, Warren R. *And the Poor Get Welfare: The Ethics of Poverty in the United States*. Nashville: Abingdon, 1994.

Cornish, Audie. "'The Atlantic's' Ta-Nehisi Coates Builds 'A Case for Reparations.'" NPR, May 23, 2014. https://www.ualrpublicradio.org/post/atlantics-ta-nehisi-coates-builds-case-reparations

Cortright, David. *Peace: A History of Movements and Ideas*. New York: Cambridge University Press, 2008.

Countryman, L. William. *Dirt, Greed, and Sex: Sexual Ethics in the New Testament and Their Implications for Today*. 2nd ed. Minneapolis: Fortress, 2007.

Craig, David M. *Health Care as a Social Good: Religious Values and American Democracy*. Washington, DC: Georgetown University Press, 2014.

"Criminal Justice Facts." The Sentencing Project. Accessed January 4, 2021. https://www.sentencingproject.org/criminal-justice-facts/.

"Criminal Justice Fact Sheet." NAACP. Accessed January 4, 2021. http://www.naacp.org/criminal-justice-fact-sheet.

Dahl, Robert. *A Preface to Economic Democracy*. Berkeley: University of California Press, 1985.

Daly, Herman E., and Joshua Farley. *Ecological Economics: Principles and Applications*. 2nd ed. Washington, DC: Island, 2011.

Davis, Angela Y. *Are Prisons Obsolete?* New York: Seven Stories Press, 2003.

Davis, Ellen F. *Scripture, Culture, and Agriculture: An Agrarian Reading of the Bible*. New York: Cambridge University Press, 2009.

Dawn, Marva J. *Sexual Character: Beyond Technique to Intimacy*. Grand Rapids: Eerdmans, 1993.

"Death Penalty and Race." Amnesty International, May 18, 2017. https://www.amnestyusa.org/issues/death-penalty/death-penalty-facts/death-penalty-and-race/.

De Gruchy, John W. *Christianity and Democracy: A Theology for a Just World Order*. New York: Cambridge University Press, 1995.

———. *Reconciliation: Restoring Justice*. Minneapolis: Fortress, 2002.

Deidun, T. J. *New Covenant Morality in Paul*. Rome: Biblical Institute Press, 1981.

Delgado, Richard, and Jean Stefancic, eds. *Critical Race Theory: An Introduction*. New York: New York University Press, 2001.

———. *Critical Racial Theory: The Cutting Edge*. Philadelphia: Temple University Press, 2000.

Dell, Katharine J. "Covenant and Creation in Relationship." In *Covenant as Context: Essays in Honour of E. W. Nicholson*, edited by A. Mayes and Robert Salters, 111–34. New York: Oxford University Press, 2003.

Dembicki, Geoff. "Naomi Klein: 'We Face a Series of Radical Options.'" *Tyee*, March 11, 2016. http://thetyee.ca/Presents/2016/03/11/Naomi-Klein-Interview/.

Desilver, Drew. "Despite Global Concerns about Democracy, More Than Half of Countries Are Democratic." Pew Research Center, May 14, 2019. https://www.pewresearch.org/fact-tank/2019/05/14/more-than-half-of-countries-are-democratic/.

DeVuono-Powell, Saneta, Chris Schweidler, Alicia Walters, and Azadeh Zohrabi. "Who Pays? The True Cost of Incarceration on Families." National Institute of Corrections, 2015. https://nicic.gov/who-pays-true-cost-incarceration-families.

Dewey, John. *The Public and Its Problems: An Essay in Political Inquiry.* Edited by Melvin L. Rogers. Athens, OH: Swallow, 2016.

DiAngelo, Robin. "No, I Won't Stop Saying 'White Supremacy.'" *Yes!*, June 30, 2017. https://www.yesmagazine.org/democracy/2017/06/30/no-i-wont-stop-saying-white-supremacy/.

———. "White Fragility." *International Journal of Critical Pedagogy* 3, no. 3 (2011): 54–70.

———. *White Fragility: Why It's So Hard for White People to Talk about Racism.* Boston: Beacon, 2018.

Douglas, Kelly Brown. *Stand Your Ground: Black Bodies and the Justice of God.* Maryknoll, NY: Orbis, 2015.

Douglas, Mary. *Leviticus as Literature.* New York: Oxford University Press, 1999.

Dozier, Jason. "What Exactly Is 'Illiberal Democracy'?" *Global Risk Insights*, May 28, 2016. https://globalriskinsights.com/2016/05/what-is-illiberal-democracy/.

Dugdale, Lydia S., ed. *Dying in the Twenty-First Century: Toward a New Ethical Framework for the Art of Dying Well.* Cambridge, MA: MIT Press, 2015.

Dulles, Avery. *Models of Revelation.* Garden City, NY: Doubleday, 1983.

Dumbrell, William. *Covenant and Creation: An Old Testament Covenant Theology.* Nashville: Nelson, 1984.

Dunlap, Bridgette. "Three Constitutional Basics Every Abortion Rights Supporter Should Know." *Rewire News*, June 17, 2016. https://rewire.news/article/2016/06/17/three-constitutional-basics-every-abortion-rights-supporter-know/.

Dunn, James. *The Epistle to the Galatians.* Peabody, MA: Hendrickson, 1993.

Edwards, Jonathan. *A Treatise concerning Religious Affections: In Three Parts.* New York: Cosimo, 2009.

Eglinton, James. *Trinity and Organism.* New York: T&T Clark, 2012.

Eichrodt, Walther. *Theology of the Old Testament.* Vol. 1. Philadelphia: Westminster, 1961.

Elazar, Daniel J. *Covenant and Civil Society: The Constitutional Matrix of Modern Democracy.* New Brunswick, NJ: Transaction, 1998.

———. *Covenant and Commonwealth: From Christian Separation through the Protestant Reformation.* New Brunswick, NJ: Transaction, 1996.

———. *Covenant and Constitutionalism: The Great Frontier and the Matrix of Federal Democracy*. New Brunswick, NJ: Transaction, 1998.

———. *Covenant and Polity in Biblical Israel: Biblical Foundations and Jewish Expressions*. The Covenant Tradition in Politics, vol. 1. New Brunswick, NJ: Transaction, 1995.

———. "Federal Models of (Civil) Authority." *Journal of Church and State* 22, no. 2 (Spring 1991): 231–54.

———, ed. *Kinship and Consent: The Jewish Political Tradition and Its Contemporary Uses*. Washington, DC: University Press of America, 1983.

Elshtain, Jean Bethke. "Reflections on Abortion, Values and the Family." In *Abortion: Understanding Differences*, edited by Sidney Callahan and Daniel Callahan, 47–72. New York: Plenum, 1984.

Emerson, Michael O., and Christian Smith. *Divided by Faith: Evangelical Religions and the Problem of Race in America*. New York: Oxford University Press, 2000.

Estelle, Bryan D. *Echoes of Exodus: Tracing a Biblical Motif*. Downers Grove, IL: IVP Academic, 2018.

Evans, Donald. *The Logic of Self-Involvement: A Philosophical Study of Everyday Language with Special Reference to the Christian Use of Language about God as Creator*. New York: Herder & Herder, 1969.

"Facts about the Death Penalty." Death Penalty Information Center, updated May 31, 2019. https://files.deathpenaltyinfo.org/legacy/documents/FactSheet.pdf.

Farley, Margaret. *Just Love: A Framework for Christian Sexual Ethics*. New York: Continuum, 2006.

Fee, Gordon. *Paul, the Spirit, the People of God*. Grand Rapids: Baker Academic, 2011.

Feil, Ernst. *The Theology of Dietrich Bonhoeffer*. Philadelphia: Fortress, 1985.

Fileva, Iskra. Review of *Tolerance among the Virtues*, by John R. Bowlin. *Notre Dame Philosophical Review*, April 5, 2017. https://ndpr.nd.edu/news/tolerance-among-the-virtues/.

Finn, Daniel. *The Moral Ecology of Markets: Assessing Claims about Markets and Justice*. New York: Cambridge University Press, 2006.

Fishbane, Michael A. *Biblical Interpretation in Ancient Israel*. Oxford: Clarendon, 1988.

Flanders, Henry Jackson, Robert W. Crapps, and David A. Smith. *The People of the Covenant: An Introduction to the Hebrew Bible*. New York: Oxford University Press, 1996.

Fletcher, Joseph H. "Indicators of Humanhood: A Tentative Profile of Man." *Hastings Center Report* 2, no. 5 (November 1972): 1–4.

———. *Situation Ethics: A New Morality*. Louisville: Westminster John Knox, 1997.

Ford, Matt. "Can Bipartisanship End Mass Incarceration?" *Atlantic*, February 25, 2015. www.theatlantic.com/politics/archive/2015/02/can-bipartisanship-end-mass-incarceration/386012/.

Foucault, Michel. *A History of Sexuality*. Vol. 1. New York, Pantheon, 1978.

Fougère, Martin. "Corporations as Political and Unpolitical Actors." *Electronic Journal of Business Ethics and Organization Studies* 16, no. 2 (2011): 12–21.

Freedman, David Noel, ed. *Anchor Bible Dictionary*. 6 vols. New York: Doubleday, 1992.

———. "Divine Commitment and Human Obligation: The Covenant Theme." *Interpretation* 18, no. 4 (1964): 419–31.

Fretheim, Terence. *Exodus*. Louisville: Westminster John Knox, 2010.

———. "אוד." In *New International Dictionary of the Old Testament Theology and Exegesis*, edited by Willem VanGemeren, 2:413. Grand Rapids: Zondervan, 1997.

Frizell, Sam. "This Is How Much More Popular Same-Sex Marriage Is Today Than in 1989." *Time*, October 1, 2014. http://time.com/3449788/gay-marriage-1989/.

Fukuyama, Francis. "Against Identity Politics: The New Tribalism and the Crisis of Democracy." *Foreign Affairs*, September/October 2018. https://www.foreignaffairs.com/articles/americas/2018-08-14/against-identity-politics-tribalism-francis-fukuyama.

Fung, Archon. "Deliberation before the Revolution: Toward an Ethics of Deliberative Democracy in an Unjust World." *Political Theory* 33, no. 3 (2005): 397–419.

Galloway, Allan D. "Creation and Covenant." In *Creation, Christ, Culture: Studies in Honor of T. F. Torrance*, edited by Richard McKinney, 108–18. Edinburgh: T&T Clark, 1976.

Garrett, Duane A. *Proverbs, Ecclesiastes, and Song of Songs*. The New American Commentary. Nashville: Broadman, 1993.

Geisler, Norman L. *Christian Ethics: Contemporary Issues & Options*. 2nd ed. Grand Rapids: Baker Academic, 2010.

Gelman, Barry. "Tzedakah and Chesed: Preparing the Month of Elul by, Rosh Kehilah Dina Najman, Marta d'Atra of." *Jewish Journal*, August 13, 2009. https://jewishjournal.com/culture/religion/jewish_thought/71849/tzedakah-and-chesed-preparing-for-the-month-of-elul-by-rosh-kehilah-dina-najman-marta-datra-of/.

Gentry, Peter J., and Stephen J. Wellum. *Kingdom through Covenant: A Biblical-Theological Understanding of the Covenants*. 2nd ed. Wheaton, IL: Crossway, 2018.

George, Susan. "A Short History of Neoliberalism." Transnational Institute, March 24, 1999. https://www.tni.org/en/article/short-history-neoliberalism.

George, Timothy, ed. *God the Holy Trinity: Reflections on Christian Faith and Practice*. Grand Rapids: Baker Academic, 2006.

Geyer, Alan. "Toward an Ecumenical Political Ethics: A Marginal View." In *Perspectives on Political Ethics: An Ecumenical Enquiry*, edited by Koson Srisang. Geneva: WCC, 1983.

Gilliard, Dominique Dubois. *Rethinking Incarceration: Advocating for Justice That Restores*. Downers Grove, IL: IVP, 2018.

Girard, René. *The Scapegoat*. Baltimore: Johns Hopkins University Press, 1986.

———. *Violence and the Sacred*. Baltimore: Johns Hopkins University Press, 1977.

"Global Prison Trends 2017." Penal Reform International. Accessed January 4, 2021. https://www.penalreform.org/resource/global-prison-trends-2017/.

Glueck, Nelson. *Hesed in the Bible*. 1967. Reprint, Eugene, OR: Wipf & Stock, 2011.

Goldingay, John E., Grant R. LeMarquand, George R. Sumner, and Daniel A. Westberg. "Same-Sex Marriage and Anglican Theology: A View of the Traditionalists." *Anglican Theology Review* 93, no. 1 (Winter 2011).

Goodstein, Laurie. "Utah Passes Antidiscrimination Bill Backed by Mormon Leaders." *New York Times*, March 12, 2015. https://www.nytimes.com/2015/03/12/us/politics/utah-passes-antidiscrimination-bill-backed-by-mormon-leaders.html.

Gorman, Michael. *The Death of Messiah and the Birth of the New Covenant: A (Not So) New Model of the Atonement*. Eugene, OR: Cascade, 2014.

———. *Inhabiting the Cruciform God: Kenosis, Justification, and Theosis in Paul's Narrative Soteriology*. Grand Rapids: Eerdmans, 2009.

Grad, Frank P. "The Constitution of the World Health Organization." *Bulletin of the World Health Organization* 80, no. 12 (2002): 981–84. https://www.who.int/bulletin/archives/80(12)981.pdf.

Grant, J. A. "Wisdom and Covenant." In *Dictionary of the Old Testament Wisdom, Poetry, and Writings*, edited by Tremper Longman III and Peter Enns, 858–63. Downers Grove, IL: IVP Academic, 2008.

———. "Wisdom and Covenant: Revisiting Zimmerli." *European Journal of Theology* 12, no. 2 (2003): 103–13.

Grant, Jonathan. *Divine Sex: A Compelling Vision for Christian Relationships in a Hypersexualized Age*. Grand Rapids: Brazos, 2015.

Grenz, Stanley J. *Sexual Ethics: An Evangelical Perspective*. Louisville: Westminster John Knox, 1997.

———. *The Social God and the Relational Self: A Trinitarian Theology of the* Imago Dei. Louisville: Westminster John Knox, 2001.

Griffin, James. *On Human Rights*. Oxford: Oxford University Press, 2009.

Gunton, Colin. *The One, the Three, and the Many*. New York: Cambridge University Press, 1993.

Guroian, Vigen. "Learning How to Die Well: Lessons from the Ancient Church." In *On Moral Medicine: Theological Perspectives on Medical Ethics*, 3rd ed., edited by M. Therese Lysaught and Joseph Kotva, 1071–78. Grand Rapids: Eerdmans, 2012.

Gushee, David P., and Glen H. Stassen, *Kingdom Ethics: Following Jesus in Contemporary Context*. 2nd ed. Grand Rapids: Eerdmans, 2016.

Gustafson, James M. *Theology and Ethics*. Philadelphia: United Church Press, 1974.

Habermas, Jürgen. *The Theory of Communicative Action*. Vol. 1, *Reason and the Rationalization of Society*. Cambridge: Polity, 1984.

Hacker, Andrew. *Two Nations: Black and White, Separate, Hostile, Unequal.* New York: Ballantine Books, 1993.

Hahn, Scott. "Covenant in the Old and New Testaments: Some Current Research (1994–2004)." *Currents in Biblical Research* 3, no. 2 (2005): 263–92.

Hansen, James, et al. "Target Atmospheric CO_2: Where Should Humanity Aim?" Last revised October 15, 2008. https://arxiv.org/vc/arxiv/papers/0804/0804.1126v2.pdf.

Hanson, Paul. *The People Called: The Growth of Community in the Bible.* Louisville: Westminster John Knox, 1986.

Hargrave, Terry D., and Franz Pfitzer. *The New Contextual Therapy: Guiding the Power of Give and Take.* New York: Routledge, 2003.

Harrington, James. *The Commonwealth of Oceana.* London: George Routledge and Sons, 1887.

Harris, Leslie M. "Higher Education's Reckoning with Slavery." American Association of University Professors, Winter 2020. https://www.aaup.org/article/higher-education%E2%80%99s-reckoning-slavery#.Xw37AB17knU.

Hartman, David. *A Living Covenant: The Innovative Spirit in Traditional Judaism.* New York: Free Press, 1985.

Harvey, David. *A Brief History of Neoliberalism.* Oxford: Oxford University Press, 2005.

Harvey, Jennifer. *Dear White Christians: For Those Still Longing for Racial Reconciliation.* Grand Rapids: Eerdmans, 2014.

Hauerwas, Stanley. "On the 'Right' to Be Tribal." *Christian Scholar's Review* 16, no. 3 (1987): 238–41.

———. "Salvation and Health: Why Medicine Needs the Church." In *On Moral Medicine: Theological Perspectives on Medical Ethics*, 3rd ed., edited by M. Therese Lysaught and Joseph Kotva, 43–51. Grand Rapids: Eerdmans, 2012.

Hayes, Cressida. "Identity Politics." In *The Stanford Encyclopedia of Philosophy*, edited by Edward N. Zalta. Fall 2020. https://plato.stanford.edu/cgi-bin/encyclopedia/archinfo.cgi?entry=identity-politics.

Hays, Richard. *The Moral Vision of the New Testament: A Contemporary Introduction to New Testament Ethics.* San Francisco: HarperSanFrancisco, 1996.

Heppe, Heinrich. *Reformed Dogmatics.* Grand Rapids: Baker Academics, 1978.

Heschel, Abraham. *The Prophets.* New York: Perennial, 2001.

Hill, Wesley. "Christ, Scripture, and Spiritual Friendship." In *Two Views on Homosexuality, the Bible, and the Church*, edited by Preston M. Sprinkle et al., 124–47. Grand Rapids: Zondervan, 2016.

Hillers, Delbert R. *Covenant: The History of a Biblical Idea.* Baltimore: Johns Hopkins University Press, 1969.

Hoekendijk, Johannes. "Mission—a Celebration of Freedom." *Union Seminary Quarterly* 21, no. 2 (1966): 135–44.

Holland, Joe, and Peter Henriott. *Social Analysis: Linking Faith with Action*. Maryknoll: Orbis, 1987.

Hollenbach, David. *Claims in Conflict: Retrieving and Renewing the Catholic Human Rights Tradition*. New York: Paulist, 1979.

———. *The Common Good and Christian Ethics*. New York: Cambridge University Press, 2002.

Hollinger, Dennis. *Choosing the Good: Christian Ethics in a Complex World*. Grand Rapids: Baker Academic, 2002.

Holmes, Stephen R. "Listening to the Past and Reflecting on the Present." In *Two Views on Homosexuality, the Bible, and the Church*, edited by Preston M. Sprinkle et al., 166–94. Grand Rapids: Zondervan, 2016.

Horsley, Richard. *Covenant Economics: A Biblical Vision of Justice for All*. Louisville: Westminster John Knox, 2005.

———. *Jesus and Empire: The Kingdom of God and the New World Disorder*. Minneapolis: Fortress, 2003.

Horton, Michael. *Covenant and Eschatology: The Divine Drama*. Louisville: Westminster John Knox, 2002.

———. *God of Promise: Introducing Covenant Theology*. Grand Rapids: Baker Books, 2006.

———. "Image and Office: Human Personhood and the Covenant." In *Personal Identity in Theological Perspective*, edited by Richard Lints, Michael S. Horton, and Mark R. Talbot, 178–203. Grand Rapids: Eerdmans, 2006.

Houghton, John. *Global Warming: The Complete Briefing*. 4th ed. Cambridge: Cambridge University Press, 2009.

Hunter-Bowman, Janna L. "Constructive Agents under Duress: Alternatives to the Structural, Political, and Agential Inadequacies of Past Theologies of Nonviolent Peacebuilding Efforts." *Journal of the Society of Christian Ethics* 38, no. 2 (2018): 149–68.

Huyssteen, J. Wentzel van. *Theology and the Justification of Faith: Constructing Theories in Systematic Theology*. Grand Rapids: Eerdmans, 1989.

"Inmate Calling Rates: Overcharged or Pay Too Much Per Minute or Per Call for Prison Calls or Jail Calls?" TelephoneComplaintConnect.com. Accessed March 31, 2020. https://telephonecomplaintconnect.com/calls/overcharged-inmate-calling-rates-prison-jail-calls/.

Jennings, Willie. "To Be a Christian Intellectual." Yale Divinity School, October 30, 2015. https://divinity.yale.edu/news/willie-jennings-be-christian-intellectual.

Jenson, Robert W. "The Triunity of Common Good." In *In Search of the Common Good*, edited by Patrick D. Miller and Dennis P. McCann. New York: T&T Clark, 2005.

Jeschke, Marlin. *Discipling the Brother: Congregational Discipline according to the Gospel.* Scottdale, PA: Herald, 1972.

Jocz, Jakób. *The Covenant: A Theology of Human Destiny*. Grand Rapids: Eerdmans, 1968.

Johnson, Todd E. "Doing God's Story: Theatre, Christian Initiation, and Being Human Together." In *Theatrical Theology: Explorations in Performing the Faith,* edited by Wesley Vander Lugt and Trevor Hart. Eugene, OR: Cascade, 2014.

Jones, Gregory. *Transformed Judgment: Toward a Trinitarian Account of the Moral Life.* Eugene, OR: Wipf & Stock, 2008.

Jones, J. M. "The Concept of Racism and Its Changing Reality." In *The Impact of Racism on White Americans,* edited by B. P. Bowser and R. G. Hunt, 27–49. Beverly Hills, CA: Sage Publications, 1981.

Jones, Matthew. "Homosexuality and Sexual Identity." In *Discerning Ethics: Diverse Responses to Divisive Moral Issues,* edited by Hak Joon Lee and Tim A. Dearborn, 144–61. Downers Grove, IL: IVP Academic, 2020.

Jones, Rachel K., Elizabeth Witwer, and Jenna Jerman. "Abortion Incidence and Service Availability in the United States, 2017." Guttmacher Institute, September 2019. https://www.guttmacher.org/report/abortion-incidence-service-availability-us-2017.

Jones, Robert P. "Self-Segregation: Why It's So Hard for Whites to Understand Ferguson." *Atlantic,* August 21, 2014. https://www.theatlantic.com/national/archive/2014/08/self-segregation-why-its-hard-for-whites-to-understand-ferguson/378928/?single_page=true.

Julian, Kate. "Why Are Young People Having So Little Sex?" *Atlantic,* December 2018. https://www.theatlantic.com/magazine/archive/2018/12/the-sex-recession/573949/.

Kaczor, Christopher. *The Ethics of Abortion: Women's Rights, Human Life, and the Question of Justice*. New York: Routledge, 2015.

Kapic, Kelly M. *Communion with God: The Divine and the Human in the Theology of John Owen*. Grand Rapids: Baker Academic, 2007.

Keen, Karen R. *Scripture, Ethics, and the Possibility of Same-Sex Relationships*. Grand Rapids: Eerdmans, 2018.

Keesmaat, Sylvia, and Brian Walsh. *Romans Disarmed: Resisting Empire, Demanding Justice*. Grand Rapids: Brazos, 2019.

Kelsey, David H. *The Use of Scripture in Recent Theology*. Philadelphia: Fortress, 1975.

Khushf, George. "Illness, the Problem of Evil, and the Analogical Structure of Healing: On the Difference Christianity Makes in Bioethics." In *On Moral Medicine: Theological Perspectives on Medical Ethics,* 3rd ed., edited by M. Therese Lysaught and Joseph Kotva, 21–29. Grand Rapids: Eerdmans, 2012.

Kim, Claire Jean. "The Racial Triangulation of Asian Americans." *Politics and Society* 27, no. 1 (1999): 105–38.

Kimelman, Reuven. "Judaism, War, and Weapons of Mass Destruction." In *Ethics and Mass Destruction: Religious and Secular Perspective*, edited by Sohail H. Hashmi and Steven P. Lee, 363–84. New York: Cambridge University Press, 2004.

King, Martin Luther, Jr. "An Experiment in Love." In *A Testament of Hope: The Essential Writing and Speeches of Martin Luther King, Jr.*, edited by James M. Washington. New York: HarperCollins, 1986.

———. "False Gods We Worship." In *Advocate of the Social Gospel, September 1948–March 1963*, vol. 6 of *The Papers of Martin Luther King, Jr.*, edited by Clayborne Carson et al. Berkeley: University of California Press, 2007.

———. "Letter from Birmingham City Jail." In *A Testament of Hope: The Essential Writing and Speeches of Martin Luther King, Jr.*, edited by James M. Washington. New York: HarperCollins, 1986.

———. "The Power of Nonviolence." In *A Testament of Hope: The Essential Writing and Speeches of Martin Luther King, Jr.*, edited by James M. Washington. New York: HarperCollins, 1986.

———. *Stride toward Freedom: The Montgomery Story*. Boston: Beacon, 2010.

———. *Where Do We Go from Here: Chaos or Community?* Boston: Beacon, 2010.

———. "Where Do We Go from Here?" In *A Testament of Hope: The Essential Writing and Speeches of Martin Luther King, Jr.*, edited by James M. Washington. New York: HarperCollins, 1986.

Kinnaman, David, and Gabe Lyons. *UnChristian: What a New Generation Really Thinks about Christianity . . . and Why It Matters*. Grand Rapids: Baker Books, 2012.

Kinsler, Ross, and Gloria Kinsler. *The Biblical Jubilee and the Struggle for Life: An Invitation to Personal, Ecclesial, and Social Transformation*. Maryknoll, NY: Orbis, 1999.

Klempa, William. "The Concept of Covenant in Sixteenth- and Seventeenth-Century Continental and British Reformed Theology." In *Major Themes in the Reformed Tradition*, edited by Donald K. McKim, 94–107. Grand Rapids: Eerdmans, 1992.

Kline, Meredith. *By Oath Consigned: A Reinterpretation of the Covenant Signs of Circumcision and Baptism*. Grand Rapids: Eerdmans, 1975.

Kochhar, Rakesh, and Richard Fry. "Wealth Inequality Has Widened along Racial, Ethnic Lines Since End of Great Recession." Pew Research Center, December 12, 2014. https://www.pewresearch.org/fact-tank/2014/12/12/racial-wealth-gaps-great-recession/.

Kotsko, Adam. *Neoliberalism's Demons: On the Political Theology of Late Capital*. Stanford, CA: Stanford University Press, 2018.

Küng, Hans. *A Global Ethic for Global Politics and Economics*. New York: Oxford University Press, 1998.

Lambelet, Kyle B. T. "Just Peacemaking: Practices, Norms, and Ends after Twenty-Five

Years." Paper presented at the annual meeting of the Society of Christian Ethics, Portland, OR, January 2018.

Lederach, John Paul. *The Moral Imagination: The Art and Soul of Building Peace*. New York: Oxford University Press, 2010.

Lee, Hak Joon. "Covenant as a Historical Drama for Incarnational Discipleship: A Covenantal Reinterpretation of Glen Stassen's Thicker Jesus." In *Justice and the Way of Jesus: Engaging Glen Stassen's Incarnational Discipleship Ethics*, edited by David Gushee and Reggie Williams. Maryknoll, NY: Orbis, 2020.

———. *God and Community Organizing: A Covenant Approach*. Waco, TX: Baylor University Press, 2020.

———. *The Great World House: Martin Luther King, Jr., and Global Ethics*. Cleveland: Pilgrim, 2011.

———. "Public Theology." In *The Cambridge Companion to Christian Political Theology*, edited by Craig Hovey and Elizabeth Phillips, 44–65. New York: Cambridge University Press, 2015.

Lehmann, Paul. *Ethics in a Christian Context*. New York: Harper & Row, 1963.

Leith, John H. *An Introduction to the Reformed Tradition: A Way of Being the Christian Community*. Atlanta: John Knox, 1981.

Lemberg, David. "Distributive Justice—Bioethics in Medical Practice." Albany Medical College, August 30, 2011. http://www.amc.edu/BioethicsBlog/post.cfm/distributive-justice-bioethics-in-medical-practice.

Lilly, Ingrid Esther. "Developing a Moral Vision for Climate Change." *Sojourners*, June 9, 2014. http://sojo.net/blogs/2014/06/09/developing-moral-vision-climate-change.

Loader, William. "Homosexuality and the Bible." In *Two Views on Homosexuality, the Bible, and the Church*, edited by Preston M. Sprinkle et al., 17–48. Grand Rapids: Zondervan, 2016.

Loder, James E. *The Logic of the Spirit: Human Development in Theological Perspective*. San Francisco: Jossey-Bass, 1998.

———. *The Transformation Moment*. Colorado Springs: Helmers & Howard, 1989.

Lohfink, Gerhard. *Jesus and Community: The Social Dimension of Christian Faith*. Minneapolis: Fortress, 1984.

Lohfink, Norbert F. *Option for the Poor: The Basic Principles of Liberation Theology in the Light of the Bible*. North Richland Hills, TX: BIBAL Press, 1995.

Lopez, German. "Report: Black Men Get Longer Sentences for the Same Federal Crime as White Men." *Vox*, November 17, 2017. https://www.vox.com/identities/2017/11/17/16668770/us-sentencing-commission-race-booker.

Manzo, Anthony V., et al. "Dialectical Thinking: A Generative Approach to Critical/Creative Thinking." Education Resources Information Center, December 1992. https://eric.ed.gov/?id=ED352632.

Marshall, Christopher. *Beyond Retribution: A New Testament Vision for Justice, Crime, and Punishment*. Grand Rapids: Eerdmans, 2001.

———. "Divine Justice as Restorative Justice." Center for Christian Ethics, Baylor University, 2012. https://www.baylor.edu/content/services/document.php/163072.pdf.

———. "Prison, Prisoners and the Bible." A paper delivered to Prison Fellowship New Zealand's Breaking Down the Walls Conference, June 14–16, 2002. http://restorativejustice.org/10fulltext/marshall-christopher.-prison-prisoners-and-the-bible.pdf.

Mason, Steven. *"Eternal Covenant" in the Pentateuch: The Contours of an Elusive Phrase*. New York: T&T Clark, 2008.

Materstvedt, Lars Johan, et al. "Euthanasia and Physician Assisted Suicide: A View from EAPC Ethics Task Force." *Palliative Medicine* 17 (2003): 97–101.

May, William. "Moral Leadership in the Corporate Setting." In *Profits and Professions: Essays in Business and Professional Ethics*, edited by W. L. Robison et al., 183–213. Clifton, NJ: Humana, 1983.

———. *The Physician's Covenant: Images of the Healer in Medical Ethics*. Louisville: Westminster John Knox, 2000.

———. *Testing the Medical Covenant: Active Euthanasia and Health Care Reform*. Grand Rapids: Eerdmans, 1996.

———. *Testing the National Covenant: Fears and Appetites in American Politics*. Washington, DC: Georgetown University Press, 2011.

Mays, James Luther. *Amos: A Commentary*. Philadelphia: Westminster, 1969.

McCann, Dennis. "The Good to Be Pursued in Common." In *The Common Good and US Capitalism*, edited by Oliver F. Williams and John W. Houck, 158–78. Lanham, MD: University Press of America, 1987.

McCarthy, Eli Sasaran, and William O'Neill. *Becoming Nonviolent Peacemakers: A Virtue Ethic for Catholic Social Teaching and US Policy*. Eugene, OR: Wipf & Stock, 2012.

McCarthy, Niall. "No Country Incarcerates More Women Than the US." Statista: The Statistics Portal, September 25, 2014. www.statista.com/chart/2755/no-country-incarcerates-more-women-than-the-us/.

McCarthy, Thomas. "Translator's Introduction." In Jürgen Habermas, *The Theory of Communicative Action*, vol. 1, *Reason and the Rationalization of Society*. Cambridge: Polity, 1984.

McComiskey, T. E. *The Covenants of Promise: A Theology of the Old Testament Covenants*. Grand Rapids: Baker Books, 1985.

McConville, Gordon J. "בְּרִית." In *New International Dictionary of the Old Testament Theology and Exegesis*, edited by Willem VanGemeren. Grand Rapids: Zondervan, 1997.

McCormick, Richard. "Physician-Assisted Suicide: Flight from Compassion." *Christian Century* 108, no. 35 (1991): 1132–34.

McDonald, Suzanne. *Re-imaging Election: Divine Election Representing God to Others and Others to God*. Grand Rapids: Eerdmans, 2010.

McDonough, Mary. *Can a Health Care Market Be Moral? A Catholic Vision*. Washington, DC: Georgetown University Press, 2007.

McFague, Sallie. *Metaphorical Theology: Models of God in Religious Language*. Philadelphia: Fortress, 1982.

McGill, Arthur C. *Suffering: A Test of Theological Method*. Eugene, OR: Wipf & Stock, 2006.

McIntosh, Peggy. "White Privilege: Unpacking the Invisible Backpack." National Consortium of Interpreter Education Centers, March 2016. http://www.interpretereducation.org/wp-content/uploads/2016/03/white-privilege-by-Peggy-McIntosh.compressed.pdf.

McKenzie, Steven L. *Covenant*. St. Louis: Chalice, 2000.

Meilaender, Gilbert C. *The Theory and Practice of Virtue*. Notre Dame: University of Notre Dame Press, 1984.

"Mental Health." The Equality Trust. Accessed January 26, 2021. https://www.equalitytrust.org.uk/mental-health.

Migliore, Daniel. *Faith Seeking Understanding: An Introduction to Christian Theology*. 3rd ed. Grand Rapids: Eerdmans, 2014.

Miller, David. "Justice." In *The Stanford Encyclopedia of Philosophy*, edited by Edward N. Zalta. Fall 2017. https://plato.stanford.edu/archives/fall2017/entries/justice/.

Miller, Patrick. *Israelite Religion and Biblical Theology: Collected Essays*. Sheffield: Sheffield Academic Press, 2000.

Miller, Perry. *Errand into the Wilderness*. Cambridge: Belknap Press of Harvard University Press, 1981.

———. *The New England Mind: The Seventeenth Century*. Boston: Beacon, 1968.

Moltmann, Jürgen. *Ethics of Hope*. Translated by Margaret Kohl. Minneapolis: Fortress, 2012.

———. *God for a Secular Society: The Public Relevance of Theology*. Translated by Margaret Kohl. Minneapolis: Fortress, 1999.

———. *God in Creation: A New Theology of Creation and the Spirit of God*. Translated by Margaret Kohl. Minneapolis: Fortress, 1993.

Moot, Glenn. *Politics Reformed: The Anglo-American Legacy of Covenant Theology*. Columbia: University of Missouri Press, 2010.

Morgan, David. *The Embodied Eye: Religious Visual Culture and the Social Life of Feeling*. Berkeley: University of California Press, 2017.

Mott, Stephen. *Biblical Ethics and Social Change.* New York: Oxford University Press, 1982.

Mount, Eric. *Covenant, Community, and the Common Good: An Interpretation of Christian Ethics.* Cleveland: Pilgrim, 1999.

Mouw, Richard J. *The God Who Commands.* Notre Dame: University of Notre Dame Press, 1990.

Myers, Bryant L. *Walking with the Poor: Principles and Practices of Transformational Development.* Maryknoll, NY: Orbis, 2011.

Nash, Elizabeth, and Joerg Dreweke. "The US Abortion Rate Continues to Drop: Once Again, State Abortion Restrictions Are Not the Main Driver." Guttmacher Institute, September 18, 2019. https://www.guttmacher.org/gpr/2019/09/us-abortion-rate-continues-drop-once-again-state-abortion-restrictions-are-not-main.

Nashville Statement. Coalition for Biblical Sexuality, August 29, 2017. https://cbmw.org/nashville-statement/.

National Centers for Environmental Information (NOAA). "Global Climate Report—Annual 2019." https://www.ncdc.noaa.gov/sotc/global/201913.

Newbigin, Lesslie. *The Gospel in a Pluralist Society.* Grand Rapids: Eerdmans, 1989.

Nicholson, Ernest W. *God and His People: Covenant and Theology in the Old Testament.* Oxford: Oxford University Press, 1986.

Niebuhr, H. Richard. "The Idea of Covenant and American Democracy." *Church History* 23, no. 2 (1954): 126–35.

———. *The Responsible Self: An Essay in Christian Moral Philosophy.* Louisville: Westminster John Knox, 1999.

Niebuhr, Reinhold. *The Children of Light and the Children of Darkness: A Vindication of Democracy and a Critique of Its Traditional Defense.* New York: Scribner's Sons, 1960.

———. *Moral Man and Immoral Society.* Louisville: Westminster John Knox, 2002.

———. *The Nature and Destiny of Man: A Christian Interpretation.* Vol. 2. Louisville: Westminster John Knox, 1996.

———. *Reinhold Niebuhr on Politics: His Political Philosophy and Its Application to Our Age as Expressed in His Writings.* Edited by Harry R. Davis and Robert C. Good. New York: Scribner's Sons, 1960.

Novak, Michael. *The Spirit of Democratic Capitalism.* New York: Simon & Schuster, 1982.

Nussbaum, Martha C. *Love's Knowledge: Essays on Philosophy and Literature.* New York: Oxford University Press, 1990.

———. *Sex and Social Justice.* New York: Oxford University Press, 1999.

O'Donovan, Oliver. "Sanctification and Ethics." In *Sanctification: Explorations in Theology and Practice,* edited by Kelly M. Kapic, 150–66. Downers Grove, IL: IVP Academic, 2014.

"On Views of Race and Inequality, Blacks and Whites Are Worlds Apart." Pew Research

Center, June 27, 2016. https://www.pewsocialtrends.org/2016/06/27/1-demographic-trends-and-economic-well-being/.

Oppel, Richard A., Jr., and Jugal K. Patel. "One Lawyer, 194 Felony Cases, and No Time." *New York Times*, January 31, 2019. https://www.nytimes.com/interactive/2019/01/31/us/public-defender-case-loads.html.

Organization for Economic Co-operation and Development. *Growing Unequal? Income Distribution and Poverty in OECD Countries.* Paris: Organization for Economic Co-operation and Development, 2008.

Oswalt, John N. *The Book of Isaiah, Chapters 40–60*. New International Commentary on the Old Testament. Grand Rapids: Eerdmans, 1998.

Ottati, Douglas F. "The Reformed Tradition in Theological Ethics." In *Christian Ethics: Problems and Prospects*, edited by Lisa Sowle Cahill and James F. Childress, 45–59. Cleveland: Pilgrim, 1996.

Paeth, Scott, E. Harold Breitenberg, and Hak Joon Lee, eds. *Shaping Public Theology: Selections from the Writings of Max L. Stackhouse.* Grand Rapids: Eerdmans, 2014.

Patrick, Dale. *The Rendering of God in the Old Testament.* Philadelphia, Fortress, 1981.

Pedersen, Johannes. *Israel: Its Life and Culture.* Vol. 1. London: Oxford University Press, 1959.

Pelikan, Jaroslav. "Christianity as an Enfolding Circle." *US News & World Report*, June 26, 1989.

Perdue, Leo G. *Wisdom Literature: A Theological History*. Louisville: Westminster John Knox, 2007.

Peterson, David G. *Transformed by God: New Covenant Life and Ministry*. Downers Grove, IL: IVP Academic, 2012.

Phan, Peter. "Betwixt and Between: Doing Theology with Memory and Imagination." In *Toward an Autobiographical Theology in American-Asian Perspective*, edited by Peter Phan and Jung Young Lee, 113–33. Collegeville, MN: Liturgical Press, 1999.

Philpott, Daniel. *Just and Unjust Peace: An Ethic of Political Reconciliation*. New York: Oxford University Press, 2012.

Pilch, John. *Healing in the New Testament: Insights from Medical and Mediterranean Anthropology.* Minneapolis: Fortress, 2000.

Pinnock, Clark. *Flame of Love: A Theology of the Holy Spirit*. Downers Grove, IL: IVP, 1996.

Plantinga, Cornelius. *Not the Way It's Supposed to Be: A Breviary of Sin*. Grand Rapids: Eerdmans, 1995.

Pohl, Christine. "Abortion: Responsibility and Moral Betrayal." In *Bioethics and the Future of Medicine: A Christian Appraisal*, edited by John Frederic Kilner et al., 212–23. Grand Rapids: Eerdmans, 1995.

———. *Living into Community: Cultivating Practices That Sustain Us*. Grand Rapids: Eerdmans, 2012.

Porter, Jean. *The Recovery of Virtue: The Relevance of Aquinas for Christian Ethics*. Louisville: Westminster John Knox, 1990.

"President Woodrow Wilson's 14 Points (1918)." OurDocuments.gov. Accessed January 11, 2021. https://www.ourdocuments.gov/doc.php?doc=62.

"Public Opinion on Abortion: Views on Abortion, 1995–2019." Pew Research Center, August 29, 2019. http://www.pewforum.org/fact-sheet/public-opinion-on-abortion/.

"Race and the Drug War." Drug Policy Alliance. Accessed January 4, 2021. https://www.drugpolicy.org/issues/race-and-drug-war.

Rad, Gerhard von. *Old Testament Theology*. Vol. 1. New York: Harper & Row, 1962.

Radner, Ephraim. *A Time to Keep: Theology, Mortality, and the Shape of Human Life*. Waco, TX: Baylor University Press, 2016.

Rae, Scott, and Paul Cox. *Bioethics: A Christian Approach in a Pluralistic Age*. Grand Rapids: Eerdmans, 1999.

Rah, Soong-Chan. *The Next Evangelicalism: Releasing the Church from Western Cultural Captivity*. Downers Grove, IL: IVP, 2019.

Ramsey, Paul. *The Patient as Person: Explorations in Medical Ethics*. New Haven: Yale University Press, 1974.

Rasmussen, Larry. *Earth Community, Earth Ethics*. Maryknoll, NY: Orbis, 1997.

———. *Earth-Honoring Faith: Religious Ethics in a New Key*. Oxford: Oxford University Press, 2013.

———. "Friendly Amendment." Read at the Stassen Symposium, April 2018.

Rastogi, S., et al. "2010 Census Brief: The Black Population 2010." US Census Bureau, September 2011.

Rata, Tiberius. "Covenant." In *Dictionary of the Old Testament: Prophets*, edited by Mark J. Boda and J. Gordon McConville, 100–102. Downers Grove, IL: IVP Academic, 2013.

Ratzinger, Joseph Cardinal. *Many Religions, One Covenant: Israel, the Church, and the World*. San Francisco: Ignatius, 1999.

———. *Seek That Which Is Above: Meditations through the Year*. San Francisco: Ignatius, 2007.

Regnerus, Mark, and Jeremy Uecker. *Premarital Sex in America: How Young Americans Meet, Mate, and Think about Marrying*. New York: Oxford University Press, 2011.

Reich, Robert B. *Aftershock: The Next Economy and America's Future*. New York: Vintage, 2013.

Ricoeur, Paul. *Oneself as Another*. Chicago: University of Chicago Press, 1982.

Roberts, Christopher C. *Covenant and Creation: The Significance of Sexual Difference in the Moral Theology of Marriage*. New York: T&T Clark, 2007.

Robertson, O. Palmer. *The Christ of the Covenants*. Grand Rapids: Baker Books, 1980.

Robinson, John A. T. *Honest to God*. London: SCM, 1963.

Rogland, Max. "The Covenant in the Book of Job." *Criswell Theological Review* 7, no. 1 (Fall 2009): 49–62.

Rusthoven, James, and Craig G. Bartholomew. *Covenantal Biomedical Ethics for Contemporary Medicine: An Alternative to Principles-Based Ethics*. Eugene, OR: Wipf & Stock, 2014.

Saliers, Don. "Liturgy and Ethics: Some New Beginnings." In *Liturgy and Moral Self: Humanity at Full Stretch before God*, edited by E. Byron Anderson and Bruce T. Morrill, 15–35. Collegeville, MN: Liturgical Press, 1998.

Salvatierra, Alexia, and Peter Heltzel. *Faith-Rooted Organizing: Mobilizing the Church in Service to the World*. Downers Grove, IL: IVP Academic, 2014.

Sandel, Michael. *Justice: What's the Right Thing to Do?* New York: Farrar, Straus & Giroux, 2009.

Sanders, E. P. *Paul and Palestinian Judaism: A Comparison of Patterns of Religion*. 40th anniversary ed. Minneapolis: Fortress, 2017.

Sanford, Jack A. *Healing and Wholeness*. New York: Paulist, 1977.

Santos, De Sousa. "Public Sphere and Epistemologies of the South." *African Development* 37, no. 1 (2012): 43–67.

Scherer, Andreas, and Guido Palazzo. "The New Political Role of Business in a Globalized World: A Review of a New Perspective on CSR and Its Implications for the Firm, Governance, and Democracy." *Journal of Management Studies* 48 (2011): 899–931.

Schlesinger, Kira. *Pro-Choice and Christian: Reconciling Faith, Politics, and Justice*. Louisville: Westminster John Knox, 2017.

Schlosser, Eric. "The Prison-Industrial Complex." *Atlantic*, December 1998. https://www.theatlantic.com/magazine/archive/1998/12/the-prison-industrial-complex/304669/.

Schulz, Kathryn. "From the White House to the Jailhouse to the Pulpit: Chuck Colson on Being Wrong." *Slate*, October 20, 2010. http://www.slate.com/blogs/thewrongstuff/2010/10/20/from_the_white_house_to_the_jailhouse_to_the_pulpit_chuck_colson_on_being_wrong.html.

Schüssler Fiorenza, Elisabeth. *In Memory of Her: A Feminist Theological Reconstruction of Christian Origins*. New York: Crossroad, 1994.

Selznick, Philip. *Moral Commonwealth: Social Theory and the Promise of Community*. Berkeley: University of California Press, 1994.

Sen, Amartya. "Equality of What?" The Tanner Lecture on Human Values. Stanford University, May 22, 1979.

Sider, Ronald J. *Just Generosity: A New Vision for Overcoming Poverty in America*. Grand Rapids: Baker Books, 2007.

———. *Rich Christians in an Age of Hunger: A Biblical Study*. Downers Grove, IL: IVP, 1984.

———. *The Scandal of Evangelical Politics: Why Are Christians Missing the Chance to Really Change the World?* Grand Rapids: Baker Books, 2008.

Sides, John, Michael Tesler, and Lynn Vavreck. "Five Myths about the 2016 Election." *Washington Post*, October 5, 2018. https://www.washingtonpost.com/outlook/five-myths/myths-about-the-2016-presidential-election/2018/10/05/4e07a22a-c808-11e8-b2b5-79270f9cce17_story.html?utm_term=.0dd825afe1c6.

Simon, Caroline J. *Bringing Sex into Focus: The Quest for Sexual Integrity*. Downers Grove, IL: IVP, 2012.

"68% of the World Population Projected to Live in Urban Areas by 2050, Says UN." United Nations, May 16, 2018. https://www.un.org/development/desa/en/news/population/2018-revision-of-world-urbanization-prospects.html.

Smedes, Lewis B. *Mere Morality: What God Expects from Ordinary People*. Grand Rapids: Eerdmans, 1983.

Smith, Adam. *An Inquiry into the Nature and Causes of the Wealth of Nations*. Edinburgh: University Press for T. Nelson and P. Brown, 1827.

Smith, James K. A. *Desiring the Kingdom: Worship, Worldview, and Cultural Formation*. Grand Rapids: Baker Academic, 2009.

———. "The Reformed (Transformationist) View." In *Five Views on the Church and Politics*, edited by Amy E. Black, 139–62. Grand Rapids: Zondervan, 2015.

———. *You Are What You Love: The Spiritual Power of Habit*. Grand Rapids: Brazos, 2016.

Snyder, T. Richard. *The Protestant Ethic and the Spirit of Punishment*. Grand Rapids: Eerdmans, 2001.

Song, Robert. *Covenant and Calling: A Theology of Same-Sex Relationships*. London: SCM, 2014.

Spezio, Michael. "Human or Vulcan? Theological Consideration of Emotional Control Enhancement." In *Transhumanism and Transcendence: Christian Hope in an Age of Technological Enhancement*, edited by Ronald Cole-Turner, 145–62. Washington, DC: Georgetown University Press, 2011.

Spiegel, James S. "Can a Christian Be Morally Pro-Life and Politically Pro-Choice?" *Christian Scholar's Review* 30, no. 1 (2000): 107–15.

Spohn, William C. *Go and Do Likewise: Jesus and Ethics*. New York: Continuum, 2000.

Sprinkle, Preston M. "Conclusion." In *Two Views on Homosexuality, the Bible, and the Church*, edited by Preston M. Sprinkle et al. Grand Rapids: Zondervan, 2016.

———. "What Is a Christian Sexual Ethic?" *Preston Sprinkle* (blog), January 23, 2017. https://www.prestonsprinkle.com/blog/2017/1/23/what-is-a-christian-sexual-ethic.

Spykman, Gordon. *Reformational Theology: A New Paradigm for Doing Dogmatics.* Grand Rapids: Eerdmans, 1992.

Stackhouse, Max L. "A Covenantal Justice in a Global Era." In *Shaping Public Theology,* edited by Scott Paeth, E. Harold Breitenberg, and Hak Joon Lee. Grand Rapids: Eerdmans, 2014.

———. *Covenant and Commitments: Faith, Family, and Economic Life.* Louisville: Westminster John Knox, 1997.

———. *Ethics and the Urban Ethos: An Essay in Social Theory and Theological Reconstruction.* Boston: Beacon, 1972.

———. "The Fifth Social Gospel and the Global Mission of the Church." In *Shaping Public Theology,* edited by Scott Paeth, E. Harold Breitenberg, and Hak Joon Lee. Grand Rapids: Eerdmans, 2014.

———. "General Introduction." In *Religion and the Powers of the Common Life,* vol. 1, *God and Globalization,* edited by Max Stackhouse and Peter Paris, 1–52. Harrisburg, PA: Trinity Press International, 2000.

———. "The Tasks of Theological Ethics." In *Shaping Public Theology,* edited by Scott Paeth, E. Harold Breitenberg, and Hak Joon Lee, 93–103. Grand Rapids: Eerdmans, 2014.

Stassen, Glen H. *Just Peacemaking: The New Paradigm for the Ethics of Peace and War.* 2nd ed. Cleveland: Pilgrim, 2008.

———. *A Thicker Jesus: Incarnational Discipleship in a Secular Age.* Louisville: Westminster John Knox, 2012.

Stassen, Glen H., and David P. Gushee. *Kingdom Ethics: Following Jesus in Contemporary Context.* Downers Grove, IL: IVP, 2003. For 2nd ed., see above under Gushee, David P.

"States across the Nation Are Criminalizing Poverty." Editorial. *Washington Post,* May 27, 2018. https://www.washingtonpost.com/opinions/states-across-the-nation-are-criminalizing-poverty/2018/05/27/4637b048-5df6-11e8-a4a4-c070ef53f315_story.html.

Stob, Henry. *Ethical Reflections: Essay on Moral Themes.* Grand Rapids: Eerdmans, 1978.

Stone, Ronald H. "Realist Criticism of Just Peacemaking Theory." *Journal of the Society of Christian Ethics* 23, no. 1 (2003): 255–67.

"Study: White and Black Children Biased toward Lighter Skin." CNN, May 14, 2010. http://www.cnn.com/2010/US/05/13/doll.study/index.html.

Sturm, Douglas. "Martin Luther King, Jr., as Democratic Socialist." *Journal of Religious Ethics* 18, no. 2 (Fall 1990): 79–105.

Suchman, Mark C. "Managing Legitimacy: Strategic and Institutional Approaches." *Academy of Management Review* 20 (1995): 571–610.

Sullivan, Andrew. "Christianity in Crisis." *Newsweek*, April 2, 2012.

Taylor, Charles. "The Politics of Recognition." In *Multiculturalism: Examining the Politics of Recognition*, edited by Charles Taylor and Amy Gutmann. Princeton: Princeton University Press, 1999.

Teilhard de Chardin, Pierre. *Hymn of the Universe*. New York: Harper & Row, 1965.

"Telephone Service for Incarcerated Individuals." Federal Communications Commission, last updated/reviewed October 27, 2020. https://www.fcc.gov/consumers/guides/inmate-telephone-service.

Thweatt-Bates, Jeanine. *Cyborg Selves: A Theological Anthropology of the Posthuman*. Burlington, VT: Ashgate, 2012.

Tubbs, James B. *A Handbook of Bioethics Terms*. Washington, DC: Georgetown University Press, 2009.

Tutu, Desmond. *No Future without Forgiveness*. New York: Doubleday, 2000.

United Nations. "Responsibility to Protect." https://www.un.org/en/genocideprevention/about-responsibility-to-protect.shtml.

US Bureau of Justice Statistics. "Prisoners in 2016." Updated August 2018. https://www.bjs.gov/content/pub/pdf/p16.pdf.

VanDrunen, David. "The Protectionist Purpose of the Law: A Moral Case from the Biblical Covenant with Noah." *Journal of the Society of Christian Ethics* 35, no. 2 (Fall-Winter 2015): 106.

Van Gelder, Craig. *The Ministry of the Missional Church: A Community Led by the Spirit*. Grand Rapids: Baker Books, 2007.

Vanhoozer, Kevin. *The Drama of Doctrine: A Canonical-Linguistic Approach to Christian Theology*. Louisville: Westminster John Knox, 2005.

———. *Faith Speaking Understanding: Reforming the Drama of Doctrine*. Louisville: Westminster John Knox, 2014.

———. *First Theology: God, Scripture, and Hermeneutics*. Downers Grove, IL: IVP, 2002.

———. *Remythologizing Theology: Divine Action, Passion, and Authorship*. New York: Cambridge University Press, 2012.

Verhey, Allen. *Remembering Jesus: Christian Community, Scripture, and the Moral Life*. Grand Rapids: Eerdmans, 2002.

Vogels, Walter. *God's Universal Covenant: A Biblical Study*. Ottawa: University of Ottawa Press, 1979.

Volf, Miroslav. *Exclusion and Embrace: A Theological Exploration of Identity, Otherness, and Reconciliation*. Nashville: Abingdon, 1996.

Wadell, Paul. *Friendship and the Moral Life: An Introduction to Christian Ethics*. Lanham, MD: Rowman & Littlefield, 2012.

Wagner, Peter, and Daniel Kopf. "The Racial Geography of Mass Incarceration." Prison Policy Initiative, July 2015. www.prisonpolicy.org/racialgeography/report.html.

Wagner, Peter, and Bernadette Rabuy. "Mass Incarceration: The Whole Pie 2015." Prison Policy Initiative, December 8, 2015. https://www.prisonpolicy.org/reports/pie2015.html.

Wagner, Peter, and Wendy Sawyer. "Mass Incarceration: The Whole Pie 2018." Prison Policy Initiative, March 14, 2018. www.prisonpolicy.org/reports/pie2018.html.

Walker, Alice. *The Color Purple*. New York: Harvest Books, 1982.

Wallis, Jim. *America's Original Sin: Racism, White Privilege, and the Bridge to a New America*. Grand Rapids: Brazos, 2016.

———. *God's Politics: Why the Right Gets It Wrong and the Left Doesn't Get It*. San Francisco: HarperSanFrancisco, 2006.

Walton, John H. *Covenant: God's Purpose, God's Plan*. Grand Rapids: Zondervan, 2010.

Walzer, Michael. *Exodus and Revolution*. New York: Basic Books, 1985.

———. "Gulf Crisis." *New Republic*, August 5, 1996.

———. *The Revolution of the Saints: A Study in the Origins of Radical Politics*. Cambridge: Harvard University Press, 1965.

———. *Spheres of Justice: A Defense of Pluralism and Equality*. New York: Basic Books, 1983.

———. *Thick and Thin: Moral Argument at Home and Abroad*. Notre Dame: University of Notre Dame Press, 1994.

Weir, David. *Early New England: A Covenanted Society*. Grand Rapids: Eerdmans, 2005.

Wellman, David. *Portraits of White Racism*. Cambridge: Cambridge University Press, 1993.

Wells, Louise. *The Greek Language of Healing from Homer to New Testament Times*. New York: de Gruyter, 1998.

Wells, Samuel. "Improvising Leadership," *Faith & Leadership*, March 26, 2012. https://faithandleadership.com/multimedia/samuel-wells-improvising-leadership.

Werpekowski, William. "Justice." In *The Westminster Dictionary of Christian Ethics*, edited by James Childress and John MacQuarrie. Philadelphia: Westminster, 1986.

White, Lynn, Jr. "The Historical Roots of Our Ecologic Crisis." In *The Ecocriticism Reader: Landmarks in Literary Ecology*, edited by Cheryll Glotfelty and Harold Fromm, 3–14. Athens: University of Georgia Press, 1996. Originally published in *Science* 155, no. 3767 (March 1967): 1203–7.

Wildes, Kevin. "The Stem Cell Report." *America* 181, no. 11 (October 1999): 12–14.

Wilkinson, Richard G., and Kate Pickett. *The Spirit Level: Why Greater Equality Makes Societies Strong*. New York: Bloomsbury, 2010.

Williams, Rowan. "The Body's Grace." ABC Religion & Ethics, August 24, 2011. https://www.abc.net.au/religion/the-bodys-grace/.

———. "Rights, Recognition, and the Body of Christ." Payton Lecture, Fuller Theological Seminary, April 5, 2018.

Williams, Timothy. "The High Cost of Calling the Imprisoned." *New York Times*, March 30, 2015. https://www.nytimes.com/2015/03/31/us/steep-costs-of-inmate-phone-calls-are-under-scrutiny.html.

Williamson, Marianne. "America Doesn't Just Have a Gun Crisis. It Has a Culture Crisis." *Washington Post*, September 2, 2019. https://www.washingtonpost.com/opinions/2019/09/02/marianne-williamson-us-needs-department-peace/.

Wink, Walter. *Engaging the Powers: Discernment and Resistance in a World of Domination*. Minneapolis: Fortress, 1992.

Winright, Tobias. "Just Cause and Preemptive Strikes in the War on Terrorism: Insights from a Just-Policing Perspective." *Journal of the Society of Christian Ethics* 26, no. 2 (2006): 157–81.

———. "Why I Shall Continue to Use and Teach Just War Theory." *Expositions* 12, no. 1 (2018): 142–61.

Wirzba, Norman. *The Paradise of God: Renewing Religion in an Ecological Age*. New York: Oxford University Press, 2003.

Wolfe, D. M., ed. *Leveller Manifestoes of the Puritan Revolution*. New York: Nelson, 1944.

Wolin, Sheldon. *Democracy Incorporated: Managed Democracy and the Specter of Inverted Totalitarianism*. Princeton: Princeton University Press, 2010.

Wolterstorff, Nicholas. *Hearing the Call: Liturgy, Justice, Church, and World*. Edited by Mark R. Gornik and Gregory Thompson. Grand Rapids: Eerdmans, 2011.

———. *Journey toward Justice: Personal Encounters in the Global South*. Grand Rapids: Baker Academic, 2013.

———. *Justice: Rights and Wrongs*. Princeton: Princeton University Press, 2008.

———. *Until Justice and Peace Embrace: The Kuyper Lectures for 1981 Delivered at the Free University of Amsterdam*. Grand Rapids: Eerdmans, 1983.

Woodley, Randy. "Reparations." In *Dictionary of Scripture and Ethics*, edited by Joel Green et al. Grand Rapids: Baker Academic, 2011.

"Words from Prison—Did You Know . . . ?" American Civil Liberties Union. Accessed January 4, 2021. https://www.aclu.org/other/words-prison-did-you-know/.

Wright, Christopher. *An Eye for an Eye: The Place of Old Testament Ethics Today*. Downers Grove, IL: IVP, 1983.

———. *Knowing Jesus through the Old Testament*. Downers Grove, IL: IVP Academic, 2014.

———. *Old Testament Ethics for the People of God*. Downers Grove, IL: IVP Academic, 2004.

Wright, N. T. "How Can the Bible Be Authoritative?" *Vox Evangelica* 21 (1991): 7–32.

———. *Jesus and the Victory of God*. Minneapolis: Fortress, 1996.

———. *The New Testament and the People of God*. Minneapolis: Fortress, 1992.

———. *Paul: In Fresh Perspective.* Minneapolis: Fortress, 2005.

———. *Paul and the Faithfulness of God.* 2 vols. Minneapolis: Fortress, 2013.

Yarhouse, Mark A. *Homosexuality and the Christian.* Bloomington, MN: Bethany House, 2010.

Yoder, John Howard. *The Politics of Jesus*. 2nd ed. Grand Rapids: Eerdmans, 1994.

Young, Iris Marion. "Activist Challenges to Deliberative Democracy." *Political Theory* 29, no. 5 (2001): 670–90.

Zakaria, Fareed. "The Rise of Illiberal Democracy." *Foreign Affairs* 76, no. 6 (November/December 1997): 22–43. https://www.foreignaffairs.com/articles/1997-11-01/rise-illiberal-democracy.

———. *The Post-American World.* London: Penguin Books, 2009.

Zauzmer, Julie. "'He Gets It': Evangelicals Aren't Turned Off by Trump's First Term." *Washington Post,* August 13, 2019. https://www.washingtonpost.com/politics/evangelicals-arent-turned-off-by-trumps-first-term--theyre-delighted-by-it/2019/08/11/3911bc88-a990-11e9-a3a6-ab670962db05_story.html.

Zezima, Carolyn. "Incarcerated with Mental Illness: How to Reduce the Number of People with Mental Health Issues in Prison." PSYCOM. Accessed January 4, 2021. https://www.psycom.net/how-to-reduce-mental-illness-in-prisons.

Zimmerman, Michael. "Isaiah for Our Time: To Transform the World." *Tikkun,* October 16, 2019. https://www.tikkun.org/isaiah-for-our-time-to-transform-the-world.

Index of Names and Subjects

Index of Scripture References